Frommer's®

Utah

9th Edition

by Eric Peterson

WILEY

John Wiley & Sons, Inc.

ABOUT THE AUTHOR

A Denver-based writer, **Eric Peterson** has authored numerous Frommer's guides covering the American West, including *Frommer's Montana & Wyoming* and *Frommer's Colorado*, as well as *Ramble: A Field Guide to the U.S.A.* and other Ramble titles for Fulcrum Publishing (www.fulcrum-books.com). Peterson's byline has also appeared in numerous newspapers and magazines, including the *New York Daily News*, *Denver Post*, and *Delta Sky*, and on winter-sports columns for Frommers.com. In his free time, he's an avid camper, skier, and hiker; a lifelong Broncos fan; and a part-time rock star (at least in the eyes of his niece Olivia and nephews Mitch and Sam).

Published by:

JOHN WILEY & SONS, INC.

111 River St.
Hoboken, NJ 07030-5774

ISBN 978-1-118-08607-0 (paper); ISBN 978-1-118-22341-3 (ebk); ISBN 978-1-118-23672-7 (ebk); ISBN 978-1-118-26167-5 (ebk)

Editor: Christine Ryan
Production Editor: Lindsay Conner
Cartographer: Elizabeth Puhl
Photo Editor: Richard Fox
Production by Wiley Indianapolis Composition Services
Front Cover Photo: The Organ and deadwood in Arches National Park © Jim Kruger / Vetta Collection / iStock Photo
Back Cover Photo: Salt Lake City © Utah Images / Alamy Images

For information on our other products and services or to obtain technical support, please contact our Customer Care Department within the U.S. at 877/762-2974, outside the U.S. at 317/572-3993 or fax 317/572-4002.

Wiley also publishes its books in a variety of electronic formats. Some content that appears in print may not be available in electronic formats.

Manufactured in the United States of America

5 4 3 2 1

CONTENTS

5 SALT LAKE CITY 45

6 THE NORTHERN WASATCH FRONT: UTAH'S OLD WEST 77

7 THE SOUTHERN WASATCH FRONT: WORLD-CLASS SKIING & MORE 106

8 DINOSAURS & NATURAL WONDERS IN UTAH'S NORTHEAST CORNER 150

9 UTAH'S DIXIE & THE COLORFUL SOUTHWEST CORNER 166

LIST OF MAPS

HOW TO CONTACT US

In researching this book, we discovered many wonderful places—hotels, restaurants, shops, and more. We're sure you'll find others. Please tell us about them, so we can share the information with your fellow travelers in upcoming editions. If you were disappointed with a recommendation, we'd love to know that, too. Please write to:

Frommer's Utah, 9th Edition
John Wiley & Sons, Inc. • 111 River St. • Hoboken, NJ 07030-5774
frommersfeedback@wiley.com

ADVISORY & DISCLAIMER

Travel information can change quickly and unexpectedly, and we strongly advise you to confirm important details locally before traveling, including information on visas, health and safety, traffic and transport, accommodation, shopping and eating out. We also encourage you to stay alert while traveling and to remain aware of your surroundings. Avoid civil disturbances, and keep a close eye on cameras, purses, wallets and other valuables.

While we have endeavored to ensure that the information contained within this guide is accurate and up-to-date at the time of publication, we make no representations or warranties with respect to the accuracy or completeness of the contents of this work and specifically disclaim all warranties, including without limitation warranties of fitness for a particular purpose. We accept no responsibility or liability for any inaccuracy or errors or omissions, or for any inconvenience, loss, damage, costs or expenses of any nature whatsoever incurred or suffered by anyone as a result of any advice or information contained in this guide.

The inclusion of a company, organization or Website in this guide as a service provider and/or potential source of further information does not mean that we endorse them or the information they provide. Be aware that information provided through some Websites may be unreliable and can change without notice. Neither the publisher or author shall be liable for any damages arising herefrom.

FROMMER'S STAR RATINGS, ICONS & ABBREVIATIONS

Every hotel, restaurant, and attraction listing in this guide has been ranked for quality, value, service, amenities, and special features using a **star-rating system.** In country, state, and regional guides, we also rate towns and regions to help you narrow down your choices and budget your time accordingly. Hotels and restaurants are rated on a scale of zero (recommended) to three stars (exceptional). Attractions, shopping, nightlife, towns, and regions are rated according to the following scale: zero stars (recommended), one star (highly recommended), two stars (very highly recommended), and three stars (must-see).

In addition to the star-rating system, we also use **eight feature icons** that point you to the great deals, in-the-know advice, and unique experiences that separate travelers from tourists. Throughout the book, look for:

special finds—those places only insiders know about

fun facts—details that make travelers more informed and their trips more fun

kids—best bets for kids and advice for the whole family

special moments—those experiences that memories are made of

overrated—places or experiences not worth your time or money

insider tips—great ways to save time and money

great values—where to get the best deals

warning—traveler's advisories are usually in effect

The following abbreviations are used for credit cards:

AE American Express	DISC Discover	V Visa
DC Diners Club	MC MasterCard	

TRAVEL RESOURCES AT FROMMERS.COM

Frommer's travel resources don't end with this guide. Frommer's website, **www.frommers. com,** has travel information on more than 4,000 destinations. We update features regularly, giving you access to the most current trip-planning information and the best airfare, lodging, and car-rental bargains. You can also listen to podcasts, connect with other Frommers.com members through our active-reader forums, share your travel photos, read blogs from guidebook editors and fellow travelers, and much more.

THE BEST OF UTAH

U tah is home to unfathomably beautiful natural features found within its national parks and monuments, but it also has its share of man-made wonders. Salt Lake City has a number of architectural highlights, including the city's centerpiece, the Mormon Temple. You'll also see this mix of natural and man-made at Utah's terrific ski resorts and jewel-like reservoirs, and throughout the state as you explore its rich and complicated history, a past populated by Utes, Mormon pioneers, rough-and-tumble mountain men, and others.

Cities **Salt Lake City** is the largest city in the state and home to many of its top attractions, including Temple Square and the Utah State Capitol. To the north, **Ogden** is worth a visit for its historic downtown core and proximity to three ski resorts in Ogden Valley. **Provo,** to the south, is home to Brigham Young University and the gateway to Provo Canyon and Sundance Resort.

Countryside The **Wasatch Mountains** are a playground winter and summer, featuring over 10 ski resorts (Alta and Deer Valley among them) and hundreds of miles of hiking and mountain-biking trails. Mount Timpanogos is the second highest mountain in the range and home to Timpanogos Peak National Monument. **Southern Utah** is a desert wonderland, featuring Arches, Canyonlands, Capitol Reef, Bryce Canyon, and Zion national parks.

Eating & Drinking Utah is mostly a traditional American destination in terms of culinary offerings. **Beef** and **local trout and game** are specialties. Utah was long known for having outdated **liquor laws,** but that all changed in 2009 when the state normalized its drinking laws, bringing it (mostly) in line with the rest of the country.

National Parks There may not be a better place in the United States to visit national parks. Utah has five: **Arches, Canyonlands, Capitol Reef, Bryce Canyon,** and **Zion.** In addition, it has seven national monuments: **Grand Staircase-Escalante, Natural Bridges, Rainbow Bridge, Cedar Breaks, Hovenweep, Timpanogos Cave,** and **Dinosaur.** It also has a Navajo Nation national park—**Monument Valley.**

THE best UTAH TRAVEL EXPERIENCES

- **Exploring Bryce Canyon National Park:** Among Utah's most scenic parks, Bryce Canyon is also one of the most accessible. Several trails lead down into the canyon—more like walks than hikes, so just about everyone can get to know this beautiful jewel up close. Part of the Rim Trail is even wheelchair accessible. The colorful rock formations are panoramically impressive when viewed from the rim but become fanciful works of art as you walk among them. See chapter 11.

- **Enjoying Capitol Reef National Park:** This tranquil park has an understated beauty all its own. And it's not too demanding, either: Wander through the orchards of Fruita, hike the Capitol Gorge Trail, stroll up the Grand Wash, or sit under the stars roasting marshmallows over a campfire. See chapter 12.

- **Houseboating on Lake Powell:** Kick back and relax while floating on the deep blue waters of man-made Lake Powell, with towering red rocks all around and an azure sky above. Feeling warm? Slip over the side for a dip in the cool water. Want a little exercise? Anchor yourself, and hike to the surrounding natural beauties, such as the Rainbow Bridge. See p. 254.

THE best VIEWS

- **The Narrows, Zion National Park:** The sheer 1,000-foot-high walls enclose you in a 20-foot-wide world of hanging gardens, waterfalls, and sculpted sandstone arches, with the Virgin River running beneath your boots—literally. The Narrows are so narrow that you can't walk beside the river. Instead, you have to wade right in it—but the views make it worth getting your feet wet. See p. 202.

- **Boulder Mountain Viewpoints** (btw. Escalante and Torrey): The panoramas from the road along the crest of Boulder Mountain are extraordinary. You can see Capitol Reef, miles to the east, and the valleys and lakes nestled in between. See p. 236.

- **The Queen's Garden, Bryce Canyon National Park:** Carved in stone by Mother Nature, these thousands of colorfully striped spires present a magnificent display when viewed from the rim. From the trail below, they dazzle as the early-morning sun throws them into stark relief. See p. 218.

- **Monument Valley Buttes at Sunset:** Impressive at any time, these stark sentinels of the desert take on a particularly dignified aura when the setting sun casts its deep colors over them, etching their profiles against a darkening sky. Although the park generally closes before sunset, you can arrange a sunset tour upon request—it's well worth the cost. See p. 295.

THE best FAMILY-VACATION EXPERIENCES

- **Camping at Cherry Hill Camping Resort** (Ogden): This fun-packed campground offers something for everybody: a water park with slides, pools, and even a pirate ship, plus miniature golf, batting cages, and aeroball (it's kind of like basketball). It's like staying in a theme park—a kid's dream come true. See p. 90.

- **Taking a Ride on the Heber Valley Historic Railroad:** Take a trip back in time on the "Heber Creeper," so called because of the way this historic steam train inches up the canyon from Provo. A ride on this once-proud passenger and freight line lets you experience travel the way it was in your grandparents' day. See p. 130.

- **Exploring Northeast Utah's Dinosaurland:** This is the real *Jurassic Park*—no special effects needed. First stop: Utah Field House of Natural History State Park in Vernal. Stroll through the Dinosaur Garden to admire the 18 life-size dinosaurs and other prehistoric creatures. Next, head to Dinosaur National Monument to see and touch—yes, touch—real fossilized dinosaur bones. See chapter 8.

- **Discovering Zion National Park:** The Junior Ranger Program, available at most national parks, is extensive here, with morning and afternoon activities for kids all summer. They'll have so much fun they won't notice they're learning about what makes this natural wonder so special. See p. 192.

THE best HIKING TRAILS

- **Indian Trail** (Ogden): Easily accessible from downtown Ogden, this 4.3-mile trail takes you into a thick forest of spruce and fir, and onto a mountainside that offers spectacular views of Ogden Canyon, including a beautiful waterfall. See p. 86.

- **Hidden Piñon Trail, Snow Canyon State Park** (St. George): This fairly easy self-guided nature trail has breathtaking panoramic views. Wander among lava rocks, into canyons, and over rocky flatland, along a trail lined with Mormon tea, cliffrose, prickly pear cactus, banana yucca, and other wild desert plants. See p. 173.

- **Lower Emerald Pools Trail, Zion National Park:** If green is your color, you'll love this trail—algae make three pools glow a deep, rich shade of emerald. The first part of the trail, navigable by wheelchairs with assistance, leads through a forest to the Lower Emerald Pool, with its lovely waterfall and hanging garden. The small pool just above it is so still and calm that the reflection in the water of the towering cliffs above looks like a photograph. See p. 201.

- **Navajo Loop/Queen's Garden Trail, Bryce Canyon National Park:** This not-too-difficult trail lets you truly experience magical Bryce Canyon. Start at Sunset Point and get the hardest part out of the way first. You'll pass Thor's Hammer, ponder the towering skyscrapers of Wall Street, and visit with majestic Queen Victoria herself—one of the park's most fanciful formations. See p. 218.

- **Petrified Forest Trail, Escalante Petrified Forest State Park** (Escalante): Along this steep nature trail, you'll walk through a stunted forest of junipers and piñons before reaching a field strewn with colorful chunks of petrified wood. The trail offers panoramic views of the town of Escalante and the surrounding stair-step plateaus. See p. 231.

THE best MOUNTAIN BIKING

- **Park City:** Some 350 miles of prime trails radiate out into the sage- and evergreen-laden open space surrounding Utah's best-known ski town. See p. 121.

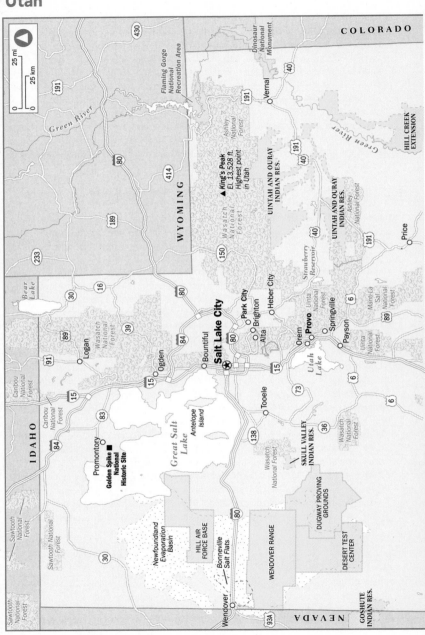

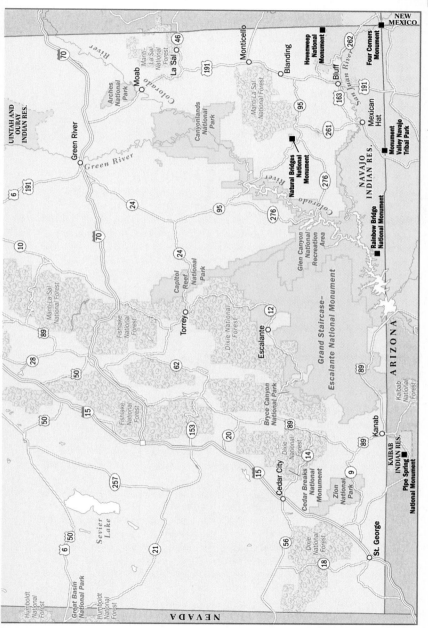

o **Brian Head Resort:** At 11,307 feet, there may not be a lot of oxygen, but the air is pure and clear, and the biking is great—especially when you can ride a chairlift up and bike down. Trails are everywhere, each with more magnificent scenery than the last. See p. 185.

o **Dave's Hollow Trail:** Just outside the entrance to Bryce Canyon National Park, this trail heads off into the national forest. The double track takes you through sun-dappled glades surrounded by tall ponderosa pines and spruce trees, all the way to fishing and camping at Tropic Reservoir. See p. 217.

o **Moab Slickrock Bike Trail:** A rite of passage for serious mountain bikers, this challenging yet rewarding trail takes 4 to 5 hours to complete. You'll enjoy breath-taking views of the Colorado River far below, the La Sal Mountains towering above, and the red sandstone formations of Arches National Park in the distance. See p. 267.

THE best DESTINATIONS FOR FISHING & WATERSPORTS

o **Strawberry Reservoir:** The number-one trout fishery in Utah for both cutthroat and rainbow, this gem of a lake is set magnificently among tall pines. You're really out in the woods here: The nearest town of any size is 30 miles away. So pick your spot and cast a line for dinner—you can't beat fresh-caught trout cooked over an open fire. See p. 135.

o **Jordanelle Reservoir** (in Jordanelle State Park, near Park City): The wide area at the dam of this boomerang-shaped reservoir is perfect for speedboats, water-skiers, and personal watercraft. The southeast end is designated for low-speed boating. Wherever you go, you'll have the beautiful Wasatch Mountains on all sides. See p. 132.

o **The Green River through Dinosaur National Monument:** The best way to see this spectacularly desolate country is from the river, the way explorer John Wesley Powell did in 1869. Crave excitement? Run the foaming rapids. Are peace and quiet your thing? Float mindlessly in the placid waters, leaving your troubles behind. See p. 158.

o **Lake Flaming Gorge:** Smaller and more intimate than Lake Powell—and located in a gloriously colorful setting—Lake Flaming Gorge is one of Utah's real hidden treasures. You can skim the water on skis or relax topside on a houseboat. As for the fishing, if you feel like the big ones always get away, this is the place for you—they're *all* big here. See p. 161.

o **Lake Powell:** This sprawling reservoir has what seems like zillions of finger can-yons reaching off the main watercourse of the Colorado River. You could spend weeks—maybe even months—water-skiing, swimming, fishing, exploring the myriad side canyons, and loafing about in the sun. See p. 250.

o **The Colorado River near Moab:** Tackle the placid stretches on your own in a canoe or kayak, or sign up with one of the outfitters and shoot the rapids. Whatever your style, a trip down the spectacular, scenic Colorado River is an adventure you won't forget. See p. 260.

THE best WILDLIFE-WATCHING

o **Rock Cliff, Jordanelle State Park** (near Park City): More than 160 species of birds, both resident and migratory, are found here. The park is an especially good place to spot eagles and other raptors that nest locally. Boardwalks and trails traverse the riparian wetlands, giving you a chance to observe wetlands life while reducing your ecological footprint. See p. 133.

o **Flaming Gorge National Recreation Area:** Take to the water to vie for a glimpse of the majestic bighorn sheep. The imposing beasts are sometimes seen on Kingfisher Island and near Hideout Canyon, on the north side of the reservoir, in spring and early summer. And keep your eyes peeled for the lovely osprey and rare peregrine falcon, occasionally spotted near their nests on the high rocky spires above the lake. See p. 159.

o **Coral Pink Sand Dunes State Park** (near Kanab): If you climb the dunes early in the morning, you're sure to see the footprints of jackrabbits, kangaroo rats, and the occasional mule deer or coyote. But the park is also a habitat for scorpions and fascinating but poisonous (and sometimes bioluminescent) arachnids that often prey on each other. Humans aren't their natural targets, but it's always best to keep your distance. See p. 188.

o **Escalante Petrified Forest State Park** (Escalante): Willows and cottonwoods line the banks of the reservoir, one of the few wetlands birding sites in southern Utah. The park is home to a wide variety of ducks, plus coots, herons, and swallows. You might also see eagles, ospreys, American kestrels, and other raptors. Cottontail and blacktail jackrabbits, squirrels, and beavers inhabit the area as well. See p. 231.

THE best DOWNHILL SKIING

o **Snowbasin** (Ogden Valley): Families love Snowbasin because there's something for everyone here, no matter what your ability. The resort is particularly popular with intermediates, who love the long, easy, well-groomed cruising runs. Experts can expect challenges, such as an abundance of untracked powder and Utah's third-highest vertical drop. See p. 97.

o **Beaver Mountain** (The Northern Wasatch Front): Visiting this small, family-oriented ski area is like going home—it's just plain comfortable. There's no glitz, no fancy anything, just lots of personal attention, plenty of snow, and great terrain with beautifully maintained trails. See p. 98.

o **Alta** (Little Cottonwood Canyon): All serious skiers must make a pilgrimage to Alta. It offers the best skiing in the state—and some of the lightest powder in the world—especially for advanced skiers willing to hike a bit for perfect conditions. If you're not up to black-diamond level yet, don't worry: Beginners and intermediates will find plenty of cruising ground, too. See p. 110.

o **Park City and Deer Valley:** These resorts offer not only excellent powder skiing on a wide variety of terrains, but also the best shopping, nightlife, lodging, and dining in all of Utah's ski areas—and for that matter, in all of Utah. Park City is the party town; Deer Valley is its grown-up, sophisticated sibling. They're less than 5 minutes apart by road, so why not take advantage of the best of both? See p. 117 for Park City and p. 116 for Deer Valley.

THE best PLACES TO DISCOVER AMERICAN INDIAN CULTURE

o **The Great Gallery in Horseshoe Canyon, Canyonlands National Park:** In a remote and hard-to-reach section of Canyonlands National Park is the Great Gallery, an 80-foot-long panel of rock art dating back several thousand years. It's one of the biggest and best prehistoric murals you'll find anywhere. See p. 286.

o **Monument Valley Navajo Tribal Park:** You've seen Monument Valley Navajo Tribal Park immortalized in movies, on TV, and in advertisements. While the Old West may be gone, many Navajos still call this area home. A Navajo guide can give you the Navajo perspective on this majestic land and take you to areas not otherwise open to visitors. See p. 295.

o **Hovenweep National Monument:** This deserted valley contains some of the most striking and isolated archaeological sites in the Four Corners: the remains of curious sandstone towers built more than 700 years ago. These mysterious structures keep archaeologists guessing. See p. 300.

o **Mesa Verde National Park (Colorado):** The largest archaeological preserve in the country is also home to the most impressive cliff dwellings in the Southwest. The sites run the gamut from simple pit houses to extensive cliff dwellings, all fascinating to explore. See p. 302.

THE best LUXURY HOTELS

o **The Grand America Hotel** (Salt Lake City; ✆ 800/621-4505; www.grandamerica. com): Built for the 2002 Olympics, the Grand America occupies an entire city block in downtown Salt Lake City and offers top-notch service, amenities, and decor. The marriage of superb design and deluxe furnishings has resulted in exquisitely comfortable guest rooms and suites. See p. 50.

o **Hotel Monaco** (Salt Lake City; ✆ 800/294-9710; www.monaco-saltlakecity. com): This hotel mixes traditional and contemporary styling in rooms that brim with an eclectic array of patterns, textures, and colors. The pet-friendly Monaco lets you bring your animal companion along, and even provides a loaner goldfish on request. See p. 52.

o **Montage Deer Valley** (Park City; ✆ 435/604-1300; www.montagedeervalley. com): Opened in 2010, the Montage Deer Valley (the first outside Southern California) looms above the resort, with luxury (and rates) similarly at the pinnacle of the resort. See p. 123.

o **Stein Eriksen Lodge** (Deer Valley; ✆ 800/453-1302; www.steinlodge.com): The Stein Eriksen is grandly elegant yet warm and welcoming, with cozy niches in the dignified lobby and lavishly comfortable suites. Attendants in the whirlpool, sauna, and fitness room are on hand to pamper you and attend to your every need, but they're so unobtrusive that you'll feel right at home—contentedly, luxuriously at home. See p. 123.

o **Amangiri** (near Lake Powell; ✆ 877/695-8999; www.amanresorts.com): A secluded, minimalist desert compound, Amangiri offers design, comfort, service, and opulence that are nothing short of superlative. Rooms are ultrachic, with two outdoor sitting areas each (the suite even has a private pool), and transcendent views. See p. 259.

THE best BED & BREAKFASTS

- **Inn on the Hill** (Salt Lake City; ✆ **801/328-1466;** www.innonthehillslc.com): Two blocks from both the Utah State Capitol and Temple Square, this stately mansion atop Capitol Hill is one of Salt Lake City's greatest B&Bs, thanks in no small part to its tremendous city and mountain views. Look for original details—such as wavy and stained-glass windows and steam heat. See p. 52.
- **Atomic Chalet** (near Ogden; ✆ **801/745-0538;** www.atomicchalet.com): Growing up in the shadow of a nuclear power plant near San Diego gave Wes Welch the inspiration for the name of his (and his wife Keri's) inn, but his experience as a professional volleyball player in the European Alps inspired its style and service. See p. 89.
- **Blue Boar Inn** (Midway; ✆ **888/654-1400;** www.theblueboarinn.com): Named for a watering hole in Robin Hood lore, the Blue Boar Inn is tucked into an upscale neighborhood in historic Midway, under the beautiful mountain vista of Wasatch Mountain State Park. This is a special property, with a dozen attractive and plush guest rooms named for poets and authors. See p. 136.
- **Hines Mansion Luxury Bed & Breakfast** (Provo; ✆ **800/428-5636;** www.hines mansion.com): A Victorian mansion ripe with vintage charm, this is a wonderful place to celebrate a wedding anniversary or romantic occasion, with complimentary sparkling cider and two-person whirlpool tubs in every room. See p. 146.
- **Green Gate Village Historic Bed & Breakfast** (✆ **800/350-6999;** www.greengate village.com): One of the most delightful lodgings in St. George, this bed-and-breakfast inn is actually 10 separate buildings—all restored pioneer homes from the late 1800s, sitting in their own flower-filled little "village" across the street from Town Square. See p. 176.
- **Stone Canyon Inn** (near Bryce Canyon National Park; ✆ **866/489-4680;** www. stonecanyoninn.com): Quiet seclusion, loads of charm, and absolutely splendid views are only three of the reasons why this inn is so highly recommended—it is also very upscale and the place to come to be pampered. Each of the six guest rooms is unique, with queen-size or king-size beds, handsome wood furnishings, and a classic Western look. The luxurious cottages each have two bedrooms and two bathrooms, a gas fireplace, full kitchen, and a private deck with a hot tub. See p. 223.
- **Sunflower Hill Luxury Inn** (Moab; ✆ **800/662-2786;** www.sunflowerhill.com): Loaded with country charm, this delightful B&B makes you feel like you're at Grandma's, where family relics surround you and handmade quilts keep you warm at night. What's more, this may be the quietest lodging in Moab, and the grassy, shady grounds are especially inviting on a hot day. See p. 271.

THE best LODGES

- **Red Canyon Lodge** (Flaming Gorge National Recreation Area; ✆ **435/889-3759;** www.redcanyonlodge.com): Not really a lodge at all, this group of delightful 1930s cabins was remodeled in the 1990s. Your choice of TV- and telephone-free accommodations ranges from rustic to luxurious. The forest setting, complete with a private lake, is spectacular. See p. 164.

○ **The Lodge at Bryce Canyon** (✆ **877/386-4383**): This handsome sandstone and ponderosa-pine lodge is the perfect place to stay while you're visiting the national park. The suites are outfitted with white wicker furniture, ceiling fans, and sitting rooms. But go for one of the cabins—the high ceilings give the impression of spaciousness, and the gas-burning stone fireplaces and log beams make them positively cozy. See p. 221.

THE best RESTAURANTS

○ **Bambara** (Hotel Monaco, Salt Lake City; ✆ **801/363-5454;** www.bambara-slc. com): An ideal setting for a romantic meal, this popular restaurant brings a host of influences to the table, from Asian to Cajun. The Utah corn bisque is delectable, and the filet mignon with roasted shallot-cabernet sauce melts in your mouth. See p. 53.

○ **Tuscany** (Salt Lake City; ✆ **801/227-9919;** www.tuscanyslc.com): Located in a quaintly elegant setting at the foot of the Wasatch Mountains and owned by the 7'4" Utah Jazz shot-blocking legend Mark Eaton, Tuscany resembles an Italian mountain lodge. The Northern Italian cuisine is tempered with Western influences, resulting in delicious dishes such as oven-roasted filet of salmon with pancetta-pesto crust served with toasted vegetable couscous. See p. 55.

○ **Glitretind Restaurant** (Park City; ✆ **435/649-3700;** www.steinlodge.com): Located in the elegant Stein Eriksen Lodge, this equally stylish restaurant is possibly the best dining experience in the entire state. The Glitretind serves innovative meals that change with the seasons but always incorporate local game. Plus, it all comes with views of the spectacular Wasatch Mountains. See p. 126.

○ **Zoom** (Park City; ✆ **435/649-9108;** www.zoomparkcity.com): Gorgeous black-and-white photos of Hollywood luminaries from the Sundance Film Festival grace the walls of this classic Park City spot, which is owned by Robert Redford. Choose from the seasonal menu of salads and delicious burgers to pasta, seafood, and ribs. See p. 129.

○ **Painted Pony** (St. George; ✆ **435/634-1700;** www.painted-pony.com): The Painted Pony is the best restaurant between Las Vegas and Salt Lake City—though its vibe is more California than Utah. The creative menu includes twists on familiar dishes such as seared ahi with wasabi aioli. See p. 178.

○ **Cafe Diablo** (Torrey; ✆ **435/425-3070;** www.cafediablo.net): Looks can be deceiving. What appears to be a simple small-town cafe in a converted home is, in fact, a very fine restaurant—among southern Utah's best—offering innovative beef, pork, chicken, seafood, and vegetarian selections, many created with a Southwestern flair. See p. 248.

THE best OF THE PERFORMING ARTS

○ **Mormon Tabernacle Choir** (Salt Lake City): Hear the glorious sounds of this world-renowned choir in its home on Temple Square. When not on tour, the choir rehearses Thursday evenings and performs Sunday mornings. Both events are open to the public, free of charge. See p. 58.

- **Utah Symphony** (Salt Lake City, Park City): Who'd expect to find one of the country's top symphony orchestras in Utah? Well, here it is: an excellent ensemble that tours worldwide and provides the soundtrack to films in the Sundance Summer series. See p. 73.
- **Utah Shakespearean Festival** (Cedar City): To go or not to go, that is the question. But if theater's your thing, by all means go. Four of the Bard's plays, plus two by other period and contemporary playwrights, are presented each summer, and they're grand entertainment. See p. 181.

UTAH IN DEPTH

U tah is certainly one of the most beautiful places in the United States. It's also one of the most misunderstood. Because of the state's once-strict liquor laws (they were normalized in 2009) and its strong association with the Church of Jesus Christ of Latter-day Saints (the Mormons), many expect Utah to be culturally at sea, so to speak. But visitors often come away with a much different notion of the Beehive State, one that includes not only beautiful places, but friendly locals and clean, well-managed cities. Visitors to Utah rightly target its parks and myriad natural wonders, but the state's fascinating history should not be ignored. Take time to delve a little into the stories of Brigham Young and the Mormon pioneers: These tales are not only unique, they're also definitively American. In this chapter, I introduce you to modern-day Utah and provide a background on the state's history and the influential Church of Jesus Christ of Latter-day Saints, while also touching on Utah's geography and its depiction in popular culture.

UTAH TODAY

Some people think Utah is stuck in the 1950s—quaintly or annoyingly so, depending on your perspective. This time warp is due in large part to the strong church influence and the corollary Mormon emphasis on family values, which make Utah a notably family-oriented state. People here are friendly, the crime rate is low, and Utah is generally a very pleasant state to visit.

But don't expect to find a lot of wild nightlife here. While alcohol laws were normalized in 2009—meaning no more memberships in private clubs—attitudes toward alcohol in Utah are considerably more conservative than what you'll find in neighboring states. Those of us who enjoy a glass of wine or beer or a mixed drink with lunch or dinner need to choose our restaurants carefully. This isn't universal, of course; in terms of nightlife, Park City can hold its own with any of the top ski resorts in Colorado, and Ogden and Moab are fun, wild-'n'-crazy kinds of places—at least by Utah standards.

Beyond the liberalization of alcohol laws, other changes are in the wind as more and more outsiders move to Utah. Many escapees from California's smog, crime, crowds, and taxes have brought their mountain bikes and West Coast philosophy to southern Utah's national park country, while others have been lured to the Wasatch Front, particularly between Salt Lake City and Provo, by the ski hills and the burgeoning high-tech industry here. These newcomers have brought demands for more services, better restaurants, upscale shops, and a greater range of activities. They're also accused by some Utahns of bringing with them the very problems they sought to escape.

The growth of tourism is causing traffic congestion problems, mainly because there are so many tourists, and because everyone wants to visit at the same time. Zion National Park has been affected the most. In 2000, in an attempt to deal with the problem, the park instituted a mandatory shuttle-bus service. Bryce Canyon National Park, too, has implemented a shuttle.

Another current issue that will affect you is the wilderness-vs.-development debate. As in many Western states, Utah endures an ongoing battle between business interests, who see federal lands as prime targets for development or resource extraction, and environmentalists, who are intent on preserving what they consider to be one of the last true wildernesses of the American West. The wilderness-preservation side sees the businesspeople as greedy land-grabbers who care nothing for the future and see the lands only as a commodity to be exploited. On the other hand, the ranchers, loggers, and miners see the environmentalists as selfish, well-off newcomers who don't care that other people need to earn a living and just want the government to designate vast wilderness areas as their personal playgrounds. To some extent, they're both right. We'll just have to wait and see what happens.

Even though its feet may be planted in the 1950s, Utah is actively looking toward the future. It's even trying to tackle such modern problems as population growth and air pollution head-on. But the story's not all grim: The Beehive State worked hard to prepare for the 2002 Winter Olympic Games, and all that work paid off with a successful Olympic Games—the legend of which continues to live on.

During the 2000s, this helped catalyze growth: Utah grew at an incredible 24% clip—more than double the national average—thanks largely to a high birth rate but also to plenty of newcomers from California and elsewhere. As of 2011, the Beehive State was also the youngest state in the U.S. (the median age is about 27 years old) and poised for even more growth in the years ahead. The current challenge for the state is to balance all of this growth (and the problems that accompany it) with the quality of life that accounts for at least some of the growth.

LOOKING BACK: UTAH HISTORY

THE FIRST PEOPLES   The first known inhabitants of Utah were the Desert Gatherers, who, from around 9000 B.C., wandered about the Great Basin and Colorado Plateau searching for food. However, being nomadic, they left little evidence of their time here. The Ancestral Puebloan (also called Anasazi) culture arose in the Four Corners region at about the time of Christ; by A.D. 1200, their villages were scattered throughout present-day Utah. For some reason—possibly drought—by 1300 the villages had been abandoned, leaving the ruins seen standing today at Hovenweep National Monument and other sites. The descendants of these early people—Shoshone, Ute, Goshute, and Paiute—were among the Native Americans inhabiting the area when the first Europeans arrived.

Another prehistoric group, the Fremont peoples, settled in central Utah, establishing small villages of pit houses. They arrived about A.D. 1200, but had disappeared by the time the first Europeans reached Utah.

Spanish explorer Juan Maria Antonio Rivera and his European expedition arrived at the Colorado River near present-day Moab in 1765. Eleven years later, two Spanish Franciscan friars reached Utah Lake and mapped it, hoping to return to establish a Spanish colony. Spain did not pursue the idea, however, and the next Europeans to explore the area were fur traders in the early 1800s. Then, in July 1847, Brigham

Young led the first Mormons (a nickname for members of the Church of Jesus Christ of Latter-day Saints) into the Salt Lake Valley, and the flood of Mormon immigrants began. These were the people who established Utah as we know it today.

MEET THE MORMONS   The Church of Jesus Christ of Latter-day Saints was born in the 1820s when Joseph Smith had a revelation: After much prayer asking which Christian church he should join, Smith was told by God and Jesus that he would be the one to restore the church that Christ established when he walked the earth. An angel named Moroni then gave Smith some ancient inscribed gold tablets that, under divine inspiration, he was able to translate into the Book of Mormon. In 1830, Smith and his followers published the Book of Mormon and founded the Church of Jesus Christ of Latter-day Saints (LDS) in upstate New York. Smith's revelations and the fervor with which his followers believed and tried to spread the word bred hostility among their more skeptical neighbors; the early Mormons were soon forced to leave New York.

Smith and his followers settled in Ohio and Missouri in the early 1830s. A few years of prosperity were followed by strife, and the growing Mormon community was once again forced to flee. They established their church headquarters at Nauvoo, Illinois, reclaiming a swampy area along the Mississippi river. Within a few years, Nauvoo was the second-largest city in Illinois, and the Mormons continued to grow and flourish. Also during these years, the practice of polygamy began slowly and quietly among church leaders. Both their nonconformism and their success bred fear and anger in their opponents, who considered Smith and his followers a political, economic, and religious threat. In 1844, a mob stormed the jail in Carthage, Illinois, where Joseph Smith and his brother Hyrum were being held on treason charges, and murdered them.

Brigham Young, a confidant of Smith, became the second leader of the church, displaying a genius for organization in the evacuation of Nauvoo and the subsequent migration westward in search of a new Zion. In 1846, the Mormons headed west from Illinois, establishing winter quarters on the far side of the Missouri River, near present-day Omaha, Nebraska.

FOUNDING ZION   In the spring of 1847, Brigham Young started out with the first group of emigrants—two children, three women, and 143 men. When the first group reached the mouth of Emigration Canyon and looked out upon the empty wasteland of Salt Lake Valley, Young reportedly said, "This is the right place." Within hours of their arrival, the pioneers had begun building an irrigation system and establishing fields for growing food. In the next few days, Young chose the site of the temple and laid out the new city in a grid system beginning at the southeast corner of Temple Square.

That first year almost ended the settlement before it had properly begun. The sod roofs leaked; provisions ran low, forcing the pioneers to eat whatever they could find, including the sego lily bulb (now the state flower); a late frost damaged the wheat and vegetables; and drought damaged more. Then a plague of crickets descended on what was left of the crops. After 2 weeks, the crickets were effectively eliminated by sea gulls (now Utah's state bird) that came from the Great Salt Lake to devour the insects by the thousands, and enough of the crops were saved to feed the pioneers. A monument in Temple Square commemorates their deliverance from famine.

By the end of 1848, almost 3,000 Mormons had arrived in the Salt Lake Valley. It was now a part of the United States, ceded to the Union by Mexico. In 1849, the Mormons petitioned to have their territory declared the State of Deseret, a name that comes from the Book of Mormon and means "honeybee." Denied statehood, the territory of Utah—named after the Ute tribe—was created in 1850, with Brigham Young as territorial governor. Although it was no longer officially run by the church, the territory was assured of its continued influence: The vast majority of voters were Mormons who elected church leaders to positions of authority in the civic domain as well.

In these years, non-Mormons—or "Gentiles," as the Mormons call them—began traveling through the valley, many on their way to or from the gold fields of California. Salt Lake City was an ideal spot for resting and resupplying before setting out again. The Mormons often bought horses, livestock, and supplies, in turn reselling what they didn't need to other travelers. The travelers who passed through to rest and trade took with them a collection of sometimes-confused ideas about the Mormons, including their fascinating practice of polygamy. The journals of these travelers gave the nation its first real knowledge—however incomplete—of Mormon faith and customs.

THE UTAH WAR In 1857, a new governor was sent from Washington to supplant Young. Fearing that he would be rejected, President Buchanan sent federal troops to escort him. The Mormons harassed the troops by driving off livestock and attacking their supply trains, forcing them to winter in western Wyoming. Although the Mormons were prepared to fight to keep the army out, neither Brigham Young nor President Buchanan wanted bloodshed. As the new governor entered Salt Lake City, Mormon families packed their belongings and awaited the order to move.

An estimated 30,000 Mormons left their homes in Salt Lake City and the northern settlements, moving south over a period of 2 months, leaving the capital virtually deserted by mid-May. The exodus drew national and international attention and placed the U.S. government in quite an unfavorable light—the government had persecuted innocent people, steamrolling over the fundamental right to religious freedom. An uneasy peace was finally established, the Mormons returned to their homes, and the two groups lived side by side until the outbreak of the Civil War, when the army was called back east.

BECOMING THE BEEHIVE STATE After the close of the Civil War, attention was again directed toward the enforcement of antipolygamy laws, and many Mormons were imprisoned. Finally, in 1890, the church leaders issued a statement: Based on a revelation from God, the church was no longer teaching plural marriage and no person would be permitted to enter into it. With this major bar to statehood removed, Utah became the 45th state on January 4, 1896.

The Depression hit Utah hard; the unemployment rate reached 35% and per capita income was cut in half. Not until World War II was industry brought back to life. Several military bases established during the war became permanent installations, and missile plants were built along the Wasatch Front. After the war, steel companies reopened, the mining industry boomed, and high-tech businesses moved in. By the mid-1960s, the economy base had shifted from agricultural to industrial.

Dams were built—including Glen Canyon Dam, creating Lake Powell, and Flaming Gorge Dam, creating Lake Flaming Gorge—to further the cause of industry and to ensure water and energy supplies, but they had an additional benefit: They provided recreational opportunities for a modern society with an increasing amount of discretionary income and free time. Ski resorts began opening in the Wasatch Mountains. In the early 1980s, after outsiders started showing interest in Utah as a recreational playground, Salt Lake City International Airport and the city's cultural center, the Salt Palace complex, expanded.

As the mining industries began winding down, tourism and service industries grew; today, they account for more of the state's economy than any other industry. In the 1990s, the state lobbied hard to be named the host of the 2002 Winter Olympics, and then built numerous venues and even roads to assure that the games would be a success. The Mormons, who spent their first decades fleeing from outsiders, are now welcoming them with open arms, and they're coming in droves.

A LOOK AT MODERN MORMONISM—OR, YES, YOU CAN GET A DRINK IN UTAH

Utah is a Mormon state. Not officially, of course—strict state and federal laws are meant to keep church doctrine out of government—and not as much as in the past, when practically all Utahns (and definitely all the decision makers) were LDS church members. But because about three-fifths of the state's population belong to the Church of Jesus Christ of Latter-day Saints, and most of them take their religion very seriously, it's hardly surprising that the teachings and values of the church have a strong influence in the voting booth and echo throughout the halls of government.

Although some conflict is inevitable as government and community leaders try to adapt to Utah's growing cultural diversity, this discord means little to most visitors, who come to Utah to experience its scenery, recreation, and history. What you'll discover is that Utah is much like the rest of the United States, although generally not as hip as California or as multicultural as New York or New Mexico.

What Mormons Believe

Mormons are Christians, believing in Jesus Christ as the son of God and the Bible as the word of God, as do all the many offshoots of Christianity. But a significant difference is the role played by the **Book of Mormon,** which they believe to be God's word as revealed to and translated by church founder Joseph Smith.

This book tells of two tribes of people who left Israel in biblical times and made their way to the Western Hemisphere. Mormons believe that these people were the ancestors of today's American Indians. The Book of Mormon teaches that after his resurrection, Christ spent about 40 days among these people, preaching, healing, and establishing his church. The Mormons believe that Joseph Smith was commanded to restore the church as organized by Christ during his ministry on earth.

The first four principles of the faith are belief in Jesus Christ, repentance, baptism by immersion, and the laying on of hands to receive "the Gift of the Holy Ghost" (in which a priest places his hands on a church member for the transference of spirituality). Another important tenet of the church is respect for the supreme authority of church leaders and the belief in the revelations from God to these leaders.

The family unit is of paramount importance to Mormons, and they believe that marriage lasts literally forever, transcending death. They believe that sex outside of marriage and homosexuality are sins. The church encourages the family to work, play, and study together, and young adults—most men and some women—generally spend 1 or 2 years as missionaries. Mormons also believe in the baptism and redemption of those already dead—hence their strong interest in genealogy.

It's practically impossible to discuss the church without discussing polygamy, which caused so much antagonism toward church members in the 19th century. But polygamy—or plural marriage, as the church dubbed it—has little to do with what the LDS church was and is. Polygamy came about as a "revelation" to church founder Joseph Smith in the 1840s, was practiced by a relatively small percentage of church members, and was outlawed by church officials in 1890. Today, polygamy is prohibited both by church doctrine and state law, although it does continue among an estimated 30,000 rebels, who have left the church to practice their own brand of fundamentalist Mormonism.

These polygamists, however, have brought unwanted media attention to Utah in recent years. The kidnapping of 14-year-old Elizabeth Smart in 2002 and a separate failed kidnapping attempt in 2003 in Salt Lake City both occurred in connection with polygamy. Smart was eventually found unharmed, and police arrested a man described as a self-proclaimed prophet and polygamist who had been thrown out of the Church of Jesus Christ of Latter-day Saints for "activity promoting bizarre teachings and lifestyle far afield from the principles and doctrines of the church."

Warren Jeffs, then leader of the Fundamentalist Church of Jesus Christ of Latter-day Saints (based just across the Utah border in Colorado City, Arizona) and self-proclaimed prophet, was placed on the FBI's Ten Most Wanted List when he went on the lam to avoid prosecution for arranging illegal marriages between his adult male followers and underage girls, sexual conduct with minors, and incest. His 2006 arrest near Las Vegas and subsequent trials in Utah and Texas made national headlines. In 2011, he was convicted of sexually assaulting underage girls and sentenced to life in prison.

What Mormonism Means for Visitors to Utah

This strong religious influence has brought about some strange laws regarding alcoholic beverages, although it's definitely not true that you can't get a drink here. Cigarettes and other tobacco products are also readily available, but smoking is prohibited by state law in all restaurants—legislation that is becoming more and more common across the United States. Although cola drinks contain caffeine, the church doesn't specifically prohibit their consumption. Some Mormons drink Coke or Pepsi; others refrain. You'll generally have no trouble at all purchasing whatever type of soft drink you want, with or without caffeine. Interestingly, there are exceptions: Although there are plenty of soda machines on the campus of church-owned Brigham Young University in Provo, they stock only decaffeinated products, and this is also true of church offices.

You might find it pleasantly surprising that, although the Mormons of Utah can be pretty tough on themselves regarding the above-mentioned "sins," virtually every Utahn encountered in researching this book—and a great many were Mormons—was tolerant of others' beliefs and lifestyles. Of course, there is no guarantee that you won't run across some holier-than-thou busybody who insists on lecturing you on the evils of Demon Rum, tobacco, promiscuity, or homosexuality, but experience has shown that they generally respect each individual's right to make his or her own moral choices.

Be forewarned, though: Mormons are practically missionaries by definition, and will, with only the slightest encouragement, want to enthusiastically help you see the wisdom of their ways.

Because the church emphasizes the importance of family, you'll see lots of kids—Utah is noted for having the highest fertility rate in the nation, year after year. This makes Utah a very kid-friendly state, with lots of family-oriented activities and attractions. Overall, prices for kids and families are often very reasonable. And because many Mormon families observe Monday evening as a time to spend together, sports facilities, amusement parks, and similar venues often offer family discounts on Mondays; if you're traveling with your family, watch for them.

Although about 60% of Utah's population are LDS church members, church membership varies greatly from community to community, so the number of Mormons you'll encounter will vary considerably. Although it's the world headquarters of the church, Salt Lake City is just under half Mormon; some of the smaller towns approach 100%. Of major cities, Provo has the strongest church influence. Although St. George was historically a major stronghold for church members, recent migration from other parts of the United States (namely Southern California) is gradually diluting that influence. You'll probably find the least church influence in Ogden, Park City, and Moab, which, in recent years, have attracted large numbers of outsiders.

> ## Impressions
>
> *TV you can make on the back lot, but for the big screen, for the real outdoor dramas, you have to do it where God put the West . . . and there is no better example of this than around Moab.*
>
> —John Wayne, while filming *The Comancheros*, in 1961

EATING & DRINKING

Utah has traditionally been a very meat-and-potatoes destination, but in recent years, there has been a boom in culinary creativity centered in Salt Lake City and the state's ski resorts. While the liquor laws were brought in line with the rest of the country in 2009, there are still some quirks: Some establishments require you to order food to get a drink and can sell only beer and other low-alcohol-content drinks. There is a flourishing microbrewery culture here and a smattering of wineries; and the first new distillery in modern times (High West Distillery in Park City) opened in 2010.

In this book, restaurants categorized as expensive typically charge $15 to $40 for a dinner main course, moderate means $10 to $20 for a dinner main course, and inexpensive indicates most main courses are under $10 for dinner.

WHEN TO GO

Deciding when to visit Utah depends on what you want to do and which places you want to see. Those traveling without children will likely want to avoid visiting during school vacations. Ski resorts are most popular during the Christmas and New Year's holidays (and the room rates accordingly shoot into the stratosphere), and national parks are inundated with visitors in July and August. The best time to visit the parks and almost everything else in southern Utah is spring or fall; summer is too hot, particularly in St. George.

Weather

Utah has four seasons, but because of the wide range of elevation—from 2,200 to 13,528 feet—conditions vary considerably across the state. Generally, as in other desert states, summer days are hot but nights are cool. Winters are cold and snowy, except in southwest Utah's "Dixie" (which includes St. George), where it seldom gets very cold and snow is rare. Mountain temperatures are always pleasantly cool and can be quite cold at night, even in summer.

Average Monthly High/Low Temperatures (°F/°C) & Precipitation (in./cm)

		JAN	FEB	MAR	APR	MAY	JUNE	JULY	AUG	SEPT	OCT	NOV	DEC
MOAB	TEMP. (°F)	37/17	42/22	53/30	65/40	75/48	87/57	92/64	89/61	82/54	68/42	49/27	39/20
	TEMP. (°C)	2/–8	5/–5	11/–1	18/4	23/8	30/13	33/17	31/16	27/12	20/5	9/–2	3/–6
	PRECIP. (IN.)	0.8	0.7	0.7	0.6	0.6	0.4	0.4	1.2	0.7	0.8	0.7	0.5
	PRECIP. (CM)	2	1.8	1.8	1.5	1.5	1	1	3	1.8	2	1.8	1.3
Elev. 4,000 ft.													
PARK CITY	TEMP. (°F)	33/12	38/17	43/22	55/30	63/36	74/44	82/50	80/50	71/41	60/31	43/21	33/13
	TEMP. (°C)	0/–10	3/–8	6/–5	12/0	17/2	23/6	27/10	26/10	21/4	15/0	6/–6	0/–10
	PRECIP. (IN.)	2.8	1.6	2.1	1.2	1.6	1.1	1.9	1.6	1.8	1.5	1.7	2.7
	PRECIP. (CM)	7.1	4.1	5.3	3	4.1	2.8	4.8	4.1	4.6	3.8	4.3	6.9
Elev. 7,000 ft.													
ST. GEORGE	TEMP. (°F)	53/24	59/29	67/35	76/42	85/49	96/57	101/65	99/63	93/53	80/41	65/30	54/24
	TEMP. (°C)	11/–4	15/–1	19/1	24/5	29/9	35/13	38/18	37/17	33/11	26/5	18/–1	12/–4
	PRECIP. (IN.)	1.4	1.6	1.6	0.9	0.6	0.3	0.8	1.1	0.8	1	0.9	1.2
	PRECIP. (CM)	3.7	4.2	4.2	2.2	1.6	0.8	2.1	2.7	2	2.6	2.3	3
Elev. 2,880 ft.													
SALT LAKE	TEMP. (°F)	37/20	43/24	52/31	62/38	72/46	83/54	92/62	90/61	80/51	66/40	50/30	39/22
CITY	TEMP. (°C)	2/–6	6/–4	11/0	16/3	22/7	28/12	33/16	32/16	26/10	18/4	10/–1	3/–5
	PRECIP. (IN.)	1.3	1.2	1.8	2	1.8	0.9	0.7	0.8	1.1	1.3	1.3	1.3
	PRECIP. (CM)	3.3	3	4.6	5.1	4.6	2.3	1.8	2	2.8	3.3	3.3	3.3
Elev. 4,330 ft.													

HOLIDAYS

Banks, government offices, post offices, and many stores, restaurants, and museums are closed on the following legal national holidays: January 1 (New Year's Day), the third Monday in January (Martin Luther King, Jr., Day), the third Monday in February (Presidents' Day), the last Monday in May (Memorial Day), July 4 (Independence Day), the first Monday in September (Labor Day), the second Monday in October (Columbus Day), November 11 (Veterans' Day/Armistice Day), the fourth Thursday in November (Thanksgiving Day), and December 25 (Christmas). The Tuesday after the first Monday in November is Election Day, a federal government holiday in presidential-election years (held every 4 years, and next in 2012). July 24 (Pioneer Day) is an official state holiday celebrated July 24 to commemorate the arrival of Brigham Young and the Mormon pioneers in 1847; many businesses and attractions are closed.

Utah Calendar of Events

For an exhaustive list of events beyond those listed here, check http://events.frommers.com, where you'll find a searchable, up-to-the-minute roster of what's happening in cities all over the world.

JANUARY

Sundance Film Festival, Park City and other locations. Sponsored by Robert Redford's Sundance Resort, this festival honors the best independent films with screenings and seminars. Visit http://festival.sundance.org for schedules and information on obtaining tickets. Late January.

FEBRUARY

Freestyle World Cup Ski Races, Deer Valley. This event is made up of sanctioned World Cup races and demonstrations. The location: the Champion and White Owl ski runs on Deer Valley's 2002 Olympic runs. Call ✆ **435/649-1000.** Early February.

Bryce Canyon Winter Festival, Bryce. This winter celebration, with snowshoe tours and other activities, takes place amid the colorful rock formations of the Bryce Canyon National Park area. Call ✆ **435/834-5341.** Mid-February.

MARCH

Hostlers Model Railroad Festival, Ogden. Fans of model trains gather at historic Union Station, where trains of all shapes and sizes are on display; model-train collectors can locate those hard-to-find items. Call ℰ **801/394-4952** or visit www.hostlers.info. Early March.

St. George Art Festival, St. George. This outdoor fine-arts festival draws artists and visitors from all over the American West. Call ℰ **435/627-4500;** otherwise visit www.sgcity.org/artfestival. Mid-March.

APRIL

Easter Rendezvous, Ogden. A gathering of mountain men at Fort Buenaventura, with black-powder shooting contests and other early-19th-century activities. Call ℰ **801/399-8099.** Early to mid-April.

April Action Car Show, Moab. A grand display of vintage hot rods, classic cars, and more, plus a Saturday night cruise down Main Street and fun contests. Call ℰ **800/635-6622** or visit http://aprilaction.moabadventurechannel.com. Late April.

MAY

Golden Spike Reenactment, Golden Spike National Historic Site, Promontory. This reenactment commemorates the moment in 1869 when rail lines from the East and West coasts were joined, linking the nation. A must for historic-railroad buffs. Call ℰ **435/471-2209,** or check out www.nps.gov/gosp. May 10.

Great Salt Lake Bird Festival, Farmington. Birders from across the country flock to this festival, which takes place at the Davis County Fair Park, midway between Salt Lake City and Ogden. Call ℰ **801/451-3286,** or visit www.greatsaltlakebirdfest.com for more information. Mid-May.

JUNE

Harmons Best Dam Bike Ride, Logan. More than 1,500 participants pedal miles along Cache Valley's back roads. The money raised goes to help in the battle against multiple sclerosis. Call ℰ **801/424-0113.** Mid-June.

Utah Shakespearean Festival, Cedar City. This professional theater festival produces several plays by William Shakespeare, plus a few contemporary offerings. Call ℰ **800/752-9849,** or check out www.bard.org. Late June through August.

JULY

Deer Valley Music Festival, Deer Valley. This festival presents a spectacular series of concerts in an equally incredible setting. Call ℰ **801/533-6683,** or visit www.deervalleymusicfestival.org for more information. July to August.

AUGUST

Railroaders' Festival, Golden Spike National Historic Site. Reenactments of the Golden Spike ceremony, which united the nation by rail, plus a spike-driving contest, railroad handcar races, and a buffalo-chip-throwing contest. Call ℰ **435/471-2209,** or visit www.nps.gov/gosp. Early or mid-August.

SEPTEMBER

Greek Festival, Salt Lake City. The music, dance, and food of Greece are featured, plus tours of the historic Holy Trinity Greek Orthodox Church. Call ℰ **801/328-9681,** or visit www.saltlakegreekfestival.com. Early September.

Moab Music Festival, Moab. Live classical, jazz, bluegrass, and other types of music are presented in a beautiful red-rock amphitheater and other locations. For more information, check out www.moabmusicfest.org, or call ℰ **435/259-7003.** Early to mid-September.

Utah State Fair, Salt Lake City. This fair has live entertainment, a horse show, rodeo, livestock judging, arts and crafts exhibits, and typical state-fair fun. Visit www.utahstate-fair.com, or call ℰ **801/538-8400.** Mid-September.

Oktoberfest, Snowbird. This is a traditional celebration, with German music, food, and, of course, beer. Call ℰ **801/933-2110,** or visit www.snowbird.com. Mid-September to mid-October.

OCTOBER

Huntsman World Senior Games, St. George. This is an extremely popular Olympics-style competition for seniors, with a variety of athletic events. Call ℰ **800/562-1268,** or check out www.seniorgames.net. Mid-October.

Bison Roundup, Antelope Island State Park. Stop by the park and watch the annual bison roundup. Take binoculars and get a close-up view of the bison as they receive their annual medical exams. Call ☏ **801/773-2941,** or visit www.stateparks.utah.gov. Late October to early November.

Ogden Christmas Parade and Christmas Village, Ogden. A parade begins the Christmas season, and the municipal park is transformed into a Christmas village, with thousands of lights, music, and animated decorations. Call ☏ **801/629-8253.** Late November through December.

Temple Square Christmas Lights, Salt Lake City. A huge, spectacular display of Christmas lights adorns Temple Square. Call ☏ **801/240-4872.** From the Friday after Thanksgiving to January 1.

Salt Lake City New Year's Eve Celebration, Salt Lake City. This New Year's Eve party animates downtown Salt Lake City with arts and crafts, entertainment, storytelling, and other family-oriented activities, with a midnight fireworks display. Visit www.eveslc.com. December 31.

LAY OF THE LAND

You can easily split Utah into three distinct regions: the Colorado Plateau, in the southern half of the state, where all those fantastic rock formations are; Rocky Mountain Utah, with rugged peaks, stately pines, deep blue lakes, and most of the state's residents; and the Great Basin Desert, the big middle-of-nowhere to which you've always wanted to send that cousin you never really liked.

Truth be told, though, certain sections of Utah do just have a whole lot of nothing. So this book is organized by destination, based on where you probably will want to go.

Eighty percent of Utah's population lives in the Rocky Mountain region of the **Wasatch Front,** the 175-mile-long north-central section of the state from Logan to Provo. **Salt Lake City** is Utah's most populous city, as well as its most cosmopolitan. It's also the international headquarters of the Church of Jesus Christ of Latter-day Saints; Temple Square is Utah's most-visited attraction. Keep in mind that Salt Lake City is still a relatively small city and not as sophisticated or glitzy as New York or Los Angeles (maybe that's what makes it so likable). As any real-estate agent will tell you, one advantage Salt Lake City has over all other Western cities its size is its location; within an hour's drive is some of the best downhill skiing in the United States. Here also is that anomaly of nature, the vast **Great Salt Lake,** eight times saltier than any of the world's oceans.

This brings you to the rest of the Wasatch Front. In this book, the section that's roughly north of Salt Lake is designated the **Northern Wasatch Front.** Here you'll find historic **Ogden; Logan,** Utah's northernmost town of any size; the national historic site where the Central Pacific and Union Pacific railroads met in 1869; and four ski resorts. The mountains that offer skiing in winter also provide numerous opportunities for hiking, horseback riding, and biking in summer.

The areas east and south of Salt Lake City are designated in this book as the **Southern Wasatch Front.** This region contains beautiful **Big** and **Little Cottonwood Canyons,** which have some of the state's best skiing, as well as great hiking and biking in the summer; **Park City,** Utah's premier ski-resort town—and a delightful destination year-round—with a historic Main Street dominated by intriguing shops and restaurants; some fun spots just outside of Park City, including a historic railroad, Strawberry Reservoir (a real gem of a lake), and several nice state parks; Robert Redford's Sundance Institute; and **Provo,** a small, conservative city that's home to Brigham Young University.

The western side of Utah, beginning west of Salt Lake City, is dominated by the vast, salty nothingness of the Great Basin Desert, which includes the pristinely white Bonneville Salt Flats, a terrain so flat that you can actually see the curvature of the earth. The Flats are also famous for the land-speed records set on them. This is not the sort of place you want to go for a picnic—it's hot, the water's undrinkable, and there's very little to see.

Northeastern Utah is home to two terrific recreational areas that creep into the adjoining states: **Flaming Gorge National Recreation Area,** which wanders into Wyoming, and nearby **Dinosaur National Monument,** which extends into Colorado. Both are what one might call "Undiscovered Utah," because they're really off the beaten path and not what most people imagine when they think of the state—consider this part of Utah well worth a visit.

The **Colorado Plateau,** which extends along the state's entire southern border and halfway up the east side, is where all five of Utah's national parks are located, and for good reason. Ancient geologic forces, erosion, oxidation, and other natural processes have carved spectacular rock sculptures—delicate and intricate, bold and stately—and painted them in a riot of color. This is quite likely why you've come to Utah in the first place, and these chapters will help you spend your time wisely and enjoyably. Check out chapter 10 on **Zion National Park** for hints on avoiding the crowds at the state's most popular national park; and see if you agree that **Bryce Canyon National Park** (chapter 11), with its marvelous stone sculptures (called hoodoos), is the West's best. Chapter 12 explains why **Capitol Reef National Park** is one of Utah's hidden treasures, and chapter 14, **"From Moab to Arches & Canyonlands National Parks,"** directs you to some of the best ways to explore eastern Utah's beautiful red-rock country.

But the Colorado Plateau isn't just national parks. This area offers historic Mormon sites; live theater, dance, and music; as well as skiing and the state's best golf. If you're heading in from Las Vegas, St. George is the first Utah town you'll see.

Utah's best destination for watersports—maybe the best in the West—is **Lake Powell and Glen Canyon National Recreation Area.** A boating vacation here is the stuff that stressed-out big-city dreams are made of.

Finally, the **Four Corners Area** is in Utah's very southeast corner. Spectacular American Indian sites, such as **Hovenweep National Monument,** make a visit here truly worth the drive through the West's vast, empty spaces.

RESPONSIBLE TOURISM

The perpetual debate continues throughout Utah: natural gas drilling and mineral extraction versus recreation and conservation. Most recently, the Bush administration opened up parcels of federal land near Canyonlands National Park for bidding to natural gas exploration in 2008; the move was condemned and quickly reversed after the Obama administration took over. Likewise, Escalante has been the center of the development-vs.-ecological-preservation debate in Utah since President Bill Clinton made it a national monument in 2000. Locals decried the move, saying it would wreck the economy, but the increased tourism has them singing a different tune today.

GENERAL RESOURCES FOR green TRAVEL

In addition to the resources for Utah listed above, the following websites provide valuable wide-ranging information on sustainable travel. For a list of even more sustainable resources, as well as tips and explanations on how to travel greener, visit www.frommers.com/planning.

- **Responsible Travel** (www.responsibletravel.com) is a great source of sustainable travel ideas; the site is run by a spokesperson for ethical tourism in the travel industry. **Sustainable Travel International** (www.sustainabletravelinternational.org) promotes ethical tourism practices, and manages an extensive directory of sustainable properties and tour operators around the world.

- In the U.K., **Tourism Concern** (www.tourismconcern.org.uk) works to reduce social and environmental problems connected to tourism. The **Association of Independent Tour Operators (AITO;** www.aito.co.uk) is a group of specialist operators leading the field in making vacations sustainable.

- In Canada, **www.greenliving online.com** offers extensive content on how to travel sustainably, including a travel and transport section and profiles of the best green shops and services in Toronto, Vancouver, and Calgary.

- In Australia, the national body that sets guidelines and standards for ecotourism is **Ecotourism Australia** (www.ecotourism.org.au). The **Green Directory**

(www.thegreendirectory.com.au), **Green Pages** (www.thegreenpages.com.au), and **Eco Directory** (www.ecodirectory.com.au) offer sustainable travel tips and directories of green businesses.

- **Carbonfund** (www.carbonfund.org), **TerraPass** (www.terrapass.org), and the **Cool Climate Network** (coolclimate.berkeley.edu) provide info on "carbon offsetting," or offsetting the greenhouse gas emitted during flights.

- The **"Green" Hotels Association** (www.greenhotels.com) recommends green-rated member hotels around the world that fulfill the company's stringent environmental requirements. **Environmentally Friendly Hotels** (www.environmentallyfriendly hotels.com) offers more green accommodation ratings.

- **Sustain Lane** (www.sustainlane.com) lists sustainable eating and drinking choices around the U.S.; also visit **www.eatwellguide.org** for tips on eating sustainably in the U.S. and Canada.

- For information on animal-friendly issues throughout the world, visit **Tread Lightly** (www.treadlightly.org).

- **International Volunteer Programs Association** (www.volunteerinternational.org) has a list of questions to help you determine the intentions and the nature of a volunteer program. For general info on volunteer travel, visit **www.volunteerabroad.org** and **www.idealist.org.**

Generally speaking, the **Wasatch Mountain Club,** 1390 S. 1100 East, Ste. 103, Salt Lake City, UT 84105-2443 (© **801/463-9842;** www.wasatchmountainclub. org), can offer a number of resources to eco-minded visitors to the Beehive State, with activities geared toward the eco-conscious outdoor lover. Many hotels and resorts in Utah have begun green initiatives, ranging from cutting down on laundry to installing solar panels, in recent years. Be sure to ask hotels about their green policies and initiatives to get a good grasp before you book a room. As for getting around in a green fashion, public transportation is great on the Wasatch Front, but nonexistent in the more remote corners of Utah.

But perhaps the best way to experience sustainability is by connecting with Utah's wild soul on a trek along the state's myriad hiking trails or a campout in one of its many campgrounds. To lessen your impact further, go off the grid on an overnight backpacking trip. **Leave No Trace** (www.lnt.org) is an educational nonprofit that expands on the backpacker's credo to leave any campsite in the same condition—or better off—as when one found it. Backpacking is a refreshing counterpoint to modern life that will give perspective on the issues of sustainability and personal energy dependence.

TOURS

Escorted tours are structured group tours, with a group leader. The price often includes everything from airfare to hotels, meals, tours, admission costs, and local transportation.

Despite the fact that escorted tours require big deposits and predetermine hotels, restaurants, and itineraries, many people derive security and peace of mind from the structure they offer. Escorted tours—whether they're navigated by bus, motor-coach, train, or boat—let travelers sit back and enjoy the trip without having to drive or worry about details. They take you to the maximum number of sights in the minimum amount of time with the least amount of hassle. They're particularly convenient for people with limited mobility, and they can be a great way to make new friends.

On the downside, you'll have little opportunity for serendipitous interactions with locals. The tours can be jam-packed with activities, leaving little room for individual sightseeing, whim, or adventure—plus they often focus on the heavily touristed sites, so you miss out on many a lesser-known gem.

Adventure & Wellness Trips

Utah is an ideal destination for an adventure- or wellness-oriented trip. The national parks are perfect for both, and the spas at Utah's numerous ski resorts and in and around St. George have deservedly earned a national reputation for excellence. See chapter 4, "The Active Vacation Planner," and individual destination chapters for more information.

Guided Tours

City Sights Bus Tours, 3359 S. Main St., Ste. 804 (**℡ 801/534-1001;** www.saltlakecitytours.org), offers several tours of Salt Lake City and the surrounding area. Offering tours to Utah's national parks and other destinations is **Tauck Tours** (**℡ 800/788-7885;** www.tauck.com).

A number of companies also offer specialized tours for outdoor-recreation enthusiasts. See chapter 4, "The Active Vacation Planner," for more information.

Volunteer & Working Trips

Home to several thousand cats, dogs, and other animals at any given time, **Best Friends Animal Sanctuary,** 5001 Angel Canyon Rd., in Kanab (© **435/644-2001;** www.bestfriends.org), offers numerous opportunities for visitors to volunteer for a few hours or an entire vacation. Thousands of folks participate annually in such volunteer activities as feeding, walking, and cleaning up after the sanctuary's furred, feathered, and scaled residents.

Volunteer trail crews offer another great opportunity for visitors to lend a hand while visiting Utah. Many state and national parks and other recreation areas have programs for volunteer trail crews; contact a specific park or area for additional information.

2

UTAH IN DEPTH | Tours

SUGGESTED UTAH ITINERARIES

3

U tah has so many worthwhile sights and attractions that you'll want to keep coming back for more. Among the highlights of a trip to Utah are splendid national parks, ski resorts, and wilderness areas; the temples, tabernacles, and historic sites of the Church of Jesus Christ of Latter-day Saints; and genuine Old West destinations, from mining towns and steam trains to saloons and shootout locales.

Like most people, however, you probably have a limited amount of vacation time. This chapter spells out some recommended itineraries that plot out the most efficient routes to Utah's must-see destinations, from a 1-week trip that squeezes in the best the state has to offer to more leisurely explorations for those with more time.

The following itineraries are all driving tours. If you plan to visit Salt Lake City only or head to a major resort to ski for a week, you can get by without a car, but most of the top destinations here—including all of the national parks—require a bit of a drive. Utah is a vast state, with its sights and attractions spread out, so you'll end up doing some driving to get from one to another. One consolation is that traffic congestion is practically nonexistent, even in cities. Services along rural highways are often limited, though, so motorists need to keep an eye on fuel levels during long-distance hauls. That hand-painted roadside sign that says NO GAS NEXT 50 MILES may be more accurate than you think.

UTAH IN 1 WEEK

Nope, it can't be done. There's no way anyone can "see Utah" in only 7 days—there's simply too much here that's really worth exploring. But if 1 week it is, then try this fun, varied vacation that will give you a good taste of what Utah is all about. This trip starts and ends in Salt Lake City, taking in historic sites, Mormon culture, and some beautiful red-rock scenery along the way.

Days 1 & 2: Salt Lake City ★

Among Salt Lake City's must-see attractions is **Temple Square,** the world headquarters of the Church of Jesus Christ of Latter-day

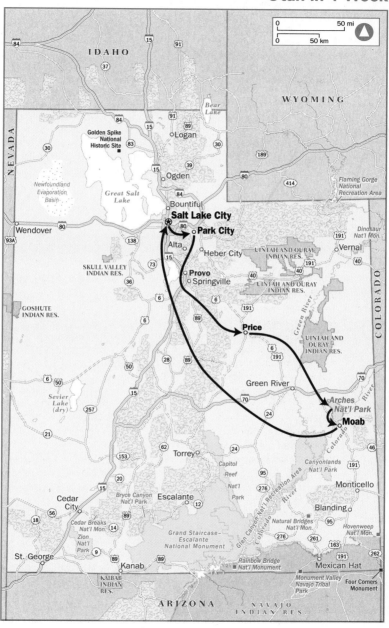

Saints (LDS). In addition to the majestic church buildings, the square houses lovely gardens and statuary, and visitor centers with exhibits on the church's history and beliefs. If possible, attend a performance of the renowned Mormon Tabernacle Choir. Then, before leaving the city, drop in at the **Beehive House,** built in 1854 as church leader Brigham Young's family home, and the **Church History Museum.** See chapter 5.

Day 3: Park City ★★

Drive to the Old West mining town of Park City, where, in winter, you can test your skills at one of three fine ski resorts. In summer, stop at the **Utah Olympic Park,** built for the 2002 Olympics. It's open year-round for tours and other activities. Next, go downtown to the **Park City Museum**—home to the old territorial jail in its basement (it's worth a look)—and pick up a copy of the *Park City Main Street Historic Walking Tour* brochure, which leads you to 45 buildings and historic sites that have managed to survive the decades. See p. 113.

Day 4: Price

Make time for a stop in Price on your way south. The town began as a railroad and coal-mining center but is now best known for its dinosaurs. Stop at the **CEU Prehistoric Museum,** operated by the College of Eastern Utah, to see huge skeletons of an allosaurus, a Utah raptor, and an intriguing duck-billed dinosaur known as the prosaurolophus. If time permits, drive about 35 miles out of town to the **Cleveland-Lloyd Dinosaur Quarry** to see excavations and the bones of more than 70 dinosaurs. See p. 291.

Days 5 & 6: Arches National Park ★★ & Moab

One of Utah's easiest-to-see national parks, **Arches** (p. 274) is prized for its mind-boggling sandstone rock formations. Explore its scenic drive and several trails, and you'll delight in the otherworldly desertscape of natural stone arches, towers, and other fanciful sandstone formations. Make the adjacent town of Moab your headquarters, and take a break and cool off at the nearby **Scott M. Matheson Wetlands Preserve** (p. 265), a lush oasis along the river that attracts more than 200 species of birds, plus river otters, beavers, and muskrats. See chapter 14.

Day 7: Back to Salt Lake City

It's a long drive back to Salt Lake City, but, if time permits, plan a stop in **Provo** (p. 140) to explore some of its fine museums, especially the excellent **Museum of Art** on the campus of Brigham Young University, or the equally renowned **Springville Museum of Art** in nearby Springville.

UTAH IN 2 WEEKS

Even 2 weeks is not enough time to see all that Utah has to offer, but in 14 days you will be able to see a bit more of everything. This tour assumes you're flying in and out of Salt Lake City and renting a car. If, on the other hand, you don't need to return to the state capital, you'll have extra time to explore the national parks. The "Utah in 1 Week" itinerary provides the base for your trip.

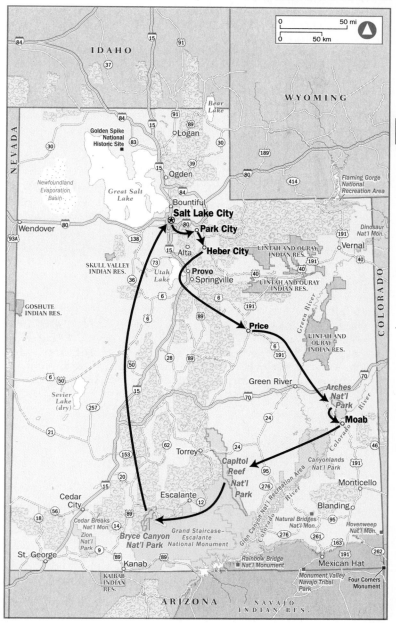

Days 1 & 2: Salt Lake City ★

Start your adventure in Salt Lake City by following the first 2 days in the "Utah in 1 Week" itinerary.

Day 3: Park City ★★

It's on to Park City, an Old West mining town. Follow the recommendations on day 3 of "Utah in 1 Week."

Day 4: Heber Valley Historic Railroad ★★

A short, pretty drive from Park City, the 100-year-old excursion train in Heber City is your ticket to Utah's past. Rides ranging from 1½ to 3 hours are offered on both steam and vintage diesel trains. See p. 130.

Day 5: Price

On your way south, spend day 5 as described on day 4 of "Utah in 1 Week."

Days 6–8: Arches National Park ★★ & Moab

Look to days 5 and 6 in "Utah in 1 Week" for suggestions on exploring the best of Arches National Park and Moab. If you have time, spend a day in Canyonlands National Park's Island in the Sky District.

Days 9 & 10: Capitol Reef National Park ★★★

This well-kept secret offers brilliantly colored, unexpectedly shaped rock formations, along with a variety of historic sites and even an orchard. The Fremont River feeds a lush oasis in this otherwise barren land; in fact, 19th-century pioneers found the soil so fertile that they established the town of **Fruita,** named for the orchards they planted. Today you can explore the buildings and even pick fruit in season. Hikers should look for the rock wall where pioneers "signed in," and explore canyons that were a favorite hide-out of famed outlaw Butch Cassidy. See chapter 12.

Days 11–13: Bryce Canyon National Park ★★★

It's an amazingly scenic drive down Utah 12 to Bryce Canyon, where you'll see thousands of intricately shaped hoodoos, those mysterious rock formations. Drive along the scenic route, stopping at the aptly named **Inspiration Point.** Then hit the colorful **Queen's Garden Trail,** named for a formation that resembles Britain's Queen Victoria, or take a leisurely stroll along the **Rim Trail** for some spectacular views. See chapter 11.

Day 14: Back to Salt Lake City

It's a long drive back to Salt Lake City, but if time permits, plan a stop in **Provo** (p. 140) to explore some fine museums, especially the excellent **Museum of Art** on the campus of Brigham Young University.

UTAH FOR FAMILIES

Utah has the family-friendly thing down pat. Admission fees for children are especially low, and many tourist attractions offer family packages priced considerably lower than the per-person rate. Attractions frequently schedule family-centric events,

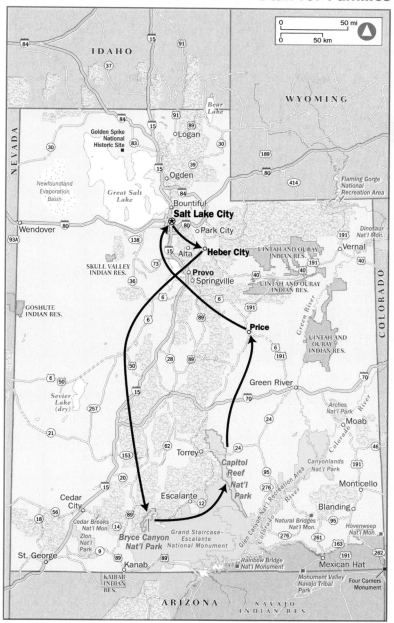

and most destinations throughout this book have special activities for kids. This 12-day itinerary, which begins and ends in Salt Lake City, has plenty for the kids while also providing lots to interest the parents.

Days 1–3: Salt Lake City

Salt Lake City has so many family attractions that it would be easy to spend a week or more here. History buffs will enjoy exploring **Temple Square** and the **Beehive House,** built in 1854 as church leader Brigham Young's family home. Other fun family stops include **Clark Planetarium,** offering star shows, light shows, and big-screen movies; **Utah's Hogle Zoo,** home to 1,100 animals; and the kid-oriented **Discovery Gateway,** home to 140 exhibits of all kinds, including a kid-size grocery store and an outdoor "flight for life" exhibit. Another option is a day trip to nearby Ogden, for the **Lagoon** amusement park, the **Treehouse Museum,** or the terrific family attractions at the **Salomon Center.** See chapters 5 and 6.

Day 4: Heber Valley Historic Railroad ★★

This 100-year-old excursion train in Heber City provides an exciting look into the past, plus lots of black smoke, cinders, and wind in your hair. Rides ranging from 1½ to 3 hours are offered on both steam and vintage diesel trains. Most kids, including the kids-at-heart, prefer the steam trains. See p. 130.

Days 5–7: Bryce Canyon National Park ★★★

This picturesque park is a long drive down I-15 and then along some back roads, but it's well worth the trip. Bryce contains thousands of intricately shaped hoodoos—those brooding rock formations that pique the imagination—colored in a palette of red, orange, and brown. Kids will especially like hiking the **Queen's Garden Trail,** where they can spot a variety of whimsical formations, such as Thor's Hammer. See chapter 11.

Days 8 & 9: Capitol Reef National Park ★★★

Heading back north, take the incredibly scenic Utah 12 to Capitol Reef, a secret gem of a national park that offers brightly colored and oddly shaped rock formations, along with a handful of historic sites. Be sure to visit the 1896 **Fruita Schoolhouse,** authentically furnished with such period pieces as wood and wrought-iron desks, a wood-burning stove, and textbooks. Nearby, the **orchards** planted by the Mormon settlers continue to thrive, tended by park workers who invite you to sample the "fruits" of their labors. See chapter 12.

Day 10: Price

If you're trying to sell children on a museum, make sure it has dinosaurs. Enter the **CEU Prehistoric Museum,** where huge skeletons of an allosaurus, a Utah raptor, and a duck-billed prosaurolophus preside. For the true dinophile, drive about 35 miles out of town to the **Cleveland-Lloyd Dinosaur Quarry,** where you'll find relics of more than 70 dinosaurs. See p. 291.

Days 11 & 12: Back to Salt Lake City

Return to Salt Lake City and catch up on attractions you missed the first time, such as **This Is the Place Heritage Park.** The park is home to **Old Deseret Village,** a pioneer village comprised of original and reproduction buildings that, in summer, becomes a mid-1800s living-history museum, complete with costumed villagers and a variety of activities, including wagon rides. Another good choice is **Liberty Park,** with trails, a small lake with ducks and paddle-boat rentals, a playground, a children's garden, a kiddie amusement park, a museum, and an excellent aviary. See chapter 5.

UTAH'S NATIONAL PARKS

Southern Utah practically bursts its seams with five delightful national parks, plus a national recreation area and monument. In addition, the Navajo Nation is home to wondrous Monument Valley park, along the Arizona state line. Visit these sites in a somewhat circuitous loop for what may very well be the best national park tour in the American West. This trip begins and ends in St. George; air travelers will probably fly to Las Vegas, Nevada, and rent a car there. It can be done in 2 weeks, but is much more satisfying done in 3 weeks as described here. With extra time you can easily add the North Rim of the Grand Canyon (see *Frommer's Grand Canyon National Park,* John Wiley & Sons, Inc.).

Day 1: St. George

Stock up on supplies in town before heading to the parks, but also make some time for the **St. George Dinosaur Discovery Site at Johnson Farm,** which showcases some 2,000 fossilized dinosaur tracks. Other noteworthy attractions include historic Mormon sites, such as the **Jacob Hamblin Home,** built in 1862, which is typical of pioneer homes throughout the West except for its two identical bedrooms—one for each of Hamblin's wives—and the exquisite 1876 **St. George Tabernacle,** with pine finished to look like exotic hardwoods, and even marble. See p. 168.

Days 2–4: Zion National Park ★★

Famous for its mammoth natural stone sculptures and unbelievably narrow slot canyon, this park begs to be explored. Hop on the shuttle bus that runs the length of the **Zion Canyon Scenic Drive,** getting off to take in the trails. Take the easy **Riverside Walk,** which follows the Virgin River down a narrow canyon through hanging gardens. Especially pleasant on hot days, the **Lower Emerald Pools Trail** traverses a forest of oak, maple, fir, and cottonwood trees, leading to a waterfall, a hanging garden, and a shimmering pool. See chapter 10.

Days 5 & 6: Glen Canyon National Recreation Area ★★★

This national recreation area is best known for **Lake Powell** and its 1,960 miles of shoreline. This is a boating destination, so you'll want to either **rent a boat** to go exploring, fishing, or swimming, or take a guided boat trip. Whichever you do, be sure to save time for **Rainbow Bridge National Monument,** which is in the recreation area and easily accessible by boat. Believed to be the largest natural bridge in the world, this "rainbow turned to stone" is considered sacred by the Navajo. See p. 250.

Days 7 & 8: Monument Valley Navajo Tribal Park

To many of us, Monument Valley *is* the Old West we've seen in movies and on TV. Part of the vast Navajo Nation, the park has a 17-mile self-guided **loop road** that lets you hit most of the major scenic attractions, or you can get a more personalized tour with a **Navajo guide.** Either way, you'll see classic Western scenery made famous in movies such as the 1939 classic *Stagecoach,* which starred a young John Wayne. Be sure to see the movie exhibits at **Goulding's Trading Post Museum.** See p. 297.

Days 9–12: Arches ★★ & Canyonlands National Parks ★★

Beloved for its captivatingly beautiful red-and-orange rock formations, this area holds two national parks that flank the lively town of Moab. **Canyonlands National Park** (p. 280) is a hikers' park. Stop at the **Grand View Point Overlook,** in the **Island in the Sky District,** and hike the **Grand View Trail,** which is especially scenic in late afternoon. **Arches National Park** (p. 274) is easier than Canyonlands to explore. Take the scenic drive and walk a few trails—on the **Devils Garden Trail** you can see 15 to 20 arches, including picturesque **Landscape Arch.**

Days 13 & 14: Capitol Reef National Park ★★★

This well-kept secret offers brilliantly colored rock formations with a bit of history. The Fremont River created a lush oasis in this otherwise barren land where 19th-century pioneers settled the town of **Fruita,** named for the orchards they planted. Today you can explore the town and even pick fruit in season. Hikers can examine **Pioneer Register,** a rock wall where traveling pioneers "signed in," and explore canyons where famed outlaw Butch Cassidy is said to have hidden out between robberies. See chapter 12.

Days 15–18: Scenic Utah 12 & Bryce Canyon National Park ★★★

From Capitol Reef, go south on Utah 12 over Boulder Mountain and through **Grand Staircase–Escalante National Monument** (p. 226); stop for a short hike to Calf Creek Falls before heading to **Bryce Canyon National Park.** Spend the night in the park or nearby so you can be on the rim of Bryce Amphitheater at sunrise—the best time to see the colorful and whimsical rock formations known as hoodoos. Top trails here include the colorful **Queen's Garden Trail,** named for a formation that resembles Britain's Queen Victoria. See chapter 11.

Days 19 & 20: Cedar Breaks National Monument ★

This small, high-altitude park has a 5-mile road that offers access to Cedar Breaks' scenic overlooks and trail heads. Hike **Spectra Point Trail** along the rim for changing views of the colorful rock formations. The fields of wildflowers, especially colorful in late July and August, and the 1,500-year-old bristlecone pines are a real treat. See p. 180.

Day 21: Back to St. George

Back in St. George, catch the historic Mormon sights you missed earlier, or possibly take in a few rounds of **golf** at one of St. George's eight splendid greens. If you want to see just one more park, drop in at one of Utah's most scenic, **Snow Canyon State Park,** which offers an abundance of opportunities for photography and hiking. See p. 173.

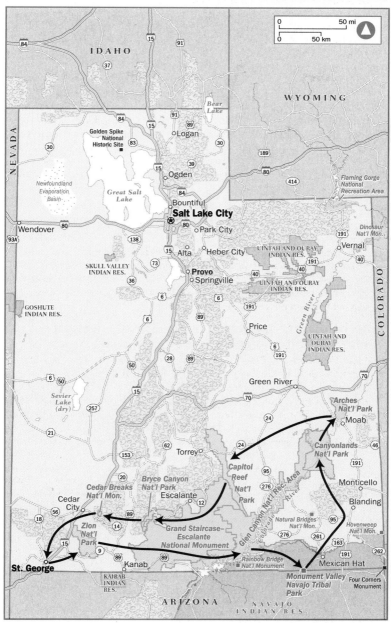

THE ACTIVE VACATION PLANNER

4

U tah is one big outdoor adventure, with millions of acres of public lands where you can cast for trout or herd cattle, go rock climbing or four-wheeling, sail or ski. The state boasts five spectacular national parks, seven national monuments, two national recreation areas, one national historic site, seven national forests, some 22 million acres administered by the federal Bureau of Land Management (BLM), and 45 state parks. But who's counting? It's enough to say that almost 80% of Utah's 85,000 square miles is yours to enjoy.

This chapter provides a primer for those folks who are new to planning active vacations or who haven't been to the state of Utah before; up-to-date information on visiting Utah's public lands; and descriptions of activities you can enjoy in Utah, including the best places to pursue your interests, and the information you need to get started. You'll find more details in the appropriate regional chapters. Have fun!

PREPARING FOR YOUR ACTIVE VACATION
What to Pack & What to Rent

Planning for a trip into the great outdoors may conjure images of vacationers loaded down with golf clubs, skis, cameras, tents, canoes, and bikes. If a car or light truck is your mode of transportation, try to keep the heaviest items between the axles and as close to the floor of your vehicle as possible; this helps improve handling. If you have a bike rack on the rear bumper, make sure the bike tires are far from the exhaust pipe; one local bike shop owner once mentioned that he does a good business replacing exhaust-cooked mountain-bike tires. Those with roof racks will want to measure the total height of their packed vehicles before leaving home. Underground parking garages often have less than 7 feet of clearance.

One alternative to carrying all that stuff is renting it. Camping equipment, ski equipment, mountain bikes, boats, and water toys are all readily available for rent in places where these activities are popular. You'll find many rental sources listed throughout this book.

ON THE TRAIL—AND IN THE MAZE—WITH
escape adventures

Located on the west side of Canyon-lands National Park, the **Maze** is one of the most spectacular places in the Lower 48. It's also one of the most remote and unforgiving places in the Lower 48, making it a good idea to have one of the state's many excellent guide services showing you the way.

Escape Adventures (℡ 800/596-2953; www.escapeadventures.com) is one such outfit, and a highly recommended one at that. I took one of its guided hiking/mountain-biking trips into the Maze in September 2008 and rank it as one of my top trips ever. With guides Rachel and Marc leading the way—and cooking up three scrumptious meals a day—we rode more than 50 miles and hiked another 20 in the span of 5 days, then caught a plane ride back to Moab from the lonely airstrip in Hite, retracing our serpentine path from the air over the course of a half-hour flight.

We started our adventure from the **Glen Canyon Recreation Area,** riding into Canyonlands and camping on the brink of the Maze on day 1. The scenery was second to none, all gnarled

sandstone in reds, oranges, tans, and whites. On the second day, the group let Marc drive the bikes around—9 miles in 6 hours—as we followed Rachel into the Maze itself. Its labyrinthine nickname is well-earned—I would not wander in there without a guide or an excellent map and plenty of water. And it's not even possible to get to the trail head without a very burly 4×4 vehicle. (As luck would have it, Escape's biodiesel-fueled truck—expertly piloted by Marc—fits that bill perfectly.)

Day 3 involved another hike, this one down to the Colorado River via an interesting geological—and archaeological—area called the **Dollhouse.** We rode the next day to our campsite above devastatingly beautiful **Cataract Canyon** before making the 25-mile ride to the Hite airstrip the following afternoon.

The trip proved doable for even my novice mountain-biking skills, but being in fairly good shape is certainly a prerequisite. The guides were excellent in every respect, and I ate better than I usually do at home.

In packing for your trip, you'll want to be prepared for a land of extremes, one that often has an unforgiving climate and terrain. Those planning to hike or bike should take more drinking water than they think they'll need—experts recommend at least 1 gallon of water per person per day on the trail—as well as high-SPF sun block, hats and other protective clothing, and sunglasses with ultraviolet protection. Summer visitors should carry rain gear for the typical afternoon thunderstorms, plus jackets or sweaters for cool evenings. Winter visitors will need not only warm parkas and hats, but also lighter clothing—the bright sun at midday, even in the mountains, can make it feel like June.

Staying Healthy & Safe in the Outdoors

The wide-open spaces and rugged landscape that make Utah such a beautiful place to explore can also be hazardous to your health, especially if you're not accustomed to the extremes here; see "Health" and "Safety," in "Fast Facts: Utah," in chapter 16, for details on dealing with desert climes and high altitudes. The isolation of many of the areas that you'll seek out means there may be no one around to help out in an emergency. So, like any good Boy or Girl Scout, be prepared. Also, be sure to carry a basic first-aid kit that includes a pair of tweezers—very handy for removing tiny cactus spines from tender flesh. Most important of all, check with park offices, park rangers, and other local outdoor specialists about current conditions before heading out.

Outdoor Etiquette

Many of the wonderful outdoor areas you'll explore in Utah are quite isolated; although you're probably not the first human being to set foot here, you may feel as if you are. Not too long ago, the rule of thumb was to "leave only footprints"; these days, some of us are trying to not even do that. Being a good outdoor citizen is mostly common sense: Pack out all trash, stay on established trails, be careful not to pollute water, and, in general, do your best to have as little impact on the environment as possible. The best among us go even further, carrying a small trash bag to pick up what others have left behind.

ADVENTURE TRAVEL

Opportunities for adventure travel are plentiful in Utah—as are some terrific outfitters to help you plan and execute your trip. You can take part in a cattle drive, thrill to the excitement of white-water rafting on the Green or Colorado rivers, scale a sheer rock wall in Zion National Park, or head out into some of the most spectacular scenery in the country in a four-wheel-drive vehicle. The variety of tours available seems almost endless, but the tour operators can help you find the one for you. In many cases, you can work with an operator to plan your own customized trip—all it takes is money.

Below are some of the most respected national companies operating in Utah. Most specialize in small groups and have trips geared to various levels of ability and physical condition. They also offer trips in a range of price categories, from basic to luxurious, and of varying length. Numerous local outfitters, guides, and adventure travel companies are discussed throughout this book. For a complete list of outfitters in Utah, as well as a lot of other useful information and Web links, contact the **Utah Office of Tourism,** 300 N. State St., Salt Lake City, UT 84114 (© **800/200-1160** or 801/538-1030; www.utah.com).

- **AdventureBus,** 375 S. Main St., 240, Moab, UT 84532 (© **888/737-5263** or 909/633-7225; www.adventurebus.com), offers trips on customized buses with an emphasis on outdoor adventures, including multisport and mountain biking tours in the Arches, Zion, and Bryce Canyon national parks areas, as well as Hovenweep National Monument.

- **Austin-Lehman Adventures,** P.O. Box 81025, Billings, MT 59108-1025 (© **800/575-1540** or 406/655-4591; www.austinlehman.com), offers guided multiday mountain biking, hiking, and combination tours in the Zion, Bryce Canyon, and Canyonlands national parks areas.

- **Backroads,** 801 Cedar St., Berkeley, CA 94710-1800 (© **800/462-2848** or 510/527-1555; www.backroads.com), offers a variety of guided multiday road biking, mountain biking, and hiking tours in the areas surrounding southern Utah's national parks.

- **Bicycle Adventures,** 29700 SE High Point Way, Issaquah, WA 98027 (© **800/443-6060** or 425/250-5540; www.bicycleadventures.com), offers guided multiday hiking and biking excursions in the Zion and Bryce Canyon national parks areas.

- **Escape Adventures,** 8221 W. Charleston Ave., 101, Las Vegas, NV 89117 (© **800/596-2953;** www.escapeadventures.com), offers guided multiday hiking, mountain biking, road cycling, and multisport trips in the Canyonlands, Arches, Bryce Canyon, Zion, and Capitol Reef national parks areas.

○ **Ski the Rockies,** 4901 Main St., Downers Grove, IL 60515 (© **800/291-2588** or 630/969-5800; www.skitherockies.com), provides customized skiing and snowboarding packages at many of Utah's major resorts.

○ The **World Outdoors,** 2840 Wilderness Place, Ste. D, Boulder, CO 80301 (© **800/488-8483** or 303/413-0946; www.theworldoutdoors.com), offers a variety of trips, including multisport adventures that include hiking, mountain biking, and kayaking to the Canyonlands area, plus hiking/biking trips in the vicinities of Bryce Canyon, Zion, and the north rim of the Grand Canyon.

UTAH'S NATIONAL PARKS

For many people, the best part of a Utah vacation is exploring the state's **five national parks** (www.nps.gov). Unfortunately, these beautiful national treasures have become so popular that they're being overrun by visitors at a time when the federal government is cutting budgets, making it difficult for the parks to cope with their own success.

The parks are busiest in summer, when most children are out of school, so try to visit at almost any other time. Fall is usually best. Spring is okay, but it can be windy and there may be snow at higher elevations. Winter can be delightful if you don't mind snow and cold. If you have to travel in summer, be patient. Allow extra time for traffic jams and lines, and try to hike some of the longer and lesser-used trails (ask a ranger for recommendations).

PASSES = paid admission ON MOST FEDERAL LANDS

Those who enjoy vacationing at national parks, national forests, and other federal lands have opportunities to save quite a bit of money by using the federal government's annual passes. The **America the Beautiful—National Parks and Federal Recreational Lands Pass** costs $80 for 1 year from the date of purchase for the general public. It provides free admission for the pass holder and those in his or her vehicle to recreation sites that charge vehicle entrance fees on lands administered by the National Park Service, U.S. Forest Service, U.S. Fish and Wildlife Service, Bureau of Land Management, and Bureau of Reclamation. At areas that charge per-person fees, the passes are good for the pass holder plus three additional adults. Children 15 and under are admitted free.

The **Senior Pass** is available for U.S. citizens and permanent residents 62 and older for a lifetime fee of $10, and the **Access Pass** is available for U.S. citizens and permanent residents with disabilities for free. The Senior and Access passes also provide 50% discounts on some fees, such as camping.

The Senior and Access passes must be obtained in person at national parks, U.S. Forest Service offices, and other federal recreation sites, but the general public version (the $80 one) can be purchased in person, by phone (© **888/ 275-8747,** ext. 1), or online at http://store.usgs.gov/pass, a website that also provides complete information about the passes.

OUTDOOR ACTIVITIES A TO Z

Utah offers a surprisingly wide range of outdoor activities, from desert hiking and four-wheeling to fishing and, of course, skiing. Among the many online outdoor recreation information sources are the very informative and user-friendly Public Lands Information Center website, **www.publiclands.org**, and the **GORP** (Great Outdoor Recreation Page) website, at **www.gorp.com**. Another excellent website is **www.outdoorutah.com**, where you can order a free copy of the annual *Outdoor Utah Adventure Guide*, and connect to its other websites (www.bicycleutah.com and www.backcountryutah.com).

This is truly a do-it-yourself kind of state, and you'll have no trouble finding detailed topographic maps—essential for wilderness trips—plus whatever equipment and supplies you need. Plus, every single ranger encountered in researching this book was happy to help visitors plan their backcountry trips. In addition, many sporting-goods shops are staffed by area residents who know local activities and areas well. In almost all cases, if you ask, there will be someone willing and able to help you make the most of your trip.

BOATING   For a state that's largely desert, Utah certainly has a lot of lakes and reservoirs, from huge **Lake Powell** in the south to **Lake Flaming Gorge** in the north. Both of these lakes are national recreation areas and have complete marinas with boat rentals. Don't forget the state parks, such as **Jordanelle,** which is near Park City, and **Quail Creek**—with the state's warmest water—near St. George. A favorite is the picturesque but chilly **Strawberry Reservoir,** southeast of Park City in the Uinta National Forest. For information on boating in state parks, contact **Utah State Parks** (📞 800/322-3770 or 801/538-7378; www.stateparks.utah.gov).

CAMPING   Utah is the perfect place to camp; in fact, at some destinations, such as **Canyonlands National Park,** it's practically mandatory. Just about every community of any size has at least one commercial campground, and campsites are available at all the national parks and national recreation areas (they're often crowded in summer). Those who can stand being without hot showers can often find free or very reasonable campsites just outside the national parks, in national forests, and on Bureau of Land Management lands. Other good bets are Utah's state parks, especially **Kodachrome,** just outside Bryce Canyon National Park; **Coral Pink Sand Dunes,** just west of Kanab; and **Snow Canyon,** near St. George.

A growing number of state and federal campgrounds allow visitors to reserve sites, although often only in the busy summer months. Throughout Utah are more than 100 national forest campgrounds and numerous state parks that will also reserve sites. To check on campground reservation possibilities for federal properties, contact the new **Recreation.gov,** which combined the old **ReserveUSA** and **National Park Reservation Service** into one portal (📞 800/444-6777; www.recreation.gov), or use the link from the individual park's website. For reservations for campgrounds in state parks, contact **Utah State Parks** (📞 800/322-3770; www.stateparks.utah.gov).

CATTLE DRIVES   Opportunities abound for you to play cowboy on cattle drives that last from a single day to a week or longer. You can actually take part in the riding and roping, though the conditions are generally much more comfortable than what real cowboys once experienced on cattle drives. Each cattle drive is different, so you'll want to ask very specific questions about food, sleeping arrangements, and other conditions before plunking down your cash. It's also a good idea to book your trip as early as possible. A good company is **Rockin' R Ranch,** located north of Bryce Canyon National Park, with a business office at 10274 S. Eastdell Dr., Sandy, UT 84092 (*©* **801/733-9538;** www.rockinrranch.com).

FISHING Utah has more than 1,000 lakes, plus countless streams and rivers, with species that include rainbow, cutthroat, Mackinaw, and brown trout, plus striped bass, crappie, bluegill, walleye, and whitefish. **Lake Flaming Gorge** and **Lake Powell** are both great fishing lakes, but **Strawberry Reservoir** is Utah's premier trout fishery. Fly-fishing is especially popular in the Park City area and in the streams of the **Wasatch-Cache National Forest** above Ogden. Contact the **Utah Division of Wildlife Resources,** 1594 W. North Temple (P.O. Box 146301), Salt Lake City, UT 84114-6301 (*©* **801/538-4700;** www.wildlife.utah.gov), for the weekly statewide fishing report.

Fishing licenses are available from state wildlife offices, sporting-goods stores, and the Division of Wildlife Resources website (www.wildlife.utah.gov). Keep in mind that several fishing locations, such as Lake Powell and Lake Flaming Gorge, cross state lines, and you'll need licenses from both states.

FOUR-WHEELING The Moab area, and Canyonlands National Park in particular, are probably the best-known four-wheeling destinations in Utah, but there are also plenty of old mining and logging roads throughout the national forests and on BLM land. Those with dune buggies like to head for **Coral Pink Sand Dunes State Park,** west of Kanab. For information on four-wheeling, contact **Utah State Parks,** the **U.S. Forest Service,** and the **Bureau of Land Management** (p. 321).

GOLF Utah's golf courses are known for their beautiful scenery and variety of challenging terrains. They range from mountain courses set among the beautiful forests of the Wasatch to desert courses with scenic views of red-rock country. The warm climate of St. George, in Utah's southwest corner, makes this area a perfect location for year-round golf, and St. George has become the premier destination for visiting golfers—the area's **Sunbrook Golf Course** is probably Utah's best public course. In northern Utah, the course at the **Homestead Resort** near Park City is well worth the trip. A free directory of the state's 80-plus courses is available from the **Utah Office of Tourism** (p. 321), or check out the Utah Golf Association at **www.uga.org**.

HIKING Hiking is the best—and sometimes only—way to see many of Utah's most beautiful and exciting areas. Particularly recommended destinations include all five of Utah's national parks. You'll find splendid forest trails and wilderness at **Flaming Gorge National Recreation Area** and in the Wasatch Mountains around Ogden and Logan. Those looking for spectacular views won't do better than the trails on **BLM land** around Moab. In **Grand Staircase–Escalante National Monument,** east of Bryce Canyon, numerous undeveloped, unmarked hiking routes explore some of the nation's most rugged country. State parks with especially good trails include **Kodachrome,** near Bryce Canyon National Park; **Jordanelle,** near Park City; **Dead Horse Point,** just outside the Island in the Sky District of Canyonlands National Park; and **Escalante,** in the town of Escalante.

Keep weather conditions in mind when hiking, such as the brutal summer heat around St. George and the likelihood of ice and snow on high mountain trails from fall through spring. Because of loose rock and gravel on trails in the southern part of the state, wear good hiking boots with aggressive soles and firm ankle support.

4

THE ACTIVE VACATION PLANNER | Outdoor Activities A to Z

LIFE ON THE open road: PLANNING AN RV OR TENTING VACATION

One of the best ways to explore Utah, especially in the warm months, is in an RV—a motor home, truck camper, or camper trailer—or a tent, if you don't mind roughing it. If you own an RV, have the mechanical systems checked out before you go as there are some very steep grades in Utah. After that's done, pack up and go. If you don't have an RV or a tent, why not rent one for your Utah trip?

Why Camp?   One advantage to this type of travel is that many of the places you'll want to go, such as Canyonlands National Park, have no lodging. If you can't accommodate yourself, you'll end up sleeping 30 or 40 miles away and missing the spectacular sunrises and sunsets and that feeling of satisfaction that comes from living the experience rather than merely visiting it. If you have special dietary requirements, you won't have to worry about trying to find a restaurant that can meet your needs; you'll be able to cook for yourself, either in your motor home or trailer or on a camp stove.

There are disadvantages, of course. Tents, small trailers, and truck campers are cramped, and even the most luxurious motor homes and trailers provide somewhat close quarters. Facilities in most commercial campgrounds are less than what you'd get in moderately priced motels, and if you cook your own meals, you miss the opportunity to experience the local cuisine. But, all this aside, camping is just plain fun—especially in a setting as spectacular as this.

Renting an RV   Camping to save money is possible if you limit your equipment to a tent, a pop-up tent trailer, or a small pickup-truck camper, but renting a motor home will probably end up costing as much as driving a compact car,

staying in moderately priced motels, and eating in family-style restaurants. That's because motor homes go only a third (or less) as far on a gallon of gas as compact cars, and they're expensive to rent— generally between $1,000 and $1,500 per week in midsummer, when rates are highest.

If you're flying into the area and renting an RV upon arrival, choose your starting point carefully. Because most of Utah's national parks are closer to Las Vegas than Salt Lake City, you could save by starting and ending your trip in Vegas. The country's largest RV rental company, with outlets in Las Vegas and Salt Lake City, is **Cruise America** (© **800/671-8042;** www.cruiseamerica. com). RV rentals are also available from **El Monte RV** (© **888/337-2214;** www. elmonte.com). Information on additional rental agencies, as well as tips on renting, can be obtained online from the **Recreation Vehicle Rental Association** (www.rvra.org).

Choosing a Campground   After you get a rig or a tent, you'll need a place to put it. Camping in national parks, federal lands, state parks, and more is discussed in the relevant sections of this book. For a brochure on the campgrounds in Utah's state parks, contact **Utah State Parks** (p. 321). Members of the **American Automobile Association (AAA)** can request the club's free *Southwestern CampBook,* which includes campgrounds and RV parks in Utah, Arizona, Colorado, and New Mexico. Major bookstores carry several massive campground directories, including *Trailer Life Directory* (www.trailerlifedirectory.com) and *Woodall's North American Campground Directory* and other Woodall's titles (www.woodalls.com).

HORSEBACK RIDING It's fun to see the Old West the way the pioneers did—from the back of a horse. Although you won't find many dude ranches in Utah, you can find plenty of stables and outfitters who lead rides lasting from an hour to several days. Try a ride at **Bryce** and **Zion** national parks—it's hard to beat the scenery—although you'll likely be surrounded by lots of other riders and hikers. If you'd like a bit more solitude, head north to the mountains around Logan in the **Wasatch Front** or to **Flaming Gorge National Recreation Area.**

HOUSEBOATING Among the best ways to experience either **Lake Powell** or **Flaming Gorge Lake** is from the comfort of a houseboat. Marinas at each lake rent them, although you'll find the best selection at Lake Powell. Houseboats provide all the comforts of home—toilets, showers, sleeping quarters, and full kitchens—but in somewhat tighter quarters. Some of the larger ones have facilities for up to 12 people. You don't have to be an accomplished boater to drive one: Houseboats are easy to maneuver, and can't go very fast. No boating license is required, but you'll need to reserve your houseboat in advance, especially in summer, and send in a sizable deposit.

MOUNTAIN BIKING Although there are a few areas where road biking is popular (especially in Zion National Park), Utah really belongs to mountain bikers. With some of the grades you'll find, be sure you have plenty of gears. **Moab** claims to be Utah's mountain biking capital, but there's no dearth of opportunities in other parts of the state, either. Be aware that mountain bikes must remain on designated motor-vehicle roads in most national parks, but are welcome almost everywhere in areas administered by the U.S. Forest Service and the BLM. In addition to the exciting and often challenging slickrock trails of Moab, you'll find excellent trail systems just outside of **Zion** and **Bryce Canyon** national parks. The warm-weather biking at **Brian Head Resort,** near St. George, is another great option.

RIVER RAFTING, KAYAKING & CANOEING The Green and Colorado rivers are among the top destinations in the United States for serious white-water as well as flat-water rafting; they're also popular with kayakers and canoeists. A favorite river trip, with plenty of white water, is down the Green River through **Dinosaur National Monument.** Trips on the Green also start in the town of Green River, north of Moab. The Colorado River sees more boaters than the Green, and has a greater range of conditions, from flat, glassy waters to rapids so rough they can't be run at all. Most Colorado River trips start in **Moab.** Several companies rent rafts, canoes, or kayaks, and give you some instruction. They'll also help you decide which stretches of river are suitable for your abilities and thrill-seeking level, and can arrange for a pickup at the takeout point. See chapter 14 for details on contacting these outfitters.

A worthwhile and lesser-known river trip is along the **San Juan River** in Bluff. This relaxing excursion will take you to relatively unknown archaeological sites and striking rock formations. See chapter 15.

A report on statewide river flows and reservoir information is available from the **Colorado Basin River Forecast Center** (© **801/539-1311** for recorded information; www.cbrfc.noaa.gov).

ROCK CLIMBING This dizzying sport is growing so much in Utah that several popular areas have imposed moratoriums on bolting, and allow climbers to use existing bolt holes only. Among the more dramatic rock-climbing spots is **Zion National Park,** where climbing is as much a spectator sport as a participatory activity. You'll also find some inviting walls in **Snow Canyon State Park** near St. George, in **Logan Canyon, Ogden Canyon,** and throughout the **Wasatch Mountains** in the Salt Lake City area.

SKIING & OTHER WINTER SPORTS   Utahns like to brag that their state has "the greatest snow on earth"—and one winter trip just might convince you they're right. Utah's ski resorts are characterized by absolutely splendid powder, runs as scary or mellow as you'd like, and a next-door-neighbor friendliness many of us thought was extinct. With a few notable exceptions—particularly **Park City, Deer Valley,** and **Snowbird**—you won't find the posh atmosphere and high-end amenities that dominate many of the ski resorts next door in Colorado, but you won't find the high prices, either. What you will discover are top-notch ski areas that are surprisingly easy to reach—half are within an hour's drive of Salt Lake City Airport. And they're relatively uncrowded, too: Utah generally receives about a third as many skiers as Colorado, so you'll see fewer lift lines and plenty of wide-open spaces.

Cross-country skiers can break trails to their hearts' content in Utah's national forests, or explore one of the developed cross-country areas. Particularly good are the mountains above **Ogden** and the old logging and mining roads southeast of Moab. Several downhill resorts, including **Brian Head, Sundance,** and **Solitude,** offer groomed cross-country trails, and some of the hiking trails at **Bryce Canyon National Park** are open to cross-country skiers in winter. Snowmobilers can generally use the same national forest roads as cross-country skiers, and both head to **Cedar Breaks National Monument** in winter, when those are the only ways to get into the park.

Growing in popularity is snowshoeing, which is not only easy but cheap. **Bryce Canyon National Park** is one of the best parks for this sport.

Call ✆ **888/999-4019** for the daily avalanche and mountain weather report from the U.S. Forest Service (www.wrh.noaa.gov/slc), ✆ **866/511-8824** for statewide road conditions (http://commuterlink.utah.gov), and ✆ **801/524-5133** for weather information. Contact **Ski Utah,** 150 W. 500 South, Salt Lake City, UT 84101 (✆ **800/754-8824** or 801/534-1779; www.skiutah.com), for statewide ski resort information.

WILDLIFE-VIEWING & BIRDING   The great expanses of undeveloped land in Utah make it an ideal habitat for wildlife, and, in most cases, it isn't even necessary to hike very far into the backcountry to spot creatures. There's plenty for you to see— water birds at many lakes and reservoirs, elk and antelope in the Wasatch Mountains, lizards and snakes in the red-rock country of the south, and deer and small mammals practically everywhere. All of the national parks and many state parks have excellent wildlife-viewing possibilities: **Coral Pink Sand Dunes** near Kanab is known for its luminescent scorpions, and **Escalante State Park** is the best wetlands bird habitat in southern Utah. Hikers on **Boulder Mountain,** near Escalante, are likely to see deer, elk, and wild turkeys, and birders will enjoy the wide variety of songbirds found here.

The mountains above **Ogden** and **Logan** are especially good places to spot elk, deer, and even moose. The relatively remote **Flaming Gorge National Recreation Area** is one of the best areas in the state to find wildlife, so don't be surprised if a pronghorn (an antelopelike creature) joins you at your campsite. Birders have a good chance of seeing ospreys, peregrine falcons, swifts, and swallows along the cliffs; and hikers on the **Little Hole National Recreation Trail,** just below Flaming Gorge Dam, should watch for a variety of birds, including bald eagles in winter. **Antelope Island State Park** in the Great Salt Lake is another good destination for bird-watchers.

SALT LAKE CITY

Nestled between the Wasatch Mountains on the east and the Great Salt Lake on the west, at an elevation of 4,330 feet, lies Salt Lake City. Utah's capital and major population center is small as far as American cities go, with a population of just over 180,000. (The entire metropolitan area is about 1.2 million strong.) But travelers come from around the world to visit magnificent Temple Square, world headquarters of the Church of Jesus Christ of Latter-day Saints (LDS), and to hear the inspired voices of the unequaled Mormon Tabernacle Choir. The city is also a base for a growing community of outdoor enthusiasts.

Things to Do The can't-miss attraction is **Temple Square,** featuring a host of historic buildings with soaring spires. Salt Lake is also home to several excellent **museums,** the **University of Utah** campus, and plenty of shopping and sightseeing.

Active Pursuits Salt Lake City's location is enviable for outdoors enthusiasts: To the east are the **Wasatch Mountains,** with skiing, biking, and hiking; to the west are the **Great Salt Lake** and **Antelope Island State Park.** The nearest ski and snowboard resorts are in Big and Little Cottonwood Canyons, and within an hour's drive of downtown: **Alta, Snowbird, Solitude,** and **Brighton.**

Restaurants & Dining Salt Lake City has a good dining scene that's only getting better. Creative **New American** cuisine is prominent, as are **American** standbys like steaks and hamburgers. **Downtown** is a prime dining district, as is the **Cottonwood Heights** area to the southeast.

Nightlife & Entertainment The highly acclaimed **Utah Symphony & Opera** and **Ballet West** are among the country's best. With the state's now-normalized liquor laws, it's not hard to get a drink in Salt Lake City. **Downtown** bustles with all sorts of nightlife, from all-ages music venues to exclusive martini bars. There are also bar strips on **South State Street** and **Sugar House.**

5

ORIENTATION

Arriving

BY PLANE Direct flights connect Salt Lake City to almost 70 cities in the United States and Canada (Delta Air Lines even offers nonstop service between Salt Lake City and Paris). **Salt Lake City International Airport** (✆ **800/595-2442** or 801/575-2400; www.slcairport.com) is located just north of I-80 at exit 115, on the west side of the city.

The Salt Lake City International Airport has a growing **collection of art** that travelers can peruse while cruising the airport's moving sidewalks. It's a multimedia assemblage of art that the airport has been accruing since 1977. See something you like? Contact (© **801/575-2096** for additional details on the artworks on display and the artists represented on the airport walls.

The airport is a main hub for **Delta Air Lines.** Other airlines flying in and out of Salt Lake City include **American Airlines, Continental Airlines, Frontier Airlines, JetBlue Airways, Southwest Airlines, United Airlines,** and **US Airways.** See chapter 16 for the websites for these airlines.

BY CAR   Salt Lake City is 303 miles north of St. George, 238 miles northwest of Moab, 45 miles north of Provo, and 35 miles south of Ogden. You can reach it from the east or west via I-80 and from the north or south via I-15.

BY TRAIN   Amtrak's California Zephyr stops in Salt Lake City on its route from Emeryville, California, to Chicago. The station is at 340 S. 600 West (© **800/872-7245;** www.amtrak.com).

5 Visitor Information

The **Salt Lake Convention and Visitors Bureau (CVB)** has an information center downtown in the Salt Palace Convention Center, 90 S. West Temple (© **800/541-4955** or 801/534-49090; www.visitsaltlake.com). It's open daily from 9am to 7pm (closed major holidays).

There are additional information centers, staffed 9am to 9pm daily, in the baggage areas in Salt Lake City International Airport Terminals I and II. A state information center is located downtown at Council Hall, 300 N. State St. (© **801/538-1030**), open Monday through Friday from 8am to 5pm, and Saturday and Sunday from 10am to 5pm.

City Layout

Salt Lake City is laid out in a simple grid system centered on Temple Square. The roads surrounding the Square are North Temple, South Temple, West Temple, and Main Street, with the center of town at the southeast corner (the intersection of Main and South Temple), which is the site of the Brigham Young Monument. The numbers in the road names increase from here by 100s in the four cardinal directions, with West Temple taking the place of 100 West, 100 North called North Temple, and 100 East known as State Street.

Addresses may seem confusing at first, but are really quite clear once you get accustomed to them. For instance, 1292 S. 400 West lies almost 13 blocks south of Temple Square and 4 blocks west, and 243 N. 600 East is about 2 blocks north and 6 blocks east.

A variety of detailed city maps can be purchased at most bookstores. The *Salt Lake Visitors Guide,* available free at the visitor center, includes maps showing the approximate location of many restaurants, motels, and attractions. There is also a free *Ski Salt Lake Vacation Planner.*

Salt Lake City Neighborhoods

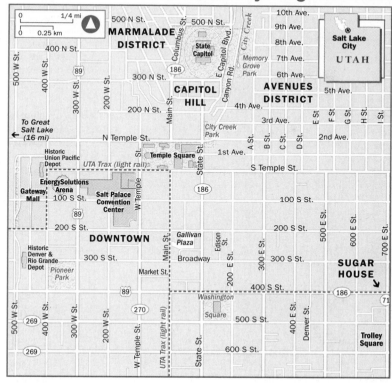

Neighborhoods in Brief

Downtown This is most likely where you'll spend the bulk of your time. The downtown area, centered on Temple Square, is both a business district and the administrative center for the LDS Church. Church offices, the Family History Library, the Church History Museum, and other church buildings surround the Square. Within a few blocks south, west, and east are hotels, restaurants, stores, and two major shopping centers. Within a couple of blocks are the Salt Palace Convention Center, the Maurice Abravanel Concert Hall, and the Capitol Theatre. The new City Creek development opened in March 2012, bringing upwards of 1,000 new residents downtown and an open-air retail area with a retractable roof.

Capitol Hill The Capitol Hill district lies north of the Square and encompasses the 40 acres around the Utah State Capitol Building and Council Hall. Some lovely old homes are located in the blocks surrounding the Capitol.

Marmalade District The blocks west of the Capitol to Quince Street are known as the Marmalade District. The streets in this small area were named for the nut and fruit trees brought in by early settlers, and the houses represent a variety of the city's early architectural styles.

Sugar House Southeast of downtown, Sugar House was named for a never-completed sugar mill and is one of the valley's longest-standing neighborhoods. Today, it's populated by the young and hip and features a quirky collection of stores, galleries, and eateries.

Avenues District   The Avenues District lies east of the Capitol and north of South Temple. Most of the larger homes here date from the silver boom in Little Cottonwood Canyon, when they were built by successful miners and merchants. Today, the tenants are mostly college students and young professionals.

GETTING AROUND

BY CAR   This is an easy city to explore by car, in large part because of the wide streets and abundant parking. National car-rental companies here include **Advantage** (© **800/777-5500** or 801/322-6090; www.advantage.com), **Alamo** (© **800/462-5266** or 801/575-2211; www.alamo.com), **Avis** (© **800/331-1212** or 801/575-2847; www.avis.com), **Budget** (© **800/527-0700** or 801/575-2821; www.budget.com), **Dollar** (© **800/800-4000** or 801/575-2580; www.dollar.com), **Enterprise** (© **800/261-7331** or 801/537-7433; www.enterprise.com), **Hertz** (© **800/654-3131** or 801/575-2683; www.hertz.com), **National** (© **800/227-7368** or 801/575-2277; www.nationalcar.com), and **Thrifty** (© **800/847-4389** or 801/265-6677; www.thrifty.com). The main **ground transportation desk** at the airport is © **801/575-2477.** All of these companies either have offices at the airport or will deliver a car to the airport for you.

Many public parking lots are situated in the downtown area, costing from $1 to $7 per day. Some lots are free with validation from participating merchants or restaurants. Street parking downtown is metered, costing 25¢ per half-hour, and is usually limited to 2 hours. Parking for larger RVs and motor homes is limited; you can park for $2 to $6 per hour in one large lot—the entire block between North and South Temple and 200 and 300 West. You might also try the lot behind the Capitol, with its few designated large-vehicle spaces; East Capitol Street, which is not metered, is a possibility as well.

BY PUBLIC TRANSPORTATION   The **Utah Transit Authority** (© **888/743-3882** or 801/743-3882; www.rideuta.com) provides **bus service** throughout the city, with a "free fare zone" in the downtown area, roughly from 400 South to North Temple, continuing up Main Street to 500 North to include the State Capitol, and between 200 East and West Temple. You can ride free within this zone, getting on and off as many times as you'd like. The fee for traveling in the other zones is $2.25 per person, $1.10 for seniors and those with disabilities, or $5.50 for a day pass. Two children 5 and under can ride free with a fare-paying adult. Some buses are wheelchair accessible, and all have bicycle carriers. **Trax,** a light-rail system also operated by the Utah Transit Authority, with the same contact information and same rates as the Utah Transit Authority's bus service (albeit free in the downtown area), runs 15 miles from the Sandy Civic Center (in the Salt Lake City suburb of Sandy) north to EnergySolutions Arena in downtown Salt Lake City, with another line running east to the University of Utah; in 2013, a line connecting downtown to the airport is slated to open. The trains are wheelchair accessible and bicycles are permitted. The **FrontRunner** train connects Ogden to Salt Lake City and its south suburbs; fares vary from about $2 to $5 based on the distance traveled. Route schedules and maps for both the buses and light rail are available at malls, libraries, and visitor centers.

BY TAXI   For a taxi, contact the **City Cab** (© **801/363-5550**), **Yellow Cab** (© **801/521-2100**), or **Ute Cab** (© **801/359-7788**), all available 24 hours a day.

Getting Around

SALT LAKE CITY

[FastFACTS] SALT LAKE CITY

Emergencies Dial 𝒞 **911** for police, fire, or ambulance.

Hospitals LDS Hospital, 8th Avenue and C Street (𝒞 **801/408-1100;** www. ldshospital.com), and **Salt Lake Regional Medical Center,** 1050 E. South Temple (𝒞 **801/350-4111;** www.saltlakeregional.com), both have 24-hour emergency rooms.

Newspapers & Magazines The two major daily newspapers are the market-leading *Salt Lake Tribune* (www.sltrib.com) and the LDS-owned *Deseret*

Morning News (www. deseretnews.com). *Salt Lake City Magazine* (www.salt lakemagazine.com) is a slick publication with a section on current events. The *Salt Lake City Weekly* (www. slweekly.com) is the local alternative paper.

Police For emergencies, call 𝒞 **911.** The nonemergency police phone number is 𝒞 **801/799-3000.**

Post Office The main post office is at 1760 W. 2100 South; the branch closest to downtown is at 230 W. 200 South (𝒞 **800/ 275-8777;** www.usps.com

for hours and locations of other post offices).

Road & Traffic Conditions For statewide road and traffic conditions, call 𝒞 **866/511-8824** or 511, or visit www.utahcommuter link.com.

Taxes Sales tax in Salt Lake City is 6.85%; restaurant tax totals 7.85%; lodging taxes total about 12.6% within the city limits, about 11% to 13% in Salt Lake County outside the municipal boundaries.

Weather Call 𝒞 **801/ 575-7669** for weather reports.

WHERE TO STAY

Finding comfortable, conveniently located accommodations in Salt Lake City, usually at relatively reasonable rates, is no trouble at all. In fact, a building boom of new rooms for the 2002 Olympics resulted in a surplus of lodging, so if you check around, you're likely to find rates that are significantly lower than those listed here.

Among the more affordable major chains and franchises (usually charging about $50–$100 for two persons) with locations in Salt Lake City are **Howard Johnson Express Inn,** 121 N. 300 West (𝒞 **888/637-4861** or 801/521-3450; www.hojo. com), **Econo Lodge,** 715 W. North Temple (𝒞 **877/233-2666** or 801/363-0062; www.choicehotels.com), and **Rodeway Inn,** 616 S. 200 West (𝒞 **801/534-0808;** www.rodewayinn.com).

In the $100-to-$200 range are **Comfort Suites Airport,** 171 N. 2100 West (𝒞 **800/424-6423** or 801/715-8688; www.choicehotels.com), **Hampton Inn Downtown,** 425 S. 300 West (𝒞 **800/426-7866** or 801/741-1110; http://hampton inn1.hilton.com), and **Radisson Hotel Salt Lake City Airport,** 2177 W. North Temple (𝒞 **800/333-3333** or 801/364-5800; www.radisson.com).

A bit more expensive (generally in the $200–$300 range), the **Salt Lake City Marriott City Center,** 220 S. State St. (𝒞 **866/961-8700** or 801/961-8700; www. marriott.com), and the **Hilton Salt Lake City Center,** 255 S. West Temple (𝒞 **800/445-8667** or 801/328-2000; www.hilton.com), are among the best full-service chain options downtown.

If you're basing yourself in metro Salt Lake to ski, you might want to consider the **Residence Inn Salt Lake City Cottonwood,** 6425 S. 3000 East (at I-215) (𝒞 **88/ 236-2427** or 801/453-0430; www.marriott.com), which has excellent access to the resorts in Big and Little Cottonwood Canyons. Winter rates start at $179 (including a hearty buffet breakfast) for studios with queen beds and pullouts and full kitchens.

You can often find the lowest hotel rates available online through the Salt Lake Convention and Visitors Bureau website, **www.visitsaltlake.com.**

Very Expensive

The Grand America Hotel ★★★   Built for the Olympics, this opulent downtown hotel is the place to stay for those who want the utmost in service and accommodations, and are willing to pay for it. Occupying an entire city block in downtown Salt Lake City, the Grand America is reminiscent of majestic European hotels, with ornate Italian chandeliers and plenty of hand-tooled marble and granite. The exquisitely designed rooms include 880-square-foot deluxe executive suites and beautifully appointed deluxe rooms with patios and balconies overlooking the pool and garden areas. The concierge floor has a lounge. All rooms are equipped with large-screen TVs, three telephones, and the finest quality furnishings.

555 S. Main St., Salt Lake City, UT 84111. www.grandamerica.com. (C) **800/621-4505** or 801/258-6000. Fax 801/258-6911. 775 units, including 395 suites. $189–$429 double; $339–$5,000 suite. AE, DISC, MC, V. **Amenities:** 2 restaurants; concierge; executive level; fitness center; indoor Jacuzzi; 1 indoor and 1 outdoor heated pool; room service; sauna. *In room:* A/C, TV, hair dryer, minibar, Wi-Fi (free).

Expensive

The Anniversary Inn–Fifth South ★ 🛏   A favorite with local couples, the Anniversary Inn makes for a fun romantic getaway, with themed rooms like the Jungle Safari (which features an elephant-trunk shower), and the treehouse-themed Swiss Family Robinson. The most popular is the luxurious Romeo and Juliet Suite, complete with marble, columns, and a sweeping circular staircase. Built on the site of an early-20th-century brewery in a quiet, shady nook east of downtown, the inn has fun details in every room, as well as fireplaces, two-person jetted tubs, and surround-sound systems. Cheesecake and sparkling cider are waiting in your room at check-in; continental breakfast is delivered in the morning. You might also check out the 14-room **Anniversary Inn** in the historic Kahn Mansion, 678 E. South Temple, which shares a website, a phone, and a similar sensibility with its larger sister property.

460 S. 1000 East, Salt Lake City, UT 84102. www.anniversaryinn.com. (C) **800/324-4152** or 801/363-4900. 36 themed suites. $139–$299 double. Lower weekday rates. Rates include continental breakfast. AE, DISC, MC, V. *In room:* A/C, TV/DVD player, Wi-Fi (free).

The Armstrong Mansion Bed & Breakfast ★★   This stately mansion exudes an atmosphere of splendor and luxury. The B&B is an opulent Queen Anne–style Victorian home decorated with antiques and reproductions. It features such architectural delights as stained-glass windows and an intricately carved oak staircase. The four-story mansion, built in 1893 and listed on the National Register of Historic Places, was renovated in 1994 and now has an elevator. Rooms feature one king or one queen bed, and all but two have jetted tubs. The stencils on the walls are reproductions of the mansion's original decorative patterns, discovered during renovation. The full all-you-can-eat breakfast buffet—served between 7:30 and 10am—consists of a hot dish, homemade croissants, and a variety of fruit.

667 E. 100 South, Salt Lake City, UT 84102. www.armstrongmansion.com. (C) **800/708-1333** or 801/531-1333. Fax 801/531-0282. 13 units. $99–$249 double. Children 15 and under stay free in cottage unit with parents. Rates include full breakfast. AE, DISC, MC, V. *In room:* A/C, TV, Wi-Fi (free).

Where to Stay

SALT LAKE CITY

Where to Stay & Eat in Downtown Salt Lake City

HOTELS ■

Anniversary Inn–
  Fifth South **25**

The Armstrong Mansion
  Bed & Breakfast **24**

Econo Lodge **2**

Grand America Hotel **22**

Hampton Inn Downtown **18**

Hilton Salt Lake City Center **8**

Hotel Monaco **9**

Howard Johnson Express Inn **4**

Inn on the Hill **5**

Little America Hotel **21**

Metropolitan Inn **20**

Peery Hotel **13**

Rodeway Inn **19**

Salt Lake City Marriott
  City Center **10**

RESTAURANTS ◆

Bambara **9**

The Beerhive Pub **6**

Cafe Trang **16**

Caputo's Deli **17**

Copper Onion **23**

Crown Burgers **3**

Desert Edge Brewery
  at the Pub **26**

Lamb's Grill Cafe **7**

Market Street Grill/
  Downtown **11**

Metropolitan **14**

The New Yorker **12**

Red Iguana **1**

Settebello **15**

Spencer's for Steaks
  and Chops **8**

Hotel Monaco ★★   Effortlessly combining a generous dose of class with just a dash of quirk, Salt Lake City's Hotel Monaco occupies the 14-story former Continental Bank Building, built in 1924 and home of the world's first drive-through teller. The colorful lobby mixes classic and contemporary, as do the flamboyant rooms, which captivate with an eclectic array of patterns and colors. Many rooms have spectacular city views. There's complimentary wine at 5pm nightly. Pets are allowed; the hotel will even provide a goldfish for your room if you'd like. The Monaco is also home to an excellent restaurant, **Bambara.**

15 W. 200 South, Salt Lake City, UT 84101. www.monaco-saltlakecity.com. © **800/294-9710** or 801/595-0000. Fax 801/532-8500. 225 units, including 20 suites. $139–$209 double; $219–$349 suite. Lower weekend rates often available. AE, DISC, MC, V. Valet parking $17. Pets accepted (free). **Amenities:** Restaurant (Bambara; see review, p. 53); lounge; concierge; exercise room; room service. *In room:* A/C, TV, hair dryer, MP3 docking station, Wi-Fi (free).

Inn on the Hill ★★   Two blocks from both the Utah State Capitol and Temple Square, this stately 11,000-square-foot mansion atop Capitol Hill—built by a local luminary in 1905—has been a B&B since the 1990s and is a city gem. Most rooms are on the first and third floors, with one king-size or queen-size bed, a large television, and a private bathroom with jetted tub. The fourth floor is occupied by the attractive Topaz Mountain, King's Peak, and Escalante rooms; I prefer King's Peak, with a sitting area and a great attic-turned-bathroom with a sunken jetted tub and adjacent shower. You'll find plenty of original architectural details, such as wavy and stained-glass windows and steam heat, and you'll enjoy tremendous city and mountain views.

225 N. State St., Salt Lake City, UT 84132. www.innonthehillslc.com. © **801/328-1466.** Fax 801/328-0590. 14 units, including 1 carriage house. $135–$179 double; $220 carriage house. Rates include continental or full breakfast. AE, MC, V. *In room:* A/C, TV/DVD, movie library, Wi-Fi (free).

Little America Hotel ★ ☺   While now overshadowed by the majesty of its sister property, the Grand America, across the street, the Little America is still among Salt Lake City's finest hotels, offering a wide variety of rooms, all individually decorated. Choices range from standard courtside units to extra-large deluxe tower suites in the 17-story high-rise—all are gracefully yet comfortably appointed in French Provincial style. The locally popular coffee shop opens at 6am; there's also a steakhouse and lounge on-site. The hotel has a second-floor sun deck with an indoor/outdoor pool plus an additional beautifully landscaped outdoor pool.

500 S. Main St., Salt Lake City, UT 84101. www.littleamerica.com/slc. © **800/453-9450** or 801/596-5700. Fax 801/596-5911. 850 units, including 2 suites. $99–$129 double; $189–$2,000 suite. AE, DC, DISC, MC, V. **Amenities:** 2 restaurants; lounge; concierge; health club; Jacuzzi; 2 pools (outdoor heated, indoor/outdoor heated); room service; sauna. *In room:* A/C, TV, Wi-Fi (free).

Peery Hotel ★★ 🛏   A top choice for those who appreciate the ambience of a vintage property, the Peery is the only truly historic hotel in downtown Salt Lake City. Completed in 1910, it has been fully renovated and restored to its former European-style elegance, offering comfortable, tastefully decorated accommodations. The lobby is delightful, with old-style pigeonholes for letters and a grand staircase to the upper floors. Each unique, handsomely appointed room contains period furnishings and pedestal sinks with antique brass fixtures in the bathroom. And it keeps getting better, with a new replica of the original sign on the roof, an awning that doubles as a deck, and a recent upgrade of the rooms and the exterior. Some units have fridges, and a few suites have jetted tubs. The entire hotel is nonsmoking.

110 W. 300 South (Broadway), Salt Lake City, UT 84101. www.peeryhotel.com. © **800/331-0073** or 801/521-4300. Fax 801/575-5014. 73 units. $99–$159 double; $149–$229 suite. Rates include continental breakfast. AE, DC, DISC, MC, V. Parking fee $10 per day self or $12 valet. **Amenities:** Restaurant; concierge; exercise room. *In room:* A/C, TV, hair dryer, MP3 docking station, Wi-Fi ($10 per day).

Moderate

Metropolitan Inn   This one-time chain motel is now a first-rate independent, clad in colorful stucco and equipped with stylish guest rooms. Art Deco reproductions and prints of *Wizard of Oz* characters hang above the beds (the Wicked Witch of the West excluded). Rooms have either one king-size bed or two queen-size, and the suite has a microwave, fridge, and two couches. The dinky outdoor pool is summer-only, and a computer is available in the lobby for guests traveling without their own.

524 S. West Temple, Salt Lake City, UT 84101. www.metropolitaninn.com. © **801/531-7100.** Fax 801/359-3814. 60 units, including 1 suite. $67–$99 double; $109–$150 suite. Rates include continental breakfast. AE, DISC, MC, V. **Amenities:** Outdoor heated seasonal pool. *In room:* A/C, TV, Wi-Fi (free).

Camping

Salt Lake KOA/VIP   This huge, well-maintained campground is the closest camping and RV facility to downtown Salt Lake City. Facilities include two pools, a hot tub, two playgrounds, Wi-Fi, a video arcade, two coin-operated laundries, several bathhouses, a convenience store with RV supplies, propane, an RV/car wash, well-maintained grassy areas for tents, and large shade trees. It offers 14 instant phone hookups, 200 sites with 50-amp power, and a jogging/pet-walk/bicycle trail behind the campground.

1400 W. North Temple, Salt Lake City, UT 84116. www.campvip.com. © **800/562-9510** or 801/355-1214. Fax 801/355-1055. 390 sites, 2 cabins. Campsites $24 tents and $42–$50 RVs; camping cabins $58. MC, V. Advance reservations recommended May–Sept. Pets accepted (free). **Amenities:** Jacuzzi; 2 outdoor pools; Wi-Fi (free).

WHERE TO EAT

Salt Lake City restaurants are more casual than those in most major American cities. The service is generally excellent and very friendly.

Expensive

Bambara ★★ NEW AMERICAN   A favorite lunch destination for the downtown business crowd, Bambara's slick dining room is the ideal pre- or post-theater dinner spot, or the perfect setting for a romantic meal. It's also conducive to people-watching, with windows on the busy (for Salt Lake City, that is) intersection of Main and 200 South. The menu brings a host of influences to the table, from Japanese to Italian to French, intermingling them without any one tradition overwhelming the others. The dinner menu changes regularly but always includes a delectable Utah corn bisque, a nice selection of beef and seafood, and a vegetarian dish. Breakfast is fairly traditional, and lunch brings sandwiches, steaks, and a scrumptious burger topped with local cheddar cheese and horseradish aioli. Popular three-course lunch specials go for $13. Service is understated and excellent. Full liquor service is available.

In the Hotel Monaco (p. 52), 202 S. Main St. ☏ **801/363-5454.** www.bambara-slc.com. Reservations recommended. Breakfast $9–$13, lunch $9–$16, dinner $20–$41. AE, DISC, MC, V. Mon–Fri 7–10am and 11am–2pm; Sat 8–11am; Mon–Thurs 5:30–10pm; Fri–Sat 5:30–10:30pm; Sun 8am–noon and 5:30–9pm.

Log Haven ★★ NEW AMERICAN   Located in a historic log mansion (1920) 4 miles up Millcreek Canyon in the Wasatch National Forest (about 20 min. from downtown), Log Haven has garnered a reputation as Salt Lake City's most romantic restaurant. The seasonally changing menu is creative and diverse, with sushi, game, and more traditional fare—steak and potatoes—to be expected. On a recent visit, the menu included a grilled bison bavette steak with caramelized cauliflower and house-cured pancetta; tomato pappardelle pasta with olives, kale, fava beans, and ricotta; and "alpine nachos," featuring Yukon gold potato chips, raclette cheese, and forest mushrooms. The waterfall- and view-laden property effortlessly blends rustic elements with elegant sensibilities while also maintaining a sense of history but pushing the culinary envelope—not an easy task. Service is impeccable, and full liquor service is available.

6451 E. Millcreek Canyon Rd. ☏ **801/272-8255.** www.log-haven.com. Reservations recommended. Main courses $20–$41. AE, DISC, MC, V. Daily 5:30–9pm.

Market Street Grill/Downtown ★★ SEAFOOD/STEAK   Open for 30 years, the Market Street Grill is quite possibly Utah's best seafood restaurant. Expect a wait before you're led into the bustling dining room. The checkerboard-floored eatery is packed for good reason: Fresh fish is flown in daily from around the world, and the Grill knows how to do it up right. I loved the Alaskan halibut Oscar, topped with snow crab, fresh asparagus, and béarnaise sauce; and the cioppino, a seafood stew of shrimp, crab, mussels, halibut, and scallops—or choose one of about two dozen other seafood offerings. You can also choose from a good variety of dinner salads, pastas, and excellent steaks. Until 7pm nightly, the restaurant offers a fixed-price early-bird dinner special: a choice of roasted prime rib, Alaska halibut, or Atlantic salmon for $21. Look for all the standard breakfast choices, plus, fittingly, a seafood omelet; lunch includes salads, sandwiches, pasta, steaks, a variety of seafood dishes, and a daily special. Sunday brunch is great here, too. Full liquor service is available.

A similar lunch, dinner, and Sunday brunch menu is served at the **Market Street Grill/Cottonwood,** 2985 E. 6580 South (☏ **801/942-8860**), **Market Street Broiler,** 260 S. 1300 East (☏ **801/583-8808**), and **Market Street Grill/South Jordan,** 10702 S. River Front Pkwy. (☏ **801/302-2262**).

48 W. Market St. ☏ **801/322-4668.** www.gastronomyinc.com. Breakfast $6–$13, lunch $8–$49, dinner $16–$56. AE, DISC, MC, V. Mon–Thurs 6:30am–3pm and 5–9pm; Fri 6:30am–3pm and 5–10:30pm; Sat 8am–3pm and 4–10:30pm; Sun 9am–3pm and 4–9pm.

Metropolitan ★★★ CONTEMPORARY AMERICAN   The Metropolitan wouldn't be out of place in San Francisco, with its see- (with city views) and-be-seen (at the industrial-chic bar) vibe. Instead, it's right at home in Salt Lake City and offers inspired fare prepared by a team of two chefs. Choose from a seasonally changing selection of dishes with European and Asian influences, gorgeous presentations, and sumptuous flavors. On a previous visit, the meal started with oysters with red peppers and asparagus soup with pancetta, cracked pepper, and olive oil before moving on to a main course of risotto with plump tiger prawns. Diners on a tighter budget might opt for the "bar bites" menu of sliders, mac 'n' cheese, and other comfort foods, or taste-size portions of soups and salads for $8 to $12. For lunch, the bison burger is a standout; panini and pizzas are also on the menu. Full liquor service is available.

173 W. Broadway. © **801/364-3472.** www.themetropolitan.com. Reservations recommended. Main courses lunch $6–$12, dinner $17–$40. AE, DISC, MC, V. Mon–Fri 11:30am–2pm; daily 6–10pm. Bar opens at 5:30pm.

The New Yorker ★★ AMERICAN Among Utah's finest restaurants since it opened in 1978, the New Yorker maintains an air of quiet sophistication, with rich woods, understated elegance, excellent food, and impeccable service. From the continually evolving dinner menu, start with the delectable coconut-panko crab cakes, which are as good as you'll find on the coasts; the certified Angus beef New York sirloin with Gouda potatoes au gratin; or the roasted rack of Dijon-crusted lamb. Lunch brings dishes such as deep-fried Gulf white shrimp, served with fries and slaw; a two-course prix-fixe option for $15; and a variety of sandwiches and salads. The dinner menu also offers scaled-down fare, such as a bacon-and-avocado burger, crispy fried Camembert and pear with red pepper jelly, and an excellent Cobb salad. Full liquor service is available; the wine list is terrific and the cocktails are inspired.

60 W. Market St. © **801/363-0166.** www.newyorkerslc.com. Reservations recommended. Main courses $10–$22 lunch, $14–$48 dinner. AE, DISC, MC, V. Mon–Thurs 11:30am–2pm and 5:30–9:30pm; Fri 11:30am–2pm and 5:30–11pm; Sat 5:30–11pm.

Spencer's for Steaks and Chops ★★ STEAK/CHOPS This sophisticated steakhouse is the perfect spot to celebrate a special occasion, or to just sit back and enjoy a truly excellent steak. The handsome dining room is reminiscent of a library in a British lord's country home, with dark wood, tapestrylike wall coverings, vintage photos, and intimate and comfortable booths. Beef is king here—aged, well-marbled USDA prime beef that is simply and perfectly prepared. The New York strip and the super-tender filet mignon come heartily recommended. Other dinner selections served a la carte include bison rib-eye, peppercorn-seared ahi, double-cut lamb chops, and free-range chicken. Don't miss the delectable loaded hash browns topped with applewood bacon, sharp white cheddar, chives, and sour cream. The lunch menu includes the same steaks, as well as burgers, chicken sandwiches, and entree salads. Spencer's also has an extensive list of wines and single malt Scotches.

Located in Hilton Salt Lake City Center, 255 S. West Temple. © **801/238-4748.** www.spencersfor steaksandchops.com. Reservations recommended. Lunch items $12–$26, dinner main courses $30–$58. AE, DISC, MC, V. Mon–Thurs 11:30am–10pm; Fri 11:30am–11pm; Sat 5–11pm; Sun 5–10pm.

Tuscany ★★★ NORTHERN ITALIAN Located in a quaintly elegant setting at the foot of the Wasatch Mountains and owned in part by the 7'4" Utah Jazz shot-blocking legend Mark Eaton, Tuscany resembles an Italian mountain lodge, with massive beams, cathedral ceilings, an extensive use of rock, old-world murals, stained glass, and four enormous fireplaces. The Northern Italian cuisine has been tempered with Western influences, resulting in delicious dishes such as a hardwood-grilled, double-cut pork chop with scallion mashed potatoes, balsamic roasted onions, and pan juices; pulled pork and beef meatloaf with Parmesan mashers; and oven-roasted filet of salmon with pancetta-pesto crust served with toasted vegetable couscous. And be sure to save room for one of the homemade desserts, such as rich old-fashioned chocolate cake or vanilla bean crème brûlée with fresh berries. In summer, you can dine alfresco in the lovely garden. Under the same management and likewise highly recommended is the adjacent **Franck's,** 6263 Holladay Blvd. (© **801/274-6264;** www.francksfood.com), dishing up ultra-creative American-French fusion dishes and comfort food ranging from meatloaf to foie gras. Full liquor service is available at both restaurants.

2832 E. 6200 South. ⓒ **801/277-9919.** www.tuscanyslc.com. Main courses lunch $8–$15, main courses dinner $15–$30. AE, DISC, MC, V. Mon–Fri 11:30am–1:30pm; Mon–Thurs 5:30–9pm; Fri–Sat 5:30–9:30pm; Sun 10:30am–1:30pm brunch (summer only) and 5:30–8:30pm.

Moderate

Archibald's Restaurant AMERICAN   Archibald's is housed in a restored 1877 flour mill that's listed on the National Historic Register. In each booth is a picture and brief discussion of one of Mormon pioneer Archibald Gardner's 11 wives. Menu items here range from American standards—burgers, top sirloin steak, salmon—to more creative fare, such as fried green tomatoes with creamy salsa. Recommended dishes include the halibut and chips, traditional turkey dinner, or the ginger chicken salad—grilled chicken and almonds over lettuce, with olives, green onions, mushrooms, snow peas, and a sesame-ginger dressing. Beer and wine are available.

1100 W. 7800 South, West Jordan (in Gardner Village, p. 69). ⓒ **801/566-6940.** www.gardner village.com. Reservations accepted only for parties of 8 or more. Main courses $8–$19. AE, DISC, MC, V. Mon–Thurs 11am–9pm; Fri–Sat 11am–10pm. Closes 1 hr. earlier in winter.

The Copper Onion NEW AMERICAN   Featuring one of Salt Lake's most creative menus, the Copper Onion serves an eclectic array of dishes in a classic but casual atmosphere. Dinners include pasta dishes, meat loaf, and heirloom chicken, with a nice array of seasonal side dishes like sautéed spinach with cashews and raisins or cauliflower with anchovy cream and capers. Lunch and brunch strike a similar note, ranging from house-made pasta dishes to huevos rancheros. There is a full bar that mixes specialty cocktails like cucumber gimlets and brandy Alexanders.

111 E. Broadway. ⓒ **801/355-3282.** www.thecopperonion.com. Reservations recommended. Main courses $8–$18 lunch and brunch, $11–$22 dinner. AE, DISC, MC, V. Mon–Thurs 11:30am–10pm; Fri 11:30am–11pm; Sat 10:30am–11pm; Sun 10:30am–10pm.

Lamb's Grill Cafe ★★ 🍴 AMERICAN/CONTINENTAL   Opened in 1919 in the northern Utah town of Logan by Greek immigrant George Lamb, this restaurant moved to Salt Lake City's Herald Building in 1939 and has been serving the who's who of Utah ever since. But this isn't one of those fancy places that you go to just to be seen; Lamb's is successful because it consistently serves good food at reasonable prices, with friendly, efficient service.

The extensive menu offers mostly basic American and Continental fare, although the restaurant's Greek origins are also evident. In a tip of the hat to the restaurant's moniker, several lamb dishes appear on the menu, including broiled French-style lamb chops and barbecued lamb shank. Other popular dinner selections—all available after 11:30am and cooked to order—include broiled New York steak topped with blue cheese, grilled baby-beef liver with sautéed onions, steamed finnan haddie (smoked haddock), Greek-style broiled chicken breasts with oregano, and grilled fresh rainbow trout. Or choose from a good selection of sandwiches and salads, daily pasta and salad specials, and a variety of desserts, including an extra-special rice pudding. Full liquor service is available.

169 S. Main St. ⓒ **801/364-7166.** http://lambsgrill.com. Main courses $5–$26. AE, DISC, MC, V. Mon–Fri 7am–9pm; Sat 8am–9pm.

Inexpensive

In addition to the choices below, I'm quite fond of the garlic burgers at the low-key watering hole known as the **Cotton Bottom,** 2820 E. 6200 South (ⓒ **801/273-9830**), the Neapolitan-style pizzas at **Settebello,** 260 S. 200 West

(𝄆 **801/322-3556;** www.settebello.net), and the Swiss fare and beer selection at the **Beerhive Pub,** 128 S. Main St. (𝄆 **801/364-4268**), with a bar featuring a narrow trough of frost to keep your pint cold to the last swig. For quick, cheap, and family-friendly food, head to one of the **Crown Burgers** locations in the metro area, including downtown at 377 E. 200 South (𝄆 **801/532-1155;** www.crown-burgers. com), and on the east side at 3190 S. Highland Dr. (𝄆 **801/467-6633**).

Café Trang ★ ✦ VIETNAMESE/CHINESE   Family-owned-and-operated Café Trang is known for serving some of the best Vietnamese food in the state since 1987. Recently relocated to the vicinity of the EnergySolutions Arena downtown, the restaurant also offers Chinese dishes—mostly Cantonese with some Vietnamese influences. Vietnamese paintings grace the walls, and two large aquariums add to the vibe. The menu is packed with literally hundreds of dishes. A popular vegetarian specialty is the fried bean curd with grilled onions and crushed peanuts, served with rice papers, a vegetable platter, and peanut sauce. It's hard to pick just one, but the top choice here just might be the spicy *bun ga xao* (rice vermicelli noodles with sautéed chicken and lemon grass, served with grilled onions and peanuts). Beer and wine are available.

307 W. 200 South. 𝄆 **801/539-1638.** www.cafetrangrestaurant.com. Reservations recommended in winter. Main courses $8–$15. AE, DISC, MC, V. Mon–Thurs 11:30am–9:30pm; Fri–Sat 11:30am–10pm; Sun noon–9:30pm.

Caputo's Deli ★ ✦ DELICATESSEN   A stalwart lunch stop, Caputo's is located in an upscale market on the west side of downtown. Order at the counter, take a seat in the semi-industrial interior or on the parkside patio out front, and wait for your number to be called. The sandwiches and salads are terrific, made with fresh and flavorful ingredients, with an emphasis on Italian standbys. New Orleans–style muffulettas, meatball subs, and roasted peppers on focaccia are among the mouthwatering selections. Salads, pasta dishes, and daily specials are available. There's a second location, **Caputo's on 15th,** 1516 S. 1500 East (𝄆 **801/486-6615**).

314 W. 300 South. 𝄆 **801/531-8669.** www.caputosdeli.com. Sandwiches and salads $6–$9, dinner main courses $13–$20. AE, DISC, MC, V. Mon–Sat 9am–8pm.

Desert Edge Brewery at the Pub ☺ MICROBREWERY   This isn't your average microbrewery: It's in a mall, it's family-friendly, and it's got an in-house coffee bar. A Trolley Square stalwart for 35 years, "the Pub" offers a nice mix of American and Mexican standards as well, and such salads as grilled tuna with basil vinaigrette. The beers are uniformly excellent, with about eight on tap at any given time, and the granite bar is a great place to watch a game.

273 Trolley Square. 𝄆 **801/521-8917.** Main courses $7–$10. AE, DISC, MC, V. Mon–Thurs 11am–midnight; Fri–Sat 11am–11pm; Sun noon–10:30pm. (Limited menu after 10pm.)

Red Iguana ★ ♟ MEXICAN   Another local favorite, owned and operated by the Cardenas family, the Red Iguana is one of the few Mexican joints anywhere that specializes in mole—the spicy sauce named for a Nahuatl (Aztec) word meaning concoction. Just as the colorful dining room nearly overwhelms the eyes, the *amarillo* mole served over chicken nearly overwhelms the taste buds with its fiery combination of *aji amarillo* and *guajillo* peppers, vegetables, and spices. Other enticing variations of mole include *verde, negro,* red *pipian* with peanuts and pumpkinseeds, and several more. The menu doesn't begin and end with mole, however: A full slate of Mexican standards, seafood, and egg dishes is available, as are beer and wine. There's a second location at 866 W. South Temple (© **801/214-6050**), and a takeout version, **Taste of Red Iguana,** at the City Creek Food Court, 28 S. State St. (© **801/ 214-6350**).

736 W. North Temple. © **801/322-1489.** www.rediguana.com. Most dishes $7–$15. AE, DISC, MC, V. Mon–Thurs 11am–10pm; Fri 11am–11pm; Sat 10am–11pm; Sun 10am–9pm. From downtown, follow North Temple west under the I-15 overpass; the restaurant is on your right.

EXPLORING TEMPLE SQUARE

This is sacred ground for members of the Church of Jesus Christ of Latter-day Saints (LDS), also known as Mormons. (See chapter 2, "Utah in Depth," to learn about the history of the church and modern Mormonism.) The 10-acre **Temple Square ★★★** is enclosed by 15-foot walls, with a gate in the center of each. In addition to the church buildings, the square houses lovely gardens and statuary, and the North and South visitor centers, which have exhibits on the church's history and beliefs, interactive videos, and films. Also in the North Center is an 11-foot-tall replica of the awe-inspiring sculpture *Christus,* a statue of Christ by the Danish artist Bertel Thorvaldsen.

The majestic **Temple** is used only for the LDS church's most sacred ceremonies and is not open to the public. Brigham Young chose the site within 4 days of entering the valley, and work began on the six-spired granite structure in 1853. It took 40 years to complete.

The oval **Tabernacle** seats about 3,500 people and has one of the West's largest unsupported domed roofs. The Tabernacle has fantastic acoustics and has served as the city's cultural center for over a century.

On Thursday evenings at 8pm, you can listen to the **Mormon Tabernacle Choir ★★★** rehearse (except when they're on tour; call © **801/240-4150,** or visit www.mormontabernaclechoir.org for schedules), and on Sunday mornings you can attend their broadcast from 9:30 to 10am (you must be seated by 9:15am). The choir, composed entirely of volunteers, was formed shortly after the first pioneers arrived; many husband-and-wife members and families participate, sometimes over several generations. The Tabernacle organ has been rebuilt a number of times, and has grown from the original 2,000 pipes and two manuals to 11,623 pipes and five manuals. The organ is said to have an instantly recognizable signature sound. Half-hour organ recitals take place year-round, Monday through Saturday at noon, Sunday at 2pm. At peak times, an additional 2pm recital is often scheduled Monday through Saturday. Admission to these performances is free.

The Gothic-style **Assembly Hall** was constructed in 1880 from leftover granite from the Temple and has lovely soaring white spires and stained-glass windows. Free concerts are offered here most weekends; inquire at a visitor center for schedules. Two monuments stand in front of the Assembly Hall: One depicts a pioneer family arriving with a handcart filled with their belongings, and the second commemorates the salvaging of the first crops from a plague of crickets (sea gulls swooped down and ate the insects).

Guided tours of the square, lasting approximately 30 minutes and available in 30 languages, leave every few minutes from any of the gates; personnel in the visitor center can direct you. Tour guides provide a general history of the church (touching upon the church's doctrine) and take you around the square, briefly explaining what you are seeing. The Tabernacle tour includes a fascinating demonstration of the incredible acoustics: the group is ushered to the last row of seats while someone stands at the podium and drops three pins—the sound is as clear as a bell!

The square is bounded by Main Street on the east and North, South, and West Temple streets. The LDS Church recently purchased the stretch of Main Street on the square's east side, closed it to traffic, and transformed it into a lovely park with trees, flowers, walking paths, and benches; a large reflecting pool dominates the area, displaying a mirror image of the magnificent Temple.

Across North Temple Street from the Square is the **Conference Center of the Church of Jesus Christ of Latter-day Saints** (✆ **801/240-0075**). This huge complex has a main auditorium for worship services, meetings, and cultural events, seating 21,000 people.

When the church leaders realized there would be 4 acres of **roof** over the conference center, they decided to do something special with it. And boy did they—the designers have created a wild landscape reminiscent of a Utah mountain on top of the roof. Among the flora are bristlecone pines, aspens, Serbian spruces, 21 native meadow grasses, and 300 varieties of Utah wildflowers. An immense fountain flows in four directions and eventually into the Conference Center spire, from which it cascades 67 feet down the south face of the building. The roof is a serene oasis in the middle of a busy modern city—people sit or stroll and enjoy the views of the city set against the Wasatch Mountains.

The Conference Center is usually open Monday through Saturday from 9am to 9pm (the roof closes at 8:30pm); free guided tours of the complex are offered except during special events.

Visitor centers are also open daily from 9am to 9pm; tours are given between 9:15am and 8:15pm. Hours are reduced on Christmas. Call ✆ **800/363-6027** or 801/240-1706 for more information, or browse **www.visittemplesquare.com** or **www.lds.org**. The Trax train stops right out front, at the Temple Square station. Allow 1 to 3 hours to tour the square.

MORE TO SEE & DO IN & AROUND SALT LAKE CITY

Church History Museum This collection of church art and artifacts, started in 1869, includes Utah's earliest Mormon log home, rare 1849 Mormon gold coins, and a scale model of Salt Lake City in 1870. The history of the LDS Church is related in the exhibits that describe each of the church presidents, from Joseph Smith to present; activities include multimedia programs, films, and puppet shows. There's also a museum shop (closed Sun). Allow 1 hour.

45 N. West Temple. ✆ **801/240-3310** or 240-4615. www.lds.org/churchhistory/museum. Free admission. Mon–Fri 9am–9pm; Sat–Sun and most holidays 10am–7pm. Trax: Temple Square.

Family History Library ★★ This incredible facility contains what is probably the world's largest collection of genealogical records under one roof. You can easily spend hours here immersed in discovering the whos, whats, wheres, and whys of your family history. The growing collection is composed of a substantial number of records from around the United States, fairly comprehensive data from the British Isles, and vital record information from 110 other countries. Most of the records, which date from about 1550 to 1930, are from governments, various churches and other organizations, and individuals.

The Mormons believe that families are united for eternity through marriage and other sacred ordinances given in the temples. These ordinances, such as baptism ceremonies, can be done on behalf of ancestors—hence the interest in tracing all deceased family members.

When you enter the library, help is available to assist with your research. There are forms you can fill out with any and all data you already know (so come prepared with copies of whatever you have), and you will be directed from there. An orientation is given to newcomers and includes a handout and a map of the library. Volunteers are stationed around the library to help with anything you need.

Some of the records are in books, and many have been converted to microfilm, microfiche, and computer files. The volunteers will show you how to use any unfamiliar machines. One of the easiest ways to begin a search is to start with the place where your ancestors lived, because records are organized first by the geographical origin.

35 N. West Temple. ℗ **866/406-1830** or 801/240-2584. www.familysearch.org. Free admission. Mon 8am–5pm; Tues–Sat 8am–9pm. Closed Sun, major holidays, and July 24. Trax: Temple Square.

University of Utah   Members of the Church of Jesus Christ of Latter-day Saints opened the University of Deseret in 1850, just 2½ years after they arrived in the Salt Lake Valley. It closed 2 years later, due to lack of funds and the greater need for primary education, but reopened in 1867 as a business academy. The name changed in 1892, and the growing school moved to its present location in 1900. The university now sprawls over 1,500 acres on the east side of the city (from the center of town, take Utah 186 east to the campus).

The University is also home to the **Utah Museum of Fine Arts** and the **Natural History Museum of Utah** (both below).

University of Utah. General information line ℗ **801/581-7200.** www.utah.edu. Trax: University Line.

Historic Buildings & Monuments

Beehive House ★   This house was built in 1854 as Brigham Young's family home. Young also kept an office here and entertained church and government leaders on the premises. Young, a lover of New England architecture, utilized much of that style in his house, including a widow's walk for surveying the surrounding desert. Today, visitors can get a glimpse of the lifestyle of this famous Mormon leader by taking a guided half-hour tour of the house. It has been decorated with period furniture (many pieces original to the home) to resemble its appearance when Young lived here, as described in a journal kept by his daughter Clarissa. Young's bedroom is to the left of the entrance hall. The Long Hall, where formal entertaining took place, is

What to See & Do in Downtown Salt Lake City

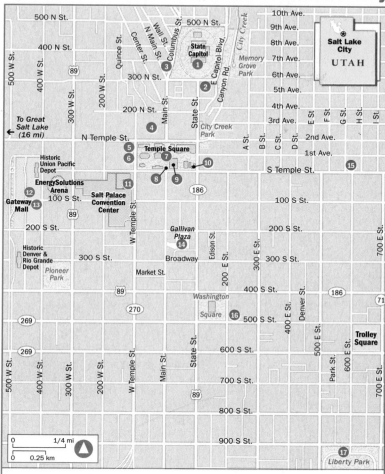

Beehive House **10**

Brigham Young Monument **8**

Capitol Building, Capitol Hill **1**

Church History Museum **5**

Clark Planetarium **13**

Conference Center of the Church of Jesus Christ of Latter-day Saints **4**

Council Hall **2**

Discovery Gateway **12**

Family History Library **6**

Gallivan Plaza **14**

Governor's Mansion **15**

Joseph Smith Memorial Building **9**

The Leonardo **16**

Liberty Park **17**

Pioneer Memorial Museum **3**

Temple Square **7**

Utah Museum of Contemporary Art **11**

on the second floor; it was also used as a dormitory to house visitors. Young's children gathered in the sewing room, where they helped with chores, bathed by the stove, and studied Christian principles. Only one of Young's 27 wives lived in the Beehive House at a time; the rest, with some of the children, lived next door in the **Lion House** (now a banquet facility and restaurant open Mon–Sat from 11am–8pm) or in other houses. Built of stuccoed adobe in 1855 through 1856, the Lion House was named for the stone lion guarding its entrance.

Before you leave, stop at **Eagle Gate,** a 76-foot gateway that marked the entrance to the Brigham Young homestead, located at the corner of State Street and South Temple. It's been altered several times over the years, and the original wooden eagle has been replaced by a 4,000-pound metal version with a 20-foot wingspan. Allow about an hour.

67 E. South Temple. ✆ **801/240-2681.** www.lds.org/placestovisit. Free admission. Daily 9:30am–8:30pm (last tour at 8:15pm). Trax: Temple Square; walk a half-block east.

Brigham Young Monument   This marker, near the southeast corner of Temple Square, was placed here to honor Young, the other pioneers who accompanied him here in 1847, and the countless Native Americans and fur trappers who preceded them.

At Main and South Temple sts.

Capitol Building ★   Built between 1912 and 1916 of unpolished Utah granite and Georgia marble—and restored and earthquake-proofed from 2004 to 2008—the Utah State Capitol, considered one of the finest examples of Renaissance Revival style in the West, rests on a hill in a beautifully landscaped 40-acre park. The state symbol, the beehive (representing industry and cooperation), is a recurring motif both inside and out. Those who don't want to take the free tour can walk through on their own.

The **Rotunda,** which stretches upward 165 feet, is decorated with murals painted during the WPA years (the four largest depict important scenes in the state's early history) and houses several busts of prominent historical figures, including Brigham Young and Philo T. Farnsworth, the man whom we can all thank for bringing us television. The chandelier is astounding—it weighs 6,000 pounds and hangs from a 7,000-pound chain.

Other rooms include the State Reception Room, known as the Gold Room because the walls are made from locally mined gold-traverse marble; the offices of the governor and lieutenant governor; the Hall of Governors, a portrait gallery that honors all those who have served as governor of Utah since statehood in 1896; and the offices of Utah's attorney general. Downstairs are a small souvenir shop and additional exhibits, including a large topographical map of Utah.

The third floor houses the Senate, House of Representatives, and Supreme Court of Utah. You can either climb one of the two marble staircases or take the elevator. The state legislature meets for 45 days in January and February. In front of the House of

---

Bigger than Texas?

Brigham Young proposed the state of Deseret to the U.S. government in 1849. The vision included parts of modern-day California (including San Diego), Nevada, Utah, Idaho, Arizona, and New Mexico. Needless to say, the proposal didn't fly.

More to See & Do in & around Salt Lake City

SALT LAKE CITY

Representatives is a replica of the Liberty Bell, one of 53 bronzed and cast in France in 1950. Allow at least an hour to explore here.

Capitol Hill, at the north end of State St. ⓒ **801/538-1800.** www.utahstatecapitol.utah.gov. Free admission and tours. Building daily 8am–8pm; guided tours Mon–Fri 9am–4pm. Bus: 23 up Main St.

Council Hall   Completed in 1866, Council Hall is a fine example of Federal Greek Revival architecture. Originally located downtown, it first served as City Hall and the meeting place for the Territorial Legislature; in the early 1960s, it was dismantled and reassembled—block by sandstone block, 325 of them—in its present location. Today, it houses the **Utah Travel Council** (www.utah.com) upstairs; the ground floor contains a bookstore and gift shop. Allow 45 minutes.

Capitol Hill, 300 N. State St. ⓒ **800/200-1160** or 801/538-1030. Free admission. Mon–Fri 8am–5pm; Sat–Sun and holidays 10am–5pm. Bus: 23 to the Capitol.

Governor's Mansion   Silver magnate Thomas Kearns started building this palatial home in 1898, sparing no expense to make it as lavish as possible. African and Italian marble and exotic woods from around the world were used extensively throughout. Kearns's widow deeded it to the state in 1937, and the 36-room mansion is now the governor's residence. It suffered a devastating fire just before Christmas 1993, but has been fully restored to its 1902 appearance (1902 was the year that the Kearns family first moved in). The best time to see the mansion is in December, when it's elaborately decorated for Christmas. Allow about half an hour.

603 E. South Temple. ⓒ **801/538-1005.** Free admission. June–Aug and Dec Tues and Thurs 2–4pm; call for hours at other times. Trax: Trolley Square.

Joseph Smith Memorial Building   Between 1911 and 1987, this building served as the world-renowned Hotel Utah. Since renovated and converted into offices, meeting spaces, restaurants (www.diningattemplesquare.com), and reception areas (very popular for wedding receptions), the architectural details have been lovingly restored. The lobby retains its art-glass ceiling and massive marble pillars—it's worth a stop for a peek inside. The **FamilySearch Center** (ⓒ **801/240-4085**) has 100 computers and a staff to help you discover your family's roots. A big-screen 500-seat **theater** (ⓒ **801/240-4383**) offers free showings of an hour-long movie about the life of LDS founder Joseph Smith. Allow between a half-hour to an hour and a half.

15 E. South Temple. ⓒ **800/537-9703** or 801/240-1266. www.visittemplesquare.com. Free admission. Mon–Sat 9am–9pm. Trax: Temple Square.

Museums

Clark Planetarium ★ ☺   This state-of-the-art planetarium presents laser light shows and big-screen movies in a 3-D IMAX theater. It also contains a variety of interactive exhibits ranging from a display about the names of the planets to a Foucault pendulum, plus a rotating relief globe. Allow up to 3 hours.

110 S. 400 West. ⓒ **801/456-7827.** www.clarkplanetarium.org. Free admission to museum; shows $8 adults, $6 children 12 and under. Sun–Thurs 10:30am–10pm; Fri–Sat 10:30am–11pm. Trax: Energy-Solutions Arena.

Gallivan Plaza   Some call this Salt Lake City's outdoor living room, with its intimate spaces, performances, food, all kinds of characters and activities, and good vantage points for watching the goings-on. Wander through the large art exhibit and the gigantic outdoor chessboard with waist-high pieces, and enjoy the pond, amphitheater, outdoor ice-skating rink (call or visit the website for hours and rates), and aviary. Allow 30 minutes; more if you plan to go skating or dine here.

239 S. Main St. (the entire block btw. Main and State sts., and 200 and 300 South). ⓒ **801/535-6110.** www.gallivanevents.com. Free admission. Daily 7am–10pm. Trax: Gallivan Plaza.

The Leonardo Opening in fall 2011, "The Leo" (named for Leonardo da Vinci) is a science and technology museum with a wide range of exhibits dedicated to innovation. Cutting-edge displays compellingly meld art and science, showcasing technological advancements in prostheses, biofuels, and architecture. (The building is a contemporary work of art in itself.) Philip Beesley's "Hylozoic Veil," an evolving environment subtly responds to outside factors, is a particularly captivating installation.

209 E. 500 South. ⓒ **801/531-9800.** www.theleonardo.org. Admission $14 adults, $12 seniors, $10 kids 6 to 17. Wed–Thurs and Sat 11am–7pm; Fri 11am–10pm; Sun 11am–5pm.

Natural History Museum of Utah ★ ☺ Moved to a stunning new building in 2011, this museum covers more than 200 million years of natural history with a focus on Utah. All-new exhibits—including intriguing dinosaur exhibits—describe the geologic and natural history of Utah right up to the present. Allow 1 hour.

At the University of Utah, 301 Wakara Way. ⓒ **801/581-6927.** www.umnh.utah.edu. Admission $9 adults, less for seniors 62 and older and children. Daily 10am–5pm (Wed until 9pm). Trax: S. Campus Dr.

Pioneer Memorial Museum 👜 Operated by the Daughters of Utah Pioneers, this museum, housed in a Grecian-style building, contains an immense collection of pioneer portraits and memorabilia, 200,000 artifacts in all. All six stories are packed with relics of Utah's history, such as paintings, photos, and the personal effects of church leaders Brigham Young and Heber C. Kimball. The collection also includes exhibits on spinning, weaving, railroading, mining, and guns; a restored 1902 steam fire engine; and a few unusual relics like hair wreaths, temple replicas, and a stuffed two-headed calf. You can walk through on your own or with the aid of a guide sheet; tours are also available with advance arrangements. A short film is shown throughout the day. Allow 1 hour.

300 N. Main St. ⓒ **801/532-6479.** www.dupinternational.org. Free admission; contributions welcome. Mon–Sat 9am–5pm; June–Aug also Sun 1–5pm. Closed major holidays. Trax: Temple Square.

Utah Museum of Contemporary Art ★ Changing exhibits feature contemporary works by local, regional, and national artists. There are generally several simultaneous exhibitions in a variety of mediums, including paintings, photographs, sculptures, and ceramics. Allow at least 1 hour, and check the schedule for lectures, poetry readings, concerts, and workshops.

20 S. West Temple. ⓒ **801/328-4201.** www.utahmoca.org. Free admission; donations welcome. Tues–Thurs and Sat 11am–6pm; Fri 11am–9pm. Trax: Temple Square.

Utah Museum of Fine Arts ★★ This is among the very best art museums in the state, housing a permanent collection of more than 18,000 objects. Changing displays might include Greek and Egyptian antiquities, Italian Renaissance works, art by European masters, Early American art, 20th century lithographic prints and photography, and art objects from Southeast Asia, China, Japan, and African and pre-Columbian cultures. Exhibits highlight shows from other institutions and private

City Sights Tours (© 801/531-1001; www.saltlakecitytours.org) offers several tours of the city and surrounding areas, including Park City and the Great Salt Lake. A 4-hour tour of the city and Mormon Trail costs $50, and a 4-hour tour to Kennecott's Bingham Canyon Mine, which includes a stop at the beach on the Great Salt Lake, is $55. A Sunday city tour that includes a Mormon Tabernacle Choir concert also costs $55.

collections. The 74,000-square-foot museum has over 20 galleries, a bookstore, a cafe, a community education center, and a sculpture garden. Allow 2 to 4 hours.

At the University of Utah, 410 Campus Center Dr. © **801/581-7332.** www.umfa.utah.edu. Admission $7 adults, $5 seniors and children 6–18, free for children 5 and under. Tues–Fri 10am–5pm (Wed until 8pm); Sat–Sun 11am–5pm. Closed Mon and major holidays. Trax: S. Campus Dr.

Parks & Gardens

Gilgal Garden ★ 🏛 Folk-art aficionados won't want to skip this collection of ornate, bizarre, and often abstract sculptures, the handiwork of the late Thomas Child, a mason and devout Mormon. Child's beliefs shine through in his works, which include a sphinxlike Joseph Smith, and his *Monument to the Trade*, in honor of bricklaying. The sculptures almost went the way of the dodo before locals fought to restore the property and turned it into a city park in 2000. Allow about 1 hour.

749 E. 500 South. © **801/582-0432.** www.gilgalgarden.org. Free admission. Apr–Sept daily 8am–8pm; rest of year daily 9am–5pm. Bus: 209.

International Peace Gardens ★ Begun in 1939 by the Salt Lake Council of Women, the Peace Gardens have expanded over the years and now belong to the city. Take a stroll along the Jordan River, through the gardens, and past statuary and displays representing different countries (such as Buddha statues, windmills, and Viking tomb replicas). Benches are scattered about for moments of rest and contemplation. Allow about 1 hour.

Jordan Park, 1060 S. 900 West. © **801/938-5326.** www.internationalpeacegardens.org. Free admission. May–Sept daily dawn–dusk. Bus: 209.

Liberty Park ★★ ☺ This delightful city park has trails for walking and jogging, tennis courts, a small lake with ducks and paddle-boat rentals, picnic facilities, a playground, a children's garden, a children's amusement park, a museum, and an excellent aviary. Covering 100 acres, this is a favorite gathering spot for locals, as well as one of the best dog-walking areas in the city (dogs must be leashed and owners must clean up after them). In the park, the **Chase Home Museum of Utah Folk Arts** (© **801/533-5760**), in the historic Brigham Young/Chase home, contains exhibits of pioneer art, American Indian art, and folk art. Allow a half-hour. **Tracy Aviary** (© **801/596-8500**; www.tracyaviary.org), in the southwest section of the park, has more than 400 birds, including a number of endangered species. There are special exhibits of cuckoos and pelicans (you can feed the latter with a keeper for $3), and free-flying bird shows are presented during the summer (call for schedule). Allow at least 1 hour.

Btw. 500 and 700 East, and 900 and 1300 South. Entrances from 900 and 1300 South. © **801/972-7800** for the city parks department. Park and museum free admission; Tracy Aviary admission $7

Greater Salt Lake Valley

Wasatch National Forest

City Creek Canyon Rd.

EMIGRATION CANYON

To Wyoming

80

MILL CREEK CANYON

215

10

University of Utah and Medical Center

Sunnyside Ave.

2300 E St.

171

6

7

9

Highland Dr.

5

1300 S St.

4

Gilgal Sculpture Garden

4th Ave.

186

181

1300 S St.

Sugar House Park

80

71

4500 S. St.

Utah State Capitol

SALT LAKE CITY

Liberty Park

Fairmount Park

700 E St.

89

Temple Square

400 S St.

State Street

UTA Trax (light rail)

15

Victory Rd.

15

80

Map continues on inset

600 N St.

186

Jordan River

Redwood Rd

3

N Temple St.

Indiana Ave.

8

2100 S. St.

SOUTH SALT LAKE

2100 S. St.

Meadowbrook Expressway

4700 S. Expressway

215

215

215

15

2200 N St.

1 2

Salt Lake City International Airport

80

500 S St.

900 S St.

California Ave.

Bangerder Hwy.

3600 W St.

4000 W St.

4800 W St.

5400 W St.

5600 W St.

4700 W St.

3600 W St.

MAGNA

Continued from main map

BOUNTIFUL

Bountiful Blvd.

Chase Lane

Porter Lane

Page Lane

Orchard Dr.

Davis Blvd.

Main St.

89

91

15

To Ogden

CENTERVILLE

WEST BOUNTIFUL

800 W St.

89

91

1100 W St.

1800 W St.

Cudahy Lane

15

215

3100 S St.

3500 S St.

4100 S St.

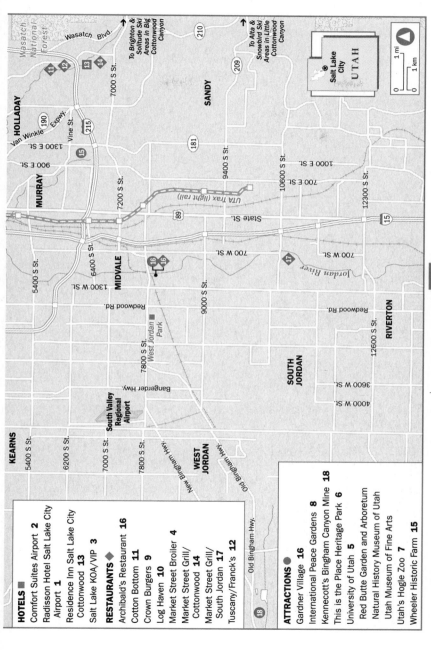

HOTELS
Comfort Suites Airport **2**
Radisson Hotel Salt Lake City
Airport **1**
Residence Inn Salt Lake City
Cottonwood **13**
Salt Lake KOA/VIP **3**

RESTAURANTS ◆
Archibald's Restaurant **16**
Cotton Bottom **11**
Crown Burgers **9**
Log Haven **10**
Market Street Broiler **4**
Market Street Grill/
Cottonwood **14**
Market Street Grill/
South Jordan **17**
Tuscany/Franck's **12**

ATTRACTIONS ●
Gardner Village **16**
International Peace Gardens **8**
Kennecott's Bingham Canyon Mine **18**
This is the Place Heritage Park **6**
University of Utah **5**
Red Butte Garden and Arboretum
Natural History Museum of Utah
Utah Museum of Fine Arts
Utah's Hogle Zoo **7**
Wheeler Historic Farm **15**

5

SALT LAKE CITY | More to See & Do in & around Salt Lake City adults, $6 students and seniors 65 and older, $4 children 3–12, free for children 2 and under. Park daily 6am–11pm (dawn–dusk in winter). Museum Mon–Fri 8am–5pm. Tracy Aviary daily 9am–5pm. Bus: 9, 205, 307, or 320.

Red Butte Garden and Arboretum ★★   This Arboretum on the University of Utah campus features 100 acres of display gardens and another 100 acres in their natural state, with 4 miles of nature trails. Located in the foothills of the Wasatch Mountains, this is a terrific spot to take a break or catch a summer concert. Allow 2 hours.

300 Wakara Way. ℭ **801/585-0556.** www.redbuttegarden.org. Admission $8 for adults, $6 for children 3–17 and seniors 65 and over. May–Aug daily 9am–9pm; shorter hours the rest of the year. From downtown, drive east on 400 South, past the university entrance, continuing until 400 South becomes Foothill Dr.; turn east on Wakara Way.

This Is the Place Heritage Park   Brigham Young and the Mormon pioneers got their first glimpse of the Salt Lake Valley at the site of this historic park. A tall granite and bronze sculpture was erected in 1947 to commemorate the centennial of their arrival. The park, which covers more than 1,600 acres, offers hiking along part of the trail used by the pioneers, with opportunities for cross-country skiing in winter. This is a good place for wildlife viewing and birding in winter and spring, with additional songbirds and raptors present in summer and fall. There's a picnic area, but no camping, and a visitor center contains exhibits depicting the Mormon pioneers' trek from Illinois to the Great Salt Lake Valley in 1847.

Also in the park, **Heritage Village** is a pioneer village comprised of original buildings from across the state along with some reproductions. In summer and during special events, it becomes a living-history museum of the period from 1847 to 1869, with costumed villagers and a variety of demonstrations and activities, including wagon rides. For a week each December the village re-creates a pioneer Christmas celebration. Allow 1 to 2 hours.

2601 E. Sunnyside Ave. ℭ **801/582-1847.** www.thisistheplace.org. Free admission to park and visitor center. Admission to Heritage Village $10 adults, $7 children 3–11 and seniors 62 and over (less on Sun and late Aug–June). Mon–Sat 9am–5 or 6pm; Sun 10am–5pm. Bus: 228.

Utah's Hogle Zoo ★ ☺   This 42-acre, modern zoo near the entrance to Emigration Canyon is home to 1,100 animals representing over 250 species. Take a stroll through a solarium with exotic plants and birds, tropical gardens, rare Grevy's zebras, and a giraffe house with a balcony so you can look eye-to-eye with the tall-necked creatures. In summer, rides on a small replica of an 1869 steam train are offered for $1.50, or you can ride a hand-carved animal on the Conservation Carousel for $2. As with any zoo, it's best to visit in a cooler season, or at least the coolest part of the day, when more animals are out and about. Allow 1 to 2 hours.

2600 E. Sunnyside Ave. ℭ **801/582-1631.** www.hoglezoo.org. Admission $9 adults, $7 children 3–12 and seniors 65 and older, free for children 2 and under. Mar–Oct daily 9am–5pm (grounds close 6:30pm); Nov–Feb daily 9am–4pm (grounds close 5:30pm). Closed Christmas and New Year's Day.

Especially for Kids

In addition to what's listed below, the **Clark Planetarium** (p. 63), **Utah's Hogle Zoo** (above), **Liberty Park** (p. 65), **Natural History Museum of Utah** (p. 64), and **Kennecott's Bingham Canyon Mine** (see below) are great places to visit with kids.

Discovery Gateway ★★ ☺ With more than 140 permanent exhibits, this 60,000-square-foot, three-story facility in the Gateway development on the west side of downtown is the place for kids of all ages to explore: Children can play a marimba, make a stop-motion animated video, or engineer a paper plane to throw in a wind tunnel. The museum also features a child-size grocery store where kids can be both shoppers and checkers, and an outdoor "flight to life" exhibit with a real helicopter now serving as a simulator. Allow 1 to 3 hours.

444 W. 100 South. ✆ **801/456-5437.** www.discoverygateway.org. Admission $8.50, $6 seniors 65 and over, free for children 1 and under. Mon–Thurs 10am–6pm; Fri–Sat 10am–8pm; Sun noon–6pm. Call for holiday hours. Trax: EnergySolutions Arena.

Wheeler Historic Farm ☺ This living-history dairy farm, where you can see demonstrations of farming and daily activities from the late 19th century, features hundred-year-old farm buildings, a small petting zoo, and a nature preserve. Activities include experiencing various farm chores (such as egg gathering and cow milking), farmhouse tours, and tractor-driven wagon rides. A variety of annual events is also offered, including a scarecrow masquerade, a holiday lights festival, breakfast with Santa, and a summer camp week. Allow 1 to 2 hours.

In Cottonwood Regional Park, 6351 S. 900 East (just north of I-215 exit 9). ✆ **801/264-2241.** www.wheelerfarm.com. Free admission to farm; 50¢–$10 fees for tours and other activities. Daily dawn–dusk. Bus: 209.

Nearby Attractions

Gardner Village This quaint village is a cluster of restored historic homes and buildings surrounding Gardner Mill, a flour mill built by Scottish immigrant Archibald Gardner in 1877. Brass plaques tell the stories of each of the historic structures. The mill, which is on the National Historic Register, now houses a large store specializing in country furniture and gift items, as well as **Archibald's Restaurant** (p. 56). Close to two dozen shops in the other historic buildings sell a wide range of items, including art, crafts, clothing, candy, quilts, dolls, and home furnishings. The village also has a spa, a bakery, and a picturesque duck pond. Plan to spend at least an hour here.

1100 W. 7800 South, West Jordan. ✆ **801/566-8903.** www.gardnervillage.com. Free admission. Shops Apr–Dec Mon–Sat 10am–8pm; Jan–Mar Mon–Thurs 10am–6pm, Fri–Sat 10am–8pm. The village is 12 miles southwest of downtown. From I-15, take exit 297 and head west on 7200 South, turn left (south) onto Redwood Rd. and left again on 7800 South; it's on the left (north) side of the road. From I-215, take exit 13 for Redwood Rd. and follow directions above. Trax: Midvale Center.

Kennecott's Bingham Canyon Mine ★ ☺ The world's largest open-pit copper mine, at 2½ miles wide and ¾ mile deep, is quite a sight to see; almost as fascinating are the huge—gigantic even—trucks that transport the ore. The visitor center, 2,000 feet above the floor of the open-pit mine, offers a spectacular view, and you might even see an explosion as rock is blasted away to expose more copper ore. In addition to the observation area, the visitor center has interactive exhibits—including 3-D microscopes for examining minerals—and a 16-minute video presentation that recounts the mine's history and geology and describes its operations. Proceeds from admission fees are donated to local charities. Allow about 1 hour.

Utah 48 (7200 South), about 25 miles southwest of Salt Lake City outside Copperton. ✆ **801/204-2025.** www.kennecott.com. Admission $5 per vehicle. Apr–Oct daily 8am–8pm. Closed Nov–Mar. Take I-15 south to exit 297 for Midvale; head west on Utah 48 to the mine.

OUTDOOR PURSUITS & SPECTATOR SPORTS

Outdoor Pursuits

Salt Lake City is an excellent base for skiing and snowboarding (see chapters 6 and 7), and plenty of opportunities for hiking and other warm-weather activities lie just outside the city in the 1.3 million acres of the Wasatch-Cache National Forest. For maps and detailed trail information, contact the **Uinta-Wasatch-Cache National Forest,** 125 S. State St. (© **801/236-3400;** www.fs.fed.us/r4/uwc). Another good source of information is the nonprofit **Public Lands Information Center** (© **801/466-6411**) located in the REI building (see below).

Sports Authority outlets (www.sportsauthority.com) can meet most of your recreational equipment needs. The Salt Lake City area has several locations, including the Utah Sportscastle at 5550 S. 900 East, Murray (© **801/263-3633**), and 10453 S. State St., Sandy (© **801/572-0157**). **Recreational Equipment, Inc. (REI),** 3285 E. 3300 South (© **801/486-2100;** www.rei.com), offers a wide range of sporting goods, both sales and rentals. A good source for sales and rentals of ski and golf equipment, bikes, and in-line skates is **Utah Ski & Golf,** 134 W. 600 South, in downtown Salt Lake City (© **801/355-9088;** www.utahskigolf.com), and at several other locations.

BIKING A number of bikeways are strung along city streets, some separate from but running parallel to the road, some a designated bike lane on the road, and others sharing the road with motor vehicles. From mid-May through September, City Creek Canyon, east of Capitol Hill, is closed to motor vehicles. It's open to hikers and in-line skaters at any time, and bicyclists can use the road on odd-numbered days. For information on the best places to bike, as well as rentals and repairs, stop at **Canyon Sports,** 1844 E. Fort Union Blvd. (© **800/736-8754;** www.canyonsports.com), or **Guthrie Bicycle,** in Sugarhouse at 803 E. 2100 South (© **801/484-0404;** www.guthriebike.com), established in 1888, making it quite possibly the nation's oldest operating bike shop.

BOATING The Great Salt Lake, at the city's front door, has marinas on the south shore and on Antelope Island (p. 75).

DIVING & SNORKELING South of the Great Salt Lake, **Bonneville Seabase,** 1390 W. Utah 138, Grantsville (© **435/884-3874;** www.seabase.net), has three diving bays up to 60 feet deep. All have exotic sea life, and one has a boat wreck. Rentals and classes are available; day use fees are $20.

FISHING Trout populate the rivers feeding into the Great Salt Lake, although no fish can live in the lake itself. Popular spots include Big and Little Cottonwood creeks and Mill Creek. Fishing licenses are required; you can get one, along with maps and suggestions, at most sporting-goods stores.

GOLF Salt Lake City has ranked as *Golf Digest's* number-one golf city in the United States in years past. The central contacts for general information and reservations for the city's nine courses are © **801/485-7730,** or 484-3333 for the automated tee-time reservation system (first call the main number to get an access code), and the excellent website, **www.slc-golf.com.** Rates range from $7 to $16 for 9 holes and $26 to $30 for 18 holes, and all courses require reservations. The 18-hole, par-72 **Bonneville,** 954 Connor St. (© **801/583-9513**), has hills, a large ravine, and a

Drive less than an hour from downtown Salt Lake City and you can be skiing the resorts in Big and Little Cottonwood Canyons: Alta, Snowbird, Brighton, and Solitude. Although you can stay in lodges and hotels in and around the canyons, many visitors base themselves in Salt Lake City proper to cut costs. If you're looking to ski several of the resorts, get a **Ski Salt Lake Super Pass** (www.visitsaltlake.com/ski/superpass), offered by the **Salt Lake Convention and Visitors Bureau.** It's good at all four of the resorts in the canyons and is a value at $60 a day. For more on the variety of activities in the canyons, see chapter 7.

But the outdoor opportunities extend beyond Big and Little Cottonwood Canyons. For the record, 11 of 14 of Utah's ski resorts are within 70 miles of Salt Lake City International Airport. You can easily spend the day skiing Alta, not to mention Ogden and/or Park City, and be back downtown for dinner and a Jazz game.

creek. The 9-hole, par-36 **Forest Dale,** 2375 S. 900 East (📞 **801/483-5420**), is a redesigned historic course with huge trees and challenging water hazards. The 18-hole, par-72 **Glendale,** 1630 W. 2100 South (📞 **801/974-2403**), features fine bent grass greens and splendid mountain views. The **Jordan River** course, 1200 N. Redwood Rd. (📞 **801/533-4527**), is a challenging executive par-3, 9-hole course that meanders along the banks of the Jordan River. Two 18-hole courses are located at **Mountain Dell** (📞 **801/582-3812**), in Parley's Canyon east on I-80: the par-71 lake course and the par-72 canyon course, with breathtaking views and a strong likelihood of seeing deer, elk, moose, and other wildlife. The 9-hole, par-34 **Nibley Park,** 2730 S. 700 East (📞 **801/483-5418**), is a good beginner course. The 18-hole, par-72 **Rose Park,** 1386 N. Redwood Rd. (📞 **801/596-5030**), is flat but challenging. The city's top course is the 18-hole, par-72 **Wingpointe,** 3602 W. 100 North, near the airport (📞 **801/575-2345**), a very challenging links-style course designed by Arthur Hills.

JOGGING   Memory Grove Park and City Creek Canyon are both great places for walking and jogging. The park is on the east side of the Capitol, and the canyon follows City Creek to the northeast. In town, you can go to one of the city parks, such as Liberty Park (p. 65).

Spectator Sports

The National Basketball Association's **Utah Jazz** (📞 **801/325-2500;** www.utahjazz.com) usually packs the house, so get your tickets early. They play at the EnergySolutions Arena, 301 W. South Temple.

The **Utah Grizzlies** (📞 **801/988-8000;** www.utahgrizzlies.com), of the East Coast Hockey League, play in the Maverik Center, 3200 S. Decker Lake Dr., West Valley City (off I-215 exit 20).

Real Salt Lake (📞 **801/727-2700;** www.realsaltlake.com), the city's professional soccer team, plays at Rio Tinto Stadium, 9256 S. State St., in Sandy.

If you want to take in a minor league baseball game, the Pacific Coast League's **Salt Lake Bees** (📞 **801/325-2273;** www.slbees.com), a Triple-A affiliate of the Anaheim Angels, play at Franklin Covey Field, at 77 W. 1300 South.

5

SALT LAKE CITY

Outdoor Pursuits & Spectator Sports

The **Utah Blaze** (📞 888/992-5293; www.utblaze.com) plays Arena Football League opponents March through July indoors at EnergySolutions Arena.

The **University of Utah's Runnin' Utes** and **Lady Utes** (📞 801/581-8849; www.utahutes.com) compete in the Mountain West Conference. The women's gymnastics team is phenomenal, and men's football and basketball have been growing in stature nationally. Tickets are usually available on fairly short notice, although it's best to call far in advance for football games.

SHOPPING

It may not be as interesting a shopping destination as places like Park City, but Salt Lake City does offer plenty of retail opportunities. Many Salt Lake City stores are closed on Sundays (the influence of the LDS Church); typical store hours are Monday through Saturday from 9am to 6pm. Shopping malls are often open Sunday afternoons from noon to 5 or 6pm, and also stay open a few hours later on weeknights.

The most popular shopping destination in the city is the **Gateway,** 18 N. Rio Grande St. (📞 801/456-0000; www.shopthegateway.com), a large, open-air shopping mall and entertainment and dining center. It covers 2 city blocks near EnergySolutions Arena and features 90 shops (anchored by Barnes & Noble and Dick's Sporting Goods), plus movie theaters, museums and other attractions, and restaurants. The historic Union Pacific Railroad Depot serves as the main entrance.

Near **Temple Square,** the LDS-owned ZCMI Center and Crossroads Mall were redeveloped as the indoor/outdoor **City Creek Center** (📞 801/613-2816; www.shopcitycreekcenter.com), anchored by Macy's and Nordstrom. The mixed-use development features about 20 high-end stores and restaurants.

Also downtown, **Sam Weller's,** 254 S. Main St. (📞 801/328-2586; www.samwellers.com), is Utah's largest bookstore, selling both new and used titles as well as coffee. Nearby, **Ken Sanders Rare Books,** 268 S. 200 East (📞 801/521-2606; www.kensandersbooks.com), is another can't-miss for book lovers.

Mormon Handicraft, in the Family Center Deseret Book at 1110 E. Fort Union Blvd. (📞 800/843-1480 or 801/561-8777; www.deseretbook.com/mormonhandicraft), was born during the Depression to encourage home industry and preserve pioneer arts. It carries a large inventory of quilting fabrics and supplies, as well as handmade quilts. It also stocks a wide variety of other crafts, plus religious books, movies, and toys.

Another central shopping destination is **Historic Trolley Square,** 600 South at 700 East (📞 801/521-9877; www.trolleysquare.com), with modern shops, galleries, and restaurants in an old-fashioned setting. You'll also see two of the city's original trolley cars, a historic water tower, and two of the city's first streetlamps.

Movie buffs will like the **Jordan Commons** complex, encompassing 2 city blocks at 9400 S. State St., south of downtown Salt Lake City in Sandy. The complex boasts 17 movie theaters surrounding a food court offering cuisines from Chinese to Mexican, plus a deli, coffee shop, and, of course, popcorn. The theaters are equipped with chairs large enough to accommodate food trays, so you can bring your dinner in with you! Call 📞 801/304-4577 or check the Web at www.megaplextheatres.com for movie information and tickets.

Although you couldn't yet call Salt Lake City an arts center, it does have a growing arts community, along with 20 or so galleries; on the third Friday of each month, there is an evening **Gallery Stroll.** One of the oldest galleries in Salt Lake City, the **Phillips Gallery,** 444 E. 200 South (📞 801/364-8284; www.phillips-gallery.com), represents over 100 artists, most of whom are Utahns, displaying everything from traditional to contemporary paintings, sculptures, and ceramics. The **"A" Gallery,** 1321 S. 2100 East (© **801/583-4800;** www.agalleryonline.com), is a large, long-standing contemporary art gallery featuring a sculpture garden. The **Hope Gallery,** 151 S. Main St. (© **801/532-1336;** www.hopegallery.com), is a 15,000-square-foot facility focusing on late-19th- and early-20th-century European and Scandinavian fine art, with an emphasis on religious works. At 177 E. Broadway, edgy and contemporary **Kayo Gallery** (© **801/532-0080;** www.kayogallery.com) shares a space with **Frosty Darling** (© **801/532-4790;** www.frostydarling.com), a purveyor of retro clothing, vintage kitsch, and often unusual local arts and crafts.

SALT LAKE CITY AFTER DARK

Salt Lake City is working hard to lose its image as a quiet town where the sidewalks are rolled up at night. Check the Friday editions of the *Salt Lake Tribune* or *Deseret Morning News* for listings of upcoming events. For additional entertainment news and listings, pick up one of the city's free papers, including the *Salt Lake City Weekly,* which also offers alternative news articles. The Salt Lake Convention and Visitors Bureau (p. 46) also publishes event calendars.

The Performing Arts

Tickets for performances at a variety of venues can be obtained from **Art Tix** (© **888/451-2787** or 801/355-2787; www.arttix.org).

The highly acclaimed **Utah Symphony & Opera ★★★** (© **801/533-6683;** www.usuo.org) combines one of the country's top symphony orchestras and the well-respected Utah Opera Company. It presents four operas a year plus a year-round

THE NORMALIZATION OF UTAH'S
drinking laws

The cumbersome private-club-membership requirements for entry into bars, nightclubs, and some restaurants are a thing of Utah's past, thanks to legislation that went into effect on July 1, 2009. Tipplers no longer need to pay membership fees or fill out applications before entering an establishment to buy an alcoholic drink.

But perceptions are hard to change, and several things about Utah's liquor laws beg for explanation. Much of the confusion comes from the terms used to define the different types of liquor licenses held by different businesses. There are three primary types of liquor licenses: **tavern, restaurant,** and **private club.** Taverns serve beer only;

restaurants serve beer, wine, and liquor; and private clubs—which are no longer private—*also* serve beer, wine, and liquor.

In a press release, the Salt Lake Convention and Visitors Bureau had this to say: "Utah's liquor laws are becoming more normalized and the perceptions about 'not being able to get a drink' should no longer be used as a reason for not taking full advantage of all that Utah has to offer. Rest assured, however, that we are not looking to 'normalize' the Greatest Snow on Earth, nor are we going to try and 'normalize' our incredible scenery." For more details, see "Drinking Laws" under "Fast Facts" on p. 313.

symphony season at Abravanel Hall, 123 W. South Temple, an elegant 2,800-seat venue known for its excellent acoustics.

The nationally acclaimed **Ballet West ★★** (© 801/869-6900; www.balletwest. org) performs at the historic Capitol Theatre, 50 W. 200 South. The October-to-May season usually brings four or five productions, ranging from classical to contemporary, as well as holiday stagings of *The Nutcracker*. Modern dance is presented by the **Repertory Dance Theatre** (© 801/534-1000; www.rdtutah.org) and the **Ririe-Woodbury Dance Company** (© 801/297-4241; www.ririewoodbury.com), with performances at the Rose Wagner Performing Arts Center, located at 138 W. 300 South, and other venues.

The **Pioneer Theatre Company,** 300 S. 1400 East (© 801/581-6961; www. pioneertheatre.org), is Utah's resident professional theater. Located on the university campus, the Pioneer has a repertoire that ranges from classical to contemporary plays and musicals. Recent productions have included *Next to Normal* and *Annie*. Producing edgier contemporary fare, the **Salt Lake Acting Company,** 168 W. 500 North (© 801/363-7522; www.saltlakeactingcompany.org), stages about six plays by local and national playwrights annually. The family-oriented **Hale Centre Theatre,** 3333 S. Decker Lake Dr., West Valley City (© 801/984-9000; www.halecentretheatre. org), features locally produced and performed plays and musical comedies.

The Club & Music Scene

As Salt Lake City grows, it's shedding its strait-laced image and beginning to cater to the party crowd. Some of the following establishments were once so-called private clubs, but as of July 2009 you no longer have to buy a short-term membership to imbibe (see "The Normalization of Utah's Drinking Laws," above).

One of the city's more with-it and cosmopolitan nightspots is **Mynt Lounge,** 63 W. 100 South (© 801/355-6968), an upscale bar with an extensive martini menu. This place attracts one of Salt Lake City's hippest crowds. The **Jackalope,** 372 S. State St. (© 801/359-8054), is a funky, edgy bar attracting the tattooed and restless. **Squatters Pub Brewery,** 147 W. Broadway (© 801/363-2739; www.squatters.com), brews top-notch suds and thumbs its nose at local conservatism with such beer names as Provo Girl and Chasing Tail. The **Red Rock Brewing Company,** 254 S. 200 West (© 801/521-7446; www.redrockbrewing.com), is another solid downtown brewpub, and a good spot to eat if you're looking for pub grub. The **Poplar Street Pub,** 242 S. 200 West (© 801/532-2715; www.poplarstreetpub.com), offers a neighborhood vibe and great *chile verde*.

For one of the best martinis around, stop at **Kristauf's Martini Bar,** 16 W. Market St. (© 801/366-9490; www.martinibarslc.com), a favorite of business types and other well-dressed tipplers. On the other end of the cultural spectrum, **Burt's Tiki Lounge,** 726 S. State St. (© 801/521-0572), is a punk-rock dive, with kitsch-bedecked walls and loud music most every night. **Urban Lounge,** 241 S. 500 East (© 801/746-0557; www.theurbanloungeslc.com), books local and national indie and hip-hop acts. For dueling pianos and perhaps too much revelry, hit **Keys on Main,** 242 S. Main St. (© 801/363-3638; www.keysonmain.com).

On the east side, the **Porcupine Pub & Grill,** 3690 Fort Union Blvd. (© 801/942-5555; www.porcupinepub.com), is an après-ski hot spot, with excellent food and 24 beers on tap. The **Canyon Inn,** 3200 E. 7200 South (© 801/942-9801), is another long-standing favorite of the après-ski-and-snowboard crowd, and makes a pretty good pizza to boot. It's also a good place to catch a game, and the dance floor is the place to see and—more importantly—be seen.

THE GREAT SALT LAKE & ANTELOPE ISLAND STATE PARK

You wouldn't expect to come across what is essentially a small ocean in the middle of the desert, but there it is: the Great Salt Lake. The lake is all that's left of ancient Lake Bonneville, which once covered most of western Utah and parts of Idaho and Nevada. Unlike its mother lake, the Great Salt Lake has no outlet, so everything that flows into it—some 2 million tons of minerals annually—stays here until someone or something—usually brine flies, brine shrimp, birds, or humans—removes it. Minerals, including salt, potassium, and magnesium, are mined here; don't be surprised to see front-end loaders moving huge piles of salt to the Morton Salt facility along I-80, on the lake's south shore.

This natural wonder might be worth checking out, but don't expect much. Although Salt Lake City residents enjoy spending weekends at the lake, it isn't really a major tourist destination, and facilities are limited. Boaters should bring their own boats, as no rentals are available. Despite its salinity, this is a relatively flat lake—kind of like a big puddle—so don't pack your surfboard.

Antelope Island State Park ★

The largest of 10 islands in the Great Salt Lake, measuring about 5 miles wide and 15 miles long, Antelope Island was named by Kit Carson and John Frémont in 1843 for the many pronghorns they found here. Hunting wiped out the herd by the 1870s, but buffalo were introduced in 1893—500 of them now make the island their home—and pronghorn have recently been reintroduced. The beaches of Antelope Island don't have the fine-grained sand and shells of an ocean beach; rather, they're a mixture of dirt and gravel. But the water is a great place to relax; because of its high salinity, you don't have to work hard to stay afloat.

ESSENTIALS

GETTING THERE   Antelope Island is about 30 miles northwest of Salt Lake City and about 16 miles southwest of Ogden. Take I-15 to exit 332, go 6½ miles west to the park entrance, and cross the 7½-mile causeway to the island.

VISITOR INFORMATION   Contact **Antelope Island State Park,** 4528 W. 1700 South, Syracuse, UT 84075-6868. The visitor center (© **801/773-2941;** www. stateparks.utah.gov), open daily in summer from 9am to 6pm and in winter daily from 9am to 5pm, has exhibits and information on the Great Salt Lake and the island's wildlife and migratory birds.

FEES & REGULATIONS   Day-use fees are $9 per vehicle and $3 for pedestrians, bicyclists, or in-line skaters. The marina offers dock rental overnight. Pets are welcome in the park but must be leashed.

OUTDOOR PURSUITS

BIKING, HIKING & HORSEBACK RIDING   More than 30 miles of hiking trails and bike and horse paths traverse the island, most of which are closed to vehicular traffic. Although generally unmarked, trails follow old ranch roads. Check at the visitor center or talk with a ranger before heading out; they can fill you in on current conditions and tell you where you're most likely to spot wildlife.

The 3-mile **Lake Side Trail** leaves the Bridger Bay Campground and follows the beach around the northwestern tip of the island to the group camping area on White Rock Bay. The walk is magnificent at sunset. Other trails take you away from the crowds, where you might catch a glimpse of a buffalo or other wildlife.

BOATING Boaters will find a marina with restrooms, docks, and fresh water for cleaning boats, but little else.

SWIMMING The largest beach is at Bridger Bay, with picnic tables and restrooms with outdoor showers to wash off the salt.

WILDLIFE-WATCHING You can drive to the buffalo corral and see these great shaggy creatures fairly close-up. If you head into the less-traveled areas, you might spot pronghorns, deer, buffaloes, bobcats, elk, coyotes, and bighorn sheep.

The annual bison roundup takes place in late November and early December. You can usually see wranglers herding the bison into corrals on the last weekend of November (binoculars are helpful) and get a close-up view the next weekend as the bison receive their annual checkups. Call for exact dates.

CAMPING

The park has two campgrounds: **Bridger Bay Campground** offers primitive camping, or you can use the parking area at **Bridger Bay Beach.** Although neither offers hookups, each area does have restrooms with showers; Bridger Bay Beach has picnic tables as well. The cost is $13 per night. Reservations are available at ✆ **800/322-3770** or www.stateparks.utah.gov.

MORE TO SEE & DO

Ten miles south of the visitor center, down a paved road, is the **Fielding Garr Ranch House.** The original three-room adobe house, built in 1848, was inhabited until the state acquired it in 1981. In addition to the ranch house is a small building that served as a schoolroom by day and sleeping quarters for the farmhands at night, plus a spring house, the only freshwater source.

The ranch has a snack bar (open only when the ranch is open), as well as a large, shady picnic area. Half-hour wagon rides are available. Check with the visitor center for current ranch hours as well as schedules and rates for wagon rides.

Great Salt Lake State Marina

This is a good spot to launch your boat (assuming you brought one; there are no rentals here), but not what one would call a great destination. A less-than-exciting stretch of muddy/sandy beach greets you, but the expanse of water and distant islands can be lovely, especially at dusk or early in the morning. Prickly pear cactuses bloom along the shore in the late spring. And for those susceptible to the lure of the sea, this huge inland ocean is mysteriously irresistible any time of year. Sailing and watersports are the main attractions here—although you can also laze on the beach. Facilities include picnic tables, open showers for washing off salt and sand, and restrooms.

Be forewarned, though. The air can be heavy with the stench of rotting algae at times, making even a brief stroll on the beach quite unpleasant. At other times, when the wind is right or the lake is high enough, trekking out to the water's edge is downright enjoyable.

ESSENTIALS

Great Salt Lake State Park is 16 miles west of Salt Lake City. Take I-80 west to exit 104; head east on the frontage road about 2 miles to the park entrance. The marina is open year-round, and the beach is open daily in summer from dawn to dusk (8am–5pm Oct–Mar), with admission fees of $2 per car. Boat slips and a launching ramp are available, but there are no boat rentals. Contact **Great Salt Lake State Marina,** P.O. Box 16658, Salt Lake City, UT 84116-0658 (✆ **801/250-1898;** www.stateparks.utah.gov). Park headquarters are located at the marina.

SALT LAKE CITY | The Great Salt Lake & Antelope Island State Park

THE NORTHERN WASATCH FRONT: UTAH'S OLD WEST

I n the mountains north of Salt Lake City lies another world. Ogden, which owes its prosperity to the transcontinental railroad, is a good starting point for discovering northern Utah's Old—and surprisingly Wild—West heritage. Ogden is also a great home base for outdoor recreation: You can ski at three nearby resorts in the winter, or hike, fish, and ride horses in the summer. Mandatory for all railroad buffs is a pilgrimage to Golden Spike National Historic Site, the point at which the East and West coasts of the United States were joined by rail in 1869. North of Ogden is the pretty little town of Logan, home to Utah State University and a similarly bountiful outdoor-recreation hot spot. For a color **map** of the Wasatch Front, see the inside back cover of this book.

OGDEN: UTAH'S WEST AT ITS WILDEST

35 miles N of Salt Lake City

In the deltas of the Ogden and Weber rivers, Ogden has always been a city apart from the rest of Utah. Founded by Mormon pioneers and home to a sizable Mormon population, Ogden really began as a popular meeting place for mountain men and fur trappers in the 1820s, and became— much to the chagrin of the church—a seriously rowdy railroad town in the 1870s. It retains some of that devil-may-care attitude today.

But Ogden's current popularity has little to do with its sinful beginnings. Like other Wasatch Front communities, the bustling city of about 80,000 has fine little museums and historic sites, as well as good restaurants and hotels. More important, at an elevation of 4,300 feet, Ogden is a perfect base for enjoying the surrounding mountains for skiing, snowboarding, snowmobiling, hiking, mountain biking, horseback riding, or boating. Mt. Ben Lomond Peak, which lies to the north of the city, may look familiar—it's said to have inspired the famous Paramount Pictures logo.

Essentials

GETTING THERE   Ogden is easily accessible from the north and south via I-15, and from the east and northwest on I-84. Shuttle service to and from Salt Lake International Airport is $30 to $40 one-way; try **Xpress Shuttle** (© **800/397-0773;** www.xpressshuttleutah.com) or **Wasatch Crest Shuttle** (© **877/475-4829;** www. wcshuttle.com), which will also take you up to the local ski resorts. For the best service, call at least 24 hours in advance. A commuter train called the **UTA Front-Runner** (© **801/743-3882;** www.rideuta.com) runs from Salt Lake City to Ogden. The fare for a one-way trip is $4.75, and the train runs from early morning to about midnight.

VISITOR INFORMATION   The **Ogden/Weber Convention & Visitors Bureau** maintains an information center at Union Station, 2438 Washington Blvd., Ogden, UT 84401 (© **866/867-8824** or 801/778-6250; www.visitogden.com). From I-15 North/I-84 West, take exit 341 and head east to Washington Boulevard; turn north (left) and continue for about 6 blocks. The information center is open Monday through Friday 8am to 5pm.

For information on the area's national forests, contact the **Ogden Ranger District,** Uinta-Wasatch-Cache National Forest, 507 25th St., Ogden, UT 84401 (© **801/625-5112;** www.fs.fed.us/r4/uwc). You can also inquire at the forest's visitor center at Union Station, 2501 Wall Ave. (© **801/625-5306**).

GETTING AROUND   Driving is the easiest way to explore Ogden. The streets are laid out in typically neat Mormon-pioneer fashion, but with a slightly different nomenclature than, say, Salt Lake City. The streets running east to west are numbered from 1st Street in the north to 47th in the south, and north-south streets are named for U.S. presidents and other historical figures. Most people define the city center as the intersection of 25th Street and Washington Boulevard.

For car rentals, try **Enterprise** (© **866/799-7965** or 801/399-5555; www. enterprise.com) or **Hertz** (© **800/654-3131** or 801/614-5005; www.hertz.com).

The **Utah Transit Authority** (© **888/743-3882** or 801/743-3882; www.rideuta. com) provides bus transport throughout greater Ogden, daily with limited service on Sunday. Exact fares are required; schedules are available at the information center. For 24-hour taxi service, call **Yellow Cab Co.** (© **801/394-9411**).

FAST FACTS   The **McKay-Dee Hospital Center,** 4401 Harrison Blvd. (© **801/ 627-2800**), has a 24-hour emergency room. The **main post office** is at 3680 Pacific Ave. (© **800/275-8777;** www.usps.com for additional locations and hours). The local **newspaper** is the *Standard Examiner.* **Sales tax** is 6.6%.

What to See & Do

Eccles Community Art Center   Built in 1893, this two-and-a-half-story turreted mansion was the home of David and Bertha Eccles. Throughout her life, Bertha made it known to her family that she wished the house to be used for education and cultural enrichment. It became the home of the Ogden Community Arts Council in 1959.

Changing exhibits in the Main House feature works by local, regional, and national artists in a variety of mediums. The Carriage House gallery offers local arts and crafts, such as paintings, pottery, fabric art, and jewelry. The Renaissance Complex presents ongoing educational programs and houses the ticket office for the Ogden Symphony and Ballet West. Outside is a sculpture and flower garden complete with a fountain

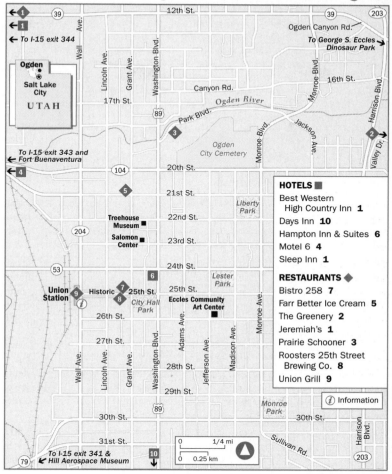

HOTELS ■
Best Western
  High Country Inn **1**
Days Inn **10**
Hampton Inn & Suites **6**
Motel 6 **4**
Sleep Inn **1**

RESTAURANTS ◆
Bistro 258 **7**
Farr Better Ice Cream **5**
The Greenery **2**
Jeremiah's **1**
Prairie Schooner **3**
Roosters 25th Street
  Brewing Co. **8**
Union Grill **9**

ⓘ Information

and benches where you can sit and enjoy the view. Allow an hour and a half, and call ahead for a schedule of events and information on classes in the visual arts and dance.
2580 Jefferson Ave. ⓒ **801/392-6935.** www.ogden4arts.org. Free admission. Mon–Fri 9am–5pm; Sat 9am–3pm. Closed major holidays. From I-15, take exit 342 and head east on 24th St. to Jefferson Ave.; turn right (south) and go 2 blocks.

Fort Buenaventura ★ With a replica of an 1846 fort and trading post, and exhibits depicting the local mountain men and fur trade of the 1820s, this park shows what life was like back in the day. Built in 1846 by fur trapper and horse trader Miles Goodyear, the fort was the first permanent Anglo settlement in the Great Basin. The Mormons bought the fort when they arrived in 1847, and Ogden grew up around it.

Rangers lead tours of the reconstructed fort (included in the admission fee), and the park has ponds, canoes for rent ($5 per hour), a picnic area, and a pleasant campground ($18–$23 per night). A 2-mile hiking trail meanders around the park, and fishing in the Weber River is permitted with a license. The park also has a kids' fishing pond, open only to children 12 and younger, no license required. The visitor center has exhibits of American Indian artifacts typical of the area. Allow at least 1 hour.

Fort Buenaventura hosts several traditional mountain-man rendezvous each year, with music, Dutch-oven food, and a variety of contests that typically include a tomahawk throw, a canoe race, a shooting competition, and footraces, with all competitors in pre-1840s dress. The rendezvous are usually scheduled on Easter (with a non-denominational sunrise service and egg hunt) and Labor Day weekends. A Pioneer Skills Festival takes place on July 24. Mountain-man supplies are available in a shop at the fort every Saturday.

444 24th St. ℂ **801/399-8099.** www.co.weber.ut.us/parks/fortb. Admission $1 per person; free for children 4 and under. Apr–Sept daily 8am–8pm; call for hours Oct–Mar. From downtown Ogden, take 24th St. west across the railroad tracks.

George S. Eccles Dinosaur Park ★ ☺

Wander among life-size reproductions of more than 100 prehistoric creatures from the Cretaceous and Jurassic periods in this 5-acre fantasyland playground. The smallest is about the size of a turkey, and the enormous tyrannosaurus rex is 30 feet high, 49 feet long, and weighs about 7 tons. Other cold-blooded friends include a 33-foot-long parasaurolophus (a duck-billed dinosaur), a triceratops, and a winged lizard, or pteranodon. There's even a replica of a 65-million-year-old volcano. Also on-site is the Elizabeth Dee Shaw Stewart Museum, with exciting hands-on exhibits of the latest dinosaur finds from Utah and around the world. It includes a sand pit where budding paleontologists can excavate real dinosaur bones. Other activities include gold-panning (fool's gold) and hunting for gems in a cave (real gems). There is a basic restaurant here as well. Allow 2 hours.

1544 E. Park Blvd., Ogden River Pkwy. ℂ **801/393-3466.** www.dinosaurpark.org. Admission $7 adults, $6 students with IDs and seniors 62 and older, $5 children 2–12, free for children 1 and under. Memorial Day to Labor Day Mon–Sat 10am–8pm, Sun noon–6pm; rest of year Mon–Sat 10am–6pm, Sun noon–6pm. Closed Easter, Thanksgiving, and Christmas, as well as Sun Nov–Mar. From exit 344, take 12th St. east 5 miles.

Hill Aerospace Museum ★

Get a close-up view of more than 90 planes, missiles, and aerospace vehicles at this museum. Aircraft on display include the rare B-17G "Flying Fortress," one of the few P-38s around, the SR-71C "Blackbird" spy plane, a Soviet MiG-21 fighter, and two aircraft that are still flyable: a JN-4 "Jenny" and a Piper L-4J "Grasshopper," painted and marked to look like one that flew in support of the Allied invasion of North Africa in November 1942. Other exhibits include a World War II chapel, an exhibit of historic Air Force uniforms, a fire truck, a Gatling gun, thermonuclear missiles (decommissioned, thankfully), and a Norden bombsight. Displays illustrate the history of the Air Force, how aircraft fly, and what the Air Force does today. The gift shop offers a wide range of Air Force–related items. Allow 1 hour.

7961 Wardleigh Rd., Hill Air Force Base. ℂ **801/777-6868** or 777-6818. www.hill.af.mil/library/museum. Free admission; donations welcome. Daily 9am–4:30pm. Closed New Year's Day, Thanksgiving, and Christmas. From I-15, take exit 338 to the museum.

Salomon Center ★★ ☺

Brand-new in 2007, this one-of-a-kind, $19-million facility has become the centerpiece of downtown Ogden, featuring a Gold's Gym as a second-floor anchor. The highlights here are the three stand-alone training grounds for extreme sports: the Flowrider (a wave simulator for surfers), a 50-foot climbing wall, and iFly (a sky-diving simulator). The impressive complex also houses an arcade and two restaurants (Mexican and pizza), and there's a 13-screen cinema complex right next door. Prices vary from activity to activity—2 minutes in the iFly costs $49; an hour on the Flowrider is $20.

2261 Kiesel Ave. ℂ **801/399-4653.** www.salomoncenter.com. Free admission; various fees for sky-diving and wave simulators and other activities. Daily; hours vary activity to activity. Located on Washington btw. 22nd and 23rd sts.

Treehouse Museum ★★ ☺ In this excellent reading-oriented museum you can climb into a two-story faux tree with a spiral staircase in its trunk, participate in daily arts and crafts activities, or "step into stories" by authors from near and far. The American Dream exhibit boasts an impressive giant floor map of the United States and a kid-size Oval Office with exhibits on U.S. presidents. In the Utah Heritage area, kids explore a pioneer schoolhouse and store, and try their hands at creating American Indian pictographs. Events include hourly storytelling programs and seasonal plays in the 132-seat theater; call for showtimes. Allow at least 1 hour.

347 22nd St. ℂ **801/394-9663.** www.treehousemuseum.org. Admission $4 adults, $5 children from walking age to 15. Mon 10am–3pm (until 5pm June–Aug and holidays); Tues–Thurs and Sat 10am–5pm; Fri 10am–8pm. Closed New Year's Day, July 4, July 24, Thanksgiving, and Dec 25. Located just north of the Salomon Center.

Union Station This stately depot faces historic 25th Street, with lovely flowers and a fountain gracing the cobbled courtyard in front. Built in 1924 to replace the original depot, which was destroyed by fire, the station now houses several museums, an art gallery, a gift shop, the **Union Grill** (p. 92), a Forest Services information center, and the Ogden/Weber Convention and Visitor's Bureau. Plan to spend an hour or two here.

The restored **lobby** is the place to start. The immense room is graced with murals at each end commemorating the building of the railroad and the linking of east and west. Both 12×50-foot murals were done in the late 1970s by Edward Laning, based on ones he painted in 1935 for New York's Ellis Island Immigration Building.

The **Utah State Railroad Museum** displays gas-turbine locomotive designs and has an extensive HO-gauge layout that depicts the construction and geography of the 1,776-mile transcontinental route. Wander around on your own, or let a railroad buff guide you through, describing the whys and wherefores of what you're seeing. The **Browning Firearms Museum** displays Browning guns from 1878 to present, a replica of an 1880s gun shop, and a film describing the Browning legacy. The **Browning-Kimball Car Museum** features beautiful examples of classic cars, mostly luxury models. You can see about a dozen vehicles from the early 1900s, including a 1901 curved-dash Oldsmobile, Pierce-Arrows from 1909 and 1931, and a 1932 Lincoln. The **Gallery at the Station** exhibits a variety of art through invitational and competitive shows. Outside, the **Eccles Rail Center** pays tribute to the Goliaths of the rails—locomotives designed to pull long trains through the steep mountains of the West. On display are a burly "Big Blow," a gas turbine rated at more than twice the horsepower of typical modern locomotives (one of only two on display anywhere), and a commemorative car used in the torch relay for the 2002 Winter Olympics.

2501 Wall Ave. ℂ **801/393-9886.** www.theunionstation.org. Admission to museums $5 adults, $4 seniors 65 and over, $3 children 11 and under, $12 family. Mon–Sat 10am–5pm. Closed New Year's Day, Thanksgiving, and Christmas. Take exit 341A off I-15 and follow 31st St. east to Wall Ave.; go north 6 blocks.

WALKING TOUR: HISTORIC DOWNTOWN OGDEN—A WALK THROUGH THE HISTORY OF THE AMERICAN WEST

START: **2148 Grant Ave.**

FINISH: **2539 Washington Blvd.**

TIME: **1–2 hours.**

BEST TIMES: **Any.**

WORST TIMES: **None, although windy days in winter can be biting cold.**

Begin your tour at 2148 Grant Ave., on Tabernacle Square, where you'll find:

1 Miles Goodyear Cabin & Daughters of Utah Pioneers Museum

This cottonwood log cabin was built in 1845 on the Weber River at Fort Buenaventura, which is now a county-run park (p. 79). The cabin is believed to be the first permanent pioneer home in Utah. Next door, the 1902 Gothic-style brick Relief Society Building now houses the **Daughters of Utah Pioneers Museum** (✆ **801/393-4460;** www.weberdupmuseum.org), containing pioneer photographs, artifacts, and memorabilia. Both the museum and cabin are open during summer only.

Now head south on Grant Avenue for 3 blocks to 298 24th St., the:

2 Ogden Post Office

This is one of two fine examples of Classical Revival Federal architecture in Utah (the other is the Salt Lake City post office). This building, constructed between 1905 and 1909, held a post office, a courthouse, and offices until 1974. The lobby, elevator, second-floor courtroom, and much of the beautiful woodwork have been lovingly restored. The building now houses a reception center and other offices.

Turn east on 24th Street; a block down the street, at 385 24th St., is the:

3 Eccles Building

Now the Hampton Inn and Suites (p. 88), this steel-framed, brick-faced, boxlike 1913 building with "Chicago-style" windows combines elements of Prairie style with classical details, evident in the terra-cotta figurines and geometric motifs along the second- and eighth-floor cornices.

Turn south onto Washington Boulevard, and continue to 2415 Washington Blvd. to see:

4 Peery's Egyptian Theater

Built as a movie theater in the Egyptian Revival style in 1924, the cinema reopened in 1997 after extensive renovation. The facade has four fluted columns, with two sculpted pharaohs between each, plus two sculptures of deities perched on the roof. The interior is equally exotic: The proscenium is decorated with paintings of Egyptian figures and colorful columns. Getting a tour of the theater can be difficult and depends on the whim of the staff. The best way to see the theater is to attend a performance. The theater doesn't show movies regularly, but hosts live productions and film festivals.

Cross the street to 2510 Washington Blvd., where you'll find the:

5 Ben Lomond Hotel

This Italian Renaissance Revival hotel, built in 1927 on the remains of the 1890 Reed Hotel, is a handsome reminder of the opulent 1920s, and is listed on the National Register of Historic Places.

Cross again to 2539 Washington Blvd., to see the:

6 Municipal Building

One of the finest representations of the Art Deco style of architecture in Utah, this building is also an excellent example of a WPA project. Built in 1939, the building is composed of a series of rectangular brick blocks with glazed terra-cotta trim, symmetrically tapered to the tall central mass—grand and awe-inspiring.

7 Historic 25th Street

Finally, take a few minutes to walk along Historic 25th Street, once known nationwide as "Two-Bit Street" because of its rowdy nature. The largest remaining group of turn-of-the-20th-century storefronts in the state has enjoyed a dandy of a renovation over the last decade. Many of the old businesses moved out to suburban shopping centers, and shops, restaurants, and pubs have since taken over.

What to See & Do Nearby

HUNTSVILLE: "THE SIN & SALVATION TOUR"

Locals jokingly refer to visiting Huntsville as taking the "Sin and Salvation Tour." Founded in 1860, this tiny town, somewhat removed from the civilization of Ogden below, is known best as the home of the state's oldest operating watering hole. The town is about 15 miles east of Ogden on Utah 39; it'll take you 20 to 25 minutes to get there, but it's well worth the drive.

First, stop at the **Shooting Star Saloon ★★**, 7350 E. 200 South (© **801/745-2002**), for a draft beer and one of the best—and sloppiest—hamburgers in the state, the knockwurst-topped Star Burger. Established in 1862, this is said to be the oldest continuously operating saloon in Utah. The decor is eclectic, to say the least—dollar bills are pinned to the ceiling; the walls are decorated with animal-head trophies, steer skulls, a stuffed St. Bernard's head (Buck), and cowboy art; the handsome oak back bar was built in 1895. A pool table and a jukebox round out the fun. The Shooting Star is open Wednesday through Saturday from noon and Sunday from 2pm; it usually closes around 9pm, depending on business. Operating under Utah's liquor laws as a tavern, the only alcoholic beverage Shooting Star serves is beer, and no one under 21 (not even with parents) is permitted in the saloon.

Now that you've done a bit of sinning, head to the **Abbey of Our Lady of the Holy Trinity Trappist Monastery,** 1250 S. 9500 East (© **801/745-3784;** www. holytrinityabbey.org), for a bit of saving. To get here, take Utah 39, turn southeast (right) at the Huntsville American Legion Hall, and follow the signs. This community of about two dozen monks established themselves here in 1947 to live "an austere and simple life of prayer and manual labor." They farm; raise Herefords; and sell books, freshly made peanut butter, preserves, and their renowned honey. The reception room and chapel are open to the public, and visitors are welcome to attend any of the scheduled services. Call for the current schedule.

For a delightful escape from civilization, visit the **Ogden Nature Center,** 966 W. 12th St. (© **801/621-7595;** www. ogdennaturecenter.org), a 152-acre wildlife sanctuary and rehabilitation center where injured birds are treated and released back into the wild. There are trails (including one fully accessible trail) for warm-weather strolling or, when snow blankets the ground, snowshoeing and cross-country skiing. Watch for golden eagles, prairie falcons, goshawks, red-tailed hawks, great horned owls, and long-eared owls. A Learning and Visitors Center houses hawks, ravens, and other birds, plus a variety of exhibits and a gift shop. The center sponsors naturalist-led educational programs; call ahead or check online for a schedule. Admission is $4 for ages 12 through 54, $2 seniors 55 and over and children 2 through 11, and free for children 1 and under. Hours are Monday through Friday 9am to 5pm and Saturday 9am to 4pm. To get here from I-15, take exit 344 and head east on 12th Street. Allow at least 2 hours.

A HISTORIC FAMILY-FUN CENTER IN FARMINGTON

Lagoon, 375 N. Lagoon Dr., Farmington (© **800/748-5246** or 801/451-8000; www.lagoonpark.com), is a delightful combination of amusement park, water park, and historical park. Swimming was the original attraction; then, in 1906, an early version of a roller coaster opened. Next came a carousel of 45 hand-carved animals (still in operation today). Now the park is filled with more than 125 rides, including Wicked, a twisting coaster that rockets riders to the top of the first hill at 40 mph—not for the faint of heart! The park also has a midway with games, shops, food courts, and more. **Lagoon's Pioneer Village** represents Utah's past, with one of America's finest collections of horse-drawn carriages, plus a gun collection and exhibits of pioneer and American Indian artifacts. You can also browse through 19th-century shops and ride a stagecoach or train. If it's water you want, visit the **Lagoon A Beach,** with a 65-foot twisting, turning, enclosed tube ride, three serpentine slides, and whitewater rapids. The less intrepid can enjoy a lazy river with crystal-clear waterfalls, exotic tunnels, steamy hot tubs, and sultry lagoons.

Admission costs $44 for adults and children 51 inches and taller, $39 for children 4 and older but under 51 inches tall and seniors 65 and over, and $28 for toddlers 3 and under. The parking fee is $8 for cars and pickups, and $10 for oversize vehicles and vehicles with trailers. The park is open daily, usually from 10 or 11am, between Memorial Day and Labor Day, and weekends from mid-April to May and the month of September; hours vary so call for the current schedule. The park is closed in winter, but opens for a special Halloween event for 3 or 4 weeks in October. To get here, from I-15 northbound, take exit 322; southbound, take exit 325.

Lagoon has an RV park and campground with more than 200 shady sites, both pull-through with hookups and grassy tent sites. The campground has a ministore, and campers receive Lagoon admission discounts. Rates range from $28 for tent and no-hookup RV sites up to $34 for pull-through RV sites with full hookups.

Sports & Outdoor Pursuits

The nearby Wasatch-Cache National Forest offers plenty of opportunities for outdoor recreation (see "Visitor Information," on p. 78). For camping and other equipment and supplies, stop by **Sports Authority,** in the Newgate Mall, 36th Street and Wall Avenue (© **801/392-5500**).

BIKING The **Ogden River Parkway** ★★ (www.weberpathways.org) is a 3.4-mile paved, wheelchair-accessible path along the Ogden River, extending from the mouth of Ogden Canyon west to Washington Boulevard. It's excellent for walking, jogging, and bicycling; it also leads to Big D Sports Park (with playground and sporting fields), Lorin Farr Park (p. 87), and George S. Eccles Dinosaur Park (p. 80).

East of Ogden are two strenuous road rides. The **Trappers Loop Road** winds 9 miles along Utah 167 from Mountain Green (exit 92 off I-84) north to Huntsville. This route alternates between wide-open meadows backed by high mountain peaks and tall evergreens and aspens that seem to envelop you.

The second ride, along **Snowbasin Road,** climbs more than 2,000 feet over 10 miles from Pineview Reservoir. Your efforts will be rewarded with stunning views of the ski runs and towering peaks. Now open in summer, **Snowbasin,** 3925 E. Snowbasin Rd. (© **888/437-5488**; www.snowbasin.com), is a mountain-biking destination, with more than 25 miles of trails that gain nearly 3,000 feet in elevation and connect to a network of Forest Service trails. Rentals are available on-site. The resort is open from the last Sunday in June through the first Sunday in October, Friday to Sunday, 9am to 6pm. Trail passes are $14 for hikers and $18 for bikers daily.

You can get additional trail information at the Forest Service visitor center in Union Station (p. 81)—ask for the excellent *Pathways in Weber County* map and brochure. For bicycle repairs and accessories, stop at **Bingham Cyclery,** 1895 Washington Blvd. (© **801/399-4981;** www.binghamcyclery.com). In Eden, **Diamond Peak Mountain Sports,** at the junction of Utah highways 158 and 162 (© **801/745-0101;** www.peakstuff.com), offers rentals, repairs, and sales of bikes, boards, and skis.

CLIMBING Ogden is a rock-climbing mecca, with many popular routes in the rugged country in and around Ogden Canyon. Waterfall Canyon is among the most accessible destinations. At the Salomon Center (p. 80), the **iRock** climbing wall (© **801/399-4653;** www.irockutah.com) costs $10 adults, $7.50 for kids 11 and under.

FISHING Brown, rainbow, cutthroat, brook, and lake trout thrive in the waters of the Wasatch-Cache National Forest around Ogden. You might also find perch, bass, catfish, whitefish, and crappie. Popular spots to wet your line are Pineview Reservoir, Causey Reservoir, and the Ogden and Weber rivers. For supplies, licenses, and tips on where they're biting, stop at **Anglers' Den,** 5296 S. Freeway Park Dr. (© **801/773-1166**). The shop can also refer you to local guides.

GOLF Golfers will find an abundance of opportunities in the Ogden area, which boasts challenging courses with spectacular views of the surrounding mountains. Public courses include the **Mount Ogden Golf Course,** 1787 Constitution Way (© **801/629-0699**), an 18-hole, par-71 championship course located on the east side of the city against the mountains, which charges $33 to $40 for 18 holes, cart included, and **El Monte Golf Course,** 1300 Valley Dr. (© **801/629-0694**), a scenic 9-hole, par-35 course of rolling hills and old-style greens in Ogden Canyon, with fees of $13 for 9 holes, and an extra $7 for a cart.

For one of the finest practice areas around, try **Toad's Fun Zone,** 1690 W. 400 North, exit 346 off I-15 (© **801/392-4653;** www.toadsfz.com), with two 18-hole miniature golf courses (one indoor and one outdoor), a year-round driving range, and a new 9-hole par-3 course. An indoor glow-in-the-dark minigolf course is located at Fat Cats in the **Salomon Center** (p. 80).

HIKING   The **Ogden River Parkway ★★** (p. 85) is great for walking. Several hiking trails are accessible from the east side of downtown Ogden. **Indian Trail ★** takes off from the parking area at 22nd Street and Buchanan Avenue, and the narrow path winds about 4.3 miles through thick stands of oak, spruce, and fir trees. The trail offers some of the finest views of Ogden Canyon from above—particularly of the waterfall at the mouth of the canyon—before dropping down to the parking area on Utah 39. This moderately difficult trail takes about 4 hours one-way.

A little over a half-mile along Indian Trail, **Hidden Valley Trail** cuts off sharply to the south. The route is difficult, climbing steadily through the old Lake Bonneville terraces, and is surrounded by dense stands of oak, maple, and aspen. After a mile and a half, you reach a turnaround; from here, enjoy a clear view of the rugged face of Mt. Ogden to the southeast. The hike takes about 2 hours one-way.

An easy 1½-hour hike is the **Mt. Ogden Park Trail,** linking the parking lots at 29th and 36th streets. It's mostly flat and surfaced with bark chips. The trail follows the east edge of a golf course much of the way, encountering splashing streams and even occasional wildlife. The views are inspiring at sunrise and sunset.

For additional trail information, ask for the *Pathways in Weber County* brochure at the Forest Service's visitor information center in Union Station (p. 81) or visit the excellent website, **www.weberpathways.org**.

ICE-SKATING & CURLING   The **Ice Sheet,** 4390 Harrison Blvd., in the southeast part of the city (© **801/778-6300;** www.co.weber.ut.us/icesheet), offers year-round ice-skating, a learn-to-skate program, hockey and figure-skating clinics, clinics on curling (this was the curling venue for the 2002 Olympics), and skate rentals. Call for current rates and schedules.

WATERSPORTS   Willard Bay State Park and Pineview Reservoir (below) are your destinations for boating, water-skiing, and swimming. Also check out the kayak parks on the Ogden River Parkway (p. 85), Lagoon (p. 84), and Lorin Farr Park (p. 87).

WINTER SPORTS   Deep snow turns the mountains surrounding Ogden into a winter playground, with four delightful family-oriented ski resorts (see "Ogden Valley & the Northern Wasatch Front," later in this chapter) and seemingly unlimited forest trails for cross-country skiers, snowshoers, and snowmobilers.

An exciting way to ski some of the best snow in the West is to get away from the groomed trails, lift lines, and parking lots and take to the skies with **Diamond Peaks Heli-ski Adventures** (© **801/745-4631;** www.diamondpeaks.com), based in Ogden. Helicopters fly you to the tops of several privately owned mountains with no developed trails, just pure snow. A six-run heli-ski tour, with lunch, costs $895; ask about one-drop packages at Powder Mountain.

Parks & Recreation Areas

For boating and water-skiing, head 10 miles north to **Willard Bay State Park,** 900 W. 650 North, No. A, Willard (© **435/734-9494;** www.stateparks.utah.gov). In addition to watersports, 9,900-acre Willard Reservoir offers birding and wildlife viewing. There are two marinas, restrooms with showers, 131 campsites (some with RV hookups), and an RV dump station. A trail leads to a wide, sandy beach for swimming and sunbathing. Some campsites are along the waterfront, but most are along a meandering access road among the abundant cottonwoods and willows along Willard

Creek. The day-use fee is $10 per vehicle; camping costs $16 to $25. Take I-15 exit 351 to South Marina, or exit 357 for North Marina.

In the Ogden Ranger District of the Uinta-Wasatch-Cache National Forest (© 801/625-5112; www.fs.fed.us/r4/uwc), **Pineview Reservoir** is 6 miles east of Ogden via Utah 39. Surrounded by towering mountains and forested hillsides, the 2,874-acre reservoir is a popular watersports destination. Created by the construction of an earth-and-rock dam in 1937, it has two boat ramps and two designated swimming areas. Anglers catch smallmouth and largemouth bass, black bullhead catfish, crappie, bluegill, yellow perch, and tiger muskie. The **North Arm Wildlife Viewing Trail,** accessible from Utah 162 where the North Fork of the Ogden River enters the reservoir, is an easy .7-mile round-trip walk through a riparian wetland, where you're likely to see northern orioles, yellow warblers, and white-crowned sparrows, plus ducks, geese, hawks, and mule deer. The best viewing times are spring and early summer.

The Forest Service's **Anderson Cove Campground,** at 5,000 feet elevation along the south edge of the reservoir, has paved roads and 68 sites, and costs $18 per night. It's usually open from May through September, and has vault toilets and drinking water. For reservations, contact the **National Recreation Reservation Service** (© 877/444-6777; www.recreation.gov).

If you need to cool off, head to **Lorin Farr Park,** 769 Canyon Rd., Ogden River Parkway (© 801/629-8284, or 801/629-8259 for pool). Facilities include water slides, a swimming pool, a playground, a skateboard park, and a picnic area with grills. The park is open year-round, but the pool is open in summer only. Admission to the park is free, but there are charges for swimming (call for current rates and schedules).

MTC Learning Park, 1750 Monroe Blvd. (© 801/629-8284), is home to a nice botanical garden featuring indigenous plants and wildflowers and includes a stretch of the trail that's part of the Ogden River Parkway.

Spectator Sports

Weber State University, southeast of downtown, belongs to the Big Sky Athletic Conference and the Mountain West Athletic Conference. Football games kick off at **Stewart Stadium** at the south end of campus, while basketball and women's volleyball take place at **Dee Events Center,** 4400 Harrison Blvd. Contact the school's athletic department (© 801/626-6500; www.weberstatesports.com) for schedules.

Ogden also has a minor league baseball team. A short season "A" team affiliate of the Los Angeles Dodgers, the **Raptors** play from mid-June to early September at **Lindquist Field,** 2330 Lincoln Ave. (© 801/393-2400; www.ogden-raptors.com).

Shopping

At one time a bawdy collection of saloons, rooming houses, brothels, and opium dens, Ogden's 25th Street has become the "in" place to shop and eat. Within its historic buildings are several antiques shops, specialty stores, restaurants, and bars. Among the best stops here is **IndigoSage Furniture Gallery,** 195 25th St. (© 801/621-7243), for all sorts of furnishings and decor. Kids will get a kick out of **Queen Bee,** 270 25th St. (© 801/791-0241), with games, toys, and chocolate on its shelves. Also worth a look are **Gallery 25,** 268 25th St. (© 801/334-9881; www.gallery25 ogden.com), a cooperative gallery featuring the work of local artists.

At the mouth of Ogden Canyon is **Rainbow Gardens,** 1851 Valley Dr. (✆ **801/621-1606;** www.rainbowgardens.com); dubbing itself as Utah's largest gift shop, it has everything from flowers and Olympic souvenirs to a restaurant (p. 90) and a trail head out back.

Those searching for specialty shops or their favorite stores will enjoy **Newgate Mall,** 36th Street and Wall Avenue (✆ **801/621-1161;** www.newgatemall.com), with boutiques, department stores, abundant eateries, and a 14-screen movie theater. The mall is open Monday through Thursday from 10am to 9pm, Friday and Saturday from 10am to 9pm, and Sunday from noon to 6pm.

Where to Stay

In addition to the choices below, the Ogden area is home to a number of affordable chain motels. **Motel 6,** 1206 W. 21st St. (✆ **800/466-8356** or 801/393-8644; www.motel6.com), **Days Inn,** 3306 Washington Blvd. (✆ **800/329-7466** or 801/399-5671; www.daysinn.com), and **Sleep Inn,** 1155 S. 1700 West (✆ **801/731-6500;** www.sleepinn.com), usually charge between $60 and $80 double.

Room tax totals about 12%. Pets are not allowed unless otherwise noted.

Alaskan Inn ★★   Discover the wilds of Alaska in this enchanting bed-and-breakfast, where the unique rooms and cabins whisk you to a land of tundra, snowcapped peaks, tall pines, grizzly bears, and cascading waterfalls. Stay in the handsome 12-room log lodge or one of the 11 cabins. All units have whirlpool tubs for two; the cabins also have free-standing showers, and one has a kitchenette. In the popular Northern Lights room, you can enjoy a light show of the Aurora Borealis while lounging in bed or soaking in the tub. Or perhaps you'd prefer the Bears' Den, with a cozy cavelike atmosphere. Cabins are more simply furnished, but continue the Alaska theme; you can dwell in a trapper's cabin or listen to the call of the bull moose along the Kenai River.

Located some 15 minutes from downtown Ogden, the inn is nestled among tall pines along the Ogden River, with easy access to hiking trails in the national forest. Full breakfasts are served in your room or cabin. Free tours of the inn are offered daily from 1 to 2pm. Smoking is not permitted.

435 Ogden Canyon Rd., Ogden, UT 84401. www.alaskaninn.com. ✆ **801/621-8600.** Fax 801/394-4054. 23 units. Sun–Thurs $125–$180 double; Fri–Sat and holidays $140–$195 double. Rates include full breakfast. AE, DISC, MC, V. Not suitable for children 17 and under. *In room:* A/C, TV/DVD or VCR, movie library, fridge, kitchenette (in one), Wi-Fi (free).

Best Western Plus High Country Inn ★   Located just off I-15, this above-average motel offers comfortable, attractive rooms with a bright, airy feel and modern mission-style decor. Guests have a choice of one or two queen-size beds or one king-size. Amenities include Wi-Fi, ski lockers and ski tuning, and the very popular **Jeremiah's** restaurant.

1335 W. 12th St., Ogden, UT 84404. www.bestwestern.com. ✆ **800/594-8979** or 801/394-9474. Fax 801/392-6589. 109 units, including 4 suites. $79–$99 double; $109–$139 suite. AE, DISC, MC, V. Just off I-15 exit 344. Pets accepted with a deposit. **Amenities:** Restaurant (Jeremiah's; see review, p. 91); exercise room; indoor Jacuzzi; outdoor heated pool. *In room:* A/C, TV, fridge, hair dryer, Wi-Fi (free).

Hampton Inn and Suites ★★   This eight-story Art Deco–style structure, built in 1913, was renovated in 2002 for the Olympics. More like a boutique hotel than a chain, its standard rooms are well-appointed, with top-quality furnishings and a comfortably refined atmosphere. The junior one-room "suites" are much more spacious, with upgraded amenities and sleeper sofas, and the 12 two-room executive suites are top of the line, with just about every amenity you can imagine. The hotel has secure covered parking, same-day dry cleaning, a business center, and a nice balance of historic architecture and reliable modernity.

2401 Washington Blvd., Ogden, UT 84401. www.ogdensuites.hamptoninn.com. ⓒ **801/394-9400.** Fax 801/394-9500. 124 units. $99–$159 double; $129–$229 junior and full suite; lower weekend rates. Rates include continental breakfast. AE, DISC, MC, V. **Amenities:** Fitness center. In room: A/C, TV, Internet (free).

HUNTSVILLE

Atomic Chalet ★★ 🖼 Growing up in the shadow of a nuclear power plant in Orange County, California, gave Wes Welch the inspiration for his inn's name, but his experience as a professional volleyball player in the European Alps inspired its style and service. The Atomic Chalet, which housed the U.S. Ski Team during the 2002 Winter Olympics, is a two-story, cedar-clad lodge with a pool table in the parlor and a hip sensibility throughout. The rooms have one king-size or queen-size bed, plus a ladder up to a loft with one or two twins. The soft color scheme accents unfinished pine furnishings, marble-laden bathrooms, and mountain views. There are boot warmers and glove driers, and you can rent cruiser bicycles ($2.50 per hour) and kayaks ($15 per half-day). Breakfast includes home-baked bread, yogurt, granola, and fresh fruit. Other perks: Avid skier Welch has insider's tips for the slopes and he's known for throwing parties during ski season.

6917 E. 100 South, Huntsville, UT 84317. www.atomicchalet.com. ⓒ **801/745-0538.** 4 units. Winter $105–$130 double; spring–fall $85–$95 double. Rates include continental breakfast and après-ski specialties. MC, V. **Amenities:** Outdoor Jacuzzi. In room: TV/VCR, hair dryer, fridge, no phone.

Jackson Fork Inn ★ A delightful alternative to standard hotels, this unique little inn was formerly an old family barn, believed to have been constructed in the 1930s. It is now in its third location. Each unit has a spiral staircase leading to an upstairs bedroom loft. All accommodations are bright and cheery, and two rooms have whirlpool tubs. The charming Jackson Fork Inn **restaurant** serves dinner and Sunday brunch; next door is **Chris Cafe,** a low-key beer bar that serves three meals a day. The inn is completely nonsmoking.

7345 E. 900 South (Utah Hwy. 39), Huntsville, UT 84317. www.jacksonforkinn.com. ⓒ **800/255-0672** or 801/745-0051. 7 units. $85–$150 double. Rates include continental breakfast. AE, DISC, MC, V. Pets accepted ($20 1-time fee). **Amenities:** Restaurant (see review, p. 93); room service. In room: A/C, TV/DVD, DVD library, no phone, Wi-Fi (free).

EDEN

Basinview Lodging (ⓒ **877/686-4733;** www.basinviewlodging.com), offering a wide variety of condos and vacation homes, is a good one-stop shop for ski-oriented lodging in the Ogden Valley. Condos start around $100 double a night and homes start at $200. Another solid option is **Red Moose Lodge and Spa,** 2547 N. Valley Junction Dr. (ⓒ **801/745-6667;** www.theredmooselodge.com), with a "New West" sensibility and rates from $99 to $199 a night in ski season.

Snowberry Inn Bed & Breakfast ★ The Snowberry, built in 1992, is a large, comfortable log-cabin-style inn within 15 minutes of three ski areas and convenient to outdoor activities in the surrounding national forest. Each room is accented with antiques and collectibles related to its theme (Canyons, Wasatch Winter, Pioneer, and so on). The Pioneer room is wheelchair accessible, and the Sundance Suite is the best family option. Each room has its own bathroom, some with shower only; the

Monte Cristo has a claw-foot tub with a shower. Amenities include a game room with a pool table, foosball, and darts. The inn has an open, friendly atmosphere and great breakfasts—a signature dish is crème brûlée French toast. Smoking is not permitted inside.

1315 N. Utah Hwy. 158, Eden, UT 84310. www.snowberryinn.com. ⓒ **888/746-2634** or 801/745-2634. Fax 801/745-3140. 8 units. $109–$129 double. Rates include breakfast. MC, V. From Ogden, follow Utah 39 east about 8 miles and turn north on Utah 158; the inn is about 2½ miles up on the west side of the road. Pets accepted with prior approval. **Amenities:** Outdoor Jacuzzi. *In room:* No phone, Wi-Fi (free).

Camping

In addition to the following options, the national forest offers camping in the Pineview Recreation Area, discussed above under "Parks & Recreation Areas," which also covers camping at Willard Bay State Park. Additional camping is found at Fort Buenaventura (p. 79) and at Lagoon (p. 84).

Century RV & Mobile Home Park   This campground, conveniently located near the interstate and downtown Ogden, has shade trees, grass, and pull-through and back-in gravel sites. There's also a large tent camping area, a bathhouse with hot showers, a dump station, a convenience store, a coin-operated laundry, a playground, free Wi-Fi, and a heated outdoor pool and hot tub. Cable TV hookups are available.

1399 W. 2100 South (1 block west of I-15 exit 343), Ogden, UT 84401. www.centuryparkrv.com. ⓒ **801/731-3800.** Fax 801/731-0010. 166 sites. $28–$38. AE, DISC, MC, V.

Cherry Hill Camping Resort ★ ☺   This immaculately maintained, remarkably comprehensive campground is part of a large complex containing a water park ($18), miniature golf course ($6), and batting cages ($4). You'll find manicured lawns, shade trees, and paved interior roads, along with a heated pool, recreation hall, and game room. The campground offers complete RV hookups, a dump station, a convenience store, and loads of sites for tent camping. Note that some recreational and camping services are limited from November to April. Call ahead.

1325 S. Main St. (2 blocks south of I-15 exit 328), Kaysville, UT 84037. www.cherry-hill.com. ⓒ **888/446-2267** for reservations, or 801/451-5379. Fax 801/451-2267. 182 sites. $30–$38; lower rates Nov–Apr. DISC, MC, V.

Where to Eat

Bistro 258 AMERICAN/EUROPEAN   This casual, airy restaurant is in one of the oldest buildings in this part of Ogden, built in 1888 and restored in 1984. It has a narrow dining room and a magnificent old wooden bar complete with mirrors behind the glassware, a large atrium dining room, and a flower- and shrub-filled outdoor patio for warm-weather dining. The changing menu blends American and European cuisines, with choices such as New York steak with Gorgonzola and balsamic vinegar and coconut-macadamia-crusted halibut. Desserts are terrific; choose from daily baked cheesecake and "fuzzy peaches": batter-fried peach halves served with ice cream and drizzled with raspberry sauce. The bistro also offers a children's menu and full liquor service.

258 25th St. ⓒ **801/394-1595.** Main courses $7–$10 lunch, $8–$26 dinner. AE, DISC, MC, V. Mon–Thurs 11am–9pm; Fri–Sat 11am–10pm.

The Greenery AMERICAN   A local lunch favorite, this pleasant eatery has a green-and-white color scheme, checkerboard floors, nice canyon views, and—of course—plenty of greenery inside and out. The menu (while the same for lunch and dinner) is diverse, and the food is good. Try the fresh-baked Mormon Muffin, made from a pioneer recipe and served with Utah honey butter. Other house specialties include Chinese chicken salad, the Fowl Play sandwich (turkey, avocado, and melted mozzarella), and caramel apple pie. Bottled beer is available.

In Rainbow Gardens (p. 88), 1851 Valley Dr. ℂ **801/392-1777** or 801/621-1606. www.rainbow gardens.com. Main courses $7–$15. AE, DISC, MC, V. Mon–Thurs 11am–9:30pm; Fri–Sat 11am–10pm; Sun 11am–9pm. From downtown, take Washington Blvd. north to 12th St. and head west to the mouth of Ogden Canyon.

Jeremiah's ★ 🏚 AMERICAN   For some of the best burgers in northern Utah, as well as a wide variety of basic American dishes and great breakfasts, head to Jeremiah's. A local favorite—due in part to its large portions and reasonable prices—this attractive Western restaurant has consistently won "Best Breakfast in Northern Utah" in the *Salt Lake City Weekly*'s readers' poll. In addition to about a dozen styles of burgers—including a buffalo burger and a meatless burger—you can also order up a sirloin steak, salads and sandwiches, and several chicken dishes. The extensive breakfast menu includes a dozen omelets, various meat and egg options, and pancakes. Early birds can catch the break-of-dawn breakfast special between 6 and 8am, a carb-heavy, all-you-can-eat bargain for $6. The huge, popular scones and cinnamon rolls are served all day. Full liquor service is available.

Best Western High Country Inn (p. 88), 1307 W. 1200 South. ℂ **801/394-3273.** www.jeremiahs utah.com. Main courses $7–$17. AE, DISC, MC, V. Mon–Sat 6am–10pm; Sun 7am–9pm.

The Oaks ★ 🏚 AMERICAN   This restaurant's delightful location—tucked among the pines in Ogden Canyon, with patio dining over the bubbling and crashing Ogden River—just can't be beat. The Oaks moved to its present spot way back in 1933, when it evolved into a hamburger and hot dog takeout joint. In 1981, Keith and Belinda Rounkles turned it into a full-service sit-down eatery and ice-cream parlor. Today, the family-friendly, home-style eatery has a rugged Western decor, accented by old photos, maps, and postcards. Food is good, solid, American fare, made mostly from scratch. Breakfast, served until noon, features the usuals, along with huevos rancheros and some exotic omelets. The lunch and dinner menus bring a variety of burgers and sandwiches, including the house specialty: sliced sirloin smothered with mushrooms, onions, and green peppers and topped with mozzarella and American cheese, served on a French bun. Dinner specials, such as charbroiled steak, chicken, or salmon, are also available; the pasta of the day is available at lunch and dinner. Utah microbrews and other beer and wine are served with meals.

750 Ogden Canyon (Utah Hwy. 39). ℂ **801/394-2421.** www.theoaksinogdencanyon.com. Main courses breakfast $5–$12, lunch $5.50–$12, dinner $15–$25. AE, DISC, MC, V. Summer daily 8am–10pm; shorter hours rest of year.

Prairie Schooner ☺ STEAK   On the south side of the Ogden River, the Prairie Schooner is so named because every dining table is modeled after a prairie schooner—that's a covered wagon for you Eastern folk. The Western theme doesn't end there; the dining room features life-size campfire dioramas, a stuffed wolf, and a facade modeled after Old West storefronts. But what's kept the place in business for 30 years are the steaks, including a monster 24-ounce porterhouse and a 16-ounce T-bone, as well as those of the chicken-fried, sirloin, and prime-rib varieties. There is also a full selection of seafood and surf-and-turf combos, and a smattering of chicken. Lunch is composed of sandwiches and a few items from the grill. Full liquor service is available.

445 Park Blvd. ℭ **801/392-2712.** www.prairieschoonerrestaurant.com. Main courses $8–$22 lunch, $10–$50 dinner. AE, DISC, MC, V. Mon–Fri 11am–2pm; Mon–Thurs 4–9pm; Fri–Sat 4–10pm; Sun 2–8pm. From downtown, drive north on Washington Blvd. and turn right (east) just before the arch at Park Blvd.

Rickenbacker's Bistro ★★ STEAK/SEAFOOD Rickenbacker's—named for the World War I flying ace and decked out with vintage airplane memorabilia—is located, fittingly, at the Ogden airport, with views of the runways and the mountains to the east. The attractively decorated space, featuring white tablecloths and plenty of style, serves as an apt backdrop for the creative takes on standards like barbecued pork chops with avocado salad and garlic mashers or pistachio-crusted halibut on a bed of butternut squash and goat cheese ravioli. Lunches are sandwiches and smaller portions of the dinner entrees. Full liquor service is available.

4282 S. 1650 West, in the KempJet Center at Ogden-Hinckley Airport. ℭ **801/627-4100.** www. rickenbackersbistro.com. Main courses $7–$17 lunch, $12–$40 dinner. AE, DISC, MC, V. Mon–Fri 11am–2pm; Mon–Thurs 5–9pm; Fri–Sat 5–10pm. From I-15, take exit 341B and drive west and south to the airport.

Roosters 25th Street Brewing Co. ★ AMERICAN This two-story, redbrick brewpub, with its prominently displayed brewing vats and intriguing metal and wood tables, is popular for both its eclectic menu and its beers. Pizzas come in several varieties, including a vegetarian option with mushrooms, peppers, asparagus, spinach, and sun-dried tomatoes. The beer-battered fish and chips is light and crisp. For an appetizer, try the crunchy Onion Loops, onion slices fried in a homemade beer batter. Fish tacos, turkey enchiladas, pasta, steaks, great soups, and excellent specialty sand-wiches are also available. Weekends bring a brunch menu that includes a killer *chili verde* omelet. Request the patio seating if the weather is nice. As you might expect, freshly brewed beer is served—try the Junction City Chocolate Stout—and full liquor service is available.

253 25th St. ℭ **801/627-6171.** www.roostersbrewingco.com. Reservations not accepted. Main courses $7–$15 brunch and lunch, $9–$22 dinner. AE, DC, DISC, MC, V. Mon–Thurs 11am–10pm; Fri 11am–11pm; Sat 10am–11pm; Sun 10am–10pm.

Union Grill ★★ AMERICAN/ECLECTIC Set in historic Union Station, the Union Grill has a lively decor of Art Deco–style stained glass and bright colors, with a contemporary touch of industrial chic. Take a peek outside: The windows look out on a view of trains rumbling by. The menu includes fresh fish, pasta, homemade soups, salads, and sandwiches, along with daily specials. Spicy Cajun dishes are especially tasty, as is the fresh flame-broiled salmon. The desserts, especially the cara-mel bread pudding, are hard to resist. Full liquor service is available.

Union Station, 2501 Wall Ave. ℭ **801/621-2830.** www.uniongrillogden.com. Reservations recom-mended for large parties. Main courses $7–$26. AE, DC, DISC, MC, V. Mon–Thurs 11am–10pm; Fri–Sat 11am–10:30pm; shorter winter hours.

HUNTSVILLE & EDEN

Beyond the options that follow, I'm also a fan of the burgers over at the **Shooting Star Saloon** (p. 83).

Carlos and Harley's Fresh-Mex Cantina ★ 🏠 MEXICAN This funky little Mexican joint, located in the old (built in 1880) Eden General Store building, is fun for all ages, with an inviting bar and eclectically decorated walls. The log cabin atmo-sphere is homey and social, perfect for enjoying the excellent south-of-the-border specialties plated up by the kitchen, such as spicy poblano chicken, seafood

Farr Better Ice Cream

Choose from over 50 flavors of ice cream and a wide range of malts, shakes, sundaes, frozen yogurt, sherbets, and homemade fudge at **Farr Better Ice Cream—Utah's Original Ice Cream Shoppe,** 286 21st St. (✆ **801/393-8629,** ext. 20), in business since 1920. Cones start at $2. Hours are Monday through Saturday 10am to 10pm (summer hours: 9am–10pm Mon–Thurs and 9am–11pm Fri–Sat).

enchiladas, and fajitas. Tuesdays bring all-you-can-eat tacos; Thursday is chile relleno night. There is a full bar.

5510 E. 2200 North (in the Historic Eden General Store), Eden. ✆ **801/745-8226.** www.carlosandharleys.com. Main courses $9–$21. AE, DISC, MC, V. Daily 11:30am–9pm.

Jackson Fork Inn ★ CONTINENTAL   A charming country atmosphere pervades this inn, housed in a converted barn. The menu includes excellent petite sirloin and slow-roasted prime rib; chicken teriyaki; seafood selections such as salmon, mahimahi, and coconut shrimp; and a changing vegetarian entree. Sunday brunch features some of the best blueberry pancakes in the West. Wine and beer are available.

Jackson Fork Inn (p. 89), 7345 E. 900 South (Utah Hwy. 39), Huntsville. ✆ **801/745-0051.** www.jacksonforkinn.com. Reservations recommended. Main courses $9–$19 dinner, $6–$11 brunch. AE, DC, DISC, MC, V. Mon–Sat 5–9pm; Sun brunch 10am–2pm.

Ogden After Dark

All summer long, Monday through Saturday, the outdoor **Ogden Amphitheater,** 343 25th St. (✆ **801/393-3866;** www.ocae.org), hosts free and paid events, including movies, community theater, open-mic nights, and concerts. Events at the historic **Peery's Egyptian Theater,** 2415 Washington Blvd. (✆ **801/395-3200;** www.peerysegyptiantheater.com), include ballet and organ performances. During the school year, Weber State University's Department of Performing Arts (✆ **801/626-6437;** www.weber.edu/performingarts/default.html) presents regular live entertainment at various venues; call ✆ **800/978-8457** for tickets or check the website for a schedule.

For classical offerings, contact the **Ogden Symphony and Ballet,** 638 E. 26th St. (✆ **801/399-9214;** www.symphonyballet.org), which presents a variety of performances, ranging from solo violin recitals and pops concerts to ballets, such as *The Nutcracker,* at various venues.

The **Golden Spike Event Center,** 1000 N. 1200 West (✆ **801/399-8798;** www.goldenspikeeventcenter.com), has surround seating for more than 6,000 people and hosts concerts, rodeos, horse races, demolition derbies, circuses, auctions, and other special events. Call for current events. If you're lucky, you might get to see a chariot race—remember Ben Hur?—or a monster truck rally.

There are also more bars per capita in Ogden than any other city in Utah. (It's sometimes called "Utah's liver.") For after-hours entertainment, the **City Club,** 264 25th St. (✆ **801/392-4447;** www.thecityclubonline.net), offers good eats and walls plastered with Beatles memorabilia, while **Brewski's,** 244 25th St. (✆ **801/394-1713;** www.brewskisonline.net), features lots of local bands and rock 'n' roll. You can catch live comedy at **Wiseguys Comedy Cafe,** 269 25th St. (✆ **801/622-5588;** www.wiseguyscomedy.com), with shows on Friday and Saturday nights. **Diamond Lounge,** 2510 Washington Blvd., at Hotel Ben Lomond (✆ **801/627-1900**), is a dueling piano bar.

WHERE EAST MET WEST: GOLDEN SPIKE

50 miles NW of Ogden, 90 miles NW of Salt Lake City

If you love steam trains, you won't want to miss the **Golden Spike National Historic Site ★★**. On May 10, 1869, the Central Pacific met the Union Pacific at Promontory Summit, and America's East and West coasts were finally joined by rail. The nation's second transcontinental telegraph had been strung along the track as it was laid, and as the final spike was driven home, the signal "Done" raced across the country—and jubilation erupted from coast to coast. A ragged town of tents quickly sprang up along the track at Promontory Summit, but within 8 months the railroads moved their terminal operations to Ogden. In 1904, the Lucin Cutoff bypassed Promontory altogether, and in 1942 the rails were torn up for use in military depots.

Although today less than 2 miles of track are here, they are laid on the original roadbed, where you can see fully functional replicas of the two engines, the Central Pacific's "Jupiter" and Union Pacific's "119," that met here in 1869. From mid- to late spring into early October, the magnificent machines are on display and make short runs (inquire at the visitor center for a schedule). Presentations are given track-side.

Essentials

Admission for up to a week is $7 per vehicle ($4 per pedestrian/bicyclist/motorcyclist) from May through mid-September and $5 per vehicle ($3 per pedestrian/bicyclist/motorcyclist) the rest of the year. There are no camping facilities. Outside attractions are open daily during daylight hours.

GETTING THERE   From Ogden, head north on I-15 to exit 365, turn west on Utah 83 for 29 miles to a sign for Golden Spike, turn south, and go 7½ miles.

INFORMATION/VISITOR CENTER   Contact **Golden Spike National Historic Site,** P.O. Box 897, Brigham City, UT 84302-0897 (© **435/471-2209, ext. 29;** www.nps.gov/gosp). The park's visitor center is open daily year-round from 9am to 5pm (closed Thanksgiving, Christmas, and New Year's Day). Restrooms, picnic areas, and a bookstore are located at the visitor center, which also offers slide programs, films, and museum exhibits detailing the linking of the nation. Ranger programs take place daily; check at the visitor center for the current schedule.

SPECIAL EVENTS   The park has several special events throughout the year, with free admission. On May 10 is a reenactment of the original **Golden Spike Ceremony,** with food, souvenirs, and handicrafts. Reenactments are also held on Saturdays and holidays from May into October. On the second Saturday in August, the **Annual Railroaders' Festival** features reenactments of the Golden Spike ceremony, a spike-driving contest, and handcar races and rides. Hot food, crafts booths, and live music add to the festivities. Although not free (regular entrance fees apply), the **Annual Railroaders' Film Festival and Winter Steam Demonstration,** held during the Christmas season, is a lot of fun, with classic Hollywood railroad films and a special appearance by one of the two resident steam locomotives.

Exploring the Historic Site

BY CAR

Die-hard railroad buffs can drive the self-guided **Promontory Trail Auto Tour** along 7 miles of the historic railroad grades. A booklet explaining the markers along

The Great Train Race

A transcontinental railroad had been a dream for Americans since railroads first appeared in the 1830s. By the time the Civil War began, numerous rail lines crisscrossed the Eastern seaboard, but the West remained relatively disconnected, and no rails linked the coasts. Finally the government selected two companies to receive loans and land for each mile of track laid. One company would start in Nebraska and head west, while the other would start in California and head east.

With trains carrying supplies following the workers as they laid down track, the race became ridiculous—opposing crews actually passed each other, furiously building parallel roadbeds, in sight of each other, in opposite directions! An end to this silliness finally came when Congress named Promontory, Utah, as the meeting spot. In 1869, four symbolic spikes (two golden, one silver, and one gold-plated silver) were driven in with a silver-plated hammer to mark the occasion, and the country was finally united by rail.

the tour is available at the visitor center. Notice the two parallel grades laid by the competing companies (see box below), clearings for sidings, original rock culverts, and many cuts and fills. Allow about 1¼ hours.

ON FOOT

The **Big Fill Trail** is a 1.5-mile loop along part of the original rail beds to the Big Trestle site and the Big Fill. The Big Fill was created when some 250 dump-cart teams and more than 500 workers—mostly Chinese immigrants—dumped load after load of rock and dirt into a ravine to create the 170-foot-deep, 500-foot span of fill required to lay the Central Pacific's track. The Union Pacific built their trestle just 150 feet away. It was never intended to be a permanent structure; speed was the goal, rather than strength. Constructed by hand by Irish and Mormon crews in 1869, the last spike went into the 85-foot-high, 400-foot-long trestle on May 5, just 36 days after it was begun.

You can hike on either the Central Pacific or Union Pacific rail bed, although the Central Pacific rail bed is an easier walk. Markers along both grades point out cuts and fills, quarries, vistas, and caves.

This is the desert, so bring water, wear a hat, and be prepared for mosquitoes and ticks. Rattlesnakes are rare, but be alert and stay clear if you see one. And be glad that you weren't one of the workers in that backbreaking effort of 1869.

OGDEN VALLEY & THE NORTHERN WASATCH FRONT

You'll find splendid powder skiing, low prices, few lift lines, and friendly people in abundance at the relatively undeveloped ski areas of northern Utah. Don't expect fancy lodges (at least not yet), but do be prepared for breathtaking scenery, a wide variety of fine terrain, and a relaxed family atmosphere.

The Ogden Valley Resorts

These resorts are just northwest of Ogden; to reach any of them, take I-15 exit 344 onto 12th Street and follow Utah 39 east. **Wolf Mountain** and **Powder Mountain** are just off Utah 158, and **Snowbasin** is off Utah 226.

6

THE NORTHERN WASATCH FRONT: UTAH'S OLD WEST

Ogden Valley & the Northern Wasatch Front

WOLF MOUNTAIN SKIING & TUBING

Family-oriented **Wolf Creek Utah Ski Resort,** 3567 Nordic Valley Way, Eden, UT 84310 (*C* **801/745-3511;** www.wolfcreekutah.com), formerly called Nordic Valley Ski Area, is Utah's smallest and least expensive ski area; it has among the best night-lighting systems in the state. Refreshingly informal and casual, Wolf Mountain has been a favorite of Ogden-area families because it's a good place to learn to ski, with enough variety to keep everyone satisfied. The terrain is rated about 25% beginner, 50% intermediate, and 25% advanced. Annual snowfall averages 300 inches. The resort also has a terrain park, and several runs have been designed specifically for snowboarders.

Wolf Creek has a double and a triple chairlift as well as a Magic Carpet serving 20 runs on 85 acres, and snow-making on 50 acres. The vertical drop is 1,000 feet from the top elevation of 6,400 feet. The ski area is generally open mid-December to early April, with lifts operating from 10am to 9pm Monday through Thursday and 9am to 9pm Friday and Saturday.

GETTING THERE   From I-15, follow Utah 39 east about 11 miles, turn north (left) onto Utah 158 for about 3 miles, then turn west (left), following signs to the ski area.

LIFT TICKETS   Day passes (9am–4pm) for adults cost $31 to $33 and kids are $19 to $21. Night skiing (4–9pm) costs $15 to $20; combination day and night passes are available.

LESSONS & PROGRAMS   The **ski school** offers private and group lessons; call for rates and information. The ski shop has equipment for rent and accessories for sale. No child-care facilities are available.

WHERE TO STAY & EAT   The mountain has no overnight lodging; see "Where to Stay," in the Ogden section earlier in this chapter, for nearby accommodations. The lodge serves hot sandwiches, homemade soups, pizza, and hot and cold beverages. You can relax around the fireplace on a cold day or outside on the deck when it's sunny and warm.

POWDER MOUNTAIN RESORT

This is a family ski area in two respects: It was founded in 1972 by the Cobabe family, who still own and run it, and it's aimed at providing a variety of skiing opportunities to suit everyone in your family. Among the 7,000 skiable acres—the most of any resort in the country—are plenty of beginner runs, which seem to grade upward in difficulty as you move from the Sundown area to the Timberline area and then the Hidden Lake area; so by the time you're skiing Three Miles, you can consider yourself an intermediate and try cruising over the big, swooping blue fields. There's no dearth of expert and powder skiing in the wilds, either. Powder Mountain uses snow cats and shuttle buses to transport skiers to more than 2,800 acres of spectacular powder that is not served by lifts—it's an out-of-bounds, backcountry skier's dream come true. A bonus is the view: On a clear day, you can see across the Great Salt Lake and sometimes all the way to Park City.

Powder Mountain is also a favorite among snowboarders; boarding is allowed everywhere.

Powder Mountain Resort, P.O. Box 450, Eden, UT 84310 (*C* **801/745-3772,** or 801/745-3771 for snow conditions; www.powdermountain.com), has two quads, one triple and one double chair, two surface lifts, and one platter lift, servicing 2,800 acres of packed runs and powder skiing, plus nearly that much in backcountry acreage—making the skiable acreage the highest in the country. The terrain is rated 25%

beginner, 40% intermediate, and 35% advanced. There are also two terrain parks. With more than 500 inches of snowfall annually, Powder Mountain doesn't have—or need—any snow-making. The elevation at the summit is 9,422 feet; the lift-served vertical drop is 2,205 feet. The season is generally mid-November to mid-April, with day skiing from 9am to 4:30pm and night skiing until 9pm.

GETTING THERE   From I-15, follow Utah 39 east about 11 miles, turn north (left) onto Utah 158, and drive about 8 miles to the ski area.

LIFT TICKETS   An all-day lift ticket is $60, a half-day ticket is $50, a kid's (ages 7–12) all-day ticket is $33, and a kid's half-day ticket is $28; night-skiing passes are $18 for adults and $15 for children. Seniors 62 to 69 pay $48 for a day pass; those 70 and over pay just $27. Kids 6 and under ride the lift free. Each snow cat ride costs backcountry skiers an extra $18; a guided "Snowcat Powder Safari" runs $350 per person in peak season.

LESSONS & PROGRAMS   The **ski school** offers a full range of ski and snow-boarding lessons and other activities, both group and private, from half-day to multi-day. These include children's lessons, a program designed especially for and taught by women, and guided Alpine tours. Private lessons start at $100 for an hour; group lessons cost $75 per person for 3 hours. Powder Mountain Lodge and Sundown Lodge both have ski shops where skis and snowboards are available for rent and accessories are for sale. No child-care facilities are available.

WHERE TO STAY & DINE   Most skiers stay in Ogden or Ogden Valley (see "Where to Stay," in the Ogden section earlier in this chapter), but for those who want to sleep slope-side, the **Columbine Inn** (*©* **801/745-1414;** www.columbineinn utah.com) has five rooms with a pleasant ski-chalet atmosphere, as well as a number of adjacent condo units that sleep as many as a dozen people. Rooms are located next to the lodge off the main parking lot. Doubles cost $80 to $150 in ski season, with condominiums going for $150 to $680. Smoking is not permitted.

As for dining, the **Powder Keg** in the basement of Timberline Lodge serves sand-wiches and draft beer around a cozy fireplace; there is also a cafeteria. **Hidden Lake Lodge** serves lunch at the summit. **Sundown Lodge** offers burgers, sandwiches, and soups.

SNOWBASIN ★★

Among America's oldest ski areas (it opened in 1939), Snowbasin remained a local secret until it hosted the downhill and Super G competition at the 2002 Olympics. Word of the area's great terrain got out, and skiers have been flocking to the resort ever since. Particularly popular for its top-to-bottom intermediate runs, Snowbasin offers plenty of untracked powder; long, well-groomed trails; and Utah's third-largest vertical drop. Beginners have plenty of terrain on which to develop their ski-legs, and some great transitional runs off the Wildcat lift will help them graduate from novice to intermediate status. With its wide-open powder bowls and Olympic downhill courses, expert skiing at Snowbasin has been growing by leaps and bounds.

Snowbasin Resort, P.O. Box 460, Huntsville, UT 84317 (*©* **801/620-1000,** or 620-1100 for snow conditions; www.snowbasin.com), has 108 runs, rated 20% begin-ner, 50% intermediate, and 30% advanced. Included in its 3,000 acres are beautiful powder bowls and glade skiing. Snowbasin has two high-speed quads, one handle tow, one Magic Carpet, and four triple chairlifts, plus two high-speed eight-passenger gondolas and a tram that serves the starting point for the downhill racecourses. The lift-served vertical drop is 2,950 feet from the 9,350-foot summit. All lifts are open to snowboarders, with retaining devices required. With about 400 inches of annual snowfall, Snowbasin has not really needed snow-making equipment, although snow-making has been added to assure an early season opening. The ski season generally runs from Thanksgiving to mid-April, with lifts operating daily from 9am to 4pm. The resort is also now open in summer, when it transforms into a hiking, biking, and horseback-riding mecca (p. 85).

GETTING THERE   Take I-15 to exit 324, then go north on U.S. 89 for about 10 miles. At the mouth of Weber Canyon, merge onto I-84 eastbound, which you take several miles to exit 92 for Mountain Green. Head east about 2 miles and turn north (left) onto Utah 167 (Trapper's Loop). Go about 5 miles to Utah 226, where you turn left and drive 3 miles to the resort.

LIFT TICKETS   All-day adult lift tickets cost $72, half-day tickets are $60; for ages 7 to 12, an all-day ticket is $44, a half-day ticket is $35; seniors over 65 pay $59 for a full day and $43 for a half-day. Kids 6 and under can ride the lift free; seniors 75 and over are $14.

LESSONS & PROGRAMS   The **ski school** (© 801/620-1016) offers both pri-vate and group skiing and snowboarding lessons for all ages and abilities, with rates starting at $48 for a 2-hour group lesson and $145 for a 2-hour private lesson. Chil-dren's lessons are also available. The Grizzly Center at the base offers ski and snow-board equipment rental and repair, plus clothing and accessories for sale. No child-care facilities are available.

WHERE TO STAY & EAT   No lodging is available at the ski area itself; most skiers stay near Ogden (see "Where to Stay," in the Ogden section, earlier in this chapter). In preparation for the Olympics, Snowbasin built three handsome restaurants—one at the base and two on the mountain. All serve American fare in a mountain lodge atmosphere; the on-mountain restaurants are preferable for their wondrous views.

Northern Wasatch Front (Near the Idaho Border)

BEAVER MOUNTAIN SKI AREA ★
Skiing at **Beaver Mountain Ski Area** is like going home to see the folks. Located at the top of beautiful Logan Canyon in the Wasatch-Cache National Forest, this small resort has been operated by the Seeholzer family since 1939. The emphasis is on friendliness, personal attention, and, as Ted Seeholzer puts it, "helping skiers find the right runs for them." Beaver Mountain gets plenty of snow and has a good mix of terrains, well-maintained slopes, and a northeast exposure that makes morning runs a warm, sunny experience. Snowboarders are welcome. Both bump skiers and snow-boarders like the steep Lue's Run (named for Ted's mother, Luella), while hot-doggers are directed to Harry's Hollow (named for Ted's father), which has plenty of bumps—and is located right under a lift so everyone can see you showing off.

   Beaver Mountain Ski Area, 1351 E. 700 North (P.O. Box 3455), Logan, UT 84321 (© **435/753-0921,** or 435/753-4822 for ski reports; www.skithebeav.com), receives an average of 400 inches of snow annually and has a top elevation of 8,800 feet and a vertical drop of 1,600 feet. Two double chairlifts, a surface lift, and two triple chairlifts service 664 total skiable acres. The terrain is 35% beginner, 40% intermediate, and 25% advanced, and there are 30 runs. The season runs from early December through March, with the lifts operating daily from 9am to 4pm. The mountain is closed on Christmas Day.

GETTING THERE Take I-15 to exit 362, then go east on U.S. 89 about 50 miles through Logan and Logan Canyon, and take the turnoff to the ski area.

LIFT TICKETS All-day adult lift tickets cost $45; the cost for children 11 and under and seniors 65 and older is $35. Half-day tickets are $35 for adults and $30 for kids and seniors.

LESSONS & PROGRAMS The **ski school** offers group and private lessons. Private lessons start at $55 per hour; group lessons are also available. The lodge is the place to find ski rentals, lockers, and a small shop that sells clothing and accessories. No child-care facilities are available.

WHERE TO STAY & DINE Most lodging and restaurants can be found 27 miles west in Logan (see "Logan," below). A cafeteria at the day lodge sells hamburgers, sandwiches, and soft drinks.

Nearby places to stay include **Beaver Creek Lodge,** P.O. 139, Millville (© **800/ 946-4485** or 435/946-3400; fax 435/946-3620; www.beavercreeklodge.com), a half-mile east of the ski area along U.S. 89. Open year-round, this 11-room log lodge offers all the modern conveniences in a spectacular mountain setting surrounded by the national forest. Spacious guest rooms contain log furnishings, handmade bed quilts, TVs and DVD players, and whirlpool tubs with showers. A large common room offers a stone fireplace and big-screen TV with DVD players, and the decks offer panoramic views. Hiking, mountain biking, horseback riding, and snowmobiling are all available on the property and in the surrounding national forest (see "Sports & Outdoor Pursuits," later in this chapter). Room rates are $129 to $149 in winter and $109 to $129 in summer, with Friday- and Saturday-night rates the highest; meals are available during ski season at an additional charge. No smoking is permitted.

A small **RV park** (© **435/563-5677**) with 23 sites for RVs and tents is open at Beaver Mountain Ski Area in summer, with showers and lots of trees. RV sites with hookups cost $25; tent sites are also available. A large tent and a yurt are available from April through November (call for details).

LOGAN

46 miles N of Ogden, 81 miles NE of Salt Lake City

Nestled in the fertile Cache Valley, at an elevation of 4,525 feet, Logan is flanked by the rugged Wasatch and Bear River mountains. Once part of prehistoric Lake Bonneville, then home to the Blackfoot, Paiute, Shoshone, and Ute Indians, the valley is now a rich farming area known for its cheeses and high-tech businesses. Mountain men arrived in the 1820s to trap beaver in the Logan River, caching (hence the valley's and county's name) the pelts in holes they dug throughout the area. Then, in 1856, Mormon pioneers established several villages in the valley.

With a population of about 49,000, Logan is a small city, but with many of the attractions of its larger neighbors to the south. Particularly worthwhile are visits to the LDS Church's Tabernacle and Temple, both handsome 19th-century structures, and a drive out to the American West Heritage Center for a trip through 100 years of Western history: 1820 to 1920. Thanks in part to Utah State University, Logan suffers from no lack of art exhibits, live music, or theater.

But nobody who comes to Logan really wants to spend much time indoors. Beautiful Logan Canyon and the nearby mountains are a delightful escape for hikers, mountain bikers, equestrians, anglers, and rock climbers.

Essentials

GETTING THERE   From Salt Lake City and Ogden, take I-15 north to exit 362, then follow U.S. 89/91 northeast about 24 miles to downtown Logan. Those flying to Salt Lake City can arrange transportation with the **Cache Valley Airport Shuttle** (© **800/658-8526** or 435/563-6400; www.loganshuttle.com). Two days' notice is recommended; round-trip fare is $56.

VISITOR INFORMATION   The **Cache Valley Visitors Bureau** has a **Visitor Information Center** located in a beautifully restored 1883 courthouse at 199 N. Main St., Logan, UT 84321 (© **800/882-4433** or 435/755-1890; www.tourcache valley.com). It's open Monday through Friday from 8am to 5pm.

GETTING AROUND   As with most Utah cities, Logan is laid out on a grid, with the center at the intersection of Main Street (north to south) and Center Street (east to west). Tabernacle Square is the block to the northeast of the intersection. U.S. 89/91 enters town on a diagonal from the southwest, along the golf course at the south end of town. Utah State University is located on the northeast side of town, north of U.S. 89 between 700 and 1400 East.

The **Cache Valley Transit District,** or CVTD (© **435/752-2877;** www.cvtd bus.org), is a **free** citywide bus service. Buses run Monday through Friday 5am to 7:10pm and Saturday 10:15am to 7:10pm, except major holidays. A route map is available at the visitor center on Main Street (see above). For a cab, call **Logan Transportation** (© **435/753-3663**).

Car-rental agencies in Logan include **Enterprise,** 2026 N. Main St. (© **800/261-7331** or 435/755-6111; www.enterprise.com), and **Avis,** 900 N. Main St. (© **800/ 331-1212** or 435/753-3575; www.avis.com).

FAST FACTS   The **Logan Regional Hospital,** 500 E. 1400 North (© **435/716-1000**), has a 24-hour emergency room. The **main post office** is at 75 W. 200 North (© **800/275-8777;** www.usps.com).

What to See & Do

Although it's not open to the general public, you can still view the outside of the handsome **LDS Temple,** 175 N. 300 East (© **435/752-3611**), and its beautiful grounds. The temple was completed in 1884, and its octagonal towers give the four-story limestone structure the appearance of a medieval castle. Because it sits on a slight rise, it can be seen from just about anywhere in the valley.

American West Heritage Center   This living history museum, covering 160 acres, tells the story of the Old West from 1820 to 1920. It includes the **Jensen Historical Farm,** an authentic 1917 farm where visitors can learn about farming in the early 20th century, and the **Pioneer Era Area** (1845–70), which describes homesteading and life in a dugout or log cabin. There are also depictions of life in Shoshone Indian villages and mountain-man encampments. Allow 2 hours. The **seasonal festivals** (special fees apply), held several times a year, feature arts and crafts demonstrations and Western reenactments, competitions, music, and food.

4025 South U.S. 89/91 (6 miles south of Logan), Wellsville. © **800/225-3378** or 435/245-6050. www.awhc.org. Admission $6 adults, $4 children 3–11 and seniors 55 and over, free for children 2 and under; festival admission varies. Historic sites June–Aug Tues–Sat 11am–4pm. Welcome Center June–Aug Mon 9am–3pm, Tues–Fri 9am–5pm; rest of year Mon–Fri 9am–3pm. Some seasonal variations. Closed New Year's Day, Thanksgiving, and Christmas.

Cache Museum—Daughters of Utah Pioneers This small museum displays pioneer artifacts from 1859 to 1899—basically the first 40 years of Mormon settlement in the area. You can see guns, musical instruments (including the first organ used in the LDS Tabernacle), handmade pioneer furniture, clothing, and kitchenware. On exhibit are several pieces of furniture made by Brigham Young for his daughter Luna Young Thatcher, who lived in Logan. Allow 30 minutes.

160 N. Main St. ℂ **435/752-5139.** Free admission. May–Sept Tues–Fri 10am–4pm; by appointment rest of year.

LDS Tabernacle The Tabernacle was built from locally quarried stone in a style that's an amalgam of Greek, Roman, Gothic, and Byzantine. The main stone, quartzite, is from Green Canyon, 8 miles northeast of Logan; the white limestone used for the corners and trimmings came from Idaho. Construction started in 1865 and took almost 27 years to complete. The main hall and balcony can accommodate about 1,800 people, and the pipe organ is a work of art. The pillars are made of wood that has been expertly painted to simulate marble, a technique widely used throughout pioneer Utah. The extensive genealogical library is open to the public. Allow 30 minutes.

50 N. Main St. ℂ **435/755-5598.** Free admission. June–Aug daily 9am–5pm.

Utah State University Founded in 1888, Utah State University (USU) is situated on a bench that was once the shore of the great Lake Bonneville. Established through the Federal Land Grant Program as the Agricultural College of Utah, USU has about 20,000 students and an international reputation for research and teaching.

Old Main was the first USU building, and is the oldest building in continuous use on any Utah college campus. At various times, it has housed nearly every office and department of the school. Its tall bell tower is a campus landmark.

The **Museum of Anthropology,** Room 252, Old Main (ℂ **435/797-7545;** http://anthromuseum.usu.edu), has exhibits on the early inhabitants of the Great Basin as well as on the peoples of Polynesia and other areas around the world. It's open Monday through Friday from 8am to 5pm and on Saturday from 10am to 4pm year-round; admission is free. Allow 45 minutes.

The **Nora Eccles Harrison Museum of Art,** 650 N. 1100 East (ℂ **435/797-0163;** http://artmuseum.usu.edu), displays a fine collection of ceramics and offers changing multimedia exhibits. It's open Tuesday through Saturday from 11am to 4pm. Allow 1 hour. Admission is free; there is a suggested donation of $3.

The **Nutrition & Food Science Building,** 750 N. 1200 East (ℂ **435/797-2112**), sells locally famous Aggie Ice Cream in a wide variety of flavors, as well as cheese. Call the **store** (ℂ **888/586-2735** or 435/797-2109; http://aggieicecream. usu.edu) for more information.

102 Old Main. ℂ **435/797-1000.** www.usu.edu. The 400-acre campus lies north of U.S. 89 and mostly east of 800 East. To get to the campus, drive north on I-15 and take exit 362. Drive east through Brigham City and the Canyon. The highway turns into Main St. Turn right on 500 North. When you get to the hill, turn left up the slope. Parking is just past the traffic light on the right.

Willow Park Zoo ☺ This small but intriguing zoo is home to a variety of animals, from lemurs to elk to bobcats, plus one of the best collections of birds in the region, with about 100 species (including wild avians who nest here). Children are invited to feed the ducks, geese, and trout. The attractive grounds have a lovely, grassy play and picnic area shaded by tall trees. Allow 1½ hours.

419 W. 700 South. ℂ **435/716-9265.** www.loganutah.org. Admission $2 adults, $1 children 3–12, and free for kids 2 and under. Daily 9am–dusk. Closed New Year's Day, Thanksgiving, and Christmas, with possible seasonal closures. From Main St., head west on 600 South for 3 blocks, turn south (left) onto 300 West for 1 block, then west (right) onto 700 South.

Sports & Outdoor Pursuits

The Wasatch-Cache National Forest, which covers almost 2 million acres of northern Utah, offers many opportunities for outdoor recreation. For maps and other information, contact the **Logan Ranger District** office, 1500 E. U.S. 89, Logan, UT 84321 (ℂ **435/755-3620;** www.fs.fed.us/r4/uwc). For outdoor equipment and supplies, as well as knowledgeable staff to help you find the best spot for your activity, stop by **Sports Authority,** 1050 N. Main (ℂ **435/752-4287**), or **Al's Sporting Goods,** 1617 N. Main (ℂ **435/752-5151;** www.alssports.com).

Excellent watersports, fishing, and wildlife viewing can all be had at **Bear Lake State Park** (ℂ **435/946-3343;** www.stateparks.utah.gov), along the Utah-Idaho border about 40 miles northeast of Logan via U.S. 89. The state's second-largest freshwater lake (20 miles long and 8 miles wide), Bear Lake is known for the azure blue of its water, caused by the suspension of calcium carbonate (limestone) particles in the lake. Facilities include boat ramps and rentals, a marina, picnic areas, campgrounds, and a 4.2-mile paved walking and biking trail. Deer are often seen in the park, and birdwatchers may spot ducks, geese, white pelicans, herons, and sandhill cranes, among other species. Anglers catch lake trout and huge cutthroat trout; an alleged Loch Ness–style monster, 90 feet long and dating back to local tribal legend, is said to inhabit the lake. Elevation is 5,900 feet. The day-use fee is $8 per vehicle ($5 on the east side); camping costs $10 to $25. Contact the marina at **Cisco's Landing** in Garden City (ℂ **435/946-2717;** www.ciscoslanding.com) for boat rentals and lake tours.

BIKING Cache Valley's patchwork of farms and villages offers excellent road biking through the countryside on well-maintained roads, and mountain bikers have plenty of opportunities in the Wasatch-Cache National Forest. For tips on the best biking spots, contact the visitors bureau or the ranger district office (above). Each June the Utah Multiple Sclerosis Society (ℂ **801/424-0113;** http://bikeutu.nationalms society.org) sponsors the 2-day **Harmons Best Dam Bike Ride,** in which more than 1,500 participants pedal up to 150 miles a day along Cache Valley's back roads. Funds support the battle against multiple sclerosis.

BIRDING Northern Utah has great birding, especially from spring through early fall in the area's wetlands. Two particularly good spots are along the Bear River west of Logan, and Cutler Marsh. These spots offer opportunities to see great blue herons, snowy egrets, white pelicans, western grebes, and a variety of other wetlands species.

FISHING Logan River and Bear River offer wonderful fly-fishing, and streams throughout the area are popular for rainbow, albino, cutthroat, and brook trout. Bear Lake (above) offers great lake fishing (including ice-fishing in winter) for trophy cutthroat and lake trout. For tips on where they're biting, stop at **RoundRocks Fly Fishing,** 530 S. Main St. (ℂ **800/992-8774;** www.roundrocks.com), a full-service fly shop and guide service—and home to the world's largest fly (32 ft. long and 3 tons).

HIKING Numerous hiking possibilities abound in the Wasatch-Cache National Forest east of Logan, and Logan Canyon in particular offers spectacular scenery. Among the easy hikes is the **Spring Hollow Trail,** about 6.5 miles up Logan Canyon, which leads a half-mile to one of the area's most photographed rivers. Stop at the visitors bureau or the Logan Ranger District office (p. 102) for a free brochure and other information.

HORSEBACK RIDING   The **Beaver Creek Lodge,** in Logan Canyon (✆ **800/946-4485;** www.beavercreeklodge.com), is about 25 miles northeast of Logan on U.S. 89 just east of Beaver Mountain Ski Resort (see "Ogden Valley & the Northern Wasatch Front," earlier in this chapter). One- to 4-hour guided rides are available for beginner through expert levels, costing from $35 to $89. Trails include a wide range of terrains, from mountaintops to rolling hills covered with aspens, pine trees, and wildflowers. The challenging rides to the top of a mountain reward you with panoramic views of the forest and Bear Lake. Reservations are recommended. See p. 99 for more information on Beaver Creek Lodge.

ROCK CLIMBING   The sheer rock walls of Logan Canyon make this one of the most challenging climbing areas in the West. An abundance of vertical and overhanging limestone and quartzite faces wait for eager climbers, and more than 275 routes have been developed—most are bolt-protected sport climbs. For practice, classes, information, and climbing advice, stop at the **Rockhaus Climbing Gym,** 1780 N. 200 East (✆ **435/713-0068;** www.rockhausgym.com).

SNOWMOBILING & OTHER WINTER FUN   Snowmobiling opportunities can be found throughout the Wasatch-Cache National Forest. Rentals are available at **Beaver Creek Lodge** (p. 99), which offers access to more than 300 miles of groomed snowmobile trails. Full-day rental rates are $179 to $219 for one rider, and $30 more for two riders. Guided day trips run an additional $350. Another popular activity is taking a sleigh ride among a herd of about 400 elk at the **Hardware Ranch Wildlife Management Area** (✆ **435/753-6206;** www.hardwareranch.com), about 20 miles southeast of Logan ($5 adults, $3 kids; cash only). Information on snowmobiling, snowshoeing, and cross-country skiing can be obtained from the Uinta-Wasatch-Cache National Forest's **Logan Ranger District** office (p. 102). Downhill skiing is at **Beaver Mountain Ski Area** (p. 98).

Spectator Sports

A member of the Western Athletic Conference, **Utah State University** competes in all major sports, winning conference championships in football, men's basketball, and women's outdoor track in recent years. Contact the school's ticket office (✆ **888/878-2831** or 435/797-0305; www.utahstateaggies.com) for information.

Where to Stay

Among the reliable chains in Logan that usually charge around $100 to $150 for two people are **Best Western Baugh Motel,** 153 S. Main St. (✆ **800/462-4154** or 435/752-5220; www.bestwestern.com), and the new-in-2009 **Holiday Inn Express,** 2235 N. Main St. (✆ **888/465-4329** or 435/752-3444; www.hiexpress.com). In the $50-to-$100 range are **Comfort Inn,** 447 N. Main St. (✆ **800/228-5150** or 435/752-9141; www.choicehotels.com), and **Super 8,** 865 S. U.S. 89/91 (✆ **800/800-8000** or 435/753-8883; www.super8.com). On the campus of Utah State, the **University Inn,** 4300 Old Main Hill (✆ **800/231-5634** or 435/797-0017; www.usu.edu/univinn), offers hotel-style rooms and suites with double rates of $79 to $119. In nearby Providence (just south of Logan), the **Providence Inn** (✆ **800/480-4943** or 435/725-3432; www.providenceinn.com) is a standout B&B located in "the Old Rock Church" (it dates back to 1871) with rates of $109 to $229 double.

Rates are highest in summer and lowest usually during the first 3 or 4 months of the year. Lodging tax totals 10.6%.

The Riter Mansion Located right off the main drag in the center of town, this 1899 Greek Revival mansion, built by a prominent Logan pharmacist, has long been central to the area population's social life. As a lodging, it's a splendid alternative to the motels on Main Street, and features a nice variety of rooms. I like the Library Suite (with 500 books and a four-poster queen bed) and the Parlor Suite (with hardwoods and a jetted tub in the bathroom).

168 N. 100 East, Logan, UT 84321. www.theritermansion.com. (C) **800/478-7459** or 435/752-7727. 6 units. $99–$169 double. AE, DISC, MC, V. *In room:* A/C, TV/DVD, Wi-Fi (free).

Where to Eat

Beyond the choices listed below, it's hard to beat **Angie's,** 690 N. Main St. ((C) **435/752-9252**), for a family-oriented, value-priced diner. It's known for its Kitchen Sink, a sundae comprised of seven scoops of ice cream and every imaginable topping. Also recommended is **Cafe Sabor** in historic Union Station at 600 W. Center St. ((C) **435/752-8088;** www.cafesabor.com), serving solid Mexican dishes like enchiladas and chimichangas as well as steaks, chicken, and pasta.

The Beehive Grill ★ AMERICAN Touting itself as "Logan's only root beer brew pub," the new-in-2009 Beehive Grill is just that—and a lot more. It also serves draft beers from the Moab Brewery, makes gelato in-house, and offers a diverse selection of food, ranging from plump burritos and fish tacos to barbecue and burgers. It also has a nice slate of vegetarian specials, including a burrito stuffed with walnuts, pineapple, and artichoke hearts. It has two distinct seating areas in the bar and dining room, and the atmosphere is casual but contemporary, attracting a cross section of Loganites: Utah State students and faculty, families, and blue-collar types. The bar has some great nightly specials and full liquor service.

255 S. Main St. (C) **435/753-2600.** www.thebeehivegrill.com. Main courses $7–$22. AE, DISC, MC, V. Sun–Thurs 11:30am–10pm; Fri–Sat 11:30am–11pm.

The Bluebird ☺ AMERICAN The Bluebird opened in 1914 as a candy shop and soda fountain. Today, the Bluebird continues to offer fountain treats along with good food. The decor, reminiscent of the 1920s, features the original marble behind the soda fountain and a mural depicting Logan from 1856 to modern times. The lunch menu offers sandwiches, such as a patty melt and barbecue pork, plus several full meal offerings, including a 6-ounce sirloin steak, pineapple chicken, and a filet mignon. In addition to a few sandwiches, the dinner menu brings such options as vegetarian pasta primavera, chicken-fried steak, and the popular slow-roasted prime rib. No alcohol is served.

19 N. Main St. (C) **435/752-3155.** Main courses $7–$16. AE, DISC, MC, V. Mon–Thurs 11am–9:30pm; Fri–Sat 11am–10pm. Just north of Center St.

Hamilton's ★ STEAKS/CONTINENTAL This swank, rugged, and masculine joint has the best steaks in the Cache Valley. Situated on either side of a massive fireplace—and likely in view of the open kitchen—the stark dark-wood tables with no tablecloths offer an excellent tableau for the steaks, all from USDA Stockyards (corn-fed, hand-cut, and broiled at 1,600°F/871°C). Beyond the beef, the menu has an excellent selection of seafood dishes, chicken, and pasta. Lunches are mostly burgers, but also include steaks, pasta, and seafood.

2427 N. Main St. ℂ **435/787-8450.** www.hamiltonssteakhouse.com. Reservations recommended for dinner. Main courses $7–$15 lunch, $12–$52 dinner. AE, DISC, MC, V. Mon–Thurs 11am–10pm; Fri 11am–11pm; Sat noon–11pm. Main St. north about 3 miles from the city center.

Logan After Dark

Logan was once known as "the Athens of the West" for its cultural slate, and the tradition is still going strong. The **Utah Festival Opera Company,** 59 S. 100 West (ℂ **800/262-0074** or 435/750-0300, ext. 106; www.ufoc.org), presents a summer series of grand operas, light operettas, and musicals at the historic **Ellen Eccles Theatre,** 43 S. Main St. (ℂ **435/752-0026;** www.centerforthearts.us), a dazzling piece of restoration. Recent productions have included such operas as *Faust, Tosca,* and *Kiss Me, Kate.* The Ellen Eccles Theatre also stages other productions, ranging from modern dance performances to big band concerts. Call for the current schedule.

One of the few true professional repertory companies anywhere, the **Old Lyric Repertory Company,** 28 W. Center St. (ℂ **435/752-1500** or 797-8022 for the box office; http://arts.usu.edu/lyric), founded at Utah State University in 1967, presents a variety of comedies, dramas, and musicals, with equity actors, during its 8-week summer season.

THE SOUTHERN WASATCH FRONT: WORLD-CLASS SKIING & MORE

7

This is the heart of Utah's terrific ski country. Set amid majestic mountain scenery southeast of Salt Lake City, nestled between some of the country's top ski resorts—including Deer Valley, Snowbird, and Alta—is an abundance of natural wonders, such as Timpanogos Cave National Monument and Provo Canyon. The towns in this area run the gamut from Park City—aka "Sin City" to some—to Provo, one the most conservative cities in the state, and the home of Brigham Young University. Over the mountains from Park City, the Heber Valley is a spectacular sight from land or air (take a balloon ride for the latter), and a hint of Hollywood even glitters in this remarkable mountain landscape, thanks to Robert Redford's Sundance Resort near Provo and the annual hullabaloo in Park City, the Sundance Film Festival.

This chapter is arranged geographically from north to south, from the Cottonwood Canyons and Park City resorts to Provo and nearby Timpanogos Cave National Monument, with a few stops in between, including pristine Strawberry Reservoir, Sundance Resort and Institute, and even an antique train.

For a **map** of the Wasatch Front, see in the inside back cover of this book.

THE COTTONWOOD CANYONS RESORTS

30 miles SE of downtown Salt Lake City

You say you want some snow? Here it is, some 500 inches of it piling up every year, just waiting for you powder-hungry skiers to make that short drive from Salt Lake City. Brighton and Solitude ski resorts are in Big Cottonwood Canyon, and Alta and Snowbird ski resorts are in its sister canyon, Little Cottonwood.

If you're skiing on a budget, stay at the more affordable Salt Lake City lodgings rather than at the resorts themselves. The resorts are so close—less than an hour's drive—that city dwellers sometimes even hit the slopes before or after a day (okay, make that a half-day) at the office.

But this area is more than just a winter playground. Big Cottonwood Canyon, cut by ancient rivers over more centuries than you can imagine, is a spectacular setting for warm-weather picnicking, camping, mountain biking, and hiking. Rugged, glacier-carved Little Cottonwood Canyon is filled with lush fields of summer wildflowers, the brilliant hues of autumn, and then a winter blanket of powder snow.

Getting There

BY CAR   From Salt Lake City, take I-215 south to exit 7, then follow Utah 210 south. Turn east onto Utah 190 to reach Solitude and Brighton in Big Cottonwood Canyon; continue on Utah 210 south and east to Snowbird and Alta in Little Cottonwood Canyon. From Salt Lake City International Airport, it'll take about an hour to reach any of the four ski areas.

BY BUS   The **Utah Transit Authority** (*✆* **888/743-3882** or 801/743-3882; www.rideuta.com) provides bus service from downtown Salt Lake City hotels and various park-and-ride lots throughout the city into Big and Little Cottonwood Canyons during ski season. The cost is $7 round-trip or $1.75 for a ride between Brighton and Solitude.

BY SHUTTLE   All Resort Express (*✆* **877/658-3999** or 435/649-3999; www. allresort.com) offers shuttles from the airport and major Salt Lake City hotels ($37 per person each way, with a two-person minimum). **Wasatch Crest Shuttle** (*✆* **877/754-8294;** www.wcshuttle.com), also offers shuttles starting at $85 round-trip for up to four people.

Big Cottonwood Canyon

Each turn along your drive to the summit of this 15-mile-long canyon brings you to yet another grand, dizzying vista. Rock climbers love these steep, rugged canyon walls—watch for them as you drive.

BRIGHTON SKI RESORT ★

In operation since 1936, the low-key, family-friendly **Brighton Ski Resort,** 12601 Big Cottonwood Canyon Rd., Brighton, UT 84121 (*✆* **800/873-5512** or 801/532-4731; www.brightonresort.com), is where many Utahns learn to ski and snowboard thanks to the highly regarded ski and snowboard school. Children 8 and under stay and ski free with their parents, and teens particularly enjoy the bumps of Lost Maid Trail as it winds through the woods. But don't let its reputation as a beginner's mountain fool you: Brighton's slopes are graced with a full range of terrain, all the powder you can imagine, and virtually no crowds. More Utahns than out-of-staters hit the slopes here—Brighton is located just 35 miles from downtown Salt Lake City at the top of Big Cottonwood Canyon, and visitors tend to stay away because of the paucity of area lodgings. Elbow room is plentiful on the intermediate and advanced slopes, even on the weekends, and you may have them all to yourself on weekdays. Snowboarders will delight to know that this is one of the state's top snowboarding destinations. Plus, you needn't leave after dark: Brighton lights up 200 acres for night skiing.

Brighton has six quad lifts, one triple, and a Magic Carpet serving over 1,050 acres in the Wasatch-Cache National Forest. The lift-served vertical drop is 1,745 feet, accessible by hiking. Base elevation is 8,755 feet. Of the 66 runs, 21% are rated

The Cottonwood Canyons Resorts

The Ski Salt Lake Super Pass

If you want to experience all of the Cottonwood Canyons resorts, your best deal is the **Ski Salt Lake Super Pass,** starting at $192 adults and $105 children ages 7 to 12 for 3 days of access to the four resorts including transportation on UTA buses. Four- to 6-day passes are also available, as are 1- and 2-day passes in conjunction with lodging. Visit **www. ski-saltlake.com** to buy a pass or learn more.

beginner, 40% intermediate, and 39% advanced. Lifts are open daily from 9am to 4pm, mid-November to mid-April, with night skiing and snowboarding Monday through Saturday from 4 to 9pm from early December to March. The resort can make snow on 200 acres, but with 500 inches of average snowfall per year, the man-made stuff isn't usually necessary.

Brighton has a beautiful day lodge, with ticket windows, restrooms, a common area, a ski rental and repair facility, and a convenient bus depot.

LIFT TICKETS   Adult all-day passes cost $62; night skiing is $34. Children 8 to 12 are $29, but those 8 and under ski free with an adult (with a maximum of two kids per paying adult). Seniors 70 and over are $35.

LESSONS & PROGRAMS   **Brighton Ski & Snowboard School** (✆ **800/873-5512,** ext. 209), in the Alpine Rose building, offers both private and group lessons. Group lessons cost $45 for adults and private lessons start at $85 for 1 hour. Night skiing lessons cost $45, including a lift ticket. The ski and snowboard school also offers a variety of workshops and clinics, including a telemark series as well as adult parallel, senior, children's, and women's workshops.

WHERE TO STAY & EAT   **Brighton Lodge,** at the ski resort (✆ **800/873-5512,** ext. 120; www.brightonresort.com), has 20 units, ranging from dorm-style rooms (which sleep up to four) to luxurious suites, with rates of $129 to $209 double. The lodge's large outdoor Jacuzzi will help loosen those sore muscles for your next day of skiing. Room tax is about 12%. You'll find cafeteria-style dining for all three meals and a bar that opens for lunch and stays open through après-ski and dinner. Another option is **Mount Majestic Properties** (✆ **801/824-4700;** www.mountmajestic. com), which rents all manner of mountain homes and condominiums for $150 a night and up.

WARM-WEATHER FUN   Mountain biking and hiking are popular activities, but note that lifts are not open in summer.

SOLITUDE MOUNTAIN RESORT

Solitude, 12000 Big Cottonwood Canyon, Solitude, UT 84121 (✆ **800/748-4754** or 801/534-1400; snow report 801/536-5777; www.skisolitude.com), is a friendly, family-oriented resort that hasn't been "discovered" yet, so lift lines are virtually nonexistent. The snow is terrific, and it's easy to reach—it's in Big Cottonwood Canyon, just 28 miles from downtown Salt Lake City. Like its next-door neighbor, Brighton—which is connected to Solitude via the Solbright Trail—Solitude enjoys excellent powder and few crowds. Its 1,200-plus acres of skiable terrain range from well-groomed, sunny beginner and intermediate trails to gently pitched bowls and glades. The mountain is well designed, with runs laid out so beginners won't suddenly find themselves in more difficult terrain. Intermediates have wide-open bowls in which to cruise and practice their powder skiing, several excellent forest runs, and some great bumpy stretches on which to hone their mogul skills. Advanced skiers have many long fall lines, open powder areas, and steeply graded chutes.

Solitude is the state's only downhill ski area with a world-class Nordic center out its back door: The University of Utah and U.S. Olympic teams train here. The resort also has an ice-skating rink.

Three high-speed quad lifts, two fixed-grip quads, one triple, and two doubles service 65 runs and three bowls. Runs are rated 20% beginner, 50% intermediate, and 30% advanced/expert. The resort is open from early November to late April, daily from 9am to 4pm. With a summit elevation of 10,035 feet and a vertical drop of 2,047 feet, Solitude receives an average yearly snowfall of more than 500 inches.

LIFT TICKETS   All-day passes cost $68 for adults, $45 for seniors 70 and older, $42 for kids 7 to 14, and those 6 and under ski free. Afternoon half-day adult lift tickets are $56.

LESSONS & PROGRAMS   Solitude's **ski school** offers group and private lessons. Adult group classes (lift ticket included) are $80 for a half-day, $95 for all day; call for rates for customized private lessons (✆ **801/536-5730**). The **Moonbeam Kid's Program,** for kids 4 through 12, offers an all-day learn-to-ski program, including lunch, lift ticket, and rental, for $135; the afternoon-only program is $75.

WHERE TO STAY & EAT   The **Inn at Solitude** (✆ **877/517-7717;** www.innatsolitude.com) is a full-service luxury hotel, with 46 rooms and nightly rates from $209 to $449 during ski season (lower in summer). Its restaurant, **St. Bernard's,** offers fine dining with a menu from Europe's Alpine regions. Breakfast and dinner are served.

The resort also manages numerous **condo units and private homes,** with ski season prices ranging from $236 to over $1,000.

Adjacent to the Apex Chairlift and with terrific views of the mountain, the day lodge **Last Chance Mining Camp** offers hearty lunches, and après-ski refreshments. The **Moonbeam Lodge** has a cafeteria for breakfast and lunch and a pub for dinner and libations. **Kimi's Mountainside Bistro** is nestled on the canyon floor and offers gourmet dinners and weekend brunches. The **Thirsty Squirrel** is a pub in the base village with an in-house sushi bar open weekend nights. Also in the village is **Stone Haus,** serving pizza and ice cream for lunch and dinner.

For an unusual experience, reserve dinner at the **Yurt** (✆ **801/536-5709**), in the forest above the main lodge. You can either cross-country ski or snowshoe through the evergreens to get to your elegant five-course gourmet meal for $100 per person,

Great Cross-Country Skiing

Solitude Nordic Center ★★ is Utah's oldest cross-country ski area. It has about 12 miles of groomed trails, including a children's trail. The center is located between Solitude and Brighton at 8,700 feet and connects the two downhill resorts. Trails pass through alpine forests and meadows and around frozen Silver Lake. The **Silver Lake Day Lodge** offers rentals, equipment for sale, lessons, and light snacks. Trail passes for ages 11 to 69 cost $17 for a full day, $12 for a half-day. Those 10 and under or 70 and over ski free.

served at a table set with linen, silver, and crystal. Dress is casual, but the meal isn't. Advance reservations are recommended after mid-October.

Room tax in this area is 13.6%.

WARM-WEATHER FUN   Solitude remains open in summer, offering chairlift rides, mountain bike and scooter rentals, 18-hole mountainside disc golf, and a place to hike or just kick back and watch the wildflowers grow.

Little Cottonwood Canyon

With towering peaks rising 11,000 feet above the road on both sides, Utah 210 takes you on a lovely scenic drive through the canyon. Located at the junction of Utah 209 and Utah 210, the mouth of Little Cottonwood Canyon is where pioneers quarried the granite used to build the LDS Church's Salt Lake City Temple.

ALTA SKI AREA ★★★

Alta, P.O. Box 8007, Alta, UT 84092-8007 (*C* **801/359-1078;** snow report 801/572-3939; www.alta.com), is famous for its snow—over 500 inches per year of some of the lightest powder in the world—and at $72 for an all-day lift ticket, it's an excellent value. Located about 45 minutes southeast of Salt Lake City, at the top of Little Cottonwood Canyon, Alta is an excellent choice for serious skiers of all levels. Beginners have their share of runs, and the more adventurous novices can even try a bit of easygoing tree skiing through the woods. Intermediates will find plenty of open cruising ground, forested areas, and long, arcing chutes to glide through, plus opportunities to work on their bumps technique (try Challenger for a moderately pitched set) or practice their turns in the powder. Experts will find an abundance of the Cottonwood Canyons' famous powder and spectacular runs, like steep, long Alf's High Rustler. Alta offers much for the expert and the extreme skier—far too much to cover here—but hard-core skiers should know that you'll have to step out of the bindings and do a bit of hiking to get to some of the longest drops and best powder-laden runs. And this is a true skier's mountain: Alta is one of the few Western ski areas left that forbids snowboarding.

Alta's fans are many and loyal. That's because the emphasis here is on quality skiing, and to protect that quality, Alta has chosen to limit its uphill capacity. This is a classic ski resort, with both European-style terrain *and* sensibilities. This means that people are turned away on those occasions when the ski gods determine there are already enough skiers on the mountain. An announcement is made on 530 AM radio about a half-hour before the closure.

More than 100 runs are served by two detachable quads, one detachable triple, one triple, three doubles, three surface tows, and a moving conveyor. Alta has 2,200 skiable acres, with snow-making on 50 acres. Although it's famous for its expert runs, Alta also has fine beginner and intermediate trails. The breakdown is 25% beginner, 40% intermediate, and 35% advanced, with a base elevation of 8,530 feet rising to 10,550 feet at the top, yielding a vertical drop of 2,020 feet. Alta is generally open from mid-November to mid-April, with lifts operating daily from 9:15am to 4:30pm.

Alta Ski Lifts Company owns and operates only the ski area; all other businesses and services are privately run. At the base of Albion and Sunnyside lifts is a day lodge with a cafeteria, lift-ticket sales, day care, the ski school, and rentals. Two more cafeterias are located on the mountain. A transfer tow connects the Albion and Wildcat lift areas; in this base area, there are four lodges with dining facilities, ski rentals, and kids' programs.

LIFT TICKETS All-day, all-lift tickets cost $72, with half-day tickets at $60. Beginner lifts only are $38, as are children 12 and under. Combination lift tickets are available for both Alta and Snowbird. The area also has a "Ski Free After 3" ticket, which allows beginners to test out some of the easiest terrain in Albion Basin for an hour and a half at the end of the day.

LESSONS & PROGRAMS Founded in 1948 by Alf Engen, the highly regarded **ski school** (© 801/799-2271) is recognized for its contribution to the development of professional ski instruction. Two-hour group lessons cost $50; private instruction starts at $95 for a 1-hour lesson. The **Children's Ski Adventures** program, for ages 4 to 12, offers fun skill development, and lessons in ski etiquette. Choose either a half- or all-day program.

Alta's **day-care program** (© 801/742-3042; www.altachildrenscenter.com) is open to children ages 2 months to 10 years old; reservations are encouraged. Call for current rates.

WHERE TO STAY & EAT The best places to stay in Alta are slope-side. The following accommodations add a 15% service charge to your bill in lieu of tipping; room tax adds about 13%.

Alta Lodge (© 800/707-2582 or 801/742-3500; www.altalodge.com) is perhaps the quintessential mountain ski lodge—simple and rustic, with a touch of class. The lodge has Jacuzzis, saunas, a general store, a kids' program, a bar, and a restaurant with superb food. The comfortable units range from small and basic dormitory rooms to handsome corner rooms with fireplaces and a balcony. Rates, including breakfast and dinner, range from $290 to $554 for two, or $108 to $146 per bed (less for kids) in a dorm room.

Rustler Lodge (© 888/532-2582 for reservations, or 801/742-2200; www. rustlerlodge.com) is elegant yet relaxed, with a great mountain-lodge ambience, a spa, and rooms that range from basic to deluxe (several two-room suites are available). Rates, including full breakfast and dinner, range from $270 to $950 for two; a bed for one in a dorm room, with breakfast and dinner, costs $150 to $200.

The value here is the **Alta Peruvian** (© 800/453-8488 or 801/742-3000), featuring lodging and three meals for $107 to $132 in dorms, $119 to $158 double with shared bathroom, and $150 to $204 double with private bathroom. Suites are $169 to $276 double. The funky bar here is the best après-ski spot on the mountain.

SNOWBIRD SKI & SUMMER RESORT ★★

The combination of super skiing and snowboarding plus super facilities lures both hard-core enthusiasts seeking spectacular powder, and those who enjoy the pampering that accompanies a stay at a full-service resort. Consistently rated among America's top-10 ski resorts, **Snowbird,** P.O. Box 929000, Snowbird, UT 84092-9000 (© 800/232-9542 or 801/933-2222, and 801/933-2100 for snow conditions; www. snowbird.com), is Alta's "younger, slicker sister." The same wonderful snow falls here, but this resort has a wider range of amenities, including Snowbird's extremely popular spa and salon—worth the trip even if you don't ski. Some, however, find Snowbird's dense, modern village and resort atmosphere cold compared to Alta's historic, European-style lodges and classic, ruggedly Western atmosphere and attitude.

Many expert skiers absolutely worship Snowbird, however, with plunging cliff runs like Great Scott, one of the steepest runs in the country. Mogul-meisters will want to take the Peruvian or Gad II lifts to a great variety of fall lines on some steep and sinuous runs.

Off the Slopes at Snowbird

Don't miss the popular **Cliff Spa** (☎ **801/933-2225**), which offers a lap pool and huge whirlpool, aerobic and weight-training rooms, and individual treatment rooms for massages, body wraps, mud baths, and hydrotherapy. The **Snowbird Canyon Racquet Club** (☎ **801/947-8200**), 15 minutes from the slopes, features 23 tennis courts (10 indoor), racquetball, and aerobic and cardiovascular facilities. Snowbird provides a variety of facilities for children, including a state-licensed day-care center and a youth camp; call for details.

But beginners and intermediates haven't been forgotten, and their runs are also top-notch. There are even some "family-only" ski zones. Novices might want to head over to explore West Second South, set in a woodsy glade, or the less crowded Baby Thunder area. Intermediates will enjoy the excellent runs coming off the Gad II lift; if you decide to take the tram, wait around a bit at the top while your fellow riders take off so that you'll have these blue runs all to yourself—the next tramload won't get dumped off for another 5 minutes.

The entire mountain is open to snowboarders, and the resort also provides snowmobile adventures and cat skiing and snowboarding.

Snowbird has 85 runs on 2,500 acres, rated 27% beginner, 38% intermediate, and 35% advanced. The ski season generally runs from mid-November to mid-May, although the record 783 inches—that's over 60 feet—of snow that fell in 2010–11 allowed Snowbird to keep the lifts running through the Fourth of July—the latest lift-served skiing ever in Utah. From a base elevation of 7,760 feet, the vertical rise of 3,240 feet reaches Hidden Peak at 11,000 feet.

An aerial tram transports 125 skiers and boarders at a time up 2,900 vertical feet to Hidden Peak in about 7 minutes. It's quick, but can feel like a crowded New York City subway car. Snowbird also has four high-speed detachable quads, six doubles, and two conveyor lifts, giving it a total uphill capacity of 17,400 skiers per hour. The tram and lifts operate between 9am and 4:30pm daily, except for one that operates until 8:30pm for night skiing Wednesdays, Fridays, and Saturdays.

LIFT TICKETS   Adult lift tickets cost $72 for a full day and $62 for a half-day for lifts only; for both lifts and tram, the cost is $78 and $68, respectively. Children 7 to 12 are charged $42 including tram, and seniors 65 and over are charged $65, or $59 half-day. Children 6 and under can ride the lifts for free and the tram for $15. Combination lift tickets are available for both Snowbird and Alta.

LESSONS & PROGRAMS   The **ski and snowboarding school** (☎ 801/947-8222) offers an all-day class (which includes lunch); a package for first-timers; and specialized workshops for racers, women, snowboarders, half-pipe riders, and seniors. Two-and-a-half-hour workshops start at $100.

Established in 1977, Snowbird's **Wasatch Adaptive Sports Program** (☎ 801/933-2188; www.wasatchadaptivesports.org) is among the best special-needs sports programs in the country. Using state-of-the-art adaptive ski devices and a team of specially trained instructors, the program is available to children and adults alike. Sit-skis, mono-skis, and outriggers are available at no extra cost.

HELI-SKIING   Between December 15 and April 15, helicopter skiing is available on more than 40,000 acres from **Wasatch Powderbird Guides** (☎ 800/974-4354 or 801/742-2800; www.powderbird.com). Daily rates (seven runs, a continental breakfast, and lunch) are $980 to $1,000 per person from mid-January through the third week of March, and $875 to $910 per person at other times.

WHERE TO STAY & EAT   The approximately 900 rooms at Snowbird range from standard lodge units to luxurious condominiums with kitchens and fireplaces; almost every unit has a terrific view. **Snowbird Central Reservations** (✆ **800/453-3000**) books all lodging for the resort and can also arrange ground transportation. Room tax adds about 11.6%; resort fees add another $6 to $20 per night.

The **Cliff Lodge & Spa** is located in a ski-in, ski-out pedestrian mall. Practically all of the 511 rooms, with mission-style furnishings, have splendid views of the mountain or canyon. Choose a standard or extra-large room, or a one- or two-bedroom suite. You'll find a splendid spa, restaurants, shops, and practically anything else you might want. Rooms are $189 to $389 double in ski season, and suites start around $500.

The **Lodge at Snowbird,** the **Inn,** and **Iron Blosam Lodge** are condominium properties, offering rooms, efficiencies, studios, and one-bedroom and one-bedroom-with-loft units. Many have Western decor with Murphy beds and/or sofa beds. Winter rates range from $139 to $299 for a room at the Inn to $350 or more for a deluxe room in the Lodge at Snowbird.

The **Aerie Restaurant** (✆ **801/933-2160**), on the top floor of the Cliff Lodge, features New American dining with spectacular views, and serves a skier's breakfast buffet in the winter, and sushi and "gastro-pub" specialties for dinner year-round. Entree prices range from $20 to $40. Also in the Cliff Lodge, **El Chanate** (✆ **801/933-2025**) serves Mexican seafood for lunch and dinner in the summer, dinner-only in winter. Dinner prices range from $8 to $25. On level B of the Cliff Lodge is the **Atrium** (✆ **801/933-2140**), with tremendous alpine views. It features a buffet lunch in winter and a light breakfast buffet in summer, with prices from $12 to $22. The Atrium Espresso Bar is open daily.

For steak and seafood, try the **Steak Pit** (✆ **801/933-2260**), in the Snowbird Center, open for dinner daily. Prices range from $19 to $45. Also in the Snowbird Center is the **Forklift Restaurant** (✆ **801/933-2440**), serving breakfast and lunch daily. Prices range from $7 to $11.

The **Lodge Bistro** (✆ **801/933-2145**) is on the pool level in the Lodge at Snowbird, offering an eclectic dinner menu in an intimate setting. Italian fare is offered for dinner daily at Iron Blosam's **Wildflower** (✆ **801/933-2230**). Entrees at both range from $10 to $35.

WARM-WEATHER FUN   After the skiers go home for the season, Snowbird is still active with hikers and mountain bikers. A lift hauls mountain bikers up the slopes. Snowbird's summer music program includes several annual festivals; call or visit the website for details.

PARK CITY: UTAH'S PREMIER RESORT TOWN ★★

31 miles E of Salt Lake City

Utah's most sophisticated resort community, Park City, is reminiscent of Aspen, Colorado, and Taos, New Mexico—other historic Western towns that have made the most of excellent ski terrain while evolving into popular year-round vacation destinations, offering a casual Western atmosphere with a touch of elegance.

Step Back in Time

Be sure to pick up a copy of the *Park City Main Street Historic Walking Tour* brochure at the visitor information center. It will lead you to 45 buildings and historic sites that have somehow managed to survive fires, hard times, and progress through the decades. The historic walk, complete with engaging anecdotes, really brings the town's lively past to life.

A silver boom brought thousands to Park City in the 1870s, and that boom continued for 50 years, giving Park City a population of 10,000 at its height, with more than 30 saloons along Main Street and a flourishing red-light district. Then came the Depression and plummeting mineral prices, leaving Park City to doze in the summer sun and under a blanket of winter snow. In 1963, the area's first ski lift was built (rates were $2.50 for a weekend of sledding and skiing), and Park City was on the road to becoming one of the West's most popular ski towns. The 2002 Olympics helped cement its reputation internationally.

Today's visitors will find three separate ski areas, lodgings that range from basic to luxurious, some of the state's most innovative restaurants and best shops, an abundance of fine performing arts events, many of Utah's liveliest nightspots, and plenty of hiking, mountain biking, fishing, and other outdoor opportunities.

As in many tourist towns, prices here can be a bit steep; if you're watching your wallet, avoid visiting during the Christmas season or the Sundance Film Festival in mid- to late January, when Hollywood takes over. Those who are really pinching pennies might want to stay in Salt Lake City and drive to Park City in the morning for a day of skiing, exploring, or adventuring.

Essentials

GETTING THERE   Most visitors fly into Salt Lake City International Airport and drive or take a shuttle to Park City. Driving time from the airport is about 35 minutes. At I-80 exit 145, take Utah 224 into Park City.

Park City Transportation (© 800/637-3803 or 435/649-8567; www.park citytransportation.com) offers frequent shuttles from the Salt Lake City airport and hotels ($78 round-trip). **All Resort Express** (© 877/658-3999 or 435/649-3999; www.allresort.com) and **Wasatch Crest Shuttle** (© 877/754-8294; www. wcshuttle.com) also serve the area.

VISITOR INFORMATION   The **Park City Chamber of Commerce/Convention and Visitors Bureau,** 1910 Prospector Ave. (P.O. Box 1630), Park City, UT 84060 (© 800/453-1360 or 435/649-6100; www.visitparkcity.com), is open Monday through Friday from 8am to 5pm. It operates a visitor information center in Kimball Junction near the entrance to the Utah Olympic Park near I-80, open Monday through Saturday from 9am to 5pm and Sunday from 10am to 5pm, and another at 333 Main St., open Monday through Saturday from 10am to 7pm and Sunday from noon to 6pm; both have shorter hours in the off season.

GETTING AROUND   Parking in Park City is limited, especially in the historic Main Street area, and it is just plain awful if you're driving a motor home or pulling a trailer. If you've arrived in a car, the best plan is to park it and ride the free city bus.

The Park City Area

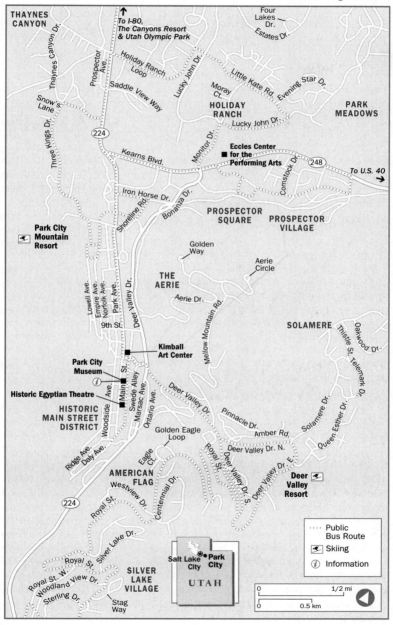

THAYNES CANYON

To I-80, The Canyons Resort & Utah Olympic Park

Four Lakes Estates Dr.

Thaynes Canyon Dr.

Prospector Ave.

Holiday Ranch Loop

Saddle View Way

Lucky John Dr.

Little Kate Rd.

Evening Star Dr.

Moray Ct.

HOLIDAY RANCH

PARK MEADOWS

Snow's Lane

Three Kings Dr.

224

Kearns Blvd.

Monitor Dr.

Lucky John Dr.

Eccles Center for the Performing Arts

248

To U.S. 40

Iron Horse Dr.

Shoreline Rd.

Bonanza Dr.

Comstock Dr.

PROSPECTOR SQUARE

PROSPECTOR VILLAGE

Park City Mountain Resort

Golden Way

Aerie Circle

THE AERIE

Aerie Dr.

SOLAMERE

Lowell Ave.

Empire Ave.

Norfolk Ave.

Park Ave.

Deer Valley Dr.

9th St.

Mellow Mountain Rd.

Thistle St.

Oakwood Dr.

Telemark Dr.

Kimball Art Center

Park City Museum

Historic Egyptian Theatre

Main St.

Swede Alley

Marsac Ave.

Ontario Ave.

Woodside Ave.

HISTORIC MAIN STREET DISTRICT

Deer Valley Dr.

Pinnacle Dr.

Amber Rd.

Solamere Dr.

Queen Esther Dr.

Golden Eagle Loop

Deer Valley Dr. N.

Ridge Ave.

Daly Ave.

AMERICAN FLAG

Eagle Ct.

Royal St.

Deer Valley Dr. S.

Deer Valley Dr. E.

Deer Valley Resort

Westview Dr.

224

Royal St.

Centennial Dr.

Royal St.

Silver Lake Dr.

Royal St. W.

Woodland View Dr.

SILVER LAKE VILLAGE

Sterling Dr.

Stag Way

Salt Lake City

Park City

UTAH

Public Bus Route

Skiing

Information

0   1/2 mi

0   0.5 km

7

THE SOUTHERN WASATCH FRONT | Park City: Utah's Premier Resort Town

115

Main Street has metered parking (in effect daily 11am–8pm); fairly large parking lots are situated near both the upper and lower ends of Main Street.

If you still want to rent a car and brave the parking problems, rental agencies here include **All Resort Car Rental,** 1821 Sidewinder Dr. (© **877/658-3999** or 435/649-3999; www.allresort.com), and **Enterprise,** 2720 W. Rasmussen Rd. (© **800/261-7331** or 435/655-7277; www.enterprise.com).

Park City's very efficient free transit system offers several routes throughout Park City and the surrounding area, daily from 7:30am until 10:30pm. The **Main Street Trolley** links Main Street and Park City Mountain Resort, and **public buses** travel to the outlying areas. Pick up the *Transit System Guide* brochure for a good route map and specific schedules. The weekly booklet *This Week in Park City* contains helpful info plus several area maps, including one of Main Street. Both are available at the visitor centers and many lodgings.

FAST FACTS   To take care of injury or illness, go to **Park City Healthcare,** 1665 Bonanza Dr. (© **435/649-7640;** www.parkcityclinic.com). The main **post office** is at 450 Main St. (© **800/275-8777;** www.usps.com). The local **newspaper** is the *Park Record* (www.parkrecord.com), published twice weekly.

Skiing the Park City Area Resorts

The three area ski resorts, all within a few minutes' drive of each other, are vastly different. There's something for everyone here: Posh **Deer Valley** is Utah's version of very upscale Beaver Creek, Colorado, and big and lively **Park City** is the party resort. The **Canyons** is casual and friendly. Snowboarders are welcome at Park City Mountain Resort and the Canyons, but not Deer Valley.

Many skiers try all three resorts, and if you're going to do so, it will pay to do a bit of advance planning. The **Silver Passport** is a discounted multiday package for use at all three resorts. Various restrictions apply, though, including that the passport *must* be purchased before your arrival in Park City, and that it must be purchased in conjunction with lodging (3-night minimum). Contact the Park City Chamber of Commerce (p. 114) for details.

DEER VALLEY RESORT ★★★

If you're looking for a first-class experience in every way, this is the spot for you. Unquestionably Utah's most elegant and sophisticated resort, **Deer Valley,** P.O. Box 889, Park City, UT 84060 (© **800/424-3337** or 435/649-1000, or 435/649-2000 for snow conditions; www.deervalley.com), offers perfectly manicured slopes, guest service attendants, heated sidewalks, and some of the state's finest dining and lodging. Along with all this, you get fantastic skiing—especially if you crave long, smooth, perfectly groomed cruising runs that let you enjoy the spectacular mountain scenery around you. Although half of the terrain is rated intermediate, beginners love Success, a long run that gives them the feeling they're actually getting somewhere. In addition, much of the intermediate terrain is fit for advancing novices, as the entire mountain is kept very skiable. Experts will find some steep, exhilarating-enough trails on top, through majestic aspen and evergreen glades, plus plenty of woodsy terrain to explore. Deer Valley is primarily a pampering resort experience, meant for cruising the wide lanes of impeccably groomed snow all day, then hobnobbing all evening with the rich—and often famous—over gourmet meals in the plush lodges.

Six bowls and 100 runs are spread over Empire Canyon, Deer Crest, Flagstaff, Bald, and Bald Eagle mountains, served by a total of 21 chairlifts—11 high-speed quad lifts, a high-speed gondola, two fixed-grip quads, five triples, and two double chairs. The base is at 6,570 feet with the summit at 9,570 feet, yielding a 3,000-foot vertical drop. The ski season generally runs from early December to mid-April, with lifts operating daily from 9am to 4:15pm. The 2,026 skiable acres are rated 15% beginner, 50% intermediate, and 35% advanced. Deer Valley has snow-making on over 660 acres.

GETTING THERE   From Utah 224, head southeast on Deer Valley Drive to the resort.

LIFT TICKETS   All-day lift tickets cost $96 for adults ($100 during holidays), $60 for children 4 to 12, $21 for children 3 and under, and $69 for seniors 65 and older. Half-day and multiday packages are available.

LESSONS & PROGRAMS   The **ski school** (© 435/645-6648) at Deer Valley offers private and group lessons, workshops, and clinics. Group lessons for 3 hours cost about $155 for adults (not including lift ticket); private lessons are also available.

The licensed **child-care center,** open daily from 8:30am to 4:30pm, costs $115 to $120 per day for kids ages 2 months to 12 years, and includes lunch.

WHERE TO EAT ON THE MOUNTAIN   Snow Park Lodge (© 435/645-6632), at the base, has a bakery, two restaurants, and a lounge. The **Seafood Buffet,** open Monday through Saturday evenings, offers hearty hot meals, a salad and seafood buffet, and fancy desserts. **Snow Park Lounge** serves hors d'oeuvres after 3:30pm.

Silver Lake Lodge (© 435/645-6715), midway up the mountain, serves a variety of quick-and-easy food all day, including continental breakfasts (with fresh-baked pastries), salads, grilled fare, and pizzas. You can also choose from two fine-dining rooms, the **Mariposa,** open evenings only, and **Royal Street Café,** open for lunch, après-ski, and dinner. **Fireside Dining** at **Empire Canyon Lodge** (© 435/645-6632) is a unique alpine dining room offering Continental lunch and dinner menus, while also serving as a base for moonlight sleigh rides and snowshoe treks.

PARK CITY MOUNTAIN RESORT ★★

Park City Mountain Resort, 1345 Lowell Ave. (P.O. Box 39), Park City, UT 84060 (© **800/222-7275** or 435/649-8111, or 435/647-5449 for snow reports; www.park-citymountain.com), one of Utah's largest and liveliest resorts, is where the U.S. Ski and Snowboard Olympic team comes to train. It's an official training site of the U.S. Ski and Snowboard Association as well. What brings them here? Plenty of dependable, powdery snow and a variety of terrain and runs that offers something for everyone. Surveys continually rank Park City among the country's top resorts for both its terrain and its challenging runs. And, because it's located right in the heart of Park City, what more could you ask for in terms of amenities?

Beginners will find plenty of great training ground, blessedly free of that frequent mountain problem—hordes of advanced skiers whizzing their way right through the green runs on their way to the bottom. After they have a good handle on the sport, beginners and novices can head up the lift to Summit House and then glide down their own scenic 3½-mile green run. Intermediates will find good cruising ground and powder runs; experts can delight in some 750 acres of wide-open bowls and hair-raising narrow chutes. After a good storm, the locals know to rise early, race to the top of the Jupiter Bowl, and carve their way back down through fresh powder.

The resort has four six-passenger high-speed lifts, three high-speed quads, seven triples, and two double chairs servicing 114 runs on 3,300 acres, plus two Magic Carpet people movers in the children's learning area. There's even a triple-chair access lift directly from Park City's Old Town onto the mountain, as well as two runs (Quit 'n' Time and Creole) that lead back into town, so those staying in Park City proper don't have to ride back and forth to the base resort every day. Trails are rated 17% beginner, 52% intermediate, and 31% expert. With a base elevation of 6,900 feet and summit of 10,000 feet, the vertical drop is 3,100 feet. The season generally runs from late November to mid-April, with lifts operating daily between 9am and 4pm. Night operations usually run from Christmas through late March from 4 to 7:30pm, and include a snowboard park. Park City has snow-making capabilities on 500 acres.

The **Resort Center,** at the base of the mountain, houses the ski school, equipment sales and rentals, a restaurant and bar, lockers, and a ticket office.

GETTING THERE   The resort is off of Main Street, Park City.

LIFT TICKETS   All-day lift ticket fees vary throughout the season, but typically run $90 to $95 for adults, $55 for children 7 to 12, and $60 for seniors. Night skiing is in the $40 to $60 range. Half-day rates are also available. Children 6 and under ski free.

LESSONS & PROGRAMS   The **Park City Mountain Resort Ski and Snowboard School** (© **800/227-2754**) offers a wide variety of choices for every level, plus a **Kids Signature Program** for ages 3 to 14 that includes equipment rental, a snack, lunch, and lessons. Group lessons start at $80 for 3 hours, a half-day private lesson starts at around $400, and a full day for kids starts at about $150. Customized packages are available.

WHERE TO EAT ON THE MOUNTAIN   In addition to the wide variety of options in Park City (see "Where to Eat," later in this chapter), you'll find the following slope-side facilities. Only Viking Yurt requires reservations.

The **Food Court,** at the Legacy Lodge, offers homemade breakfast and dinner buffets. For lunch, it offers soups and stews, sandwiches, pizza, a salad bar, and fresh roasted meats. **Legends Bar & Grill** offers lunch and après-ski refreshments.

Mid-Mountain Lodge is at the base of Pioneer Lift on the Mid-Mountain Ski Run, at 8,700 feet. Built around 1898, the lodge may be the oldest original mine building in Park City. It's open daily for lunch, serving vegetarian dishes, homemade soups and stews, salads, burgers, sandwiches, and pizza.

Summit House, at the top of the Bonanza chairlift, serves lunch and boasts an outdoor deck with magnificent panoramic views and a cozy fireplace inside. The **Snow Hut,** at the bottom of the Silverlode six-passenger lift, serves breakfast and lunch daily.

The most refined and recommended eatery here is the **Viking Yurt,** accessible by sleigh ride. It's open from 6 to 10pm and serves a five-course, prix-fixe dinner for $125. Advance reservations are required. Call © **435/615-9878,** or visit www.vikingyurt.com for additional information.

THE CANYONS

The **Canyons Resort,** 4000 The Canyons Resort Dr., Park City, UT 84098 (© **888/226-9667** or 435/649-5400, or snow report 435/615-3456; www.thecanyons.com), the state of Utah's largest ski area, offers a wide variety of terrain on eight distinct mountains, with an excellent people-moving system to get you to the ski runs quickly

SKI THEM ALL IN JUST 1 day

Ski Utah's **Interconnect Adventure Tour** is unique. Six full-time guides take a dozen skiers on journeys to the slopes of four to six of Utah's renowned resorts—and about 20 miles of untracked back-country in between.

"If you're a good skier and looking for a day of adventure, come out with us," says Deb Lovci, one of the guides and owner of the Old Town Guest House in Park City (see "Where to Stay" in Park City, below). "It's an awesome way to see how the whole Wasatch is connected."

Tours visit the Deer Valley, Park City Mountain, Solitude Mountain, Brighton, and Snowbird resorts, and the Alta Ski Area, and use the backcountry routes to navigate between the resorts. These rarely used routes offer incredible views of some of the most majestic terrain in the Rockies.

Interested skiers should know a few things before making reservations. Skiers should be advanced, comfortable with skiing a variety of terrains and snow conditions, and in good physical condition. "It's a long day," Lovci notes. Be sure to make reservations in advance—these popular tours fill up around holidays and on weekends. Tours are done completely with alpine gear.

The trip is offered daily from mid-December to mid-April, weather permitting, departing from either Deer Valley Resort (Sun–Mon, Wed, and Fri; p. 123) or Snowbird Ski & Summer Resort (Tues, Thurs, and Sat; p. 111), and costs $295, including lunch, lift tickets at all resorts, guide service, and transportation—and a much-deserved finisher's pin. Participants must be at least 16, and snowboarding is not permitted.

For additional information, call **Ski Utah** at ✆ **801/534-1907,** or visit www.skiutah.com/interconnect.

and efficiently. In the past few years, intermediate and expert terrains have been greatly expanded. The large beginners' area offers gentle slopes and grand views.

The resort has 182 runs, 4,000 skiable acres, serviced by two high-speed gondolas, one high-speed six-pack, four high-speed quad chairs, five fixed-grip quad chairs, one triple chair, one double chair, one eight-person Cabriolet, and two surface lifts. It receives an average of 355 inches of snow a year, and has snow-making on 400 acres. The vertical drop serviced by lifts is 3,190 feet, from a base elevation of 6,800 feet. The summit elevation is 9,990 feet. Runs are rated 10% beginner, 44% intermediate, and 46% advanced. The season usually runs from early December to mid-April, with lifts operating daily from 9am to 4pm.

The resort offers ski and snowboard rentals and a day-care center.

GETTING THERE   The Canyons is on the west side of Utah 224 a few miles south of I-80.

LIFT TICKETS   Adult lift tickets start at $96 for a full day; children 7 to 12 and seniors pay $57. Kids 6 and under ride the lifts free. Deals are available for those who book online or for multiple days; holiday prices are a bit higher.

LESSONS & PROGRAMS   The **ski school** (✆ **877/472-6306**) offers lessons for both skiing and snowboarding, starting at $83 for a 2½-hour group clinic. Private lessons start at about $400 for 3 hours.

WHERE TO STAY & EAT ON THE MOUNTAIN   You'll find a nice range of lodging options at the resort proper, including the **Grand Summit Hotel, Sundial Lodge,** and **Waldorf Astoria Park City.** The ski-season rates range from $340 for a double

Park City's $100-million **Utah Olympic Park,** 3000 Bear Hollow Dr. (© **435/658-4200;** www.olyparks.com), constructed for the 2002 Olympics, has six state-of-the-art ski jumps, a 1,335m bobsled/luge track, a freestyle aerials training and competition hill, a day lodge, a ski museum, and an exhibit on the 2002 games. The U.S. Ski Team uses the facility regularly, and it's open year-round for both guided and self-guided tours. In summer, extreme types can try out riding a pair of ziplines on the ski jumps ($15–$20 for the first ride, subsequent rides are half price) or an alpine slide ($15 for the first, $7.50 for the second), the first on the continent made of stainless steel. On summer Saturdays, national team members demonstrate freestyle aerials and ski jumping. The Olympic Park also offers piloted bobsled runs ($60 for the first ride, $30 for a second run) and skeleton rides ($50), and schedules workshops on freestyle aerials and ski jumping, even for amateurs (call for schedules and rates). Besides the fees for the assorted activities, admission is free.

room at Sundial to $1,758 for a four-bedroom suite at the Waldorf Astoria. Among the ski area's restaurants are the **Red Pine Lodge,** featuring lunches of pizza, fresh grilled entrees, hearty soups, and a salad bar; **Lookout Cabin,** specializing in Rocky Mountain cuisine for lunch and featuring spectacular views from its perch atop Lookout Peak; and the **Farm,** featuring New American cuisine at the foot of the Red Pine Gondola.

More Winter Fun

CROSS-COUNTRY SKIING   White Pine Nordic Center (© 435/649-6249; www.whitepinetouring.com) operates Park City's cross-country ski center, with more than 12 miles of groomed trails on the Park City Golf Course on Utah 224, on the north side of town. The center offers rentals, instruction (including skating and telemark lessons), guided tours, and sales and service. The terrain is rated 60% beginner, 20% intermediate, and 20% advanced. Full-day trail passes cost $18 for adults, $8 for kids 6 to 12; children 5 and under and seniors 65 and over ski free. White Pine is open daily from 9am to 6pm, usually from mid-November through March.

SNOWMOBILE & SLEIGH RIDES   Guided snowmobiling tours and sleigh rides are available at the scenic Rockin' R Ranch, east of Park City in Weber Canyon, from **Rocky Mountain Recreation** (© 800/303-7256 or 435/645-7256; www.rocky mtnrec.com). A sleigh ride, with dinner, costs about $80 for adults, $60 for children 12 and under. Snowmobile trips range from $95 to $198 for the driver ($20–$48 for a passenger), depending on length. Also offering a variety of snowmobile tours is Deer Valley's **Summit Mountain Adventures** (© 888/896-7669 or 435/645-7669; www.utahsnowmobiling.com), with similar rates.

Warm-Weather Fun in & Around Park City

ALPINE SLIDE   In addition to the stainless steel slide at the Utah Olympic Park (see above), a plastic bobsledlike track over a half-mile long is housed at **Park City Mountain Resort** (p. 117). Riders control the speed of their sleds. Cost is $11 to $12 for adults and $3 for passengers ages 2 to 6; those 1 and under cannot ride. The resort also has an alpine coaster ($20–$22 adults, $7–$8 kid passengers), ziplines ($14–$20 per ride), and other adrenaline-pumping amusements.

BALLOONING Call **Park City Balloon Adventures** (© 800/396-8787 or 435/645-8787; www.pcballoonadventures.com) for bird's-eye views of the mountains. Prices start at $200 per person for an hour-long flight.

FLY-FISHING Anglers have plenty of opportunities for fishing in the streams in the mountains around Park City, either on their own or with local guides. For tips on where they're biting, as well as equipment and information on guided trips, check with **Jans Mountain Outfitters,** 1600 Park Ave. (© 435/649-4949; www.jansfly shop.com), or **Park City Fly Shop,** 2065 Sidewinder Dr., Prospector Square (© 435/645-8382; www.pcflyshop.com). The **Canyons** (p. 118) has a reservoir stocked with native trout.

HIKING & MOUNTAIN BIKING With more than 350 miles of trails crisscrossing the mountains around Park City, opportunities abound for hiking and mountain biking. For a short hike with a variety of terrains and good views of both mountains and town, try the 1.5-mile **Sweeny Switchbacks Trail,** accessible from near the base of the town lift.

The 30-mile **Historic Union Pacific Rail Trail State Park** hiking and biking path follows the old Union Pacific railroad bed from Park City to Echo Reservoir. It offers wonderful views of meadows, the volcanic crags of Silver Creek Canyon, the Weber River, Echo Reservoir, and the steep walls of Echo Canyon. You might spot deer, elk, moose, and bald eagles along the trail. An end-of-the-trail pickup service is available from **Daytrips** (© 888/649-8294; www.daytrips.com).

More than 30 miles of dirt roads and single-track trails at **Park City Mountain Resort** (p. 117) are open to hikers and mountain bikers, who can ride the PayDay chairlift up, and then bike or hike down. Tickets cost $11 to $12 for a single ride, or $18 to $20 for an all-day pass. **Deer Valley Resort** (p. 123) offers more than 50 miles of panoramic trails for both hikers and bikers, with chairlift access in summer ($12–$20 a ride or $20–$34 a day). As you might expect, the terrain is steep and beautiful. The **Canyons** (p. 118) also has hiking trails and a bike park, and runs both the gondola and a chairlift during its summer season; tickets are $15 adults, $10 seniors and kids 7 to 12.

For bike rentals ($30–$40 a day), guided rides and hikes (as well as climbs), and even mountain biking clinics, get in touch with **White Pine Touring Center,** 1790 Bonanza Dr. (© 435/649-8170; www.whitepinetouring.com). For a good description of area trails, pick up a copy of the free *Park City Hiking & Biking Trail Map* at either visitor center and at sporting-goods shops. The website of the **Mountain Trails Foundation** (www.mountaintrails.org) is another good resource.

HORSEBACK RIDING Guided trail rides are available from several outfitters in the area. **Rocky Mountain Recreation** (p. 120) operates stables at Park City Mountain Resort, at Deer Valley Resort, and at 2,300-acre Rockin' R Ranch. It operates daily from late May to late October. Rates start at $61 for adults and $56 for children for a 1-hour ride. Rides with meals and overnight trips are also offered; call for details.

More to See & Do in Park City

Kimball Art Center ★ This highly respected center for visual arts, housed in a historic 1929 building, has three galleries with changing exhibits, both classic and contemporary, that include national and international traveling shows, as well as works by local artists. This nonprofit community art center also sponsors classes, workshops, and seminars throughout the year. Each summer, on the first weekend in August, it produces the Park City Arts Festival, an outdoor exhibit featuring works by about 200 fine artists, and is open daily leading up to and during the event. Allow about 45 minutes.

638 Park Ave., at the bottom of Main St. ✆ **435/649-8882.** www.kimballartcenter.org. Free admission; donations accepted. Mon–Thurs 10am–5pm; Fri 10am–7pm; Sat noon–7pm; Sun noon–5pm. All bus loops stop here.

Park City Museum   Following a major 2-year expansion and renovation, the museum reopened in fall 2009. The original territorial jail downstairs is a must-see—the dark, tiny cells were state of the art in 1886! Featuring plenty of new exhibits, the upstairs is a bit more civilized, displaying a stagecoach, 19th-century mining equipment, vintage photographs, and early ski gear. Allow about 1½ hours.

518 Main St. ✆ **435/649-7457.** www.parkcityhistory.org. Admission $10 adults, $8 seniors, $5 children 7–17, free for children 6 and under. Mon–Sat 10am–7pm; Sun noon–6pm. Main St. Trolley.

Shopping

Historic Main Street is lined with galleries, boutiques, and a wide variety of shops, with transportation conveniently provided by the Main Street Trolley. You won't find many bargains here, but prices aren't too far out of line for a tourist and ski town, and are downright reasonable when compared to places like Aspen and Santa Fe.

No Place Like Home, in Park City Plaza at 1685 Bonanza Dr. (✆ **435/649-9700**), is the place to go for kitchen and home accessories. Choose from glassware, gadgets, gourmet coffee beans, bed and bath items, and lots more. Get reading material of all kinds at **Dolly's Bookstore,** 510 Main St. (✆ **435/649-8062;** www.dollysbookstore.com).

Bargain hunters will want to head to the **Tanger Factory Outlets,** 6699 N. Landmark Dr. (✆ **435/645-7078;** www.tangeroutlet.com). From downtown Park City, take Utah 224 north to I-80, but don't get on; instead, go west on the south frontage road to the mall. Among the best outlet malls around, this place houses more than 60 stores, including Banana Republic, Carter's, Gap, Levi's, Nike, Old Navy, Polo Ralph Lauren, Samsonite, and Tommy Bahama.

Where to Stay

The Park City area offers a wide variety of places to stay, and it's probably home to the largest portion of the state's deluxe accommodations. Even some of the most luxurious properties, however, lack air-conditioning, but at this elevation—6,900 feet in Park City and higher in the mountains—it's seldom needed. For those skiers interested in renting a condo, check out the offerings online at **www.parkcitylodging.com**, **www.resortpropertymanagement.com**, and **www.utahvacationhomes.com**. For central reservations at Deer Valley, call ✆ **800/558-3337.**

Among the franchise properties in Park City are the **Best Western Plus Landmark Inn,** 6560 N. Landmark Dr. (✆ **800/548-8824** or 435/649-7300; www.bwlandmarkinn.com), with ski-season rates for two from $119 to $259, and **Hampton Inn and Suites,** 6609 N. Landmark Dr. (✆ **800/426-7866** or 435/645-0900; www.hamptoninn.com), with ski-season rates of $89 to $199 double. You can save some money by staying in Kimball Junction and taking the free shuttle into Park City. Try the **Newpark Resort,** 1456 Newpark Blvd. (✆ **877/649-3600** or 435/649-3600; www.newparkresort.com), with winter rates of $200 to $500 for two people, or **Holiday Inn Express Hotel & Suites,** 1501 W. Ute Blvd. (✆ **888/465-4329** or 435/658-1600; www.holidayinn.com), with peak rates of $169 to $199 for two.

A Helping Hand for Room Reservations

Although it's possible to book reservations directly with individual lodges, many people find it more convenient to go the one-stop-shopping route, making all their arrangements directly with one of the resorts. See the contact information earlier in this chapter under "Skiing the Park City Area Resorts."

Listed rates indicate rack rates for peak seasons, excluding special events. Rates are almost always higher—sometimes dramatically so—during ski season, and rates during Christmas week and the Sundance Film Festival can be absurd. The best bargains are in spring and fall. Sales and lodging taxes in Park City total about 10.5%. Pets are not allowed, unless otherwise noted.

DEER VALLEY RESORT

Goldener Hirsch Inn ★★ This château-style inn combines warm hospitality with European charm reminiscent of the inn's sister hotel in Salzburg, the Hotel Goldener Hirsch. Austrian antiques dot the common areas and decorate the walls. Guest rooms are elegantly furnished with hand-painted-and-carved Austrian furniture, king-size beds with down comforters, and minibars stocked with snacks and nonalcoholic beverages. Suites boast wood-burning fireplaces and small private balconies. The excellent restaurant is Austrian in decor and features European-inspired fare. In summer, you can dine outdoors on the flower-filled deck.

7570 Royal St. E., Silver Lake Village, Deer Valley (P.O. Box 859), Park City, UT 84060. www.goldener hirschinn.com. © **800/252-3373** or 435/649-7770. Fax 435/649-7901. 20 units. Winter (including continental breakfast) $299–$1,399 double; summer $155–$300 double. AE, MC, V. Closed mid-Apr to mid-June and Oct–Nov. **Amenities:** Restaurant. *In room:* TV, hair dryer, minibar, MP3 docking station, Wi-Fi (free).

Montage Deer Valley ★★★ Opened in 2010, the Montage Deer Valley (the first outside Southern California) looms above the resort, with a level of luxury that is similarly high. The views are staggering: You can see all the way to Wyoming from many rooms. Interiors are likewise impressive, featuring art of local flora and fauna (including several original Remingtons) and superlative furnishings and decor. The bedding is plush and marshmallow-soft; the bathrooms have soaking tubs and rain shower heads. The facilities are also a cut above, from Utah's largest spa (35,000 sq. ft.!) to the kid's art program to the zinc bar in the lounge. There's an incredible game room with a commercial Wii installation, pool tables, foosball tables, four bowling lanes, and vintage arcade games. This is a true ski-in, ski-out experience: There are three lifts right out the door.

9100 Marsac Ave. (P.O. Box 4680), Park City, UT 84060. www.montagedeervalley.com. © **435/604-1300.** Fax 435/604-1310. 220 units, including 66 suites and residences. Winter (including full breakfast) $845–$1,410 double, from $2,295 suite/residence suite; mid-Apr to late Nov $345–$600 double, from $695 suite/residence. AE, DISC, MC, V. **Amenities:** 4 restaurants; concierge; exercise room; 3 outdoor and 3 indoor Jacuzzis; outdoor heated pool; room service; sauna; spa. *In room:* TV/DVD, fridge, hair dryer, Wi-Fi ($15 per day).

Stein Eriksen Lodge ★★★ Opened in 1982 under the direction of Stein Eriksen, the Norwegian 1952 Olympic gold medalist, this standout hotel retains both the striking decor and the intimate charm of his original plan. The lobby is most impressive, with a magnificent three-story stone fireplace fronted by an elegant seating area.

The main lodge has 13 rooms, with the remaining units in nearby buildings. The connecting sidewalks are heated, and the grounds are beautifully landscaped. Spacious deluxe rooms, each individually decorated, contain one king- or two queen-size beds, plenty of closet space, a whirlpool tub, and tasteful, solid wood furniture; suites have full kitchens. The three large mountain chalet–style town-house suites each have a stone fireplace, full kitchen with service for eight, and private deck. The lodge has two dining venues: the **Glitretind Restaurant,** serving three meals daily, and the more casual **Troll Hallen Lounge.** Under the same management is the **Chateaux at Silver Lake,** a full-service condo property in Silver Lake Village.

Stein Way (P.O. Box 3177), Park City, UT 84060. www.steinlodge.com. ✆ **800/453-1302** or 435/649-3700. Fax 435/649-5825. 180 units. Winter (including buffet breakfast) $630–$1,160 double, from $1,395 suite; mid-Apr to late Nov $200–$300 double, from $325 suite. AE, DISC, MC, V. **Amenities:** 2 restaurants (see Glitretind Restaurant review, p. 126); babysitting; concierge; exercise room; outdoor Jacuzzi; outdoor heated pool; room service; sauna; spa. *In room:* TV/VCR or DVD, DVD library, fridge, hair dryer, MP3 docking station, Wi-Fi (free).

PARK CITY

Chateau Après Lodge ✦   For those on a budget, this lodge is a good option close to the slopes—150 yards away, to be exact. It looks like a Swiss Alps–style lodge from the outside—simple but attractive—with a large central fireplace in the lobby. Rooms are basic and clean, each with a queen-size bed or a double and a single, plus a private shower-only bathroom. The dorms have a shared bathroom. The entire facility is nonsmoking.

1299 Norfolk Ave. (P.O. Box 579), Park City, UT 84060. www.chateauapres.com. ✆ **800/357-3556** or 435/649-9372. Fax 435/649-5963. 32 units. Winter $110 double; dorm rooms $40 per bed. Rates include continental breakfast. Closed in summer except for groups requiring 8 rooms or more. AE, DISC, MC, V. *In room:* TV, Wi-Fi (free).

Hotel Park City ★★★   This is one of the most posh places to hang your hat in the area, if not the entire state. Drawing inspiration from the grand lodges of the national park system, the brain trust behind Hotel Park City spared no expense, from the masculine guest rooms, all with sublime mountain views, to the year-round pool in the central courtyard. Half of the suites are located in the main lodge, with the rest in 10 structures on the Park City Golf Course (the clubhouse is in the hotel and transforms into a cross-country center come winter). The rooms all feature king-size beds, two TVs, kitchenettes, washers and dryers, and Western decor; the bathrooms are superb, with big jetted tubs and separate three-headed showers. The on-site spa is top-rate. The Silver Star lift to Park City Mountain Resort is easily accessible from the hotel.

2001 Park Ave. (P.O. Box 683120), Park City, UT 84068. www.hotelparkcity.com. ✆ **435/200-2000.** Fax 435/940-5001. 100 suites. Winter $399–$3,000 double; summer $179–$1,500 double. AE, DC, DISC, MC, V. **Amenities:** Restaurant; lounge; concierge; outdoor Jacuzzi; outdoor heated pool; room service; sauna; spa. *In room:* A/C, TV/DVD player, hair dryer, kitchenette, Wi-Fi (free).

Old Town Guest House ★ 🛏   This cozy little B&B is perfect for outdoor enthusiasts—innkeeper Deb Lovci is a backcountry ski guide in winter and avid hiker and mountain biker in summer—and it's affordable to boot. The inn is within easy walking distance of both the Park City Mountain Resort and Main Street. The delightfully homey living room retains its original 1910 fireplace. The decor is country, with pine furniture and hardwood floors throughout, and as with most historic bed-and-breakfasts, each guest room is unique. Treasure Hollow has a queen-size bed and private bathroom with shower. McConky's Suite, upstairs, contains a queen-size bed in one room and bunk beds in another, a tub, and a shower. Two smaller rooms in back have private bathrooms, but share a shower. Guests can use the outdoor deck and Jacuzzi, not to mention a stock of head lamps, day packs, and water bottles. Lovci also offers regular fitness "camps" focused on biking or skiing.

1011 Empire Ave., Park City, UT 84060. www.oldtownguesthouse.com. © **800/290-6423,** ext. 3710, or 435/649-2642. 4 units. Winter (including breakfast) $129–$229 double; summer $99–$129 double. AE, MC, V. **Amenities:** Outdoor Jacuzzi. *In room:* TV/VCR/DVD player in most rooms, Wi-Fi (free).

Sky Lodge ★★ Opening its doors in December 2007, the Sky Lodge is Park City's first LEED-certified hotel and features oodles of contemporary style to boot. Located in a historic spot just off Main Street, the hotel exudes outstanding attention to detail in everything from the timbers recycled from a trestle over Salt Lake to the underwater surround sound in the lap pool to the bathroom doors, which are fitted with copper weavings made in Africa to help fund AIDS research. The rooms are large condominium-style units in several different configurations; most feature a deck and a hot tub, and some have a billiards table. The bars and restaurants are a cut above—I especially like Sky Blue, which has a hot tub and fire pits on the deck and sparkling mine tailings under glass on the bar itself.

201 Heber Ave. (P.O. Box 683300), Park City, UT 84068. www.theskylodge.com. © **888/876-2525** or 435/658-2500. 33 units, including 22 suites. Winter $325–$1,999 for 1- to 3-bedroom units, $1,500–$3,000 penthouse suite; lower rates spring–fall. AE, DISC, MC, V. **Amenities:** 2 restaurants; 2 lounges; concierge; outdoor Jacuzzi; small indoor lap pool. *In room:* A/C, TV/DVD, hair dryer, kitchen, Wi-Fi (free).

Treasure Mountain Inn ★ Originally built in 1963, the Treasure Mountain Inn was reborn after new ownership took over in 2002, and it has since won accolades as Park City's most environmentally conscious lodging (thanks to its green supplies, recycling program, and salt-based hot tub). With studios and one- and two-bedroom condominium units decorated in spare contemporary style, the rooms feature flatscreen TVs, iPod docking stations, full kitchens, and a king-size bed or two queens. The courtyard is especially attractive, centered on the aforementioned hot tub and a faux waterfall.

255 Main St. (P.O. Box 1570), Park City, UT 84060. www.treasuremountaininn.com. © **800/344-2460** or 435/655-4501. Fax 435/655-4504. 56 units. Winter $145–$515 double; spring–fall $112–$260 double. AE, DISC, MC, V. **Amenities:** Fitness center; outdoor Jacuzzi. *In room:* A/C, TV/DVD, DVD library, MP3 docking station, Wi-Fi (free).

Washington School House ★★★ Nestled against the Wasatch Mountains, this 1889 limestone schoolhouse turned inn has been reborn as a boutique hotel. The exterior has been faithfully restored to its late-19th-century appearance, but the interior was gutted and reinvented in 2011, with impressive results. Slick but classic rooms are individually decorated with antiques and reproductions, as well as modern American art. Facilities include ski storage and a new heated pool and Jacuzzi.

543 Park Ave. (P.O. Box 536), Park City, UT 84060. www.washingtonschoolhouse.com. © **800/824-1672** or 435/649-3800. Fax 435/649-3802. 12 units. Winter $700–$1,850 double; lower rates spring to fall. Rates include full breakfast. AE, MC, V. **Amenities:** Outdoor Jacuzzi; outdoor heated pool. *In room:* TV, hair dryer, Wi-Fi (free).

Where to Eat

For a smallish town, Park City has a wonderful selection of very good restaurants. Several menu guides are available free at the visitor centers. Two-for-one main courses are often available at Park City restaurants, especially in the off season; check the *Park Record* for information and coupons. For coffee, baked goods, and Internet access, try **Park City Coffee Roaster,** 738 Lower Main St. (✆ **435/649-0051;** www.parkcitycoffeeroaster.com). If you're on a budget, head to either **El Chubasco,** 1890 Bonanza Dr. (✆ **435/645-9114;** www.elchubascopc.info), with great Mexican eats beloved by local mountain bikers and ski bums, and one of the best salsa bars this side of the border, or local favorite **Davanza's,** 690 Park Ave. (✆ **435/649-2222;** www.davanzas.com), a family-friendly pizzeria with a huge beer collection and posters of 1970s icons like Bob Marley and Farrah Fawcett lining its walls. Another local favorite, **Good Karma,** 1782 Prospector Ave. (✆ **435/658-0958;** www.good karmarestaurants.com), offers Indo-Persian cuisine and American breakfasts.

Cafe Terigo ★ EUROPEAN/CONTINENTAL

This upscale eatery is a good choice when you want innovative cuisine in a classy atmosphere. In fine weather, you can eat outdoors; otherwise, dine in the simple yet elegant European-style cafe, which is outfitted with black upholstered booths, white tablecloths, fresh flowers, and wrought-iron chandeliers. The lunch menu offers burgers and a variety of sandwiches, such as a grilled vegetable sandwich composed of sweet onions, zucchini, mushrooms, roasted red peppers, and provolone cheese on homemade focaccia. Dinner brings such main courses as herb-encrusted Utah rainbow trout; beef tenderloin with gorgonzola polenta, shiitake mushrooms, and red chard; and almond-encrusted salmon, served with green beans and a shallot salad. A variety of pastas and pizzas (with toppings such as shrimp and artichoke hearts) are also available, not to mention a delectable bread pudding for dessert. The cafe sells espresso and has full liquor service.

424 Main St. ✆ **435/645-9555.** www.cafeterigo.com. Main courses $11–$15 lunch, $16–$29 dinner. AE, DISC, MC, V. Daily 11:30am–2:30pm and 5:30–10pm. Closed Sun spring and fall. Main St. Trolley.

The Eating Establishment ☺ AMERICAN

Probably the oldest continuously operating restaurant on Park City's historic Main Street (since 1972), the Eating Establishment is casual and comfortable, a solid choice for families or anyone who wants a heaping serving of comfort food at a reasonable price. The dining room is accented with brick and light wood, fireplaces, and scenic photos of Utah. The enclosed patio was recently remodeled in an airy Southwest style. The extensive menu features breakfast until 3:30pm (a variety of omelets, skillet dishes, eggs, Belgian waffles, fruit-filled crepes, and lox and bagels). Lunch choices, served from 11am until closing, include wonderful charbroiled burgers, fish and chips, salads, a variety of sandwiches, and barbecued pork, beef, or chicken. Dinners are served from 5pm, with choices including salads, excellent barbecued baby back ribs, a certified Kansas City Angus strip steak, several pasta selections, and fresh seafood specials. Desserts, such as the mud pie and New York–style cheesecake, are made in-house. Full liquor service is available.

317 Main St. ✆ **435/649-8284.** www.theeatingestablishment.net. Main courses $7–$14 breakfast and lunch, $9–$23 dinner. AE, DISC, MC, V. Daily 8am–9pm. Closed 3:30–5pm Mon–Thurs spring–fall. Main St. Trolley.

Glitretind Restaurant ★★★ REGIONAL AMERICAN

Located in the elegant Stein Eriksen Lodge, this equally stylish restaurant is a top pick for a romantic dinner in the Park City area. The Glitretind serves innovative, impeccably prepared meals in a charming and airy dining room with views of the spectacular Wasatch Mountains. The menu changes with the seasons, and reflects the New American style of Executive Chef Zane Holmquist. Breakfast offerings include French toast, pancakes, a fruit plate, and omelets; for lunch choose a soup, salad, sandwich, or full meal. At lunch and dinner, Stein's Wild Game Chili, with wild boar, buffalo, and elk, is a stalwart on the ever-changing menu, which usually offers an array of creative preparations of seafood, steaks, Utah lamb, and other game dishes. The restaurant has an excellent wine list and also offers full liquor service.

Stein Eriksen Lodge (p. 123), Deer Valley. © **435/645-6455**. www.steinlodge.com. Reservations requested. Main courses $12–$20 breakfast, $14–$22 lunch, $25–$40 dinner. AE, DISC, MC, V. Mon–Sat 7–10am and 11:30am–2:30pm; brunch Sun 11am–2:30pm; daily 6–9pm. Bus: Deer Valley Loop.

Grappa Italian Restaurant ★★ ITALIAN   At this elegant, award-winning restaurant, everything is made from scratch, using the freshest herbs and vegetables available—preparing the tomato sauce alone requires cases of Roma tomatoes each day. In a century-old building at the top of Main Street, Grappa's feels like a Tuscan farmhouse. The restaurant has three floors, with a small patio on the ground floor and a larger second-floor deck with a delightful view of historic Main Street and the surrounding mountains. Baskets of fresh fruit and vegetables decorate the dining area. The menu changes frequently, but popular dishes include a terrific rib-eye, horseradish-crusted salmon, and numerous pasta dishes. The meats, such as the *osso buco,* are seasoned in the style of southern French and Italian cooking, then grilled or rotisseried over a wood-burning flame. Aside from the choices on the excellent wine list, full liquor service is also available.

151 Main St. © **435/645-0636**. www.grapparestaurant.com. Reservations required. Main courses $25–$40. AE, DISC, MC, V. Winter daily 5–10pm; summer Thurs–Mon 5–10pm. May close several weeks in Nov and Apr. Main St. Trolley.

High West Distillery ★★ NEW AMERICAN   This is Utah's first new distillery since the Church of Latter-day Saints shuttered a few church-owned stills a century ago. It's also a heck of a place to get a bite to eat. With a rollicking barroom and more refined dining areas in an attached historic house, the space is a converted livery (1907) that served as a garage for most of the 20th century. Reimagined as an eatery that makes whiskey and vodka, the food here is as creative as any fare you'll find in the Rockies, from gourmet mac and cheese, bacon-wrapped shrimp, and bourbon-bacon-cashew-caramel popcorn to bison rib-eyes and Idaho elk. Distillery tours are free; tastings are $18. Specialty cocktails are excellent; the Dead Man's Boots, with house rye, tequila, fresh lime, and ginger beer, is a revelation.

703 Park Ave. © **435/649-8300**. www.highwest.com. Reservations recommended in winter. Small plates $8–$13, large plates $14–$55. AE, DISC, MC, V. Winter daily 2–10pm; shorter hours rest of year.

Jean Louis ★ CONTEMPORARY/ECLECTIC   After guiding the restaurant at the Goldener Hirsch Inn at Deer Valley, Jean Louis Montecot opened his own place in downtown Park City in 2006, and the results are electrifying. Centered on an amber onyx bar, the casual, contemporary space is dimly lit and attractive to the barhopping crowd, but it prides itself on providing a fine-dining experience at the same time. The diverse menu ranges from fish tacos to rack of New Zealand lamb. With side dishes of such comfort foods as onion rings and corn mashed potatoes, the results are reliably dazzling. Full liquor service is available.

136 Heber Ave. © **435/200-0260**. www.jeanlouisrestaurant.com. Main courses $14–$20. AE, DISC, MC, V. Daily 5–11pm (10pm in summer/off season). Bar open later.

Purple Sage ★★ AMERICAN   Serving what they call "American Western cuisine," this upscale dinner restaurant is owned and operated by the same people who do such a great job at nearby Cafe Terigo (p. 126). The atmosphere could be described as "refined casual Western," and the menu offers innovative and sometimes fascinating variations on American favorites. The grilled shrimp in chipotle-and-leek sauce, served on golden polenta cakes, and fried chicken with mashers and bacon-pepper gravy are highly recommended. The restaurant offers full liquor service.

434 Main St. ☎ **435/655-9505.** www.purplesageparkcity.com. Main courses $18–$29 dinner. AE, MC, V. Daily 5:30–10pm. Closed Sun in spring and fall. Main St. Trolley.

350 Main ★★ CONTEMPORARY GLOBAL   A rich, romantic setting for an excellent meal, 350 Main is one of Park City's most reliable eateries. That's not to say it isn't creative—Chef Michael LeClerc's preparations are adventurous and bold, dabbling in French and Asian traditions while coming up with distinct and bold flavors. He utilizes primarily local, organic, and antioxidant-rich ingredients; many items on the menu also list the caloric content. Start your meal with the Tower of Ahi, one of the most strikingly delicate presentations encountered anywhere; the grilled lentil cakes are also recommended. The main courses run the gamut from black-pepper-crusted venison medallions to the Ono-Ono (Pacific ono prepared two ways: grilled or wasabi-seared). For dessert, the rich mocha pot au crème tantalizes the taste buds—the creation is topped with a meringue born of the improbable marriage of chipotle and cinnamon. Full liquor service (including a wine list beloved by *Wine Spectator*) is available.

350 Main St. ☎ **435/649-3140.** www.350main.com. Reservations recommended. Main courses $23–$38. AE, DISC, MC, V. Dec–Apr 5:30–10pm; May–Nov Wed–Sun 5:30–10pm. Main St. Trolley.

Wahso—An Asian Grill ★ ASIAN   This distinctively elegant restaurant boasts an Art Deco and Victorian interior furnished with authentic Asian screens, an ebony fireplace, and carvings and pictures from around the world. The food is equally unique, an amalgamation of traditional Asian ingredients with French cooking style, which gives rise to deliciously light and healthy offerings. Entrees change frequently, but might include specialties such as Szechuan-style grilled filet mignon, pan-seared pork with Utah Bing cherries or sweet corn, and miso-glazed Alaskan cod. Be sure to save room for the dessert specialty—crème brûlée in a coconut shell. Premium sake, imported beer, liquor, and an extensive wine list are available.

577 Main St. ☎ **435/615-0300.** www.wahso.com. Main courses $29–$38. AE, DISC, MC, V. Winter daily 5–10pm; spring–fall Sun–Thurs 6–9pm, Fri–Sat 6–10pm. Main St. Trolley.

Wasatch Brew Pub ★ AMERICAN   Views of the brewing area and Main Street dominate the scene in this popular brewpub, which courts controversy with such beers as Polygamy Porter (tag line: "Why have just one?"). Beyond the liquid refreshments, you can get well-prepared pub grub for lunch, including fish and chips, burgers, pulled pork sliders, various pizzas, and a mean pastrami Reuben melt. The dinner menu offers many of the same lunch items but adds some more adventurous selections, such as fresh Idaho trout with a hazelnut-caper brown butter sauce, Niman Ranch pot roast, and shrimp and andouille sausage jambalaya.

250 Main St. ☎ **435/649-0900.** www.wasatchbeers.com. Reservations not accepted. Main courses $8–$13 lunch, $10–$18 dinner. AE, DISC, MC, V. Daily 11am–10pm; kitchen closes at 9:30pm Sun–Thurs spring–fall. Bar open later. Main St. Trolley.

Zoom ★★ CONTEMPORARY AMERICAN   Robert Redford owns this classic Park City joint, complete with rough-hewn floors, rustic antique chandeliers, and gorgeous black-and-white photos of Hollywood luminaries from the Sundance Film Festival over the years. The menu offers something for all pocketbooks, from salads and delicious burgers to pasta, seafood, and ribs. The offerings change seasonally— you might find pumpkinseed-crusted trout or buffalo filet mignon—but the Double R Ranch ribs are the true standby, served with poppy-seed slaw and corn bread. Full liquor service is available.

660 Main St. ⓒ **435/649-9108.** www.zoomparkcity.com. Reservations not accepted. Main courses $7–$30 lunch, $11–$36 dinner. AE, DISC, MC, V. Daily 11:30am–2:30pm and 5–9pm. Main St. Trolley.

Movies, Music & More in the Mountains: Sundance & the Performing Arts

For 10 days every January, the Hollywood glitterati and the paparazzi who follow them descend on Park City in droves for the star-studded **Sundance Film Festival** ★★★ (ⓒ **435/776-7878;** www.sundance.org/festival). The slate includes cutting-edge indies as well as blockbuster premieres, and the event has grown into the top festival of its kind in the country; there are screenings in Park City as well as Sundance Resort, Kimball Junction, and Salt Lake City. (It's also a great time to hit the slopes, as everyone else is jammed like sardines into the theaters!) Unlike the film festival in Cannes, getting tickets is neither particularly difficult nor prohibitively exclusive, though it does require advance planning. Tickets go on sale (and sell out) during a slim window of time at the end of October, although a handful of tickets are made available the day of a screening, and more comprehensive packages go on sale in September. Go online or call the film festival for details.

Throughout the summer, **concerts** are presented at a variety of venues. Past **Sundance films** are also screened for free in City Park on summer Thursday nights. The **Park City Film Series** (www.parkcityfilmseries.com) screens independent movies at the Park City Library for $6 to $12; there are also free screenings.

The **Deer Valley Music Festival** ★★ (ⓒ **801/533-66833;** www.deervalley musicfestival.org) takes place in July and August. The program includes classical masterpieces like Tchaikovsky's *1812 Overture,* plus jazz and popular works by composers such as Gilbert and Sullivan and John Philip Sousa. There are also concerts by pop acts of all stripes. The stage faces the mountainside; bring a chair or blanket and relax under the stars. Call the box office for schedule and ticket information.

The **Park City & SLC International Music Festival** (ⓒ **435/649-5309;** www.pcmusicfestival.com) presents classical performances in the summer and fall. Classical musicians from around the world attend, and programs feature soloists, chamber music, and full orchestras.

The 1,300-seat **Eccles Center for the Performing Arts,** 1750 Kearns Blvd., and the outdoor **Snow Park Amphitheatre** at Deer Valley (ⓒ **435/655-3114;** www. ecclescenter.org), present a wide variety of top national performing arts companies. Recent productions and concerts have included Willie Nelson, Joss Stone, and Trisha Yearwood.

The **Historic Egyptian Theatre,** 328 Main St. (ⓒ **435/649-9371;** www. egyptiantheatrecompany.org), was built in 1926 in the popular Egyptian Revival style. Originally used for vaudeville and silent films, this was the first theater in Park City to offer the "new talking pictures." Today, the Egyptian is the home of the

Egyptian Theatre Company, which presents a variety of dramas, comedies, musicals, and other productions throughout the year.

Park City After Dark: The Club Scene

Known as Utah's "Sin City," Park City probably has the best nightlife in the state. And with the 2009 normalization of liquor laws, you no longer have to "join a private club" (more like paying a cover charge) to drink legally in bars and nightclubs. The following are busiest during ski season, and generally have fewer nights of live music at other times.

The **Spur,** 350½ Main St. (✆ **435/615-1618;** www.thespurbarandgrill.com), is a contemporary Western joint that has regular live music. **Cisero's,** downstairs at 306 Main St. (✆ **435/649-6800;** www.ciseros.com), with a large dance floor, hosts good bands. **O'Shucks,** 427 Main St. (✆ **435/645-3999**), is one of those low-key places where beers are available in 32-ounce schooners and you can chuck your peanut shells on the floor. The burgers are pretty good, too. "Helping people forget their name since 1903," **No Name Saloon,** 447 Main St. (✆ **435/649-6667;** www.nonamesaloon.net), is another fun place to drink, an old redbrick with lots of TVs, a constant crowd, and a nice rooftop patio. More Hollywood than Utah, **Sky Blue** (✆ **435/658-2500**) at the Sky Lodge (p. 125) is a great place to people-watch—or be seen.

HEBER VALLEY HISTORIC RAILROAD, STRAWBERRY RESERVOIR & SOME GREAT STATE PARKS

The southern Wasatch Front isn't just about skiing. The wonderful lakes and parks near Park City are still some of Utah's best-kept secrets, but they're getting more and more popular by the year. To the northeast is Rockport State Park, a man-made lake that attracts watersports enthusiasts, from swimmers to ice-fishermen, year-round. Not far from Park City is Jordanelle State Park, which is a great boating lake, and Wasatch Mountain State Park, which is Utah's second-largest state park and a major golf destination. Heading southeast from Park City, you'll reach **Heber City,** whose main claim to fame is its historic steam train. A bit farther afield along U.S. 40 is pristine Strawberry Reservoir, a favorite water playground.

Heber Valley Railroad

Those who love old trains, who want to see firsthand some of the history of the American West, or who simply enjoy beautiful scenery, should go for a ride on the **Heber Valley Railroad ★★**. This 100-year-old excursion train provides an exciting step back into the past, while also offering a fun ride through a delightful diversity of landscapes. Excursions ranging from 1½ to 3 hours are offered on both steam and vintage diesel trains, and a number of special-event trips are scheduled, including murder mysteries, sunset excursions, and the "Polar Express" Christmas trip. Train cars have restrooms, snack bars, and souvenir shops.

The views along the shores of Deer Creek Lake and through beautiful Provo Canyon are wonderful at any time, but fall is one of the prettiest seasons to ride the train, when the mountainsides are decorated with the rich hues of changing leaves.

The train depot is in Heber City, 20 miles south of Park City via Utah 248 and U.S. 40. Round-trip tickets cost $24 to $30 for adults, $16 to $20 for children 3 to 12, and $19 to $25 for seniors 60 and older. Rates are higher for special events and meal and entertainment excursions; one-way tickets are also available (call for rates). There are also combination rafting and horseback riding train expeditions ($89) and a trip that ends with a zipline ride ($99). The ticket office is open daily from 9am to 5pm. For information, contact **Heber Valley Railroad,** 450 S. 600 West, Heber City (© **800/888-8499,** 435/654-5601, or 801/581-9980 from Salt Lake City; www. hebervalleyrailroad.org).

Rockport State Park

Rockport, one of the Utah State Park system's man-made lakes, is a great destination offering a full range of outdoor activities, from windsurfing to wildlife-watching. In the winter, add ice-fishing and cross-country skiing. Facilities at the half-mile-wide, 3-mile-long lake include a marina, a boat ramp and courtesy docks, a picnic area, and camping spots in a variety of settings. The Wanship Dam, at the north end of the lake, is an important water-storage and flood-control dam on the Weber River, which has its headwaters high in the Uinta Mountains.

ESSENTIALS

GETTING THERE   From Park City, head east on I-80 for about 11 miles to exit 156, then go 5 miles south on Utah 32 along the western bank of Rockport Lake to the access road. The park entrance is at the lake's southern tip. Turn east to the park entrance, and then follow the road around to the north along the eastern bank.

INFORMATION, FEES & REGULATIONS   Contact **Rockport State Park,** 9040 N. Utah 302, Peoa, UT 84061-9702 (© **435/336-2241;** www.stateparks.utah. gov). Open year-round, the park has a day-use fee of $9 per vehicle. Pets are allowed, but must be confined or leashed.

OUTDOOR PURSUITS

CROSS-COUNTRY SKIING   Groomed cross-country ski trails run through the open sagebrush, and these offer a better chance of seeing wildlife than the more forested areas in the surrounding national forest.

HIKING & WILDLIFE-WATCHING   A 4-mile round-trip hike takes off from Juniper Campground. This easy, relatively flat walk among juniper and sagebrush offers an opportunity to glimpse mule deer, yellow-belly marmots, badgers, raccoons, weasels, skunks, and ground squirrels. Less visible are elk, moose, coyotes, bobcats, and cougars. Birds abound, and sometimes you can spot Western grebes, Canada geese, whistling swans, great blue herons, and golden and bald eagles. More frequently seen are ducks, red-tailed hawks, magpies, scrub jays, and hummingbirds.

WATER ACTIVITIES   The day-use area, located about 3½ miles north of the park entrance, offers the best swimming. The lake is also popular for boating, windsurfing, water-skiing, sailing, kayaking, and fishing. Both the lake and river are home to rainbow and brown trout, yellow perch, and smallmouth bass. Unfortunately, there are no equipment outfitters nearby.

CAMPING

A number of RV and tent campsites are located in five areas around the lake. The first campground is to the right of the access road, along the Weber River rather than the lake. Sites are shady and provide easy access to a trail along the river, handy for fishermen. The remainder of the sites lies between the road and the lake, along its eastern bank, and most have vault toilets only. One campground, Juniper, has sites with water and electric hookups, a dump station, and modern restrooms. Sites cost $10 to $20; yurts are $60. The park generally fills on weekends, but reservations can be made by calling ✆ **800/322-3770,** or through the state parks website (www.stateparks.utah.gov).

Jordanelle State Park ★★

Two recreation areas provide access to **Jordanelle Reservoir** in the beautiful Wasatch Mountains. Both areas are great for boating, fishing, picnicking, and camping. The reservoir is shaped rather like a boomerang, with the dam at the elbow. The Perimeter Trail connects the highly developed **Hailstone Recreation Site** to the more primitive **Rock Cliff Recreation Site.** Hailstone is on the terraced peninsula poking into the upper arm just above the dam; Rock Cliff is at the southeastern tip of the lower arm of the reservoir. Hailstone's camping and picnicking areas face the widest part of the reservoir, which is perfect for speedboats, water-skiing, and personal watercraft. The narrow arm reaching down to Rock Cliff is designated for low-speed water use. Trails—27 miles of them—circle the reservoir and connect to other area trails. They're open to hikers, mountain bikers, horseback riders, and cross-country skiers.

ESSENTIALS

GETTING THERE   For Hailstone, from Park City, head east on Kearns Boulevard (Utah 248) for about 3¾ miles; at U.S. 40, go southeast 4 miles to exit 8 and follow the entrance road east into Hailstone. From Heber City, take U.S. 40 northwest about 6 miles.

For Rock Cliff, from Park City, continue southeast on U.S. 40 past Hailstone for about 2 miles to Utah 32, then east about 6 miles to the entrance. From Heber City, follow U.S. 40 northwest for about 4 miles, then head east onto Utah 32 for about 6 miles to the entrance.

INFORMATION, FEES & REGULATIONS   Contact **Jordanelle State Park,** Utah 319, No. 515, Box 4, Heber City, UT 84032 (✆ **435/649-9540** for Hailstone or 435/782-3030 for Rock Cliff; www.stateparks.utah.gov). Stop at the **visitor center** at Hailstone or the **Nature Center** at Rock Cliff, a nature-oriented visitor center, for information and trail maps. The exhibit room in the visitor center at Hailstone presents an overview of human history in the area.

The park is open year-round at Hailstone, and May through September at Rock Cliff. Day-use hours in summer are 7am to 10pm; from October through March, they are 8am to 5pm. The visitor centers are open April through September from 9am to 6pm. The day-use fee is $10 per vehicle (or $7 for Rock Cliff only).

In order to protect the abundance of wildlife, particularly birds, pets are not allowed at Rock Cliff. They're welcome at Hailstone, but must be confined or leashed. Bicycling is permitted on established public roads, in parking areas, and on the Perimeter Trail.

HAILSTONE RECREATION SITE

At Hailstone are three camping areas and a group pavilion, along with a swimming beach and a picnic area available for day use. The 76-slip marina offers camping, picnicking supplies, boat rentals, a small restaurant, an amphitheater, boat ramps, a wheelchair-accessible fishing deck, and a fish-cleaning station.

OUTDOOR PURSUITS A concessionaire at **Jordanelle Marina** (✆ **435/655-9919;** www.jordanellemarina.com) rents ski boats, jet skis, and fishing boats.

CAMPING Hailstone's three camping areas have walk-in tent sites, RV/tent sites without hookups, and RV sites with water and electric hookups. Facilities include modern restrooms, showers, a small coin-op laundry, and a playground. Cost is $16 to $20. For reservations, call ✆ **800/322-3770,** or log on to the Utah State Parks' website (www.stateparks.utah.gov).

ROCK CLIFF RECREATION SITE

Rock Cliff contains three walk-in camping areas; picnic tables; the **Nature Center,** which offers maps, environmental programs, and exhibits on the various habitats of the area and how man's activities impact them; and the **Jordanelle Discovery Trail,** a boardwalk interpretive trail that winds through the Provo River riparian terrain.

BIRDING Rock Cliff offers great opportunities for **birding ★**, with more than 160 species either living here or passing through, and eagles and other raptors nesting in the area. Situated as it is among numerous riparian wetlands, Rock Cliff is designed to protect these sensitive habitats. Trails and boardwalks traverse the area, and bridges cross the waterways at four points, enabling you to get quite close to a variety of wetland life without inadvertently doing any harm to their habitats.

CAMPING The recreation area has three walk-in campgrounds with a total of 50 sites and two modern restrooms with showers. These sites are more nature-oriented than those at Hailstone and are scattered over 100 acres, providing great privacy. Cost is $16. The site doesn't have any areas for RVs. For reservations, call ✆ **800/322-3770,** or log on to the Utah State Parks' website, **www.stateparks.utah.gov**.

Wasatch Mountain State Park

The second-largest of Utah's state parks (after Antelope Island), at 21,592 acres, Wasatch Mountain State Park is also Utah's most developed state park, and among its most popular. This year-round destination is well maintained, well serviced, and easy to enjoy, and it just keeps getting better. This is a terrific golf and camping destination, and trails are continually being expanded to meet the demands of hikers and mountain bikers. In winter, a network of groomed cross-country skiing and snowmobiling trails lead from the park into the surrounding forest, and both cross-country-ski and snowmobile rentals are available. Wasatch Mountain's rangers offer a variety of instructive and interpretive programs. Fall is the best time to visit: The incomparable juxtaposition of rich reds, ochers, and deep evergreens will exceed your expectations.

ESSENTIALS

GETTING THERE It's about 5½ miles from Heber City to the park: From downtown, turn west on Utah 113 (100 South) to Midway; following signs for the state park, jog north on 200 West, then west on 200 North, and finally north again on Homestead Drive. The visitor center is located on Homestead Drive (where it becomes Snake Creek Rd.), in the park.

INFORMATION/VISITOR CENTER For advance information, contact **Wasatch Mountain State Park,** P.O. Box 10, Midway, UT 84049-0010 (✆ **435/654-1791;** www.stateparks.utah.gov). The visitor center, on Homestead Drive (where it becomes Snake Creek Rd.), also serves as a lounge for golfers. It's open daily from 8am to 5pm and includes a large mountain-lodge-style room with comfortable seating. Rangers are on hand to discuss park activities and provide trail maps and other information.

FEES & REGULATIONS   The day-use fee is $5 per vehicle. Pets are welcome in the park, but must be confined or leashed.

RANGER PROGRAMS   Interpretive programs take place most Friday and Saturday summer nights at the amphitheater, and a junior ranger program is offered Saturday mornings. The stocked pond adjacent to the visitor center provides fishing fun for children 15 and under in summer; call for details.

OUTDOOR PURSUITS

CROSS-COUNTRY SKIING   A 7½-mile Nordic ski track, with both diagonal stride and skating lanes, is laid out on the golf course. Neither dogs nor snowmobiles are allowed on the track, which is open from 8am to 5pm. At the southern end of the park, **Soldier Hollow** (© **435/654-2002;** www.soldierhollow.com) was the 2002 Olympics site for biathlon and cross-country-skiing competitions, and is available for cross-country skiing, snowshoeing, tubing, and other nonmotorized winter sports; in summer, mountain biking and horseback riding are popular. Day passes are $18 for adults and $9 for kids 7 to 17. Cross-country skis are available for rent at the golf course pro shop.

GOLF   With the USGA-sanctioned 36-hole, par-143 **Lake** and **Mountain** courses, golfing is the most popular pastime here. Ten lakes are scattered throughout the tree-lined fairways, and the views of the lovely Heber Valley are grand. Another 36 holes, at the **Soldier Hollow Golf Course** at the southern end of the park, opened in summer 2004. Facilities include a full-service pro shop, driving range, practice greens, and a cafe. Fees for adults are $15 for 9 holes, $29 for 18 holes. For juniors and seniors, the fees for 18 holes are $22 and $24, respectively, and $29 on weekends. Carts are available for an additional $13. Tee times may be reserved (© **435/654-0532**) a week in advance.

HIKING & WILDLIFE-WATCHING   **Pine Creek Nature Trail** is just over a mile in length and encompasses three smaller loops. Many songbirds make their homes in the trees along the trail, so watch for Steller's jays, chickadees, wrens, robins, and Western tanagers. You might also see the tracks of mule deer along the creek, where they come to forage. From the large parking area in Pine Creek campground, follow the half-mile trail to the Pine Creek trail head, which lies just north of the Oak Hollow loop. The trail begins at an elevation of 6,100 feet and climbs 220 feet, crossing Pine Creek four times and traversing several boulder ridges. The trail guide describes some of the plants you'll see on this hike. Don't attempt the trail after a rain, as it becomes quite muddy and slick. No bikes or motorized vehicles are allowed. Be sure to take water, a sun hat, and binoculars. Literature describing the plant and animal life of the park is available at the camp manager's office near the entrance to the campground and at the visitor center.

MOUNTAIN BIKING   An 18-mile loop affords great fun for mountain bikes. The road leaves the visitor center and heads west, winding through magnificent wooded country and offering occasional breathtaking views of the valley.

SNOWMOBILING   The park's 90 miles of groomed trails, very popular among snowmobilers, take you into Pine Creek, Snake Creek, and American Fork canyons. Warming stations are located at the clubhouse and visitor center.

CAMPING

Four camping loops in the **Pine Creek Campground** provide a total of 139 sites, including about 80 that are off-limits to tenters. All have modern restrooms, and all except Little Deer Creek, the smallest loop, have showers. Some sites are nestled among trees and are quite shady; others are more open. All except Little Deer Creek have paved parking pads, water, electricity, picnic tables, and barbecue grills; some also have sewer hookups. A dump station is located near the entrance to the campground. Camping fees are $13 at Little Deer Creek and $20 to $25 in the other three loops. Reservations are advised and can be made by calling ✆ **800/322-3770,** or through the state parks website (www.stateparks.utah.gov).

Strawberry Reservoir ★★

Located along U.S. 40 in the eastern portion of the Uinta National Forest, the jewel-like Strawberry Reservoir is a terrific water playground offering amazing fishing, as well as boating, hiking, and mountain biking. It's also great for cross-country skiing, ice-fishing, and snowmobiling in winter.

Utah's premier trout fishery—indeed, one of the premier trout fisheries in the West—Strawberry Reservoir is home to huge cutthroat and rainbow trout and kokanee salmon, so it's no surprise that fishing is the number-one draw. Fishing boats with outboard motors are available at **Strawberry Bay Marina** (✆ **435/548-2261;** www.strawberrybay.com); call for current rates.

Strawberry Reservoir has four marinas, with the largest at Strawberry Bay. This is the only one that provides year-round services, including a restaurant and lodging at **Strawberry Bay Lodge** (✆ **435/548-2500;** www.strawberrybay.com), with rooms for $65 for one full-size bed to $220 for a suite with four queens; the others offer limited services.

Campgrounds are located at each of the four marinas on the reservoir. Sites in the Strawberry Bay campgrounds have hookups; Soldier Creek, Aspen Grove, and Renegade do not. The fee is $17 per vehicle. Boat ramps and fish-cleaning facilities are located adjacent to each campground. Reservations can be made for a limited number of designated campsites in summer by contacting the National Recreation Reservation Service (✆ **877/444-6777;** www.recreation.gov).

To get to Strawberry Reservoir from Heber City, drive 22 miles southeast on U.S. 40 and turn south onto the access road. After about a half-mile, you'll come to the USFS visitor center for Strawberry Reservoir.

For information, contact the **Heber-Kamas Ranger District,** 2460 S. U.S. 40, P.O. Box 190, Heber City, UT 84032 (✆ **435/654-0470;** www.fs.fed.us/r4/uwc), or stop by the **Strawberry Visitor Center** (✆ **435/548-2321**). Day use is free in some parts of the complex, but there's a $5 fee in most areas.

Where to Stay & Eat

Heber City has a number of motels and inns, including **Holiday Inn Express,** 1268 S. Main St. (✆ **435/654-9990;** www.hiexpress.com), with rates from $89 to $129 for two people. The Swiss-themed **Zermatt Resort & Spa,** 784 W. Resort Dr., Midway (✆ **866/643-2015;** www.zermattresort.com), targets the convention crowd but has terrific facilities for weekend visitors. Rates start around $169 for a double room and go north of $1,000 a night for three-bedroom suites. The **Homestead Resort,** 700 N. Homestead Dr., Midway (✆ **888/327-7220;** www.homestead resort.com), has a wide variety of options (double rooms are typically $129–$199 and suites, condos, and cottages are $250 and up) in myriad buildings on a golf course, as well as the 55-foot volcanic Homestead Crater, its interior developed for soaking, diving, or snorkeling in the 90°F (32°C) water.

In downtown Midway, the **Café Galleria,** 101 W. Main St. (© **435/657-2002;** www.cafegalleriapizza.com), serves wood-fired pizza, bagel sandwiches, and salads. Home to a terrific model railway, the **Dairy Keen,** 199 S. Main St., Heber City (© **435/654-5336**), is a good bet for families, focusing on juicy burgers and thick milkshakes.

Blue Boar Inn ★★★ Winner of the prestigious Utah's "Best of State" award in the B&B category every year it's been given, the Blue Boar Inn is tucked into an upscale neighborhood under the beautiful mountain vista of Wasatch Mountain State Park. Owned by Adobe Systems founder John Warnock, this is a special property, with a dozen attractive and plush guest rooms named for poets and authors. All of the rooms have their own unique charms, from the elephant-embroidered pillows in the Rudyard Kipling room to the leather sleigh bed in the Charles Dickens to the rugged motif in the Robert Frost; the William Shakespeare room is very European with a rococo hand-carved king-size bed from Italy. Each room has a fireplace and a jetted tub. Named for a watering hole in Robin Hood lore, the Blue Boar Inn is also home to one of the region's best restaurants, with contemporary chef Eric May's Continental menu heavy on fresh seafood and a superlative 3,000-bottle wine cellar. Main courses are typically $30 to $40. Through the entire property, every detail, from the fascinating antiques (including 600-year-old crossbows) to the impeccable landscaping, hits the mark.

1235 Warm Springs Rd., Midway, UT 84049. www.theblueboarinn.com. © **888/654-1400** or 435/ 654-1400. Fax 435/654-6459. 12 units. $175–$295 double. Rates include full breakfast. AE, DISC, MC, V. **Amenities:** Restaurant; bar. *In room:* A/C, TV, Wi-Fi (free).

SUNDANCE RESORT

14 miles NE of Provo, 50 miles SE of Salt Lake City

Situated in beautiful Provo Canyon, at the base of 12,000-foot Mt. Timpanogos, Sundance is a year-round resort that emphasizes its arts programs as much as its skiing and outdoor activities. That should come as no surprise—it's owned by actor/ director Robert Redford, who bought the property in 1969 and named it after his character in the classic film *Butch Cassidy and the Sundance Kid.* You might recognize the area: Redford and director Sydney Pollack set their 1972 film *Jeremiah Johnson* here.

The goal for Sundance was to create a place where the outdoors and the arts could come together in a truly unique mountain community, and it seems to be a success. The rustic yet elegant, environmentally friendly retreat is a full-service ski resort in winter. During the summer, you can explore great hiking trails and participate in other warm-weather outdoor activities.

Essentials

GETTING THERE   Sundance is less than an hour's drive from Salt Lake City via I-15. From Park City, take U.S. 189 south to Sundance. From Provo, take I-15 to exit 272, go east on Utah 52 for 5½ miles, turn north on U.S. 189 up Provo Canyon for 7 miles, and turn north on Utah 92 for about 2 miles to Sundance. In winter, the road beyond Sundance is often closed by snow.

A van shuttle service connects Sundance with both Salt Lake International Airport and Provo Airport. Call **Sundance Resort** (see below) for information and to arrange for pickup.

SO YOU WANNA BE IN PICTURES: THE sundance FILM FESTIVAL

Forget Cannes; forget Hollywood. If you want to be (or at least be up on) the next art-house cinema sensation, go to Utah.

Tired of waiting for the next Great American Novel, many people have traded their reading glasses for tubs of popcorn, and are packing the movie houses to catch the latest work of the new creative hero: the American independent filmmaker. These next Tarantinos have to start somewhere—and that somewhere is, more often than not, the Sundance Film Festival.

For more than 20 years, the hottest independent films have been discovered at this 10-day January event, hosted by Robert Redford's Sundance Institute. The festival doesn't actually take place at Sundance; it's held 30 miles away, in Park City, covered earlier in this chapter. There are screenings here during the festival, however, as well as lodging packages and shuttles that take guests back and forth.

The festival has seen the rise to glory of many pictures, including *sex, lies, and videotape; Reservoir Dogs; Slacker; Like Water for Chocolate; Hoop Dreams; The Station Agent; The Aristocrats;* and *Napoleon Dynamite*—and that's just the short list.

Hosting the nation's premier annual film festival is only part of the Sundance Institute's role in the world of American cinema. Since Robert Redford founded the Institute, it has brought some of the finest and most well-respected directors, actors, and producers to Utah to serve as advisors while students rehearse, shoot, and edit their works.

Admission to the festival—as a filmmaker or as an audience member—is non-exclusive; that means you and I can rub shoulders with the rich and famous and up-and-coming. To receive a free guide, or to learn how to purchase tickets, contact the **Sundance Institute** (© **435/658-3456** or 435/776-7878; www.sundance.org).

VISITOR INFORMATION   For information on all facilities and activities, plus lodging reservations, contact **Sundance Resort,** R.R. 3, Box A-1, Sundance, UT 84604 (© **800/892-1600** or 801/225-4100; www.sundanceresort.com).

Skiing Sundance

Sundance is known for its quiet, intimate setting and lack of lift lines. It offers runs for all levels—some quite challenging—including several delightfully long cruising trails for novices. The area is gaining a reputation as a good place to learn to ski or snowboard. The two levels of skiing are pretty well separated from each other: The beginner areas and some of the intermediate terrain are on the front mountain, whereas the prime blue runs and all of the expert slopes are on the back mountain. The expert crowd will be pleased with the steep glades, precipitous bump runs (due to the general lack of traffic, the mountain never really bumps up too high, though), and untracked snow on the back mountain, where you'll have to work at it to run into another skier.

The terrain is rated 20% beginner, 40% intermediate, and 40% advanced, with a total of 41 runs over 450 skiable acres. One quad and two triple chairlifts, plus a handle tow, serve the mountain, which has a vertical drop of 2,150 feet, from a base elevation of 6,100 feet to the top at 8,250 feet. Sundance is usually open from mid-December to early April, and has state-of-the-art snow-making equipment on the entire front mountain. Lifts operate daily from 9am to 4:30pm and on Monday, Wednesday, Friday, and Saturday nights from 4:30 to 9pm.

Bearclaw's Cabin, the only mountaintop day lodge in Utah, offers snacks and hot drinks, as well as stupendous views. **Creekside** day lodge, at the base of the ski area, serves excellent quick lunches during ski season. Equipment rental and sales are available.

LIFT TICKETS   Adult all-day lift tickets cost $49, children 6 to 12 are $27, 5 and under ski free, and seniors 65 and over pay $15. Night skiing is $25 for adults and $18 for children. If you're staying at the resort, the lift ticket is included in your room rate.

LESSONS & PROGRAMS   The **ski school** (✆ **801/225-4140**) offers private and group lessons daily, as well as specialized workshops. Three-hour private lessons start at $240; group lessons start at $67 for 2 hours.

Sundance Kids ski school offers several programs, including group lessons and all-day programs that include supervision, lunch, and instruction. The resort has no day-care facility.

CROSS-COUNTRY SKIING & SNOWSHOEING   Sundance's excellent **Cross Country Center ★★★** is 1½ miles north of the main Sundance entrance. It has about 21 miles of groomed Nordic and snowshoe trails. Classic, skating, and telemark rentals and lessons are available. Trail passes for adults cost $16 for a full day, or $12 after 2pm. Children 12 and under and seniors 65 and over ski free.

Warm-Weather Fun

An abundance of warm-weather activities and spectacular scenery make Sundance just as popular a destination in the summer as during the winter. A quad ski lift operates in warm weather (usually from late May through late Oct), carrying hikers and bikers to upper trails, and offering scenic rides to anyone. Lift rides cost $11, $9 for kids 6 to 12, $8 for seniors 65 and older, and are free for children 5 and under accompanied by an adult.

FLY-FISHING   The **Provo River** provides great fly-fishing just 10 minutes away for rainbow, cutthroat, and German brown trout. Licenses and information are available at the Sundance General Store (p. 139). Sundance offers guided fishing trips, including equipment rentals. Rates start at $160 for group, $240 for private, half-day fly-fishing trips.

HIKING & MOUNTAIN BIKING   Sundance is home to a terrific network of close to a dozen trails, some of which connect to the Uinta National Forest, 88 W. 100 North, Provo (✆ **801/342-5100**; http://fs.usda.gov/uwcnf). The resort's trails range from hour-long nature walks to all-day affairs, and include three routes to the summit of Mt. Timpanogos.

The **Sundance Nature Trail,** a 1- to 1½-hour round-trip hike, winds through groves of spruce, oak, and maple and across alpine meadows before reaching a cascading waterfall. The **Great Western Trail,** one of the Wasatch Front's most spectacular trails, climbs nearly 4,000 feet to some amazing scenic vistas. It starts at the base of Aspen Grove, winds to the crest of North Fork and American Fork canyons, and ends at the top of Alta ski area. This is an 8- to 10-hour round-trip hike.

Mountain bikers will find the mountain trails at Sundance fun and challenging. Bikers can minimize some of the work by taking their bikes up the lift and pedaling down. The mountain biker's trail-use fee is $12, which includes one lift ride; a full-day pass, including unlimited use of the lift, costs $20.

Contact the resort for a comprehensive trail guide.

HORSEBACK RIDING The **Sundance Stables** offer guided mountain rides of 1 hour and up, starting at $59 per person. Call the main number at Sundance for information.

Shopping

The **General Store** (✆ **801/223-4250**) in the Sundance Resort was the inspiration for the Sundance Catalog; it may have come to you in the mail at some time or another. If so, you may recognize the American Indian art and jewelry, local crafts, and high-end Southwest-style clothing and outdoor wear that line the shelves. You can also browse through hiking and fishing apparel and gear (including licenses and rentals) in warm weather, ski accessories in winter, and fresh-baked goodies year-round. At **Sundance Mountain Outfitters** (✆ **801/223-4121**), you can also browse through hiking and fishing apparel and gear (including licenses and rentals) in warm weather, ski accessories in winter.

Where to Stay

Sundance offers standard rooms, studios, and cottage suites that range from $279 to $600 per night, as well as larger mountain suites and several luxury mountain homes that cost from $350 to over $1,000 per night. Each suite is outfitted with well-crafted handmade furnishings that match the rustic luxury of the entire resort, as well as American Indian crafts, stone fireplaces, and outdoor decks; most have fully equipped kitchens. Contact the **Sundance Resort,** R.R. 3, Box A-1, Sundance, UT 84604 (✆ **800/892-1600** or 801/225-4100; www.sundanceresort.com), for information and reservations.

Where to Eat

The Sundance restaurants' culinary approach stresses the use of natural, seasonal ingredients, and dishes are often prepared with such locally raised products as lamb, fresh trout or chicken, and lots of seasonal fruit and vegetables. Dinner reservations are recommended, particularly in season. Full liquor service is available.

The **Tree Room** ★★ (✆ **801/223-4200** for reservations), the resort's most elegant dining room for over 25 years, is the place for relaxing, romantic dinners with wine and candlelight in a room decorated with American Indian art and artifacts from Redford's private collection. Seasonal menus might include wild Alaskan salmon with collard greens and roasted beets, grilled buffalo tenderloin with wild mushroom au gratin, and a signature pepper steak with buttermilk mashed potatoes and mango chutney. It's open daily from 5pm, with dinner entree prices from $24 to $47.

The **Foundry Grill** (✆ **801/223-4220**), a less formal eatery offering seasonal ranch-style cuisine, serves three meals Monday through Saturday and brunch and dinner on Sunday. Wood is the predominant feature in both decor and food—a wood oven and wood-fired grill and rotisserie are the main cooking methods. Lunch main courses range from $10 to $17; dinner entrees run $12 to $35.

The **Owl Bar** (✆ **801/223-4222**) is just next door. This is the same 1890s bar frequented by Butch Cassidy's Hole-in-the-Wall Gang, moved here from Wyoming, stripped of shag, and refinished—but now locals and resort guests belly up to the

Victorian rosewood bar to order their favorite tipple. A limited grill menu is available ($14–$35); it's open from 5pm weekdays and noon weekends.

PROVO & ENVIRONS

45 miles S of Salt Lake City, 258 miles NE of St. George

The second-largest metropolitan area in Utah, **Provo** (elevation 4,500 ft.) and its adjacent communities have a population of over 500,000. The main draw here is Brigham Young University, with its museums, cultural events, and spectator sports. Provo also makes a good base for exploring the nearby mountains, Timpanogos Cave National Monument, and the quite spectacular gardens and other attractions at Thanksgiving Point, in nearby Lehi. The Ute Indian tribe reigned here until Mormon leader Brigham Young sent 30 families south from Salt Lake City in March 1849 to colonize the area. Today, the city remains primarily Mormon; many restaurants, stores, and attractions are closed Sundays.

South of Provo lies **Springville,** a town of about 30,000 that likes to refer to itself as "Utah's Art City." Although not a major tourist destination, it is home to one of the state's finest art museums. **Orem,** which abuts Provo on the northwest, is a tech industry hub. Utah Lake State Park, just west of downtown Provo, is great for boating, and the surrounding Wasatch Mountains abound with natural beauty and recreational opportunities.

Essentials

GETTING THERE   Provo and Orem are easily accessible from the north or south by I-15. If you're driving in from the east on I-70, take exit 156 at Green River and follow U.S. 6 northwest to I-15 north.

Amtrak (© **800/872-7245;** www.amtrak.com) offers passenger service to Provo on the Chicago-to-Emeryville California Zephyr line. The train station is located at 600 South and 300 West.

The **Utah Transit Authority** runs about a dozen bus routes in and around the Provo area, with connections to Salt Lake City, Lehi, and Springville. For schedule information, call © **801/743-3882** or check the Web, **www.rideuta.com**. Route maps and schedules are also available at the visitor center in the county courthouse. The FrontRunner train will run south to here from Salt Lake City by 2015.

VISITOR INFORMATION   The **Utah Valley Convention and Visitors Bureau** runs a visitor center at 111 S. University Ave., Provo, UT 84601 (© **800/222-8824** or 801/851-2100; www.utahvalley.org/cvb). The visitor center is open 8:30am to 5pm Monday through Friday and 9am to 3pm on Saturday.

For information on the surrounding national forest, contact the **Uinta National Forest,** 88 W. 100 North, Provo, UT 84601 (© **801/342-5100;** http://fs.usda.gov/uwcnf).

GETTING AROUND   The easiest way to get around is by car. The streets are organized in a numbered grid pattern, beginning at the intersection of Center Street and University Avenue in Provo. From here, the blocks increase by 100 in all four directions, such as 100 South, 200 West, 700 North, and so forth. University Parkway cuts diagonally northwest across the grid from Brigham Young University to connect with 1300 South (I-15 exit 269) in Orem. The center of Orem is the intersection of Center Street (I-15 exit 271) and Main Street. State Street (U.S. 89) crosses the city diagonally.

Where to Stay & Eat in Downtown Provo

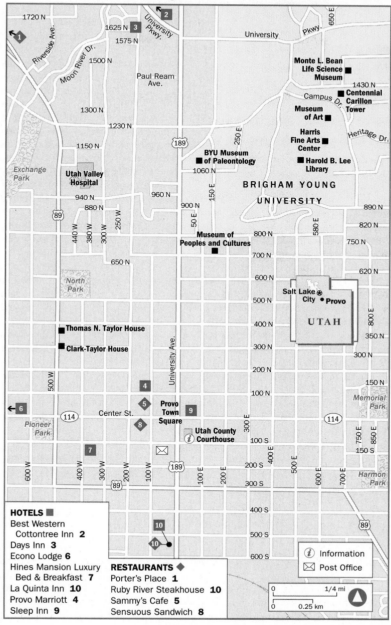

1720 N

1625 N **3**
1575 N

2

University Pkwy.

University Pkwy.

650 N

Riverside Ave.

Moon River Dr.

1500 N

Paul Ream Ave.

1300 N

1230 N

1150 N

189

Monte L. Bean Life Science Museum ■

Campus Dr.

1430 N

■ Centennial Carillon Tower

Museum of Art ■

Harris Fine Arts ■ Center

Heritage Dr.

BYU Museum ■ of Paleontology

1060 N

■ Harold B. Lee Library

Exchange Park

Utah Valley Hospital ■

BRIGHAM YOUNG

UNIVERSITY

940 N
880 N

89

960 N

900 N

150 E

250 E

50 E

890 N

820 N

440 W

380 W

300 W

250 W

Museum of Peoples and Cultures ■

800 N

580 E

750 N

650 N

North Park

700 N

600 N

620 N

Salt Lake City ⊛ • Provo

500 N

■ Thomas N. Taylor House

400 N

800 E

350 N

■ Clark-Taylor House

University Ave.

300 N

UTAH

200 N

300 N

500 W

100 N

150 N

4

Memorial Park

5

Provo Town Square

9

114

Center St.

114

8

Utah County ⓘ Courthouse

300 E

100 S

750 E

850 E

150 S

Pioneer Park

Harmon Park

← **6**

7

600 W

400 W

300 W

200 W

100 W

100 E

200 E

400 E

500 E

600 E

700 E

150 S

189

89

200 S

300 S

400 S

HOTELS ■
Best Western
   Cottontree Inn **2**
Days Inn **3**
Econo Lodge **6**
Hines Mansion Luxury
   Bed & Breakfast **7**
La Quinta Inn **4**
Provo Marriott **4**
Sleep Inn **9**

10

10

500 S

600 S

89

RESTAURANTS ◆
Porter's Place **1**
Ruby River Steakhouse **10**
Sammy's Cafe **5**
Sensuous Sandwich **8**

ⓘ Information
⊠ Post Office

0   1/4 mi
0   0.25 km

Major car-rental agencies include **Avis** (✆ **800/238-4898** or 801/494-1529; www.avis.com) and **Enterprise** (✆ **800/261-7331** or 801/375-7755; www.enterprise.com).

FAST FACTS   The main hospital in Provo is **Utah Valley Regional Medical Center,** 1034 N. 500 West (✆ **801/357-7850**), with a 24-hour emergency room. The main **post office** is at 95 W. 100 South (✆ **800/275-8777;** www.usps.com). The local newspaper is the *Daily Herald* (www.heraldextra.com). The **sales tax** totals 6.25%.

Exploring Brigham Young University

Founded in 1875 by Brigham Young, Brigham Young University is the nation's largest church-owned private university, sponsored by the Church of Jesus Christ of Latter-day Saints. Home to more than 30,000 students, the beautiful 638-acre campus is located on the east side of Provo at the base of the Wasatch Mountains.

For information, contact Brigham Young University, Public Affairs and Guest Relations, Provo, UT 84602 (✆ **801/422-4678;** www.byu.edu). To get to the university from I-15 north, take exit 269, University Parkway, and travel east through Orem into Provo to the northwest entrance of the campus.

Free 40-minute **tours** of the campus, beginning at the visitor center, are offered Monday through Friday on the hour from 9am to 4pm. Allow at least 1 hour. Admission to campus museums is free unless otherwise noted; allow 1 to 2 hours for each of the BYU museums.

The 112-foot-tall **Spencer W. Kimball Tower,** a campus landmark, houses 52 bells that toll at intervals throughout the day.

The **Monte L. Bean Life Science Museum,** 645 E. 1430 North, just east of the Marriott Center (✆ **801/422-5051;** http://mlbean.byu.edu), houses extensive collections of insects, plants, reptiles, fish, shells, mammals, and birds from around the world, with an emphasis on Utah's wildlife. It's open Monday through Friday from 10am to 9pm and Saturday from 10am to 5pm. Admission is free.

The **BYU Museum of Paleontology,** 1683 N. Provo Canyon Rd., west of LaVell Edwards Football Stadium (✆ **801/422-3680**), houses one of Utah's largest collections of dinosaur bones from the Jurassic period. Guided tours are available by appointment. Hours are Monday through Friday from 9am to 5pm and there is no admission charge.

The **Harris Fine Arts Center,** Campus Drive (✆ **801/422-2881** or 801/422-4322 for the ticket office), houses galleries featuring American and European artists. The B. F. Larsen Gallery and Gallery 303 feature student and faculty exhibitions. The center also hosts theatrical and musical performances in its five theaters; call for the schedule and ticket prices.

The state-of-the-art **BYU Museum of Art ★★**, north of the Fine Arts Center at 492 E. Campus Dr. (✆ **801/422-8287;** http://moa.byu.edu), is one of the largest museums in the West. Its 17,000-plus-piece collection includes something for everyone, from ceramics to sculpture, paintings to pottery. The galleries hold everything from etchings by Rembrandt and Monet to jade and ivory from Asia. The museum also contains a gift shop and a cafe that serves lunch. Hours are Monday through Saturday from 10am to 6pm (until 9pm Thurs–Fri). Admission is charged for special exhibitions only.

The **Museum of Peoples and Cultures,** in Allen Hall, 100 E. 700 North (✆ **801/422-0020;** http://mpc.byu.edu), focuses on the cultures of the Western

Hemisphere, but also looks at Colombian, Egyptian, Israeli, Polynesian, and Syrian societies. It's open Monday through Friday from 9am to 5pm (until 7pm Tues and Thurs) and admission is free.

The **Harold B. Lee Library** (© **801/422-2927;** http://lib.byu.edu) is the largest library in Utah, with more than three million bound volumes. Library hours are Monday through Friday from 7am to midnight and Saturday from 8am to midnight. The second floor houses one of the world's largest **genealogical libraries** (© **801/422-6200**), with free services to all.

More to See & Do in the Provo Area

Here in Provo, home of Brigham Young University, are a number of stately homes that once belonged to well-to-do church officials, as well as commercial buildings constructed to serve the growing community. Stop at the **visitor center** (p. 140) for a booklet describing the city's dozens of historic buildings. Nearby, the **Utah County Courthouse** is well worth a visit. This magnificent structure was built of Manti limestone in the 1920s. Notice the marble floors and detailing, the fine collection of artwork displayed on the walls, and the overall feeling of grandeur emanating from the classical balance of the design.

The **Provo Town Square,** at the intersection of University Avenue and Center Street, contains the core of Provo's business community, which began to develop and grow in the 1890s. Here you'll see the 1900 **Knight Block,** a big red building with a large clock; the **Gates & Snow Furniture Co.,** to the east of the Knight Block, with one of Utah's best pressed-tin fronts; and the **Zion Bank,** at the northwest corner, situated in what was originally the Bank of Commerce building. West along Center Street sits a row of period storefronts, with the newer businesses now occupying them.

An interesting historic home is the **Thomas N. Taylor House,** 342 N. 500 West. "T.N.T.," as he was known, was manager of the Taylor Brothers Store and served as mayor of Provo and president of the Utah Stake of the LDS Church. His home, built in the first decade of the 20th century, exemplifies the kind of house most second-generation Utahns aspired to have. Nearby is the **Clark-Taylor House,** 310 N. 500 West, thought to be the oldest home in Utah Valley still standing on its original site. The adobe structure was built in 1854, with later additions of the two-story front, the trim around the windows, and the gables. Neither of these houses is open for tours.

Heading out of town, a turnout on U.S. 189, about 4 miles north and east of Provo, affords awe-inspiring views of **Bridal Veil Falls,** a double cataract waterfall that drops 607 feet to the Provo River. This is also a good spot to begin hikes into Provo Canyon.

Hutchings Museum   Born in 1889, John Hutchings had an insatiable curiosity about the world around him. He collected and studied numerous objects, discussing his observations with friends and family. His collections are the core of this museum, which houses mineral displays and rare specimens of variscite and crystal aluminum, and describes their links to mining districts of the region. Also on display are dinosaur bones, flamingo tracks from Spanish Fork Canyon, a piece of tusk from a woolly mammoth, tools and pottery from early man, and artifacts from Utah's early residents, including a shotgun owned by famed outlaw Butch Cassidy. Allow 45 minutes.

55 N. Center St., Lehi. © **801/768-7180.** www.hutchingsmuseum.org. Admission $4 adults; $3 seniors, students, and children 3–12; free for children 2 and under; $12 family. Tues–Sat 11am–5pm. From I-15 exit 279, take Main St. west to Center St. and turn right.

Provo Beach Resort ★ ☺ Featuring a mind-boggling array of diversions (indoor surfing to outdoor beach cruiser bicycles, not to mention Pinewood Derby, minigolf, and a boardwalk complete with a carousel), this attraction is located at an upscale mall on the north side of Provo proper. Allow at least 1 hour for your visit.

4801 N. University Ave., Provo. ☏ **801/224-5001.** www.provobeachresort.com. Admission varies by activity; cruisers are $6–$8 an hour, surfing $20 an hour, carousel rides $1. Mon–Thurs 11am–10pm; Fri 11am–11pm; Sat 10am–11pm. Closed Sun and legal holidays.

Springville Museum of Art ★★ The art of Utah is the cornerstone of this fine museum, housed in part in a 1937 Spanish Colonial Revival–style building. The museum contains one of the finest displays of Utah art available, arranged in chronological order to illustrate the development of art in the state. Of its nine galleries, four are reserved for changing exhibits of historical and contemporary art of Utah. The museum also has an excellent (and little-known) collection of Russian and Soviet Socialist Realism. The museum contains a research library and bookstore, and offers a series of lectures. Allow about 1 hour for your visit.

126 E. 400 South, Springville. ☏ **801/489-2727.** www.sma.nebo.edu. Free admission; donations accepted. Tues–Sat 10am–5pm (Wed to 9pm); Sun 3–6pm. Closed Mon and legal holidays. From I-15 exit 260, go east to Springville, entering town on 400 South.

Thanksgiving Point ★★ ☺ This huge complex, developed by the cofounders of WordPerfect software as an expression of gratitude to their community, includes a splendid dinosaur museum—the **Museum of Ancient Life.** Billed as the largest dinosaur museum in the world, it houses some of the longest and tallest dinosaur replicas ever put on display, plus fossils and related exhibits on paleontology. The museum contains a children's discovery room, a fossil lab where you can see paleontologists at work, a widescreen theater, and a museum store selling practically everything dinosaur related. Allow 2 hours.

Elsewhere at Thanksgiving Point are the delightful **Thanksgiving Point Gardens**—55 acres of themed gardens, including topiary, butterfly, fragrance, herb, and English rose gardens, plus an unusual waterfall garden, all connected by some 2 miles of landscaped brick pathways. The Children's Discovery Garden, designed to encourage children's imaginations, contains a large Noah's Ark, an underground exhibit area, and a hedge maze. Allow 2 hours. Kids will also enjoy **Farm Country,** with an animal park and exhibits on the farming life (allow 1–2 hr.). Other attractions include an amphitheater, a golf course (p. 145), numerous shops, and several restaurants. Wagon and carriage rides are also offered.

3003 N. Thanksgiving Way, Lehi. ☏ **888/672-6040** or 801/768-2300. www.thanksgivingpoint.com. Admission to museum $10 adults, $8 children 3–12 and seniors 65 and over, free for children 2 and under. Call for fees for gardens and other sites and activities. Grounds Mon–Sat; call for hours for specific venues. Closed New Year's Day, Thanksgiving, and Christmas. From I-15 exit 284, go west to Thanksgiving Way.

Sports & Outdoor Pursuits

One of the top spots for fishing, boating, and swimming in this area is **Utah Lake State Park ★★**, 4400 W. Center St. (☏ **801/375-0731;** www.stateparks.utah.gov), Utah's largest freshwater lake. The 96,600-acre lake is especially popular with owners of speedboats, personal watercraft, and sailboats, although the occasional canoe or kayak can be seen gliding by. Mountains dominate the view in all directions, and at night, the lights of the city illuminate the panorama to the east. Anglers catch channel catfish, walleye, white bass, black bass, and several species of panfish. While there are boat-launching ramps, there are no boat rentals. Although the park itself has no hiking or biking trails, the **Provo River Parkway Trail** leads from the edge of the park into Provo Canyon (see below).

The park's 54-site campground is open April through October only; the park is open for day use year-round. The campground has no RV hookups, but it does have a dump station as well as modern restrooms with showers. Day-use hours are 6am to 10pm in summer, 8am to 5pm in winter. Day use costs $9 per vehicle. Camping costs $20; reservations can be made by calling ℭ **800/322-3770,** or through the state parks website (www.stateparks.utah.gov). Take I-15 exit 268, Center Street west; it's about 3 miles to the park.

Outdoor recreation enthusiasts also head into the **Uinta National Forest,** which practically surrounds Provo and offers hundreds of miles of hiking, mountain biking, and horseback riding trails. Check with the **Forest Supervisor's office,** 88 W. 100 North (ℭ **801/377-5780;** http://fs.usda.gov/uwcnf), for maps and tips on where to go.

Right in town, the 15-mile **Provo River Parkway Trail** winds from Utah Lake to Provo Canyon, following the Provo River part of the way. This slag trail (slag is the rock left over when a metal is mined) is open to both bikers and hikers.

Among the public golf courses in the area are **Thanksgiving Point Golf Club** in Lehi (p. 144; ℭ **801/768-7400**), an 18-hole, par-72 championship course designed by golf pro Johnny Miller, with greens fees of $29 to $85 for 18 holes, cart included; **Cascade Golf Course,** 1313 E. 800 North, Orem (ℭ **801/225-6677;** www.cascadegolfcenter.com), which has a driving range and 9 holes and is par-35, with greens fees of $12 to $13, plus $7 per person for a cart; and **East Bay Golf Course,** 1860 S. Eastbay Blvd. (ℭ **801/373-6262**), on the south side of the city, which is an 18-hole, par-71 course with greens fees of $11 to $13 for 9 holes ($14 for a cart) and $27 for 18 holes, cart included.

Lehi is home to a huge (150,000-sq.-ft.!) **Cabela's,** 2502 W. Grand Terrace Pkwy. (ℭ **801/766-2500;** www.cabelas.com), selling every kind of outdoor gear imaginable. They've even got a restaurant, horse corrals, and an indoor archery range.

Water & Ice Fun

Seven Peaks Water Park   This is the place for a wide variety of water fun: Dozens of heated water attractions on 26 acres are set against the mountains. The facilities include a large wave pool, winding slides, children's pools, an activity pool, large pavilions and shaded cabanas, plenty of grass, a gift shop, and food vendors. Tubes are available for rent. The adjacent **Peaks Ice Arena** (ℭ **801/852-7465**), built for the 2002 Olympics, contains two Olympic-size ice-skating rinks that are open to the public. Skate rental is available. The arena is open year-round; call for the current rates and schedule.

1330 E. 300 North. ℭ **801/377-4386.** www.sevenpeaks.com. All-day admission to the Water Park $25 adults, $20 children under 48 in. tall, free for seniors 65 and older and toddlers 3 and under; half-day (after 4pm) $16 ages 4–64. Water Park late May to early Sept Mon–Sat 11am–8pm. From I-15 exit 265, head east on Center St.

Spectator Sports

Brigham Young University is part of the Mountain West Conference. The **Cougars football** team plays at the 65,000-seat LaVell Edwards Football Stadium; tickets are hard to come by, so call as far in advance as possible. The **basketball** team plays in the 23,000-seat Marriott Center; you usually won't have too much trouble getting tickets, especially now that Jimmer Fredette has moved on to the NBA. For general information on all BYU sports teams, call ☎ **801/422-2096,** or check the athletic department's website at www.byucougars.com. For tickets, call ☎ **800/322-2981** or 801/422-2981, or buy online at www.byutickets.com.

Where to Stay

In addition to the following listings, affordable chain and franchise motels in Provo include **Best Western Plus Cottontree Inn,** 2230 N. University Pkwy. (☎ **800/662-6886** or 801/373-7044; www.bestwestern.com), **Days Inn,** 1675 W 200 North (☎ **800/329-7466** or 801/375-8600; www.daysinn.com), **Econo Lodge,** 1625 W. Center St. (☎ **800/553-2666** or 801/373-0099; www.choicehotels.com), **La Quinta Inn,** 1460 S. University Ave. (☎ **800/753-3757** or 801/374-9750; www.lq.com), and **Sleep Inn,** 1505 S. 40 East (☎ **800/753-3746** or 801/377-6597; www.choicehotels.com). Rates are typically $60 to $120 for a double at these properties.

Rates are highest in summer, lowest in late winter and early spring. Rates are often significantly higher during Brigham Young University special events, and rooms can be very scarce at graduation time. Tax added to lodging bills is 11%. Pets are not allowed unless otherwise noted.

Hines Mansion Bed & Breakfast ★★ Built in 1895 for pharmacist and mining magnate Russell Spencer Hines, this Victorian-style mansion is a true gem. It makes a wonderful spot to celebrate a special occasion or to simply relax and soak up some historical charm. Innkeepers Sandy and John Rowe have retained the mansion's historical ambience and integrity while adding numerous modern touches. Every room is unique, but each has a queen- or king-size bed, robes, and a two-person whirlpool tub plus a separate private bathroom. The penthouse, which occupies the entire top floor of the mansion, boasts a king-size bed, a 46-inch TV with a DVD player, and spectacular views of the city and nearby mountains from the tub. Fresh-baked cookies and fresh fruit are served each evening. Breakfasts feature fruit, yogurt, and a hot dish such as baked egg puffs or pecan pancakes. Smoking is not permitted.

383 W. 100 South, Provo, UT 84601. www.hinesmansion.com. ☎ **800/428-5636** or 801/374-8400. Fax 801/374-0823. 9 units. $129–$235 double. Rates include full breakfast. AE, MC, V. Not recommended for children. *In room:* A/C, TV/VCR or DVD, movie library, Wi-Fi (free).

Provo Marriott This well-regarded high-rise hotel in downtown Provo provides comfortable—even luxurious—accommodations with splendid views (especially from the upper floors) and all the amenities you could want, including coffeemakers, irons and ironing boards, hair dryers, and wireless high-speed Internet access in the rooms. Public areas and bedrooms are handsomely appointed, decorated primarily in light earth tones. Some in-room fridges are available, and some units have whirlpool tubs. Allie's American Grille serves three meals daily.

101 W. 100 North, Provo, UT 84601. www.provomarriott.com. ☎ **888/825-3162** or 801/377-4700. Fax 801/377-4708. 330 units, including 6 suites. $89–$149 double; $299–$500 suite. AE, DC, DISC, MC, V. **Amenities:** Restaurant; concierge-level rooms; fitness center; Jacuzzi; 2 heated pools (indoor and outdoor); room service; sauna; Wi-Fi (free). *In room:* A/C, TV, hair dryer, Wi-Fi ($10 per day).

CAMPING

Lakeside RV Campground Situated along the Provo River, this campground offers the best of both worlds—it's close to the attractions and restaurants of Provo, and it offers a quiet camping experience with trees, flowers, grassy areas, ducks, and geese. In addition to the usual bathhouse, dump station, and RV hookups, the campground has a self-serve laundry, free Wi-Fi access, heated pool, nature walk, horseshoe pits, volleyball area, playground, and game room. A store sells groceries, and propane is available. You can fish in the Provo River, or head to Utah Lake, just a quarter-mile away.

4000 W. Center St., Provo, UT 84601. www.lakesidervcampground.com. © **801/373-5267.** Fax 801/373-8624. 130 sites (all RV sites, most with full hookups). $20–$30 for 2 people. DISC, MC, V. From I-15 exit 265B, go west 3 miles. Pets welcome.

Where to Eat

Provo is a conservative, family-oriented city; many restaurants do not serve alcohol, and a number are closed on Sundays. In addition to the restaurants discussed below, try the recommended **Tree Room,** at the nearby Sundance Resort (p. 136) and **Sammy's Cafe,** 27 N. 100 West (© **801/805-9208;** http://sammyscafe.blogspot. com), an old-school burger joint that stays open later than every place else in town— midnight most nights and 2am on Friday and Saturday. Burgers are $5 to $7.

Porter's Place ★★ ☺ STEAK/AMERICAN   One of Utah's more colorful and controversial characters, Porter Rockwell served as a bodyguard for LDS church leaders Joseph Smith and Brigham Young; was accused but acquitted of attempting to assassinate the lieutenant governor of Missouri; and was blamed for, but not charged with, other murders. Named in Rockwell's honor, Porter's Place is an Old West–style restaurant with a large regional following. Housed in a 1915 building, the restaurant has the look of an old saloon, with redbrick walls, heavy wood tables, and old photos. The counter (actually a bar from an 1883 Montana saloon) has tractor seats for stools.

Porter's specializes in thick steaks and fresh fish. The lunch menu features a variety of sandwiches and burgers, including a buffalo burger and a huge 1-pound beef burger. Especially popular at dinner are the top sirloin steaks, ranging from 5 to 24 ounces, and the buffalo steaks. Portions are generally large, but the dinner menu also offers 10 "lite dinners" with smaller portions. A local bakery provides the breads and pastries; fountain treats such as old-fashioned sodas, malts, and banana splits are available as well. Despite the saloonlike appearance and handsome old bar, no alcohol is served.

24 W. Main St., Lehi. © **801/768-8348.** www.porterrockwellutah.com. Main courses $7–$10 lunch, $9–$35 dinner. AE, DISC, MC, V. Mon–Thurs 10am–10pm; Fri–Sat 10am–11pm. From I-15 exit 279, go west on Main St.

Ruby River Steakhouse ★ STEAK   If a thick, juicy, sizzling steak is your idea of the perfect meal, then Ruby River is for you. Decor is strictly Western, with a large painting of galloping wild horses, a rock fireplace, and a bar with tall tables and buckets of peanuts. Beef is USDA Choice, aged 21 days, hand-cut, seasoned, and double-broiled at 1,600°F (871°C). Choices range from the New York cut (voted Utah's best steak in various polls) to tender filet mignon, rib-eye, T-bone, and porterhouse. The very tasty prime rib is slow-roasted and served with fresh-grated horseradish and sour cream. The restaurant also does an admirable job with slow-roasted baby back ribs in Louisiana-style barbecue sauce, and several chicken and seafood dishes. Side dishes include a baked potato that's deep-fried in garlic batter and a baked yam that's deep-fried in cinnamon batter. There is a full bar, a rarity in these parts.

1454 S. University Ave. (in the La Quinta Inn). © **801/371-0648.** www.rubyriver.com. Reservations not accepted, but you can call ahead to get on the waiting list. Main courses $7–$18 lunch, $12–$35 dinner. AE, DISC, MC, V. Mon–Thurs 11am–10pm; Fri–Sat 11am–11pm; Sun 1–9pm. Just north of I-15 exit 269.

Sensuous Sandwich 🍴 SANDWICHES   At this speedy, kitsch- and Polaroid-laden sandwich shop, you can eat at one of the tables, clad in cartoons and unusual news clippings, or you can take your selection to go. All sandwiches come with the usual condiments, including spicy brown mustard and lettuce, as well as extras such as horseradish, olives, avocado, green pepper, and cheese. Top of the line is, of course, the Sensuous Sandwich, with ham, turkey, roast beef, and jack cheese. Also available are veggie, pastrami, crab, chicken breast, and tuna, as well as salads. No alcohol is served. This downtown spot is especially busy; a second location is at 378 E. University Pkwy., Orem (© **801/225-9475**).

163 W. Center St. © **801/377-9244.** www.sensuoussandwich.com. Sandwiches by the inch: $2.70–$12 (4–24 in.). MC, V. Mon–Sat 10:30am–8pm. From I-15 exit 265A, follow Center St. east.

Provo After Dark

The **Brigham Young University Theatre,** on the BYU campus (© **801/422-4322;** www.byuarts.com), presents more than a dozen theatrical productions each year.

From summer through early fall, you can see live musicals and concerts under the stars at the **SCERA Shell Theatre,** 699 S. State St., in SCERA Park, Orem (© **801/ 225-2569;** www.scera.org). The season usually includes several locally produced Broadway musicals, plus a variety of concerts, from pop to country to classical.

There is a downtown bar and rock venue, **A. Beuford Gifford's Libation Emporium,** 190 W. Center St. (© **801/373-1200;** www.abgsbar.com).

TIMPANOGOS CAVE NATIONAL MONUMENT

20 miles N of Provo, 35 miles S of Salt Lake City

This national monument is actually composed of three caves—Hansen, Middle, and Timpanogos—that are linked together by man-made tunnels. Martin Hansen discovered the first cavern in 1887 while tracking a mountain lion. The other two were reported in the early 1910s, and the connecting tunnels were constructed in the 1930s. The caves are filled with 47 kinds of formations, from stalactites and stalagmites to draperies and helictites. The caves aren't easy to reach, but their beauty and variety make them worth the rough 1½-hour trek to the mouth.

Essentials

The caves are accessible only on guided tours from early May to mid-October, daily from 7:30am to 4:30pm (8am–3:30pm after Labor Day). The caves close in winter because snow and ice make the access trail too hazardous. The steep trail is not navigable by wheelchair or stroller.

GETTING THERE/ACCESS POINTS   From Provo, head north on I-15 to exit 284, then east on Utah 92 to the visitor center, which is on the south side of the road. For a beautiful but slow drive, when you leave the caves, continue east and then south on Utah 92 through American Fork Canyon, which is narrow and winding, and turn west on U.S. 189 back to Provo. From Salt Lake City, take I-15 south to exit 287, and proceed as above.

INFORMATION/VISITOR CENTER   Contact **Timpanogos Cave National Monument** at R.R. 3, Box 200, American Fork, UT 84003 (© **801/756-5238** or 801/756-5239 in winter; www.nps.gov/tica). The visitor center is on the south side of

Utah 92. It is open May to Labor Day daily from 7am to 5:30pm, and Labor Day to mid-October daily from 8am to 5pm.

Note that parking at the visitor center is limited for large vehicles, such as motor homes over 20 feet. Although small, the visitor center offers a short film about the caves, a few explanatory displays and booklets, and postcards for sale. A snack bar and gift shop are next to the center, as well as two picnic areas located along the shady banks of the American Fork River. One is across from the visitor center; a larger one, with fire grills and restrooms, is about a quarter-mile west.

FEES & REGULATIONS   One-hour cave tours cost $7 for adults, $5 for children 6 to 15, $3 for children 3 to 5, and free for children 2 and under; 90-minute "Introduction to Caving" tours, available only to those 14 and older, cost $15 per person. The U.S. Forest Service also charges a $6 per vehicle fee to enter American Fork Canyon, where the national monument is located. Pets are not allowed on the trail or in the caves.

Exploring the Monument

The only way to see the caves is on a ranger-guided tour. Allow about 3 hours total for the basic cave tour—1½ hours hiking up, an hour in the caves, and 30 to 45 minutes hiking back down. The tours are limited to 20 persons and often fill up early in the morning, so it's best to call ahead and reserve your space with a credit card. The "Introduction to Caving" tours are about a half-hour longer and are limited to five people. Reservations are required. The temperature inside the caves is around 45°F (7°C; about the same as a refrigerator), so take a jacket or sweatshirt.

THE HIKE TO THE CAVES   The change in elevation between the visitor center (at about 5,600 ft.) and the cave entrance is 1,065 feet, and the steep, albeit paved, trail is 1.5 miles long; it's a physically demanding walk, but quite rewarding. The trail should not be attempted by anyone with breathing, heart, or walking difficulties. Wear good walking shoes and carry water and perhaps a snack.

This is a self-guided hike, so you can travel at your own pace, stopping at the benches along the way to rest and enjoy the views of the canyon, the Wasatch Range, and Utah Valley. A trail guide, available at the visitor center, will help you identify the wildflowers growing amid the Douglas fir, white fir, maple, and oak trees. You'll also spot chipmunks, ground squirrels, lizards, and myriad birds along the way. Restrooms are available at the cave entrance, but not inside the cave or along the trail.

TOURING THE CAVES   The basic ranger-guided cave tour is along a surfaced, well-lit, and fairly level route. You enter at the natural entrance to Hansen Cave and continue through Hansen, Middle, and Timpanogos Caves. Nature decorated the limestone chambers with delicately colored stalactites, stalagmites, draperies, graceful flowstone, and helictites (curvy formations for which the caves are famous), all in soft greens, reds, yellows, and white. The huge cave formation of linked stalactites at the Great Heart of Timpanogos is quite impressive, and the profusion of bizarre, brilliant white helictites in the Chimes Chamber of Timpanogos is stunning. Mirrorlike cave pools reflect the formations. The "Introduction to Caving" tours ($15 per person) take you to less developed sections, and require some crawling through tight places.

Bring high-speed film or a flash if you're taking photos; tripods are not allowed. Remember that the formations are fragile and easily damaged, even by a light touch of your hand. Also note that the oils from your skin will change the chemical makeup of the formations.

DINOSAURS & NATURAL WONDERS IN UTAH'S NORTHEAST CORNER

U tah has more than its share of natural treasures, with Zion and Bryce Canyon national parks and the other wonderful red-rock areas of southern Utah springing to mind first. But tucked away in the state's far northeastern corner, more rugged and less accessible, lies a playground of great scenic beauty, filled with fascinating historic (and prehistoric) sites. And you won't have to fight throngs of tourists here: This land where the dinosaurs once roamed is still relatively undiscovered and unspoiled.

VERNAL: GATEWAY TO DINOSAUR NATIONAL MONUMENT

175 miles E of Salt Lake City

A perfect base for exploring Dinosaur National Monument—just 20 miles from town—and Ashley National Forest, Vernal (at 5,280 ft. in elevation) is the largest community in the region. You'll find all the services you might need, as well as a few attractions that serve as a good introduction to the compelling geologic and natural history of the area. It's also emerging as a mountain-biking destination for those who have ridden southern Utah's slickrock and are looking for new terrain to pedal.

Essentials

GETTING THERE From Heber City, U.S. 40 leads east, past Strawberry Reservoir (there's world-class fishing here if you have time to stop; p. 135) and through Duchesne and Roosevelt, each of which has

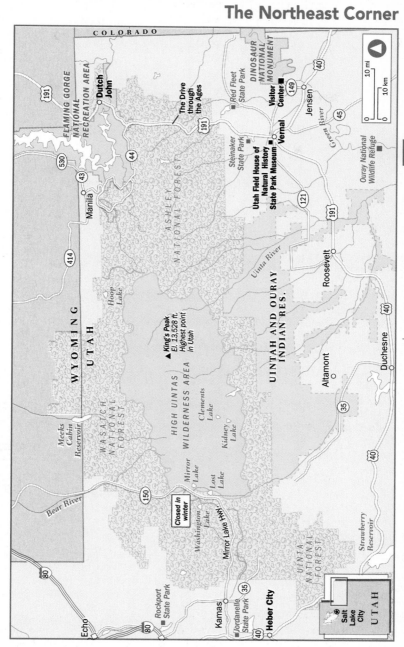

a few motels, restaurants, and services, before reaching Vernal (158 miles from Heber City).

From I-70, take exit 157 west of Green River and follow U.S. 6/191 north 68 miles through Price and Helper, branching northeast above Helper to follow U.S. 191 for 44 beautiful, mountainous miles to Duchesne. Then take U.S. 40 east for 58 miles to Vernal.

The **Vernal Regional Airport** (© 435/789-3400) is located about 1½ miles southeast of the center of town, with flights to and from Denver year-round on **Great Lakes Airlines** (© 800/554-5111 or 307/433-2899; www.greatlakesav.com).

VISITOR INFORMATION Information on area lodging, dining, and recreational facilities can be obtained from **Northeastern Utah's Dinosaurland Travel Board,** 134 W. Main St., Ste. 101, Vernal, UT 84078 (© 800/477-5558 or 435/781-6765; www.dinoland.com), open Monday through Friday from 8am to 5pm. You can also get information at the **Utah Welcome Center** in Jensen, about 13 miles southeast of Vernal on U.S. 40 (© 435/789-6932), which is open in summer daily from 8am to 8pm and in winter daily from 9am to 5pm.

GETTING AROUND Car rentals are available at the airport from **Enterprise** (© 800/261-7331 or 435/781-3008) and **All Save** (© 435/789-4777; www.allsavecarrental.com). Local transportation is available 24 hours a day from **Vernal City Cab** (© 435/790-1212).

Outdoor Pursuits

In addition to the outdoor recreation areas discussed here, see the sections "Dinosaur National Monument" and "Flaming Gorge National Recreation Area," later in this chapter. **Basin Sports,** 511 W. Main St., in Vernal (© 435/789-2199), is a good place to stock up on gear.

ASHLEY NATIONAL FOREST

This vast forest encompasses more than a million acres of beautiful mountain country, including Flaming Gorge National Recreation Area (p. 159) and the High Uintas Wilderness, which is home to **Kings Peak,** Utah's tallest mountain, at 13,528 feet. Throughout the national forest are numerous opportunities for hiking, backpacking, fishing, camping, cross-country skiing, and other activities. The Forest Service also rents out its guard stations and yurts, which make an excellent base for exploring the mountains north of Vernal (see "Where to Stay," below).

The two major access points are along U.S. 191 from Vernal and Utah 44 from Manila. Information is available from the **Vernal Ranger District office,** 355 N. Vernal Ave., Vernal, UT 84078 (© 435/789-1181; www.fs.fed.us/r4/ashley), open Monday through Friday from 8am to 5pm.

OURAY NATIONAL WILDLIFE REFUGE

Hundreds of species of migratory birds and waterfowl make their home in this 11,987-acre wetlands refuge, which lies south of Vernal along the Green River. A 12-mile car tour route begins at the visitor contact station, which also has hiking trails and an observation tower. In addition to a variety of birds, you're likely to see mule deer.

To get here from Vernal, take U.S. 40 west about 14 miles and turn left (south) onto Utah 88 for about 14 miles to the refuge entrance. The visitor contact station is about a mile from the entrance. Entry is free. The refuge is open daily year-round,

The Drive Through the Ages

One of the most scenic drives in the state is the Flaming Gorge–Uintas Scenic Byway—U.S. 191 from Vernal up to Manila and Flaming Gorge National Recreation Area—one of the first designated national scenic byways in the United States. The 67-mile route climbs through foothills covered with pine and juniper trees into the Uinta Mountains; signs along the way explain the evolution of the intriguing geologic formations visible along the drive. Near Flaming Gorge, you pass the billion-year-old rock core of the Uinta Mountains. Stop at some of the many turnouts for scenic views, short walks, and wild-life viewing—watch for bighorn sheep, elk, mule deer, and moose, especially in spring.

from an hour before sunrise to an hour after sunset; camping is not allowed in the refuge. Contact the refuge office, HC 69, Box 232, Randlett, UT 84063-2042 (© **435/545-2522;** http://ouray.fws.gov), for more information.

RED FLEET STATE PARK

Located 10 miles north of Vernal, at 4335 N. U.S. 191, this scenic park—which looks like a junior version of Lake Powell—offers fishing, boating, swimming, and camping, plus about 200 well-preserved dinosaur tracks. The 750-acre Red Fleet Reservoir was named for three large deep-red sandstone rock formations that resemble the hulls of ships. You'll encounter sandy beaches, rock cliffs, and plenty of open water; wildlife such as rabbits, ground squirrels, mule deer, and the occasional bobcat; and good fishing for rainbow and brown trout, bluegill, and bass. On chilly mornings, golden eagles are sometimes spotted sunning themselves on rock outcroppings; other birds that frequent the park include hawks, vultures, owls, and bluebirds.

The **dinosaur tracks,** which are about 200 million years old, are found on a large slab of rock that slants down into the water and is located across the reservoir from the park's boat ramp. The greatest number of tracks can be seen when the water level is low, from late summer through winter. You can reach the tracks by boat or by swimming (wear a life jacket so you can return easily), or via a 1.5-mile hike (one-way) from a Bureau of Land Management road. To reach the BLM road, continue north along U.S. 191 1 mile past the turnoff to Red Fleet. Turn right (east) just past mile marker 212, cross a cattle guard, and drive 2⅓ miles on the paved road to the trail head, a small turnout with a sign at the trail; a stock tank sits across the road, partly hidden by bushes and trees. Allow about 2 hours for the moderate hike over low, sandy hills. In winter, when the reservoir is frozen, it's a quick walk from the boat ramp across the ice to the tracks (provided it's thick enough to cross—please use caution).

Park facilities include the boat ramp, fish-cleaning stations, an RV dump station, and a 29-site campground. Although the campground is essentially a parking lot, it does offer splendid panoramic views across the lake. There are also five sites with full hookups, grassy areas for tents, plus tables and fire pits, and modern restrooms but no showers. Camping costs $13 for tents or $25 for RV hookups; the day-use fee is $7 per vehicle. Gates are open daily from 6am to 10pm in summer, 8am to 5pm in winter. Call © **435/789-4432** for information, 800/322-3770 for campsite reservations. The Utah State Parks website is www.stateparks.utah.gov.

STEINAKER STATE PARK

Steinaker offers a sandy swimming beach, good fishing for rainbow trout and large-mouth bass, and an attractive campground, just 7 miles north of Vernal at 4335 N. U.S. 191. This reservoir, which covers 780 acres when full, is also popular with water-skiers and boaters. Unfortunately, no rental facilities are nearby.

Wildlife here includes mule deer, jackrabbits, cottontails, ground squirrels, porcupines, and an occasional elk or bobcat. Migratory waterfowl are often seen in spring and fall, and the park also attracts American robins, pheasants, and golden eagles. The landscape is composed primarily of juniper and sagebrush, with cottonwoods and aspen trees near the lake. Spring usually brings out an abundance of wildflowers, such as Indian paintbrush, larkspur, and sego lily. Several unmarked hiking trails—ask a ranger for directions—and additional hiking opportunities are nearby on property managed by the Bureau of Land Management.

Facilities include a boat ramp, fish-cleaning station, and RV dump station. The tree-shaded campground contains 31 sites (five with RV hookups) and modern restrooms with hot showers. Picnic tables, barbecue grills, and fire pits are available. Camping costs $13 for tents or $25 for a site with RV hookups; the day-use fee is $7. Gates are open daily from 6am to 10pm in summer, from 8am to 5pm in winter. Call ⓒ **435/789-4432** for information, 800/322-3770 for campsite reservations. The Utah State Parks website is www.stateparks.utah.gov.

What to See & Do in Town

Daughters of Utah Pioneers Museum   This small museum offers a display of pioneer relics and photos, and a history of the settling of the area from the mid-1800s. Allow half an hour.

186 S. 500 West. ⓒ **435/789-0352.** www.dupinternational.org. Donations requested. June–Aug Tues–Sat 10am–4pm. Closed rest of year.

Utah Field House of Natural History State Park Museum ★ ☺   Centered around a 22,000-sq.-foot museum with a theater, this park gives visitors a close-up look at a huge dinosaur skeleton and a number of exhibits on paleontology, geology, and the Fremont and Ute cultures. Kids will love the **Dinosaur Garden ★★**, with 18 life-size models of dinosaurs and other prehistoric creatures in a delightful garden that simulates the dinosaurs' actual habitat. Start your visit at the theater for a short film about paleontologists at work in the field. The gift shop sells dinosaur-related souvenirs and books. Allow at least 1 hour.

496 E. Main St. ⓒ **435/789-3799.** www.stateparks.utah.gov. $6 adults, $3 children 6–12, free for children 5 and under. Mon–Sat 9am–5pm. Closed Thanksgiving, Christmas, and New Year's Day.

Western Heritage Museum ★   This well-organized and attractive museum is a good stop for those interested in the prehistoric Fremont Indians—in fact, it contains one of the country's best collections of Fremont Indian objects. It also has 1880s Ute artifacts and displays of historic rifles, fossils, and rocks. Pioneer life is depicted in a country store; a blacksmith shop with tack and saddles; a one-room schoolhouse; a barbershop; and a bedroom, kitchen, and parlor. Clothing fashions from 1880 to 1930 are also on display. The museum features changing art exhibits, and early horse-drawn wagons and farm equipment are on display outside. Allow an hour.

Western Park, 328 E. 200 South. ⓒ **435/789-7399.** Free admission. Memorial Day to Labor Day Mon–Fri 9am–6pm, Sat 10am–4pm; rest of year Mon–Fri 9am–5pm, Sat 10am–2pm.

Where to Stay

The town of Vernal has more than a dozen motels, including chain and franchise properties such as **Best Western Antlers,** 423 W. Main St. (© 800/780-7234 or 435/789-1202; www.bestwestern.com), **Best Western Dinosaur Inn,** 251 E. Main St. (© 800/780-7234 or 435/789-2660; www.bestwestern.com), **Holiday Inn Express,** 1515 W. Main St. (© 800/718-8466 or 435/789-4654; www.hiexpress. com), and **Super 8,** 1624 W. Main St. (© 800/800-8000 or 435/789-4326; www. super8.com). Among the independents, the best option is the **Weston Plaza Hotel,** 1684 W. Main St. (© 435/789-9550; www.westonplazavernal.com). Rates for double rooms range from $70 to $150, with the highest rates in summer. A good budget option is the **Sage Motel,** 54 W. Main St. (© 800/760-1442 or 435/789-1442; www.vernalmotels.com), with double rates of $40 to $70. There is also a B&B, the **Jensen Inn,** 5056 S. 9500 East, Jensen (© 435/789-5905; www.thejenseninn. com), not far from the boundary to Dinosaur National Monument. Rooms start at $95 for two people (the suite runs $150 and up), breakfast included, and it also has a tepee and a campground. Room tax adds about 9%.

Another lodging option in this area is to stay at one of the **U.S. Forest Service's guard stations or yurts ★**, located in spectacular forest settings north of Vernal in the Ashley National Forest. Rates range from $25 to $40 per night, and the facilities offer a range of amenities and sleeping capacities and are available year-round. For information, contact the Vernal Ranger District office (© 435/789-1181; www.fs.fed.us/r4/ashley); for reservations, call © 877/444-6777 or visit www. recreation.gov.

CAMPING

Among the area campgrounds with full RV hookups and hot showers is **Dinosaurland KOA,** 930 N. Vernal Ave., Vernal (© 435/789-2148; www.dinokoa.com), which is open from April through October. It has 65 RV sites and 15 grassy tent sites, with rates from $25 for tent sites and $32 to $38 for RV sites. This KOA also has seven cabins for $60 double and two deluxe cottages for $130 double and up. Both **Red Fleet State Park** (p. 153) and **Steinaker State Park** (p. 154) also have camping.

Where to Dine

Bakeries and delicatessens can be found at **Davis Jubilee,** 575 W. Main St. (© 435/789-2001), and **Smith's,** 1080 W. Main St. (© 435/789-7135).

Betty's Cafe ★ ♦ AMERICAN   This simple, down-home cafe is a local favorite, and it's easy to see why. It serves well-prepared homemade food at reasonable prices. Breakfast, which includes all the usual offerings, is served all day. Lunch fare is sandwiches, half- and quarter-pound burgers, plus such choices as chicken-fried steak, liver and onions, catfish, and hamburger steak. No alcoholic beverages are served, but the pie selection is great.

416 W. Main St. © **435/781-2728.** Main courses $4–$13. MC, V. Mon–Fri 6am–2pm; Sat–Sun 6am–noon.

Dino Brew Haus ♦ AMERICAN   A bare-bones beer joint with Salt Lake's Squatters microbrew on tap, the Dino Brew Haus isn't much to look at—with concrete walls, a pool table, and a slightly woodsy feel—but it serves reasonably good burgers and barbecue, as well as salads and sandwiches, including a portobello mush-room. It also has a patio out back and serves as the home base for a river-rafting company, **Dinosaur Expeditions** (℡ **800/345-7238;** www.dinoadv.com).

550 E. Main St. ℡ **435/781-0717.** Main courses $8–$17. AE, DISC, MC, V. Daily 11am–9pm.

7-11 Ranch Restaurant ★ AMERICAN A good family restaurant offering home-style food in a comfortable, Western-style setting, the 7-11 Ranch Restaurant had its beginnings in 1933, when Warren "Fat" Belcher sold a cow and bought a hot dog stand. Now owned by Belcher's daughter Connie and her husband, Jerry Pope, the restaurant has changed a bit—you won't even find hot dogs on the menu—but you can count on friendly service and a wide range of American favorites. Choose from a variety of burgers—including a huge 1-pound killer—plus hot and cold sand-wiches, deep-fried and grilled halibut and other seafood, excellent chef's salads, homemade chili, pork chops, and chicken in a variety of forms. There are also steaks, barbecued beef or pork ribs, and prime ribs on Fridays. Breakfasts consist of the usual American favorites. There is a large gift shop in the front with all sorts of dinosaur souvenirs.

77 E. Main St. ℡ **435/789-1170.** Main courses $3–$8.50 breakfast, $6–$19 lunch and dinner. AE, DISC, MC, V. Mon–Sat 6am–10pm.

DINOSAUR NATIONAL MONUMENT

20 miles E of Vernal, 195 miles E of Salt Lake City

In some ways, this park is two separate experiences: a look at the lost world of dino-saurs on one hand, and a scenic wonderland of colorful rock, deep river canyons, and a forest of Douglas fir on the other.

About 150 million years ago, the region was a warm land of ferns, conifers, grasses, ponds, and rivers. This made it a suitable habitat for dinosaurs, including vegetarians such as diplodocus, apatosaurus, and stegosaurus; and sharp-toothed carnivores, such as allosaurus, that hunted their vegetarian cousins. When these huge creatures died, most of their skeletons decayed and disappeared, but in at least one spot, flood-waters washed dinosaur carcasses into the bottom of a river. Here they were pre-served in sand and covered with sediment, creating the largest quarry of Jurassic-period dinosaur bones ever discovered.

But visitors who limit their trip to the Dinosaur Quarry, fascinating as it is, miss quite a bit. Encompassing 325 square miles of stark canyons at the confluence of two rivers, the monument also offers hiking trails, pioneer homesteads, thousand-year-old rock art, spectacular panoramic vistas, wildlife-watching opportunities, and the thrills of white-water rafting.

The Yampa, Green, and smaller rivers are responsible for the area's fertility, creat-ing microclimates that support hanging gardens of mosses and ferns, cottonwoods, and even an occasional Douglas fir—all just yards from the predominant landscape of sagebrush, cactus, and dwarfed piñon and juniper trees. Wildlife includes species that can survive the harsh extremes of the high desert climate—bighorn sheep, coy-otes, rabbits, and snakes—as well as mule deer, beavers, and porcupines along the riverbanks. Birds that are occasionally spotted include peregrine falcons, sage grouse, and Canada geese.

Essentials

GETTING THERE/ACCESS POINTS/VISITOR CENTERS Straddling the Utah-Colorado state line, Dinosaur National Monument is accessible via two main roads—one from each state—that don't connect inside the monument.

The **visitor center** is 20 miles east of Vernal. To get here, take U.S. 40 to Jensen and head north on Utah 149 for 7 miles. The main visitor center at the Dinosaur Quarry closed in 2006 due to structural concerns and was replaced by a stunning new facility that opened in fall 2011. It is open daily from 9am to 5pm, with extended summer hours if staffing allows. It is closed New Year's Day, Thanksgiving, and Christmas.

Administrative offices and a small **visitor center** are located about 2 miles east of the town of Dinosaur, Colorado, at the intersection of U.S. 40 and Harpers Corner Drive. This visitor center offers a short slide program; hours are daily 9am to 4pm in summer (closed in winter). The center is closed for federal holidays.

Several other monument entrances exist, all without visitor centers: At the far eastern edge of the monument off U.S. 40, an entry road leads to Deerlodge Park (open in summer only); at the northern tip, off Colo. 318, a road goes to the Gates of Lodore; just inside the Utah border at Jones Hole Fish Hatchery, a road leads into the park via the Jones Hole Road from Vernal; and at the Rainbow Park section, you'll find a park entry road off Island Park Road (impassable when wet) from the monument's western edge.

INFORMATION Contact **Dinosaur National Monument,** 4545 E. U.S. 40, Dinosaur, CO 81610-9724 (✆ **435/781-7700** or 970/374-3000; www.nps.gov/dino). In addition, the nonprofit **Intermountain Natural History Association,** 1291 E. U.S. 40, Vernal, UT 84078 (✆ **800/845-3466;** www.inhaweb.com), offers numerous publications, maps, posters, and videos on the park and its geology, wildlife, history, and dinosaurs. Information on area lodging, dining, and recreational facilities can be obtained from the **Dinosaurland Travel Board** (p. 152).

FEES, BACKCOUNTRY PERMITS, REGULATIONS & SAFETY The entry fee, charged only at the main Utah entrance, is $10 per vehicle or $5 per person for those on foot, motorcycle, or bicycle, for up to 1 week. Camping fees are additional (free–$12 a night); backcountry overnight camping permits, although free, are required and available from park rangers.

Regulations forbid damaging or taking anything, particularly fossils and other natural, historical, and archaeological items. Off-road driving is not permitted. Dogs must be leashed at all times. Pets are not allowed in buildings, on trails, more than 100 feet from developed roads, or on river trips.

Rangers warn that the rivers are not safe for swimming or wading; the water is icy cold, and the current is stronger than it appears.

SEASONS/AVOIDING THE CROWDS Summer is the busiest and hottest time of the year at Dinosaur National Monument, with daytime temperatures often soaring into the upper 90s (30s Celsius). Winters are a lot quieter but can be cold, with fog, snow, and temperatures below zero (−18°C). The best times to visit are spring, although you should be prepared for rain showers, and fall—perhaps the very best time—when the cottonwood trees turn a brilliant gold.

RANGER PROGRAMS Rangers present a variety of activities in summer, including evening campfire programs; check the schedules posted at either visitor center.

Seeing the Highlights

Those with only a short amount of time should make their first stop the shiny new **Quarry Exhibit Hall,** accessible via shuttles departing from the (likewise new) Quarry Visitor Center. This is the only place in the monument where you can see dinosaur bones. This area is believed to be one of the world's most concentrated and accessible deposits of the fossilized remains of dinosaurs, crocodiles, turtles, and clams. The exhibit hall's fossil wall—which looks like a long slab of frozen pudding with bones sticking out of it—contains some 1,500 fossils. Models show what pale-ontologists believe these dinosaurs looked like when they still had their skin, and other exhibits detail life in the Jurassic.

After spending about an hour in the quarry area, drive the **Tour of the Tilted Rocks,** which takes an hour or two. Then, if time remains, or if you're heading east into Colorado anyway, take another few hours to drive the scenic **Harpers Corner Drive** (see the next section for descriptions of both drives).

Exploring by Car

Drives in both the Utah and Colorado sections of the park allow motorists to see spectacular scenery in relative solitude. Brochures for each of the following drives are available at the visitor centers.

From the quarry area on the Utah side of the park, the **Tour of the Tilted Rocks** along Cub Creek Road is a 26-mile round-trip drive that's suitable for most passenger cars. This route takes you to 1,000-year-old rock art left by the Fremont people, a pioneer homestead, and views of nearby mountains and the Green River. Watch for prairie dogs both alongside and on the road. Although mostly paved, the last 2 miles of the road are dirt and narrow, and may be dusty or muddy. Allow 1 to 2 hours.

For the best scenic views, drive to Colorado and take the **Harpers Corner Drive.** This paved, 62-mile round-trip has several overlooks offering panoramic views into the gorges carved by the Yampa and Green rivers, a look at the derby-shaped Plug Hat Butte, and close-ups of a variety of other colorful rock formations. The drive also provides access to the easy .25-mile round-trip Plug Hat Nature Trail and the mod-erately difficult 2-mile round-trip Harpers Corner Trail (p. 159). Allow about 2 hours for the drive, more if you plan to do some hiking.

Outdoor Pursuits

BOATING   To many people, the best way to see this beautiful, rugged country is from the river, where you can admire the scenery while crashing through thrilling white water and floating over smooth, silent stretches. About a dozen outfitters are authorized to **run the Yampa and Green rivers ★** through the monument, offering trips ranging from 1 to 5 days, usually from mid-May to mid-September. Among companies providing river trips are **Hatch River Expeditions** (✆ **800/342-8243** or 435/789-4316; www.donhatchrivertrips.com) and **Dinosaur River Expeditions** (✆ **800/345-7238** or 435/781-0717; www.dinoadv.com). Prices start at about $80 for a 1-day trip. A complete list of authorized river-running companies is available from monument headquarters (see "Visitor Information" on p. 152).

FISHING   The catch is mostly catfish in the Green and Yampa rivers, although there are also some trout. Several endangered species of fish—including the razor-back sucker and humpback chub—must be returned unharmed to the water if caught. Either a Utah or Colorado fishing license (or both) is required, depending on where you plan to fish.

HIKING   Because most visitors spend their time at the quarry and along the scenic drives, hikers willing to exert a little effort can discover spectacular and dramatic views of the colorful canyons while enjoying an isolated and quiet wilderness experience. The best times for hiking are spring and fall, but even then, hikers should carry at least a gallon of water per person, per day.

In addition to several developed trails, experienced backcountry hikers with the appropriate maps can explore miles of unspoiled canyons and rock benches. Ask rangers about the numerous possibilities.

In the Utah section of the park, you can search out extreme solitude along the **Sound of Silence Trail,** a moderate-to-difficult 3-mile hike that leaves Cub Creek Road about 2 miles east of the Dinosaur Quarry. This trail is designed to help you learn how to find your own way in the desert, and is not always easy to follow.

The **Desert Voices Nature Trail,** a self-guided nature trail near the quarry, offers sweeping panoramic views and a section with signs created by kids for kids. This 1.5-mile (round-trip) hike is moderately difficult.

Visitors to the Colorado side of the park enjoy the **Cold Desert Trail,** which begins at the headquarters' visitor center. This easy .5-mile round-trip trail offers a good introduction to the natural history of this arid environment.

Panoramic vistas await visitors on the **Plug Hat Nature Trail,** an easy .25-mile round-trip hike that introduces you to the interactions between plants and animals in the piñon juniper forest. It's located along the Harpers Corner Scenic Drive.

The very popular **Harpers Corner Trail ★** begins at the end of the Harpers Corner Scenic Drive. This 2-mile round-trip hike is moderately difficult but highly recommended for a magnificent view of the deep river canyons.

Camping

The **Green River Campground,** 5 miles east of the Dinosaur Quarry within park boundaries, has 80 RV and tent sites, modern restrooms, drinking water, tables, and fireplaces, but no showers or RV hookups. Park rangers often give campfire talks. Cost is $12 per night; it's open mid-April into October and reservations are not available.

Several smaller campgrounds with limited facilities are also available in the monument, with fees ranging from nothing to $8; check with the visitor centers.

FLAMING GORGE NATIONAL RECREATION AREA ★★

41 miles N of Vernal, 210 miles E of Salt Lake City

Tucked away in the far northeast corner of Utah and stretching up into Wyoming is **Flaming Gorge National Recreation Area,** one of the region's most scenic areas and a wonderful place for outdoor recreation. A dam was built on the Green River for flood control, water storage, and the generation of electricity, but a wonderful side effect was the creation of a huge and gorgeous lake—some 91 miles long, with more than 300 miles of shoreline—that has become one of the prime fishing and boating destinations of the region.

Here is some of the best fishing in the West, well over 100 miles of hiking and mountain-biking trails, and hundreds of camp and picnic sites. It's a boater's paradise, filled with everything from kayaks and canoes to ski and fishing boats to pontoons to gigantic houseboats with everything on board (including the kitchen sink).

Named by Major John Wesley Powell during his exploration of the Green and Colorado rivers in 1869, Flaming Gorge has a rugged, wild beauty that comes alive when the rising or setting sun paints the red rocks surrounding the lake in a fiery, brilliant palette. It's a land of clear blue water, colorful rocks, tall cliffs, dark forests, hot summer sun, and cold winter wind. It'll take more than a dam to tame Flaming Gorge.

Essentials

Flaming Gorge National Recreation Area lies in the northeast corner of Utah, crossing into the southwest corner of Wyoming. The dam and main visitor center, in the southeast section of the national recreation area, are 41 miles north of Vernal (210 miles east of Salt Lake City via U.S. 40).

GETTING THERE   From Vernal and other points south, take U.S. 191 north to its intersection with Utah 44 at the southern edge of the reservoir. U.S. 191 goes up the east side of the reservoir, leading to the dam and the community of Dutch John; Utah 44 goes around the reservoir on the west side, eventually ending at the village of Manila. Both of these towns offer accommodations, restaurants, fuel, and other services.

From I-80 in Wyoming, follow U.S. 191 south around the reservoir's east side to the dam; or Wyo. 530 and Utah highways 43 and 44 to Manila and the west and south sides of the reservoir.

INFORMATION/VISITOR CENTER   The recreation area is administered by the Ashley National Forest. For information, contact the **Flaming Gorge National Recreation Area,** P.O. Box 279, Manila, UT 84046 (© **435/784-3445;** www. fs.usda.gov/r4/ashley). The **Intermountain Natural History Association,** 1291 E. U.S. 40, Vernal, UT 84078 (© **800/845-3466;** www.inhaweb.com), sells maps, books, and other publications.

The **Flaming Gorge Dam Visitor Center** (© **435/885-3135**), along U.S. 191 on the east side of the recreation area, is open daily 8am to 6pm in summer, 9am to 5pm spring and fall, and is open weekends only November through March. You can get information on the geology, history, flora, and fauna of the area; the construction of the dam; and facilities and recreation possibilities. Free dam tours lasting 45 minutes to an hour are conducted from 9am to 3pm in summer only.

FEES & REGULATIONS   Entry to the recreation area is $5 for 1 day or $15 for up to 7 days. Administered by the U.S. Forest Service, regulations here are based mostly on common sense, and are aimed at preserving water quality and protecting the forest and historic sites. Utah and Wyoming fishing and boating regulations apply in those states' sections of the recreation area, and the appropriate fishing licenses are required. Dogs are allowed on hiking trails but are not permitted in buildings and should be leashed at all times.

SEASONS/AVOIDING THE CROWDS   As one would expect, summer is the busy season at this major boating destination, when both the air and water are at their warmest. This is the best time to come for watersports, and with elevations from 5,600 to over 8,000 feet, it never gets as hot here as it does in many other parts of Utah. Although summer is the busiest time of year, this remains a relatively undiscovered destination, and you will likely have no trouble finding campsites, lodging, or boat rentals. Hikers will enjoy the area in fall. During the cold, snowy winter, this is a popular snowshoeing, cross-country skiing, and ice-fishing destination.

Exploring Flaming Gorge by Car

Numerous viewpoints are situated along U.S. 191 and Utah 44 in the Utah section of Flaming Gorge; especially dramatic is the **Red Canyon Overlook** on the southern edge, where a rainbow of colors adorns 1,000-foot-tall cliffs. Another great overlook is **Dowd Mountain.** In Wyoming, highways are farther from the lake, offering few opportunities to see the river and its canyons.

Sheep Creek Canyon, south of Manila on the western side, has been designated a special geological area by the Forest Service because of its dramatically twisted and upturned rocks. A mostly paved 11-mile loop road cuts off from Utah 44, offering a half-hour tour of this beautiful, narrow canyon, with its lavish display of rocks that have eroded into intricate patterns, a process that began with the uplifting of the Uinta Mountains millions of years ago. This loop may be closed in winter; check at the visitor center before heading out.

Outdoor Pursuits

BIKING A number of mountain-biking trails provide splendid views of the recreation area's scenery, especially in the Utah section. Bikes are permitted in most of Flaming Gorge and adjacent Ashley National Forest, except in the High Uintas Wilderness, where all wheeled vehicles are prohibited. Bikes are also restricted from Memorial Day to Labor Day on a section of the Little Hole National Recreation Trail along the Green River below the dam, due to very heavy use by anglers and hikers. Keep in mind that mountain bikers here often share trails with hikers, horses, and four-wheelers. A free mountain-biking brochure is available at visitor centers.

For a scenic and fairly easy ride, try the 5-mile one-way **Red Canyon Rim Trail.** This single track follows the south rim of the canyon, providing terrific views of the lake 1,700 feet below. Deer and elk are frequently seen in the forested areas. Watch also for interpretive signs on area wildlife and the ecosystem. Trail heads and parking are located at Red Canyon Visitor Center, Red Canyon Lodge, and Greendale Overlook.

Death Valley Trail, a moderately difficult 15-mile round-trip ride, offers good views of the Uinta Mountains and ends with a fine view of the lake from the top of Sheep Creek Hill. The trail head is located along Utah 44, south of Manila, at milepost 16.5.

Rentals of full-suspension mountain bikes are available at **Red Canyon Lodge,** in Dutch John (© **435/889-3759;** www.redcanyonlodge.com), at rates of $10 for 1 hour, $20 for a half-day, and $35 for a full day. The lodge also sponsors a mountain-bike festival each year in August. In Vernal, head to **Altitude Cycle,** 580 E. Main St. (© **435/781-2295;** www.altitudecycle.com), for gear, service, and advice.

BOATING & HOUSEBOATING Boaters get to enjoy a unique perspective of some memorable scenery, with magnificent fiery red canyons surrounding the lake in the Utah section, and the wide-open Wyoming badlands farther north.

Three marinas on **Lake Flaming Gorge** provide boat rentals, fuel, launching ramps, and boating and fishing supplies. **Cedar Springs Marina** (© **435/889-3795;**

Flaming Gorge is one of the best places in Utah to see a wide variety of wildlife. Boaters should watch for osprey, peregrine falcons, swifts, and swallows along the cliffs. Bighorn sheep are sometimes spotted clambering on the rocky cliffs on the north side of the lake in spring and early summer. On land, be on the lookout for pronghorn antelope year-round along the west side of the lake, particularly in Lucerne Valley and in the campground. Hikers on the Little Hole National Recreation Trail should keep their eyes peeled for a variety of birds, including bald eagles in winter.

www.cedarspringsmarina.com) is located 2 miles west of Flaming Gorge Dam; **Lucerne Valley Marina** (✆ 435/784-3483; www.flaminggorge.com) is on the west side of the lake, 7 miles east of Manila; and **Buckboard Marina** (✆ 307/875-6927; www.buckboardmarina.com) is also on the west side of the lake, off Wyo. 530, 22 miles north of Manila.

Nine boat ramps serve those who bring their own craft; boat and water-ski rentals are available at all three marinas. Although types of boats and costs vary, a 14-foot fishing boat with a small outboard motor usually costs about $130 per day, a 17- or 18-foot ski boat with a powerful outboard motor costs about $250 to $350 per day, and a 24-foot pontoon boat with a 50-horsepower outboard motor will cost about $225 to $250 per day. Partial-day rentals are also available. At Lucerne Valley Marina, a 36-foot houseboat costs about $1,000 for 3 nights during the summer, with discounts in spring and fall; a 52-footer is also available for about $2,000 for 3 nights in the summer. For all boat rentals, life jackets are included but fuel is extra.

Nonmotorized boating is permitted on a 20-acre private lake at Red Canyon Lodge (p. 164), where you can rent canoes, rowboats, and paddle boats. Rates start at $10 an hour and range up to $50 for a day.

Dinosaur River Expeditions (✆ 800/345-7238 or 435/781-0717; www.dinoadv.com), in Vernal, offers a 1-day raft trip for $75 for adults and $54 for kids 7 to 12.

FISHING You might want to bring along a muscular friend if you plan to fish Lake Flaming Gorge, which is famous as a place to catch record-breaking trout, such as the 51-pound, 8-ounce lake (Mackinaw) trout caught in 1988; the 26-pound, 2-ounce rainbow caught in 1979; and the 33-pound, 10-ounce German brown caught in 1977. You'll encounter other cold-water species such as smallmouth bass and kokanee salmon. Fishing is popular year-round, although ice-fishermen are warned to make sure the ice is strong enough to hold them.

Cedar Springs and Lucerne Valley marinas (see "Boating & Houseboating," above) offer a variety of fishing guide services. Typical rates for one or two people in a guided trip aboard a sportfishing boat are $300 for a half-day, including fishing gear but not fishing licenses. Also providing guided fishing trips, in a 28-foot sportfishing boat with state-of-the-art fish-finding and GPS equipment, is Kyle Edwards of **Conquest Expeditions ★★** (✆ 801/244-9948; www.conquestexpeditions.com). Rates for a 4-hour fishing trip, with all equipment (but not fishing licenses), are $275 for one or two people and $425 for three or four people. Rates for an 8-hour fishing trip are $550 for one or two people, $650 for three or four.

Trout fishing on the Green River below the dam is also outstanding. **Flaming Gorge Recreation Services,** based in Dutch John (☎ **435/885-3191;** www.fglodge.com), offers guided fishing trips for one or two people, with rates of $350 for a half-day float trip, $425 for a full day. A complete list of guides is available at the Flaming Gorge Dam Visitor Center (p. 160).

Two private stocked lakes are also at **Red Canyon Lodge** (p. 164), one with a fully accessible fishing pier, and both open to catch-and-release fishing only. No state fishing license is needed, but a Red Canyon Lodge permit is required (free for guests, $5 for nonguests). A free kids' fishing pond is in front of the lodge's restaurant.

HIKING   Many of the trails here offer spectacular scenic views of the reservoir and its colorful canyons. Remember, though, that in most cases the trail is shared with mountain bikers and in some cases horses and four-wheel-drive vehicles as well.

The **Red Canyon Rim Trail** runs 5 miles (one-way) from the Red Canyon Visitor Center to the Greendale Rest Area, accessible from either of those points or at Green's Lake or Canyon Rim campgrounds. The trail wanders through a forest of Douglas fir and pine, with stops along the canyon rim providing outstanding views of the lake far below (see also "Biking," above).

For an easy 3-mile round-trip hike to an overlook offering a fine view of the lake, try the **Bear Canyon Bootleg Trail,** which starts just off U.S. 191 opposite Fire-fighters Memorial Campground, 3 miles south of the dam.

One trail popular with hikers is the **Little Hole National Recreation Trail,** which runs about 7 miles from the dam spillway downstream to Little Hole, with its fishing platforms and picnic areas. The trail is easy to moderate and offers splendid vistas of the Green River, which appears to be a mere ribbon of emerald when seen from the cliffs above. This is a good trail for birders, who may spot osprey in summer and bald eagles in winter.

Hikers can also use the mountain-biking trails listed above. A free hiking-trails brochure is available at the visitor centers.

HORSEBACK RIDING   Many of the more than 100 miles of trails in Flaming Gorge are open to riders. Guided rides are available from **Red Canyon Stables** at Red Canyon Lodge (p. 164), with prices starting at about $20 for a 1-hour ride and $70 for a half-day. Children must be at least 6 years old to go on rides.

SWIMMING   Sometimes you've just got to dive right in, even though the water is pretty cold. Lake Flaming Gorge has two designated swimming areas: Sunny Cove, just north of the dam, and Lucerne Beach, a mile west of Lucerne Campground. Neither has a lifeguard.

WINTER SPORTS   Ice-fishing is popular, but check with rangers first for ice conditions. Also popular from mid-January until the snow melts are cross-country skiing, snowshoeing (an excellent way to see wildlife), and snowmobiling. At Red Canyon Lodge, you can rent snowshoes for $5 per hour, $10 per half-day, or $15 per day (poles are $2 extra), and Flaming Gorge Resort rents cross-country ski packages in winter. See p. 164 for the lodges' contact information.

Man-Made Attractions

FLAMING GORGE DAM & POWER PLANT

Completed in 1963 at a cost of $50 million for the dam and another $65 million for the power plant, Flaming Gorge is part of the Colorado River Storage Project, which also includes Glen Canyon Dam on the Colorado River along the Arizona-Utah border, Navajo Dam on the San Juan River in New Mexico, and a series of three dams on the Gunnison River in Colorado. At full capacity, the lake is 91 miles long and holds almost 4 million acre-feet of water. The dam, constructed in an arch shape for strength, is 1,285 feet long and stands some 450 feet tall; its three turbine generators can produce 152,000 kilowatts of electricity, enough to take care of the needs of 210,000 people.

The dam and power plant are open for free guided tours 9am to 4pm daily from mid-March to mid-October. The total round-trip walking distance is just under half a mile. Check at the visitor center for the hours and times of the hour-long guided tours. You'll walk along the crest of the dam, and then take an elevator ride to the power plant below, where you get to see the inner workings of the hydroelectric plant, with its huge transformers, generators, and turbines.

SWETT RANCH HISTORIC SITE

This homestead, listed on the National Register of Historic Places, was constructed by Oscar Swett starting in 1909, and contains two cabins, a five-room house, a meat house, a root cellar, sheds, a granary, and a barn, built and improved upon over a period of 58 years. Swett and his wife, Emma, raised nine children here, running the 397-acre ranch using only horse and human muscle power, before selling the property in 1968. From Utah 44, take U.S. 191 north for a half-mile and turn west (left) onto Forest Road 158, which you follow 1½ miles to the ranch. The unpaved Forest Road is muddy when wet and not recommended for large RVs or trailers at any time. The ranch is open daily 10am to 5pm from Memorial Day to Labor Day; guided tours are available. Admission is free. Allow about an hour.

Where to Stay

In addition to the lodging suggestions below, see the "Where to Stay" section in "Vernal: Gateway to Dinosaur National Monument," earlier in this chapter.

Flaming Gorge Resort A location close to everything you'll want to do makes this well-maintained property a good choice for those seeking a modern motel room or a one-bedroom condominium. Motel rooms come with two queen-size beds and an optional rollaway; condo units contain one queen bed, a single, and a hide-a-bed, plus a fully equipped kitchen. There is also a "trailer suite" and a four-bedroom suite for those needing a little more room. Facilities include a restaurant that serves three meals daily, a gas station, a liquor and convenience store, and a fly and tackle shop. Guided fishing and rafting trips on the Green River are available, and the lodge offers nonmotorized watercraft rentals and mountain-bike rentals in the summer.

155 Greendale, U.S. 191 (4 miles south of Flaming Gorge Dam), Dutch John, UT 84023-9702. www. flaminggorgeresort.com. ☏ **877/348-7688** or 435/889-3773. Fax 435/889-3788. 48 units, including 27 suites. Apr–Oct $119–$159 double, $159–$249 condo or suite; Nov–Mar $99–$129 double, $129–$219 condo or suite. AE, DISC, MC, V. **Amenities:** Restaurant; bike rentals. *In room:* A/C, TV/ DVD/VCR, kitchen in condos, Wi-Fi (free).

Red Canyon Lodge ★ Open since 1930, this secluded cabin resort offers a variety of delightful handcrafted log cabins. All have private bathrooms, two queen-size beds, a separate living room, minifridges, limited cooking facilities, vaulted ceilings, and covered porches. Some also have free-standing woodstoves (firewood provided), kitchenettes, and custom wood furniture. Lower-priced units have showers only; the more expensive rooms have tub/shower combos. The lodge offers two private lakes plus a kids' fishing pond, boat and mountain-bike rentals, hiking and mountain-biking trails, horseback rides (p. 163), a restaurant, and a gift shop.

2450 W. Red Canyon Lodge (turn off Utah 44 at milepost 3.5), Dutch John, UT 84023. www.red canyonlodge.com. © **435/889-3759.** Fax 435/889-5106. 18 units. $110–$140 double. AE, DISC, MC, V. Dogs allowed (free). **Amenities:** Restaurant (see review below); bike rentals; Wi-Fi (free). *In room:* Fridge, hair dryer, kitchenette (in some), no phone.

CAMPING

U.S. Forest Service campgrounds are located throughout Flaming Gorge Recreation Area and range from primitive sites to modern facilities with showers (open in summer only) and flush toilets, but no RV hookups. Some are open year-round, others in summer only. Most sites cost $10 to $20. The more developed (and expensive) sites, including a favorite campground, Deer Run, include use of the showers (those camping in the cheap spots have to pay for a shower—bring quarters). Campsite reservations are available through the **National Recreation Reservation Service** (© **877/ 444-6777;** www.recreation.gov). Dispersed forest camping (with no facilities) is free; check with forest service personnel for suggested locations. RV dump stations are located in several locations in the recreation area (check at the visitor center).

Commercial campgrounds with full RV hookups are located in Vernal (see section 1, earlier in this chapter). A **KOA campground** (© **800/562-3254** or 435/784-3184; www.utahidahokoa.com), located in Manila, is open from mid-April through mid-October, and charges about $22 to $27 for tent sites and $32 to $37 for RV sites. It also has cabins at $45 to $65 per night double.

Where to Eat

Red Canyon Lodge Dining Room AMERICAN   For locals and visitors alike, this is a popular spot—especially the patio on nice summer days. The dining room maintains a classic mountain-lodge atmosphere, along with views of tall pines and a small lake. Top choices here include the buffalo rib-eye and the elk medallions with black cherry–burgundy sauce. The menu also features pastas, salads, steaks, chicken (try the mildly spicy Szechuan chicken pasta), fish, and slow-roasted prime rib. Nightly fine-dining specials include a broiled salmon filet with hollandaise sauce. You'll also find standard American breakfasts, and burgers and sandwiches at lunch. Full liquor service is available.

In Red Canyon Lodge (see above), 2450 W. Red Canyon Lodge (turn off Utah 44 at milepost 3.5), Dutch John. © **435/889-3759.** Reservations accepted for large parties only. Main courses $4–$10 breakfast and lunch, $8–$25 dinner. AE, DISC, MC, V. Apr to mid-Oct daily 8am–9pm; mid-Oct to Mar Fri 4–9pm, Sat 8am–9pm, Sun 8am–4pm.

UTAH'S DIXIE & THE COLORFUL SOUTHWEST CORNER

S mall lakes and big rocks, golf courses and ski areas, Shake-speare and the latest special effects—you'll find it all in the southwest corner of Utah, dubbed "Color Country" by the locals for its numerous and colorful rock formations. In addition to the attractions, another reason to visit is the warm winter weather: The region's largest city, St. George, and its immediate surroundings are known as "Utah's Dixie" for the mild climate as well as the area's previous life as a Civil War–era cotton-growing region. Color Country is a terrific winter playground; there's no need to ever put away the golf clubs or swimsuits in this neighborhood.

The range of elevations here means you can often lounge around the pool in the morning and build a snowman that same afternoon. From the scorching desert at St. George, it's only 74 miles—and almost 7,500 feet up—to the cool mountain forest at Cedar Breaks National Monument. Home to a variety of scenic and recreation areas (including a ski resort), a surprising number of historic attractions, and excellent performing arts events (such as the Utah Shakespearean Festival in Cedar City), this region also serves as the gateway to several of the area's spectacular national parks.

Here, you can step back more than a hundred years at Mormon leader Brigham Young's winter home or cheer on the Dixie State College Red Storm football team. Of course, the favorite stops are all outdoors: the rugged red-rock cliffs at Snow Canyon State Park, the ruddy sands of Coral Pink Sand Dunes State Park, and the panoramic views from Cedar Breaks National Monument. This area is also a good base for those visiting the area's national parks, including Grand Canyon (pick up a copy of *Frommer's Grand Canyon* [John Wiley & Sons, Inc.]), Great Basin, and Zion (see chapter 10).

In recent years, St. George has been booming, with Washington County's population jumping over 50% from 2000 to 2010; it's now home to about 140,000 people. More than a few Californians have retired here after falling in love with the climate—and the real estate prices. But the growth hasn't changed everything: The space is still wide open, the winters still mild, and the surroundings still starkly beautiful.

GETTING OUTDOORS IN UTAH'S COLOR COUNTRY

This is Utah's playground, a year-round mecca for hikers, mountain bikers, golfers, boaters, anglers, and anybody else who just wants to get outdoors. Among the top spots for experiencing nature at its best are Cedar Breaks National Monument, a high-mountain oasis of towering pines and firs, with wildflowers galore, and state parks such as Snow Canyon, Coral Pink Sand Dunes, and Quail Creek.

The best seasons for outdoor activities here are based on elevation. In St. George and other lowlands, spring and fall are best, winter's okay, and summer is worst, because temperatures soar well over 100°F (38°C). However, not everyone says no to St. George in summer: Its desert climate makes it the **golfing** capital of Utah. The Sunbrook is considered one of the state's best courses, with a challenging layout and spectacular views of the White Hills, but you can stay a week in St. George and play a different course each day. On the other side of the seasonal coin, don't try to drive up the mountains to Cedar Breaks until June at the earliest or mid-October at the latest; the roads will be closed by snow.

A good way to see this part of Utah is on foot. **Hiking** trails abound throughout the Dixie and Fishlake national forests north of St. George. Several of the best trails are in state parks, particularly Snow Canyon State Park near St. George, and in the nearby national parks.

Biking here generally means **mountain biking.** Even when riding in the city, you never know when you're going to discover a great little trail turning off into the red-rock desert or up into alpine meadows. The best mountain biking is at Brian Head Resort. Both road and mountain bikes can take you to beautiful areas in and around Snow Canyon State Park near St. George.

For an area with so much desert, there's a lot of **boating** here: Utahns have created reservoirs to provide the desert and its residents with drinking and irrigation water. The best boating is at Quail Creek State Park near St. George; for a bit more solitude try the relatively undeveloped Gunlock State Park, also near St. George, or Minersville State Park, west of Beaver. The top **fishing** hole in these parts is Quail Creek State Park, but there are plenty of smaller lakes and hidden streams in the national forests.

Off-road vehicles can simply be a means to get to an isolated fishing stream or hiking trail, or the adventure itself. The old mining and logging roads in the national forests are great for four-wheel exploring. Visitors with dune buggies will want to challenge the shifting dunes at Coral Pink Sand Dunes State Park, just outside Kanab.

An abundance of **wildlife** makes its home in this part of the state. Sure, you'll encounter deer, squirrels, chipmunks, and other furry creatures at Cedar Breaks National Monument and the area's national parks, but there's also animal life in the desert, including everyone's favorites: the luminescent scorpions at Coral Pink Sand Dunes State Park and the Gila monster at Snow Canyon State Park, also home to numerous songbirds.

It may be hot down in the desert, but plenty of snow is perched up on those mountaintops, and the **skiing** is great at Brian Head Resort and newly reopened Eagle Point. In winter, cross-country skiers and snowshoers will want to head to nearby Cedar Breaks National Monument after the snow closes the roads to cars.

ST. GEORGE: GATEWAY TO THE WONDERS OF THE SOUTH

120 miles NE of Las Vegas, Nevada; 305 miles SW of Salt Lake City

In the fall of 1861, Brigham Young sent 309 families to establish a cotton-growing community in the semiarid Virgin River Valley. Today, St. George has more than 70,000 inhabitants. Life in St. George, known as one of Utah's more conservative communities, is still strongly influenced by the Mormon church. At an elevation of 2,800 feet, the town is also a winter home to many snowbirds—not the feathered variety, but humans who annually flee the cold of more northern climes for this region's gentle winters. Despite the climate, this desert city appears quite green, with tree-lined streets and lovely grassy areas. St. George also has more than a half-dozen golf courses, along with recreational and cultural facilities to suit most every taste.

St. George is also the gateway to some of the most spectacular scenery in the West. Zion, Bryce, and Grand Canyon national parks are within relatively easy driving distance, as are Cedar Breaks and Pipe Springs national monuments and Snow Canyon, Gunlock, and Quail Creek state parks. Depending on your itinerary, St. George may be the largest town that you stop in en route to Lake Powell and Glen Canyon National Recreation Area, Capitol Reef National Park, and the prehistoric Indian sites in the Four Corners area.

Essentials

GETTING THERE   The closest major airport is **McCarran International Airport,** in Las Vegas, Nevada (✆ **702/261-5211;** www.mccarran.com). Most major airlines fly into McCarran, where you can rent a car from most major car-rental companies and drive the 120 miles northeast on I-15 to St. George.

The **St. George Shuttle** (✆ **800/933-8320** or 435/628-8320; www.stgshuttle. com) provides daily van service to and from the Las Vegas airport ($30 each way or $50 round-trip), and also offers transportation between St. George and Salt Lake City ($55 one-way, $100 round-trip; reservations are required).

The new-in-2011 **St. George Municipal Airport,** 4550 S. Airport Pkwy., south of the city (✆ **435/627-4080;** www.sgcity.org/airport), is served by **United** to Los Angeles and **Delta** to Salt Lake City. Both routes are operated by **SkyWest Airlines.** Airline websites are listed in chapter 16.

St. George is on I-15. Take exit 2 (Airport Pkwy.).

VISITOR INFORMATION   Before your trip, contact the **St. George Area Chamber of Commerce** (✆ **435/628-1658;** www.stgeorgechamber.com) for a visitor's guide. When you get into town, stop in at the information center operated by the chamber in the historic Pioneer Courthouse, 97 E. St. George Blvd. It's open Monday through Friday from 9am to 5pm.

For information on the state and national parks in the area, as well as Dixie National Forest and land administered by the National Park Service and the Bureau of Land Management, stop by the **Interagency Office and Visitor Center,** 345 E. Riverside Dr. (✆ **435/688-3246;** www.fs.fed.us/r4; www.nps.gov; www.ut.blm.gov). This is a good place to ask questions about the area's public lands, get trail recommendations, and pick up backcountry permits for the Grand Canyon. A variety of free brochures are available, and maps, books, posters, and videos are for sale. To get

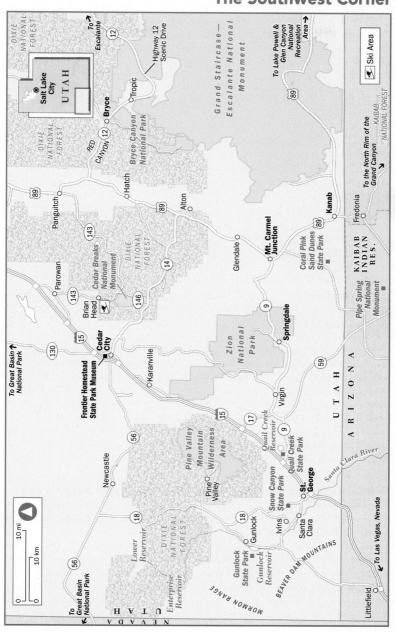

there, take I-15 exit 6 and turn east. The center is open Monday through Friday 7:45am to 5pm and Saturday 10am to 3pm; it's closed Sundays.

GETTING AROUND The street grid system is centered on the point at which Tabernacle Street (running east-west) crosses Main Street (running north-south), with numbered streets increasing in each direction by hundreds. St. George Boulevard takes the place of 100 North, Bluff Street runs along a bluff at the western edge of the city, I-15 cuts through in a northeast direction (from exit 6 at the south end of Bluff St. to exit 8 at the east end of St. George Blvd.), and River Road lies at the eastern edge, becoming Red Cliffs Road north of St. George Boulevard. Other than that, the system stays true to the grid.

Car-rental agencies with offices in St. George include **Avis** (© **435/627-2002;** www.avis.com), **Budget** (© **435/673-6825;** www.budget.com), and **Hertz** (© **435/ 652-9941;** www.hertz.com), all at St. George Municipal Airport, and **Enterprise,** 289 E. St. George Blvd. (© **435/634-1556;** www.enterprise.com).

Free on-street parking is available in much of the city, and many streets are tree-lined and shady.

For a taxi, call **AAA Quality Cab** (© **435/656-5222**) or **Taxi USA** (© **435/ 656-1500**).

FAST FACTS One of the larger hospitals in this part of the state is **Dixie Regional Medical Center,** 1380 E. Medical Center Dr. (© **435/251-1000;** www. intermountainhealthcare.org), which provides 24-hour emergency care. The **post office** is located at 180 N. Main St. (© **800/275-8777** for hours and other information; www.usps.com). The regional **newspaper** is the *Spectrum* (www.thespectrum. com).

What to See & Do

Most visitors head to St. George for rest and relaxation at the spas, golf courses, and area parks, but there's also a good deal of history in these parts, not to mention prehistory: The **St. George Dinosaur Discovery Site at Johnson Farm,** 2180 E. Riverside Dr. (© **435/574-3466;** www.dinotrax.com), showcases 2,000 fossilized tracks left by dinosaurs of all kinds when the area sat on the edge of a vast lake. It's open Monday through Saturday from 10am to 6pm; admission is $6 adults, $3 kids, and those 3 and under are free. In Kayenta, outside Ivins north of St. George, is the **Desert Rose Labyrinth and Sculpture Garden** (© **435/634-0510**), featuring a labyrinth made of local red rock and intriguing outdoor art. Admission is free; it is open dawn to dusk.

DISCOVERING MORMON HISTORY IN & AROUND ST. GEORGE

Because the LDS Church was the primary driving force in the settlement of St. George, it should come as no surprise that most of the sightseeing in town is church-related. At the town's historic buildings, staffed by knowledgeable church members, you'll learn about the church as well as the specific sites; expect a little sales pitch on the benefits of Christianity in general and the Mormon faith in particular.

Brigham Young Winter Home Historical Site Church leader Brigham Young was one of St. George's first snowbirds. He escaped the Salt Lake City cold during the last few winters of his life by coming south to this house. In addition to its obvious religious importance, this home is a handsome example of how the well-to-do of the late 19th century lived. Allow about a half-hour for the guided tour.

St. George & Environs

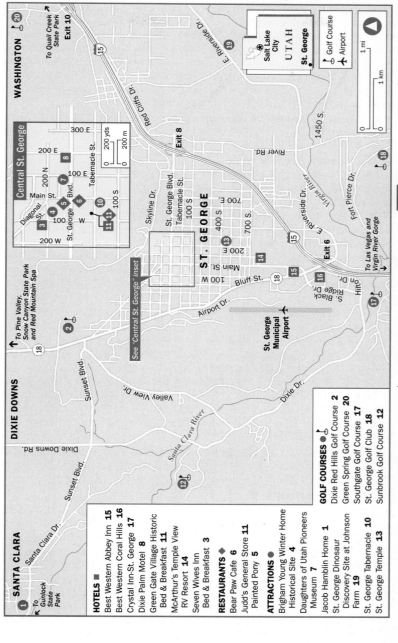

HOTELS ■
Best Western Abbey Inn **15**
Best Western Coral Hills **16**
Crystal Inn-St. George **17**
Dixie Palm Motel **8**
Green Gate Village Historic
Bed & Breakfast **11**
McArthur's Temple View
RV Resort **14**
Seven Wives Inn
Bed & Breakfast **3**

RESTAURANTS ◆
Bear Paw Cafe **6**
Judd's General Store **11**
Painted Pony **5**

ATTRACTIONS ●
Brigham Young Winter Home
Historical Site **4**
Daughters of Utah Pioneers
Museum **7**
Jacob Hamblin Home **1**
St. George Dinosaur
Discovery Site at Johnson
Farm **19**
St. George Tabernacle **10**
St. George Temple **13**

GOLF COURSES ●
Dixie Red Hills Golf Course **2**
Green Spring Golf Course **20**
Southgate Golf Course **17**
St. George Golf Club **18**
Sunbrook Golf Course **12**

9

UTAH'S SOUTHWEST CORNER | St. George: Gateway to the Wonders of the South

171

67 W. 200 North. © **435/673-5181.** www.stgeorgetemplevisitorscenter.org. Free guided tours. Summer daily 10am–7pm; rest of year daily 10am–5pm. Last tour at 6:30pm summer and 4:30pm winter. From I-15 exit 8, head west on St. George Blvd., turn right (north) onto Main St., and turn left (west) onto 200 North.

Daughters of Utah Pioneers Museum   This museum contains an eclectic collection of items that belonged to the pioneers—including a bed used by Brigham Young, plus spinning wheels, an 1894 loom, guns, tools, musical instruments, and other relics from bygone days. Vintage photos, mostly of pioneer families, are on display, and copies are available for purchase. Guided tours are given by volunteers from the Daughters of Utah Pioneers. Allow at least a half-hour.

145 N. 100 East. © **435/628-7274.** www.dupstgeorge.org. Free admission; donations accepted. Fall and spring Mon–Tues and Thurs–Sat 10am–5pm; shorter hours rest of year. Closed Wed, Sun, and all of Dec. From I-15 exit 8, head west on St. George Blvd. and turn right (north) at 100 East.

Jacob Hamblin Home ★   This stone-and-pine house, built in 1862, is closer to what you'd think of as a pioneer home than most of the refined houses of St. George, and it's typical of pioneer homes throughout the West—except for one aspect that is definitively Mormon: It has two identical bedrooms, one for each of Hamblin's wives. Note also that the dining table is set in typical Mormon fashion, with plates upside down and chairs facing away from the table to facilitate kneeling for before-meal prayers. The guided tour lasts about a half-hour.

3325 Hamblin Dr., Santa Clara. © **435/673-5181.** www.stgeorgetemplevisitorscenter.org. Free guided tours. Summer daily 10am–7pm; rest of year daily 10am–5pm. Last tour at 6:30pm summer and 4:30pm winter. From St. George, go 3 miles west on Sunset Blvd. to the community of Santa Clara; watch for sign.

Pine Valley Chapel   This handsome white chapel was built in 1868 by Ebenezer Bryce (for whom Bryce Canyon National Park was named) and Lorenzo and Erastus Snow (for whom Snow Canyon State Park was named). The settlers of the Pine Valley logging and saw-milling community wanted to build a church that would also function as a school and community building. Bryce was approached to design it, and because of his experience as a shipbuilder, he laid out the structure as an upside-down boat. Each of the walls was constructed flat on the ground, then lifted up and tied at the corners with strips of rawhide. The chapel was constructed of local pine and ponderosa and set on a foundation of granite and red limestone. Today it is the oldest LDS chapel in continuous use.

50 W. Main St., Pine Valley. © **435/574-3202.** www.lds.org. Free guided tours. Memorial Day to Labor Day daily 11am–5pm. Closed rest of year. From St. George, go north on Utah 18 to Central and head east on Forest Rd. 035.

St. George Tabernacle ★   This is the most beautiful building in St. George—an excellent example of fine old-world craftsmanship, from the hand-quarried red stone walls to the intricate interior woodwork. Its craftsmen finished pine, which was all they had, to look like exotic hardwoods and even marble. Completed in 1876 after 13 years of work, the Tabernacle served as a house of worship and town meeting hall. During the 1880s, when a nearby silver strike brought many Catholics to the area, the Tabernacle was used for a Roman Catholic High Mass led by a Roman Catholic priest, but with music from the liturgy sung by the local Mormon choir—in Latin. Today, the Tabernacle functions as a community center, presenting free weekly concerts and other cultural events (see "St. George After Dark," later in this chapter). The guided tour takes about half an hour.

18 S. Main St. at Tabernacle St. ℂ **435/673-5181.** www.stgeorgetemplevisitorscenter.org. Free guided tours. Daily 10am–5pm. Last tour at 4:30pm. From I-15 exit 8, head west on St. George Blvd. and turn left at Main St.

St. George Temple   Completed in 1877, St. George Temple was the first Mormon temple in Utah, and is the world's oldest still in use today. The majestic white temple is not open to the general public, but you can walk among the beautiful gardens and stop at the visitor center south of the temple for a tour of the center's exhibits and a multimedia program on the beliefs of the Church of Jesus Christ of Latter-day Saints.

490 S. 300 East. ℂ **435/673-5181.** www.stgeorgetemplevisitorscenter.org. Temple not open to the public; free guided tours of visitor center exhibits. Daily 9am–9pm. From I-15 exit 8, head west on St. George Blvd. to 200 East, turn left (south) and go about 6 blocks.

SNOW CANYON STATE PARK ★★★

Among Utah's most scenic state parks, **Snow Canyon** offers an abundance of opportunities for photography and hiking. The park is surrounded by rock cliffs and walls of Navajo sandstone in shades of red, layered with white and black from ancient lava flows. Hike the trails and discover shifting sand dunes, mysterious lava caves, colorful desert plants, and a variety of rock formations. You can also hike to an attractive cactus garden and several ancient petroglyphs (ask park rangers for directions).

Because the summers here are hot—well over 100°F (38°C)—the best time to visit is any other time. Winters are mild, but nights can be chilly. Spring and fall are usually perfect weather-wise, and therefore the busiest. By the way, don't come looking for snow—Snow Canyon was named for pioneers Lorenzo and Erastus Snow, who discovered the canyon.

Essentials

GETTING THERE   The park is 11 miles northwest of St. George, off Utah 18.

INFORMATION, FEES & REGULATIONS   For a copy of the park's brochure, contact **Snow Canyon State Park,** 1002 Snow Canyon Dr., Ivins, UT 84738 (ℂ **435/628-2255;** www.stateparks.utah.gov). Day-use fee is $6. As in most state parks, dogs are welcome, even on trails, but must be leashed. The park is open from 6am to 10pm.

Outdoor Pursuits

HIKING   The best way to see Snow Canyon is on foot. Several short trails make for easy full- or half-day hikes. The **Hidden Piñon Trail ★** is a 1.5-mile round-trip self-guided nature trail that wanders among lava rocks, through several canyons, and onto rocky flatlands, offering panoramic views of the surrounding mountains. The trail begins across the highway from the park's campground; you can pick up a brochure at the park office/entrance station. The walk is fairly easy, but allow at least an hour, especially if you're planning to keep an eye out for local vegetation such as Mormon tea, cliffrose, prickly pear cactus, and banana yucca.

An easy 2-mile round-trip is **Johnson Canyon Trail.** It begins just south of the campground, passes the popular rock-climbing wall (see below) and some low sand dunes, and then leads into Johnson Canyon and a view of Johnson Arch (both named after pioneer wife Maude Johnson), spanning 200 feet high above.

The **Lava Flow Overlook Trail,** a 1.5-mile round-trip, starts just north of the campground. Caves can be found for about a half-mile along the trail, but watch carefully—it's easy to miss them. The caves were formed from liquid lava, and Native

American tribes, at times, have occupied the large rooms. Another quarter-mile past the caves is the **West Canyon Overlook,** with a breathtaking view into West Canyon.

Several longer and steeper trails lead to spectacular views of the canyons and distant vistas; check with park rangers for details.

MOUNTAIN BIKING   Bicycling is only allowed on the 7-mile round-trip Whiptail Trail and the unpaved West Canyon Road. The latter 8-mile round-trip road lies just west of the park; ask park rangers for directions. You can rent bikes at **Bicycles Unlimited** (p. 175).

ROCK CLIMBING   Climbers love the tall wall of rock on the east side of the road just south of the campground. Check with the park office for information.

WILDLIFE-WATCHING   You're likely to see cottontail rabbits, ground squirrels, and songbirds; luckier visitors may also spot desert mule deer, bobcats, coyotes, kit foxes, eagles, and owls. Although it's unlikely, you may see a desert tortoise (a federally listed threatened species) or a Gila monster. Snow Canyon is also home to some rattlesnakes.

Camping

The 36-site campground is one of the best in the state. One section has rather closely spaced sites with electric hookups; those not needing electricity can set up camp in delightful little side canyons, surrounded by colorful red rocks and Utah juniper. The views are spectacular no matter where you choose to set up. Facilities include hot showers, modern restrooms, and an RV dump station. Campsites with water and electricity cost $20, while those without are $16. Reservations are recommended from February through May and September through November; call ✆ **800/322-3770,** or visit www.stateparks.utah.gov.

More Outdoor Pursuits in the St. George Area

In addition to the outdoor opportunities that Snow Canyon State Park offers, great hiking, biking, and fishing can be enjoyed in the Dixie National Forest and on nearby lands administered by the Bureau of Land Management. For information, contact the Interagency Office (p. 168).

FISHING   Quail Creek and Gunlock state parks are the local fishing holes. For equipment, licenses, and tips on where they're biting, visit **Hurst Ace Hardware & Sports Center,** 160 N. Bluff St. (✆ **435/673-6141;** www.hurststores.com).

GOLFING   Utah's golf capital attracts golfers from around the country to a variety of public courses, known for their challenging designs, well-maintained fairways and greens, and spectacularly scenic settings. Rates given below are for winter; summer rates are usually lower. The area's best course, encompassing three 9-hole, par-36 courses, is the 27-hole **Sunbrook Golf Course,** 2366 W. Sunbrook Dr. (✆ **435/627-4400;** www.sgcity.org/golf), tops in both design and magnificent scenery. Greens fees are $26 summer and $51 to $56 fall to spring for 18 holes, cart included. Also highly rated, and considered by many to be the area's second-best course, is **Green Spring Golf Course,** 588 N. Green Spring Dr., Washington (✆ **435/673-7888;** www.golfgreenspring.com), several miles northeast of St. George. Challenging Green Spring is an 18-hole, par-72 course, with fees of $40 to $64 for 18 holes, cart included, likewise with the lowest fees in the summer.

GETTING IN SHAPE WITH the biggest loser

You can make your vacation count in terms of calories at the **Biggest Loser Resort at Fitness Ridge,** 260 S. 200 West, Ivins (✆ **435/673-3330;** www. biggestloserresort.com). Named for the television program, the resort offers structured programs that combine indoor and outdoor activities with healthy meals. These "fitness getaways" are fairly intensive: Your day starts with a hike around 6:30am and doesn't end until dinner at 5:45pm. In between are several cardiovascular workouts, lectures on healthy living, kickboxing, swimming, and much more. Meals top out at 1,200 calories a day and cooking demos round out the curriculum. Programs last at least a week and start around $2,000 if you stay on-site or $1,200 if you do not.

Other 18-hole courses include the par-73 **St. George Golf Club,** 2190 S. 1400 East (✆ **435/627-4404**), and the par-70 **Southgate Golf Course,** 1975 S. Tonaquint Dr. (✆ **435/627-4440**). Fees at these city-owned courses are $19 to $33 for 18 holes, cart included. The par-34, 9-hole **Dixie Red Hills Golf Course,** 645 W. 1200 North (✆ **435/627-4444**), charges $13 to $21 for 9 holes.

You can play the renowned private **Entrada at Snow Canyon Country Club,** 2537 Entrada Trail (✆ **435/986-2200;** www.golfentrada.com), if you stay at the **Inn at Entrada** (see "Where to Stay," later in this chapter). Rates run $75 to $175 a night per person, including an 18-hole round of golf on the Johnny Miller–designed course.

A marketing cooperative dubbed the **Red Rock Golf Trail** (✆ **888/345-5551;** www.redrockgolftrail.com) offers golfers a number of packages that start at about $70 per day for 18 holes and a room in an area hotel, based on double occupancy.

HIKING   Some of the best hiking in the area is at Snow Canyon State Park (p. 173) and in the Dixie National Forest to the north, which has some 200 miles of trails. Check with forest rangers for current trail conditions and be sure to carry detailed maps on any long hikes, especially if you're venturing into the Pine Valley Wilderness Area. Stop at the **Interagency Office and Visitor Center** (p. 168) for maps and details.

MOUNTAIN BIKING & ROAD BIKING   With hundreds of miles of trails in the St. George area, mountain biking has been rapidly gaining in popularity. For information on the best mountain-biking areas, plus maps, mountain-biking trail guides, bike repairs, bike accessories, and rentals, stop at **Bicycles Unlimited,** 90 S. 100 East (✆ **888/673-4492** or 435/673-4492; www.bicyclesunlimited.com); it's open Monday through Saturday 8am to 7pm. Top-quality road and mountain bikes rent for $55 to $74 per day; ask about multiday rates.

A popular road-biking trip is the scenic **24-mile loop** from St. George through Santa Clara, Ivins, and Snow Canyon State Park. The route follows paved roads with narrow shoulders but generally little traffic. Allow 2 to 3 hours. Head north out of St. George on Bluff Street (Utah 18) and follow it to its intersection with U.S. 91. Turn west (left) and go about 6 miles to the village of Santa Clara, where you can visit the Jacob Hamblin Home (p. 172). From Santa Clara, continue west about a mile before turning north (right); follow the signs to Ivins and the Tuacahn Amphitheater. At Ivins, turn east (right) onto the Snow Canyon Road, following signs for Snow Canyon

State Park, where you can easily spend from several hours to several days exploring the red-rock formations, lava pools, and sand dunes. From the park, continue east to Utah 18, turn south (right), and pedal back into St. George.

Spectator Sports

The **Dixie State College Red Storm** are the ones to root for in St. George. The football, women's volleyball, women's soccer, men's and women's basketball, men's baseball, men's golf, and women's softball teams at this community college are often nationally ranked. You're not likely to have any trouble getting tickets to join the 5,000 students in Hansen Stadium or Burns Arena. Tickets are available at the Athletic Department offices (© **877/546-7327** or 435/879-4295; www.dixieathletics.com).

Where to Stay

St. George has a good selection of lodgings. Most are on St. George Boulevard and Bluff Street, within easy walking distance of restaurants and attractions. Summer is the slow season here—people tend to head to the mountains when the temperature hits 115°F (46°C)—so prices are lowest then. High seasons are spring and fall. Golfers should ask about special golf packages.

Reliable chain properties in the area, almost all clustered around exits 6 and 8 off Hwy. 15, include a pair of top-notch Best Westerns: the **Best Western Plus Abbey Inn,** 1129 S. Bluff St. (© **888/222-3946** or 435/652-1234; www.bwabbeyinn. com), with rates of $89 to $119 double and $109 to $139 suite, and the **Best Western Coral Hills,** 125 E. St. George Blvd. (© **800/542-7733** or 435/673-4844; www.coralhills.com), with rates of $69 to $119 double.

Also in town near I-15 is **Crystal Inn,** 1450 S. Hilton Dr. (© **877/688-7177** or 435/688-7477; www.crystalinnstgeorge.com), with rates of $65 to $135 double. There are numerous inexpensive chain properties, including **Motel 6,** 205 N. 1000 East (© **800/466-8356** or 435/628-7979; www.motel6.com), and **Quality Inn,** 1165 S. Bluff St. (© **877/424-6423** or 435/628-4481; www.qualityinn.com). Rooms at these properties typically run $40 to $65 double, higher during special events.

Room tax adds about 12% to your lodging bill. Pets are generally not accepted unless otherwise noted.

EXPENSIVE & MODERATE

Green Gate Village Historic Bed & Breakfast ★★   One of the most delightful lodgings in St. George, this bed-and-breakfast inn is actually 10 separate buildings—all restored pioneer homes from the late 1800s, sitting in their own flower-filled little "village" across the street from Town Square. Each has a different floor plan (most have one king bed); breakfast is served in the central 1876 Bentley House. Outside are the green gates of the establishment's name. It seems Brigham Young ordered white paint for the St. George Temple in 1877, but got a shipment of green instead. He couldn't send it back, so Young gave the green stuff to locals for their gates and fences. Only one original green gate remains: It's on display in the inn's garden.

76 W. Tabernacle St., St. George, UT 84770. www.greengatevillageinn.com. © **800/350-6999** or 435/628-6999. Fax 435/628-6989. 15 units. $99–$259 double. Rates include full breakfast. AE, DISC, MC, V. From I-15 exit 8, head west to Main St., turn left (south) 1 block to Tabernacle St., and turn right (west) to Green Gate Village. **Amenities:** Outdoor Jacuzzi; small outdoor heated pool. *In room:* A/C, TV/VCR or DVD, movie library, Wi-Fi (free).

The Inn at Entrada ★★   Located on an exclusive golf course north of downtown St. George, the Inn at Entrada offers a place to get away from it all right in the thick of an upscale residential development. The high-tech units feature automatic shades and touch-control lighting as well as plenty of Southwestern-inspired style. The recreational facilities make the place: Besides access to the Entrada at Snow Canyon Country Club with purchase of a golf package (lodging and 18 holes for $75–$175 per night), guests have the run of a rec center with a full gym, pools, and sand volleyball courts. All units have kitchens; all but the studios have washers and dryers.

2588 Sinagua Trail, St. George, UT 84770. www.innatentrada.com. ℭ **435/634-7100.** 23 units. $79–$129 double. Rates include access to gym, pool, and golf course. AE, DISC, MC, V. **Amenities:** Restaurant; exercise room; 18-hole golf course; 1 indoor and 1 outdoor Jacuzzi; 1 indoor and 1 outdoor heated pool; tennis courts. *In room:* A/C, TV/DVD, hair dryer, kitchen, Wi-Fi (free).

Red Mountain Resort ★★   One of the largest destination spa resorts in the country, Red Mountain is also among the best, and it serves as an excellent base for all sorts of adventures in southwestern Utah. Guests can stay in either stylishly chic hotel-style rooms or condolike villas, all done in earth tones with a contemporary style. Located in a concrete geodesic dome, the centerpiece is the spa, with a sublime view of adjacent Snow Canyon State Park and a terrific staff. Other on-site activities include fitness classes, special events, indoor and outdoor pools, guided hikes on nearby trails, and a terrific restaurant focused on healthy cuisine.

1275 E. Red Mountain Circle, Ivins, UT 84738. www.redmountainresort.com. ℭ **435/673-4905.** Fax 435/673-1363. 106 units, including 24 villas. $230–$619 per person per night. Rates include all meals and numerous activities. Room only $175–$445 double. AE, DISC, MC, V. Located about 7 miles north of St. George via Utah 18 and Utah 8. **Amenities:** Restaurant; bike rentals; exercise room; Jacuzzi; indoor and outdoor pools; spa. *In room:* A/C, TV, Wi-Fi (free).

Seven Wives Inn Bed & Breakfast ★   While no polygamists are hiding in the attic of Seven Wives Inn anymore—as there were in the 1880s after polygamy was outlawed—it's fascinating to imagine what things must have been like in those days. Decorated with antiques, mostly Victorian and Eastlake, the inn consists of two historic abodes: the main house, built in 1873, where the polygamists hid, and the president's house next door, a four-square Victorian built 10 years later that played host to many of the LDS Church's early presidents. Each room has a deck or balcony, and private bathroom; most units have DVD players, four have a functioning fireplace, and four have two-person whirlpool tubs—one is installed in a Model T Ford! A separate wheelchair-accessible cottage furnished with replica pioneer furniture, an extra-large shower, a two-person whirlpool, a king-size bed, a kitchenette, and a gas fireplace is also available. Tours are offered by appointment; smoking is not permitted.

217 N. 100 West, St. George, UT 84770. www.sevenwivesinn.com. ℭ **800/600-3737** or 435/628-3737. Fax 435/628-5646. 13 units, including 2 suites. $99–$150 double; $185–$195 suite. Rates include full breakfast. AE, DISC, MC, V. **Amenities:** Outdoor pool. *In room:* A/C, TV/DVD, hair dryer, Wi-Fi (free).

INEXPENSIVE

Dixie Palm Motel 🔥   Travelers on tight budgets should head to the Dixie Palm for basic lodging at bargain-basement rates. Located right in the center of town, within walking distance of several restaurants and attractions, this motel is clean and well maintained—and the price is right. All rooms have fridges and micro-waves, some units have full kitchens, and some are "family suites" with plenty of room and up to three beds.

185 E. St. George Blvd., St. George, UT 84770. www.dixiepalmmotel.com. © **866/651-3997** or 435/673-3531. 15 units. $35–$55 double; $55–$70 family suite. AE, DISC, MC, V. **Amenities:** Restaurant. *In room:* A/C, TV, kitchen, Wi-Fi (free).

CAMPING

Snow Canyon, Quail Creek, and Gunlock state parks also have campgrounds.

McArthur's Temple View RV Resort This large RV park is right in town and has an attractive outdoor pool and hot tub, as well as an exercise room, a shuffleboard court, Wi-Fi near the clubhouse, and a putting/chipping green.

975 S. Main St., St. George, UT 84770. www.templeviewrv.com. © **800/776-6410** or 435/673-6400. 260 sites. $38–$42. AE, DISC, MC, V. Just off I-15 exit 6.

Where to Eat

In addition to the restaurants discussed below, the **Bear Paw Coffee Company,** 75 N. Main St. (© **435/634-0126**; www.bearpawcafe.com), serves great breakfasts ranging from steak and eggs to French toast. Also don't miss **Judd's General Store,** a century-old business at **Green Gate Village** (see "Where to Stay," earlier in this chapter), with sandwiches and soups for lunch as well as ice cream, candy, and one of the widest selections of bottled soft drinks in the state.

Painted Pony ★★ STEAK/SEAFOOD From a lively contemporary space over-looking Ancestor Square, Randall Richards's excellent eatery is easily the best restaurant in St. George, and probably the best between Vegas and Salt Lake. Infused with a sensibility that's more California than Utah, Richards's creative menu includes familiar dishes with fresh preparations, seafood (seared ahi with wasabi aioli is particularly good), expertly grilled steaks (you could slice the tenderloin with a spoon), and an excellent bacon-wrapped duck with apple stuffing and purée of celery root. The room, with a curving bar and a colorful equine motif, nicely complements the menu. Lunch offerings include gourmet sandwiches and salads. Full liquor service is available.

The Tower at Ancestor Square, 1 W. St. George Blvd., No. 22. © **435/634-1700**. www.painted-pony.com. Main courses $9–$11 lunch, $26–$34 dinner. AE, DC, DISC, MC, V. Mon–Sat 11:30am–10pm; Sun 4–9pm.

Xetava Gardens Cafe ★ NEW AMERICAN Located amid the galleries at Coyote Gulch Art Village, Xetava Gardens Cafe serves creative fare in a chic space with a terrific courtyard north of St. George. The cafe morphs from counter-service coffee shop for breakfast and lunch into an upscale restaurant for dinner 3 nights a week. The menu includes waffles, parfaits, and egg sandwiches for breakfast, then salads and bagel and ciabatta sandwiches for lunch. Dinner is more refined, with chili-garlic rack of lamb, spicy shrimp, and steaks. There are also vegetarian selections for every meal.

815 Coyote Gulch Court, Ivins. © **435/656-0165**. www.xetava.com. Main courses $7–$14 lunch, $12–$32 dinner. AE, DISC, MC, V. Daily 8am–5pm; Thurs–Sat 5:30–9pm. Located 7 miles west of St. George via Sunset Blvd.

St. George After Dark

St. George, with its large nondrinking Mormon population, isn't one of the West's hot spots as far as bar scenes go. Locals going out on the town will often attend a performing arts event, and perhaps stop in for a nightcap at one of the local restaurants that serve alcohol or a hotel restaurant. Keep in mind that you'll have to buy something to eat in order to purchase a drink.

Dixie State College's **Avenna Center,** 425 S. 700 East (ticket office ☎ **435/652-7800;** http://tickets.dixie.edu), is St. George's primary performing arts venue. The four-building complex hosts a wide range of performances, from country and rock concerts to symphony, ballet, and opera performances—and even sports games.

Dixie State College, 225 S. 700 East (☎ **435/652-7500;** www.dixie.edu), offers a variety of events throughout the school year. The Celebrity Concert Series, running from October through April, has developed a strong following for its programs of music, ballet, modern dance, and performing arts presented by national and international performers. Tickets are typically $20. Recent offerings have included performances by the Osmonds–Second Generation and the Red Star Red Army Band and Chorus.

Not to be outdone, the college's music and drama departments offer numerous performances, including student recitals; band, chamber singer, and jazz ensemble concerts; and theater that runs the gamut from musicals to dramas—and maybe even a Greek tragedy. Admission usually costs between $8 and $12 per person; most performances are presented at **Cox Auditorium.** Call the box office (☎ **435/652-7800;** http://tickets.dixie.edu) to find out what's scheduled during your visit.

Music lovers will enjoy St. George's own **Southwest Symphonic Chorale and Southwest Symphony,** the only full symphony orchestra between Provo and Las Vegas. Its repertoire includes classical, opera, and popular music. Get tickets early for the annual Christmas production of Handel's *Messiah*—it usually sells out. Concerts are usually scheduled from October to May (☎ **435/688-8183;** www.southwest symphony.org).

Broadway musicals and plays are presented in a September-through-April season by **St. George Musical Theater,** 735 E. Tabernacle (☎ **435/628-8755;** www. sgmt.org). Recent productions have included *Annie Get Your Gun* and *Singing in the Rain;* tickets cost $10 to $15.

The **St. George Tabernacle** (p. 172) presents free concerts (including half-hour organ recitals) on Saturday at 12:15pm and Wednesday at 7pm. For information on these and other programs, call ☎ **435/673-5181.**

Not far from St. George, at 1100 Tuacahn Dr., in Ivins, is the **Tuacahn Amphitheatre and Center for the Arts** (☎ **800/746-9882** or 435/652-3300; www. tuacahn.org). Surrounded by towering red-rock cliffs, this 2,000-seat state-of-the-art outdoor theater presents original and Broadway productions from June through September, and at other times is the venue for big-name music acts, such as Kenny Rogers. It also hosts the annual Christmas Festival of Lights, during which Christmas lights illuminate the buildings and grounds at Tuacahn. Reservations are recommended. Tickets for the musicals vary, but are generally in the range of $20 to $60 for adults and $20 to $40 for children 11 and under. Dutch-oven dinners are served before the productions ($13 for adults and $9.50 for children).

Those looking for more lowbrow nightlife should check out **Jazzy's Rock 'n' Roll Grill,** 285 N. Bluff St. (☎ **435/674-1678;** www.jazzysrocknrollgrill.com), offering beers, burgers, and live music of all kinds.

CEDAR BREAKS NATIONAL MONUMENT

Cedar City: 53 miles NE of St. George, 251 miles SW of Salt Lake City; Cedar Breaks National Monument: 21 miles E of Cedar City

This great little area is home to some unheralded—and uncrowded—natural gems. Cedar Breaks National Monument is like a miniature Bryce Canyon—a stunning multicolored amphitheater of stone, with hiking trails, camping, and a plateau ablaze with wildflowers in summer. Brian Head is Utah's southernmost ski resort, but because it has the highest base elevation of any of the state's ski areas, it gets about 450 inches of powder each winter. Where else but southern Utah can you be on the links in the morning and on the slopes by the afternoon? And because Brian Head Resort is off the average skier's beaten track, lift lines are usually nonexistent.

But this area is more than an outdoor play land—with Frontier Homestead State Park Museum and the nationally renowned Utah Shakespearean Festival, Cedar City happens to be a great place to experience a little history as well as some great theater. Even if neither of these attractions appeals to you, you'll probably end up in Cedar City anyway—it's home to most of the area's accommodations and restaurants.

Basing Yourself in Cedar City

The community of Cedar City (elevation 5,800 ft.) is a good base for those exploring this area, especially because Cedar Breaks National Monument has no lodging or dining facilities. If you're here to ski and you'd like to save money on accommodations, Cedar City also offers an economical alternative to Brian Head's more expensive condos, and it's only 28 miles from Brian Head's slopes (but beware: it can be a mean 28 miles when the weather's bad). In addition to the facilities mentioned below, a good selection of motels, restaurants, campgrounds, gas stations, grocery stores, and other services is strung along I-15 at exits 57, 59, and 62.

ESSENTIALS

GETTING THERE   **Delta** flies into **Cedar City Regional Airport** (© 435/867-9408; www.cedarcity.org) from Salt Lake City; car-rental agencies include **Avis** (© 435/867-9898; www.avis.com), **Hertz** (© 435/586-9806; www.hertz.com), and **Enterprise** (© 435/865-7636; www.enterprise.com).

VISITOR INFORMATION   Contact the **Cedar City-Brian Head Tourism Bureau,** 581 N. Main St., Cedar City, UT 84720 (© 800/354-4849 or 435/586-5124; www.scenicsouthernutah.com). The visitor center is open Monday through Friday 8am to 5pm, and Saturday and Sunday from 9am to 5pm.

FAST FACTS   This area is served by Cedar City's **Valley View Medical Center,** 1303 N. Main St. (© 435/868-5000). The **post office** is located at 333 N. Main St. (© 800/275-8777 for hours and other information; www.usps.com).

WHERE TO STAY & EAT

Lodging possibilities in Cedar City include the **Abbey Inn,** 940 W. 200 North (© 800/325-5411 or 435/586-9966; www.abbeyinncedar.com), **Best Western El Rey Inn,** 80 S. Main St. (© 800/688-6518 or 435/586-6518; www.bwelrey.com), **Best Western Town & Country,** 189 N. Main St. (© 800/493-0062 or 435/586-9900; www.bwtowncountry.com), **Days Inn,** 1204 S. Main St. (© 800/329-7466 or 435/867-8877; www.daysinn.com), **Motel 6,** 1620 W. 200 North (© 800/466-8356

THE UTAH shakespearean FESTIVAL

Cedar City hosts Utah's premier theater event—the highly acclaimed **Utah Shakespearean Festival ★★★**, which has been presenting professionally staged works by Shakespeare and others since 1962.

The season, which runs from late June through October, includes eight plays—usually three by Shakespeare and five by others—in which top actors perform in true Elizabethan style in an open-air replica of the original Globe Theatre and in a modern enclosed theater. Productions scheduled for 2012 include Shakespeare's *The Merry Wives of Windsor, Titus*

Andronicus, and *Hamlet,* plus *Stones in His Pockets* by Marie Jones and *To Kill a Mockingbird* by Christopher Sergel, based on the novel by Harper Lee.

You can also take a backstage tour for $8 per person in the summer. A variety of other programs and special events are scheduled.

The festival is held on the Southern Utah University campus, 351 W. Center St., Cedar City. Ticket prices range from $22 to $71. For tickets and information, call ✆ **800/752-9849** or 435/586-7878; or check out the festival's website, **www. bard.org**.

or 435/586-9200; www.motel6.com), **Quality Inn,** 250 N. 1100 West (✆ **800/627-0374** or 435/586-2082; www.qualityinncedarcity.com), and **Super 8,** 145 N. 1550 West (✆ **800/800-8000** or 435/586-8880; www.super8.com). All of the above charge less than $100 for doubles in winter; rates are slightly higher in summer. Room tax adds about 10% to lodging bills.

Cedar City KOA Campground, 1121 N. Main St., Cedar City (✆ **800/562-9873** or 435/586-9872) is open year-round and charges $25 to $50 per site.

The local favorite since 1956, **Milt's Stage Stop,** 5 miles east of town on Utah 14 (✆ **435/586-9344;** www.miltsstagestop.com), offers steak and seafood for dinner only, from $15 to $50, with complete liquor service. For lighter fare, try the **Pastry Pub,** 86 W. Center St. (✆ **435/867-1400;** www.cedarcitypastrypub.com), a cafe offering sandwiches, tostadas, egg dishes, and baked goods in a Shakespearean-themed space.

Those planning trips into the nearby mountains—perhaps for a few days at Cedar Breaks National Monument, described below—can pick up supplies in Cedar City at **Albertson's Food & Drug,** 905 S. Main St. (✆ **435/586-4433;** www.albertsons.com), or **Smith's Food & Drug Center,** 633 S. Main St. (✆ **435/586-1203;** www.smithsfoodanddrug.com).

A BRIEF LOOK AT CEDAR CITY'S PIONEER PAST

Frontier Homestead State Park Museum   Horse-drawn wagons are the main focus at this state park and museum, the site of the original Mormon iron works in Utah, with several dozen on display. In addition to the usual buckboards, a bullet-scarred Old West stagecoach, and some elaborate, for-the-very-very-rich-only coaches, you'll see an original Studebaker White Top Wagon (predecessor of the present-day station wagon) and several hearses, as well as the only artifact dating back to the original foundry, the town bell.

Also on exhibit are Native American and pioneer artifacts from the region, as well as a diorama depicting the 1850s iron furnace and equipment for which the park is named. Demonstrations of pioneer crafts, such as weaving, spinning, candle making, cooking, and toy making, are held periodically. Changing exhibits feature the work of local artists. Allow about an hour.

The museum also manages Old Iron Town, an 1860s-to-1870s iron foundry west of Cedar City. Ask at the desk for information and directions.

635 N. Main St., downtown Cedar City. © **435/586-9290.** www.stateparks.utah.gov. Admission $3, free for children 5 and under. Mon–Sat 9am–5pm. Closed Thanksgiving, Christmas, and New Year's Day.

Cedar Breaks National Monument ★★

A delightful little park, Cedar Breaks is a wonderful place to spend a few hours or even several days, gazing down from the rim into the spectacular natural amphitheater, hiking the trails, and camping among the spruce, fir, and wildflowers that blanket the plateau in summer.

This natural coliseum, reminiscent of Bryce Canyon, is more than 2,000 feet deep and over 3 miles across; it's filled with stone spires, arches, and columns shaped by the forces of erosion and painted in ever-changing reds, purples, oranges, and ochers. But why "Cedar Breaks"? Well, the pioneers who came here called such badlands "breaks," and they mistook the juniper trees along the cliff bases for cedars.

ESSENTIALS

At more than 10,000 feet elevation, it's always pleasantly cool at Cedar Breaks. It actually gets downright cold at night, so bring a jacket or sweater, even if the temperature is scorching just down the road in St. George. The monument opens for its short summer season only after the snow melts, usually in late May, and closes in mid-October—unless you happen to have a snowmobile or a pair of cross-country skis or snowshoes, in which case you can visit year-round.

GETTING THERE   Cedar Breaks National Monument is 21 miles east of Cedar City, 56 miles west of Bryce Canyon National Park, and 247 miles south of Salt Lake City.

From I-15, drive east of Cedar City on Utah 14 to Utah 148, turn north (left), and follow Utah 148 into the monument. If you're coming from Bryce Canyon or other points east, the park is accessible from the town of Panguitch via Utah 143. From the north, take the Parowan exit off I-15 and head south on Utah 143. It's a steep climb from whichever direction you choose, and vehicles prone to vapor lock or loss of power on hills (such as motor homes) may have some problems.

INFORMATION/VISITOR CENTER   For advance information, contact the Superintendent, Cedar Breaks National Monument, 2390 W. Utah 56, Ste. 11, Cedar City, UT 84720-4151 (© **435/586-9451;** www.nps.gov/cebr).

A mile from the south entrance gate is the **visitor center,** open 9am to 6pm daily from late May to mid-October, with exhibits on the geology, flora, and fauna of Cedar Breaks. You can purchase books and maps here, and rangers can help plan your visit.

FEES & REGULATIONS   Admission is $4 per person per week for those 16 and older (charged only in summer). Regulations are similar to those at most national parks: Leave everything as you find it. Mountain bikes are not allowed on hiking trails. Dogs, which must be leashed at all times, are prohibited on all trails, in the backcountry, and in public buildings.

HEALTH & SAFETY   The high elevation—10,350 feet at the visitor center—is likely to cause shortness of breath and tiredness, and those with heart or respiratory conditions should consult their doctors before going. Avoid overlooks and other high, exposed areas during thunderstorms; they're often targets for lightning.

RANGER PROGRAMS   During the monument's short summer season, rangers offer campfire talks at the Point Supreme campground several nights a week, daily talks on geology and other subjects, and several guided hikes. There are also special programs on the monument's wildflowers, and, in recent years, stargazing programs have become especially popular. All ranger programs are free. A complete schedule is posted at the visitor center and the campground.

EXPLORING CEDAR BREAKS BY CAR

The 5-mile road through Cedar Breaks National Monument offers easy access to the monument's scenic overlooks and trail heads. Allow 30 to 45 minutes to make the drive. Start at the visitor center and nearby **Point Supreme** for a panoramic view of the amphitheater. Then drive north, past the campground and picnic ground turnoff, to **Sunset View** for a closer view of the amphitheater and its colorful canyons. From each of these overlooks, you can see out across Cedar Valley, over the Antelope and Black mountains, into the Escalante Desert.

Continue north to **Chessman Ridge Overlook,** so named because the hoodoos directly below look like massive stone chess pieces. Watch for swallows and swifts soaring among the rock formations. Then head north to **Alpine Pond,** a trail head for a self-guided nature trail (see "Hiking," below) with an abundance of wildflowers. Finally, you'll reach **North View,** which offers the best look into the amphitheater. The view here is reminiscent of Bryce Canyon's Queen's Garden, with its stately statues frozen in time.

OUTDOOR PURSUITS

HIKING   No trails connect the rim to the bottom of the amphitheater, but the monument does have two high-country trails. The fairly easy 2-mile **Alpine Pond Trail** loop leads through woodlands of bristlecone pines to a picturesque forest glade and pond surrounded by wildflowers, offering panoramic views of the amphitheater along the way. A printed trail guide is available for purchase at the trail head.

A somewhat more challenging hike, the 4-mile round-trip **Spectra Point/Ramparts Overlook Trail** follows the rim more closely than the Alpine Pond Trail, offering changing views of the colorful rock formations. It also takes you through fields of wildflowers and by bristlecone pines that are more than 1,600 years old. Be especially careful of your footing along the exposed cliff edges, and allow yourself some time to rest—there are lots of ups and downs along the way.

 Late-Summer Bonanza: The Cedar Breaks Wildflowers

During its brief summer season, Cedar Breaks makes the most of the warmth and moisture in the air with a spectacular wildflower show. The rim comes alive in a blaze of color—truly a sight to behold. The dazzling display begins practically as soon as the snow melts and reaches its peak in mid-July. The annual 2-week **Wildflower Festival,** which celebrates the colorful display, starts the weekend closest to Independence Day. Watch for mountain bluebells, spring beauty, beard tongue, and fleabane early in the season; those beauties then make way for columbine, larkspur, Indian paintbrush, wild roses, and other flowers.

The 1-mile round-trip **Campground Trail** connects the campground with the visitor center, providing views of the amphitheater along the way. It is the only trail in the monument where pets are permitted.

There are no trails from the rim to the bottom of the amphitheater completely within the monument, but there are trails just outside the monument that go into the amphitheater. Check with the visitor center for details and directions.

WILDLIFE-WATCHING Because of its relative remoteness, Cedar Breaks is a good place for spotting wildlife. You're likely to see mule deer grazing in the meadows along the road early and late in the day. Marmots make their dens near the rim and are often seen along the Spectra Point Trail. Ground squirrels, red squirrels, and chipmunks are everywhere. Pikas, which are related to rabbits, are here, too, but it's unlikely you'll see one because they prefer the high, rocky slopes.

In the campground, birders should have no trouble spotting the Clark's nutcracker, with its gray torso and black-and-white wings and tail. The monument is also home to swallows, swifts, blue grouse, and golden eagles.

WINTER FUN The monument's facilities are shut down from mid-October to late May due to the blanket of snow that covers the area. The snow-blocked roads keep cars out, but they're perfect for snowmobilers, snowshoers, and cross-country skiers, who usually come over from the Brian Head ski area (see below) nearby. Snowshoers and cross-country skiers have several different trails to choose from, but snowmobiles are restricted to the main 5-mile road through the monument, which is groomed and marked.

CAMPING

The 28-site campground, **Point Supreme,** just north of the visitor center, is open from June to mid-September, with sites available on a first-come, first-served basis. It's a beautiful high-mountain setting, among tall spruce and fir. Facilities include restrooms, drinking water, picnic tables, grills, and an amphitheater for the ranger's evening campfire programs. No showers or RV hookups are available. The camping fee is $14 per night. Keep in mind that even in midsummer, temperatures can drop into the 30s (single digits Celsius) at night at this elevation, so bring cool-weather gear.

Brian Head Resort

Like the ski areas in the Ogden and Logan areas, the reasons to visit Brian Head Resort are terrain and snow; the wide range of amenities found in Park City, Deer Valley, and Snowbird just don't exist here. In summer, mountain bikers and hikers converge on Brian Head.

Brian Head has the distinction of being Utah's southernmost ski resort, just a short drive from the year-round short-sleeve warmth of St. George. Its location makes it particularly popular with skiers from the Las Vegas area and Southern California. But with the highest base elevation of any of the state's ski areas (9,600 ft.), it receives over 400 inches of powdery snow each winter. Another plus is the scenery: The only ski resort in Utah's famed red-rock country, Brian Head Resort offers stunning views.

On Giant Steps Mountain, you'll find challenging intermediate, advanced, and expert-only runs and terrain parks for a family's more advanced skiers and boarders. Giant Steps sits just below 11,307-foot Brian Head Peak, where expert-level skiers and snowboarders enjoy hike-accessed, backcountry bowls. Intermediates will enjoy fine cruising runs a little farther down the mountain, and beginners can ski Navajo

After the snow melts, bikers and hikers claim the mountain. With elevations of 9,600 to 11,307 feet, Brian Head is stunningly beautiful and always cool and crisp. For those who want to see the mountains without the sweat, chairlift rides are offered in summer Friday to Sunday ($10 adults, $6 children 4–12, free for kids 3 and under). Evenings are busy, too, with live musical entertainment ranging from jazz and country to bluegrass and classical.

Brian Head is fast becoming a major destination for serious and dedicated mountain bikers. This is a wonderful place for **mountain biking ★**, with endless trails, superb scenery, and about the freshest air you're going to find. What's more, mountain biking here can be oh-so-very easy: A chairlift hauls you and your bike up the mountain ($24 for a full-day pass), or you can take a shuttle to and from several locations ($17)—leaving only the fun parts to pedal. Bike rentals start at $35 to $54 per day for adults, $20 for kids 11 and under, and helmets are $5. Contact the **Brian Head Resort Mountain Bike Park** (✆ **866/ 930-1010,** ext. 212), **Brianhead Sports** (✆ **435/677-2014;** www.brianhead sports.com), or **George's Bike Shop** (✆ **435/677-2013;** www.georgsskishop. com) for details.

Other summer on-mountain activities including mountain biking, hiking, disc golf, and the new self-guided "Brian Head Family Adventure," earth-science- and natural-history-focused activities ranging from orienteering to learning about petroglyphs.

All of these activities are offered on Fridays, Saturdays, and Sundays through Labor Day and then Saturdays and Sundays through September. Hours are 9:30am to 4:30pm (weather conditions permitting) and can be accessed via the Giant Steps chairlift.

Mountain, dedicated solely to children and beginning skiers and snowboarders. The terrain is rated 40% beginner, 40% intermediate, and 20% advanced on 65 runs. One double chair and seven triples service 650 skiable acres. The vertical drop is 1,320 feet, 1,548 feet if you hike a little. There are snow-making capabilities on 170 acres. The ski season generally runs from mid-November to mid-April, with lifts operating daily from 10am to 4:30pm. On weekends and holidays, night skiing and tubing is available until 9pm.

Snowboarders are welcome, with four terrain parks of varying ability levels, plenty of free riding terrain, and a half pipe, conditions permitting. The resort also has a snow tubing park.

For information, contact **Brian Head Resort,** 329 S. Utah 143, P.O. Box 190008, Brian Head, UT 84719 (✆ **435/677-2035;** www.brianhead.com), or **Brian Head Chamber of Commerce & Visitor Services,** P.O. Box 190325, Brian Head, UT 84719 (✆ **888/677-2810** or 435/677-2810; www.brianheadchamber.com).

From Cedar City, it's 28 miles to Brian Head; take I-15 to exit 75 and head south on the very steep Utah 143 about 12 miles.

LIFT TICKETS   An adult all-day lift ticket is $49 regular season and an all-day child's (ages 6–12) or senior's (ages 65 and over) ticket is $35 regular season; half-day tickets are $40 and $29, respectively. Kids 5 and under ski free with a paying adult. Night skiing or snowboarding costs $15. Snow tubing is $15 for 2 hours, including tube rental.

9

UTAH'S SOUTHWEST CORNER

Cedar Breaks National Monument

eagle point: TWO RESORTS REBORN AS ONE

Skiers and snowboarders take note: Southern Utah now has another ski area in **Eagle Point,** located 18 miles east of Beaver, via exit 109 or 112 on I-15 (𝄃 **855/324-5378** or 435/438-3700; www.skieaglepoint.com). Nestled in the scenic Tushar Mountains, the resort is not exactly new (it's comprised of the former Elk Meadows and Mount Holly ski areas) but the freshly minted ownership has breathed plenty of new life into the place, which gets a full 450 inches of snow annually on its 625 acres. There are 42 runs here with a 1,500-foot vertical rise served by one quad chair, one triple, two doubles, and a platter. There are plenty of steeps (45% expert) to complement the beginner (20%) and intermediate (35%) terrains. There is also a pair of terrain parks and a tubing area. Lift tickets are a bargain at $50 for adults for a full day, $35 for kids 7 to 17 and seniors 65 and up. There are condos available on the mountain starting at $150 nightly, as well as a restaurant serving three meals daily in winter.

LESSONS & PROGRAMS   The **ski school** offers private and group lessons, as well as clinics, snowboard classes, and children's ski instruction. Day care is available for children and infants; also available are packages combining day care and ski lessons. Call 𝄃 **435/677-2049** for current rates.

CROSS-COUNTRY SKIING   There are numerous cross-country options in Cedar Breaks National Monument (p. 180). Lessons and rentals are available at **Brianhead Sports** (𝄃 **435/677-2014;** www.brianheadsports.com); there's no charge for trail use.

WHERE TO STAY & DINE   The Brian Head area offers a variety of lodging possibilities, with winter rates ranging from about $150 to $300 per night (higher at Christmas; lower in summer). Contact the **Brian Head Chamber of Commerce** (𝄃 **888/677-2810;** www.brianheadchamber.com) or **Brian Head Reservation Center** (𝄃 **800/845-9781** or 435/677-2042; www.brianheadtown.com/bhrc). Room tax is about 10%. You can also stay in Cedar City, 28 miles away (see "Basing Yourself in Cedar City," earlier in this chapter).

Cedar Breaks Lodge & Spa ★, 2223 Hunter Ridge Rd., Brian Head (𝄃 **888/ 282-3327** or 435/677-3000; www.cedarbreakslodge.com), near the base of Navajo Mountain, recently underwent an extensive multimillion-dollar renovation. It offers more than 100 studio, parlor, and master "villas" ranging from $95 to $480 in winter, $80 to $205 in summer. All rooms have whirlpool tubs, wet bars, refrigerators, microwaves, coffeemakers, and hair dryers; some also have fireplaces. Facilities include a 24-hour front desk, two restaurants, a lounge, an indoor pool, a fireside Jacuzzi, a fitness center, a sauna, and a steam room. Boasting one of Utah's top spas, the lodge has several massage therapists available, offering Swedish full-body massage, deep tissue massage, sports massage, reflexology, aromatherapy baths, hydrating facials, salt glows, and herbal wraps. New in 2009, the **Grand Lodge at Brian Head ★**, 314 Hunter Ridge Rd. (𝄃 **435/677-9000;** www.grandlodgebrianhead.com), is another posh spot to hang your hat at the resort, offering rooms and suites with earth tones and subtle contemporary furnishings. Facilities include a restaurant, bar, fitness center, concierge, game room, and spa.

Quick breakfasts and lunches are served at several places at Brian Head, including the **Giant Steps** and **Navajo Lodge** grills, with meals from $5 to $10. The **Double Black Diamond Steak House** at Cedar Breaks Lodge & Spa (see above) offers fine dining daily in winter, with steaks, prime rib, and several seafood and pasta dishes in the $15-to-$30 range. Reservations are recommended (© 435/677-4242). Also at Cedar Breaks Lodge & Spa, the **Cedar Breaks Café** serves a breakfast buffet plus a la carte menu each morning, and offers casual dinners each evening. Prices range from $8 to $18. The **Cedar Breaks Bar & Grill** is a local gathering place, with a full bar and the option of ordering from the Cedar Breaks Café menu. The Grand Lodge at Brian Head (see above) has **Leany's Steakhouse** (breakfast and dinner) and the hip **Lift Bar & Patio.**

KANAB: CINEMA, SAND DUNES & GRAND CANYON GATEWAY

82 miles E of St. George, 303 miles S of Salt Lake City, 79 miles N of the Grand Canyon

Another southern Utah town founded by Mormon pioneers sent by Brigham Young in the 1870s, Kanab is best known for its starring role in the movies and on TV. This is the Wild West many of us recognize from old TV shows like *Gunsmoke, The Lone Ranger, Death Valley Days,* and *F Troop,* and from the big screen in *Buffalo Bill, Sergeants 3, Bandolero!,* and *The Outlaw Josey Wales.*

But Kanab (4,925 ft. elevation) lives on more than just memories of the Old West: It's also a stopping point for travelers on their way to southern Utah's major sights. Visitors coming from Arizona are likely to pass through on their way to Zion and Bryce Canyon national parks. And with the Grand Canyon's north rim directly to the south, Kanab is a good choice for a home base. True, none of these natural wonders are all that close to Kanab, but in Utah terms, they're "just around the corner."

Essentials

GETTING THERE Kanab is 82 miles east of St. George, 80 miles south of Bryce Canyon National Park, 42 miles east of Zion National Park, 68 miles west of Lake Powell and Glen Canyon Recreation Area, 79 miles north of the Grand Canyon, and 303 miles south of Salt Lake City. The town is located on U.S. 89 at the junction of U.S. 89A, which crosses into Arizona just 7 miles south of town.

VISITOR INFORMATION Contact the **Kane County Visitors Center,** 78 S. 100 East (U.S. 89), Kanab, UT 84741 (© **800/733-5263** or 435/644-5033; www. kaneutah.com), which is open April through November Monday to Friday 9am to 7pm and Saturdays 9am to 6pm, with shorter hours in the winter.

GETTING AROUND Kanab is laid out on a grid, with the heart of town at the intersection of Center and Main streets. U.S. 89 enters from the north on 300 West Street, turns east onto Center Street, south on 100 East Street, and finally east again on 300 South. U.S. 89A follows 100 East Street south to the airport and into Arizona.

FAST FACTS The **Kane County Hospital** is at 355 N. Main St. in Kanab (© **435/644-5811;** www.kanecountyhospital.net). The **post office** is at 39 S. Main St. (© **800/275-8777** for hours and other information; www.usps.com).

Coral Pink Sand Dunes State Park

Long a favorite of dune-buggy enthusiasts (off-road-vehicle users lobbied hard to have this designated a state park), Coral Pink Sand Dunes has recently been attracting an increasing number of campers, hikers, photographers, and all-around nature lovers. While big boys—and some big girls—play with their expensive motorized toys, others hike; hunt for wildflowers, glow-in-the-dark scorpions, and lizards; or just wiggle their toes in the smooth, cool sand. The colors are especially rich at sunrise and sunset. Early-morning visitors will find the tracks of yesterday's dune buggies gone, replaced by the tracks of lizards, kangaroo rats, snakes, and the rest of the park's animal kingdom, who venture out in the coolness of night, after all the people have departed.

ESSENTIALS

GETTING THERE   From downtown Kanab, go about 8 miles north on U.S. 89, then southwest (left) on Hancock Road for about 12 miles to the park.

INFORMATION/VISITOR CENTER   For copies of the park brochure and off-highway-vehicle regulations, contact the **park office** at P.O. Box 95, Kanab, UT 84741-0095 (© **435/648-2800;** www.stateparks.utah.gov). At the **park entry station,** there's a small display area with sand from around the world, local fossils, and live scorpions, lizards, and tadpoles.

FEES & REGULATIONS   The day-use fee is $6 per vehicle. The standard state park regulations apply, with the addition of a few extra rules due to the park's popularity for off-roading: Quiet hours are from 10pm to 9am, later in the morning than in most parks. Dunes are open to motor vehicles between 9am and 10pm and to hikers at any time. Vehicles going onto the dunes must have safety flags, available at the entry station; while on the dunes, they must stay at least 10 feet from vegetation and at least 100 feet from hikers. Dogs are permitted on the dunes but must be leashed.

OUTDOOR PURSUITS

FOUR-WHEELING   This giant 3,700-acre sandbox offers plenty of space for **off-road-vehicle enthusiasts,** who race up and down the dunes, stopping to perch on a crest to watch the setting sun. Because the sand here is quite fine, extra-wide flotation tires are needed; lightweight dune buggies are usually the vehicle of choice. Adjacent to the park on Bureau of Land Management property are hundreds of miles of trails and roads for off-highway vehicles.

HIKING   The best time for hiking the dunes is early morning. It's cooler then, the lighting at and just after sunrise produces beautiful shadows and colors, and there are no noisy dune buggies until after 9am. Sunset is also very pretty, but you'll be sharing the dunes with off-road vehicles. Keep in mind that hiking through fine sand can be very tiring, especially for those who go barefoot. A self-guided .5-mile loop nature trail has numbered signs through some of the dunes; allow half an hour.

Several other hikes of various lengths are possible within and just outside the park, but because there are few signs—and because landmarks change with the shifting sands—it's best to check with park rangers before setting out. Those spending more than a few hours in the dunes will discover that even their own tracks disappear in the wind, leaving few clues to the route back to park headquarters.

CAMPING

The spacious and mostly shady 22-site campground, open year-round, offers hot showers, modern restrooms, and an RV dump station, but no hookups. Camping costs $16. Call © **800/322-3770** or visit www.stateparks.utah.gov for reservations.

best friends ANIMAL SANCTUARY

If you're an animal lover, one of the highlights of a trip to this part of Utah is a stop at the **Best Friends Animal Sanctuary,** near Kanab. Whether you volunteer, or just stop for a look, you won't soon forget a visit to this 5,000-acre spread, home to more than 2,000 cats, dogs, rabbits, horses, birds, and other animals. Founded in the 1980s, the Best Friends Animal Society's mission is simple: to bring the number of pets being euthanized to "essentially zero."

You can see the group's deep commitment to animals at the sanctuary, set amid the red rock of Angel Canyon. The staff works tirelessly to get these often abused or abandoned animals ready for adoption. Their efforts have been chronicled on National Geographic Channel's show *Dog Town.* At Best Friends, every animal has a home for life.

Free guided tours are available daily; call ahead for a reservation. Many people come and stay for a week or more, and you can rent cottages ($95–$120 double per night), smaller cabins ($60–$75 per night), and RV sites ($45 per night) on the property. You don't need to volunteer in order to stay—some people simply take advantage of the amazing setting, with its network of hiking trails.

Volunteers sign up to help with everything from walking dogs to socializing cats to feeding birds; you can pick which critters you'd like to work with. Volunteers must be at least 6 years of age, and those 17 and under must be accompanied at all times by an adult. You must make arrangements to volunteer before your visit. Specialized workshops on animal-related topics are also available.

The entrance to Best Friends is about 5 miles north of Kanab on the east side of U.S. 89. The Welcome Center is open daily from 8am to 5pm. Call ✆ **435/644-2001** or visit **www.bestfriends.org** for more information.

More to See & Do in the Kanab Area

Frontier Movie Town Hollywood's vision of the Wild West lives on, with a jail, bunkhouse, bank, ranch house, and numerous other set creations for movies filmed in the Kanab area (once nicknamed "Little Hollywood") over the years. On display are buildings from the sets of Disney's 1973 comedy-drama *One Little Indian,* starring James Garner and Vera Miles; the 1948 classic Western *Black Bart,* with Yvonne De Carlo and Dan Duryea; the 1994 Western *Maverick,* with Mel Gibson, Jodie Foster, and James Garner; and Clint Eastwood's 1976 hit *The Outlaw Josey Wales,* among others.

On the grounds is a large gift/souvenir shop, offering a wide variety of Native American arts and crafts, cowboy hats, coonskin caps, and the like. Call to see if a chuck-wagon dinner is scheduled during your visit. Allow about an hour to tour the whole town.

297 W. Center St. ✆ **435/644-5337.** www.frontiermovietown.com. Free admission. Summer daily 8:30am–9pm; shorter hours rest of year.

Heritage House Of the 16 historic houses in the downtown area of Kanab, this is the only one open to the public. Built in 1894, this handsome Victorian was purchased by Thomas H. Chamberlain in 1897, and by the city in 1975. The house has been restored to its original appearance and contains household items from the late 1800s, some belonging to the original owners. Allow about 45 minutes.

At 100 South and Main sts. ✆ **435/644-3966.** www.kanabheritage.com. Admission by donation. June–Sept Mon–Fri 1–5pm. A block south of the intersection of Center and Main sts.

Moqui Cave American Indians known as the Moqui are believed to have used this cave to store food 800 to 900 years ago. Times have changed since then, and so has the cave—the ancient Moqui would be amazed by what they'd find here today. The Chamberlain family, descendants of Thomas and Mary Chamberlain (see Heritage House, above), bought the cave in 1951, and the following year opened a tavern and dance hall in it. Although you can't order a drink today, the unique bar is still here, along with a huge collection of objects and artifacts that ranges from authentic dinosaur tracks (more than 140 million years old) to a beautiful fluorescent mineral display. You'll also see Native American pottery, spear points, and other art and artifacts. A large gift shop specializes in Native American arts and crafts.

1508 S. Kanab Creek Dr., on the east side of U.S. 89, about 5½ miles north of Kanab. © **435/644-8525.** www.moquicave.com. Admission $5 adults, $4.50 seniors 61 and over, $3.50 ages 13–17, $3 children 6–12, free for children 5 and under. Memorial Day to Labor Day Mon–Sat 9am–7pm; winter Mon–Sat 10am–4pm, but check on possible closures.

Where to Stay

In addition to the properties described below, you might consider the moderately priced **Best Western Red Hills,** 125 W. Center St. (© 800/780-7234 or 435/644-2675; www.bestwesternredhills.com), with rates of $70 to $130 double; the **Holiday Inn Express & Suites,** 217 S. 100 East (© 888/465-4329 or 435/644-3100; www.hiexpress.com), with rates of $89 to $149 double; or the **Rodeway Inn,** 70 S. 200 West (© 877/424-6423 or 435/644-5500; www.rodewayinn.com), with rates of $99 to $109 double.

Room tax adds 12%. Pets are not accepted unless otherwise noted.

Parry Lodge ★ Now on the National Register of Historic Places, this is where the stars stayed—Frank Sinatra, Dean Martin, John Wayne, Roddy McDowall, James Garner, and Anne Bancroft, to name just a few—while filming in Kanab. In 1931, Chauncey Parry decided to open a motel for the film people who were regularly coming to town. Two chandeliers from Paris hang in the lobby, while about 200 autographed photos of movie stars are scattered about the public areas of the colonial-feel lodge. Doors to the original guest rooms, which make up about a third of all rooms, are each adorned with the name of an actor who stayed here. The newer rooms are larger, but lack the charm of the older, smaller rooms. In summer, free movies that were filmed in Kanab are screened in the lodge's theater.

89 E. Center St. (U.S. 89), Kanab, UT 84741. www.parrylodge.com. © **800/748-4104** or 435/644-2601. Fax 435/644-2605. 89 units, including 3 family units. Summer $72–$95 double, $105–$120 family unit or kitchen apt; winter $49 double, $69 family unit or kitchen apt. Rates include discounted breakfast buffet in summer and continental breakfast in winter. AE, DISC, MC, V. Pets accepted ($10 per night). **Amenities:** Restaurant; outdoor heated pool; room service; Wi-Fi (free). *In room:* A/C, TV, kitchen.

Quail Park Lodge ★ This vintage motel is something of a blast from the past (built in 1963)—with the exception of the slick modern rooms and their understated contemporary vibe. A 2010 renovation returned the place to its 1960s splendor, from the dinky pool out front to the landscaping to the unmistakable vintage sign. Rooms feature one or two queens with premium bedding and plush robes; suites have electric fireplaces in the bedrooms. The amenity list is long and cutting-edge and free cruiser bicycles are available for guests.

125 N. 300 West, Kanab, UT 84741. www.quailparklodge.com. © **435/215-1447.** 13 units, including 2 suites. Summer $79–$119 double, $139 suite; winter $69–$79 double, $99 suite. Rates include

continental breakfast. AE, DISC, MC, V. **Amenities:** Complimentary bikes; small heated outdoor pool (seasonal). *In room:* A/C, TV/DVD, DVD library, hair dryer, MP3 docking station, Wi-Fi (free).

CAMPING

Kanab RV Corral   Open summer only, this well-kept RV park makes a good base camp for exploring the region. The sites—half back-in and half pull-through—are a bit close together, and you do get some highway noise; however, the bathhouses are exceptionally nice (with extra-large shower stalls), the coin-operated laundry is kept spotless, and the small, kidney-shaped pool is pleasant. Additional extras include free Wi-Fi access, a dog run, and horseshoe pits.

483 S. 100 East, U.S. 89A, Kanab, UT 84741. www.kanabrvcorral.com. (C) **435/644-5330.** 41 sites. $30. MC, V. Closed Nov to mid-Mar.

Where to Eat

Nedra's Too MEXICAN   Southwest home-style cooking in a friendly, casual atmosphere is what Nedra's is known for. Choose from tables in the dining room, decorated in Southwestern style, and booths in the adjacent coffee shop. The original Nedra's opened in 1957 in Fredonia, Arizona (7 miles south of Kanab), and this restaurant, which opened in 1990, carries on the legacy with the first location now closed. The delightful breakfasts, served all day, include the usual ham and eggs, omelets, and pancakes, but there's also an eye-opening chorizo and eggs, which is made with Mexican sausage, and a delicious huevos rancheros. Lunch and dinner menus offer a variety of charbroiled burgers, such as the Philly (with Swiss cheese, grilled red and green peppers, and Bermuda onions) and several sandwiches. Other options include steaks and seafood, fried chicken, and a wide choice of Mexican dishes, from burritos to enchiladas to fajitas. The house-made salsa is excellent; beer and wine coolers are available with meals.

300 S. 100 East. (C) **435/644-2030.** www.nedrascafe.com. Main courses $7–$13 breakfast, $7–$20 lunch and dinner. AE, DISC, MC, V. Summer daily 7am–10pm; rest of year daily 8am–9pm.

Rewind Diner ☺ AMERICAN   This diner—bedecked in sparkly red vinyl and plenty of 1950s nostalgia—is the best family restaurant in the vicinity, offering up a nice selection of salads, sandwiches, and pasta dishes for lunch. Dinners include a spicy Cajun rib-eye, chicken dishes, salmon, and barbecue ribs; there are also a few vegetarian options. Beer and wine are served.

18 E. Center St. (C) **435/644-3200.** Main courses $5–$11 lunch, $15–$22 dinner. AE, MC, V. Tues-Fri 11am–9pm; Sat 5:30–9pm.

Rocking V Cafe ★★ NEW AMERICAN   After 25 years in the television industry, Vicky and Victor Cooper switched gears, bought the old 1892 mercantile in downtown Kanab, and opened this delightfully artsy eatery. The "slow food" prepared in the Rocking V's kitchen is loaded with fresh ingredients, with an emphasis on great produce—vegan dishes are available. Dinner entrees, such as Thai curry, red trout crusted with cornmeal and pumpkinseeds, and deep-dish enchiladas topped with chili-tomatillo sauce, give you an idea of the breadth of influences driving the menu. Meat-eaters, don't be discouraged—try the buffalo tenderloin. Everything is made in-house, from the breads to the soups to the mouthwatering desserts. (Top pick: the Key lime pie.) The Coopers' place is a feast for the eyes as well as the taste buds: Original art hangs on the walls and in the second-story Rafters Gallery, showcasing regional talent.

97 W. Center St. (C) **435/644-8001.** www.rockingvcafe.com. Main courses $15–$38. MC, V. Late Mar to late Apr Thurs–Mon 5–9pm; late Apr to Oct daily 5–10pm. Usually closed Nov to late Mar; check the website for current hours.

ZION NATIONAL PARK

Early Mormon settler Isaac Behunin is credited with naming his homestead "Little Zion" because it seemed to be a bit of heaven on earth. Today, some 150 years later, **Zion National Park ★★** still casts a spell over visitors who gaze upon its sheer multicolored walls of sandstone, explore its narrow canyons, hunt for hanging gardens of wildflowers, and listen to the roar of the churning, tumbling Virgin River.

It's easy to conjure up a single defining image of the Grand Canyon or the delicately sculpted rock hoodoos of Bryce, but pinning down Zion is more difficult. It's not simply the towering Great White Throne, deep Narrows Canyon, or cascading waterfalls and emerald green pools. You'll discover an entire smorgasbord of sights, sounds, and even smells here. Take time to discover Zion's trails, visiting viewpoints at different times of the day to see the changing light, and let the park and nature work its magic.

Because of its extreme range of elevations (3,666–8,726 ft.) and weather (with temperatures soaring over 100°F/38°C in summer and a landscape carpeted by snow in winter), Zion harbors a vast array of plants and animals. Over 900 native species of plants have been found: cactus, yucca, and mesquite in the hot, dry desert areas; ponderosa pines on the high plateaus; and cottonwoods and box elders along the rivers and streams. Of the 14 varieties of cactus that grow in the park, keep an eye out for the red claret cup, which blooms spectacularly in spring. Wildflowers common to the park include manzanita, with tiny pink blossoms; buttercups; and the bright red hummingbird trumpet. You'll also see the sacred datura—dubbed the "Zion Lily" because of its abundance in the park—with its large funnel-shaped white flowers that open in the cool of night and often close by noon.

While exploring Zion, be sure to watch for "spring lines," areas where water seeps out of rock, and for the "hanging gardens" that accompany them. Because sandstone is porous, water can percolate down through the rock until it's stopped by a layer of harder rock. Then the water changes direction, moving horizontally to the rock face, where it seeps out, forming the "spring line" that provides nutrients to whatever seeds the wind delivers, which sprout into "hanging gardens"—plants and flowers you can see clinging to the sides of cliffs.

Aside from the variety of vegetation, Zion is a veritable zoo, with mammals ranging from pocket gophers to mountain lions, hundreds of birds

HOW NATURE painted ZION'S LANDSCAPE

Zion National Park is many things to many people: a day hike down a narrow canyon, a rough climb up the face of a massive stone monument, a moment of quiet appreciation as the sun sets with a red glow over majestic peaks. At least to some degree, each of these experiences is possible only because of rocks—their formation, uplifting, shifting, breaking, and eroding. Of Zion's nine rock layers, the most important in creating the park's colorful formations is Navajo sandstone—at up to 2,200 feet, the thickest rock layer in the park. This formation was created some 200 million years ago during the Jurassic period, when North America was hot and dry. Movements in the earth's crust caused a shallow sea to rise up and cover sand dunes. Minerals from the water, including lime from the shells of sea creatures, glued sand particles together, eventually forming sandstone. Later crust movements caused the land to lift, draining away the sea but leaving rivers that gradually carved the relatively soft sandstone into the spectacular shapes seen today.

So where do the colors come from? Essentially, from plain old rust. Most of the rocks at Zion are stained by iron or hematite (iron oxide), either contained in the original stone or carried into the rocks by groundwater. Although iron often creates red and pink hues, seen on many of Zion's sandstone faces, it can also result in shades of brown, yellow, black, and even green. Sometimes the iron seeps into the rock, coloring it through, but it can also stain just the surface, often in vertical streaks. Deposits of salt left by evaporating water frequently cause white streaks, and rocks are also colored by bacteria that live on their surfaces. These bacteria ingest dust and expel iron, manganese, and other minerals, which stick to the rock and produce a shiny black, brown, or reddish surface called desert varnish.

(including golden eagles), lizards of all shapes and sizes, and a dozen species of snakes (only the Great Basin rattlesnake is poisonous, and it usually slithers away from you faster than you can run from it). Mule deer are common, and although seldom seen, there are also a few shy elk and bighorn sheep, plus foxes, coyotes, ringtail cats, beavers, porcupines, skunks, and plenty of squirrels and bats. Practically every summer visitor sees lizards, often the colorful collared and whiptail varieties, and it's easy to hear the song of the canyon wren and the call of the piñon jay.

ESSENTIALS

Located in southwest Utah, at elevations ranging from 3,666 feet to 8,726 feet, Zion National Park has several sections: **Zion Canyon,** the main part of the park, where everyone goes, and the less-visited **Kolob Terrace** and **Kolob Canyons** areas.

GETTING THERE/ACCESS POINTS   St. George and Cedar City (see chapter 9) are the closest towns with airport service. From either airport, it's easy to rent a car and drive to Zion. Utah 9 connects with Zion National Park, giving the main section of the park two entry gates—south and east. The drive into Zion Canyon (the main part of the park) from I-15 on the park's western side, following Utah 9 or Utah 17, and then Utah 9 to the south entrance at Springdale, is by far the more popular, with

Zion National Park

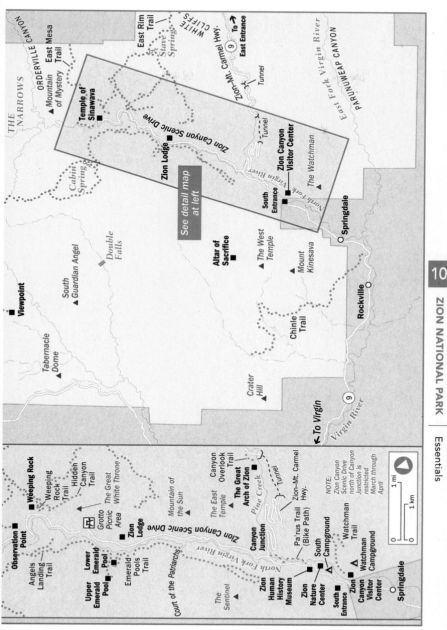

THE NARROWS

ORDERVILLE CANYON

Mountain of Mystery Trail

East Mesa Trail

East Rim Trail

WHITE CLIFFS

To → 9 East Entrance

Stave Spring

Zion-Mt. Carmel Hwy.

Tunnel

Temple of Sinawava

Cabin Spring

Zion Canyon Scenic Drive

Tunnel

Tunnel

Zion Lodge

Zion Canyon Visitor Center

Virgin River

North Fork

The Watchman

South Entrance

Springdale

East Fork Virgin River

PARUNUWEAP CANYON

See detail map at left

Guardian Angel

South

Double Falls

Altar of Sacrifice

The West Temple

Mount Kinesava

Viewpoint

Tabernacle Dome

Chinle Trail

Crater Hill

Rockville

10

ZION NATIONAL PARK | Essentials

← To Virgin

9

Virgin River

Observation Point

Angels Landing Trail

Weeping Rock

Weeping Rock Trail

Hidden Canyon Trail

The Great White Throne

Grotto Picnic Area

Zion Lodge

Mountain of the Sun

Canyon Overlook Trail

The East Temple

The Great Arch of Zion

Pine Creek

Zion-Mt. Carmel Hwy.

Tunnel

Upper Emerald Pool

Lower Emerald Pool

Emerald Pools Trail

Court of the Patriarchs

Zion Canyon Scenic Drive

North Fork Virgin River

Canyon Junction

Pa'rus Trail (Bike Path)

NOTE: Zion Canyon Scenic Drive north of Canyon Junction is restricted March through April

The Sentinel

Zion Human History Museum

Zion Nature Center

South Entrance

South Campground

Zion Canyon Visitor Center

Watchman Trail

Watchman Campground

Springdale

0   1 mi

0   1 km

two-thirds of park visitors arriving there. Most area lodgings and restaurants are found in Springdale, and the park's two campgrounds and the Zion Canyon Visitor Center are located just inside the south entrance. This approach has the added advantage of avoiding possible delays at the Zion–Mt. Carmel Tunnel. However, this approach is much less scenic than the eastern approach.

From the east, it's a spectacularly scenic 24-mile drive from Mt. Carmel on Utah 9, reached from either the north or south via U.S. 89. However, be aware that this route into the park drops over 2,500 feet in elevation, passes through the mile-long Zion–Mt. Carmel Tunnel, and winds down six steep switchbacks. The tunnel is too small for two-way traffic for any vehicles larger than standard passenger cars and pickup trucks. Buses, large trucks, and most recreational vehicles must be driven down the center of the tunnel, and therefore, all oncoming traffic must be stopped. This applies to all vehicles over 7 feet 10 inches wide (including mirrors) or 11 feet 4 inches tall (including luggage racks, and so on). Information is available at park entrances or by calling park headquarters (℃ **435/772-3256**). Affected vehicles must pay a $15 fee before entering the tunnel, good for two trips through the tunnel for that vehicle during a 7-day period. All vehicles over 13 feet 1 inch tall and certain other particularly large vehicles are prohibited from driving anywhere on the park road between the east entrance and Zion Canyon.

Kolob Terrace Road, with additional viewpoints and trail heads, heads north off Utah 9 from the village of Virgin, about 15 miles west of the park's southern entrance. This road is closed in the winter.

The Kolob Canyons section, in the park's northwest corner, can be reached via the short Kolob Canyons Road off I-15 exit 40.

Some helpful distances: The park is 83 miles southwest of Bryce Canyon National Park; 120 miles northwest of the north rim of Grand Canyon National Park, in northern Arizona; 309 miles south of Salt Lake City; and 158 miles northeast of Las Vegas, Nevada.

INFORMATION/VISITOR CENTERS   Contact Zion National Park, Springdale, UT 84767 (℃ **435/772-3256;** www.nps.gov/zion). Officials will mail you information (they request that you write rather than call, at least a month before your planned visit), but you will find everything they will send you and more at the park website. You can purchase books, posters, maps, DVDs, and CDs related to the park from the nonprofit **Zion Natural History Association,** Zion National Park, Springdale, UT 84767 (℃ **800/635-3959** or 435/772-3265; www.zionpark.org). Some publications are available in foreign languages. Those wanting to help the nonprofit association can join ($45 single or $60 family annually) and get a 20% discount on purchases, a 20% discount on most Zion Canyon Field Institute classes, and discounts at most other nonprofit bookstores at national parks, monuments, historic sites, and recreation areas.

The park has two visitor centers. The **Zion Canyon Visitor Center,** near the south entrance to the park, has a wide variety of outdoor exhibits. Rangers answer questions and provide backcountry permits; free brochures are available; and books, maps, videos, postcards, and posters are sold. In summer, it is open daily from 8am to 7:30pm, with shorter hours the rest of the year. The **Kolob Canyons Visitor Center,** in the northwest corner of the park, right off I-15, provides information, permits, books, and maps. It is open from 8am to 6pm in summer, with shorter hours the rest of the year.

Essentials

ZION NATIONAL PARK

The **Zion Human History Museum,** located about 1 mile inside the south entrance, offers museum exhibits, park information, and an orientation program, plus a bookstore. It's open daily in summer from 9am to 7pm, with shorter hours at other times.

Both visitor centers and the museum are closed on Christmas Day.

FEES, BACKCOUNTRY PERMITS & REGULATIONS Entry into the park (for up to 7 days), which includes unlimited use of the shuttle bus, costs $25 per private car, pickup truck, van, or RV, or $12 per individual 16 or older on motorcycle, bicycle, or foot (maximum charge of $25 per family). America the Beautiful National Parks and Federal Recreational Lands Passes are honored. Oversize vehicles are charged $15 for use of the Zion–Mt. Carmel Tunnel on the east side of the park (see "Getting There/Access Points," above).

Backcountry permits, available at either visitor center, are required for all overnight hikes in the park as well as for any slot canyon hikes. Permits cost $10 for 1 or 2 persons, $15 for 3 to 7, and $20 for 8 to 12 people. Camping costs $16 per night for basic campsites and $18 to $20 per night for sites with electric hookups (located in Watchman Campground).

Bicycles are prohibited in the Zion–Mt. Carmel Tunnel, the backcountry, and on trails, except the Pa'rus Trail. Feeding or disturbing wildlife is forbidden, as are vandalism and disturbing any natural feature of the park. Pets, which must be leashed at all times, are prohibited on all trails (except the Pa'rus Trail, where leashed pets are permitted), in the backcountry, and in public buildings.

SEASONS/AVOIDING THE CROWDS The park is open year-round (though visitor centers are closed Christmas Day), 24 hours a day, although weather conditions may limit some activities at certain times. For instance, avoid long hikes in midsummer, when the park bakes under temperatures that can exceed an unbearable 110°F (43°C), or during and immediately after winter storms, when ice and snow at higher elevations can make trails dangerous.

If possible, try to avoid the peak months of June, July, and August, when Zion receives almost half of its annual visitors. The quietest months are December, January, and February, but, of course, it's cold then; you may have to contend with some snow and ice. A good compromise is to visit in spring or fall, when the weather is usually good and the park is less crowded.

The best way to avoid crowds is to simply walk away from them, either taking the longer and more strenuous hiking trails or hiking into the backcountry. It's sad but true—most visitors never bother to venture far from the road, and their loss can be your gain. If you're willing to expend a little energy, you can enjoy a wonderful solitary experience. You can also avoid hordes of tourists by spending time in spectacular Kolob Canyons, in the far northwest section of the park; it receives surprisingly little use, at least compared to Zion Canyon.

RANGER & EDUCATIONAL PROGRAMS Rangers present a variety of free programs and activities. Evening programs, which last about 45 minutes, take place most evenings from April through September at the Watchman Campground Amphitheater and Zion Lodge Auditorium. They usually include a slide show, and cover topics such as the animals or plants of the park, geology, the night sky, mankind's role in the park, or some unique aspect of Zion, like slot canyons. Rangers also give short talks on similar subjects during the day at various locations, including the Zion Lodge

10

ZION NATIONAL PARK | Essentials

auditorium and the Zion Human History Museum. Ranger-guided hikes and walks, which may require reservations, might take you to little-visited areas of the park, on a trek to see wildflowers, or on a night hike under a full moon. These range from easy to very difficult. Rangers also lead shuttle tours during summer. The 2-hour "Ride with a Ranger" trip offers an opportunity to see the scenic drive and learn about Zion Canyon from a park ranger's perspective. Schedules of the various activities are posted on bulletin boards at the visitor centers, campgrounds, and other locations.

Children up to 12 years old can join the **Junior Rangers/Explorers ★★** and participate in a variety of hands-on activities, earning certificates, pins, and patches. Morning and afternoon sessions, each lasting 1½ to 2½ hours, take place daily from Memorial Day through Labor Day, with children meeting at the Zion Nature Center, near the entrance to South Campground.

The **Zion Canyon Field Institute,** operated by the nonprofit Zion Natural History Association, Zion National Park, Springdale, UT 84767 (© **800/635-3959,** 435/772-3265, or 435/772-3264 for the Field Institute; www.zionpark.org), offers a variety of single and multiday outdoor workshops and classes, including the highly recommended photo workshops, which are led by institute director Michael Plyler. Fees for most of the 1-day programs start at $35, and multiday programs cost from $100 to $300.

SEEING THE HIGHLIGHTS

The best way to see Zion is to spend a week here, starting by exploring the visitor center displays and programs, and then riding the shuttle bus to the various viewpoints (or driving in the off season). Gradually work up from short hikes and walks to full-day and overnight treks into the backcountry. That's the ideal, but for most visitors, time and finances dictate a shorter visit.

If you have only a day or two at the park, head first to the **Zion Canyon Visitor Center** for the orientation video and exhibits, and then talk with a ranger about the amount of time you have, your abilities, and interests. A brief visit to the **Zion Human History Museum** will give you a little more insight into humanity's role—historically and currently—in Zion. Because Zion offers such a variety of landscapes and activities, you can easily create your own itinerary. If your goal is to see as much of the park as possible in 1 full day, consider the following:

After a quick stop at the visitor center, hop on the free **shuttle bus,** which runs during the high season and takes you to the major roadside viewpoints. You can get off, look at the formations, take a short walk if you like, and then catch the next shuttle for a ride to the next stop.

You can get off the shuttle at the **Temple of Sinawava** and take the easy 2-mile round-trip **Riverside Walk,** which follows the Virgin River through a narrow canyon past hanging gardens. Then take the shuttle back to Zion Lodge (total time: 2–4 hr.).

 Wildlife Viewing

The earlier in the day you get out on the Zion Canyon Scenic Drive, the better chance you'll have of seeing wildlife.

At the lodge, stop by the gift shop and perhaps have lunch in the excellent restaurant.

Near the lodge is the trail head for the **Emerald Pools ★.** Especially pleasant on hot days, this easy walk through a forest of oak, maple, fir, and cottonwood trees leads to a waterfall, hanging garden, and the shimmering lower pool. This part of the walk should take about an hour round-trip, but those with a bit more time may want to add another hour and another mile to the loop by taking the moderately strenuous hike on a rocky, steeper trail to the upper pool. If you still have time and energy, head back to the south park entrance and stop at **Watchman** (east of Watchman Campground), for the 2-mile, 2-hour round-trip, moderately strenuous hike to a plateau with beautiful views of several rock formations and the town of Springdale. In the evening, try to take in a campground amphitheater program.

EXPLORING ZION BY SHUTTLE OR CAR

If you enter Zion from the east, along the steep **Zion–Mt. Carmel Highway,** you'll travel 13 miles through the park to the **Zion Canyon Visitor Center,** passing **Checkerboard Mesa,** a massive sandstone rock formation covered with horizontal and vertical lines that make it look like a huge fishing net. Continuing on, a fairyland of fantastically shaped rocks of red, orange, tan, and white, as well as the **Great Arch of Zion,** carved high in a stone cliff, will come into view.

A **shuttle-bus** system has been implemented in the main section of the park to reduce traffic congestion and the resultant problems of pollution, noise, and damage to park resources. The shuttle system consists of two loops: one in the town of Springdale and the other along Zion Canyon Scenic Drive, with the loops connecting at the visitor center. From April through October, access to the Zion Canyon Scenic Drive (above Utah 9) is limited to shuttle buses, hikers, and bikers. The only exception: overnight Zion Lodge guests and tour buses connected with the lodge, which have access as far as the lodge. Shuttles run frequently—about every 6 minutes at peak times—and have room for packs, coolers, strollers, and two bicycles. In winter, when the fewest number of visitors are here, you are permitted to drive the full length of Zion Canyon Scenic Drive in your own vehicle.

Those driving into the park at the northwest corner will find a short scenic drive open year-round. The **Kolob Canyons Road** (about 45 min. from Zion Canyon Visitor Center at I-15, exit 40) runs 5 miles among spectacular red and orange rocks, ending at a high vista. Allow about 45 minutes round-trip, and get a copy of the *Kolob Canyons Road Guide* at the Kolob Visitor Center. Here's what you'll pass along the way:

Leaving **Kolob Canyons Visitor Center,** drive along the Hurricane Fault to **Hurricane Cliffs,** a series of tall, gray cliffs composed of limestone, and onward to **Taylor Creek,** where a piñon-juniper forest clings to the rocky hillside, providing a home to the bright blue scrub jay. Your next stop is **Horse Ranch Mountain,** which, at 8,726 feet, is the national park's highest point. Passing a series of colorful rock layers, where you might be lucky enough to spot a golden eagle, your next stop is **Box Canyon,** along the south fork of Taylor Creek, with sheer rock walls soaring over 1,500 feet high. Next you'll see a multicolored layer of rock, pushed upward by tremendous forces from within the earth.

Continue until you reach a canyon, which exposes a rock wall that likely began as a sand dune before being covered by an early sea and cemented into stone. Next stop is a side canyon, with large, arched alcoves crowned with delicate curved ceilings. Head on to a view of **Timber Top Mountain,** which has a sagebrush-blanketed

Exploring Zion by Shuttle or Car

desert at its base but is covered with stately fir and ponderosa pine at its peak. Watch for mule deer on the brushy hillsides, especially between October and March, when they might be spotted just after sunrise or before sunset.

From here, continue to **Rockfall Overlook;** a large scar on the mountainside marks the spot where a 1,000-foot chunk of stone crashed to the earth in July 1983, the victim of erosion. And finally, stop to see the canyon walls themselves, colored orange-red by iron oxide and striped black by mineral-laden water running down the cliff faces.

OUTDOOR PURSUITS

Guided hiking, rock climbing, and biking trips in the park and surrounding area are offered by several reliable local companies, including **Zion Adventure Company,** 36 Lion Blvd., at the corner of Lion Boulevard and Zion Park Boulevard, Springdale (© **435/772-1001;** www.zionadventures.com), and **Zion Rock & Mountain Guides,** 1458 Zion Park Blvd., Springdale (© **435/772-3303;** www.zionrockguides. com). **Zion Cycles,** 868 Zion Park Blvd., behind Zion Pizza & Noodle, Springdale (© **435/772-0400;** www.zioncycles.com), rents, repairs, and advises about mountain and road bikes. In the park, the free shuttle offers the best way to reach trail heads.

Biking & Mountain Biking

Although bikes are prohibited on all trails and forbidden to travel cross-country within the national park boundaries, two developments have helped Zion become one of America's few bike-friendly national parks.

The **Pa'rus Trail** runs 2 miles along the Virgin River from the South Campground entrance to Zion Canyon Scenic Drive, near its intersection with the Zion–Mt. Carmel Highway. Along the way, the trail crosses the North Fork of the Virgin River and several creeks, and provides good views of Watchman, West Temple, the Sentinel, and other lower canyon formations. The paved trail is open to bicyclists, pedestrians, and those with strollers or wheelchairs, but is closed to motor vehicles.

> ## Impressions
>
> *Nothing can exceed the wondrous beauty of Zion . . . in the nobility and beauty of the sculptures, there is no comparison.*
> —Geologist Clarence Dutton, 1880

Bikes are permitted on the park's established roads at any time, except in the Zion–Mt. Carmel tunnel, where they are always prohibited. From April through October, **Zion Canyon Scenic Drive** north of the Zion–Mt. Carmel Highway is open only to shuttle buses, bicyclists, and hikers, plus tour buses and motorists going to Zion Lodge. The rest of the year, the road is open to private motor vehicles, and the shuttle buses don't run. Bicyclists should stay to the right to allow shuttle buses to pass.

On Bureau of Land Management and state-owned property just outside the park, mountain bikers will find numerous rugged jeep trails that are great for mountain biking, plus more than 70 miles of slickrock cross-country trails and single-track trails. **Gooseberry Mesa,** above the community of Springdale, is generally considered the best mountain-biking destination in the area, but good trails can be found on nearby Wire and Grafton mesas.

Talk with the knowledgeable staff at **Zion Cycles** (above) about the best trails for your interests and abilities. This full-service bike shop offers maps, a full range of bikes and accessories, repairs, and rentals ($38–$55 for a full day, $28–$45 for a half-day).

For guided mountain or road bike trips, contact **Zion Adventure Company** (above). A guided hike and road bike trip into the park costs $139 for a half-day and $179 for a full day, per person for two people, with lower per-person rates for larger groups. **Zion Rock & Mountain Guides** (above) also offers guided mountain bike excursions outside the national park at similar rates.

Hiking

Zion offers a wide variety of hiking trails, ranging from easy half-hour walks on paved paths to grueling overnight hikes over rocky terrain. Hikers with a fear of heights should be especially careful when choosing trails; many include steep, dizzying drop-offs. Below are a variety of hiking suggestions.

The **Weeping Rock Trail,** among the park's shortest trails, is a .4-mile round-trip walk from the Zion Canyon Scenic Drive to a rock alcove with a spring and hanging gardens of ferns and wildflowers. Although paved, the trail is steep and not suitable for wheelchairs.

Another short hike is the **Lower Emerald Pools Trail ★★**, an easy 1-hour walk. If you want to extend your trip to a moderately strenuous 2-hour hike, you can continue along the loop. A .6-mile paved path from the Emerald Pools parking area through a forest of oak, maple, fir, and cottonwood leads to a waterfall, a hanging garden, and the Lower Emerald Pool, and is suitable for those in wheelchairs, with assistance. From here, a steeper, rocky trail (not appropriate for wheelchairs) continues past cactus, yucca, and juniper another .5 mile to Upper Emerald Pool, with another waterfall. A third pool, just above Lower Emerald Pool, offers impressive reflections of the cliffs. The pools are named for the green color of the water, which is caused by algae.

A particularly scenic hike is the **Hidden Canyon Trail,** a 2.4-mile moderately strenuous round-trip hike that takes about 3 hours. Starting at the Weeping Rock parking area, the trail climbs 850 feet through a narrow water-carved canyon, with a small natural arch upstream from the mouth of the canyon. Hidden Canyon Trail includes long drop-offs and is not recommended for anyone with a fear of heights.

Another moderately strenuous but relatively short hike is the **Watchman Trail,** which starts near the transit/visitor center. This 2.7-mile round-trip hike gets surprisingly little use, possibly because it can be very hot in midday. Climbing to a plateau near the base of the formation called the Watchman, it offers splendid views of lower Zion Canyon, the Towers of the Virgin, and West Temple formations.

For a strenuous 4-hour, 5.4-mile round-trip hike—one that's definitely not for anyone with even a mild fear of heights—take the **Angels Landing Trail** to a summit that offers spectacular views into Zion Canyon, with the Virgin River gently bending around three sides at the bottom of the canyon, the Great White Throne and Red Arch Mountain to the southeast, and the entrance to the Narrows beyond the Temple of Sinawava to the north. But be prepared: The final .5 mile follows a narrow, knife-edge trail along a steep ridge, where footing can be slippery even under the best of circumstances. Support chains have been set along parts of the trail. Shortly before reaching the head of the canyon, a series of 21 switchbacks has been built into a cleft in the wall; these are regarded as one of the engineering marvels of the park.

Hiking the **Narrows ★★** is not really hiking a trail at all, but involves walking or wading along the bottom of the Virgin River, through a stunning 1,000-foot-deep chasm that, at a mere 20 feet wide, definitely lives up to its name. Passing fancifully sculptured sandstone arches, hanging gardens, and waterfalls, this moderately strenuous 16-mile one-way hike can be completed in less than a day or in several days, depending on how quickly you want to go.

Warning: The Narrows is not an easy hike by any means. The Narrows is subject to flash flooding and can be very treacherous. Park service officials remind hikers that they are responsible for their own safety and should always check on current water conditions and weather forecasts before heading out. This hike is *not* recommended when rain is forecast. Hikers should wear sturdy boots or shoes with good ankle support that they won't mind getting wet, be prepared for cold temperatures with a sweater or jacket, and put everything in waterproof containers. Experienced Narrows hikers also recommend that you take a walking stick to help steady yourself against the strong currents. Sticks are sometimes available near the end of the Riverside Walk, but you're better off taking your own—hikers are prohibited from cutting tree branches to make walking sticks. Finally, because of the strong currents, park officials recommend that kids under 4' 8" tall not hike in the river. Permits are required for full-day and overnight hikes (check with rangers for details), but are not needed for easy, short day hikes, which you can access from just beyond the end of the **Riverside Walk,** a 2.2-mile round-trip trail that starts at the Temple of Sinawava parking area.

Horseback Riding

Guided rides in the park are available March through October from **Canyon Trail Rides** (🕿 **435/679-8665;** www.canyonrides.com), with ticket sales and information near Zion Lodge. A 1-hour ride along the Virgin River costs $40; a half-day ride on the Sand Beach Trail costs $75. Riders must weigh no more than 220 pounds, and children must be at least 7 years old for the 1-hour ride and 10 years old for the half-day ride. Reservations are advised.

Rock Climbing

Technical rock climbers like the sandstone cliffs in Zion Canyon, although rangers warn that much of the rock is loose, or "rotten," and climbing equipment and techniques suitable for granite are often less effective on sandstone. Permits ($10 for 1 or 2 persons, $15 for 3 to 7, and $20 for 8 to 12 people) are required for overnight climbs, and because some routes may be closed at times, climbers should check at the Zion Canyon Visitor Center before setting out. **Zion Adventure Company** and **Zion Rock & Mountain Guides** (above) offer a variety of guided rock climbing trips, as well as instruction. Typical per-person rates are $125 for a half-day and $160 for a full day for two people, with lower per-person rates for larger groups. Zion Rock & Mountain Guides also offers equipment rentals and sales.

Swimming

Hikers in the Narrows soon find that they are participating in a watersport, as they wade along the "trail" at the bottom of the Virgin River. Swimming and wading are prohibited in the Emerald Pools. Swimming is permitted south of South Campground amphitheater; check with the visitor center about other areas that would be safe for swimming during your visit. You can also go tubing in the river; **Zion Adventure Company** (above) rents tubes for $15.

Outdoor Pursuits | ZION NATIONAL PARK

Wildlife Viewing & Bird-Watching

It's a rare visitor to Zion who doesn't spot a critter of some sort, from mule deer to the numerous varieties of lizards, including the park's largest, the chuckwalla, which can grow to 20 inches. The ringtail cat, a relative of the raccoon, prowls Zion Canyon at night and is not above helping itself to your camping supplies. Along the Virgin River, you'll see bank beavers, so named because they live in burrows dug into riverbanks instead of building dams.

If you're interested in spotting birds, you're in luck here. The peregrine falcon, among the world's fastest birds, sometimes nests in the Weeping Rock area, where you're also likely to see the dipper, winter wren, and white-throated swift. Also in the park are golden eagles, several species of hummingbirds, ravens, and piñon jays.

> **Impressions**
>
> *You can't see anything from your car. You've got to get out of the damn thing and walk!*
>
> —Author Edward Abbey

Snakes include the poisonous Great Basin rattler, found below 8,000 feet elevation, as well as nonpoisonous kingsnakes and gopher snakes. Tarantulas are often seen in the late summer and fall. Contrary to popular belief, the tarantula's bite is not deadly, although it can be somewhat painful.

Remember, it's illegal to feed the wildlife.

CAMPING

The best places to camp are at one of the **national park campgrounds ★★★** just inside the park's south entrance. Both of Zion's main campgrounds have paved roads, well-spaced sites, and lots of trees. Facilities include restrooms with flush toilets but no showers, a dump station, a public telephone, and sites for those with disabilities. The fee is $16 per night for basic sites, or $18 to $20 per night for sites with electric hookups.

South Campground has 127 sites (no hookups) and is usually open from early March through October only. Reservations are not accepted and the campground often fills by noon in summer. Some campers stay at nearby commercial campgrounds their first night in the area, then hurry into the park the next morning, circling like vultures until a site becomes available.

Watchman Campground (✆ 877/444-6777 or www.recreation.gov for reservations) has 164 sites. Of those, 95 have electric hookups and 69 are available only to those camping in tents. Watchman is open year-round (reservations available spring through fall only).

Lava Point, with only six sites, is located on the Kolob Terrace. It has fire grates, tables, and toilets, but no water and no fee. Vehicles are limited to 19 feet, and it's usually open from June through mid-October.

Outside the Park

Just outside the east and south park entrances are commercial campgrounds with hot showers and RV hookups. Note that the park's visitor center, campgrounds, and most of its attractions are closer to the south entrance.

East Zion Riverside RV Park is located in the Best Western East Zion Thunderbird Lodge complex in Mt. Carmel Junction, about 13 miles east of the east entrance to the national park (at the junction of Utah 9 and U.S. 89; ✆ **435/648-2203;** www.zionnational-park.com). Especially good for self-contained RVs, the park sits along the banks of the Virgin River in the shade of cottonwood trees, and offers campers use of the pool, hot tub, and other amenities at the adjacent Thunderbird Lodge. It has 12 sites, all with hookups, and a dump station. It's open year-round. The fee is $15 per night.

Zion Canyon Campground ★ is at 479 Zion Park Blvd., Springdale, a half-mile south of the park's south entrance (✆ **435/772-3237;** www.zioncamp.com). It's open year-round and offers 200 tent and RV sites, many of which are shaded. Although it gets quite crowded in summer, the campground is clean and well maintained. There are some especially large sites for big RVs, and it has a dump station, a swimming pool, a game room, a playground, and a store. Rates range from $30 to $35 for two people.

WHERE TO STAY

The only lodging actually in Zion National Park is Zion Lodge. The other properties listed here are all in Springdale, a village at Zion's south entrance. Pets are not accepted unless otherwise noted. Room tax adds 10.2% in the park and 12.8% outside the park. For additional information about lodging, dining, and other services in the area, contact the **Zion Canyon Visitors Bureau,** P.O. Box 331, Springdale, UT 84767 (✆ **888/518-7070;** www.zionpark.com).

In the Park

Zion Lodge ★★★ This handsome lodge is a wonderful place to stay, but the main draw is its location. Built in 1925 by the Union Pacific Railroad, the lodge was destroyed by fire in 1966, then rebuilt and restored to its historic appearance. It's the only lodging inside the park, and it sits in a valley with spectacular views of the park's rock cliffs. The charming and genuinely historic cabins are our first choice here. Each has a private porch, stone (gas-burning) fireplace, two queen-size or double beds, and pine walls. The comfortable modern motel units have two queen-size beds and a private porch or balcony. The plush motel suites are spacious, with one king-size bed, a separate sitting room with a queen-size hide-a-bed, and a refrigerator. Ranger programs are presented in the lodge auditorium in summer. All units are nonsmoking.

Zion National Park, UT. www.zionlodge.com. ✆ 435/772-7700. Information and reservations: Xanterra Parks & Resorts, Central Reservations, 6312 S. Fiddlers Green Circle, Ste. 600N, Greenwood Village, CO 80111. ✆ 888/297-2757 or 303/297-2757. Fax 303/297-3175. 121 units. Mid-Mar to Nov motel rooms $170 double; cabins $180 double; suites $186 double. Discounts (sometimes up to 50% off) and packages available at other times. AE, DISC, MC, V. **Amenities:** 2 restaurants, the Red Rock Grill and Castle Dome Cafe (see reviews, p. 208). *In room:* A/C.

Nearby

Best Western East Zion Thunderbird Lodge ★ A well-maintained two-story motel with Southwest decor, the Thunderbird offers quiet, spacious, comfortable rooms, with king- or queen-size beds, wood furnishings, photos or artwork depicting area scenery, and a private balcony or patio. The lodging has a gas station and a convenience store on the premises. All rooms are nonsmoking. Also under the same management, with the same contact information, is a nearby house with two bedrooms, each with their own bathroom, a living room with a fireplace and vaulted ceiling, and a large fully equipped kitchen for $295 for up to six people (minimum

2-day rental). The complex also includes a campground, the East Zion Riverside RV Park. (See "Camping," above.)

At the junction of Utah 9 and U.S. 89 (P.O. Box 5536), Mt. Carmel Junction, UT 84755. www.zion national-park.com. © **888/848-6358** or 435/648-2203. Fax 435/648-2239. 61 units. May–Oct $114–$129 double; Nov–Apr $73–$83. AE, DC, DISC, MC, V. **Amenities:** Restaurant, Thunderbird Restaurant; 9-hole golf course; Jacuzzi; large outdoor heated pool (Apr–Oct only). *In room:* A/C, TV, fridge (in some), hair dryer, free Wi-Fi.

Best Western Zion Park Inn ★

This is a good choice for those who are seeking an upscale, reliable chain motel. Rooms in the handsome two-story complex, located 1½ miles from the park, are tastefully appointed in Southwest style, with two queen- or one king-size bed, artwork depicting the area, and solid wood furnishings. Especially appealing are the units with pitched, high ceilings, with windows that capture the views of the colorful rock formations outside.

1215 Zion Park Blvd., Springdale, UT 84767. www.zionparkinn.com. © **800/934-7275** or 435/772-3200. Fax 435/772-2449. 120 units. Mar–Oct $115–$135 double, $140–$180 suite or family unit; Nov–Feb $68–$85 double, $90–$130 suite or family unit. Children 17 and younger stay free in parent's room. AE, DC, DISC, MC, V. 1 pet accepted, for an extra fee of $25. **Amenities:** Restaurant; sports bar; putting green; Jacuzzi; heated outdoor pool (Mar–Oct only). *In room:* A/C, TV, hair dryer.

Canyon Ranch Motel

Consisting of a series of two- and four-unit cottages set back from the highway, this motel's buildings simply ooze charm, with the look of 1930s-style cabins on the outside and modern motel rooms inside. Rooms are either new or newly remodeled, and options include one queen- or king-size bed, two queen-size beds, or one queen-size and one double. Some rooms have showers only, while others have tub/shower combos. Room no. 13, with two queen-size beds, offers spectacular views of the Zion National Park rock formations; views from most other rooms are almost as good. The units surround a lawn with trees and picnic tables. All units are nonsmoking.

668 Zion Park Blvd. (P.O. Box 175), Springdale, UT 84767. www.canyonranchmotel.com. © **866/946-6276** or 435/772-3357. 22 units. Apr–Oct $99–$119 double, $139 kitchenette; Nov–Mar $69–$89 double, $109 kitchenette. AE, DISC, MC, V. Pets accepted in some units, only 1 or 2 dogs per unit ($24 fee 1st night, $12 2nd night, $6 3rd night). **Amenities:** Jacuzzi; outdoor pool (Apr–Oct only). *In room:* A/C, TV, kitchenette (some units), Wi-Fi (free).

Cliffrose Lodge & Gardens ★

With delightful river frontage and 5 acres of lawns, shade trees, and flower gardens, the Cliffrose offers a beautiful setting just outside the entrance to Zion National Park. The architecture is Southwestern adobe style, with redwood balconies, and the outdoor rock waterfall whirlpool tub is a delight, especially in the evening. Modern, well-kept rooms have all the standard motel appointments, and unusually large bathrooms. We especially like the four very luxurious Canyon View Suites, which sleep up to six guests each. On the lawns, you'll find comfortable seating, a playground, and a lawn swing. All units are nonsmoking.

281 Zion Park Blvd., Springdale, UT 84767. www.cliffroselodge.com. © **800/243-8824** or 435/772-3234. 50 units. Apr–Oct and holidays $149–$199 per unit; rates lower at other times. AE, DISC, MC, V. **Amenities:** Jacuzzi; large outdoor heated pool (Apr–Oct only). *In room:* A/C, TV, fridge, Wi-Fi (free).

Desert Pearl Inn ★

This riverside property offers luxurious and comfortable accommodations with beautiful views of the area's scenery from private terraces or balconies. Spacious rooms are decorated in modern Southwest style, with either two queen- or one king-size bed, and each room also has a queen-size sofa sleeper.

Bathrooms are two rooms: One has a tub/shower combo, toilet, and bidet; the other has a closet, vanity, and sink. There are also luxurious suites. The grounds are nicely landscaped. All units are nonsmoking.

707 Zion Park Blvd., Springdale, UT 84767. www.desertpearl.com. © **888/828-0898** or 435/772-8888. Fax 435/772-8889. 61 units. Summer $158–$188 double, $298 suite; winter $98–$118 double, $198 suite. AE, DISC, MC, V. **Amenities:** Jacuzzi; huge outdoor heated pool (Apr–Oct only). *In room:* A/C, TV, fridge, hair dryer, minibar, Wi-Fi (free).

Driftwood Lodge   Beautiful lawns and gardens enhance this attractive, well-kept motel—a quiet, lush complex perfect for sitting back and admiring the spectacular rock formations that practically surround the town. The spacious rooms have wood-grain furnishings plus patios or balconies. Most standard rooms have two queen-size beds; others have one king-size. Two family suites each have one king-size and two queen-size beds, and the handsome king suites have a separate sitting room, king-size bed, and a microwave. The restaurant has a delightful outdoor patio with splendid views.

1515 Zion Park Blvd. (P.O. Box 447), Springdale, UT 84767. www.driftwoodlodge.net. © **888/801-8811** or 435/772-3262. Fax 435/772-3702. 53 units. Apr–Nov $129–$149 double, $169–$209 family unit and suite; Dec–Mar $59–$79 double, $89–$129 family unit and suite. AE, DC, DISC, MC, V. Pets accepted at management's discretion, $25 fee. **Amenities:** Restaurant; Jacuzzi; outdoor heated pool (Apr–Oct only). *In room:* A/C, TV, fridge, hair dryer, Wi-Fi (free).

Flanigan's Inn ★★   A mountain-lodge atmosphere suffuses this very attractive complex of natural wood and rock set among trees, lawns, and flowers, just outside the entrance to Zion National Park. This is a place where you will actually want to spend time relaxing. The rooms are artfully decorated in a spalike atmosphere, with top-of-the-line amenities. Most units have decks or patios and large windows overlooking a natural courtyard, including a koi pond, heated pool, and hot tub. Suites have microwaves in addition to small refrigerators, and the two completely furnished villas are beautifully decorated upscale homes separate from the main inn. A nature trail leads to a hilltop labyrinth and spectacular vistas. There is a full-service spa, including a salon and yoga exercise room, and bicycles are available for guests' use. The inn is 50% wind powered and entirely nonsmoking.

450 Zion Park Blvd., Springdale, UT 84767. www.flanigans.com. © **800/765-7787** or 435/772-3244. Fax 435/772-3396. 36 units. Mid-Mar through Nov and holidays $129–$169 double, $249–$359 suite and villa; lower rates at other times. AE, DISC, MC, V. **Amenities:** Restaurant, Spotted Dog Café (see review, p. 209); outdoor Jacuzzi; outdoor heated pool (Apr–Oct only); full-service spa. *In room:* A/C, TV, fridge, hair dryer, Wi-Fi (free).

Harvest House Bed & Breakfast at Zion ★★   Personal touches and yummy breakfasts make this B&B a fine alternative to a standard motel. Built in 1989, the house is Utah territorial-style (similar to Victorian), with a garden sitting area with a koi pond and spectacular views of the national park's rock formations. Rooms are charming, comfortable, and quiet, with king- or queen-size beds and private bathrooms. The units are furnished with an eclectic mix of contemporary items, and original art dots the walls. One upstairs room faces west and has grand sunset views, while the other two have private decks facing the impressive formations of Zion.

There's a big-screen TV in the living room with access to some 40 movie channels; and the gourmet breakfasts are sumptuous, with fresh-baked breads, fresh-squeezed orange juice, granola, fruit, yogurt, and a hot main course. All units are nonsmoking.

29 Canyon View Dr., Springdale, UT 84767. www.harvesthouse.net. © **800/719-7493** or 435/772-3880. 4 units. $100–$135 double. Rates include full breakfast. DISC, MC, V. Children 7 and older welcome. **Amenities:** Outdoor Jacuzzi. *In room:* A/C, no phone, Wi-Fi (free).

Historic Pioneer Lodge and Restaurant ★   Old West ambience and style with modern amenities and comfortable beds are what you'll find at the Historic Pioneer Lodge. Standard rooms have a homey feel with one king- or two queen-size beds and some of the quietest heating/air conditioning units around (and heating and cooling are remote control). There are 40 rooms and three suites, and all units have rustic log furnishings, good lighting, full carpeting, and granite counters. On the premises is a gift shop selling the work of Southern Utah artists, an Internet cafe, and a reasonably priced restaurant where lodge guests receive a 10% discount during their stay. All units are nonsmoking.

838 Zion Park Blvd., Springdale, UT 84767. www.pioneerlodge.com. © **888/772-3233** or 435/772-3233. 43 units. Summer $164–$186 double, $208–$329 suite; lower rates the rest of the year. AE, DISC, MC, V. **Amenities:** Restaurant; Jacuzzi; outdoor heated pool (Apr–Oct only). *In room:* A/C, TV, fridge, hair dryer, Wi-Fi (free).

Majestic View Lodge ★★   This place truly lives up to its name: virtually every room at this sprawling complex offers spectacular glimpses of the surrounding scenery. It's a lovely place to start the day, or to wrap up a long afternoon of hiking, with the added bonus of being very close to the park entrance. The lodge is actually a series of two-story stucco and log buildings, and each unit has its own balcony or patio (perfect for watching the sunset light up the rock formations). The spotless rooms are furnished with rustic aspen decor, including either a king bed or two queen beds, and the deluxe suites have kitchenettes. Spend some time at the restaurant or saloon—both sharing the excellent views—or visit the lodge's sprawling trading post and wildlife museum. There's free shuttle service to the park.

2400 Zion Park Blvd., Springdale, UT 84767. www.majesticviewlodge.com. © **866/772-0665** or 435/772-0665. 69 units. Apr–Oct $159–$169 double; Nov–Mar $89 double. AE, DC, DISC, MC, V. **Amenities:** Restaurant; bar; brewpub; Jacuzzi; heated outdoor pool. *In room:* A/C, TV, fridge, Wi-Fi (free).

Under the Eaves Inn ★★   This romantic 1931 home, located in the heart of Springdale, offers handsomely decorated historic rooms, beautiful gardens and shade trees, and spectacular views from what innkeepers Joe Pitti and Mark Chambers call "the best front porch in Utah." The units range from the basic Hiker's Room to a luxurious suite—covering 1,200 square feet, it has a vaulted ceiling, a wood-burning stove, a kitchenette, and a claw-foot tub plus separate shower. The cute Garden Cottage, built in 1928, was moved here from inside the national park. It contains two small but comfortable rooms on the main floor, and the more rustic, lower level Hiker's Room. Breakfast is off the menu at nearby Oscar's Cafe, served from 7 to 11am. All units are nonsmoking.

980 Zion Park Blvd. (P.O. Box 29), Springdale, UT 84767. www.undertheeaves.com. © **866/261-2655** or 435/772-3457. 6 units. $85–$150 double; $185 suite. Rates include full breakfast. AE, DISC, MC, V. Children allowed at management's discretion. *In room:* A/C, no phone, Wi-Fi (free).

Zion Park Motel   This economical motel is a good choice for travelers on a budget, offering comfortable, attractively furnished rooms with showers or tub/shower combos. Standard rooms are a bit small, especially with the refrigerator and microwave they all have, but the light-colored wood furnishings and walls help make them feel bigger. The one king- or two queen-size beds have colorful spreads, and art depicting the region decorates the walls. The family units sleep six. All units are nonsmoking.

865 Zion Park Blvd. (P.O. Box 365), Springdale, UT 84767. www.zionparkmotel.com. ✆ **435/772-3251.** 21 units. $84 double; $104–$149 family unit and suite. AE, DISC, MC, V. **Amenities:** Outdoor heated pool (Apr–Oct only). *In room:* A/C, TV, fridge, full kitchen (in 2 units), Wi-Fi (free).

WHERE TO EAT

With the exception of the Castle Dome Cafe and the Red Rock Grill, these restaurants are all located on the main road to the park through Springdale.

In the Park

Castle Dome Cafe ☺ SNACK BAR   Located at the north end of Zion Lodge, this simple fast food restaurant offers an outdoor dining patio serving cinnamon buns, burgers, sandwiches, hot dogs, pizza, ice cream, frozen yogurt, and similar fare. No alcoholic beverages are served.

Zion Lodge, Zion National Park. ✆ **435/772-3213.** Menu items $3.75–$9.95. No credit cards. Summer daily 7am–9pm; shorter hours the rest of the year.

Red Rock Grill ★★ AMERICAN   Try to have at least one meal here during your national park vacation. The restaurant's mountain lodge decor competes for your attention with the spectacular rock formations, visible through the dining room's large windows; for an even better view, dine on the outside patio. The menu changes periodically, but breakfasts usually offer all the usuals, including a good buffet. At lunch, you'll likely find a buffet or two, plus items such as chicken salad and grilled salmon or beef burgers. Specialties at dinner might include the excellent Santa Fe flatiron steak (grilled and topped with pico de gallo and fried onions), a bison rib-eye steak with a potato medley, grilled pork loin with prickly pear sauce, slow-cooked baby back ribs, plus seafood and pasta. We heartily recommend the lodge's specialty desserts, such as the bourbon pecan pie or turtle Bundt cake. There is full liquor service.

Zion Lodge, Zion National Park. ✆ **435/772-7760.** www.zionlodge.com. Dinner reservations required in summer. Main courses $4–$10 breakfast, $8–$12 lunch, $14–$29 dinner. AE, DC, DISC, MC, V. Daily 6:30–10:30am, 11:30am–3pm, and 5–10pm.

Nearby

Bit & Spur Restaurant & Saloon ★★ MEXICAN/SOUTHWESTERN   Rough wood-and-stone walls and an exposed-beam ceiling give this restaurant the look of an Old West saloon. It's actually much more than that, with a family dining room, patio dining, and original art decorating the walls. The food here is also a lot better than you'll find in the average saloon, closer to what we expect in an upscale Santa Fe restaurant. The menu changes seasonally, but usually includes Mexican standards such as burritos, flautas, chiles rellenos, and a traditional green-chili stew with pork and rice. You'll also often find seafood, such as grilled salmon, and our personal favorite, grilled chili-rubbed rib-eye steak with a port wine and blue cheese demiglace. The Bit & Spur has full liquor service—try the fresh fruit margaritas—an extensive wine list, and an excellent variety of microbrewed beers.

1212 Zion Park Blvd., Springdale. ✆ **435/772-3498.** www.bitandspur.com. Reservations recommended. Main courses $12–$25. AE, DISC, MC, V. Spring–fall daily 5–10pm; call for winter hours.

Spotted Dog Café ★★ AMERICAN/REGIONAL   This restaurant's art-filled interior makes the most of the scenery, with large windows for inside diners plus a Euro-style outdoor patio with spectacular views of Zion Canyon. Selections vary by season and may include Rocky Mountain trout, lamb, free-range poultry, hormone-free beef, environmentally farmed fish, hearty pastas, fresh summer salads, plus local specialties. There is also a surprisingly healthy children's menu. It offers an express breakfast buffet daily at 7am featuring country potatoes, bacon, link sausage, plus selections of eggs, cereals, pastries, yogurt, fresh fruit, French toast, waffles, and freshly baked specialties. The Spotted Dog has an excellent wine cellar, microbrewed draft beers, and complete liquor service.

At Flanigan's Inn (p. 206), 428 Zion Park Blvd., Springdale. ✆ **435/772-0700.** Reservations recommended. Main courses $12–$26. AE, DISC, MC, V. Daily 7–11am and 5–9pm; reduced hours in winter.

Zion Park Gift & Deli ★ 🍴 DELI   Want a top quality sandwich at an economical price? This is the place. You can eat at one of the cafe-style tables inside or on the patio outside, or you can carry your sandwich off on a hike or to a national park picnic ground. All baked goods, including the excellent sandwich breads and sub rolls, are made in-house. In typical deli style, you order at the counter and wait as your sandwich is prepared with your choice of bread, meats, cheeses, and condiments. This is also a good breakfast stop for those who enjoy fresh-baked cinnamon rolls, muffins, banana nut bread, and similar goodies, with a cup of espresso. Locally made candy, including 14 flavors of excellent fudge, and 24 flavors of ice cream and frozen yogurt are offered. No alcohol is served.

866 Zion Park Blvd., Springdale. ✆ **435/772-3843.** All items $4.95–$10. DISC, MC, V. Summer Mon–Sat 8:30am–9:30pm; reduced hours in winter.

Zion Pizza & Noodle ★ ☺ PIZZA/PASTA   A local favorite, this busy cafe offers good pizza and pasta in a funky atmosphere—a former Mormon church with a turquoise steeple. The dining room has small, closely spaced tables and black-and-white photos on the walls. You find your own table, place your order at the counter, and a server delivers it. The pizzas, with lots of chewy crust, are baked in a slate stone oven. Choose one of the house favorites, such as the Southwest burrito pizza or barbecue chicken pizza, or create your own by adding any of the more than 20 extra toppings, from pepperoni to green chilies to pineapple. The menu also offers pastas, calzones, and stromboli. Beer is served inside and in the delightful year-round beer garden.

868 Zion Park Blvd., Springdale. ✆ **435/772-3815.** www.zionpizzanoodle.com. Reservations not accepted. Entrees $11–$16. No credit cards. Summer daily from 4pm; call for winter hours.

WHAT TO SEE & DO IN NEARBY SPRINGDALE

Just outside the south entrance to Zion National Park, in Springdale, are two worthwhile attractions.

The **Tanner Twilight Concert Series** presents a varied performing arts program in the stunning, 2,000-seat outdoor **Tanner Amphitheater,** just off Zion Park Boulevard. Performances range from symphony orchestra concerts and dance performances to rock, jazz, and gospel concerts. Shows begin at 8pm many Saturdays throughout the summer, and cost $10 for adults and $5 for youths (18 and younger).

For information, contact **Dixie State College,** in St. George (© **435/652-7994;** www.dixie.edu/tanner/index.html).

The **Zion Canyon Theatre,** 145 Zion Park Blvd. (© **888/256-3456** or 435/772-2400; www.zioncanyontheatre.com), boasts a huge screen—some 60 feet high by 82 feet across. Here you can see the dramatic film *Zion Canyon: Treasure of the Gods,* with thrilling scenes of the Zion National Park area, including a hair-raising flash flood through Zion Canyon's Narrows and some dizzying bird's-eye views. The theater also shows a variety of other Hollywood and large-format films. Admission is $8 adults and $6 children under 12. The theater is open daily from 11am in summer; call for winter hours. The theater complex also contains a tourist information center, an ATM, a picnic area, gift and souvenir shops, restaurants, and a grocery store.

What to See & Do in Nearby Springdale

ZION NATIONAL PARK

BRYCE CANYON NATIONAL PARK

I f you can visit only one national park in your lifetime, make it **Bryce Canyon** ★★★, a place full of magic, inspiration, and spectacular beauty. The main draw of the park is the thousands of intricately shaped hoodoos: those silent rock sentinels and congregations gathered in colorful cathedrals, arranged in formations that invite your imagination to run wild.

Geologically speaking, hoodoos are simply pinnacles of rock, often oddly shaped, left standing after millions of years of water and wind have eroded the surrounding rock. But perhaps the real truth lies in a Paiute legend. These American Indians, who lived in the area for several hundred years before being forced out by Anglo pioneers, told of "Legend People" who once lived here; because of their evil ways, they were turned to stone by the powerful Coyote and even today remain frozen in time.

Whatever the cause, mythical or scientific, Bryce Canyon is certainly unique. Its intricate and often whimsical formations are on a more human scale than the impressive rocks seen at Zion, Capitol Reef, and Canyonlands national parks. And Bryce is far easier to explore than the huge and sometimes intimidating Grand Canyon. Bryce is comfortable and inviting in its beauty; by gazing over the rim, or spending even just one morning on the trail, you will feel you're on intimate terms with the park.

Although the colorful hoodoos first grab your attention, it isn't long before you notice the deep amphitheaters, with their cliffs, windows, and arches, all colored in shades of red, brown, orange, yellow, and white that change and glow with the rising and setting sun. Beyond the rocks and light are the other faces of the park: three separate life zones at the various elevations in the park, each with its own unique vegetation, and a kingdom of animals, from the busy chipmunks and ground squirrels to the stately mule deer and its archenemy, the mountain lion.

Human exploration of the Bryce area likely began with the Paiute. It's possible that trappers, prospectors, and early Mormon scouts visited here in the early to mid-1800s before Major John Wesley Powell conducted the first thorough survey of the region in the early 1870s. Shortly after Powell's exploration, Mormon pioneer Ebenezer Bryce and his wife, Mary, moved to the area and tried raising cattle. Although they stayed only a few years before moving on to Arizona, Bryce left behind his name and his oft-quoted description of the canyon as "a helluva place to lose a cow."

ESSENTIALS

GETTING THERE/ACCESS POINTS   **Bryce Canyon Airport** (Airport Code BCE; ☏ **435/834-5239;** www.brycecanyonairport.com), at 7,586 feet of elevation, is located several miles from the park entrance on Utah 12, and has a 7,400-foot lighted runway. There is no regularly scheduled airline service, but charter service is available from **Bryce Canyon Airlines** (☏ **435/834-8060;** www.rubysinn.com/bryce-canyon-airlines.html). There is a free shuttle service to local motels, and car rentals are available from **Hertz** (☏ **800/654-3131;** www.hertz.com), located at the Chevron service station in the Ruby's Inn complex.

You can also fly into St. George (130 miles southwest of the park on I-15) or Cedar City (also on I-15, about 80 miles west of the park), and rent a car (see chapter 9).

From St. George, travel north on I-15 10 miles to exit 16, then head east on Utah 9 for 63 miles to U.S. 89, north 44 miles to Utah 12, and east 13 miles to the park entrance road. The entrance station and visitor center are just 3 miles south of Utah 12. From Cedar City (I-15 exits 57, 59, and 62), take Utah 14 west 41 miles to its intersection with U.S. 89, and follow U.S. 89 north 21 miles to Utah 12, then east 17 miles to the park entrance road.

Situated in the mountains of southern Utah, the park is traversed east to west by Utah 12, with the bulk of the park, including the visitor center, accessible via Utah 63, which branches off from Utah 12 and goes south into the heart of the park. Utah 89 runs north-south west of the park, and Utah 12 heads east to Tropic and Escalante.

From Salt Lake City, it's approximately 240 miles to the park. Take I-15 south about 200 miles to exit 95, head east 13 miles on Utah 20, south on U.S. 89 for 17 miles to Utah 12, and east on Utah 12 for 13 miles to the park entrance road.

From Capitol Reef National Park, take Utah 24 west 10 miles to Torrey, and turn southwest onto Scenic Highway Utah 12 (through Boulder and Escalante) for about 110 miles, until you reach the park entrance road.

Bryce is 83 miles east of Zion National Park and 250 miles northwest of Las Vegas, Nevada.

GETTING AROUND   To alleviate congestion along the park's only road, a free **shuttle service** is in effect from early May to early October, daily from 8am until 7:40pm (until 5:40pm the last few weeks of the shuttle season). Visitors can park their cars at the parking and boarding area at the intersection of the entrance road and Utah 12, 3 miles from the park boundary, and ride the shuttle into the park. Those staying in the park at the Lodge at Bryce Canyon or one of the campgrounds can also use the shuttle. The shuttle has stops at various viewpoints, as well as Ruby's Inn, Ruby's Campground, the visitor center, Sunset Campground, and the Lodge at Bryce Canyon. It runs every 12 to 15 minutes. Note that using the shuttle is not required; you can use your own car if you wish.

INFORMATION/VISITOR CENTER   For advance information, contact the park at P.O. Box 640201, Bryce, UT 84764-0201 (☏ **435/834-5322;** www.nps.gov/brca). Officials request that you write rather than call, at least a month before your planned visit, for them to mail you information. However, you can find everything they will send you and more at the park website. You can also get information at www.twitter.com/brycecanyonnps and at www.facebook.com/brycecanyonnps. If you desire even more details to help plan your trip, you can order books, maps, posters, DVDs, and CDs from the nonprofit **Bryce Canyon Natural History Association,** P.O. Box

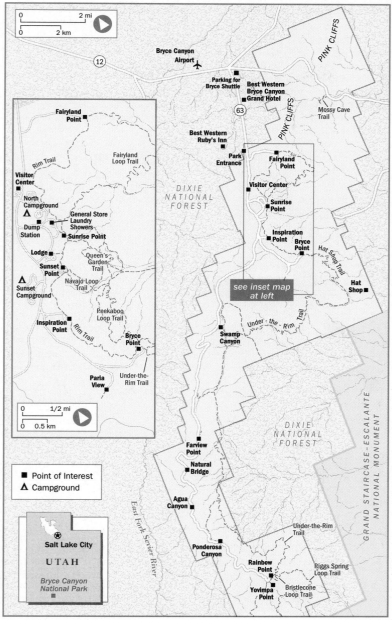

0   2 mi
0   2 km

Bryce Canyon
Airport

12

Parking for
Bryce Shuttle

Best Western
Bryce Canyon
Grand Hotel

PINK CLIFFS

63

Mossy Cave
Trail

PINK CLIFFS

Best Western
Ruby's Inn

Park
Entrance

Fairyland
Point

Visitor
Center

Sunrise
Point

DIXIE
NATIONAL
FOREST

Inspiration
Point

Bryce
Point

Hat Shop Trail

Fairyland
Point

Rim Trail

Fairyland
Loop Trail

Visitor
Center

North
Campground

General Store
Laundry
Showers

Dump
Station

Sunrise Point

Lodge

Queen's
Garden
Trail

Sunset
Point

Navajo Loop
Trail

Sunset
Campground

Peekaboo
Loop Trail

Inspiration
Point

Rim Trail

Bryce
Point

Parla
View

Under-the-
Rim Trail

0   1/2 mi
0   0.5 km

see inset map
at left

Hat
Shop

Under - the - Rim   Trail

Swamp
Canyon

GRAND STAIRCASE–ESCALANTE   NATIONAL MONUMENT

DIXIE
NATIONAL
FOREST

■ Point of Interest
▲ Campground

Farview
Point

Natural
Bridge

Agua
Canyon

East Fork Sevier River

Salt Lake City

UTAH

Bryce Canyon
National Park

Ponderosa
Canyon

Rainbow
Point

Yovimpa
Point

Under-the-Rim
Trail

Riggs Spring
Loop Trail

Bristlecone
Loop Trail

The International Astronomical Union has officially named the minor planet 49272 as **Bryce Canyon.** Hundreds of thousands of minor planets, which most of us call asteroids, orbit the sun and range in size from several yards to hundreds of miles across. The Bryce Canyon asteroid, estimated to be 3 to 5 miles across, orbits the sun between Mars and Jupiter, but is too dim to be seen with a small telescope. Even visitors who participate in the park's popular twice-weekly summertime **Astronomy Program ★** (telescopes provided; consult the visitor center for details and dates) won't be able to see the park's celestial namesake. But don't worry: On a clear night, there's always plenty to see.

640051, Bryce, UT 84764-0051 (✆ **888/362-2642** or 435/834-4782; www.bryce canyon.org). Association members (membership costs $35 single or $50 family annually) receive a 15% discount on purchases and also receive discounts at the Bryce Lodge gift shop and most other nonprofit bookstores at national parks, monuments, historic sites, and recreation areas.

The **visitor center,** at the north end of the park, has exhibits on the geology and history of the area and a short slide show on the park. Rangers can answer questions and provide backcountry permits. Free brochures are available, and books, maps, videos, and posters can be purchased. The visitor center is open daily year-round except Thanksgiving, Christmas, and New Year's Day. Summer hours are usually from 8am to 8pm, with shorter hours the rest of the year (in the dead of the winter, the visitor center will close at 4:30pm).

FEES, BACKCOUNTRY PERMITS & REGULATIONS   Entry into the park (for up to 7 days) costs $25 per private car, pickup truck, van, or RV, which includes unlimited use of the park shuttle (when it's operating). Individuals 16 and older entering the park on motorcycle, bike, or foot are charged $12 each; those 15 and under are admitted free. Campsites cost $15 per night.

Backcountry permits are required for all overnight trips into the backcountry, and for up to 7 days cost $5 for 1 or 2 people, $10 for 3 to 6 people, and $15 for 7 to 15 people (group sites only). Backcountry camping is permitted on only two trails (see "Hiking," below).

Backcountry hikers are expected to practice minimum-impact techniques, prohibited from building fires, and required to carry their own water. Bicycles are prohibited in the backcountry and on all trails. Feeding or disturbing wildlife is forbidden, as is vandalizing or upsetting any natural feature of the park. Dogs, which must be leashed at all times, are prohibited on all trails, in the backcountry, and in public buildings.

SEASONS/AVOIDING THE CROWDS   Although Bryce Canyon National Park receives only two-thirds the number of annual visitors that pour into Zion, the park can still be crowded, especially during peak season from June through September, when the campgrounds are often full by 2pm. If you visit then, head for some of the lesser-used trails (ask rangers for recommendations), and start your hike as soon after sunrise as possible.

A better time to visit, if your schedule allows, is spring or fall; if you don't mind a bit of cold and snow, the park is practically deserted from December through February—and the sight of bright red hoodoos capped with fresh white snow is something you won't soon forget.

For an unforgettable view of the canyon, contact **Bryce Canyon Airlines & Helicopters** (*(C)* **435/834-8060;** www.rubysinn.com/bryce-canyon-airlines.html) for scenic flights by helicopter or open cockpit biplane. Tours last from about 35 minutes to several hours, and the longer trips include surrounding attractions. Prices start at about $100 per person, and reservations are required.

SAFETY   While most visitors to Bryce Canyon enjoy an exciting vacation without mishap, accidents can occur, and here—possibly because of the nature of the trails—the most common injuries by far are sprained, twisted, and broken ankles. Park rangers strongly recommend that hikers—even those just out for short day hikes—wear sturdy hiking boots with good traction and ankle support. When hiking, remember that the lower you drop below the rim, the hotter it gets, so carry lots of water and dress in layers that can be removed and easily carried as the temperature rises.

Another concern in the park is bubonic plague, which, contrary to popular belief, is treatable with antibiotics if caught in its early stages. The bacteria that causes bubonic plague has been found on fleas in prairie dog colonies in the park, so you should avoid contact with wild animals, particularly prairie dogs, chipmunks, ground squirrels, and other rodents. Those taking pets into the park should first dust them with flea powder.

RANGER & EDUCATIONAL PROGRAMS   Park rangers present a variety of free programs and activities. One-hour **evening programs,** which may include a slide show, take place at the Lodge at Bryce Canyon, the visitor center, and occasionally at the North Campground amphitheater. Topics vary but may include such subjects as the animals and plants of the park, the park's geology, and the role of humans in the park's early days. Rangers also give half-hour talks several times daily at various locations in the park and lead hikes and walks, including a **moonlight hike ★★** (reservations required, so sign up at the visitor center) and a wheelchair-accessible, 1½-hour **canyon rim walk ★★**. Schedules are posted on bulletin boards at the visitor center, General Store, campgrounds, and the Lodge at Bryce Canyon. Especially popular are the park's **Astronomy Programs ★**, which are usually offered 3 evenings a week through the summer. Telescopes are provided.

The **High Plateaus Institute,** which is affiliated with Bryce Canyon Natural History Association, occasionally presents educational programs for the public. For details, check with park offices or the Bryce Canyon Natural History Association (*(C)* **888/362-2642** or 435/834-4782; www.brycecanyon.org).

During the summer, children 12 and younger can join the **Junior Rangers** for a nominal fee. Junior Rangers participate in a variety of programs, and earn certificates and patches; booklets are available at the visitor center. In addition, park rangers periodically conduct **special kids' activities**—usually lasting about an hour and a half—on subjects such as the park ecology. Reservations are required—contact the visitor center for information.

SEEING THE HIGHLIGHTS

Because Bryce Canyon is a relatively compact and easily accessible park, it is possible to see a good deal of it in a short amount of time.

Start at the **visitor center** and watch the short slide show that explains some of the area geology. Then drive the 18-mile (one-way) dead-end **park road,** stopping at viewpoints (see "Exploring Bryce Canyon by Car," below). An alternative is to take the **shuttle system** (see "Getting Around," p. 212), which will take you to most of the main viewpoints.

Whichever way you choose to get around, make sure you spend at least a little time at **Inspiration Point,** which offers a splendid (and yes, inspirational) view of **Bryce Amphitheater** and its hundreds of statuesque pink, red, orange, and brown hoodoo stone sculptures.

 Top Picnic Spot

On a hot summer day, the best spot in the park for a picnic lunch is Rainbow Point, which has picnic tables and restrooms. It's also among the coolest areas because, at 9,115 feet of elevation, it's the highest point in the park.

After seeing the canyon from the top down, walk at least partway down the **Queen's Garden Trail.** If you can spare 3 hours, hike down the Navajo Loop Trail and return to the rim via the Queen's Garden Trail (p. 218). Those not willing or physically able to hike into the canyon can enjoy a leisurely walk along the **Rim Trail,** which provides spectacular views into the canyon. The views are especially gorgeous about an hour before sunset. In the evening, try to take in the campground amphitheater program.

EXPLORING BRYCE CANYON BY CAR

The park's **18-mile scenic drive** (one-way) follows the rim of Bryce Canyon, offering easy access to a variety of views into the fanciful fairyland of stone sculptures below. Trailers are not permitted on the road, but can be left at several parking lots. All the overlooks are on your left as you begin your drive, so it's best to drive all the way to the end of the road and stop at the overlooks on your return trip. Allow 1 to 2 hours.

From the visitor center, drive 18 miles to **Yovimpa and Rainbow Point overlooks,** which offer expansive views of southern Utah, Arizona, and often even New Mexico. From these pink cliffs, you can look down on a colorful platoon of stone soldiers, standing at eternal attention. A short loop trail from Rainbow Point leads to an **1,800-year-old bristlecone pine,** believed to be the oldest living thing at Bryce Canyon.

From here, drive back north to **Ponderosa Canyon Overlook,** where you can gaze down from a dense forest of spruce and fir at multicolored hoodoos, before continuing to **Agua Canyon Overlook,** which has views of some of the best color contrasts in the park. Looking almost straight down, watch for a hoodoo known as the **Hunter,** wearing a hat of green trees.

Now continue on to **Natural Bridge,** actually an arch carved by rain and wind and spanning 85 feet. From here, go on to **Farview Point** for a panoramic view to the distant horizon and the Kaibab Plateau at the Grand Canyon's north rim. Passing through **Swamp Canyon,** turn right off the main road to three viewpoints, the first of which is **Paria View,** with views to the south of the light-colored sandstone White

Cliffs, carved by the Paria River. To the north of Paria View is **Bryce Point,** a splendid stop for seeing the awesome **Bryce Amphitheater,** the largest natural amphitheater in the park, as well as distant views of the Black Mountains to the northeast and the Navajo Mountain to the south. From here, it's just a short drive to **Inspiration Point,** offering views similar to those at Bryce Point plus the best vantage point for seeing the **Silent City,** a sleeping city cast in stone.

The Best Time to Make the Scenic Drive

The scenic drive is practically deserted in early mornings—any time before 9am. This is the best time to see deer, and the light on the hoodoos is at its richest during this time.

Return to the main road and head north to **Sunset Point,** where you can see practically all of Bryce Amphitheater, including the aptly named **Thor's Hammer** and the 200-foot-tall cliffs of **Wall Street.**

Continue north to a turnoff for your final stop at **Sunrise Point,** which has an inspiring view into Bryce Amphitheater. This is the beginning of the **Queen's Garden Trail ★★**, an excellent choice for a walk below the canyon's rim (p. 218).

OUTDOOR PURSUITS

In addition to the activities in Bryce Canyon National Park, the adjacent national forest has its own share of outdoor activities. For information, stop at the Dixie National Forest's **Red Canyon Visitor Center** (✆ **435/676-2676**), along Utah 12, about 11 miles west of the Bryce Canyon National Park entrance road. It's usually open daily from early May to early October, and offers various interpretative programs on many Saturdays. Or contact the **Dixie National Forest Information Center,** 345 E. Riverside Dr., St. George, UT 84790 (✆ **435/688-3246;** www.fs.fed.us/dxnf).

Biking & Mountain Biking

The park's established scenic drive is open to cyclists, but bikes are prohibited on all trails and forbidden from traveling cross-country within the national park boundaries.

Because mountain bikers are not welcome on national park hiking trails, you have to leave Bryce in search of trails. Fortunately, you won't have to go far. **Dave's Hollow Trail ★** starts at the Bryce Canyon National Park boundary sign on Utah 63 (the park entrance road) about a mile south of Ruby's Inn. The double-track trail goes west for about a half-mile before connecting with Forest Road 090, where you turn south and ride for about ¾ of a mile before turning right onto an easy ride through Dave's Hollow to the Dave's Hollow Forest Service Station on Forest Road 087. From here, you can retrace your route for an 8-mile round-trip ride; for a 12-mile trip, turn right on Forest Road 087 to Utah 12 and then right again back to Utah 63 and the starting point. A third option is to turn left on Forest Road 087 and follow it to Tropic Reservoir (see "Fishing," below). This part of the journey does not form a loop, so you would turn around once you've reached the reservoir.

Fishing

The closest fishing hole to the park is **Tropic Reservoir,** a large lake in a ponderosa pine forest. From the intersection of Utah 63 (the park entrance road) and Utah 12, drive west about 3 miles to a gravel road, then about 7 miles south. Facilities include a forest service campground open in summer, a boat ramp, and fishing for rainbow, brook, and cutthroat trout. Locals say the fishing can be better in streams above the lake than in the reservoir itself. For more information, contact the **Dixie National Forest** (see above).

Hiking

One of Bryce Canyon's greatest assets is that you don't have to be an advanced backpacker to really get to know the park. However, all trails below the rim have at least some steep grades, so wear hiking boots with a traction tread and good ankle support to avoid ankle injuries. During the hot summer months, go hiking either early or late in the day, carry plenty of water, and keep in mind that the deeper you go into the canyon, the hotter it gets.

Spotting Peregrine Falcons

For a good chance to see peregrine falcons, go to Paria View, sit quietly away from the crowds, and then look out over the amphitheater, where these beautiful birds can often be spotted.

The **Rim Trail,** which does not drop into the canyon but offers splendid views from above, meanders along the rim for more than 5 miles. Overlooking Bryce Amphitheater, the trail offers excellent views along much of its length. An easy to moderate walk, it includes a .5-mile section between two overlooks—Sunrise and Sunset—that is suitable for wheelchairs. This trail is a good choice for an after-dinner stroll, when you can watch the changing evening light on the rosy rocks below.

Your best bet for getting down into the canyon and seeing the most with the least amount of sweat is to combine two popular trails—**Navajo Loop** and **Queen's Garden ★★★**. The total distance is just under 3 miles, with a 521-foot elevation change, and it takes most hikers from 2 to 3 hours to complete the trek. It's best to start at the Navajo Loop Trail head at Sunset Point and leave the canyon on the less-steep Queen's Garden Trail, returning to the rim at Sunrise Point, .5 mile to the north. The Navajo Loop Trail section is considered fairly strenuous; Queen's Garden Trail is rated moderate. Along the Navajo Loop Trail section, you'll pass Thor's Hammer—wondering why it hasn't fallen—and then ponder the towering skyscrapers of Wall Street. Turning onto the Queen's Garden Trail, you'll see some of the park's most fanciful formations—including majestic Queen Victoria herself, for whom the trail was named—plus the Queen's Castle and Gulliver's Castle.

Those up for a challenge might consider the **Hat Shop Trail,** a strenuous 4-mile round-trip with a 1,336-foot elevation change. Leaving from the Bryce Point Overlook, the trail drops quickly to the Hat Shop, so-named for the hard gray "hats" perched on narrow reddish-brown pedestals. Allow 4 hours.

For die-hard hikers who don't mind rough terrain, Bryce has two backcountry trails, usually open in summer only. The **Under-the-Rim Trail** runs for some 23 miles, providing an excellent opportunity to see the park's spectacular scenery on its own terms. **Riggs Spring Loop Trail,** 8.5 miles long, offers splendid views of the pink cliffs in the southern part of the park. The truly ambitious can combine the two trails for a weeklong excursion. Permits, available at the visitor center, are required for all overnight trips into the backcountry. They cost $5 for 1 or 2 people, $10 for 3 to 6 people, and $15 for 7 to 15 people (group sites only).

Horseback Riding

To see Bryce Canyon the way the early pioneers did, you need to look down from a horse. **Canyon Trail Rides** (© **435/679-8665;** www.canyonrides.com) offers a close-up view of Bryce's spectacular rock formations from the relative comfort of a saddle. The company has a desk inside Bryce Lodge. A 2-hour ride to the canyon floor and back costs $50 per person, and a half-day trip farther into the canyon costs $75 per person. Rides are offered April through November. Riders must be at least 7 years old for the 2-hour trip, at least 10 for the half-day ride, and weigh no more than 220 pounds.

Guided horseback rides in Red Canyon are offered by several companies, including **Ruby's Inn Horse Rides** (© **866/782-0002** or 435/834-5341; www.horse rides.net), at Ruby's Inn (p. 221). Rates are $45 for a 1-hour ride, $75 to $85 for a half-day ride, and $125 for a full day, including lunch. Ruby's will also board your horse (call for rates).

Wildlife-Watching

The park is home to a variety of wildlife, ranging from mule deer to mountain short-horned lizards, which visitors often spot while hiking down into the canyon. Occasionally you might catch a glimpse of a mountain lion, most likely on the prowl in search of a mule-deer dinner; elk and pronghorn may also be seen at higher elevations.

The Utah prairie dog, listed as a threatened species, is actually a rodent. It inhabits park meadows, but should be avoided, as its fleas may carry disease (see "Safety," earlier in this chapter).

There are many birds in the park; you're bound to hear the obnoxious call of the Steller's jay. Watch for swifts and swallows as they perform their exotic acrobatics along cliff faces; binoculars will come in handy.

The Great Basin rattlesnake should be given a wide berth. Sometimes more than 5 feet long, this rattler is the park's only poisonous reptile. However, like most rattlesnakes, it is just as anxious as you are to avoid confrontation.

Winter Fun

Bryce is beautiful in the winter, when the white snow creates a perfect frosting on the red, pink, orange, and brown statues standing proudly against the cold winds. Cross-country skiers will find several marked, ungroomed trails (all above the rim), including the **Fairyland Loop Trail ★★**, which leads 1 mile through a pine and juniper forest to the Fairyland Point Overlook. From here, take the 1-mile **Forest Trail** back to the road, or continue north along the rim for another 1¼ miles to the park border.

Snowshoeing is allowed anywhere in the park except on cross-country-ski tracks. There are also connections to ski trails in the adjacent national forest.

 Winter Safety

Although the entire park is open to cross-country skiers, rangers warn that it's extremely dangerous to try to ski on the steep trails leading down into the canyon.

Stop at the visitor center for additional trail information, and go to **Best Western Plus Ruby's Inn** (p. 221), just north of the park entrance (© **866/866-6616** or 435/834-5341; www.rubysinn.com), for information on cross-country ski trails, snowshoeing, and snowmobiling opportunities outside the park. Ruby's grooms more than 30 miles of ski trails and also rents snowshoes and cross-country ski equipment.

CAMPING
In the Park

Typical of the West's national park campgrounds, the two campgrounds at Bryce offer plenty of trees for a genuine "forest camping" experience, easy access to trails, and limited facilities. **North Campground ★** has 101 sites; **Sunset Campground** has 102 sites. One section in North Campground is open year-round; Sunset Campground is open late spring through early fall only. North Campground is best because it's closer to the Rim Trail—making it easier to rush over to catch those amazing sunrise and sunset colors—but any site in either campground is fine. Neither has RV hookups or showers, but both have modern restrooms with running water. Reservations are available from early May through late September for North Campground and for 20 tent-only sites in Sunset Campground (© **877/444-6777**; www.recreation. gov) for an additional booking fee of $10, regardless of the number of days. If you don't have reservations, get to the campground early to claim a site (usually by 2pm in summer). Cost is $15 per night at both campgrounds.

Showers ($2), a coin-operated laundry, a snack bar, bundles of firewood, food and camping supplies, and souvenirs are located at the **General Store** (for information, contact the Lodge at Bryce Canyon [p. 221]; © **435/834-5361**), which is usually open daily from mid-April through October. The store is a healthy walk from either campground. The park service operates an RV dump station ($2 fee) in the summer.

Nearby

In addition to the campgrounds listed below, there is camping at Kodachrome Basin State Park; see p. 226.

King Creek Campground   Located above Tropic Reservoir, this forest service campground, at 7,900 feet elevation, has graded gravel roads and sites nestled among tall ponderosa pines. Facilities include flush toilets, drinking water, and an RV dump station ($5 fee), but no showers or RV hookups. The reservoir has a boat ramp (see "Fishing," above). To get to the campground from the Bryce Canyon National Park entrance, go north 3 miles on Utah 63 to Utah 12, turn west (left), and go 2½ miles to the King's Creek Campground Road; turn south (left) and follow signs to Tropic Reservoir for about 7 miles to the campground.

Dixie National Forest Information Center, 345 E. Riverside Dr., St. George, UT 84790. www.fs.fed. us/dxnf. © **435/688-3246**. 37 sites. $10. No credit cards. Closed Oct to mid-May.

Ruby's Inn RV Park & Campground   Ruby's is the closest campground to Bryce Canyon National Park that offers complete RV hookups, and it's also on the park's shuttle-bus route. Many sites are shaded, there's an attractive tent area, and just adjacent to the campground are a lake and horse pasture. Facilities include a swimming pool, coin-op laundry, barbecue grills, and a store with groceries and RV supplies. Also on the grounds are several camping cabins ($56 double) and tepees ($34 double), which share the campground's bathhouse and other facilities.

300 S. Main St., Bryce Canyon City, UT 84764. www.brycecanyoncampgrounds.com. © **866/878-9373** or 435/834-5301; Nov–Mar © 435/834-5341. 150 total sites. Full hookups $41; electric/water only $35; tent space $25. AE, DC, DISC, MC, V. Closed Oct–Apr.

WHERE TO STAY

Room taxes add about 11% to the cost. Pets are not accepted unless otherwise noted.

In the Park

The Lodge at Bryce Canyon ★★★ This sandstone and ponderosa pine lodge, which opened in 1924, offers the perfect atmosphere for visiting Bryce Canyon National Park. Located near the Rim Trail, the lodge provides extremely close access to the rim. The luxurious lodge suites are wonderful, with white wicker furniture, ceiling fans, and separate sitting rooms. The motel units are simply pleasant modern motel rooms, with two queen-size beds and either a balcony or a patio. The best choice here is any one of the historic cabins, restored to their 1920s appearance. They're a bit small, but have two double beds, high ceilings, stone (gas-burning) fireplaces, and log beams. The gift shop has one of the best selections of American Indian jewelry in the area. All units are nonsmoking.

Bryce Canyon National Park (P.O. Box 640041), Bryce, UT 84764. www.brycecanyonforever.com. © **877/386-4383** or 435/834-8700. 114 units, 110 in motel rooms and cabins, 3 suites and 1 studio in lodge. $130–$165 double; $175 cabin; $179 lodge suite. AE, DISC, MC, V. Closed Mid-Nov through Mar. **Amenities:** Restaurant (see review, p. 223).

Nearby

Best Western Plus Bryce Canyon Grand Hotel ★★ "Western luxury" sums up the atmosphere at this upscale hotel, which offers excellent facilities just a stone's throw from the entrance to Bryce Canyon National Park. The rooms and suites have solid wood furnishings, good lighting, and top quality beds—either one king or two queens. The hotel caters to those who want to take care of business while on vacation, with large working desks plus everything else you might want to keep in touch with the office. The large deluxe suites, at 770 square feet each, have a king bed, hide-a-bed couch, and jetted tub. The hotel is under the same management as the nearby Best Western Plus Ruby's Inn (see below). All units are nonsmoking.

31 N. 100 E. (at the entrance to Bryce Canyon), Bryce Canyon City, UT 84764. www.brycecanyon grand.com. © **866/866-6634** or 435/834-5700. Fax 435/834-5701. 162 units. Summer $150 double, $200–$290 suite; rest of year $75 double, $140–$199 suite. Rates include a hot breakfast. AE, DC, DISC, MC, V. **Amenities:** Restaurant; fitness center; Jacuzzi; heated outdoor pool (May–Oct only). *In room:* A/C, TV, fridge, hair dryer, Wi-Fi (free).

Best Western Plus Ruby's Inn ★★ ☺ Most of the hikers and canyon rim gazers visiting the park stay at this large motel, and with good reason—not only is Ruby's among the closest lodgings to the park but this is where practically everything is happening. You can arrange excursions of all sorts in the lobby, from horseback and all-terrain-vehicle rides to helicopter flights. Spread among nine buildings, the modern motel rooms contain wood furnishings and art that depicts scenes of the area. Deluxe units, located in the main building, have either jetted tubs or two-person jetted spas. Rooms at the back of the complex are a bit quieter. There is also a campground on the property. (See "Camping," above.) All units are nonsmoking.

26 S. Main St. (at the entrance to Bryce Canyon), Bryce Canyon City, UT 84764. www.rubysinn.com. ℰ **866/866-6616** or 435/834-5341. 370 units. June–Sept $135–$169 double, $195 suite; Oct–May $70–$140 double, $145 suite. AE, DC, DISC, MC, V. Pets accepted ($20 per night fee). **Amenities:** 2 restaurants (Canyon Diner and Cowboy's Buffet and Steak Room; see reviews, p. 224); concierge; 1 indoor and 1 outdoor Jacuzzi; indoor heated pool. *In room:* A/C, TV, fridge, hair dryer, Wi-Fi (free).

Bryce Canyon Pines   A modern motel with a Western flair, the Bryce Canyon Pines offers well-maintained rooms with light-colored wood furnishings and two queen-size beds in most rooms. Some units have fireplaces, some have kitchenettes, and one has its own whirlpool tub. A family suite contains one king-size bed plus two queen-size beds, each in a separate room. There are also some rustic cottages. All units are nonsmoking.

Milepost 10, Utah 12 (3 miles west of intersection with park entry road; P.O. Box 640043), Bryce, UT 84764. www.brycecanyonmotel.com. ℰ **800/892-7923** or 435/834-5441. Fax 435/834-5330. 53 units. $55–$105 double; $95–$130 cottage; $120–$325 deluxe room and suite. Highest rates are in summer. AE, DC, DISC, MC, V. **Amenities:** Restaurant; Jacuzzi; covered heated pool (Apr–Oct only). *In room:* A/C, TV, Wi-Fi (free).

Bryce Country Cabins ★   There's something special about staying in a genuine log cabin during a national park vacation, but there's also something very appealing about hot showers and warm beds. Bryce Country Cabins offers the best of both worlds, with modern log cabins and a historic pioneer cabin. The grounds are nicely landscaped, with good views, although we wish the units were farther from the highway.

The modern cabins have knotty pine walls and ceilings, exposed beams, and ceiling fans. Each has one or two queen-size beds, a table and chairs, and a porch. Bathrooms have shower/tub combos or showers only. The 1905 pioneer cabin has two spacious rooms with country-style decor. Each has two queen-size beds and a full bathroom, and the rooms can be rented together or individually. There are outdoor barbecues, a fire pit for evening gatherings, and a children's play-fort. All cabins are nonsmoking.

320 N. Utah 12 (P.O. Box 141), Tropic, UT 84776. www.brycecountrycabins.com. ℰ **888/679-8643** or 435/679-8643. 13 units. Summer $95–$135 double; lower rates at other times. AE, DC, MC, V. *In room:* A/C, TV, fridge, hair dryer, Wi-Fi (free).

Bryce Valley Inn   A member of the America's Best Value Inn & Suites franchise, the Bryce Valley Inn offers simply decorated, basic motel rooms that are a clean, well-maintained, and relatively economical choice for park visitors. Units are furnished with either one king-size bed, one or two queen-size beds, or two double beds. There are also suites with either one queen or one king bed, plus a refrigerator and microwave. All units are nonsmoking. A gift shop on the premises offers a large selection of American Indian arts and crafts, handmade gifts, rocks, and fossils.

199 N. Main St., Tropic, UT 84776. www.brycevalleyinn.com. ℰ **800/442-1890** or 435/679-8811. 65 units. Late spring to early fall $85–$115 double and suite; rates from $50 double the rest of the year. AE, DISC, MC, V. 8 miles east of the park entrance road. Pets accepted ($20 fee). **Amenities:** Restaurant. *In room:* A/C, TV, Wi-Fi (free).

Bryce View Lodge   This basic modern American motel offers the best combination of economy and location. It consists of four two-story buildings, set back from the road and grouped around a large parking lot and attractively landscaped area. The simply decorated average-size rooms are comfortable and quiet, with two queen-size beds and artwork depicting the rock formations you'll see in the park, located just down the road. Guests have access to the amenities at Ruby's Inn, across the street. All units are nonsmoking.

105 E. Center St., Bryce Canyon City, UT 84764. www.bryceviewlodge.com. © **888/279-2304** or 435/834-5180. Fax 435/834-5181. 160 units. Summer $80–$110 double; rest of year $60–$100 double. AE, DC, DISC, MC, V. Pets accepted ($20 per night fee). **Amenities:** See Best Western Plus Ruby's Inn, p. 221. *In room:* A/C, TV, Wi-Fi (free).

Stone Canyon Inn ★★★ ⊡   This charming inn is the best place to stay outside the park for those who seek upscale accommodations and fantastic views. Each room is unique, with queen- or king-size beds, colorful quilts, handsome wood furnishings, and a classic Western look. Three rooms have double whirlpool tubs and separate showers, two rooms have whirlpool tub/shower combos, and one room, partly crafted for travelers with disabilities, has a traditional tub/shower combo. The four cottages—they're much too nice to call cabins—have two bedrooms and two bathrooms, gas fireplaces, full kitchens, living rooms with TVs with VCR/DVD players, tile floors, private decks with hot tubs, and barbecue grills. The inn sits well off the main road, on the boundary of the Bryce Canyon National Park, and large windows afford views either into the park or nearby Grand Staircase–Escalante National Monument. Smoking is not permitted.

1220 W. 50 S. (P.O. Box 156), Tropic, UT 84776. www.stonecanyoninn.com. © **866/489-4680** or 435/679-8611. 10 units. Apr–Oct $145–$200 room, $330 cottage; winter rates lower. Room rates include full breakfast; cottage rates do not. AE, DC, DISC, MC, V. From Utah 12 in Tropic, take Bryce Way Rd. west 1 mile to Fairyland Lane, and follow the sign to the inn. Children 4 and under not allowed in the inn; no age restrictions for cottages. *In room:* A/C, TV, Wi-Fi (free).

WHERE TO EAT

In addition to the restaurants discussed below, **Ebenezer's Barn & Grill,** part of the huge Best Western Plus Ruby's Inn complex, at 26 South Main St., in Bryce Canyon City, offers a Western dinner and show nightly at 8pm during the summer. Diners go through a chow line and pick up their grub and then head to large tables to eat and enjoy the show, a combination of Western-style music and humor. Dinner choices include rib-eye steak, baked salmon, baked chicken, and barbecue, with prices from $26 to $32, and all meals include beans, potatoes, corn bread, dessert, and a nonalcoholic beverage. Tickets are available at Ruby's Inn; for information call © **435/834-5341,** ext. 7099.

In the Park

The Lodge at Bryce Canyon ★★ AMERICAN   The mountain-lodge atmosphere, with two handsome stone fireplaces and large windows looking out on the park, is reason enough to dine at the lodge. But the food's good, too, and reasonably priced considering that this is the only real restaurant in the park. Breakfasts offer typical American standards and a good buffet. At lunch, you'll find sandwiches, burgers, salads, and a taco bar. The menu changes periodically, but may include dinner specialties such as pan-seared Alaskan sockeye salmon topped with sun-dried tomato pesto, and perhaps a rack of lamb. Steaks are also offered, including a bison tenderloin, and other dishes frequently available include chicken with lime and chili. There are also vegetarian items, and the restaurant serves wine and beer.

Bryce Canyon National Park. © **435/834-8700.** www.brycecanyonforever.com. Main courses $5–$12 breakfast and lunch, $13–$25 dinner. AE, DC, DISC, MC, V. Daily 7–10am, 11:30am–3pm, and 5–10pm. Closed Mid-Nov through Mar.

Nearby

Canyon Diner ☺ AMERICAN   Part of the Best Western Plus Ruby's Inn complex, this self-serve restaurant offers typical fast-food fare, relatively quick and close to the park. Breakfasts, served until 11am, include bagels and several egg croissants; for lunch and dinner, you can get hoagies, burgers, hot dogs, nachos, pretty good stuffed potatoes, pizza, broiled chicken sandwiches, and salads. Specialties include a fish and chips basket. No alcohol is served.

At the Best Western Plus Ruby's Inn, 1000 S. Utah 63, Bryce Canyon City. © **435/834-8030.** www.rubysinn.com. Reservations not accepted. Individual items $4–$7; meals $6–$11. AE, DISC, MC, V. Daily 6:30am–9:30pm. Closed Nov–Mar.

Cowboy's Buffet and Steak Room STEAK/SEAFOOD   The busiest restaurant in the Bryce Canyon area, this main restaurant at the Best Western Plus Ruby's Inn moves 'em through with buffets at every meal, plus a well-rounded menu and friendly service. The breakfast buffet offers more choices than you'd expect, with scrambled eggs, fresh fruit, several breakfast meats, potatoes, pastries, and cereals. At the lunch buffet, you'll find country-style ribs, fresh fruit, salads, soups, vegetables, and breads; and the dinner buffet features charbroiled thin-sliced rib-eye steak and other meats, pastas, potatoes, and salads. Regular menu dinner entrees include prime rib, pot roast, grilled rainbow trout, grilled turkey breast, southern-style catfish, and salads. In addition to the large, Western-style dining room, an outdoor patio is open in good weather. Full liquor service is available.

At the Best Western Plus Ruby's Inn, 26 S. Main St., Bryce Canyon City. © **435/834-5341.** www.rubysinn.com. Reservations not accepted. Breakfast and lunch $3.50–$15, dinner main courses and buffets $12–$30. AE, DC, DISC, MC, V. Summer daily 6:30am–10pm; winter daily 6:30am–9pm.

Foster's Family Steak House STEAK/SEAFOOD   The simple Western decor here provides the right atmosphere for a down-to-earth steakhouse. Locally popular for its slow-roasted prime rib and steamed Utah trout, Foster's also offers several steaks (including a 14-oz. T-bone), sandwiches, a soup of the day, and homemade chili with beans. All of the pastries, pies, and breads are baked on the premises. Bottled beer is available with meals.

At Foster's motel, 1150 Utah 12, about 1½ miles west of the park entrance road. © **435/834-5227.** www.fostersmotel.com. Main courses $5–$12 breakfast and lunch, $12–$26 dinner. AE, DISC, MC, V. Mar–Nov daily 7am–10pm; call for winter hours.

WHAT TO SEE & DO JUST OUTSIDE BRYCE CANYON

The **Best Western Plus Ruby's Inn** (see "Where to Stay," earlier in this chapter), in Bryce, is practically a one-stop entertainment center for those looking for a bit of variety in their national park vacation.

Directly across Utah 63 from the inn are **Old Bryce Town Shops,** open daily 8am to 10pm from May through September, where you'll find a rock shop and a variety of other stores offering an opportunity to buy that genuine cowboy hat you've been wanting. There's a trail here especially for kids, where they can search for arrowheads, fossils, and petrified wood; or perhaps they would prefer checking out the jail.

Nearby, **Bryce Canyon Country Rodeo** (© **866/782-0002**) showcases bucking broncos, bull riding, calf roping, and all sorts of rodeo fun in a 1-hour program, from Memorial Day weekend through late August, Wednesday through Saturday evenings at 7pm. Admission is $10 for adults, $7 for children 3 to 12, and free for children 2 and under. Adventurous visitors can also ride—bulls for adults and steers and sheep for kids. Call for details.

Red Canyon

About 9 miles west of Bryce Canyon National Park, in the Dixie National Forest, is Red Canyon, named for its vermilion-colored rock formations, which are accented by stands of rich green ponderosa pine. The canyon is a favorite of hikers and mountain bikers in summer and cross-country skiers and snowshoers in winter.

Red Canyon has about a dozen trails. Some trails are open to hikers only, others to mountain bikers, horseback riders, and those with all-terrain vehicles. One especially scenic multiuse trail is the 5.5-mile (one-way) **Casto Canyon Trail,** which runs along the bottom of Casto Canyon. It connects with the 8.9-mile (one-way) **Cassidy Trail** (legend has it that outlaw Butch Cassidy used this trail) and 2.9-mile (one-way) **Losee Canyon Trail** to produce a loop of about 17 miles ideal for a multiday backpacking trip. Watch for elk in winter, and pronghorns and raptors year-round. The Casto Canyon and Losee Canyon trails are considered moderate; Cassidy Trail ranges from easy to strenuous.

For maps, specific directions to trail heads, current trail conditions, and additional information, stop at the **Red Canyon Visitor Center** (© **435/676-2676**), along Utah 12, about 11 miles west of the Bryce Canyon National Park entrance road. It's usually open daily from early May to early October, and offers various interpretive programs on many Saturdays. Information can also be obtained from the **Dixie National Forest Information Center,** 345 E. Riverside Dr., St. George, UT 84790 (© **435/688-3246;** www.fs.fed.us/dxnf).

KODACHROME BASIN: A PICTURE-PERFECT STATE PARK

Located about 22 miles from the entrance to Bryce Canyon National Park, Kodachrome Basin lives up to its name—its wonderful scenery practically cries out to be photographed. Named for the classic Kodak color slide film by the National Geographic Society after an expedition there in 1948, the park is chock-full of tall stone chimneys and pink-and-white sandstone cliffs, all set among the contrasting greens of sagebrush and piñon and juniper trees. It also abuts and makes a good base for exploring Grand Staircase–Escalante National Monument, which is discussed below.

Because temperatures get a bit warm here in summer—the park is at 5,800 feet elevation—the best times to visit, especially for hikers, are May, September, and October, when there are also fewer people.

Essentials

GETTING THERE   From Bryce Canyon National Park, go 3 miles north to the junction of Utah 63 and Utah 12, go east (right) on Utah 12 for about 12 miles to Cannonville, turn south onto the park's access road (there's a sign), and go about 7 miles to the park entrance.

INFORMATION, FEES & REGULATIONS   Contact the **park office** at P.O. Box 180069, Cannonville, UT 84718-0069 (© **435/679-8562;** www.stateparks.utah.

gov), for information. Day use costs $6 per vehicle. Dogs are permitted in the park and on trails, but must be kept on leashes no more than 6 feet long. The park office at the pay station at the entrance to the park can give you information.

Outdoor Pursuits

HIKING   Kodachrome Basin offers several hiking possibilities. Starting just south of the campground, the **Panorama Trail** is only moderately difficult, with no steep climbs. At first, it follows an old, relatively flat wagon route, and then climbs to offer views of the park's rock formations before reaching the well-named Panorama Point. Along the way are several possible side trips, including a short walk to the **Hat Shop,** so named because the formations resemble broad-brimmed hats, and **White Buf-falo Loop,** where you can try to find a formation that looks like—you guessed it—a white buffalo. The optional **Big Bear Geyser Trail** is a bit more difficult, winding past Big Bear and Mama Bear before returning to Panorama Trail. Allow 2 to 3 hours for the Panorama Trail and an extra hour for Big Bear Geyser Trail.

Fans of arches will want to drive the dirt road to the trail head for the .5-mile round-trip hike to **Shakespeare Arch.** This trail also provides views of a large chimney-rock formation.

HORSEBACK RIDING   To see Kodachrome Basin from the back of a horse, con-tact **Red Canyon Trail Rides** (✆ **800/892-7923;** www.redcanyontrailrides.com). A 1-hour ride costs $30 and a 2-hour ride costs $50.

WILDLIFE-WATCHING   Jackrabbits and chukar partridges are probably the most commonly seen wildlife in the park, although you are likely to hear the piñon jay and might see an occasional coyote or rattlesnake.

Where to Stay

CAMPING   The park's attractive 27-site campground is set among stone chimneys and scattered piñon and juniper trees. It has flush toilets, showers, drinking water, picnic tables, barbecue grills, and an RV dump station. Four sites have full RV hook-ups. Basic campsites cost $16 per night, and sites with hookups cost $25 per night. Call ✆ **800/322-3770** or 801/322-3770, or visit www.reserveamerica.com for res-ervations ($8 reservation fee).

LODGING & SUPPLIES   Located in the park along the park road (you can't miss it), **Kodachrome General Store** (✆ **435/679-8536;** www.redstonecabins.com) sells camping supplies, food items, and the like. This is also headquarters for **Red-stone Cabins,** six modern cabins. Four have two double beds and two have one king, and all six have bathrooms with showers, refrigerators, microwaves, air-conditioning, private porches with tables and chairs, and outside charcoal barbecue grills. Cost per cabin per night for up to four people is $90 from mid-April to mid-October, $70 from mid-March to mid-April, and $50 the rest of the year.

GRAND STAIRCASE–ESCALANTE NATIONAL MONUMENT & THE HIGHWAY 12 SCENIC DRIVE

Even if it didn't have a beautiful national park at each end (Bryce Canyon and Capitol Reef), the Highway 12 Scenic Byway, which passes by and through Grand

Staircase–Escalante National Monument, would be well worth the drive for the richly varied scenery: red-rock spires and canyons, dense forests of tall evergreens, pastoral meadows, colorful slickrock, and plunging waterfalls. Whether you're just passing through, pausing briefly at scenic viewpoints along the way, or stopping to explore this huge national monument, you'll have plenty to see. Those driving between Bryce Canyon and Capitol Reef national parks should allow at least 4 hours for the trip, but it can easily take longer with a stop in the small community of Escalante (see "Basing Yourself in Escalante," later in this chapter), a visit to its fine state park, and a detour through the wild areas in the Grand Staircase–Escalante National Monument and other nearby public lands.

Grand Staircase–Escalante National Monument

Known for its stark, rugged beauty, this vast land contains a unique combination of geological, biological, paleontological, archaeological, and historical resources. The area's 1.9 million acres of red-orange canyons, mesas, plateaus, and river valleys became a national monument by presidential proclamation in 1996. Although hailed by environmentalists, the president's action was not popular in Utah, largely because the area contains a great deal of coal and other resources. Utah Senator Orrin Hatch denounced Clinton's decree, calling it "the mother of all land-grabs."

Under the jurisdiction of the Bureau of Land Management, the monument is expected to remain open for grazing and possible oil and gas drilling under existing leases (although no new leases will be issued), as well as for hunting, fishing, hiking, camping, and other forms of recreation.

Unlike most other national monuments, almost all of this vast area is undeveloped—there are few all-weather roads, only one maintained hiking trail, and two developed campgrounds. But the adventurous will find miles upon miles of dirt roads and practically unlimited opportunities for camping, and hiking, horseback riding, and mountain biking on existing dirt roads.

The national monument can be divided into three distinct sections: the **Grand Staircase** of sandstone cliffs, which includes five life zones from Sonoran Desert to coniferous forests, in the southwest; the **Kaiparowits Plateau,** a vast, wild region of rugged mesas and steep canyons in the center; and the **Escalante River Canyons** section, along the northern edge of the monument, a delightfully scenic area containing miles of interconnecting river canyons.

ESSENTIALS

GETTING THERE   The national monument occupies a large section of southern Utah—covering an area almost as big as the states of Delaware and Rhode Island combined—with Bryce Canyon National Park to the west, Capitol Reef National Park on the northeast edge, and Glen Canyon National Recreation Area along the east and part of the south sides.

Access is via Utah 12 along the monument's northern boundary, from Kodachrome Basin State Park and the communities of Escalante and Boulder, and via U.S. 89 to the southwestern section of the monument, east of the town of Kanab, which is about 80 miles south of Bryce Canyon.

INFORMATION/VISITOR CENTERS   The national monument remains a very rugged area, with limited facilities, poor roads, and changeable weather. Before setting out, all visitors are strongly urged to contact one of the monument's visitor centers to get maps and other information, and especially to check on current road and weather conditions. Also see the monument's website, **www.ut.blm.gov/ monument**.

Visitor centers include the **Escalante Interagency Visitor Center,** on the west side of Escalante, at 755 W. Main St. (Utah 12), Escalante, UT 84726 (✆ **435/826-5499**), open daily 8am to 4:30pm from mid-March through mid-November, and Monday through Friday the same hours the rest of the year. You can also get information at the Bureau of Land Management's **Kanab Visitor Center,** 745 E. U.S. 89, Kanab, UT 84741 (✆ **435/644-4680**), open daily 8am to 4:30pm.

The **Cannonville Visitor Center** is open daily from 8am to 4:30pm, mid-March through mid-November only, at 10 Center St., in Cannonville (✆ **435/826-5640**), east of Bryce Canyon National Park. The **Big Water Visitor Center** is along U.S. 89, near the southern edge of Glen Canyon National Recreation Area, at 100 Upper Revolution Way, in Big Water (✆ **435/675-3200**). It is open daily from 9am to 5:30pm April through October and daily 8am to 4:30pm the rest of the year.

FEES, REGULATIONS & SAFETY   There is no charge to enter the monument; those planning overnight trips into the backcountry should obtain free permits at any of the offices listed above. Regulations are similar to those on other public lands; damaging or disturbing archaeological and historic sites in any way is forbidden.

Water is the main safety concern here, whether there's too little or too much. This is generally very dry country, so those going into the monument should carry plenty of drinking water. However, thunderstorms can turn the monument's dirt roads into impassable mud bogs in minutes, stranding motorists, and potentially fatal flash floods through narrow canyons can catch hikers by surprise. Anyone planning trips into the monument should always check first with one of the offices listed above for current and anticipated weather and travel conditions.

OUTDOOR PURSUITS

This rugged national monument offers numerous opportunities for outdoor adventures, including **canyoneering** through narrow slot canyons with the aid of ropes. You can get information on the best areas for canyoneering at the monument's visitor centers, but this is definitely not the place for beginners. To put it bluntly, people die here, and you don't want to be one of them.

Unless you are an expert at this specialized sport, go with an expert. One of the best is Rick Green, owner of **Excursions of Escalante** ★★, 125 E. Main St., Escalante (✆ **800/839-7567;** www.excursionsofescalante.com). Trips, which are available mid-March through mid-November, usually include four people with one guide, and all equipment is provided. In addition to canyoneering trips, the company offers day hiking and backpacking excursions, specialized tours, and 3-day canyoneering courses ($500–$600). Day trips include lunch. Day hiking trips cost $125 per person, canyoneering costs $145 to $165 per person, and a photo safari costs $170 per person. Overnight backpacking trips cost $250 to $275 per person per day, which includes practically everything you need, including food. Credit cards are not accepted; cash and checks are welcome. Excursions of Escalante also provides a flexible shuttle service; call for a quote.

> **Impressions**
>
> *On this remarkable site, God's handiwork is everywhere.*
> —Former President Bill Clinton, September 18, 1996

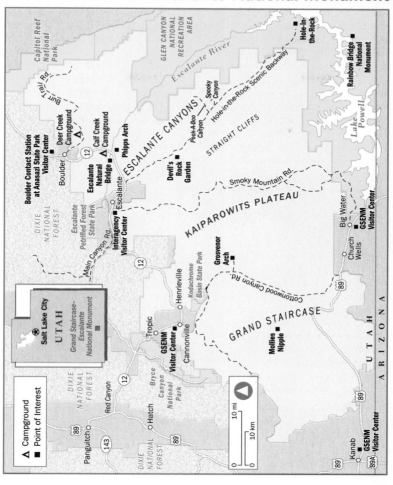

HIKING, MOUNTAIN BIKING & HORSEBACK RIDING Located about 15 miles northeast of Escalante via Utah 12, the **Calf Creek Recreation Area** has a campground (p. 231), a picnic area with fire grates and tables, trees, drinking water, and flush toilets. The tree-shaded picnic and camping area lies along the creek at the bottom of a high-walled, rather narrow rock canyon. The best part of the recreation area, though, is the moderately strenuous 6-mile round-trip hike to **Lower Calf Creek Falls.** A sandy trail leads along **Calf Creek,** past beaver ponds and wetlands, to a beautiful waterfall that cascades 126 feet down a rock wall into a tree-shaded pool. You can pick up an interpretive brochure at the trail head. Day use fee is $2 per vehicle.

Although the Calf Creek Trail is the monument's only officially marked and maintained trail, numerous unmarked cross-country routes are ideal for hiking, mountain biking (on existing dirt roads only), and horseback riding. Hikers are advised to stop at one of the visitor centers (p. 228) to get recommendations on hiking routes and to purchase topographic maps. Hikers need to remember that this is wild country and can be hazardous. Rangers recommend carrying at least 1 gallon of water per person per day and testing all water from streams before drinking. The potential for flooding is high, and hikers should check with the BLM before attempting to hike through the monument's narrow slot canyons, which offer no escape during flash floods. Other hazards include poisonous snakes and scorpions and, in the wetter areas, poison ivy. Slickrock, as the name suggests, is slippery, so hikers should wear sturdy hiking boots with traction soles.

Among the popular and relatively easy-to-follow hiking routes is the footpath to **Escalante Natural Bridge;** it repeatedly crosses the river, so be prepared to get wet up to your knees. The easy 2-mile (one-way) hike begins at a parking area at the bridge that crosses the Escalante River near Calf Creek Recreation Area, 15 miles northeast of the town of Escalante. From the parking area, hike upstream to Escalante Natural Bridge, on the south side of the river. The bridge is 130 feet high and spans 100 feet.

Also starting at the bridge parking area is a hike downstream to **Phipps Wash.** Mostly moderate, this hike goes about 1.5 miles to the mouth of Phipps Wash, which enters the river from the west. You'll find Maverick Natural Bridge in a north side drainage, and climbing up the drainage on the south side leads to Phipps Arch.

Hiking the national monument's **slot canyons** is very popular, but the importance of checking on flood potentials before starting out cannot be stressed enough. A sudden rainstorm miles away can cause a flash flood through one of the monument's narrow canyons, trapping hikers.

One challenging and very strenuous slot-canyon hike is through **Peek-a-boo** and **Spooky canyons,** which are accessible from the Hole-in-the-Rock Scenic Backway (see "Sightseeing & Four-Wheeling," below). Stop at the Escalante Interagency Office for precise directions.

SIGHTSEEING & FOUR-WHEELING Because this is one of America's least-developed large sections of public land, it offers a wonderful opportunity for exploration by the adventurous. Be aware, though, that the dirt roads inside the monument turn muddy—and impassable—when it rains.

One particularly popular road is the **Hole-in-the-Rock Scenic Backway,** which is partly in the national monument and partly in the adjacent Glen Canyon National Recreation Area. Like most roads in the monument, this should be attempted in dry weather only. Starting about 5 miles northeast of Escalante off Utah 12, this clearly marked dirt road travels 57 miles (one-way) to the Hole-in-the-Rock. This is where Mormon settlers, in 1880, cut a passage through solid rock to get their wagons down a 1,200-foot cliff to the canyon floor and Colorado River below.

About 12 miles in, the road passes by the sign to **Devil's Rock Garden,** which has classic red-rock formations and arches and a picnic area (about a mile off the main road). The road continues across a plateau of typical desert terrain, ending at a spectacular scenic overlook of Lake Powell. The first 35 miles of the scenic byway are relatively easy (in dry weather); it then gets a bit steeper and sandier, and the last 6 miles of the road require a high-clearance 4×4 vehicle. Allow about 6 hours round-trip, and make sure you have plenty of fuel and water.

Another recommended drive in the national monument is the **Cottonwood Canyon Road,** which runs from Kodachrome Basin State Park south to U.S. 89, along the monument's southern edge, a distance of about 46 miles. The road is sandy and narrow and washboard in places, but it's usually passable for passenger cars in dry weather. It mostly follows Cottonwood Wash, with good views of red-rock formations and distant panoramas from hilltops. About 10 miles east of Kodachrome Basin State Park is a short side road to **Grosvenor Arch.** This magnificent stone arch, with an opening 99 feet wide, was named for the National Geographic Society founder and editor, Gilbert H. Grosvenor, and is well worth the trip.

WILDLIFE VIEWING & BIRDING The isolated and rugged terrain here makes a good habitat for a number of species, including desert bighorn sheep and mountain lions. More than 200 species of birds have been seen, including bald eagles, golden eagles, Swainson's hawks, and peregrine falcons. The best areas for seeing wildlife are along the Escalante and Paria rivers and Johnson Creek.

CAMPING

Backcountry camping is permitted in most areas of the monument with a free permit, available at the Interagency Office in Escalante (p. 168) and BLM office in Kanab. Sites are first-come, first-served.

The monument also has two designated campgrounds. **Calf Creek Campground,** in the Calf Creek Recreation Area about 15 miles northeast of the town of Escalante via Utah 12, has 14 sites and a picnic area. Open year-round, the tree-shaded campground is situated in a steep, scenic canyon along Calf Creek, surrounded by high rock walls. There is an interpretive hiking trail (p. 230), and facilities include flush toilets and drinking water, but no showers, RV hookups, RV dump stations, or trash removal. In summer, the campground is often full by 10am. From November through March, the water is turned off and only vault toilets are available. Vehicles must ford a shallow creek, and the campground is not recommended for vehicles over 25 feet long. Campsites cost $7 per night; day use is $2 per vehicle.

The national monument's other designated campground is **Deer Creek,** located 6 miles east of the town of Boulder along the scenic Burr Trail Road. There are vault toilets, picnic tables, and grills, but no drinking water or other facilities. Camping at the seven primitive sites costs $4, and the campground is open year-round. RVs and cars can fit onto the sites here.

Escalante Petrified Forest State Park

Large chunks of colorful petrified wood decorate this unique park, which offers hiking, fishing, boating, camping, and panoramic vistas of the surrounding countryside. There's wildlife to watch, trails to hike, and a 30-acre reservoir for boating, fishing, and somewhat chilly swimming. It's open all year, but spring through fall is the best time to visit. Hikers should be prepared for hot summer days and carry plenty of water.

ESSENTIALS

GETTING THERE The park is 44 miles from Bryce Canyon. It's located about 2 miles southwest of Escalante on Utah 12 at Wide Hollow Road.

INFORMATION/VISITOR CENTER Contact **Escalante Petrified Forest State Park,** 710 N. Reservoir Rd., Escalante, UT 84726 (© **435/826-4466;** www.stateparks.utah.gov). The **visitor center,** open daily, displays petrified wood, dinosaur bones, and fossils, plus an exhibit explaining how petrified wood is formed.

rock or wood—WHAT IS THIS STUFF?

It looks like a weathered, multicolored tree limb, shining and sparkling in the light—but it's heavy, hard, and solid as a rock. Just what is this stuff? It's petrified wood.

Back in the old days—some 135 to 155 million years ago—southern Utah was not at all like you see it today. It was closer to the equator than it is now, which made it a wet and hot land, with lots of ferns, palm trees, and conifers providing lunch for the neighborhood dinosaurs.

Occasionally, floods would uproot the trees, dumping them in flood plains and along sandbars, and then bury them with mud and silt. If this happened quickly, the layers of mud and silt would cut off the oxygen supply, halting the process of decomposition—and effectively preserving the tree trunks intact.

Later, volcanic ash covered the area, and groundwater rich in silicon dioxide and other chemicals and minerals made its way down to the ancient trees. With the silicon dioxide acting as a glue, the cells of the wood mineralized. Other waterborne minerals produced the colors: Iron painted the tree trunks in reds, browns, and yellows; manganese produced purples and blues.

Sometime afterward, uplift from within the earth, along with various forms of erosion, brought the now-petrified wood to the surface in places like Escalante Petrified Forest State Park and Grand Staircase–Escalante National Monument, breaking it into the shapes of today in the process—one that's taken only a hundred million years or so to complete.

FEES & REGULATIONS Entry costs $6 per vehicle, which includes boat launching. As at most parks, regulations are generally based on common sense and courtesy: Don't damage anything, drive slowly on park roads, and observe quiet hours between 10pm and 7am. In addition, you're asked to resist the temptation to carry off samples of petrified wood. Pets are welcome, even on trails, but must be on leashes no more than 6 feet long.

OUTDOOR PURSUITS

FISHING & BOATING **Wide Hollow Reservoir,** located partially inside the park, has a boat ramp (sorry, no rentals are available) and is a popular fishing hole for rainbow trout and bluegill, plus ice-fishing in winter.

HIKING The 1-mile loop **Petrified Forest Trail ★** is a moderately strenuous hike among colorful rocks, through a forest of stunted juniper and piñon pine, past a painted desert, to a field of colorful petrified wood. The hike also offers panoramic vistas of the town of Escalante and surrounding stair-step plateaus. A free brochure is available at the visitor center. Allow about 45 minutes. An optional three-quarter-mile loop off the main trail—called **Trail of Sleeping Rainbows**—leads through a large mound of petrified wood, but is considerably steeper than the main trail.

WILDLIFE-WATCHING This is one of the best spots in the region to see **wildlife ★**. The reservoir is home to ducks, geese, and coots. Chukar partridges wander throughout the park, and you're also likely to see eagles, hawks, lizards, ground squirrels, and both cottontails and jackrabbits. Binoculars are helpful.

CAMPING

The 22-unit RV and tent **campground,** within easy walking distance of the park's hiking trails and reservoir, is open year-round. Facilities include hot showers, modern restrooms, and drinking water. There are four sites with water and electric RV hookups. Camping costs $16 per night, $20 with hookups. Reservations are available at ℂ **800/322-3770** or 801/322-3770 (www.reserveamerica.com); an $8 nonrefundable fee will be charged.

Basing Yourself in Escalante

Originally called Potato Valley, this community's name was changed in the 19th century to honor Spanish explorer and missionary Father Silvestre Velez de Escalante. But it's believed Escalante never actually visited this particular part of southern Utah on his trek from Santa Fe, New Mexico, to California, a hundred years earlier. Home to nearly 100 historic buildings (a free walking-tour map is available at the information booth and at local businesses), Escalante is your best bet for lodging, food, and supplies as you travel Utah 12. At 5,868 feet elevation, it's also a good base for exploring the nearby mountains and Grand Staircase–Escalante National Monument, or for finally taking a hot shower after a week of backpacking. Be aware, though: Services in this town of 800 are limited in winter.

ESSENTIALS

GETTING THERE   Escalante is 50 miles east of Bryce Canyon National Park and 63 miles south of Capitol Reef National Park on the Highway 12 Scenic Byway. Utah 12 becomes Main Street as it goes through town.

VISITOR INFORMATION   The National Park Service, Dixie National Forest, and Bureau of Land Management operate the **Escalante Interagency Visitor Center** that provides recreation and other tourist information year-round. It's located on the west side of Escalante, at 755 W. Main St. (Utah 12), Escalante, UT 84726 (ℂ **435/ 826-5499**), and open daily 8am to 4:30pm from mid-March through mid-November, and Monday through Friday the same hours the rest of the year.

The **Escalante Chamber of Commerce,** P.O. Box 175, Escalante, UT 84726 (ℂ **435/826-4810;** www.escalante-cc.com), can also provide area information.

WHAT TO SEE & DO

Several local companies will help you explore this rugged land. **Excursions of Escalante** (p. 228) offers guided day and overnight trips in Grand Staircase–Escalante National Monument and the nearby national forest. **Escalante Outfitters** (see "Where to Stay," below), offers guided fly-fishing trips in the national monument and on Boulder Mountain (p. 236). Cost for a full-day trip, including lunch and all gear, is $225 for one angler, $275 for two, and $300 for three. Escalante Outfitters also leads evening natural history hikes ($45 per person), and has a well-stocked store where you'll find outdoor clothing, maps, guide books, and whatever outdoor gear you might need.

But the great outdoors isn't the only reason to visit Escalante. Art lovers should schedule their visits for late September or early October, when Escalante and nearby communities join to sponsor the **Escalante Canyons Arts Festival–Everett Ruess Days,** with demonstrations, workshops, contests, exhibits, talks, music, and more. Subjects range from painting to pottery, plus quilting, ceramics, tie-dying, cowboy poetry—you name it.

Philip and Harriet Priska's **Serenidad Gallery,** 360 W. Main St. ((**888/826-4577** or 435/826-4720; www.serenidad gallery.com), offers seven rooms crammed with wild and wonderfully fun stuff. Browse among fine art, photography, antiques, collectibles, gift items, jewelry, and even locally handmade soaps and lip balms. Petrified wood and local rocks fill one room. Harriet's huge collection of buttons includes her own hand-painted porcelain creations. The Priskas carry only things they particularly like, so it's fun to talk with them about the selection of items. The gallery/shop is open daily from 8:30am to 8:30pm, with occasional meal breaks.

The festival is named for Everett Ruess, a young artist who disappeared in the rugged canyon country near here in November 1934 and whose remains were recently discovered. For additional information on the festival and on Ruess, contact the chamber of commerce (see above), or check out the festival website, **www.everett ruessdays.org**.

As a small town, Escalante has a surprising number of galleries and working artists. Pick up a free copy of the brochure *Escalante Arts & Crafts Guide,* which includes a map, at the Escalante Interagency Visitor Center (see "Visitor Information," above), or check out the chamber of commerce website, **www.escalante-cc.com**.

WHERE TO STAY

Room tax adds about 11%. Pets are not accepted unless otherwise noted.

In addition to the lodging choices discussed below, the **Shooting Star Drive-In,** 2020 W. Utah 12, Escalante ((**435/826-4440;** www.shootingstardrive-in.com), offers a unique opportunity to spend the night in a luxurious, custom-designed Airstream trailer, decorated as they might have been when movie stars had such accommodations while filming on location. There are eight Airstreams, each with a fully equipped kitchen and full bathroom, and all the amenities you would expect as the Hollywood star you obviously are. There's a drive-in theater—open to lodging guests only—where you sit in a vintage convertible to watch the latest from Cary Grant, Clark Gable, or Marilyn Monroe. Rates range from $149 to $169 double. There is also an Airstream-only RV park with 18 sites ($30–$40).

For additional information on lodging, including house rentals, contact the chamber of commerce (see above).

Escalante Outfitters   These cute little log cabins are a favorite of backpackers who want a break from sleeping on the ground. Think of this place as a cross between a motel and a campground; actually, it's closer to the auto camps of the 1930s. Built in the mid-1990s, each cabin either has one queen-size bed or a pair of bunk beds, a chair, a small table with a lamp, and two small windows. There's heat in cool weather and fans for warm weather. That's it. All guests share a simple but adequate and well-maintained bathhouse; no private bathrooms are available. On the grounds are barbecue pits, picnic tables, and horseshoe pits. There is also a camping area for about 10 tents ($16 per night). A state liquor store and outdoor gear and clothing store are on the premises.

310 W. Main St. (Utah 12), P.O. Box 575, Escalante, UT 84726. www.escalanteoutfitters.com. $\mathcal{C}$ **866/455-0041** or 435/826-4266. 7 units. $45 double. AE, DISC, MC, V. Dogs accepted for a $10 per night fee. Closed Nov–Feb. **Amenities:** Restaurant (Esca-Latte Internet Café & Pizza Parlor; see below). *In room:* No phone, Wi-Fi (free).

Escalante's Grand Staircase Bed & Breakfast Inn This beautiful B&B has spacious rooms with skylights, full private bathrooms, and beds with pillow-top mattresses. The modern country decor includes some furniture in solid wood aspen or lodgepole pine, Southwestern drum tables, and pictograph designs on the walls. The full gourmet breakfast consists of a fruit dish, juice, coffee, tea, and hot chocolate, and a main course including breakfast meats or breads. Food allergies can be accommodated with advance notice. The entire property, including the grounds, is nonsmoking.

280 W. Main St. (Utah 12), Escalante, UT 84726. www.escalantebnb.com. $\mathcal{C}$ **866/826-4890** or 435/826-4890. 8 units. Mid-Mar to Oct from $145 double; Nov–Feb from $110 double. DISC, MC, V. Children 11 and under not accepted; older children accepted with prior approval. *In room:* A/C, TV, hair dryer, Wi-Fi (free).

WHERE TO EAT

Pizza lovers should stop at the **Esca-Latte Internet Café & Pizza Parlor,** located in Escalante Outfitters, 310 W. Main St. ($\mathcal{C}$ **866/455-0041** or 435/826-4266; www. escalanteoutfitters.com). This is the place for true aficionados, where you can build your own 12- or 16-inch pizza by selecting among some 20 toppings, ranging from pepperoni to Utah goat cheese. It also has a salad bar, a variety of hot and cold coffee drinks, and Utah microbrew beer. Most lunch and dinner main courses cost from $8.50 to $13; most breakfast items range from $5.50 to $7.50. The restaurant is open daily from 8am to 9pm, and is usually closed from November through February.

For excellent burgers, including a black bean burger, and slow-smoked locally raised range-fed beef, stop at **Circle D Eatery,** 475 W. Main St., Escalante ($\mathcal{C}$ **435/ 826-4125;** www.escalantecircledeatery.com). House specialties at dinner include brisket, the steak of the day, smoked chicken, and pork ribs, or you can choose baked trout filet, a teriyaki veggie stir-fry, sandwiches, or spaghetti with homemade marinara sauce. Lunch is more burgers, sandwiches, and salads, and the breakfast menu includes egg dishes, pancakes, granola, and fruit. Hours are 7:30am to around 9:30pm daily (closed mid-Nov to early Feb). Prices for most main courses are $5 to $11 breakfast and lunch, and $7.50 to $19 dinner. Wine and an excellent selection of beer are served.

Excellent regional cuisine, prepared from organic and natural ingredients, is on the menu at **Hell's Backbone Grill** ($\mathcal{C}$ **435/335-7464;** www.hellsbackbonegrill.com), a classy but casual restaurant about 28 miles northeast of Escalante in the community of Boulder, at 20 N. Hwy. 12. It's open 7 to 11:30am and 5 to 9:30pm daily from mid-March through late November; it's closed the rest of the year. The menu changes seasonally, but for dinner you're likely to be offered chipotle meatloaf with lemony mashed potatoes and vegetables from the restaurant's own farm or skillet fried trout with blue corn, pecans, and molasses. Try to leave room for one of the yummy desserts such as the lemon chiffon cake or a chocolate chili cream pot. Breakfast items include a variety of egg dishes, French toast, homemade granola, and various breakfast meats. Dinner main courses are priced from $17 to $32, while breakfast items cost $6 to $13. Wine and beer are served.

North from Escalante Along Utah 12

Heading toward Capitol Reef National Park from the town of Escalante, the rugged mountain scenery, with forests of pine and fir producing a deep green contrast to the rosy red, orange, and brown hues of the region's rock formations, comes into view.

Picturesque **Posey Lake** (sometimes spelled Posy), under the jurisdiction of the U.S. Forest Service, is open to nonmotorized boats and offers good fishing for rainbow trout. It's in a mixed conifer forest at 8,600 feet elevation, some 16 miles northwest of Escalante via Utah 12 and gravel Forest Road 153. Facilities include a picnic area, two floating docks, fish cleaning stations, and a boat ramp. There are several trail heads, and numerous dirt roads are popular with mountain bikers and hikers in summer, cross-country skiers and snowmobilers in winter. The **Posy Lake Campground,** usually open mid-May through early September, has 20 sites (maximum RV length 24 ft.), drinking water, and restrooms, but no showers, RV hookups, or trash pickup. Camping costs $10 per night, and reservations are available (✆ **877/444-6777;** www.recreation.gov) for an additional booking fee of $10. For information on the lake and campground, contact the **Escalante Interagency Visitor Center** (see "Visitor Information," above).

Visitors to **Anasazi State Park Museum,** in the village of Boulder (about 28 miles northeast of Escalante along Utah 12), step back to the 12th century A.D., when the Kayenta Anasazi (also called Ancestral Puebloans) lived here in one of the largest communities west of the Colorado River. The 6-acre park includes the ruins of the village, a full-size six-room replica of a home, a gift shop, picnic area, auditorium, and museum. The museum is open daily from 8am to 6pm from April through October and Monday through Saturday from 9am to 5pm the rest of the year. It is closed Thanksgiving, Christmas, and New Year's Day. Admission costs $5 per person, $3 for seniors 62 and older, with a $10 maximum per family. There is no campground. For more information, contact **Anasazi State Park Museum,** 460 N. Utah 12, Boulder, UT 84716 (✆ **435/335-7308;** www.stateparks.utah.gov).

Boulder Mountain ★★ has some of the most dramatic views along Utah 12. Located northeast of Escalante at an elevation of 9,670 feet, you are practically in the clouds. From viewpoints such as **Point Lookout,** you'll gaze out over the colorful sandstone rock cliffs of Capitol Reef National Park to the imposing Henry Mountains, Navajo Mountain, and sights more than 100 miles away.

Those venturing into the backcountry by foot, four-wheel-drive, mountain bike, or horse will discover rugged, remote beauty; the area is also a trout fisherman's paradise, with dozens of secluded mountain lakes and streams hidden among the tall pines and firs. **Escalante Outfitters** (p. 234) offers guided fly-fishing trips. Don't be surprised to see mule deer, elk, and wild turkey in the open meadows. Contact the **Escalante Interagency Visitor Center** (see "Visitor Information," above) for information.

After Boulder, it's not too much farther to Capitol Reef National Park, but first is the community of Torrey, where Utah 12 intersects with Utah 24. You can turn right here and proceed to the park. See chapter 12 for complete coverage of Capitol Reef.

CAPITOL REEF NATIONAL PARK

Capitol Reef National Park is one of those undiscovered gems, its rangers quietly going about their business while visitors flock to its more famous neighbors, Bryce Canyon and Zion.

But when people do stumble across this park, they are often amazed. Capitol Reef not only offers spectacular southern Utah scenery with lots of fascinating rock formations, but it also has a unique twist and a personality all its own.

What Makes Capitol Reef So Special?

Capitol Reef is a place to let your imagination run wild. You'll see the appropriately named Hamburger Rocks, sitting atop a white sandstone table; the tall, rust-red Chimney Rock; the silent and eerie Temple of the Moon; and the commanding Castle. The colors of Capitol Reef's canyon walls draw from a spectacular palette, which is why Navajos called the area "the Land of the Sleeping Rainbow."

But unlike some of southern Utah's other parks, Capitol Reef is more than just brilliant rocks and barren desert. The Fremont River has helped create a lush oasis in an otherwise unforgiving land, with cottonwoods and willows along its banks. In fact, 19th-century pioneers found the land so inviting and the soil so fertile that they established the community of Fruita, planting orchards that have been preserved by the Park Service.

Because of differences in geologic strata, elevation, and availability of water in various sections of the park, an assortment of ecosystems and terrains, as well as a variety of activities, coexist. There are hiking trails, mountain-biking trails, and four-wheel-drive touring roads; a lush fruit orchard; desert wildflowers and rich, green forests; an abundance of songbirds; and a surprising amount of wildlife—from lizards and snakes to the bashful ringtail cat (a member of the raccoon family). Throughout the park, you'll find thousand-year-old petroglyphs, and traces of the more recent Ute and Southern Paiute, Wild West outlaws, and industrious Mormon pioneers (in the one-room Fruita Schoolhouse, their children learned the three Rs and studied the Bible and Book of Mormon).

The name Capitol Reef, which conjures up an image of a tropical shoreline, seems odd for a park composed of cliffs and canyons and situated in landlocked Utah. But many of the pioneers who settled the West were former seafaring men, and they extended the traditional meaning of the word *reef* to include these seemingly impassable rock barriers. The huge round white domes of sandstone reminded them of the domes of capitol buildings, and so this area became known as Capitol Reef.

A more accurate name for the park might be "the Big Fold." When the earth's crust lifted some 60 million years ago, creating the Rocky Mountains and the Colorado Plateau, most of the lifting was relatively even. But here, through one of those fascinating quirks of nature, the crust wrinkled into a huge fold. Running for 100 miles, almost all within the national park, it's known as the Waterpocket Fold.

ESSENTIALS

GETTING THERE   Capitol Reef National Park is 120 miles northeast of Bryce Canyon National Park, 204 miles northeast of Zion National Park, 224 miles south of Salt Lake City, and 366 miles northeast of Las Vegas, Nevada. The park straddles Utah 24, which connects with I-70 both to the northeast and northwest.

Those coming from Bryce Canyon National Park (see chapter 11) can follow Utah 12 northeast to its intersection with Utah 24, and follow that east into Capitol Reef. If you're approaching the park from Glen Canyon National Recreation Area and the Four Corners region, follow Utah 276 and/or Utah 95 north to the intersection with Utah 24, where you then head west into the park.

The closest major airport is **Grand Junction Regional Airport,** about 200 miles east in Grand Junction, Colorado (© **970/244-9100;** www.gjairport.com). It has direct flights or connections from most major cities on **Allegiant, American/American Eagle, Continental, Delta, United,** and **US Airways.** Car rentals are available at the airport from **Alamo** (© **970/243-3097;** www.alamo.com), **Avis** (© **970/244-9170;** www.avis.com), **Budget** (© **970/244-9170;** www.budget.com), **Enterprise** (© **970/254-1700;** www.enterprise.com), **Hertz** (© **970/243-0747;** www.hertz.com), and **National** (© **970/243-6626;** www.nationalcar.com).

INFORMATION/VISITOR CENTER   For advance information, contact **Capitol Reef National Park,** HC 70 Box 15, Torrey, UT 84775 (© **435/425-3791,** ext. 4111; www.nps.gov/care).

The **visitor center** is located on the park access road at its intersection with Utah 24. A path alongside the access road connects the visitor center with the campground, passing the historic Fruita blacksmith shop, the orchards, and a lovely shaded picnic ground. The visitor center, open daily from 8am to 6pm in summer (shorter hours at other times), has exhibits on the area's geology and history as well as a 10-minute introductory slide show on the park. You can ask the rangers questions, get backcountry permits, pick up free brochures, and purchase books, maps, videos, postcards, and posters. The **Ripple Rock Nature Center,** located about ¾ mile south of the visitor center along the Scenic Drive, offers exhibits and activities especially for children. It's open from Memorial Day weekend through Labor Day weekend only. Check at the visitor center for its current hours.

Books and maps are available from the nonprofit **Capitol Reef Natural History Association,** Capitol Reef National Park, HC 70 Box 15, Torrey, UT 84775 (© **435/425-4106;** www.capitolreefnha.org).

FEES, REGULATIONS & BACKCOUNTRY PERMITS   Entry to the park is free, although it costs $5 per vehicle (including motorcycles) or $3 per person on foot or bicycle to access the scenic drive beyond the main campground (pass valid for up to 7 days). Free **backcountry permits** (available at the visitor center) are required for all overnight hikes.

Capitol Reef National Park

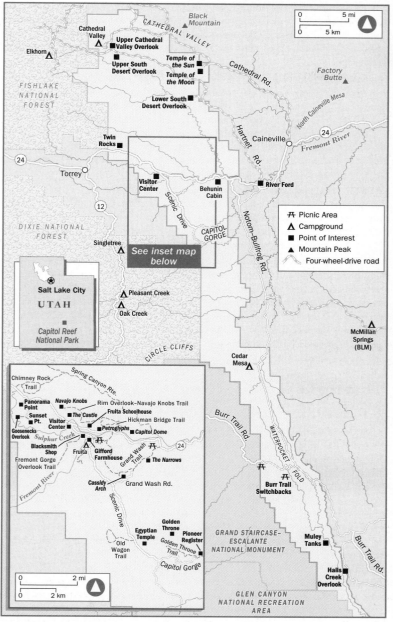

Black Mountain

CATHEDRAL VALLEY

Cathedral Valley

Upper Cathedral Valley Overlook

Elkhorn

Upper South Desert Overlook

Temple of the Sun

Temple of the Moon

Cathedral Rd.

Factory Butte

FISHLAKE NATIONAL FOREST

Lower South Desert Overlook

North Caineville Mesa

Hartnet Rd.

Caineville

24

Fremont River

Twin Rocks

Torrey

24

12

Visitor Center

Scenic Drive

Behunin Cabin

River Ford

CAPITOL GORGE

Notom-Bullfrog Rd.

🅣 Picnic Area

🅐 Campground

■ Point of Interest

▲ Mountain Peak

Four-wheel-drive road

DIXIE NATIONAL FOREST

Singletree

See inset map below

Salt Lake City

UTAH

Capitol Reef National Park

Pleasant Creek

Oak Creek

CIRCLE CLIFFS

Cedar Mesa

McMillan Springs (BLM)

Chimney Rock Trail

Spring Canyon Rte.

Panorama Point

Navajo Knobs

Rim Overlook–Navajo Knobs Trail

Fruita Schoolhouse

Sunset Pt.

The Castle

Visitor Center

Hickman Bridge Trail

Goosenecks Overlook

Sulphur Creek

Petroglyphs

Capitol Dome

Blacksmith Shop

Fruita

Gifford Farmhouse

Grand Wash Trail

Fremont Gorge Overlook Trail

Fremont River

The Narrows

24

Burr Trail Rd.

WATERPOCKET FOLD

Cassidy Arch

Grand Wash Rd.

Scenic Drive

Egyptian Temple

Golden Throne

Pioneer Register

Burr Trail Switchbacks

Old Wagon Trail

Golden Throne Trail

Capitol Gorge

GRAND STAIRCASE–ESCALANTE NATIONAL MONUMENT

Muley Tanks

Burr Trail Rd.

Halls Creek Overlook

0   2 mi
0   2 km

GLEN CANYON NATIONAL RECREATION AREA

Bicycles are prohibited in the backcountry and on all hiking trails. Feeding or otherwise disturbing wildlife is forbidden, as is vandalizing or upsetting any natural, cultural, or historic feature of the park. Because park wildlife refuse to follow park rules regarding wildlife diet, campers should be especially careful of where they store food and should dispose of garbage promptly. Dogs, which must be leashed at all times, are prohibited on all trails, more than 100 feet from any road, and in public buildings.

SEASONS/AVOIDING THE CROWDS   Although Capitol Reef receives fewer than 700,000 visitors annually—not many compared to big name parks like Grand Canyon and Yellowstone—it can still be busy, especially during the peak summer season. For this reason, the best time to visit is fall, particularly October and November, when temperatures remain warm enough for comfortable hiking and camping, but are not so hot that they'll send you constantly in search of shade. You also don't have to be as cautious about flash floods through the narrow canyons as you do during the July-through-September thunderstorm season.

SAFETY   Hikers should carry plenty of water, especially in summer, and watch out for rattlesnakes, which have been seen in the rocks of the Grand Wash and around Fruita. Afternoon thunderstorms in July, August, and September can bring flash floods, which fill narrow canyons without warning. Steep-walled Grand Wash can be particularly hazardous—avoid it whenever storms are threatening.

RANGER PROGRAMS   Rangers present a variety of free programs and activities from spring through fall. Campfire programs take place most evenings at the outdoor amphitheater next to Fruita Campground. Topics vary, but could include animals and plants, geology, and human history in and of the area. Rangers also lead hikes and walks and give short talks on history at the pioneer Fruita Schoolhouse. Schedules are posted on bulletin boards at the visitor center and campground.

Kids can become Junior Rangers or Junior Geologists—they'll learn to map ancient earthquakes, inspect water bugs, and so on. Get details at the visitor center.

SEEING THE HIGHLIGHTS BY CAR

As with most national parks, it would be easy to spend a week or more here, hiking the trails, admiring the views, and loafing about the campground. However, those with a limited amount of time, and those who prefer the comfort of a car to the demands of the hiking trail, will still find Capitol Reef relatively easy to explore.

Start at the **visitor center** and watch a short slide show explaining the park's geology and early history. From the center, the paved 25-mile round-trip **Scenic Drive** leads south into the park, offering good views of dramatic canyons and rock formations. Pick up a copy of the Scenic Drive brochure ($2 at the visitor center) and set out, stopping at viewpoints to admire the colorful cliffs, monoliths, and commanding rock formations.

If the weather's dry, drive down the gravel **Capitol Gorge Road** (5 miles round-trip) at the end of the paved Scenic Drive for a look at what many consider the best backcountry scenery in the park. If you're up for a short walk, the relatively flat 2-mile (round-trip) **Capitol Gorge Trail,** which starts at the end of Capitol Gorge Road, takes you to the historic **Pioneer Register,** a rock wall where traveling pioneers "signed in" (p. 244).

butch cassidy: UTAH'S MOST INFAMOUS SON

Robert LeRoy Parker was born into a hardworking Mormon family, in the little Southwestern Utah town of Beaver, on April 13, 1866. The oldest of 13 children, Robert was said to be a great help to his mother, and worked on the small ranch his parents bought near Circleville, about 50 miles north of Bryce Canyon.

It was in Circleville where the problems began. Teenager Robert fell in with some rather unsavory characters, including one Mike Cassidy, the ne'er-do-well role model who reportedly gave the youth his first gun, and presumably from whom young Robert took the alias "Cassidy." The boy made his way to Telluride, Colorado, worked for one of the mines there for a while, and then wandered up to Wyoming. He made his way back to Telluride—and, strangely enough, the Telluride bank was robbed. Butch Cassidy had officially begun his life of crime.

In the following years, Butch—who gained the nickname after a short stint working in a butcher shop—became an expert at rustling cattle, robbing banks, and, his ultimate glory, robbing trains. Butch wanted to call his gang the Train Robbers Syndicate, but they raised such hell in celebration of their economic successes that saloonkeepers in Vernal and other Utah towns began calling them "that wild bunch," and the name stuck. The Wild Bunch would travel through Utah, hiding out in the desolate badlands that were to become Bryce Canyon, Capitol Reef, and Canyonlands national parks. Capitol Reef's Cassidy Arch was named after Butch; this area was supposedly one of his favorite hiding places.

If you've seen the 1969 movie *Butch Cassidy and the Sundance Kid*, with Paul Newman and Robert Redford, you can't forget the spectacular scene in which Butch and his cohorts blow the door off a railroad car. Then they use way too much dynamite to open the safe, sending bills flying into the air. Apparently, the story is basically true, having taken place on June 2, 1899, near Wilcox, Wyoming. According to reports of the day, they got away with $30,000.

The Union Pacific Railroad took exception to Butch's antics. When the posse started getting a bit too close, Butch, Sundance, and Sundance's lady friend, Etta Place (Katharine Ross in the film), took off for South America, where it's said they continued a life of crime for a half dozen or so years. There are also some stories—unconfirmed—that it was in South America that Butch first killed anyone.

According to some historians (as well as the movie), Butch and Sundance were shot dead in a gun battle with army troops in Bolivia in 1908. But some believe that Butch returned to the United States, visited friends and family in Utah and Wyoming, and eventually settled in Spokane, Washington, where he lived a peaceful life under the name William T. Phillips until he died of cancer in 1937.

Another dry-weather driving option is the **Grand Wash Road,** a maintained dirt road that's subject to flash floods, but in good weather offers an easy route into spectacular backcountry. Along the 2-mile round-trip, you reach **Cassidy Arch;** famed outlaw Butch Cassidy is said to have hidden out nearby.

Utah 24, which crosses Capitol Reef from east to west, also has several viewpoints offering good looks at the park's features, such as monumental **Capitol**

Dome, which resembles the dome of a capitol building; the aptly named **Castle** formation; the historic **Fruita Schoolhouse;** and some roadside **petroglyphs** left by the prehistoric Fremont people (see below).

CAPITOL REEF'S HISTORIC SITES

Throughout the park is scattered evidence of man's presence through the centuries. The **Fremont** people lived along the river as early as A.D. 700, staying until about A.D. 1300. Primarily hunters and gatherers, the Fremont also grew corn, beans, and squash to supplement their diet; when they abandoned the area, they left little behind. They lived in pit houses, so called because they were dug into the ground—the remains of one can be seen from the **Hickman Bridge Trail.** Many of the Fremont people's petroglyphs (images carved into rock) and some pictographs (images painted on rock) are still visible on the canyon walls. If you could read them, they might even say why these early Americans left the area—a puzzle that continues to baffle historians and archaeologists.

Fast-forwarding to the 19th century, prospectors and other travelers passed through the **Capitol Gorge** section of the park in the late 1800s, leaving their names on a wall of rock that came to be known as the **Pioneer Register.** You can reach it via a 2-mile loop; see p. 244.

Mormon pioneers established the appropriately named community of **Fruita** when it was discovered that this was a good locale for growing fruit. The tiny 1896 **Fruita Schoolhouse** served as a church, social hall, and community-meeting hall, in addition to functioning as a one-room schoolhouse. The school closed in 1941, but it was carefully restored by the National Park Service in 1984 and is authentically furnished with old wood and wrought-iron desks, a woodstove, a chalkboard, and textbooks. The hand bell used to call students to class still rests on the corner of the teacher's desk. Nearby, the **orchards** planted by the Mormon settlers continue to flourish, tended by park workers who invite you to sample the "fruits" of their labors.

The historic **Gifford Farmhouse,** built in 1908, is a typical early-20th-century Utah farmhouse. Located about a mile south of the visitor center, the authentically renovated and furnished farmhouse is open daily from mid-April through September. In addition to displays of period objects, there are often demonstrations of early homemaking skills and crafts, such as quilting and rug making. Park across the road at the picnic area; a short path leads to the farmhouse.

OUTDOOR PURSUITS

Among the last areas in the continental United States to be explored, many parts of Capitol Reef National Park are still practically unknown, perfect for those who want to see this rugged country in its natural state. Several local companies offer **guide services,** both in the national park and nearby. **Hondoo Rivers and Trails,** 90 E. Main St., Torrey (✆ **800/332-2696** or 435/425-3519; www.hondoo.com), offers multiday horseback trail rides plus half- and full-day hiking and four-wheel-drive tours, including special tours for photographers and expeditions to rock art sites, plus shuttle services for hikers and mountain bikers. **Backcountry Outfitters,** 677 E. Utah 12, Torrey (✆ **866/747-3972** or 435/425-2010; www.ridethereef.com), offers a variety of guided trips, including hiking, canyoneering, biking, fishing, horseback riding, and four-wheel-drive excursions.

Four-Wheel Touring & Mountain Biking

As in most national parks, bikes and four-wheel-drive vehicles are restricted to established roads, but Capitol Reef has several so-called roads—actually little more than dirt trails—that provide exciting opportunities for those using 4×4s or pedal power. Use of ATVs is not permitted in the park.

The only route appropriate for road bikes is the 25-mile round-trip Scenic Drive, described above. However, both the Grand Wash and Capitol Gorge roads (see p. 240 for descriptions of these roads), plus three much longer dirt roads, are open to mountain bikes as well as four-wheel-drive vehicles. Note that rain can make the roads impassable, so check on current conditions with park rangers before setting out.

The **Cathedral Valley Loop** is recommended for mountain bikers and four-wheel-drivers. This road covers 60 miles on a variety of surfaces, including dirt, sand, and rock, and requires the fording of the Fremont River, where water is usually 1 to 1½ feet deep. You are rewarded with beautiful, unspoiled scenery, including bizarre sandstone monoliths and majestic cliffs, in one of the park's most remote areas. A small, primitive campground is located in Cathedral Valley. Access to the loop is from Utah 24, just outside the park, 12 miles east of the visitor center at the river ford; or 19 miles east of the visitor center on the Caineville Wash Road, though it's best to begin at the river ford to be sure you can make the crossing.

Hondoo Rivers and Trails and **Backcountry Outfitters** (see above) offer full-day four-wheel-drive **tours,** including lunch, into the national park and surrounding areas, at rates from $125 to $150 per person. Early-morning starting times are available for photographers who want to catch the light at sunrise, and specialized tours, including trips to rock art sites, are also available. Backcountry Outfitters, whose motto is "Get Out and Stay Out!," also rents mountain bikes at $32 to $42 for a half-day and $38 to $48 for a full day. Those wanting to go four-wheel-drive touring on their own can rent a 4WD vehicle for $95 to $125 per day, including 150 miles, at **Thousand Lakes RV Park & Campground** (see "Camping" below).

Hiking

Trails through the national park offer sweeping panoramas of colorful cliffs and soaring spires, eerie journeys through desolate steep-walled canyons, and cool oases along the tree-shaded Fremont River. Watch carefully for petroglyphs and other reminders of this area's first inhabitants. Little has changed from the way cowboys, bank robbers, settlers, and gold miners found it in the late 1800s. In fact, one of the best things about hiking here is experiencing the unique combination of scenic beauty, American Indian art, and Western history.

Park rangers can help you choose trails best suited to the time of year, weather conditions, and your personal physical condition; those planning serious backpacking treks will want to buy topographic maps, available at the visitor center. The summer sun is wicked, so hats and sunscreen are mandatory, and a gallon of water per person is recommended.

Among the best short hikes at Capitol Reef is the 2.5-mile round-trip **Capitol Gorge Trail.** It's easy, mostly level walking along the bottom of a narrow canyon. Starting at the end of the dirt Capitol Gorge Road, the hiking trail leads past the

Pioneer Register, where prospectors and other early travelers carved their names. The earliest legible signatures were made in 1871 by J. A. Call and "Wal" Bateman.

An easy hike that's best at sunset is the aptly named **Sunset Point Trail.** The hike is less than a half-mile but affords panoramic views of cliffs and domes at their most dramatic, at sunset. The trail head is at Panorama Point turnoff, on Utah 24, 3 miles west of the visitor center, then 1 mile on a gravel access road.

Another short hike, but quite a bit more strenuous, is the 3.5-mile round-trip **Cassidy Arch Trail.** This route offers spectacular views as it climbs steeply from the floor of Grand Wash to high cliffs overlooking the park. The trail provides several perspectives of Cassidy Arch, a natural stone arch named for outlaw Butch Cassidy, who is believed to have occasionally used the Grand Wash as a hide-out. The trail, which has an elevation change of 1,150 feet, is off the Grand Wash dirt road, which branches off the east side of the highway about halfway down the park's Scenic Drive.

Capitol Reef offers a variety of backpacking opportunities, including the 15-mile round-trip **Upper Muley Twist Canyon** route, which follows a canyon through the Waterpocket Fold and offers views of arches and narrows, as well as panoramic vistas from the top of the fold; and the 22-mile round-trip **Halls Creek Narrows,** which follows Halls Creek through a beautiful slot canyon (where you may have to wade or swim). Free backcountry permits (available at the visitor center, p. 238) are required for all overnight hikes. Discuss any plans with park rangers first, as these routes are prone to flash floods.

Guided hikes in the park and in other nearby locations are available from **Hondoo Rivers and Trails** and **Backcountry Outfitters** (see above). Prices vary, but as an example, half-day guided hiking trips cost about $90 per person, and full-day guided hikes, including lunch, cost about $125.

Horseback Riding

Horses are welcome in some areas of the park but prohibited in others; check at the visitor center for details. Multiday guided trail rides that include the national park or other areas are offered by **Hondoo Rivers and Trails** (see above), at rates of about $1,500 per person for a 6-day trip, including all food and equipment; Hondoo also leads custom trips. **Backcountry Outfitters** (see above) also provides multiday trail rides, and, in addition, offers kids' pony rides (5 and younger) for $20, plus 1-hour horseback rides for $35, 2-hour rides for $60, half-day rides for $120, and full-day rides, with lunch, for $160.

Wildlife-Watching

Although summer temperatures are hot and there's always the threat of a thunderstorm, this is a good season for wildlife viewing. Many species of lizards reside in the park; you might spy one warming itself on a rock. The western whiptail, eastern fence, and side-blotched lizards are the most common, but the loveliest is the collared lizard, dark in color but with light speckles that allow it to blend easily with lava rocks and become almost invisible to its foes. Watch for deer throughout the park, especially along the path between the visitor center and Fruita Campground. This area is also where you're likely to see chipmunks and antelope ground squirrels.

If you keep your eyes to the sky, you may spot a golden eagle, Cooper's hawk, raven, and numerous songbirds that pass through each year. Although they're somewhat shy and only emerge from their dens at night, the ringtail cat, a member of the raccoon family, also makes the park his home, as do the seldom-seen bobcat, cougar, fox, marmot, and coyote.

CAMPING

In the Park

The 71-site **Fruita Campground ★★** offers a delightful forest camping experience, with large, well-spaced sites and trees and wildlife galore. Open year-round, it offers modern restrooms, drinking water, picnic tables, fire grills, and an RV dump station (in summer only), but no showers or RV hookups. It's located along the main park road, 1 mile south of the visitor center. Camping costs $10; reservations are not accepted.

The park also has two primitive campgrounds, free and open year-round on a first-come, first-served basis. Both have tables, fire grills, and pit toilets, but no water. Check road conditions before going; unpaved roads may be impassable in wet weather. **Cedar Mesa Campground,** with five sites, is located in the southern part of the park, about 23 miles down Notom-Bullfrog Road (paved for only the first 10 miles), which heads south off Utah 24 just outside the eastern entrance to the park. **Cathedral Valley Campground,** with six sites, is located in the northern part of the park. From the visitor center, head east on Utah 24 about 12 miles to the Fremont River ford, cross the river, and turn north on unpaved Hartnet Road for about 25 miles. A high-clearance or four-wheel-drive vehicle is necessary.

> **Impressions**
>
> *The colors are such as no pigments can portray. They are deep, rich, and variegated; and so luminous are they, that light seems to flow or shine out of the rock.*
> —Geologist C. E. Dutton, 1880

Backcountry camping is permitted in much of the park with a free permit, available at the visitor center. Fires are forbidden in the backcountry.

Nearby

Sandcreek RV Park The open, grassy area in this pleasant park affords great views in all directions, and there are numerous trees. Facilities include a large, clean bathhouse; horseshoe pits; a gift shop with handmade stone and antler jewelry; a dump station; and pay laundry. There are 24 sites plus two attractive cabins that share the campground bathhouse ($30 double). There is also horse boarding ($5 per horse per night).

540 Utah 24, 5 miles west of the park entrance (P.O. Box 750276), Torrey, UT 84775. www.sandcreek rv.com. ✆ **435/425-3577.** 24 sites, 12 tent and 12 RV. $15 tent site; $21–$24 RV site. MC, V. Closed mid-Oct to Mar.

Single Tree Campground ★ Located in a forest of tall pines at an elevation of 8,200 feet, this campground features nicely spaced paved sites. Some sites are situated in the more open center area; others are set among trees along the edge of the campground. There are also sites that can accommodate large RVs. Most popular are those sites offering distant panoramic views of the national park. Facilities include a picnic table, grill, and fire ring at each site; restrooms with flush toilets but no sinks or showers; water hydrants scattered about; an RV dump station; and a horseshoe pit and volleyball court. There are no RV hookups. **Note:** The campground is part of the Dixie National Forest but is managed by the Fishlake National Forest.

Utah 12, about 16 miles south of Torrey. Fremont Ranger District, Fishlake National Forest, 138 S. Main St. (P.O. Box 129), Loa, UT 84747. www.fs.fed.us/r4. ✆ **435/836-2800.** Reservations ✆ 877/444-6777; www.recreation.gov. 26 sites. $10. No credit cards on-site. Closed Nov to mid-May.

Thousand Lakes RV Park & Campground   Good views of surrounding rock formations are one of the perks of staying at this well-maintained campground, which also has some shade trees. RV sites are gravel; tent sites are grass. Facilities include the usual bathhouse, plus a gift-and-convenience store, a coin-op laundry, a dump station, a heated outdoor swimming pool, horseshoes, barbecues, and Wi-Fi. Eight cabins ($35–$95 double) range from basic with a shared bathhouse to complete with shower and toilet, plus several upscale units. One unit sleeps six and has a kitchen and bathroom. In addition, Western dinners are offered Monday through Friday and some Saturdays ($15–$23 adults, $7.95–$9.95 children 12 and younger), and 4×4 rentals are available at $95 to $125 per day.

Utah 24, 6 miles west of Capitol Reef National Park (P.O. Box 750070), Torrey, UT 84775. www.thousandlakesrvpark.com. ✆ **800/355-8995** for reservations, or 435/425-3500. Fax 435/425-3510. 67 sites. $18 tent site; $28–$29 RV site. DISC, MC, V. Closed late Oct to late Mar.

Wonderland RV Park ★★   The closest full-service RV park and campground to the national park, Wonderland offers great views, immaculately maintained grounds and bathhouses, plus shade trees, grass, big rig sites, and croquet, horseshoes, volleyball, and basketball. Wi-Fi, cable TV, and use of gas barbecue grills are included in the rates. There are fire pits and a dump station. Also on the grounds and sharing the bathhouse are two basic camping cabins and two "mountain cabins," with two queen beds, color TVs, microwave, and fridge. There's also a cute sheep wagon ($48 double).

Junction of Utah 12 and 24 (P.O. Box 67), Torrey, UT 84775. www.capitolreefrvpark.com. ✆ **877/854-0184** or 435/425-3665. Fax 435/425-3346. 43 sites, 10 tent and 33 RV. $24 tent site; $28–$31 RV site; $28–$48 cabins. DISC, MC, V. Closed Nov–Mar.

WHERE TO STAY

The park itself has no lodging or dining facilities, but the town of Torrey, just west of the park entrance, can take care of most needs. Room tax adds 10.25% to lodging bills.

In addition to the properties discussed below, Torrey has a **Days Inn,** 825 E. Utah 24 (✆ **888/425-3113** or 435/425-3111), with rates of $79 to $94 double and $94 to $129 suite. Also see the information on cabins at **Sandcreek RV Park, Thousand Lakes RV Park & Campground,** and **Wonderland RV Park** under "Camping," above.

For additional information on area lodging, dining, and activities, contact the **Wayne County Travel Council,** P.O. Box 7, Teasdale, UT 84773 (✆ **800/858-7951** or 435/425-3365; www.capitolreef.travel), which operates a **visitor center** at the junction of Utah highways 12 and 24, from April through October, Sunday through Thursday 9am to 5pm and Friday and Saturday 8am to 7pm.

Austin's Chuck Wagon Motel   This attractive family-owned-and-operated motel offers a wide range of options. The well-maintained property includes modern motel rooms, which have Southwestern decor, phones, and two queen-size beds, and a family suite with a large living room, fully equipped kitchen, and three bedrooms that sleep six. The best choice here, however, is one of the plush (but still Western-style) cabins. Measuring 576 square feet, each cabin has two bedrooms (each with a queen-size bed), a living room with a queen-size sofa bed, a complete kitchen, a full bathroom, a covered porch, and a small yard with a barbecue grill and a picnic table. The grounds are attractively landscaped, with a lawn and large trees; also on the property is a grocery store/bakery with a well-stocked deli. All rooms are nonsmoking.

12 W. Main St. (P.O. Box 750180), Torrey, UT 84775. www.austinschuckwagonmotel.com. ℂ **800/ 863-3288** or 435/425-3335. Fax 435/425-3434. 24 units. Motel rooms $75 double; cabins $135 for up to 4; family suite $150 for up to 4. AE, DISC, MC, V. Closed Dec–Feb. **Amenities:** Deli (p. 248); Jacuzzi; outdoor heated pool. *In room:* A/C, TV, Wi-Fi (free).

Best Western Capitol Reef Resort Located a mile west of the national park entrance, this attractive Best Western is one of the closest lodgings to the park. Try to get a room on the back side of the motel, where the windows look out onto fantastic views of the area's red-rock formations. Standard units have either one king-size or two queen-size beds; minisuites have a king-size bed and a queen-size sofa sleeper, plus a refrigerator, microwave, and wet bar; full suites add a separate sitting room for the sofa sleeper, a second TV and telephone, a jetted tub, and patio. The sun deck and pool are situated out back, away from road noise, with glass wind barriers and spectacular views.

2600 E. Utah 24, Torrey, UT 84775. ℂ **888/610-9600** or 435/425-3761. Fax 435/425-3300. 97 units. June–Sept $110–$130 double, $140–$150 minisuite and suite; Oct–May $90–$109 double, $119– $129 minisuite and suite. Children 12 and under stay free in parent's room. AE, DC, DISC, MC, V. Pets accepted in designated pet rooms. **Amenities:** Restaurant; Jacuzzi; outdoor heated pool; tennis court. *In room:* A/C, TV, hair dryer, Wi-Fi (free).

Boulder View Inn 🍴 This attractive, well-maintained, modern motel is perfect for those who just want a good night's sleep without a lot of frills. Guest rooms are large and comfortable, with queen-size or king-size beds, tables with chairs, and a Southwestern motif. Smoking is not permitted.

385 W. Main St. (Utah 24), Torrey, UT 84775. www.boulderviewinn.com. ℂ **800/444-3980** or 435/ 425-3800. 11 units. Apr–Nov $75 double; Nov–Mar $40 double. Rates include continental breakfast. DISC, MC, V. *In room:* A/C, TV, Wi-Fi (free).

Capitol Reef Inn & Cafe This older, Western-style motel—small, nicely landscaped, and adequately maintained—offers guest rooms that are both homey and comfortable. The furnishings are handmade of solid wood. Facilities include a lovely desert garden and kiva. Adjacent, under the same ownership, is a good restaurant as well as a gift shop that sells American Indian crafts, guidebooks, and maps.

360 W. Main St. (Utah 24), Torrey, UT 84775. www.capitolreefinn.com. ℂ **435/425-3271.** 10 units. $53 double. Children 2 and under stay free in parent's room. AE, DISC, MC, V. Closed late Oct to mid-Mar. **Amenities:** Restaurant (see review, p. 248); large Jacuzzi. *In room:* A/C, TV, fridge.

Sandstone Inn ★★ 🍴 If you want panoramic views in all directions and an attractive, comfortable room at a very good price, this is the place. Perched high on a hill set back from the highway, the well-maintained property is peaceful and quiet. Standard motel rooms have two queen-size beds or one king, along with typical modern motel decor and some genuine wood touches. Deluxe rooms add refrigerators and microwaves, and suites have king-size beds, large whirlpool tubs, and private balconies.

955 E. Utah 24, at the junction of Utah 24 and 12 (P.O. Box 750208), Torrey, UT 84775. www.sandstone capitolreef.com. ℂ **800/458-0216** or 435/425-3775. Fax 435/425-3212. 50 units. Apr–Oct $78–$ 98 double, $125 suite; Nov–Mar $58–$78 double, $80 suite. AE, DISC, MC, V. Pets accepted, $10 per night nonrefundable fee. **Amenities:** Restaurant (see review, p. 249); Jacuzzi; indoor heated pool. *In room:* A/C, TV, hair dryer, Wi-Fi (free).

Torrey Schoolhouse Bed and Breakfast ★★ 👜   This excellent inn offers a charming alternative to the standard motel. The imposing three-story red sandstone building served as the community's school from 1917 until 1954; during its early days, it also hosted plays, boxing matches, and dances. Beautifully restored, it now houses a bed-and-breakfast inn that maintains the schoolhouse theme on the first and second floors, with furnishings such as an antique writing desk and musical instruments, while third-floor rooms have a pioneer theme. Units are spacious, with light-colored walls and high ceilings, which make them feel even bigger. The inn offers a good mix of historical ambience and modern conveniences, including top-of-the-line beds and massage recliners. The organic breakfasts, often from locally grown ingredients, might include a breakfast quiche, Belgian waffles with fruit topping, or a breakfast burrito, along with homemade muffins and breakfast meats. All units are nonsmoking.

150 N. Center St. (P.O. Box 750337), Torrey, UT 84775. www.torreyschoolhouse.com. ℂ **435/633-4643.** 10 units. Apr–Oct $110–$160 double. Rates include full breakfast. MC, V. Closed Nov–Mar. Children 12 and older welcome. *In room:* A/C, hair dryer, Wi-Fi (free).

WHERE TO EAT

In addition to the restaurants discussed below, you'll find a very good deli and bakery at **Austin's Chuck Wagon Motel,** 12 W. Main St., Torrey (ℂ **800/863-3288** or 435/425-3335; www.austinschuckwagonmotel.com), open daily with varying hours from mid-March through October (closed the rest of the year). It offers a good choice of hot and cold sandwiches, wraps, and Mexican items such as burritos and enchiladas, at prices from $3 to $7. Although primarily for takeout, the deli does have several small tables. In the same building is a grocery store.

Cafe Diablo ★★★ SOUTHWESTERN   Looks are deceiving. What appears to be a simple, Western cafe is in fact a very fine restaurant—among Utah's best—offering innovative beef, pork, chicken, seafood, and vegetarian selections, many with a Southwestern flair. The rack of glazed pork ribs, slow roasted in chipotle, molasses, and rum glaze, is spectacular. Other noteworthy dishes include pumpkinseed-crusted red trout served with cilantro-lime sauce and wild rice pancakes, and Mayan tamales—eggplant, poblano peppers, roasted tomatoes, *masa,* and Casera cheese steamed in a banana leaf. The pastries—at least eight different ones are prepared daily—and homemade ice creams are wonderful. In addition to the dining room there is a heated patio. Beer, wine, and cocktails are served.

599 W. Main St., Torrey. ℂ **435/425-3070.** www.cafediablo.net. Main lunch courses $10–$13, main dinner courses $22–$30. AE, MC, V. Daily 5–10pm. Closed late Oct to early Apr.

Capitol Reef Inn & Cafe AMERICAN   This popular restaurant offers a good selection of fresh, healthy foods, although the service can be a bit slow, especially at dinner. Known for its locally raised trout (available at every meal), the cafe is equally famous for its 10-vegetable salad. Vegetables are grown locally, and vegetarian dishes include spaghetti and mushroom lasagna. There are several steaks, including an excellent tenderloin, plus chicken. The atmosphere is casual, with comfortable seating, American Indian crafts, and large windows. The restaurant offers beer and wine.

At the Capitol Reef Inn & Cafe (p. 247), 360 W. Main St. ☏ **435/425-3271.** www.capitolreefinn. com. Main courses $6–$11 breakfast and lunch, $10–$20 dinner. AE, DISC, MC, V. Daily 7am–9pm. Closed late Oct to mid-Mar.

Rim Rock Restaurant ★★ AMERICAN   A local favorite for special occasions, this fine-dining restaurant is an excellent choice for beef—try the grilled tenderloin with cranberry demi-sauce or the blackened top sirloin with caramelized onions and button mushrooms. The smoked pork barbecue ribs are recommended, as is the smoked trout appetizer. The menu also includes a pasta of the day, pan-seared Utah trout, several chicken dishes, a few vegetarian items, and homemade pies. The casual dining room has a Western look, with lots of windows providing stupendous views and a raised outdoor dining area. Full liquor service is available.

2523 E. Utah 24. ☏ **435/425-3388.** www.therimrock.net. Main courses $15–$30. AE, DISC, MC, V. Daily 5–9:30pm. Closed Nov to late Mar.

Sandstone Restaurant ★ AMERICAN   Perched on a hill back from the highway, the Sandstone offers tremendous views of the area's famed red-rock formations plus good food at reasonable prices. The Sandstone does an especially good job with barbecue—try the tender pork ribs—and beef, including a prime rib special most Fridays and Saturdays. It also has pasta and chicken dinners, a salad bar, and excellent desserts, such as the four-layer chocolate cake and the huge brownie sundae. Breakfasts offer the usual American standards, and lunch may be served in summer (call for hours). Beer and wine are available.

In the Sandstone Inn (p. 247), 955 E. Utah 24, at the junction of Utah 24 and 12. ☏ **435/425-3775.** www.sandstonecapitolreef.com. Main dinner courses $12–$23. AE, DISC, MC, V. Apr–Nov daily 7am–noon and 5–9pm. Call for summer lunch hours if available, and all hours Dec–Mar.

Slacker's Burger Joint ☺ BURGERS/SANDWICHES   This nonfranchise fast-food restaurant serves good burgers—about a dozen varieties including one topped with pastrami!—plus sandwiches, fries, fish and chips; for those who insist on eating healthy, several salads and a garden burger are offered. A small dining room is decked out in '50s memorabilia, and a lawn is set with picnic and patio tables. A wide variety of ice-cream cones and thick milkshakes are also available; no alcohol is served.

165 E. Main St., Torrey. ☏ **435/425-3710.** All items $2–$9. MC, V. May–Aug daily 11am–9pm, closes at 8pm Sept–Oct and mid-Mar to Apr. Closed Nov to mid-Mar.

LAKE POWELL & GLEN CANYON NATIONAL RECREATION AREA

This huge canyon is a spectacular wonderland of stark contrasts—parched desert, deep blue water, startlingly red rocks, rich green hanging gardens. A joint effort by man and nature, the **Lake Powell and Glen Canyon National Recreation Area** ★★★ is a huge water park, with more shoreline than the West Coast of the continental United States. It's also a place of almost unbelievable beauty, where millions of visitors each year take to the water to explore, fish, water-ski, swim, or simply lounge in the sun.

Named for Major John Wesley Powell, a one-armed Civil War veteran who led a group of nine explorers on a scientific expedition down the Green and Colorado rivers in 1869, the lake is 186 miles long and has almost 100 major side canyons that give it 1,960 miles of shoreline. And with more than 160,000 surface acres of water when full, it has the second-largest capacity of any man-made lake in the United States after Lake Mead. Both reservoirs have been at historically low levels in recent years, but they enjoyed a strong runoff in 2011.

Glen Canyon National Recreation Area, with Lake Powell at its heart, is three parks in one: a major destination for boaters and fishermen, a treasury of scenic wonders, and an important historic site. Lake Powell is best enjoyed by boat—you can glide through the numerous side canyons among delicately sculpted sandstone formations that are intricate, sensuous, and sometimes bizarre, the work of millions of years of erosion. One rock formation that's considered a must-see for every visitor is Rainbow Bridge National Monument, a huge natural stone bridge sacred to the Navajo and other area tribes. You can also explore the 1870s stone fort and trading post at Lees Ferry, the Ancestral Puebloan (also called Anasazi) ruins of Defiance House, and the dam, which supplies water and electric power to much of the West.

Glen Canyon National Recreation Area

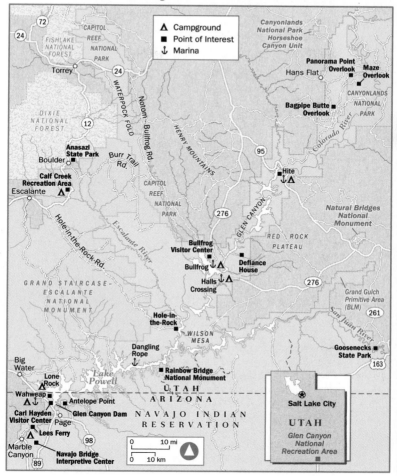

ESSENTIALS

ACCESS POINTS: THE MARINAS Located in southern Utah and northern Arizona, Lake Powell and Glen Canyon National Recreation Area has four major access points: **Wahweap Marina** and **Lake Powell Resort** (© **888/896-3829** or 928/645-2433; www.lakepowell.com and www.lakepowellmarinas.com), on the lake's south end, is the most developed area of the recreation area, with the largest number of facilities, and the closest to additional lodging, dining, and services in nearby Page, Arizona;

Bullfrog Marina (© 435/684-3000) and Halls Crossing Marina (© 435/684-7000) are midlake, and are also fairly well developed. Hite Marina (© 435/684-2278), which has been closed quite a bit in recent years because of low water, is normally the lake's northernmost access point. It is the smallest and least developed marina, with extremely limited services off season.

These four marinas, operated by Lake Powell Resorts and Marinas, are accessible by car, operate year-round, and provide boat rentals, docks, fuel, fishing and other supplies, and accommodations. A fifth marina, **Dangling Rope,** is accessible by boat only (it's 40 lake miles north of the dam and 55 lake miles south of Halls Crossing and Bullfrog marinas) and is mainly a fuel stop, though it does offer minor repairs, limited supplies, a free dump/pump-out station, emergency medical services, and some of the best soft-serve ice cream around. A sixth marina, **Antelope Point** (© 928/645-5900; www.antelopepointlakepowell.com), has a launch ramp onto the original channel of the river, small courtesy docks, a large graveled parking area, restrooms, a beach access road, a covered fuel dock, and boat rentals. This ramp may close during low-water levels. **Lees Ferry** is a popular river crossing, but does not offer direct access to Lake Powell.

GETTING THERE Wahweap Marina and Glen Canyon Dam are just off U.S. 89, 6 miles north of Page, Arizona. Wahweap is 150 miles southeast of Bryce Canyon National Park; 130 miles northeast of the north rim of Grand Canyon National Park; 65 miles east of Kanab; 267 miles east of Las Vegas, Nevada; and 381 miles south of Salt Lake City. By road, **Halls Crossing** is 220 miles northeast of Wahweap, and **Bullfrog** is 283 miles northeast (both are about 100 miles from Wahweap by boat); both are reachable via Utah 276. **Hite,** 40 miles uplake from Halls Crossing and Bullfrog, is off Utah 95.

Motorists can reach the dam and **Wahweap Marina** via U.S. 89 from Kanab or Grand Canyon National Park, and via Ariz. 98 from the east. To get to the **Lees Ferry** section, south of Wahweap, drive south on U.S. 89 and then north on U.S. 89A to Marble Canyon, where you can pick up the Lees Ferry access road.

Bullfrog and **Halls Crossing** marinas, which are connected by a toll ferry midlake, are accessible via Utah 276, which loops southwest from Utah 95. The 3-mile crossing takes about 30 minutes; it does not run in winter. For the current schedule and rates, contact either Bullfrog or Halls Crossing marinas (see "Access Points: The Marinas," above).

Flights between Page and Southwestern cities including Phoenix and Denver are available from **Great Lakes Airlines** (© 800/554-5111; www.greatlakesav.com).

INFORMATION/VISITOR CENTERS For advance information, contact Superintendent, **Glen Canyon National Recreation Area,** P.O. Box 1507, Page, AZ 86040 (© 928/608-6200; www.nps.gov/glca), or call the **Carl Hayden Visitor Center** (© 928/608-6404). Books, maps, and other materials are available from the nonprofit **Glen Canyon Natural History Association,** P.O. Box 1835, Page, AZ 86040 (© 877/453-6296 or 928/608-6358; www.glencanyonnha.org).

For lodging, tour, and boat-rental information, contact the licensed park concessionaire, **Lake Powell Resorts and Marinas,** 100 Lakeshore Dr., Page, AZ 86040 (© 888/896-3829 or 928/645-2433; www.lakepowell.com).

Numerous services, including lodging and dining, are available in nearby Page, Arizona. For information, contact the **Page–Lake Powell Tourism Bureau,** 34 N. Lake Powell Blvd. (P.O. Box 332), Page, AZ 86040 (© 888/261-7243 or

LAKE POWELL & GLEN CANYON NATIONAL RECREATION AREA | Essentials

928/660-3405; www.pagelakepowelltourism.com). It's open daily in summer from 8am to 7pm, Monday through Friday in winter from 9am to 5pm.

The **Carl Hayden Visitor Center,** at Glen Canyon Dam, 2 miles north of Page, Arizona, via U.S. 89 (© **928/608-6404**), has exhibits on the construction of the dam, local dinosaurs, and other related subjects. Audiovisual programs, free brochures, and books, maps, and videos are available. The visitor center is open daily 8am to 6pm from Memorial Day through Labor Day, the rest of the year daily 8am to 5pm.

The **Bullfrog Visitor Center,** at midlake off Utah 276 (© **435/684-7423**), has a variety of exhibits and information. It's open intermittently May through October and closed at other times. An **interpretative center** at Navajo Bridge, along U.S. 89A near Lees Ferry (© **928/355-2319**), is open from 9am to 5pm from mid-April through October and closed the rest of the year. The **Halls Crossing Boater Contact Station,** a self-serve visitor information center, is usually open daily from 8am to 6pm during the summer.

FEES & REGULATIONS   Entry into the park costs $15 per vehicle or $7 per person for up to 7 days. Boating fees are $16 for the first vessel and $8 for each thereafter, for up to 7 days. Backcountry permits (free) are required for overnight trips into the Escalante River section of the national recreation area.

The standard National Park Service regulations, such as not damaging anything and driving only on established roadways, apply here; additional regulations are aimed at protecting the water quality of the lake by prohibiting any dumping of garbage into the water, plus requiring the containment and proper disposal of human wastes within a quarter-mile of the lake. Safe-boating requirements include mandatory use of life jackets by children 12 and under. Remember, boating regulations are slightly different in Utah and Arizona; brochures of regulations are available at the marinas. Pets must be leashed at all times, except on houseboats, and are prohibited in public buildings.

SEASONS/AVOIDING THE CROWDS   The park is open year-round and is busiest in summer—when it's also the hottest, with temperatures often topping 100°F (38°C). Spring is pleasant, but can be a bit windy. October is great, when the water's still warm enough for swimming but most of the crowds have gone home. Winter can also be beautiful, with snow only rarely dusting the rocks and daytime temperatures usually in the 40s and 50s (single digits and teens Celsius). Another advantage to visiting in off season: discounts on lodging and tours November through March and on boat rentals October to May.

A Bird's-Eye View of Lake Powell

The quickest way to see the sights is by air. **Westwind Air Service** (© **480/991-5557** or 928/645-2494; www.westwind airservice.com) provides half-hour flights over the dam, Rainbow Bridge, and other scenic attractions. Longer flights take in the Grand Canyon, Canyonlands, Monument Valley, and even Bryce Canyon. Tours start at $148 per person for a 45-minute trip to Rainbow Bridge or Horseshoe Bend (two-person minimum) and go up to about $275 per person for expeditions to the Grand Canyon (three-person minimum).

RANGER PROGRAMS Amphitheater programs at Wahweap Campground take place several evenings each week in summer. Topics vary, but may include such subjects as the animals or plants of the park, geology, or the canyon's human history. Schedules are posted on bulletin boards at the campground and at the visitor center.

Kids 12 and under can become **Junior Rangers** and receive badges by completing projects in an activity book available at the Carl Hayden and Bullfrog visitor centers.

EXPLORING LAKE POWELL BY BOAT

The best way to see Lake Powell and Glen Canyon National Recreation Area is by boat, either your own or a rental, or on a boat tour. Exploring by **rented houseboat ★★** for a week and wandering among the numerous side canyons is the best way to get to know the lake.

If your time is limited, try to spend a few hours touring the dam and seeing the exhibits in the Carl Hayden Visitor Center, particularly the excellent relief map that helps you see the big picture. Then take one of the boat tours, such as the half-day trip to Rainbow Bridge. Adventurous types might want to buy some good maps, rent a boat for the day, and explore the canyons on their own. But whatever you do, try to get to Rainbow Bridge.

BRINGING YOUR OWN BOAT If you happened to bring your own boat, whether it's a one-person kayak or family-size cabin cruiser, you are sure to have a wonderful time. Boat-launching ramps are located at Wahweap, Lees Ferry, Bullfrog, Halls Crossing, and Hite (the locations of these marinas are described earlier in the chapter). Fuel, supplies, sewage pump-out stations, drinking water, and boat repairs are available at all of the above except Lees Ferry. Services and supplies are also available at Dangling Rope Marina, about 40 miles uplake from Wahweap Marina and accessible only by boat. As part of the Lake Powell Pure campaign, new facilities have been added for the disposal of human waste. You can get directions to them at the marinas or visitor center.

BOAT RENTALS **Lake Powell Resorts and Marinas** (p. 251) and **Antelope Point Marina** (✆ **800/255-5561**; www.lakepowellhouseboating.com) rent powerboats of all sizes, from two-passenger personal watercraft to luxurious 75-foot houseboats.

Late spring through early fall is the best time to be on the water, and consequently the most expensive: Rates for houseboats that sleep up to 20 people range from $2,200 to $9,000 for 4 days, or $3,700 to $15,000 for 7 days. Rates are considerably lower—sometimes by as much as 30%—in winter. Rates for small fishing boats, ski boats, and personal watercraft range from about $300 to $700 per day. Ask about packages that include boat rentals plus lodging, houseboats with smaller powerboats, and powerboats with water-skiing equipment. Nonmotorized water toys are also available for rent. Most types of boats, although not necessarily all sizes, are available at Wahweap, Bullfrog, Halls Crossing, and Antelope Point marinas. Making reservations well in advance is strongly recommended (see p. 251 for the marina telephone numbers).

You can sometimes get lower rates away from the marinas. About 12 miles northwest of Page in Big Water, Utah, is **Skylite Boat Rentals,** at U.S. 89 Mile Marker 6 (✆ **800/355-3795** or 435/675-3795; www.skylite.net), offering water toys—there are some great tubes that kids will love—and a range of powerboats.

When you're boating in the vastness of Lake Powell, basking in the sun and breathing that clear air, it seems impossible that carbon monoxide (CO) poisoning could be a threat. Yet more than a dozen people have died on Lake Powell in the last few years as a result of CO poisoning, mostly from the fumes produced by houseboat generators and boat engines. An especially dangerous area is near the rear of the boat, where carbon monoxide can accumulate under and around the rear deck. Anyone swimming or playing near this area can be overcome in a matter of minutes. Don't allow anyone to swim or play near the rear deck while engines and/or generators are running, or for an hour after they've been turned off—CO can hang around that long. Sometimes CO exhaust can literally be sucked back into a boat that's underway, a phenomenon known as the "station wagon effect." Be aware of the symptoms of CO poisoning (which can include headaches, dizziness, weakness, sleepiness, nausea, and disorientation), as well as the conditions under which CO poisoning is possible.

Generally, anybody who can drive a car can pilot a boat. The only tricks are learning to compensate for wind and currents. Be sure to spend a few minutes practicing turning and stopping; boats don't have brakes! No lessons or licenses are required; the marinas supply all the equipment needed and offer some training as well.

BOAT TOURS Year-round boat tours will take you to those hidden areas of the lake that you may never find on your own. Options range from 1½-hour trips ($32 adults, $18 children 11 and under) to all-day tours to Rainbow Bridge ($100 per adult, $72 per child). Ask about dinner cruises, float trips, and numerous packages that combine activities with lodging and/or RV spaces. For information and reservations, contact **Lake Powell Resorts and Marinas** (p. 251).

WHAT TO SEE & DO

Among the many attractions here, several deserve special mention as must-sees. Sites are arranged geographically below, from the south end of the lake to the north.

LEES FERRY Downriver from Glen Canyon Dam, Lees Ferry is a historic river crossing and the site of a stone fort built by Mormon pioneers in 1874 for protection from the Navajo. It was later used as a trading post. You can see the remains of the fort and a 1913 post office. Nearby at Lonely Dell, you'll find 19th- and early-20th-century ranch buildings, an orchard, and a blacksmith shop. Upriver, during low water, you can spot the remains of a steamboat, the *Charles H. Spencer,* a 92-foot-long paddle-wheeler that was used briefly in the early 1900s to haul coal for a gold-dredging operation.

Lees Ferry is also the starting point for white-water river trips through the Grand Canyon, and is known for its trophy trout fishing.

GLEN CANYON DAM Construction began on this U.S. Bureau of Reclamation project in October 1956. By the time the $155-million dam was completed in September 1963, almost 10 million tons of concrete had been poured, creating a wall 710 feet high and 1,500 feet long. It took until 1980 for the lake to reach its "full pool," covering much of the area that had been explored over 100 years earlier by Major

John Wesley Powell. Today, the dam provides water storage, mostly for agriculture and hydroelectric power. Its eight generators, which cost an additional $70 million, produce more than 1 million kilowatts of electrical energy per day.

RAINBOW BRIDGE NATIONAL MONUMENT ★★   This huge natural bridge is considered sacred by Native Americans. The Navajo call it a "rainbow turned to stone," and in the summer of 1995, they briefly blocked the route to the bridge to conduct a blessing ceremony and protest what they considered to be the bridge's commercialization. Located about 50 miles by boat from Wahweap, Bullfrog, and Halls Crossing marinas, the bridge is so spectacular that it was named a national monument in 1910, long before the lake was created. Believed to be the largest natural bridge in the world, Rainbow Bridge is almost perfectly symmetrical and parabolic in shape, measuring 278 feet wide and standing 290 feet above the streambed. The top is 42 feet thick and 33 feet across.

DEFIANCE HOUSE   This archaeological site 3 miles up the middle fork of Forgotten Canyon, uplake from Halls Crossing, is believed to have been occupied by a small clan of Ancestral Puebloans between A.D. 1250 and 1275. The cliff-side site includes ruins of several impressive stone rooms, food storage areas, and a kiva for religious ceremonies. The rock art panel, high along a cliff wall, includes a pictograph for which the ruin is named—an image of three warriors carrying clubs and shields. The panel also contains paintings of sheep and men.

OUTDOOR PURSUITS

Fishing

Although March through November is the most popular season, the fishing is good year-round, especially for huge rainbow trout, which are often caught in the Colorado River between the dam and Lees Ferry. Lake fishermen also catch largemouth, smallmouth, and striped bass; catfish; crappie; and walleye. Because Glen Canyon National Recreation Area lies within two states, Utah and/or Arizona fishing licenses are required, depending on where you want to fish. The marinas sell licenses as well as fishing supplies.

Hiking, Mountain Biking & Four-Wheeling

Although boating and watersports are the main activities, most of this recreation area is solid ground—actually hard rock. Lake Powell makes up only 13% of the area, so hikers and other land-based recreationists will find plenty to do. There are few marked trails, and changing water levels create a constantly shifting shoreline.

HIKING   Several short hikes lead to panoramic vistas of Lake Powell. For a view of the lake, Wahweap Bay, the Colorado River channel, and the sandstone cliffs of Antelope Island, drive half a mile east from the Carl Hayden Visitor Center, cross a bridge, and turn left onto an unmarked gravel road; follow it for about a mile to its end and a parking lot in an area locally known as the **Chains** (day-use area only). Heading north from the parking lot, follow the unmarked but obvious trail across sand, up slickrock, and across a level gravel section to an overlook that provides a magnificent view of the lake. This is usually a 10-minute walk (one-way). To extend the hike, you can find a way down to the water's edge, but beware: The steep sandstone can be slick.

Several hikes originate in the Lees Ferry area, including a moderate 2.5-mile round-trip hike through narrow **Cathedral Wash** to the Colorado River. The trail head is at the second turnout from U.S. 89A along Lees Ferry Road. This hike isn't along a marked trail, but rather down a wash, past intriguing rock formations. In wet weather, be alert for flash floods and deep pools. Allow 1 to 1½ hours for the round-trip hike.

Another relatively easy hike, the **River Trail,** starts just upriver from the Lees Ferry fort and follows an old wagon road to a ferry-crossing site, passing the historic submerged steamboat, the *Charles H. Spencer.* Allow about an hour for this 2-mile round-trip walk. A self-guiding booklet is available at Lees Ferry.

A heavy-duty 45-mile hike through the **Paria Canyon Primitive Area,** which departs from Lonely Dell Ranch at Lees Ferry, takes you through beautiful but narrow canyons. *Warning:* Flash flooding can be hazardous. This hike requires a permit from the Bureau of Land Management office in Kanab (© **435/644-4680;** www. blm.gov/ut).

Although most visitors take an easy half- or full-day boat trip to see beautiful Rainbow Bridge National Monument, it is possible to hike to it, although the 14-mile one-way trail is difficult and not maintained. It crosses the Navajo Reservation and requires a permit. Contact the **Navajo Nation Parks and Recreation Department,** P.O. Box 2520, Window Rock, AZ 86515 (© **928/871-6647;** www.navajo nationparks.org).

Serious backcountry hikers should obtain current maps of the area and discuss their plans with rangers before setting out. Hikers should carry at least 1 gallon of water per person, per day.

MOUNTAIN BIKING & FOUR-WHEELING   Mountain bikers and four-wheel-drive enthusiasts must stay on established roadways within the recreation area, but quite a few challenging dirt roads can be found both in the recreation area and on adjacent federal land. Get information from the Glen Canyon National Recreation Area office (p. 252).

In the Hite area, the **Orange Cliffs** are particularly popular among mountain bikers. The 53-mile one-way **Flint Trail** connects Hite with Hans Flat in the far-northern section of the recreation area. It's rocky, with some sandy stretches and steep grades.

For a shorter ride, the **Panorama Point/Cleopatra's Chair Trail** follows recreation area routes 744, 774, and 775 for 10 miles (one-way) from Hans Flat to Cleopatra's Chair, providing a spectacular view into Canyonlands National Park. Camping in the Orange Cliffs area requires a permit, and strict regulations apply; contact the **Canyonlands National Park** office (© **435/719-2313;** www.nps.gov/cany).

The Escalante River canyons of the national recreation area are accessible by four-wheel-drive vehicle via the 56-mile one-way **Hole-in-the-Rock Road,** which leaves Utah 12 5 miles east of Escalante, traversing part of the Grand Staircase–Escalante National Monument (chapter 11). Managed by the Bureau of Land Management (© **435/644-4680;** ww.blm.gov/ut), the dirt and sometimes rocky road passes

13

LAKE POWELL & GLEN CANYON NATIONAL RECREATION AREA

Outdoor Pursuits

257

through **Devil's Rock Garden,** an area of unique rock formations, and offers a spectacular overlook of Lake Powell. Although four-wheel-drive is not always needed, the last 6 miles of the road require a high-clearance vehicle. Regardless of what you're driving, avoid the road in wet weather. Allow at least 6 hours round-trip.

CAMPING

National recreation area concessionaire **Lake Powell Resorts and Marinas** (p. 251) operates year-round full-service RV parks at Wahweap, Bullfrog, and Halls Crossing, with complete RV hookups, modern restrooms, RV dump stations, drinking water, groceries, and LP gas. Wahweap and Halls Crossing have showers and coin-op laundries as well. Rates for two people range from $40 to $50; reservations are accepted through the concessionaire. Package deals that include RV sites and boat tours are offered.

The National Park Service operates a campground year-round at Lees Ferry, with 54 sites, flush toilets, and drinking water, but no showers or RV hookups. Reservations are not accepted; rates are $12 per site. The only camping at Hite is a primitive campground with no amenities. The cost is $6 per person or $12 per vehicle, and it's open year-round. Several other primitive campgrounds charge $6 to $12 per night.

Free dispersed camping is permitted throughout the recreation area, except within 1 mile of marinas and Lees Ferry, and at Rainbow Bridge National Monument. Those camping within a quarter-mile of Lake Powell are required to have and use self-contained or portable toilets.

WHERE TO STAY & EAT

Lake Powell Resorts and Marinas (p. 251) operates all of the recreation area's lodging facilities, as well as houseboat rentals; call to make reservations and to get additional information.

Although plenty of hotels, motels, and condominium-type units are available, the best choice for lodging is that wonderful floating vacation home, the **houseboat.** Powered by two outboard motors and complete with a full kitchen, bathrooms with hot showers, and sleeping areas for up to 22 people, houseboats serve not only as your home away from home, but also as your means of exploring the fascinating red-rock canyons that make Lake Powell the unique paradise it is. Hungry? There's a fridge, a kitchen stove with an oven, and a gas barbecue grill. For prices and additional information, see "Exploring Lake Powell by Boat," above.

In addition to the facilities described below, a variety of motels are located in Page, Arizona. For information, contact the **Page–Lake Powell Tourism Bureau** (p. 252).

At Wahweap

If you prefer a bedroom that doesn't float, consider the **Lake Powell Resort** (formerly the Wahweap Lodge), the largest (350 units) hotel in the area. Right at the Wahweap Marina, it offers good access for boat tours and rentals; has two pools, a hot tub, and sauna; and provides shuttle service into Page. Many of the rooms have spectacular views of Lake Powell. Rates for two range from $81 to $306, depending on the season. Contact Lake Powell Resorts and Marinas (p. 251).

Restaurants at Lake Powell Resort include the **Rainbow Room** (*(C)* **928/645-1162**), serving American and Southwestern dishes alongside a panoramic view of Lake Powell. All three meals are served daily (closed in winter); dinner main courses cost $15 to $32. Other dining options include a lounge, a coffee shop, and a casual grill.

Near Wahweap

Amangiri ★★★ Travelers without budgetary constraints will want to consider a stay at Amangiri, opened in 2009 as Singapore-based Amanresorts' second entry into the North American luxury market, after Amangani in Jackson Hole, Wyoming. A secluded, minimalist desert compound, Amangiri offers design, comfort, service, and opulence that are nothing short of superlative, in line with the price point. Rooms are ultra-chic, with two outdoor sitting areas each (the suite even has a private pool), and transcendent desert views. Four-digit nightly rates aside, it serves as a great base for desert recreation of all kinds. The resort itself is surrounded by trails into the surrounding desert wilderness, and the in-house Adventure Center offers everything from kayaking trips on Lake Powell to helicopter tours to Grand Canyon. Amangiri is also home to one of the best pools in the West, featuring a late Jurassic rock formation snaking down the cliffs into its crystal-clear depths.

1 Kayenta Rd., Canyon Point, UT 84741. www.amanresorts.com. *(C)* **800/477-9180** or 877/695-3999. 34 suites. $1,000–$1,600 double; $3,600 pool suite. AE, DISC, MC, V. **Amenities:** Restaurant; lounge; outdoor heated pool; spa. *In room:* A/C, TV/DVD, fridge, hair dryer, Wi-Fi (free).

At Bullfrog & the Other Marinas

The attractive **Defiance House Lodge,** at Bullfrog Marina, has 48 rooms with beautiful views of the lake; prices for two range from $86 to $185. There is a restaurant; the lodge closes down in winter.

Three-bedroom mobile-home family units are available at Bullfrog, Halls Crossing, and Hite marinas. Prices for up to six people are about $225 spring to fall, and about 30% to 40% lower in winter.

FROM MOAB TO ARCHES & CANYONLANDS NATIONAL PARKS

14

Canyonlands country they call this—a seemingly infinite high desert of rock, with spectacular formations and rugged gorges that have been carved over the centuries by the forces of the Colorado and Green rivers. Massive sandstone spires and arches that seem to defy gravity, all colored by iron and other minerals in shades of orange, red, and brown, define the national parks of southeastern Utah. This is a land that begs to be explored—if you've come to Utah for mountain biking, hiking, four-wheeling, or rafting, then this is the place. And the region holds a few surprises, too, from Ancestral Puebloan (also called Anasazi) dwellings and rock art to dinosaur bones.

MOAB: GATEWAY TO THE NATIONAL PARKS

238 miles SE of Salt Lake City

Named for a biblical kingdom at the edge of Zion, the promised land, Moab has evolved into a popular base camp for mountain bikers, four-wheel-drive enthusiasts, hikers, kayakers, and rafters eager to explore the red-rock canyon country that dominates southeastern Utah. A drive down Main Street confirms that, yes, this is a tourist town, with scores of businesses catering to visitors.

Not far from the Colorado River, Moab sits in a green valley among striking red sandstone cliffs, a setting that has lured Hollywood filmmakers for hits such as John Wayne's *The Comancheros,* the biblical epic *The Greatest Story Ever Told, Indiana Jones and the Last Crusade, Thelma & Louise,* and *City Slickers II.*

Like most Utah towns, Moab was established by Mormon pioneers sent by church leader Brigham Young. But Moab was actually founded twice. The first time, in 1855, missionaries set up Elk Mountain Mission to see to the spiritual needs of the local Ute. Apparently unimpressed with the notion of abandoning their own religion for the ways of the LDS

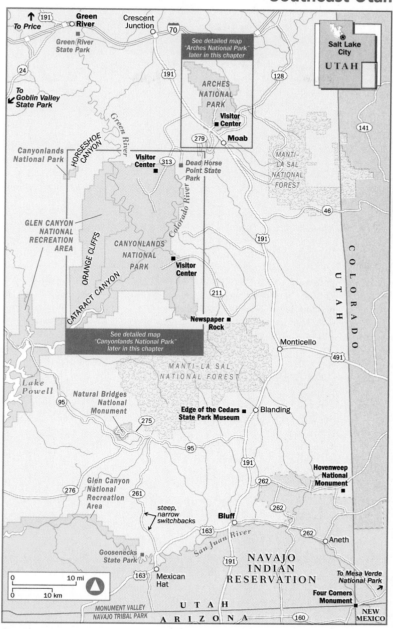

To Price ↑ 191

Green River ○

Green River State Park ■

Crescent Junction ○

70

See detailed map "Arches National Park" later in this chapter

Salt Lake City ✷

UTAH

24

To Goblin Valley State Park ↙

191

128

ARCHES NATIONAL PARK

Visitor Center ■

141

279

Moab ○

Canyonlands National Park

HORSESHOE CANYON

Green River

Visitor Center ■

313

Dead Horse Point State Park ■

MANTI-LA SAL NATIONAL FOREST

46

GLEN CANYON NATIONAL RECREATION AREA

ORANGE CLIFFS

Colorado River

191

CANYONLANDS NATIONAL PARK

Visitor Center ■

CATARACT CANYON

211

See detailed map "Canyonlands National Park" later in this chapter

Newspaper Rock ■

Monticello ○

491

MANTI-LA SAL NATIONAL FOREST

Lake Powell

95

Natural Bridges National Monument

275

Edge of the Cedars State Park Museum ■

Blanding ○

95

191

Hovenweep National Monument ■

276

Glen Canyon National Recreation Area

261

262

steep, narrow switchbacks ↙

163

Bluff ○

262

262

San Juan River

Aneth ○

Goosenecks State Park ■

163

Mexican Hat

191

NAVAJO INDIAN RESERVATION

To Mesa Verde National Park ↗

Four Corners Monument ■

NEW MEXICO

0 — 10 mi
0 — 10 km

MONUMENT VALLEY NAVAJO TRIBAL PARK

U T A H
A R I Z O N A

160

C O L O R A D O

U T A H

14

FROM MOAB TO ARCHES & CANYONLANDS | Moab

261

Church, the Ute killed several missionaries, sending the rest back to Salt Lake City in a hurry. It wasn't until 20 years later that the settlers tried again; this time, they successfully established a small farming and ranching community.

Moab (elevation 4,000 ft.) remains a relatively small town, with just under 5,000 permanent residents, but that still makes it the biggest community in southeastern Utah. Practically within walking distance of Arches National Park, Moab is also close to Canyonlands National Park and is surrounded by the Manti-La Sal National Forest and vast, open spaces under the jurisdiction of the Bureau of Land Management (BLM).

Essentials

GETTING THERE   Situated on U.S. 191, Moab is 30 miles south of I-70 (take exit 182 at Crescent Junction) and 53 miles north of Monticello. Moab is 399 miles northeast of the north rim of Grand Canyon National Park and 238 miles southeast of Salt Lake City. From Salt Lake City, follow I-15 south to Spanish Fork, take U.S. 6 southeast to I-70, and follow that east to Crescent Junction, where you'll pick up U.S. 191 south to Moab.

Sixteen miles north of downtown Moab, **Canyonlands Field** (✆ **435/259-4849;** www.moabairport.com) has daily scheduled flights between Moab and Denver and Moab and Las Vegas on **Great Lakes Airlines** (✆ **800/554-5111** or 435/259-0566; www.flygreatlakes.com) and car rentals from **Enterprise** (✆ **435/259-8505;** www. enterprise.com). Shuttle service into Moab is also available from several companies, including **Roadrunner Shuttle** (✆ **435/259-9402;** www.roadrunnershuttle.com).

The closest major airport is **Grand Junction Regional Airport,** about 112 miles east in Grand Junction, Colorado (✆ **970/244-9100;** www.gjairport.com). It has direct flights or connections from most major cities on **Allegiant, American/ American Eagle, Continental, Delta, United,** and **US Airways.** Car rentals are available at the airport from **Alamo** (✆ **970/243-3097;** www.alamo.com), **Avis** (✆ **970/244-9170;** www.avis.com), **Budget** (✆ **970/244-9170;** www.budget.com), **Enterprise** (✆ **970/254-1700;** www.enterprise.com), **Hertz** (✆ **970/243-0747;** www.hertz.com), and **National** (✆ **970/243-6626;** www.nationalcar.com).

Another option for air travelers is to fly into **Salt Lake City International Airport** (✆ **800/595-2442** or 801/575-2400; www.slcairport.com), about 240 miles from Moab, which has service from most major airlines and rental-car companies. You can rent a car at the airport and drive to Moab, or check with **Roadrunner Shuttle** (✆ **435/259-9402;** www.roadrunnershuttle.com) or **Moab Luxury Coach** (✆ **435/940-4212;** www.moabluxurycoach.com) about current shuttle rates and schedules.

Amtrak's (✆ **800/872-7245;** www.amtrak.com) California Zephyr stops in Green River, about 52 miles north of Moab, and provides service to Salt Lake City and Grand Junction, Colorado. If you plan to go from Green River to Moab, make reservations with **Roadrunner Shuttle** or **Moab Luxury Coach** (see above).

VISITOR INFORMATION   For area information, contact the **Moab Area Travel Council,** P.O. Box 550, Moab, UT 84532 (✆ **800/635-6622** or 435/259-8825; www.discovermoab.com). When you arrive, stop by the **Moab Information Center,** at the corner of Main and Center streets, open Monday through Saturday 8am to 8pm and Sunday from 9am to 7pm from mid-March through October, with shorter hours the rest of the year. This multiagency visitor center has information from the

Park Service, Bureau of Land Management, U.S. Forest Service, Grand County Travel Council, and Canyonlands Natural History Association. You can get advice, watch a number of videos on Southwest attractions, pick up brochures on local businesses and outfitters, and purchase books, videos, and other materials. A board displays current weather conditions and campsite availability.

GETTING AROUND Rentals (standard passenger cars, vans, and four-wheel-drive vehicles) are available from **Enterprise** (☎ **435/259-8505;** www.enterprise.com). Rugged four-wheel-drive vehicles are available from **Farabee's Jeep Rentals** (☎ **877/970-5337** or 435/259-7494; www.farabeejeeprentals.com); **Canyonlands Jeep Adventures** (☎ **866/892-5337** or 435/259-4413; www.canyonlandsjeep.com), which also rents regular passenger cars; and **Cliffhanger Jeep Rental** (☎ **435/259-0889;** www.cliffhangerjeeprental.com), which also rents camping trailers. Want a cab? Call **Moab Taxi** (☎ **435/210-4297**).

FAST FACTS The full-service **Moab Regional Hospital,** 450 Williams Way (☎ **435/259-7191;** www.amhmoab.org), offers 24-hour emergency care. The **post office** is at 50 E. 100 North (☎ **800/275-8777;** www.usps.com).

The best grocery store in town is **City Market,** 425 S. Main St. (☎ **435/259-5181;** www.citymarket.com), open daily from 6am to 11pm. Pick up sandwiches from the deli, mix it up at the excellent salad bar, or choose fresh-baked items from the bakery before hitting the trail. The store also sells fishing licenses, money orders, and stamps; offers photo finishing; and has a pharmacy.

Outdoor Pursuits

The Moab area is one of Utah's main outdoor playgrounds, an ideal spot for hiking, boating, camping, or just plain horsing around (with or without the horse). In addition to the nearby national parks, Arches and Canyonlands, which are covered in full later in this chapter, there's plenty of room to roam on land administered by the **Bureau of Land Management**'s Moab office, 82 E. Dogwood Ave., Moab, UT 84532 (☎ **435/259-2100;** www.blm.gov/utah/moab), and the **Manti-La Sal National Forest's Moab Ranger District,** 62 E. 100 North (P.O. Box 386), Moab, UT 84532 (☎ **435/259-7155;** www.fs.fed.us/r4). The best source for information is the **Moab Information Center** (p. 262).

Because of the extreme desert heat in summer, the best time for most outdoor activities is spring or fall—even the relatively mild winters are inviting. If you end up vacationing in the middle of summer, do your serious hiking and mountain biking early in the day, enjoy a siesta along the river or beside a swimming pool during the heat of the afternoon, and take a short hike in the evening, just before sundown.

OUTFITTERS

Although Moab has plenty for the do-it-yourselfer, more than 60 local outfitters offer guided excursions of all kinds, from lazy canoe rides to hair-raising jet-boat and four-wheel-drive adventures. The chart below lists some of the major companies that can help you fully enjoy this beautiful country, and you can get additional recommendations at the **Moab Information Center** (p. 262). All are located in Moab. Advance reservations are often required. It's best to check with several outfitters before deciding on one; in addition to asking about what you'll see and do and what it costs, it doesn't hurt to make sure the company is insured and has the proper permits with the various federal agencies. Also ask about its cancellation policy, just in case.

Outfitter	4WD	Bike	Boat	Horse	Rent
Adrift Adventures 378 N. Main St., Box 577 ☎ 800/874-4483, 435/259-8594 www.adrift.net	✓		✓	✓	
Canyon Voyages Adventure Co. 211 N. Main St., Box 416 ☎ 800/733-6007, 435/259-6007 www.canyonvoyages.com	✓	✓	✓	✓	
Dan Mick's Guided Jeep Tours 600 Mill Creek Dr., Box 1234 ☎ 435/259-4567 www.danmick.com	✓				
Escape Adventures Moab Cyclery, 391 S. Main St. ☎ 800/451-1133, 435/259-5774 www.escapeadventures.com		✓			
Magpie Cycling 497 N. Main St., Box 1496 ☎ 800/546-4245, 435/259-4464 www.magpieadventures.com		✓			
Moab Adventure Center 225 S. Main St. ☎ 866/904-1163, 435/259-7019 www.moabadventurecenter.com	✓	✓	✓	✓	✓
Moab Rafting and Canoe Co. 805 N. Main St. ☎ 800/753-8216, 435/259-7238 www.moab-rafting.com			✓		✓
Navtec Expeditions 321 N. Main St. ☎ 800/833-1278, 435/259-7983 www.navtec.com	✓		✓		✓
Sheri Griffith Expeditions 2231 S. U.S. 191, Box 1324 ☎ 800/332-2439, 435/259-8229 www.griffithexp.com			✓		
Tag-A-Long Expeditions 452 N. Main St. ☎ 800/453-3292, 435/259-8946 www.tagalong.com	✓		✓		✓
Western Spirit Cycling 478 Mill Creek Dr. ☎ 800/845-2453, 435/259-8732 www.westernspirit.com		✓			✓

FOUR-WHEELING

The Moab area has thousands of miles of four-wheel-drive roads, most left over from mining days. These roads offer a popular way to explore this scenic country without exerting too much energy.

A number of local companies (see "Outfitters," above) provide guided trips, starting at about $70 per adult and $60 per child under 16 or 17 for a half-day. You can also rent a 4×4 and take off on your own (see "Getting Around," above).

For a delightful escape from the desert heat, take a break at the **Scott M. Matheson Wetlands Preserve** ★, 934 W. Kane Creek Blvd. (📞 **435/259-4629; www.nature.org/wherewework**). Owned by the Nature Conservancy, this lush oasis attracts more than 200 species of birds and other wildlife, such as river otters, beavers, and muskrats. The preserve has a wheelchair-accessible 1-mile loop trail, boardwalks over the wet areas, and a two-story viewing blind. Guided bird walks are given (call for the current schedule), and bird and wildlife lists and self-guided tour brochures are available. In late spring and summer, visitors are advised to bring mosquito repellent. The preserve is open daily year-round from dawn to dusk, and admission is free. From downtown Moab, go south on Main Street to Kane Creek Boulevard (btw. McDonald's and Burger King), and go west about ¾ mile, passing the Moab Public Works Department, to a Y in the road. Take the left fork, and continue for about another half-mile to the preserve entrance. From the parking area, a footpath and bridge lead over Mill Creek to an information kiosk and into the preserve.

When hitting the trail on your own, either in a rental or personal 4×4, you will encounter everything from fairly easy dirt roads to "You-don't-really-expect-me-to-take-this-$50,000-SUV-up-*there*-do-you?" piles of rocks. Several four-wheel-drive trips are described in the Canyonlands section, later in this chapter, and a free brochure, available at the Moab Information Center (p. 262), covers several others.

Poison Spider Mesa Trail ★★★, which covers 16 miles of 4×4 road, providing stupendous views down to the Colorado River and Moab Valley, is a favorite of four-wheelers. It's considered difficult; a short-wheelbase high-clearance vehicle is best. Allow at least 4 hours. To reach the trail from the Moab Information Center, drive north on U.S. 191 for about 6 miles and turn west (left) onto Utah 279. Continue another 6 miles to the dinosaur tracks sign, where the trail leaves the pavement to the right, passing over a cattle guard. From here, simply follow the main trail (which is usually obvious) up switchbacks, through a sandy canyon, and over some steep, rocky stretches. From a slickrock parking area on top, you can take a short walk to Little Arch, which isn't really so little.

One easy 4×4 road is the **Gemini Bridges Trail,** which four-wheelers share with mountain bikers (see below). Those with 4×4s often drive the route in the opposite direction of the mountain bikers, starting at a dirt road departing from the west side of U.S. 191, about 10 miles north of the Moab Information Center. This involves more uphill driving, which is safer for motor vehicles—mountain bikers usually prefer going downhill.

The self-guided **Mill Canyon Dinosaur Trail** provides a close-up view of dinosaur bones and fossils from the Jurassic period, including a sauropod leg bone, vertebrae, ribs, toe bones, and the fossil remains of a large tree trunk. To reach the trail head, drive about 15 miles north of Moab on U.S. 191, then turn left at an intersection just north of highway mile marker 141. Cross the railroad tracks and follow a dirt road for about 2 miles to the trail head. Allow about 1 hour. On the south side of the canyon are the remnants of an old copper mill that operated in the late 1800s. Also nearby are the ruins of the Halfway Stage Station, a lunch stop in the late 1800s for stagecoach travelers making the 35-mile trip between Moab and Thompson, the nearest train station at that time. From the dinosaur trail head, go north as though you're returning to U.S. 191, but at the first intersection, turn right and drive to a dry wash, where you turn right again onto a jeep road that takes you a short distance to the stage station. The trail is managed by the **BLM**'s Moab office (p. 263).

GOLFING

It might be hard to keep your eye on the ball at the 18-hole, par-72 **Moab Golf Club** course, 2705 East Bench Rd. (© **435/259-6488;** www.moabcountryclub.com). Located 5 miles south of downtown Moab in Spanish Valley (take Spanish Trail Rd. off U.S. 191), the challenging course, nestled among red sandstone cliffs, offers spectacular views in every direction. Open daily year-round (weather permitting), the course has a driving range, a pro shop and lessons, and a snack bar open for breakfast and lunch. Greens fee is $42, which includes cart rental.

HIKING

The Moab area offers hundreds of hiking possibilities, many of them just a few miles from town. Get information at the Moab Information Center (p. 262) and pick up the free brochure that describes seven local trails. Hikes in nearby Arches and Canyonlands national parks are described later in this chapter.

Particularly in the summer, carry at least a gallon of water per person per day and wear a broad-brimmed hat.

A local favorite is the **Negro Bill Canyon Trail,** named for William Granstaff, who lived in the area in the late 1800s. Allow about 4 hours for this 4-mile-plus round-trip hike, which is considered easy to moderate. You may get your feet wet, depending on the level of the stream you follow up the canyon. To get to the trail head, go north from Moab on U.S. 191 to Utah 128, turn east (right), and go about 3 miles to a dirt parking area. A little over 2 miles up the trail, in a side canyon to the right, is the Morning Glory Bridge, a natural rock span of 243 feet. Watch out for the poison ivy that grows by a pool under the bridge. (In case you don't remember from your scouting manual, poison ivy has shiny leaves with serrated edges, and grows in clusters of three.)

The **Hidden Valley Trail** is a bit more challenging, taking you up a series of steep switchbacks to views of rock formations and a panorama of the Moab Valley. Allow at least 3 hours for the 4-mile round-trip. To get to the trail head, drive about 3 miles south of the Moab Information Center on U.S. 191, turn west (right) onto Angel Rock Road, and go 2 blocks to Rimrock Road. Turn north (right) and follow Rimrock Road to the parking area. The trail is named for a broad shelf, located about halfway up the Moab Rim. Many hikers turn around and head back down after reaching a low pass with great views of huge sandstone fins (the 2-mile point), but you can extend the hike by continuing all the way to the Colorado River on a four-wheel-drive road.

The highly recommended **Corona Arch Trail** offers views of three impressive arches, a colorful slickrock canyon, and the Colorado River. Allow 2 hours for this 3-mile round-trip hike, which involves a lot of fairly easy walking plus some rather steep spots with handrails and a short ladder. From Moab, go north on U.S. 191 to Utah 279, turn west (left), and go about 10 miles to a parking area on the north side of the road. A registration box and trail head are near the railroad; after crossing the tracks, follow an old roadbed onto the trail, which is marked with cairns (piles of stones).

HORSEBACK RIDING

For those who want to see the canyons from horseback, several companies lead guided rides (get current information from the Moab Information Center, p. 262), and one company, **Adrift Adventures,** offers combination rafting/horseback riding excursions, starting at $109 each for adults, $99 each for children 8 to 17 (see "Outfitters," above).

MOUNTAIN BIKING

With hundreds and hundreds of miles of trails, a wide variety of terrains, and spectacular scenery, Moab is easily the mountain-bike capital of Utah, and possibly of the United States. In addition to the mountain-biking possibilities on four-wheel-drive roads in the national parks (see sections on Arches and Canyonlands national parks, later in this chapter), there are abundant trails on Bureau of Land Management and national forest lands that are much less trafficked than national park routes.

When you get into town, stop by the Moab Information Center (p. 262) for a free copy of the *Moab Area Mountain Bike Trails* pamphlet. Discuss your plans with the very knowledgeable employees here, who can help you find the trails most suitable for your interests, ability, and equipment. You can also get information, as well as rent or repair bikes, at **Poison Spider Bicycles,** 497 N. Main St. (✆ **800/635-1792** or 435/259-7882; www.poisonspiderbicycles.com), which recommends shuttle services from **Porcupine Shuttle** (✆ **435/260-0896**). Bike rentals and repairs, plus shuttle services, will be found at **Chile Pepper Bike Shop,** 702 S. Main St. (✆ **888/677-4688** or 435/259-4688; www.chilebikes.com). Bike rentals range from $40 to $65 per day, with discounts for multiday rentals. Bike shuttle services are also available from several other companies, including **Coyote Shuttle** (✆ **435/260-2097;** www.coyoteshuttle.com) and **Roadrunner Shuttle** (✆ **435/259-9402;** www.roadrunnershuttle.com).

Several local companies (see "Outfitters," above) also offer guided mountain-bike tours, with rates starting at about $85 for a half-day and about $110 for a full day. Multiday biking/camping trips are also available.

The area's most famous trail is undoubtedly the **Slickrock Bike Trail ★★★**, a scenic but challenging 11-mile loop that crosses a mesa of heavily eroded pale orange Navajo sandstone just a few minutes from downtown Moab. Along the way, the trail offers views that take in the towering La Sal Mountains, the red-rock formations of Arches National Park, a panorama of Canyonlands National Park, and the Colorado River. The trail, open to both mountain bikes and motorcycles, is physically demanding and technically difficult and not recommended for children, novices, or anyone who is out of shape or has medical problems. Allow 4 to 5 hours, and expect to walk your bike in some areas. If you're not sure you're ready for the trail, get started on the 2¼-mile practice loop. To access the trail head from the visitor information center, take Center Street east to 400 East. Turn south (right) and follow 400 East to Mill Creek Drive. Turn east (left) and follow Mill Creek Drive to Sand Flats Road, which you take 2⅓ miles east to the BLM's Sand Flats Recreation Area and the trail head.

Those looking for a somewhat less challenging experience might try the **Gemini Bridges Trail,** a 14-mile one-way trip that shows off the area's colorful rock formations, including the trail's namesake: two natural rock bridges. Considered relatively easy, this trail follows a dirt road mostly downhill, ending at U.S. 191 just under 10 miles from the center of Moab, so it's best to arrange a shuttle (see above). To get to the trail head from the Moab Information Center, drive north along U.S. 191 to Utah 313, turn west (left), and go about 13 miles. Allow a full day, including getting to and from the trail, and be sure to watch for the magnificent view of Arches National Park from a hilltop as you approach U.S. 191 near the end of the ride.

14

FROM MOAB TO ARCHES & CANYONLANDS

Moab

Although dozens of fabulous trails are waiting for you to explore in the immediate area, mountain bikers who really want to go somewhere—perhaps all the way to Colorado—will want to check out Kokopelli's Trail and the San Juan Hut System. Winding for 142 miles across sandstone and shale canyons, deserts, and mountains, **Kokopelli's Trail** connects Moab and Grand Junction, Colorado. It combines all types of mountain biking, from demanding single track to well-maintained dirt roads, and passes primitive campsites along the way. The elevation change is about 4,200 feet. The west end of the trail is near Sand Flats Road in Moab; the east end is at the Loma Boat Launch, 15 miles west of Grand Junction. For more information contact the **Colorado Plateau Mountain Bike Trail Association,** P.O. Box 4602, Grand Junction, CO 81502 (℃ **970/244-8877;** www.copmoba.org).

The **San Juan Hut Systems,** P.O. Box 773, Ridgway, CO 81432 (℃ **970/626-3033;** www.sanjuanhuts.com), links Moab with Telluride and Durango, both in Colorado, via two 215-mile mountain-bike trail systems. Approximately every 35 miles there is a primitive cabin with eight bunks, a woodstove, a propane cooking stove, cooking gear, and groceries. The route is appropriate for intermediate-level mountain-bikers in good physical condition; more experienced cyclists will find advanced technical single tracks near the huts. The mountain-biking season generally runs from June through September. The cost for riders who plan to make either complete trip is $850 per person, which includes use of the six huts, food, sleeping bags at each hut, and maps and trail descriptions. Shorter trips and shuttles are also available.

ROCK CLIMBING

Those with the proper skills and equipment for rock climbing will find ample opportunities in the Moab area; check with the BLM (p. 263). Several companies also offer instruction and guided climbs, with rates for full-day climbs generally from $150 to $200 per adult with two people going. Contact **Desert Highlights,** 50 E. Center St., Moab (℃ **800/747-1342** or 435/259-4433; www.deserthighlights.com), **Moab Desert Adventures,** 415 N. Main St., Moab (℃ **877/765-6622** or 435/260-2404; www.moabdesertadventures.com), or **Moab Cliffs & Canyons,** 253 N. Main St., Moab (℃ **877/641-5271** or 435/259-3317; www.cliffsandcanyons.com). For climbing equipment, you'll find one of the best selections anywhere, at reasonable prices, at **Gearheads,** 471 S. Main St. (℃ **435/259-4327**), which also offers free filtered water (bring your own jugs).

WATERSPORTS: BOATING, CANOEING, RAFTING & MORE

After spending hours in the blazing sun looking at mile upon mile of huge red sandstone rock formations, it's easy to get the idea that the Moab area is a baking, dry, rock-hard desert. Well, it is. But Moab is also the only town in Utah that sits along the **Colorado River ★★**, and it's rapidly becoming a major boating center.

You can travel down the river, all the way down to Canyonlands National Park, in a canoe, kayak, large or small rubber raft (with or without motor), or a speedy, solid jet boat. Do-it-yourselfers can rent kayaks or canoes for $40 to $65 for a full day, or rafts starting at $70 for a full day. Half-day guided river trips start at about $45 per person; full-day trips are usually $55 to $75 per person. Multiday rafting expeditions, which include meals and camping equipment, start at about $300 per person for 2 days. Jet-boat trips cost about $50 for 2 hours, and from $80 for a half-day trip. Children's rates are usually 10% to 20% lower. Some companies also offer sunset or dinner trips. See "Outfitters," p. 263.

Public boat-launching ramps are opposite Lion's Park, near the intersection of U.S. 191 and Utah 128; at Take-Out Beach, along Utah 128 about 10 miles east of its intersection with U.S. 191; and at Hittle Bottom, also along Utah 128, about 24 miles east of its intersection with U.S. 191. For recorded information on river flows and reservoir conditions statewide, contact the **Colorado Basin River Forecast Center** (✆ **801/539-1311;** www.cbrfc.noaa.gov).

What to See & Do

Film Museum at Red Cliffs Lodge   Moab, and much of this part of Utah, has been a popular location for moviemaking since it was "discovered" by famed director John Ford. Ford filmed much of *Stagecoach,* starring a young John Wayne, in Monument Valley in the 1930s; in the 1940s, Ford found Moab. The Red Cliffs Ranch provided the spectacular scenery for many of Ford's movies, including *Wagon Master* and *Rio Grande.* In recent years, feature films shot in the Moab area have included *City Slickers* and *Thelma & Louise.* The museum has exhibits from the earliest films to the most recent, including props, posters, and photos—and the scenery's still spectacular. Allow 1 hour.

Red Cliffs Lodge, 14 miles east of Moab on Utah 128 (milepost 14). ✆ **866/812-2002** or 435/259-2002. www.redcliffslodge.com/museum. Free admission. Daily 8am–10pm.

Museum of Moab   This growing museum, which is also known as the Dan O'Laurie Museum of Moab, has numerous displays depicting the history of Moab from prehistoric times to the present. It starts with dinosaur skeletons and bones and also has exhibits on the geology of the area and the resultant uranium and radium mining. A hands-on testing area allows for identification of minerals. The archaeology section includes a large basket unearthed near Moab plus Ancestral Puebloan and early Fremont pottery. You can try your hand (actually your feet) at the restored player piano. Early home-medical remedies are on display, as is the first incubator, which used only a 25-watt bulb and was invented by a local doctor. There is a large hand-carved relief map of the Moab area, as well as the expected ranching and farming exhibits. Another display discusses the National Park Service, Bureau of Land Management, and U.S. Forest Service, describing their role in the area—a large one—and how they work together. Allow about an hour.

118 E. Center St. (2 blocks east of Main St.). ✆ **435/259-7985.** www.moabmuseum.org. Admission $5 for those 17 and older, free for youths 16 and under, $10 family. Mar–Oct Mon–Fri 10am–5pm, Sat noon–5pm; Nov–Feb Mon–Sat noon–5pm. Closed Thanksgiving, Christmas, and New Year's Day.

Where to Stay

Room rates are generally highest from March through October—with the highest rates often in September—and sometimes drop by up to half in winter. High season rates are listed here; call or check websites for off-season rates. A room tax of 12.25% is added to all bills. Pets are not accepted unless otherwise noted.

Most visitors are here for the outdoors and don't plan to spend much time in their rooms; as a result, many book into one of the fully adequate chain and franchise motels, most of which are located on Main Street. Franchises here include our favorite, the very well-maintained but a bit pricey **La Quinta Inn,** 815 S. Main St. (✆ **435/259-8700;** www.lq.com), which is pet friendly and charges from $169 double. Other more-than-adequate franchises, with rates in the same general area, include **Super 8,** on the north edge of Moab at 889 N. Main St. (✆ **435/259-8868;**

www.super8.com), **Best Western Plus Canyonlands Inn,** 16 S. Main St. (𝄐 **435/ 259-2300;** www.bestwesternutah.com), **Best Western Plus Greenwell Inn,** 105 S. Main St. (𝄐 **435/259-6151;** www.bestwesternutah.com), and **Comfort Suites,** 800 S. Main St. (𝄐 **435/259-5252;** www.choicehotels.com). You'll generally find lower rates at **Days Inn,** 426 N. Main St. (𝄐 **435/259-4468;** www.daysinn.com), **Motel 6,** 1089 N. Main St. (𝄐 **435/259-6686;** www.motel6.com), and **Sleep Inn,** 1051 S. Main St. (𝄐 **435/259-4655;** http://moabsleepinn.com). Alternatives include the cabins at Arch View Resort RV Camp Park, Canyonlands Campground & RV Park, and Moab Valley RV Resort (see "Camping," below).

Big Horn Lodge Spacious rooms with log furniture and knotty pine walls give the Big Horn a lodgelike atmosphere. All of the well-maintained units have two queen-size beds. Bikes are permitted in the rooms. All units are nonsmoking.

550 S. Main St., Moab, UT 84532. www.moabbighorn.com. 𝄐 **800/325-6171** or 435/259-6171. Fax 435/259-6144. 58 units. $90–$120 double. AE, DISC, MC, V. Pets permitted with $5 per-night fee. **Amenities:** Restaurant; Jacuzzi; outdoor heated pool. *In room:* A/C, TV, fridge, hair dryer, Internet (free).

Bowen Motel This older family-owned-and-operated motel offers fairly large, comfortable, clean, basic rooms with attractive wallpaper and a king-size or one or two queen-size beds. Family units sleep up to six persons each, and there is an 1,800-square-foot guest house with three bedrooms, two full bathrooms, and a complete kitchen (about $300 per night). All units are nonsmoking.

169 N. Main St., Moab, UT 84532. www.bowenmotel.com. 𝄐 **800/874-5439** or 435/259-7132. Fax 435/259-6641. 40 units. $84–$109 double. Rates include continental breakfast. AE, DC, DISC, MC, V. Pets accepted with $10 per-night fee. **Amenities:** Heated outdoor pool. *In room:* A/C, TV, fridge (some), Wi-Fi (free).

Cali Cochitta Bed & Breakfast ★★ For a delightful escape from the hustle and bustle of Moab, head to the Cali Cochitta (Aztec for "House of Dreams"), a handsomely restored late-1800s Victorian home, with great views of the surrounding mountains and red rock formations. The spacious guest rooms have queen-size beds with down comforters, handsome wood furnishings (including many antiques), and cotton robes. Our favorite room is the romantic Cane, which has a high queen-size mahogany sleigh bed and French glass doors. The cottages have refrigerators, and the suite can be rented as one or two rooms. Breakfasts include a hot entree (often prepared with herbs from the inn's garden), plus fresh muffins or other baked goods, fruit, and beverages. Bike storage is available. All units are smoke-free.

110 S. 200 E., Moab, UT 84532. www.moabdreaminn.com. 𝄐 **888/429-8112** or 435/259-4961. Fax 435/259-4964. 6 units. Mar–Oct $135–$175 double; Nov–Feb $90–$140 double. Rates include full breakfast. DISC, MC, V. **Amenities:** Heated outdoor pool. *In room:* A/C, TV, fridge (some), hair dryer, no phone, Wi-Fi (free).

Lazy Lizard International Hostel This hostel offers exceptionally clean, comfortable lodging at bargain rates on the south side of town. The main house, which is air-conditioned, has basic dorm rooms plus two private rooms. A separate building contains four private rooms, which look much like older motel units. The best facilities are the cabins, constructed of real logs, with beds for up to six. There's also a camping area (no hookups). Everyone shares the bathhouses and the phone in the main house. Guests also have use of a fully equipped kitchen; living room with TV, VCR, and movies; gas barbecue grill; and picnic tables. Groups should inquire about the nearby houses, which can be rented by the night ($120–$260 for 12–30 people).

1213 S. U.S. 191, Moab, UT 84532. www.lazylizardhostel.com. ✆ **435/259-6057.** 25 dorm beds, 10 private rooms, 8 cabins; total capacity 65 persons. $10 dorm bed; $29 private room double occupancy; $33 cabin double occupancy; $7 per person camping space. Showers $3 for nonguests. Hostel membership not necessary. AE, DISC, MC, V, but cash preferred. *In room:* A/C, no phone.

Red Stone Inn 🏌 This centrally located motel is comfortable and quiet and offers quite a bit for the price. The exterior gives the impression that these are cabins, and the theme continues inside, with log furniture and colorful posters and maps of area attractions decorating the knotty pine walls. Rooms are a bit on the small side, although perfectly adequate and spotlessly maintained. Three rooms accessible to travelers with disabilities have combination tub/showers. There is a mountain bike work stand and bike wash, and bikes are permitted in the rooms. On-site is a covered picnic area with tables and gas barbecue grills, and guests have free access to the heated outdoor pool at a sister motel across the street.

535 S. Main St., Moab, UT 84532. www.moabredstone.com. ✆ **800/772-1972** or 435/259-3500. Fax 435/259-2717. 52 units. $90–$99 double. AE, DISC, MC, V. Pets accepted ($5 fee). **Amenities:** Indoor Jacuzzi; access to heated outdoor pool. *In room:* A/C, TV, fridge, hair dryer, Internet (free).

Sunflower Hill Luxury Inn ★★★ This upscale country-style retreat, 3 blocks off Main Street, is an excellent choice for a relaxing escape. The elegant rooms are individually decorated—for instance, the Summer House Suite boasts a colorful garden-themed mural—with handmade quilts on the queen-size beds, and bathrobes and Molton Brown toiletries. Deluxe rooms have jetted tubs and private balconies. The popular French Bedroom includes a hand-carved antique bedroom set, stained-glass window, vaulted ceiling, white lace curtains, and large whirlpool tub and separate tiled shower. The lush grounds are grassy and shady, with fruit trees and flowers and a delightful swimming pool, all lending it the air of an oasis. There is locked bike storage, a swing, a picnic table, and a barbecue. The substantial breakfast buffet includes fresh-baked breads and pastries, honey-almond granola, fresh fruit, and a hot entree such as a vegetable frittata, Belgian waffles, or potato omelet. All units are nonsmoking.

185 N. 300 East, Moab, UT 84532. www.sunflowerhill.com. ✆ **800/662-2786** or 435/259-2974. Fax 435/259-3065. 12 units. Mid-Mar to Oct $169–$239 double; Nov to mid-Mar $120–$180 double. Rates include full breakfast and evening refreshments. AE, DISC, MC, V. Children 9 and under are generally not allowed. **Amenities:** Jacuzzi; outdoor heated pool. *In room:* A/C, TV, DVD/VCR player, CD player, hair dryer, no phone, Wi-Fi (free).

CAMPING

In addition to the commercial campgrounds discussed here, you can also camp at Canyonlands and Arches national parks, at Dead Horse Point State Park, and at Newspaper Rock, which are discussed elsewhere in this chapter. Pets are permitted in campgrounds unless otherwise noted. Those camping on public lands where there are no showers can get a list of businesses offering public showers from the **Moab Area Travel Council**'s website (www.discovermoab.com; "Area Info & Services" section) or at the **Moab Information Center** (p. 262). The cost runs from $2.25 to $8.

Arch View Resort RV Camp Park This well-maintained campground offers all the usual RV hookups, showers, and other amenities you'd expect in a first-class commercial RV park, plus great views into Arches National Park, especially at sunset. Located about 6 miles from the park entrance, Arch View has trees throughout the park, a grassy tent area, a convenience store, a pool, a playground, a coin-op laundry, Wi-Fi, and propane, gasoline, and diesel sales. Basic log cabins and more upscale, fully equipped cottages are available for $50 and up for two people.

U.S. 191, at the junction with U.S. 313, 9 miles north of town (P.O. Box 938), Moab, UT 84532. www. archiewresort.com. © **800/813-6622** or 435/259-7854. 83 sites. For 2 people, $23 tent, $35–$45 RV. AE, DISC, MC, V. Closed mid-Nov to mid-Mar.

Canyonlands Campground ★ This campground is surprisingly shady and quiet, given its convenient downtown location, which makes it our top choice for a commercial campground here. Open year-round, it has tent sites as well as partial and full (including cable TV) RV hookups. Facilities include a dump station, self-service laundry, convenience store, playground, and outdoor heated pool. It also offers Wi-Fi. There are also six cabins ($58 double). A City Market grocery store is within walking distance (p. 263).

555 S. Main St., Moab, UT 84532. www.canyonlandsrv.com. © **800/522-6848** or 435/259-6848. 122 sites. For 2 people, $25–$29 tent, $35–$39 RV. AE, DISC, MC, V. Dogs not permitted in cabins.

Moab Valley RV Resort Situated on the north side of Moab, near the intersection of U.S. 191 and Utah 128, this campground is just 2 miles from Arches National Park. Practically any size RV can be accommodated in the extra-large pull-through sites, and some tent sites are covered. All sites have great views of the surrounding rock formations. There are trees and patches of grass, and full RV hookups include cable TV connections. Facilities include an RV dump station, coin-op laundry, convenience store, bike wash, outdoor pool and whirlpool tub, a playground, and Wi-Fi. Eighteen cabins and cottages are available starting at $55 for two people.

1773 N. U.S. 191, Moab, UT 84532. www.moabvalleyrv.com. © **435/259-4469.** 115 sites. For 2 people, $24 tent, $31–$45 RV. MC, V. Closed Nov–Feb. Dogs permitted in RV sites, but not in tent sites or cabins.

Where to Eat

In addition to the restaurants discussed here, Moab has a 24-hour **Denny's** at 191 N. U.S. 191 (© **435/259-8839;** www.dennys.com). Also, see the Bar-M Chuckwagon and Canyonlands by Night & Day, under "Moab After Dark," below. To view the menus of practically every restaurant in town, see **www.moabhappenings.com**.

Buck's Grill House ★★ AMERICAN WESTERN Among Moab's best choices for steak, this popular restaurant also does a lot of other things well. The dining room's subdued Western decor is accented by exposed wood beams and local artwork, and there are two patios—one open air and one heated and covered. There's also a bar, the Vista Lounge. Especially good are the grilled sirloin or New York strip; the buffalo meatloaf, with black onion gravy; and the slow-cooked elk stew. Southwestern dishes include duck tamale with grilled pineapple salsa, and the ground chuck or bison burgers are an especially good deal at $10. Pasta and vegetarian items are also served. Buck's offers full liquor service and a good wine list and serves a variety of Utah microbrews.

1393 N. U.S. 191, about 1½ miles north of town. © **435/259-5201.** www.bucksgrillhouse.com. Main courses $9–$38. DISC, MC, V. Daily 5:30pm–closing.

Eddie McStiff's AMERICAN This bustling, noisy brewpub is half family restaurant and half bar, with a climate-controlled garden patio bar as well. The dining room has a Southwest decor, and the bar has the look of an Old West saloon—long bar, low light, and lots of wood. You can't beat the fresh-ground burgers here—beef, buffalo, salmon, turkey, and veggie—but the menu also includes a good variety of grill items, pasta, and excellent pizzas. Specialties include grilled Atlantic salmon and slow-smoked barbecued ribs, and prime rib is available after 4:30pm. About a dozen fresh-brewed beers are on tap, and full liquor service is available.

In McStiff's Plaza, 57 S. Main St. (just south of the information center). 🕿 **435/259-2337.** www. eddiemcstiffs.com. Main courses $8–$19. DISC, MC, V. Daily 11:30am–midnight.

Moab Brewery ★ ECLECTIC   Fresh ales brewed on-site, along with a wide variety of steaks, sandwiches, salads, soups, vegetarian dishes, and assorted house specialties, are served at this open, spacious microbrewery and restaurant on the south side of town. It's popular with families, who gobble down basic American fare such as half-pound burgers; fresh fish, including good salmon tacos; and, our top choice here, the St. Louis smoked pork ribs. The huge dining room is decorated with light woods, outdoor sports equipment—including a hang glider on the ceiling—and local artwork. Patio dining is available. You can sample the brews—from wheat ale to oatmeal stout—at the separate bar. Aside from the wares in the gift shop, you can also purchase beer-to-go in half-gallon jugs. Beer is sold in the bar; in the restaurant, diners can purchase beer, wine, or mixed drinks.

686 S. Main St. 🕿 **435/259-6333.** www.themoabbrewery.com. Main courses $7–$22. AE, DISC, MC, V. Sun–Thurs 11:30am–10:30pm; Fri–Sat 11:30am–11:30pm.

Moab Diner & Ice Cream Shoppe ★ ☺ AMERICAN/SOUTHWESTERN Late risers can get breakfast—about the best in town—all day here, featuring the usual egg dishes, biscuits and gravy, and a spicy breakfast burrito. Hamburgers, sandwiches, and salads are the offerings at lunch. For dinner, it's steak, shrimp, and chicken, plus liver and onions. The green chili is excellent. In addition to ice cream, you can get malts and shakes, plus sundaes with seven different toppings. The decor is old-time diner, with comfy red vinyl booths, a bit of neon, photos of classic cars, and old Coca-Cola ads. No alcoholic beverages are served.

189 S. Main St. 🕿 **435/259-4006.** www.moabdiner.com. Main courses $5.75–$11 breakfast and lunch, $7.25–$15 dinner. MC, V. Mon–Sat 6am–10pm. Closed New Year's, Thanksgiving, and Christmas.

Sunset Grill ★★ AMERICAN   Perched on a hill at the north edge of Moab, this fine restaurant offers the best sunset views in town. Once the home of uranium miner Charles Steen, the Sunset Grill contains four tastefully decorated dining rooms and three patios. A favorite of locals celebrating special events, the restaurant serves excellent steaks, hand-cut in-house, plus such treats as a roasted half duck with a raspberry sauce, and a grilled salmon filet with an Asian glaze served in a light soy-sherry cream sauce. Texas-style prime rib sells out often, so get here early if it's your first choice. The menu also includes a number of chicken dishes and several pasta selections. Full liquor service is available.

900 N. U.S. 191. 🕿 **435/259-7146.** www.sunsetgrillmoab.com. Main courses $14–$26. AE, DISC, MC, V. Mon–Sat 5pm–closing.

Moab After Dark

For a small town in conservative, nondrinking Utah, this is a pretty wild place. After a day on the river or in the back of a jeep, don't be surprised to see your outfitter letting his or her hair down at **Eddie McStiff's** (p. 272), a microbrewery that's part family restaurant and part bar, with several TVs and a game room with pool tables, foosball, shuffleboard, and, if you must, Wi-Fi. Another good option for beer lovers is the **Moab Brewery** (see above). The **Rio Sports Bar & Grill,** 2 S. 100 West, a block west of Main Street on Center Street (🕿 **435/259-6666**), is a longtime locals' favorite watering hole known for its large selection of alcoholic beverages. For a relaxing, somewhat sophisticated and more upscale bar, stop at **Vista Lounge,** located inside Buck's Grill House (p. 272).

Those looking for a foot-stompin' good time and a Western-style dinner will want to make their way to the **Bar-M Chuckwagon Live Western Show and Cowboy Supper,** 7 miles north of Moab on U.S. 191 (© **800/214-2085** or 435/259-2276; www.barmchuckwagon.com). Diners go through a supper line to pick up sliced roast beef or barbecued chicken, baked potatoes, baked pinto beans, cinnamon applesauce, buttermilk biscuits, cake, and nonalcoholic beverages. Vegetarian meals can be prepared with advance notice, and beer and wine coolers are available. After dinner, a stage show entertains with Western-style music, jokes, and down-home silliness from the Bar-M Wranglers. The grounds, which include a small Western village and gift shop, open at 6:30pm, with gunfights starting at 7pm, dinner at 7:30pm, and the show following supper. The Bar-M is usually open from April through mid-October, but is closed several evenings each week; call for the current schedule. Supper and the show cost $28 for adults, $14 for children 4 to 12, and free for kids 3 and younger. Reservations are strongly recommended.

Canyonlands by Night & Day (© **800/394-9978** or 435/259-5261; www.canyonlandsbynight.com) offers a variety of excursions in the area, including an evening river trip, operating spring through fall, that combines a 1½-hour sunset jet-boat ride with a Dutch-oven dinner. Cost for the boat trip and dinner is $70 for adults and $60 for children 4 to 12 (minimum age 4), with a family rate of $215 for two adults and two children. A 4-hour daytime jet-boat ride costs $80 for adults and $70 for children 4 to 12 (minimum age 4), with a family rate for two adults and two kids of $249. Reservations are recommended. The office and dock are just north of Moab at the Colorado River Bridge.

ARCHES NATIONAL PARK ★★

233 miles SE of Salt Lake City

Natural stone arches and fantastic rock formations are the defining features of this park, and they exist in remarkable numbers and variety. Just as soon as you've seen the most beautiful, most colorful, most gigantic stone arch you can imagine, walk around the next bend and there's another—bigger, better, and more brilliant than the last. It would take forever to see them all, with more than 2,000 officially listed and more being discovered or "born" every day.

Some people think of arches as bridges, but to geologists there's a big difference. Bridges are formed when a river slowly bores through solid rock. The often bizarre and beautiful contours of arches result from the erosive force of rain and snow, which freezes and thaws, dissolving the "glue" that holds the sand grains together and chipping away at the stone, until gravity finally pulls a chunk off.

Although arches usually grow slowly—*very* slowly—something dramatic happens every once in a while: like that quiet day in 1940 when a sudden crash instantly doubled the size of the opening of Skyline Arch, leaving a huge boulder lying in its shadow. Luckily, no one (that we know of) was standing underneath it at the time. The same thing happened to the magnificently delicate Landscape Arch in 1991, when a slab of rock about 60 feet long, 11 feet wide, and 4½ feet thick fell from the underside of the arch. Now there's such a thin ribbon of stone that it's hard to believe it can continue standing at all.

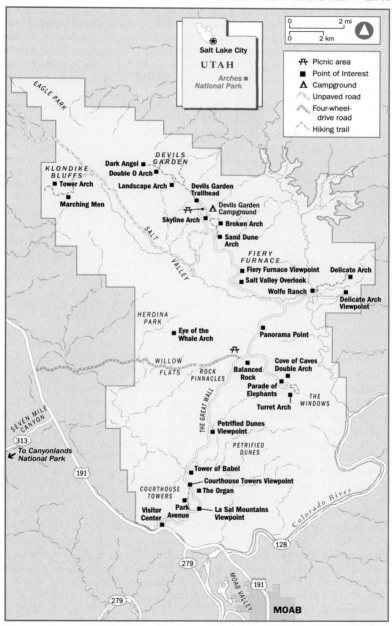

Spend a day or a week here, exploring the terrain, watching the rainbow of colors deepen and explode with the long rays of the setting sun, and gazing at the moonlight glistening on the tall sandstone cliffs. Watch for mule deer, cottontail rabbits, and bright green collared lizards as they go about the difficult task of desert living. And let your own imagination run wild among the Three Gossips, the Spectacles, the Eye of the Whale, the Penguins, the Tower of Babel, and the thousands of other statues, towers, arches, and bridges that await your discovery in this magical playground.

Essentials

See the Moab section of this chapter for camping options outside the park, plus lodging, restaurants, and other nearby services.

GETTING THERE From Moab, drive 5 miles north on U.S. 191. Arches is located 27 miles east of Canyonlands National Park's Island in the Sky Visitor Center, 233 miles southeast of Salt Lake City, 404 miles northeast of the north rim of Grand Canyon National Park in Arizona, and 371 miles west of Denver, Colorado.

INFORMATION/VISITOR CENTERS For advance information, contact **Arches National Park,** P.O. Box 907, Moab, UT 84532 (☎ **435/719-2299;** www.nps. gov/arch).

Books, maps, and videos on Arches as well as Canyonlands National Park and other southern Utah attractions can be purchased from the nonprofit **Canyonlands Natural History Association,** 3015 S. U.S. 191, Moab, UT 84532 (☎ **800/840-8978** or 435/259-6003; www.cnha.org). Some publications are available in foreign languages.

The attractive **Arches National Park Visitor Center** is just inside the entrance gate. It offers maps, brochures, and other information, and a museum explains arch formation and other features of the park. Be sure to take time to watch the orientation film, *Secrets of Red Rock,* shown in the auditorium. From April through October the visitor center is open daily from 7:30am to 6:30pm; the rest of the year it's open daily 8am to 4:30pm. On Christmas Day, the park is open but the visitor center is closed.

FEES, REGULATIONS & BACKCOUNTRY PERMITS Entry for up to 7 days costs $10 per private vehicle or $5 per person on foot, motorcycle, or bike. A $25 annual pass is also available; it's good for Arches and Canyonlands national parks as well as Natural Bridges and Hovenweep national monuments. Campsites cost $20 per night, and guided ranger walks into Fiery Furnace cost $10 for adults and $5 for children 5 to 12 (p. 279). Required permits for overnight trips into the backcountry, available at the visitor center, are free.

Backcountry hikers should practice minimum-impact techniques, packing out all trash. Feeding or otherwise disturbing wildlife is prohibited, as is vandalizing or disturbing any natural, cultural, or historic feature of the park. Wood fires are not permitted. Dogs, which must be leashed at all times, are prohibited in public buildings, on all trails, and in the backcountry.

SEASONS/AVOIDING THE CROWDS Summer days here are hot, often exceeding 100°F (38°C), and winters can be cool or cold, dropping below freezing at night, with snow possible. The best time to visit, especially for hikers, is in spring or fall, when daytime temperatures are usually between 60° and 80°F (16°–27°C) and nights are cool.

Visitation to Arches is highest from March through October, with August the peak month. Parking lots are crowded and the campground is often full by late morning. As with most popular parks, avoid visiting during school vacations if possible.

RANGER PROGRAMS From spring through fall, rangers lead guided hikes on the Fiery Furnace Trail (see "Outdoor Pursuits," below), as well as daily nature walks at various park locations. Evening campfire programs, also from spring through fall, are held on topics such as rock art, geological processes, and wildlife. A schedule of events is posted at the visitor center.

Kids between the ages of 6 and 12 can pick up a **Junior Ranger** booklet at the visitor center. After completing activities and participating in several programs, kids pick up their badge and certificate at the visitor center.

Seeing the Park's Highlights by Car

Arches is the easiest of Utah's national parks to see in a day, if that's all you can spare. An 18-mile (one-way) **scenic drive** offers splendid views of countless natural rock arches and other formations, and several easy hikes reveal additional scenery. Allow 1½ hours for the round-trip drive, adding time for optional hikes.

You can see many of the park's most famous rock formations without even getting out of your car—although venturing out and exploring on foot is always the best way to see them. You have the option of walking short distances to a number of viewpoints, or stretching your legs on a variety of longer hikes along the way (see "Outdoor Pursuits," below). The main road is easy to navigate, even for RVs, but parking at some viewpoints is limited. Please be considerate and leave trailers at the visitor center parking lot or in a Moab campground.

Start out by viewing the short slide show at the **visitor center** to get a feel for what lies ahead. Then drive north past the Moab Fault to the overlook parking for **Park Avenue,** a solid rock "fin" that reminded early visitors of the New York skyline.

From here, your next stop is **La Sal Mountain Viewpoint,** where you look southeast to the La Sal Mountains, named by early Spanish explorers who thought the snow-covered mountains looked like huge piles of salt. In the overlook area is a "desert scrub" ecosystem, composed of sagebrush, saltbush, blackbrush, yucca, and prickly pear cactus. Animals that inhabit the area include the kangaroo rat, blacktailed jackrabbit, rock squirrel, several species of lizards, and the coyote.

Continuing on the scenic drive, some of the park's major formations will come into view: At **Courthouse Towers,** large monoliths, such as Sheep Rock, the Organ, and the Three Gossips, dominate the landscape. Leaving Courthouse Towers, watch for the **Tower of Babel** on the east (right) side of the road, then proceed past the petrified sand dunes to **Balanced Rock,** a huge boulder weighing about 3,600 tons, perched on a slowly eroding pedestal. You can take an easy, .3-mile round-trip walk around the base of the pedestal from the Balanced Rock parking area. You get a great close-up view of the huge and precariously perched rock.

Continuing, take a side road to the east (right) to the **Windows.** Created when erosion penetrated a sandstone fin, they can be seen after a short walk from the parking area. Also in this area are **Turret Arch** and the **Cove of Caves.** Erosion is continuing to wear away at the back of the largest cave, which means it will probably become an arch one day. The North and South Windows are also off this trail. Once you reach them, take the loop around back and see for yourself why they are sometimes called Spectacles—the scene looks almost like a sea monster poking its large snout up into the air. A short walk from the parking lot takes you to **Double Arch,** which looks exactly like what its name implies. It is possible to climb right up underneath the arch; just take care not to disturb the delicate desert vegetation. To the right of Double Arch are several alcoves that may one day become arches. If you're visiting in the spring, look for the sego lily, Utah's state flower. It has three lovely cream-colored petals with a reddish-purple spot fading to yellow at the base. From the end of this trail, you can also see the delightful **Parade of Elephants.**

Return to the main park road, turn north (right) and drive to **Panorama Point,** which offers an expansive view of Salt Valley and the Fiery Furnace, which can really live up to its name at sunset.

Next, turn east (right) off the main road onto the Wolfe Ranch Road and drive to the **Wolfe Ranch** parking area. A very short walk leads to what's left of this ranch. John Wesley Wolfe and his son Fred moved here from Ohio in 1898, and, in 1907, were joined by John's daughter Flora, her husband, and their children. The cabin seen here was built for Flora's family (John's cabin was destroyed by a flash flood). In 1910, the family decided this was not the greatest location for a ranch, and they packed up and returned to Ohio. If you follow the trail a bit farther, you'll see some Ute petroglyphs.

More ambitious hikers can continue for a moderately difficult 3-mile round-trip excursion to **Delicate Arch,** with a spectacular view at trail's end. If you don't want to take the hike, you can still see this lovely arch, albeit from a distance, by getting back in your car, continuing down the road for 1 mile, and walking a short trail (about a 5-min. walk) to the **Delicate Arch Viewpoint.**

Returning to the park's main road, turn north (right) and go to the next stop, the **Salt Valley Overlook.** The various shades of color in this collapsed salt dome are caused by differing amounts of iron in the rock, among other factors.

Continue to the vantage point for **Fiery Furnace,** which offers a dramatic view of colorful sandstone fins. This is where 3-hour ranger-guided hikes begin.

From here, drive to a pullout for **Sand Dune Arch,** located down a short path from the road, where you'll find shade and sand along with the arch. This is a good place for kids to play. The trail leads across a meadow to Broken Arch (which isn't broken at all—it just looks that way from a distance).

Back on the road, continue to **Skyline Arch,** whose opening doubled in size in 1940 when a huge boulder tumbled out of it. The next and final stop is the often crowded parking area for the **Devils Garden Trailhead.** From here, you can hike to some of the most unique arches in the park, including **Landscape Arch,** which is among the longest natural rock spans in the world. It's a pretty easy 1.6-mile round-trip hike.

From the trail head parking lot, it's 18 miles back to the visitor center.

Outdoor Pursuits

BIKING   Bikes are prohibited on all trails and are not allowed to travel cross-country within national park boundaries. The park's established scenic drive is open to cyclists, although you need to be aware that the 18-mile dead-end road is narrow and winding in spots and can be a bit crowded with motor vehicles in summer.

Mountain bikers also have the option of tackling one of several four-wheel-drive roads (see below). For guided mountain-bike trips outside the park, as well as rentals, repairs, and supplies, see the Moab section earlier in this chapter.

FOUR-WHEELING   Arches doesn't have nearly as many four-wheel-drive opportunities as nearby Canyonlands National Park, but it has a few, including the **Salt Valley Road** and the **Willow Flats Road,** both of which can be extremely slick after a rain and are open to four-wheel-drive vehicles and mountain bikes. Check at the visitor center for directions and current conditions.

HIKING   Most trails here are short and relatively easy, although because of the hot summer sun and lack of shade, it's wise to carry a good amount of water on any jaunt of more than 1 hour.

One easy walk is to **Sand Dune Arch,** a good place to take kids who want to play in the sand. It's only .3 miles (round-trip), but you can add an extra 1.2 miles by continuing on to Broken Arch. Sand Dune Arch is hidden among and shaded by rock walls, with a naturally created giant sandbox below the arch. Resist the temptation to climb onto the arch and jump down into the sand: Not only is it dangerous, but it can also damage the arch. Those who continue to Broken Arch should watch for mule deer and kit foxes, which inhabit the grassland you'll be crossing. Allow about 30 minutes to Sand Dune Arch and back; 1 hour to Broken Arch.

From the **Devils Garden Trail,** you can see about 15 to 20 arches on a strenuous and difficult hike of 7.2 miles round-trip, or view some exciting scenery by following only part of the route. Take at least the easy-to-moderate 1.6-mile round-trip hike to **Landscape Arch ★**, a long, thin ribbon of stone that's one of the most beautiful arches in the park. Watch for mule deer along the way, and allow about an hour. Past Landscape Arch, the trail becomes more challenging but offers numerous additional views, including panoramas of the curious **Double O Arch** and a large, dark tower known as Dark Angel. From the section of the trail where Dark Angel is visible, you are 2.5 miles from the trail head. If you turn back at this point, the round-trip will take about 3 hours; if you keep going, you'll have the primitive loop almost to yourself as most people turn back at Double O Arch.

The park's best and most scenic hike, the 3-mile round-trip **Delicate Arch Trail ★★**, is a moderate-to-difficult hike, with slippery slickrock, no shade, and some steep drop-offs along a narrow cliff. Hikers are rewarded with a dramatic and spectacular view of Delicate Arch, as well as a visit to the John Wesley Wolfe ranch, and an opportunity to take a side trip to a Ute petroglyph panel that includes what may represent a bighorn sheep hunt. When you get back on the main trail, watch for collared lizards—up to a foot long—which are usually bright green with stripes of yellow or rust, with a black collar. Collared lizards feed in the daytime, mostly on insects and other lizards, and can stand and run on their large hind feet in pursuit of prey. (Very reminiscent of *Jurassic Park.*)

Continuing along the trail, watch for **Frame Arch,** off to the right. Its main claim to fame is that numerous photographers have used it to "frame" a photo of Delicate Arch in the distance. Just past Frame Arch, the trail gets a little weird—narrow and twisting—having been blasted out from the cliff. Allow 2 to 3 hours.

The **Fiery Furnace Guided Hike ★** is a strenuous 2-mile round-trip naturalist-led hike to some of the most colorful formations in the park. Guided hikes are given into this restricted area twice daily from March through October, by reservation. Cost is $10 per adult, $5 per child from 5 to 12. Children 5 to 13 must be accompanied by an adult, and children under 5 are not permitted. Reservations must be made at least 4 days in advance (no more than 6 months in advance) online at www. recreation.gov. As you hike along, a ranger describes the desert plants, points out hard-to-find arches, and discusses the geology and natural history of the Fiery Fur-nace. Rangers recommend against it, but you can hike in the Fiery Furnace on your own. You must first obtain a permit and watch a short video (get details at the visitor center). Other restrictions apply, and there are no marked trails, so it's best to join a guided hike.

Another strenuous hike is to **Tower Arch.** This 3.4-mile round-trip hike on a primitive trail starts with a steep incline to the top of the bluff and proceeds up and down, with great views of the Klondike Bluffs to the right. Beware of the slickrock that makes up part of the trail, and watch for the cairns leading the way. The hardest part is near the end, where you struggle uphill through loose sand. Your reward is a grand sight: the immense Tower Arch standing among a maze of sandstone spires. Climb up under it for a soothing view while you take a much-deserved break. In the spring, the majestic, snowcapped La Sal Mountains can be seen to the east through the arch opening.

The backcountry has no trails or campsites, and very little of the park is open to overnight camping, but backcountry hiking is permitted. Ask park rangers to suggest routes. No fires are allowed, and hikers must carry their own water and practice low-impact hiking and camping techniques. Those planning to be out overnight need free backcountry permits, available at the visitor center (p. 276).

Camping

Devils Garden Campground ★, at the north end of the park's scenic drive, is Arches' only developed camping area, offering a perfect location for exploring the park. The 50 well-spaced sites are nestled among rocks, with plenty of piñon and juniper trees, and some sites can accommodate RVs up to 30 feet long. From March through October, the campground accepts reservations (🕐 **877/444-6777**; www. recreation.gov), with a $9 additional booking fee. In summer, the campground fills very early, with people arriving early trying to garner any nonreserved sites, so reservations are strongly recommended. Sites costs $20 per night. You'll find drinking water and flush toilets, but no showers or RV hookups. See the Moab section earlier in this chapter for information on public showers and nearby commercial campgrounds.

CANYONLANDS NATIONAL PARK ★★

34 miles W of Moab, 304 miles SE of Salt Lake City

Utah's largest national park is not for the sightseer out for a Sunday afternoon drive. Instead, it rewards those willing to spend time and energy—*lots* of energy—exploring the rugged backcountry. Sliced into districts by the Colorado and Green rivers, which are the park's primary architects, this is a land of extremes: vast panoramas, dizzyingly deep canyons, dramatically steep cliffs, broad mesas, and towering red spires.

The most accessible part of Canyonlands is the **Island in the Sky District,** in the northern section of the park, where a paved road leads to sites such as Grand View Point, which overlooks some 10,000 square miles of rugged wilderness. Island in the Sky has several easy-to-moderate trails offering sweeping vistas. A short walk provides views of Upheaval Dome, which resembles a large volcanic crater but may actually have been created by the crash of a meteorite. For the more adventurous, the 100-mile White Rim Road takes experienced mountain bikers and those with high-clearance four-wheel-drive vehicles on a winding loop tour through a vast array of scenery.

The **Needles District,** in the southeast corner, offers only a few viewpoints along the paved road, but boasts numerous possibilities for serious hikers and backpackers, and those with high-clearance 4×4s or mountain bikes. Named for its tall, red-and-white-striped rock pinnacles, this diverse district is home to impressive arches,

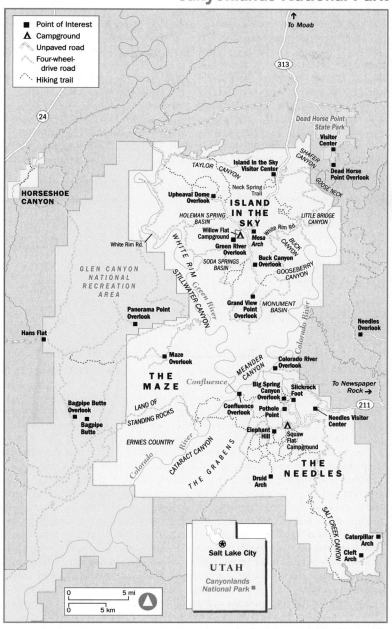

Point of Interest
Campground
Unpaved road
Four-wheel-drive road
Hiking trail

To Moab

313

24

Dead Horse Point
State Park

Visitor
Center

HORSESHOE
CANYON

TAYLOR CANYON

Island in the Sky
Visitor Center

SHAFER CANYON

Dead Horse
Point Overlook

GOOSE NECK

Neck Spring
Trail

Upheaval Dome
Overlook

ISLAND
IN THE
SKY

LITTLE BRIDGE
CANYON

HOLEMAN SPRING
BASIN

Willow Flat
Campground

White Rim Rd.

BUCK
CANYON

White Rim Rd.

WHITE RIM

Mesa
Arch

Green River
Overlook

SODA SPRINGS
BASIN

Buck Canyon
Overlook

GOOSEBERRY
CANYON

GLEN CANYON
NATIONAL
RECREATION
AREA

STILLWATER CANYON

Green River

Grand View
Point
Overlook

MONUMENT
BASIN

Panorama Point
Overlook

Colorado River

Needles
Overlook

Hans Flat

Maze
Overlook

Colorado River
Overlook

THE
MAZE

Confluence

MEANDER CANYON

To Newspaper
Rock →

Big Spring
Canyon
Overlook

Slickrock
Foot

211

Bagpipe Butte
Overlook

LAND OF
STANDING ROCKS

Confluence
Overlook

Pothole
Point

Needles Visitor
Center

Bagpipe
Butte

ERNIES COUNTRY

Elephant
Hill

Squaw
Flat
Campground

Colorado River

CATARACT CANYON

THE GRABENS

Druid
Arch

THE
NEEDLES

SALT CREEK CANYON

Caterpillar
Arch

Cleft
Arch

Salt Lake City

UTAH

Canyonlands
National Park

0   5 mi

0   5 km

including the 150-foot-tall Angel Arch, as well as grassy meadows and the confluence of the Green and Colorado rivers. Backcountry visitors will also find ruins and rock art left by the Ancestral Puebloans (also known as Anasazi) some 800 years ago.

Most park visitors don't get a close-up view of the **Maze District,** but instead see it off in the distance from Grand View Point at Island in the Sky or Confluence Overlook in the Needles District. That's because it's inhospitable and practically inaccessible. A lot of endurance and at least several days are necessary to see even a few of its sites, such as the appropriately named Lizard Rock and Beehive Arch. Hardy hikers can visit Horseshoe Canyon in 1 day, where they can see the Great Gallery, an 80-foot-long rock art panel. The Maze is a great destination, if you don't want to see many people. It's estimated that in one recent year about 40,000 people visited the Island in the Sky, about 20,000 visited the Needles, but only 546 ventured into the Maze.

The park is also accessible by boat, which is how explorer Major John Wesley Powell first saw the canyons in 1869, when he made his first trip down the Green to its confluence with the Colorado, and then even farther downstream, eventually reaching the Grand Canyon. River access is from the towns of Moab and Green River; several local companies offer boat trips (see the Moab section earlier in this chapter or the Green River section later in this chapter).

Essentials

No lodging facilities, restaurants, or stores are located inside the national park. Most visitors use Moab as a base camp.

GETTING THERE/ACCESS POINTS   To reach the Island in the Sky Visitor Center, 34 miles west of Moab, take U.S. 191 north to Utah 313, which you follow south into the park. To reach the Needles Visitor Center, 75 miles southwest of Moab, take U.S. 191 south to Utah 211, which you follow west into the park. Getting to the Maze District is a bit trickier: From I-70 west of Green River, take Utah 24 south. Watch for signs and follow two- and four-wheel-drive dirt roads east into the park.

INFORMATION/VISITOR CENTERS   Contact **Canyonlands National Park,** 2282 SW Resource Blvd., Moab, UT 84532 (✆ **435/719-2313;** www.nps.gov/cany). Books, maps, and DVDs can be purchased from the nonprofit **Canyonlands Natural History Association,** 3015 S. U.S. 191, Moab, UT 84532 (✆ **800/840-8978** or 435/259-6003; www.cnha.org). Some publications are available in foreign languages.

Canyonlands National Park operates two visitor centers—**Island in the Sky Visitor Center,** in the northern part of the park, and **Needles Visitor Center,** in the southern section—where you can get maps, free brochures on hiking trails, and, most important, advice from rangers. The terrain at Canyonlands can be extremely brutal, and it's important to know not only your own limitations, but also the limitations of your vehicle and other equipment. The Island in the Sky Visitor Center is open 8am to 6pm from late March through late October and 9am to 4:30pm the rest of the year. The Needles Visitor Center is open 8:30am to 4:30pm from November through February, with extended summer hours. Both centers are closed Christmas and New Year's Day, and close early on Thanksgiving. Those going into the Maze District can get information at the Hans Flat Ranger Station, usually open daily from 8am to 4:30pm.

FEES, REGULATIONS & BACKCOUNTRY PERMITS   Entry into the park (for up to 7 days) costs $10 per private vehicle or $5 per person on foot, bike, or motorcycle. A $25 annual pass is also available; it's good for Canyonlands and Arches national parks as well as Natural Bridges and Hovenweep national monuments. The camping fee at Squaw Flat Campground in the Needles District is $15; camping at Willow Flat Campground in the Island in the Sky District costs $10.

Backcountry permits, available at either visitor center, are required for all overnight stays in the park, except at the two established campgrounds. **Permit reservations** can be made in advance (*©* **435/259-4351;** www.nps.gov/cany). Permits for overnight four-wheel-drive and mountain-bike trips are $30, while those for overnight backpacking trips are $15. The permit for white-water boating through Cataract Canyon is $30 per group plus $20 per person; flat-water boating costs $20 per group plus $20 per person.

There is a $5 day-use fee for those taking four-wheel-drive vehicles into the Needles District.

Backcountry hikers should practice minimum-impact techniques, packing out all trash. Feeding or disturbing wildlife is prohibited, as is vandalizing or upsetting any natural, cultural, or historic feature of the park. Wood fires are also prohibited.

Dogs, which must be leashed at all times, are prohibited in public buildings, on all trails, and in the backcountry (even in vehicles on four-wheel-drive roads).

SEASONS/AVOIDING THE CROWDS Summers here are hot, with temperatures often exceeding 100°F (38°C). Winters can be cool or cold, dropping well below freezing at night, with light snow possible. The best time to visit, especially for hikers, is in spring or fall, when daytime temperatures are usually from 60° to 80°F (16°–27°C) and nights are cool. Late-summer and early-fall visitors should be prepared for afternoon thunderstorms.

Although Canyonlands does not get nearly as crowded as most other national parks in Utah, summer is still the busiest time, and reservations for backcountry permits are recommended from spring through fall. As with most parks, if you want to escape humanity, pick the longest and most difficult trail you can handle.

SAFETY Due to the extreme variety and ruggedness of the terrain, the main safety problem at Canyonlands is that people underestimate the hazards. Rangers warn hikers to carry at least 1 gallon of water per person per day, be especially careful near cliff edges, avoid overexposure to the intense sun, and carry maps when going into the backcountry. During lightning storms, avoid lone trees, high ridges, and cliff edges. Four-wheel-drive-vehicle operators should be aware of their vehicle's limitations and carry extra food and emergency equipment. Anyone heading out into the backcountry should let someone know where they're going and when they plan to return. Traveling alone in Canyonlands is not a good idea.

RANGER PROGRAMS A variety of ranger programs are presented from March through October. Several programs are offered daily in the **Island in the Sky District,** including geology presentations at Grand View Point at 10:30 and 11:30am, and talks at the visitor center at 2pm. In the **Needles District,** there are 1-hour evening programs at Squaw Flat Campground most nights of the week. In the **Maze District,** guided hikes in Horsehoe Canyon are offered most weekends in spring and fall.

Seeing the Highlights

Canyonlands is not an easy place to see in a short period of time. In fact, if your schedule permits only a day or less, you might want to simply skip the Needles and Maze districts entirely and drive directly to the **Island in the Sky Visitor Center.** After looking at the exhibits, drive to several of the overlooks, stopping along the way for a short hike or two. Make sure you stop at the **Grand View Point Overlook,** at the south end of the paved road. Hiking the **Grand View Point Trail,** which is especially scenic in the late afternoon, literally gives you the "grand view" of the park. Allow about 1 hour for this easy 2-mile walk. The 1-mile **Upheaval Dome Overlook Trail,** which should take about half an hour and takes you to a mile-wide crater of mysterious origins, is another interesting walk.

Exploring Canyonlands by Car

No driving tour has yet been designed to show off Canyonlands. The Island in the Sky District has about 20 miles of paved highway, some gravel roads accessible to two-wheel-drive vehicles, and several viewpoints. The Needles District has only 8 miles of paved roads and fewer viewpoints. Many (but not all) of Needles' viewpoints and trail heads are accessible only by high-clearance four-wheel-drive vehicles, mountain bikes, or plain old foot power. The Maze District has no paved roads. Essentially, both of the park's main roads lead to trail heads, and unless you plan to leave your car and hike for at least a half-hour or so, it would be better to skip Canyonlands and spend your time at nearby Arches National Park, which is much more accessible by car.

Of course, if your "car" happens to be a serious 4×4, and you're equally serious about doing some hard-core four-wheeling, this is the park for you (see "Outdoor Pursuits," below). Due to the constantly changing conditions of the dirt roads, however, it is strongly recommended that you discuss your plans with rangers before setting out.

Outdoor Pursuits

BIKING & MOUNTAIN BIKING

Bikes of any kind are prohibited on hiking trails or in the backcountry, except on designated two- and four-wheel-drive roads. Road bikes are of little use, except for getting to and from trail heads, viewpoints, visitor centers, and campgrounds in the Island in the Sky and Needles districts.

Mountain bikers will find themselves sharing four-wheel-drive roads with motor vehicles of every size, plus occasional hikers and horseback riders. Because some of the four-wheel-drive roads have deep sand in spots—which can turn into quicksand when wet—mountain biking may not be as much fun here as you'd expect, although it certainly is a challenge. It's wise to ask rangers about current conditions on specific roads before setting out. Roads that are popular with mountain bikers include the Elephant Hill and Colorado River Overlook jeep roads, both in the Needles District. The 100-mile White Rim Road, in the Island in the Sky District, also makes a great mountain-bike trip, especially for bikers who can arrange for an accompanying 4×4 vehicle to carry water, food, and camping gear (see "Four-Wheeling," below).

FOUR-WHEELING

Unlike most national parks, where all motor vehicles and mountain bikes must stay on paved roads, Canyonlands has miles of rough four-wheel-drive roads where mechanized transport is king, and jacked-up jeeps with oversize tires rule the day. Four-wheelers must stay on designated 4×4 roads, but keep in mind that the term "road" can mean anything from a graded, well-marked, two-lane gravel byway to a pile of loose rocks with a sign that says "that-a-way." Many of the park's jeep roads are impassable during heavy rains and for a day or two after. Rangers warn that many of the park's 4×4 roads are suitable only for high-clearance four-wheel-drive vehicles. ATVs and non-street-legal dirt bikes are not permitted.

A Bird's-Eye View of Canyonlands

Canyonlands is beautiful, but many of its most spectacular sections are difficult to get to. **Slickrock Air Guides, Inc.** (© **866/259-1626** or 435/259-6216; www.slickrockairguides.com) offers 1-hour scenic flights over Canyonlands National Park and nearby areas for $150 per person, 2-hour flights that take in Canyonlands Natural Bridges National Monument and Monument Valley Navajo Tribal Park for $270 per person, and 3-hour flights that include Canyonlands National Park and add Lake Powell, the edge of the Grand Canyon, and Capitol Reef National Park for $395 per person.

The best four-wheel-drive adventure in the Island in the Sky District is the **White Rim Road ★★**, which winds some 100 miles through the district and affords spectacular views, from broad panoramas of rock and canyon to close-ups of red and orange towers and buttes. A high-clearance 4×4 is necessary. Expect the journey to be slow, taking 2 to 3 days, although with the appropriate vehicle, it isn't really difficult. There are primitive campgrounds along the way, but reservations and backcountry permits are needed (see "Essentials," above). Mountain bikers also enjoy this trail, especially when accompanying a four-wheel-drive vehicle that can carry supplies and equipment.

Four-wheeling in the Needles District can be an end in itself, with a variety of exciting routes, or simply a means to get to some of the more interesting and remote hiking trails and camping spots. Four-wheel-drive fans will find an ultimate challenge on the **Elephant Hill** road, which begins at a well-marked turnoff near Squaw Flat Campground. Although most of the 10-mile trail is only moderately difficult, the stretch over Elephant Hill itself (near the beginning of the drive) can be a nightmare, with steep, rough slickrock, drifting sand, loose rock, and treacherous ledges. Coming down the hill, one switchback requires you to back to the edge of a steep cliff. This road is also a favorite of mountain bikers, although bikes will have to be walked on some stretches because of the abundance of sand and rocks. The route offers views of numerous rock formations, from striped needles to balanced rocks, plus panoramas of steep cliffs and rock "stairs"; side trips can add another 30 miles. Allow from 8 hours to 3 days. Backcountry permits are needed for overnight trips.

For a spectacular view of the Colorado River, the **Colorado Overlook ★** road can't be beat. This 14-mile round-trip is popular with four-wheelers, backpackers, and mountain bikers. Considered among the park's easiest 4×4 roads, the first part is very easy indeed, accessible by high-clearance two-wheel-drives, but the second half has rough and rocky sections that require four-wheel-drive. Starting at the Needles Visitor Center parking lot, the road takes you past numerous panoramic vistas to a spectacular 360-degree view of the park and the Colorado River, some 1,000 feet below.

HIKING

With little shade, no reliable water sources, and temperatures soaring to 100°F (38°C) and higher in summer, it can get hot in Canyonlands. Rangers strongly advise that hikers carry at least a gallon of water per person per day, along with sunscreen, a hat, and all the usual hiking and emergency equipment. If you expect to do some serious hiking, try to plan your trip for the spring or fall, when conditions are much more hospitable, and never hike alone. Because some of the trails may be confusing, hikers attempting the longer ones should carry good topographic maps, available at park visitor centers and at stores in Moab. Although the park offers dozens of hiking possibilities, the few below are highlighted for their variety of ability requirements, and are listed by district.

HORSESHOE CANYON   This detached section of the park was added to Canyonlands in 1971 mainly because of its **Great Gallery ★★★**, an 80-foot-long rock art panel with larger-than-life human figures, believed to be at least several thousand years old. Only one road leads into the Horseshoe Canyon Unit, and you'll have to drive some 120 miles (one-way) from Moab and then hike 6.5 miles (round-trip) to see the rock art. To get to the area by two-wheel-drive vehicle, take I-70 west from Green River about 11 miles to U.S. 24, go south about 24 miles to the Horseshoe Canyon turnoff (near the WATCH FOR SAND DRIFTS sign), turn left, and follow this maintained dirt road for about 30 miles to the canyon's west rim, where you can park. From here, it's a 1.5-mile hike down an 800-foot slope to the canyon floor, where you turn right and go 1.75 miles to the Great Gallery. There's no camping in Horseshoe Canyon, but primitive camping is available on BLM property on the rim just outside the park boundary.

ISLAND IN THE SKY   The **Mesa Arch Trail** provides the casual visitor with an easy .5-mile (round-trip) self-guided nature walk through an area forested with piñon and juniper trees, mountain mahogany, cactus, and a plant called Mormon tea, from which Mormon pioneers made a tealike beverage. The loop trail's main scenic attraction is an arch, made of Navajo sandstone, that hangs precariously on the edge of a cliff, framing a spectacular view of nearby mountains. Especially scenic at sunrise, allow about a half-hour.

Another half-hour round-trip hike, although a bit steeper and moderately strenuous, leads to the **Upheaval Dome Overlook.** Upheaval Dome doesn't fit with the rest of the Canyonlands terrain—it's obviously not the result of gradual erosion like the rest of the park, but rather a dramatic deformity in which rocks have been pushed into a domelike structure. At one time, it was believed that the dome was formed by a hidden volcano, but a more recent theory suggests that a meteorite may have struck the earth here some 60 million years ago. This hike is about 1 mile round-trip; a second overlook adds about 1 mile round-trip and at least 15 minutes.

An easy 2-mile hike, especially scenic at sunset, is the **Grand View Point Trail ★**, which follows the canyon rim from Grand View Point and shows off numerous canyons and rock formations, the Colorado River, and distant mountains. Allow about 1 hour.

Those looking for a real challenge can explore the **Lathrop Canyon Trail,** which meanders some 5 miles down into the canyon to the White Rim Road, affording beautiful views as you descend. Allow 5 to 7 hours for this strenuous hike over steep terrain and loose rock, remembering that it's another 5 miles back. It's possible to continue down to the Colorado River from here, which makes your round-trip close to 22 miles, but check with rangers about the feasibility of this overnight trip before attempting it.

THE MAZE   Getting to the trail heads in the Maze District involves rugged four-wheel-drive roads; rangers can help you with directions.

The 3-mile **Maze Overlook Trail** is not for beginning hikers or anyone with a fear of heights. It is quite steep in places, requiring the use of your hands for safety. At the trail head, you get a fine view of the many narrow canyons that inspired this district's name; the trail then descends 600 feet to the canyon bottom. The 9-mile **Pictograph Fork to Harvest Scene Loop** is a 7- to 10-hour hike (or an overnight) that leads over slickrock and along canyon washes—watch for the cairns to be sure you don't wander off the trail—to a magnificent example of rock art.

NEEDLES Trails here are generally not too tough, but keep in mind that slickrock can live up to its name, and that this area has little shade. One relatively easy hike is the **Roadside Ruin Trail,** a short (.3-mile), self-guided nature walk that takes about 20 minutes round-trip and leads to a prehistoric granary, probably used by the Ancestral Puebloans some 700 to 1,000 years ago to store corn, nuts, and other foods. Although easy, this trail can be muddy when wet.

For a bit more of a challenge, try the **Slickrock Trail,** a 2.4-mile loop that leads to several viewpoints and takes 2 or 3 hours. Slickrock—a general term for any bare rock surface—can be slippery, especially when wet. Viewpoints show off the stair-step topography of the area, from its colorful canyons and cliffs to its flat mesas and striped needles. Also, watch for bighorn sheep.

From **Elephant Hill Trailhead,** you can follow several interconnecting trails into the backcountry. The road to the trail head is gravel, but is graded and drivable in most two-wheel-drive passenger cars; those in large vehicles such as motor homes, however, will want to avoid it. The 11-mile round-trip **Elephant Canyon–Druid Arch hike** can be accomplished in 4 to 6 hours and is moderately difficult, with some steep drop-offs and quite a bit of slickrock. But the views are well worth it, as you hike through narrow rock canyons, past colorful spires and pinnacles, and on to the huge Druid Arch, its dark rock somewhat resembling the stone structures at Stonehenge.

The **Confluence Overlook Trail,** a 10-mile round-trip day or overnight hike, leads to a spectacular bird's-eye view of the confluence of the Green and Colorado rivers and the 1,000-foot-deep gorges they've carved. The hike is moderately difficult, with steep drop-offs and little shade, but it splendidly reveals the many colors of the Needles District, as well as views into the Maze District of the park. Allow 4 to 6 hours.

For those staying at Squaw Flat Campground, the **Big Spring to Squaw Canyon Trail** is a convenient, moderately difficult 7.5-mile loop that includes some sections not good for those with a fear of heights. This trail can be hiked in 3 to 4 hours. It winds through woodlands of piñon and juniper, but has some steep grades that can be dangerous when wet, and offers views of nearby cliffs and mesas as well as distant mountains. Watch for wildflowers from late spring through summer.

Camping

The park has two campgrounds, both open year-round. In the Island in the Sky District, **Willow Flat Campground** (elevation 6,200 ft.) has 12 sites, picnic tables, fire grates, and vault toilets, but no water. Maximum RV length is 28 feet; camping is $10. In the Needles District, **Squaw Flat Campground** (elevation 5,100 ft.) has 26 sites, fire grates, picnic tables, flush toilets, and year-round drinking water. Maximum RV length is 28 feet; the fee is $15 per night. Neither campground accepts reservations and both typically fill from late March through June and early September to mid-October. Primitive campsites are also available throughout the park for four-wheelers and backpackers (permits required; see "Essentials," earlier in this chapter).

Near Island in the Sky, the campground at **Dead Horse Point State Park** has electric hookups (see "More to See & Do Nearby," below). Additional camping facilities are available on nearby public lands administered by the Bureau of Land Management and U.S. Forest Service; commercial campgrounds and public showers are located in Moab (see the Moab section, earlier in this chapter).

More to See & Do Nearby

DEAD HORSE POINT STATE PARK ★

One of Utah's most scenic state parks, Dead Horse might be considered a mini-Canyonlands. The Dead Horse Point Overlook offers a splendid view across the river to the nearby national park, as well as down some 2,000 feet past seven distinctive and colorful layers of rock to the Colorado River. A strip of land only 30 yards wide connects the point with the rest of the mesa, and in the late 1800s, this natural corral was used by cowboys who herded wild horses in, roped all they wanted, and left the rest to find their way out.

From Canyonlands' Island in the Sky Visitor Center, drive north out of the park for 3½ miles to the intersection with Utah 313, and turn right. The state park's visitor center is about 7½ miles down the road. From Moab, head northwest on U.S. 191 for 9 miles, and turn south on Utah 313 for about 23 miles to the park (passing the access road for Canyonlands National Park).

For information, contact **Dead Horse Point State Park,** P.O. Box 609, Moab, UT 84532-0609 (℃ **435/259-2614;** www.stateparks.utah.gov).

The **visitor center/museum** is near the entrance to the park, with exhibits on the park's geology, history, plants, and animals. Rangers are on hand to assign campsites and answer questions; books, posters, maps, and souvenirs are available for purchase. A video presentation on the human and geologic history of the area is shown by request; in summer, nightly campfire programs and short guided walks are scheduled. Also, from late spring through early fall, the **Pony Expresso Coffee Shop,** open 8am to 5pm daily, sells snacks, sandwiches, soft drinks, and, of course, coffee.

The day-use fee is $10 per vehicle. In addition to the usual regulations requiring vehicles and bikes to stay on roads and pets to be leashed, visitors are asked to conserve water (which has to be trucked in) and to avoid stepping on cyanobacterial crusts—the fragile, bumpy, black mats composed of bacteria, algae, lichen, moss, and fungi found along trails and roads.

EXPLORING THE PARK **Dead Horse Point Overlook** is about 2 miles from the visitor center via a paved road. A short, wheelchair-accessible paved walkway leads from the parking area to a platform overlook that provides a magnificent panoramic view of the deep red canyons, the Colorado River, and distant mountains. The light is best either early or late in the day, but this is a worthwhile stop at any time.

Although you can easily drive to Dead Horse Point Overlook, it's a fun hike if you have the time. The main trail starts at the visitor center, follows the east rim of the mesa to the overlook, and returns on the west side. The fairly easy loop is 4 miles; you can add another 3 miles in side trips out to overlook points. Along the way, you pass a variety of rock formations while scrambling over the slickrock.

Another 3.5-mile loop leads from the visitor center to a series of potholes (holes in the rock that catch rainwater and may contain tadpole shrimp and other aquatic life) and a canyon overlook.

CAMPING The park's attractive campground has 21 sites, all with electric hookups and covered picnic tables, plus flush toilets and an RV dump station. However, because water must be trucked in, there are no showers, and campers are asked to conserve the small amount of water available. Electric outlets are hidden on the underside of picnic tables, which may be 50 or 60 feet from the site parking area, so those with recreational vehicles will likely need long extension cords. Camping costs $20; reservations are accepted (and encouraged Mar–Oct) with an $8 processing fee (✆ **800/322-3770;** www.reserveamerica.com).

NEWSPAPER ROCK

This site is famous for a large sandstone panel covered with petroglyphs that date from A.D. 1500 to modern times, created by a long line of humans, from the Ancestral Puebloans to the Utes. The panel also includes initials and names left by early European-American settlers, including one J. P. Gonzales of Monticello, who herded sheep in the canyon in the early 1900s. Administered by the Bureau of Land Management's **Monticello Field Office,** 365 N. Main St., Monticello, UT 84535 (✆ **435/587-1500;** www.blm.gov/ut/st/en/fo/monticello.html), the site is located in Indian Creek Corridor, along the road to Canyonlands' Needles District, Utah 211.

NORTH & WEST OF THE PARKS
Green River

Travelers heading north to Salt Lake City or west toward Nevada will undoubtedly pass through the village of Green River, which sits at an elevation of 4,100 feet, on I-70 along the banks of the Green River, about 54 miles northwest of Moab.

The **John Wesley Powell River History Museum,** 1765 E. Main St., Green River (✆ **435/564-3427;** www.jwprhm.com), details the phenomenal river expedition of explorer John Wesley Powell, a one-armed Civil War veteran who explored the Green and Colorado rivers in the late 1800s. Museum exhibits also discuss the geology of the region and the history of river running, from a replica of Powell's heavy wooden boat, the *Emma Dean,* to examples of boats and rafts used on the river since then. A 25-minute film, shown throughout the day, brings Powell's adventures to life. Admission is $6 per person 13 and older, $5 for children 5 to 12, free for those 4 and under, and a family rate of $15. From mid-May through mid-September, the museum is open daily 8am to 7pm, and the rest of the year it is usually open 9am to 5pm. You can also get information on other Green River area attractions, activities, and lodging at the museum.

Green River State Park, on Green River Road, Green River (✆ **435/564-3633;** www.stateparks.utah.gov), is a lush green oasis with big, old Russian olive and cottonwood trees. There's a **boat ramp** for launching your raft or canoe, but be aware that once you start heading downstream, you'll need a motor or mighty powerful arms to fight the current back to the park. The park also has a 9-hole championship **golf course** (✆ **435/564-8882**). Situated right along the river, it's open year-round (weather permitting) and has a pro shop, snacks, and carts. Fees are $10 for 9 holes and $18 for 18. Day-use park entry costs $5 per vehicle, which includes use of the boat ramp. The shady and spacious 40-site **campground,** open year-round, has modern bathhouses with toilets and hot showers (closed Dec–Feb), and a dump station, but no RV hookups. Camping costs $16; reservations are accepted from March through October with an $8 nonrefundable fee (✆ **800/322-3770;** www.reserve america.com).

Several river-running companies offer day and overnight trips on the Green. These include **Moki Mac River Expeditions, Inc.** (✆ **800/284-7280** or 801/268-6667; www.mokimac.com), which offers several trips on the Colorado and Green rivers. A day trip through Gray Canyon on the Green River costs $69 for adults and $55 for youths 15 and under, including lunch. Multiday trips start at $895 per adult and $675 per youth 15 and under for a 3-day excursion, including all gear and food. The outfitter also rents canoes at $25 per day, including life jackets and paddles for two persons.

A Magical State Park

Goblin Valley State Park ★★ (© **435/275-4584;** www.stateparks.utah.gov) is filled with fantasyland rock formations; hence its name. The landscape is so strange, in fact, that it starred in the 1999 sci-fi film *Galaxy Quest,* also starring Tim Allen and Sigourney Weaver. But have no fear. Although in the light of the full moon the little munchkins almost come alive, with shadows giving them facelike features, they're friendly. Bikes and motor vehicles are restricted to paved areas, but visitors are welcome to hike among the goblins, and even to climb onto them with caution. Park residents include kit foxes, rabbits, and lizards.

The 24-site **campground** is laid out in a semicircle among tall multicolored rocks of varying heights. Facilities include showers and a dump station, but no RV hookups. The day-use fee is $7 per vehicle; camping is $16. There are also several yurts (similar to camping cabins, with heat and electricity but no bathroom), that cost $60 per night. Reservations are accepted from March through November with an $8 nonrefundable fee (© **800/322-3770;** www.reserveamerica.com).

To get here from Green River, head west on I-70 for about 10 miles to exit 149, and turn south on Utah 24 for about 25 miles to Temple Mountain Junction, where you turn west and follow signs for about 12 miles to the park.

To the Dinosaurs of Price & Beyond

The town of Price, founded in 1879, began as a railroad and coal-mining center. A popular midway stopover for those traveling between southern Utah's national parks and the Salt Lake City area, Price is gaining in reputation as a destination, especially for those interested in dinosaurs.

Price (elevation 5,600 ft.) is 119 miles from Moab and 63 miles from the town of Green River. From I-70 exit 157, follow U.S. 191/6 northwest 57 miles. Take the business loop through the center of town and follow signs to the information center, located in the CEU Prehistoric Museum (see below), to pick up maps and brochures on the area, including a walking-tour brochure to the town's seven buildings listed on the National Register of Historic Places.

For advance information, contact **Castle Country Travel Region,** 81 N. 200 East, Price, UT 84501 (© **800/842-0789** or 435/636-3701; www.castlecountry.com).

One of the area's top attractions is the excellent **CEU Prehistoric Museum** ★★, 155 E. Main St. (© **800/817-9949** or 435/613-5060; http://museum.ceu.edu), operated by the College of Eastern Utah. Among the exhibits are the huge skeletons of an allosaurus, a Utah raptor, and a strange-looking duck-billed dinosaur known as the prosaurolophus. Watch for the large Colombian mammoth, with its long tusks, which resembles a modern elephant and roamed this area over 10,000 years ago. You'll also see exhibits on the early Native Americans of Utah—describing how they lived and adapted to changing environments—and displays of rare 1,000-year-old clay figures created by the Fremont people. Children will encounter a variety of interactive exhibits designed just for them, including a sandbox where they can do their own paleontological dig. The museum is open Monday through Saturday from 9am to 5pm. It's closed major holidays. Admission costs $5 for adults, $4 for seniors 65 and older, $2 for children 2 to 12, and free for infants 1 and under. There is also a family rate of $15.

To see more dinosaurs, you need to drive about 32 miles out of town. Designated a National Natural Landmark, the **Cleveland-Lloyd Dinosaur Quarry** contains the densest concentration of Jurassic Age dinosaur bones ever found, as well as the largest known collection of the bones of meat-eating dinosaurs. The visitor center has a complete allosaurus skeletal reconstruction and a stegosaurus wall mount on display. At the quarry itself—enclosed in two metal buildings—from several viewing areas, you can see bones in place where they were found, and sometimes watch scientists at work. Three easy-to-moderate trails, totaling just under 5 miles, are nearby and include a 1.4-mile loop interpretative trail, with a descriptive brochure available at the trail head, a 1.25-mile round-trip scenic trail to a viewpoint, and a one-way trail of over a mile that branches off the scenic trail and leads to another viewpoint. Leashed pets are permitted, and drinking water, restrooms, and picnic tables are available. From late March through May, the quarry is open 10am to 5pm Friday and Saturday and noon to 5pm Sunday. From May through August, it's open 10am to 5pm Monday, Thursday, Friday, and Saturday, and noon to 5pm Sunday. It is closed the rest of the year. Admission costs $5 for all those 16 and older, and free for youths 15 and under. For details, contact the Bureau of Land Management office in Price at 125 S. 600 West (© **435/636-3600;** www.blm.gov/ut/st/en/fo/price/recreation/quarry.html). To get here from Price, take Utah 10 southwest about 15 miles to Utah 155 south, following dinosaur signs to the quarry. The last 12 miles are on a gravel road; allow about 1 hour from Price.

For a look at the somewhat more recent history of the area, go north of Price 11 miles on U.S. 191/6 to the town of Helper, and follow signs to the **Western Mining and Railroad Museum,** 296 S. Main St. (© **435/472-3009;** www.wmrrm. org). Crammed into the four stories of the old Helper Hotel, built in 1913, are thousands of objects and exhibits illustrating the area's mining and railroad days of the late 1800s and early 1900s. Highlights include a complete jail cell, a simulated coal mine, mine models, wine- and whiskey-making equipment from Prohibition days, pictures of mine disasters, railroad equipment and photos, relics from outlaw Butch Cassidy's exploits in the area, and operating model trains. You can watch a video on the area's history, wander past the early mining equipment, caboose, and railroad snowplow in the outdoor displays, and browse the gift shop. The museum is open Monday through Saturday, 10am to 5pm, from mid-May through mid-September; Tuesday through Saturday, 11am to 4pm, the rest of the year. Admission is free, although donations are welcome.

THE FOUR CORNERS AREA

T he Four Corners area—where the borders of Colorado, New Mexico, Arizona, and Utah meet—is a major U.S. archaeological center (see the map of Southeast Utah, p. 261). A vast complex of ancient villages dominated this region a thousand years ago. Among the red-brown rocks, abandoned canyons, and flat mesas lies another world, once ruled by the Ancestral Puebloans (also known as the Anasazi) and today largely the domain of the Navajo.

15

Wander among the scenic splendors of Monument Valley, where Navajo people tend sheep and weave rugs, and trace the history of a civilization that vanished more than 7 centuries ago, leaving behind more questions than answers. Those particularly interested in the ancient and modern Native American tribes of the region will want to continue their travels into Arizona, New Mexico, and Colorado. Frommer's guidebooks to those states can provide additional information.

The southeast corner of Utah is sparsely populated—downright desolate and deserted, some might say—and you're not going to find your favorite chain motel, fast-food restaurant, or brand of gasoline right around every corner. That's assuming you can even *find* a corner. So, many travelers discover a place they like, rent a room or campsite for a few days, and take day trips. This chapter is laid out using the village of Bluff as a base—a series of excursions rings the tiny town. First, head southwest to Monument Valley and then northwest to Natural Bridges National Monument. Then head east, to Hovenweep National Monument and Four Corners Monument. Finally, this chapter takes you into Colorado, to visit Mesa Verde National Park, site of the most impressive cliff dwellings in the United States.

A BASE CAMP IN BLUFF

100 miles S of Moab, 338 miles SE of Salt Lake City

The tiny and very friendly village of Bluff sits near the intersection of U.S. 191 and U.S. 163, with roads leading off toward all the attractions of the Four Corners. With a population of about 300, Bluff (elevation 4,320 ft.) is one of those comfortable little places with most basic services, but not a lot more. Founded by Mormon pioneers in 1880, the town had already been the site of both Ancestral Puebloan and Navajo occupations. Local businesses distribute a free walking- and biking-tour guide that shows where ancient rock art and archaeological sites are located, and points out the locations of some of Bluff's handsome stone homes and other historic sites from the late 19th century.

For more information on Bluff, check out the website of the **Business Owners of Bluff** (www.bluffutah.org). You can also get information on Bluff and the other southeast Utah communities of Blanding, Monticello, Mexican Hat, and Monument Valley from **Utah's Canyon Country,** 117 S. Main St. (P.O. Box 490), Monticello, UT 84535 (𝄪 **800/574-4386** or 435/587-3235, ext. 4139; www.utahscanyon country.com). There is no visitor center in Bluff.

White-Water Rafting & Other Organized Tours

Situated along the San Juan River, Bluff is a center for river rafting. **Wild Rivers Expeditions,** 101 S. Main St., Bluff (𝄪 **800/422-7654** or 435/672-2244; www. riversandruins.com), offers river trips on the San Juan that are both fun and educational. Led by archaeology and geology professionals, the expeditions take boaters past dozens of Native American sites along the river, such as the spectacular Butler Wash Petroglyph Panel—a 250-yard-long wall of petroglyphs—plus fascinating rock formations. Trips, offered from March through October, range from a full day to more than a week, with rates starting at $165 per adult and $123 per child 12 or younger, including lunch.

Guided tours to scenic areas and archaeological sites such as Cedar Mesa and Comb Ridge are offered by **Far Out Expeditions,** 7th East Street and Mulberry Avenue, Bluff (𝄪 **435/672-2294;** www.faroutexpeditions.com). The company also offers custom guided backpacking trips. Day trips run $195 per person for groups of two people; backpacking trips are $225 per person per day for groups of two or three people. Far Out Expeditions also offers lodging (p. 294).

Note that both of the above companies also collect per-person user fees charged by the Bureau of Land Management.

More to See & Do

In town, check out the remains of **Historic Fort Bluff** and the **Chacoan Ruin** sites, both worthy of a quick stop or detour.

About 2¼ miles west of town is **Sand Island Recreation Site,** operated by the BLM. Located along the San Juan River among cottonwoods, Russian olives, and salt cedar, this area offers boating and fishing. Boaters must obtain river permits in advance, and because there are usually more people wanting permits than there are permits available, a lottery is held in January to determine who gets the permits. Fees are charged, based on the time of year, section of river, and number of people in your party. As early as possible, preferably in December for the following summer, contact the Bureau of Land Management, 365 N. Main St., Monticello, UT 84535 (𝄪 **435/ 587-1500,** or 435/587-1544 8am–noon Mon–Fri for permits and applications; www. blm.gov/ut). Nestled between the river and a high rock bluff are picnic tables, vault toilets, and graveled campsites; camping is $10 per night and drinking water is available. Head west from the boat launch to see a number of petroglyphs, some of which can be seen easily on foot; others require a boat to see. Unfortunately, you must have your own boat with you, as there are no nearby places to rent boats.

Goosenecks State Park, set on a rim high above the San Juan, offers spectacular views out over the twisting, turning river some 1,000 feet below. It's named for the sharp turns in the river, which meanders more than 5 miles to progress just 1 linear mile and provides a look straight down through 300 million years of geologic history.

(The park also has some Hollywood history: It served as the location for the climactic scene in *Thelma & Louise*.) A gravelly open area at the end of the paved road has picnic tables, trash cans, vault toilets, and an observation shelter, but no drinking water. The park is open around the clock and admission is free; primitive camping is permitted at no charge. The park is about 24 miles from Bluff, just off the route to Monument Valley Navajo Tribal Park. Head west on U.S. 163 for about 20 miles, turn north (right) on Utah 261 for about a mile, and then west (left) on Utah 316 for 2½ miles. For information, contact Goosenecks State Park, 660 W. 400 North, Blanding, UT 84511 (© **435/678-2238;** www.stateparks.utah.gov).

Another worthwhile area attraction is **Valley of the Gods,** a 16-mile driving loop south of Bluff proper, featuring a stunning landscape of isolated red mesas on a flat valley floor below sheer cliffs. It is located 8 miles northwest of Mexican Hat off U.S. 163; there are several hiking trails.

Where to Stay

In addition to the choices below, about 25 miles southwest of Bluff near Mexican Hat, the **San Juan Inn,** U.S. 163 (© **800/447-2022;** www.sanjuaninn.net), is a fairly nondescript roadside motel in a location that's anything but: perched above the San Juan River. Doubles are $88 summer and $68 winter. The complex includes a trading post and restaurant.

Campgrounds include **Cadillac Ranch RV Park,** 640 E. U.S. 191, Bluff (© **800/538-6195** or 435/672-2262), a down-home sort of place on the east side of town with sites around a small pond. It has 20 RV sites—all large pull-throughs—and 10 tent sites plus free Wi-Fi and restrooms with showers. The campground is open year-round, but water is turned off in winter. The cost per site is $16 for tents and $25 for RVs. Showers are $5.

Lodging tax adds about 10% to room bills in Bluff.

Desert Rose Inn ★★ Built in 1999, this imposing lodge-style building houses 30 attractively decorated motel rooms, all with coffeemakers and queen-size or king-size beds. The attractive suite has a wraparound porch, king-size bed, and separate living room. In addition there are five pleasant cabins, a bit more rustic in appearance, each with a large walk-in shower (no tubs), one king bed and a sofa sleeper, refrigerator and microwave, knotty pine walls and ceilings, porch, and cathedral ceiling with exposed beams. Smoking is not permitted.

701 W. U.S. 191 (P.O. Box 148), Bluff, UT 84512. www.desertroseinn.com. © **888/475-7673** or 435/672-2303. Fax 435/672-2217. 35 units. Apr–Oct $100–$125 double, $119–$149 cabin, $169–$189 suite; Nov–Mar $80 double, $105 cabin, $159 suite. AE, DISC, MC, V. *In room:* A/C, TV, Wi-Fi (free).

Far Out Guest House This restored historic home has two bedrooms, decorated in Southwestern style, with artwork and photos depicting scenes of the area. Each room has six bunk beds and a private bathroom. Both share a comfortable living room, screened porch, and fully equipped kitchen. Smoking is not permitted. The house is operated by Far Out Expeditions, which offers guided day tours and backcountry trips (p. 293).

7th East St. and Mulberry Ave. (P.O. Box 307), Bluff, UT 84512. www.faroutexpeditions.com. © **435/672-2294.** 2 units. $90 for 1 or 2 people; $100 for 3 or 4 people; $110 for 5 or 6 people; $200 for the entire house. MC, V.

Recapture Lodge ★ This well-kept motel, located on the main street near the center of town, has an attractive Western decor and a nature trail that follows the San

Juan River along the back of the property. Quiet, clean, attractive rooms contain evaporative cooling; several budget units, each with one double bed, are also available.

220 E. U.S. 191 (P.O. Box 309), Bluff, UT 84512. www.recapturelodge.com. © **435/672-2281.** 26 units. $70 double. AE, DISC, MC, V. Pets accepted (no fee). **Amenities:** Jacuzzi; pool. *In room:* TV, no phone.

Where to Eat

Cottonwood Steakhouse ★★ This is an Old West–style restaurant—lots of wood and a handsome stone fireplace—that knows what to do with beef and buffalo (not to mention homemade pie). The solid fare includes a lean rib-eye buffalo steak plus T-bone and rib-eye beefsteaks, barbecued chicken or ribs, shrimp, and catfish, accompanied by large salads, Western-grilled potatoes, and beans. In warm weather, diners can sit at picnic tables outside under cottonwood trees. Beer is available.

U.S. 191 on the west side of town (Main and 4th St. E). © **435/672-2282.** www.cottonwoodsteak house.com. Main courses $13–$25. MC, V. Apr–Oct daily 5:30–9:30pm. Closed in winter.

Twin Rocks Cafe In the shadow of the prominent Twin Rocks formation, the cafe has an open, airy dining room with large windows offering views of the surrounding red-rock walls. The American and Southwest selections range from half-pound burgers to barbecue plates to vegetarian specialties. You can also choose from a variety of sandwiches, New York strip steak, and grilled lemon herb chicken. But the most popular items by far are the regional dishes—the sheepherder's sandwich, Navajo taco, and beef stew with Navajo fry bread, a thick, deep-fried bread. You can also mix your cultures with a Navajo pizza—a variety of toppings served on Navajo fry bread. Breakfast items include the standard pancakes and egg dishes, plus granola and a spicy breakfast burrito. Microbrews and other beers are available with meals. While you're there, be sure to check out the museum-quality American Indian arts and crafts at Twin Rocks Trading Post, under the same management, next door.

913 E. Navajo Twins Dr. (off U.S. 191, on the east end of town). © **435/672-2341.** www.twinrocks cafe.com. Breakfast entrees $4–$10, lunch and dinner entrees $9–$22. AE, DISC, MC, V. Summer daily 7am–9pm; slightly reduced hours in winter.

MONUMENT VALLEY NAVAJO TRIBAL PARK ★★

50 miles SW of Bluff; 150 miles S of Moab; 395 miles S of Salt Lake City; 160 miles W of Cortez, Colorado

You've seen Monument Valley's majestic stone towers, delicately carved arches, lonely wind-swept buttes, forbidding cliffs, and mesas covered in sagebrush. Perhaps you didn't know you were looking at Monument Valley, instead believing it to be Tombstone, Arizona; or Dodge City, Kansas; or New Mexico; or Colorado. And possibly you couldn't fully appreciate the deep reddish-brown colors of the rocks or the incredible blue of the sky, which lost a bit of their brilliance in black and white.

For most of us, Monument Valley *is* the Old West. You've seen it dozens of times in movie theaters, on television, and in magazine and billboard advertisements. This all started in 1938, when Harry Goulding, who had been operating a trading post for local Navajo for about 15 years, convinced Hollywood director John Ford that Ford's current project, *Stagecoach*, should be shot in Monument Valley. Released the following year, *Stagecoach* not only put Monument Valley on the map, but also launched the career of a little-known actor by the name of John Wayne.

Ford and other Hollywood directors were attracted to Monument Valley by the same elements that draw visitors today. This is the genuine, untamed American West, with a simple, unspoiled beauty of carved stone, blowing sand, and rich colors, all compliments of nature. The same erosive forces of wind and water carved the surrounding scenic wonders of the Grand Canyon, Glen Canyon, and the rest of the spectacular red-rock country of southern Utah and northern Arizona. But here the result is different: Colors seem deeper, natural rock bridges are almost perfect circles, and the vast emptiness of the land around them gives the towering stone monoliths an unequaled sense of drama.

Essentials

Operated as a tribal park by the Navajo Nation (the country's largest tribe), Monument Valley (elevation 5,200 ft.) straddles the border of southeast Utah and northeast Arizona. U.S. 163 goes through the valley from north to south, and a tribal park access road runs east to west.

GETTING THERE   From Moab, Monticello, and most points in eastern Utah, take U.S. 191 south to Bluff, turn west (right), and follow U.S. 163 to Monument Valley. An alternative is to turn off Utah 95 south onto Utah 261 just east of Natural Bridges National Monument, follow Utah 261 to U.S. 163, turn southwest, and follow U.S. 163 to Monument Valley. This latter route is quite scenic, but because of switchbacks and steep grades it is not recommended for motor homes or vehicles with trailers. Those coming from Arizona can take east-west U.S. 160 to U.S. 163, turn north, and follow it into Monument Valley.

INFORMATION/VISITOR CENTER   Contact **Monument Valley Navajo Tribal Park,** P.O. Box 360289, Monument Valley, UT 84536 (© **435/727-5874** or 727-5870), or the **Navajo Nation Parks and Recreation Department,** P.O. Box 2520, Window Rock, AZ 86515 (© **928/871-6647;** www.navajonationparks.org).

The **visitor center/museum** is located about 4 miles east of U.S. 163 on the Monument Valley access road. It contains a viewing deck, exhibits on the geology and human history of the valley, restrooms, drinking water, a gift shop, and a restaurant that serves Navajo and American dishes for all three meals daily.

HOURS, FEES & REGULATIONS   The tribal park is open daily, May through September from 6am to 8pm and October through April from 8am to 5pm (closed Christmas and New Year's Day; half-day on Thanksgiving).

Admission is $5, free for children 9 and under. The park is operated by the Navajo Nation and not the U.S. government, so federal interagency passes are not accepted.

Because the park is part of the Navajo Nation, laws here differ somewhat from those in Utah, in Arizona, or on public lands. All alcoholic beverages are prohibited within the boundaries of the Navajo reservation. Visitors must stay on the self-guided Valley Drive unless accompanied by an approved guide, and rock climbing and cross-country hiking are prohibited. Although photography for personal use is permitted, permission is required to photograph Navajo residents and their property, and you will usually need to pay them.

Both Utah and Arizona are on Mountain Time, and although the state of Arizona does not recognize daylight saving time, the Navajo Nation does.

Exploring Monument Valley by Car

Driving the 17-mile self-guided loop lets you see most of the major scenic attractions of Monument Valley Navajo Tribal Park at your own pace, and at the lowest cost. The dirt road is a bit rough—not recommended for low-slung sports cars or vehicles longer than 24 feet, although it is passable for smaller motor homes. The road's first half-mile is the worst, and you have to drive it both at the beginning and end of the loop. There are no restrooms, drinking water, or other facilities along the route, and motorists should watch for livestock. Allow about 2 hours.

A brochure (free) and a more detailed booklet (fee) provide rough maps and information on 11 numbered sites, such as the Mittens—rock formations that resemble (you guessed it) a pair of mittens—and the aptly named Elephant and Camel buttes, Totem Pole, and the Thumb. You'll also see Yei Bi Chei, a rock formation that resembles a Navajo holy man, and John Ford Point, one of famed Hollywood director John Ford's favorite filming locations, where he shot scenes from *Stagecoach, The Searchers,* and *Cheyenne Autumn.* It's still popular with producers—watch for crews working on feature films, TV shows, or commercials.

Guided Tours

Guided tours are the best way to see Monument Valley—without a guide, visitors are restricted to the 17-mile scenic drive, but **Navajo guides ★** can take you into lesser-visited areas of the tribal park, give you their personal perspectives, and often arrange weaving demonstrations and other activities. Inquire at the visitor center for the types of tours (including the possibility of a sunset tour) currently available.

Tours are also available from **Goulding's** (see below), with rates of $40 for a 2½-hour tour, $50 for a 3½-hour tour, and $90 for a full-day tour that includes lunch. Discounts apply for children 8 and under. These prices include the park admission fee.

You can also see Monument Valley by horseback with Navajo-owned-and-operated **Black's Monument Valley Tours** (© **928/309-8834** or 435/739-4205; www.blacksmonumentvalleytours.com). Prices are about $60 per person for a 90-minute trail ride and $160 per person for a 6-hour ride; riders also have to pay the monument entrance fee.

More to See & Do

There is one hike you can take without a guide, the 3.2-mile **Wildcat Trail** around West Mitten Butte. Bring water and expect the hike to take about 2 hours.

Goulding's Trading Post Museum, at Goulding's Lodge (see "Where to Stay & Eat," below), is the original Monument Valley trading post opened by Harry and Leona (Mike) Goulding in 1924; it served as their home as well as a trading post for many years. Furnished much as it was in the 1920s and 1930s, the museum contains exhibits of Goulding family memorabilia, old photos of the area, Navajo and Ancestral Puebloan artifacts and crafts, and posters and other items from movies that were filmed at the trading post and in Monument Valley. It's open year-round (call the lodge for hours); a $2 donation is requested, which goes toward scholarships for local children. Allow a half-hour. Nearby, a more modern trading post sells souvenirs, books, videos, and top-quality American Indian arts and crafts.

The **Earth Spirit Multimedia Show,** in Harry and Mike's Theater, next to Goulding's Lodge (p. 298), is a 20-minute show on the valley's history and geology, utilizing magnificent photos of the area. It's shown several times nightly year-round and costs $2 (free for those who also take a Monument Valley tour with Goulding's).

Camping

Primitive **camping** in the park (meaning no running water, only portable restrooms), operated by the tribal park administration (p. 296), is available for $5 per person per night.

Goulding's Monument Valley Campground, on the Monument Valley access road about 3 miles west of its intersection with U.S. 163 (© **435/727-3231;** www.gouldings.com), offers splendid views, plus full RV hookups including cable TV, an indoor heated swimming pool, modern restrooms with showers, a playground, a self-serve laundry, and a large convenience store. The campground is open year-round, but with limited services from November to mid-March. Tent sites cost $25, RV sites are $44, and cabins are $75, with discounts in winter.

Where to Stay & Eat

New in 2008, the attractive, contemporary **View Hotel** (© **435/727-5555;** www.monumentvalleyview.com), is perched on the bluff next to the park's visitor center and nicely blends into the red-rock country. Every room has a private balcony with a drop-dead view of the Mittens and other valley landmarks. Rooms are modern, with flatscreen TVs, fridges, and other amenities. The property features an upscale restaurant that serves three meals a day, in-house guide service, and a trading post stocked with Navajo blankets and jewelry. Double rooms are $199 to $319 in summer, $149 to $199 in fall and spring, and $99 in winter.

Goulding's Lodge (© **800/874-0902** or 435/727-3231; www.gouldings.com), on the Monument Valley access road about 2 miles west of its intersection with U.S. 163, has 62 modern motel rooms, each with Southwestern decor, cable TV and VCR (John Wayne and other Western movies are available for rent), air-conditioning, hair dryer, iron and board, coffeemaker, and private patio or balcony. It has a small indoor heated pool and a restaurant serving three meals daily—American cuisine plus traditional Navajo dishes, with dinner prices in the $10-to-$30 range. Room rates for two are $190 to $230 from April to mid-October, and $80 to $100 the rest of the year. Taxes of about 12% are added to your bill.

NATURAL BRIDGES NATIONAL MONUMENT

60 miles NW of Bluff, 360 miles S of Salt Lake City

Utah's first National Park Service area, Natural Bridges was designated primarily to show off and protect its three outstanding natural rock bridges, carved by streams and other forms of erosion beginning some 10,000 to 15,000 years ago. You can see the bridges from roadside viewpoints, take individual hikes to each one, or hike a loop trail that connects all three.

Giant **Sipapu Bridge** is considered a "mature" bridge. It's 220 feet high, with a span of 268 feet, and is believed to be the second-largest natural bridge in the world, after Rainbow Bridge in nearby Glen Canyon National Recreation Area. **Owachomo Bridge,** which appears to be on the brink of collapse (then again, it could stand for centuries more), is the smallest of the three at 106 feet high, with a span of 180 feet. **Kachina Bridge,** 210 feet high with a span of 204 feet, is the thickest of the monument's bridges at 93 feet. All three bridges were given Hopi names: Sipapu means the "gateway to the spirit world" in Hopi legend; Owachomo is Hopi for "rock mound," so called for a rounded sandstone formation atop one side of the bridge; and Kachina was named as such because rock art on the bridge resembles decorations found on traditional Hopi kachina dolls.

Essentials

Natural Bridges National Monument is about 40 miles west of Blanding, 60 miles northwest of Bluff, 43 miles north of Mexican Hat, and about 50 miles east of Glen Canyon National Recreation Area's Hite or Halls Crossing marinas.

GETTING THERE   The national monument is located in southeast Utah, off scenic Utah 95 via Utah 275. From Monument Valley, follow U.S. 163 north to Utah 261 (just past Mexican Hat); at Utah 95, go west to Utah 275 and the Monument. Beware, though: Utah 261, although a very pretty drive, has 10% grades and numerous steep switchbacks. It's not recommended for motor homes, those towing trailers, or anyone who's afraid of heights. The less adventurous and RV-bound should stick to approaching from the east, via Utah 95.

Make sure you have enough fuel for the trip to Natural Bridges; the closest gas stations are at least 40 miles away in Mexican Hat or Blanding. In fact, no services of any kind can be found within 40 miles of the monument.

INFORMATION/VISITOR CENTER   For a park brochure and other information, contact **Natural Bridges National Monument,** HC 60 Box 1, Lake Powell, UT 84533-0101 (© **435/692-1234,** ext. 16; www.nps.gov/nabr).

A **visitor center** at the park entrance, open daily from 8am to 6pm May to October and 8am to 5pm the rest of the year, has exhibits and a video program on bridge formation, the human history of the area, and the monument's plants and wildlife. Rangers are available to advise you about hiking trails and scheduled activities. The visitor center is the only place in the monument where you can get drinking water.

FEES & REGULATIONS   Entry to the monument is $6 per vehicle or $3 per person on foot, bicycle, or motorcycle. Regulations are similar to those in most areas administered by the National Park Service, with an emphasis on protecting the natural resources. Be especially careful not to damage any of the fragile archaeological sites in the monument; climbing on the natural bridges is prohibited. Overnight backpacking is not permitted within the monument, and vehicles may not be left unattended overnight. Because parking at the overlooks and trail heads is limited, anyone towing trailers or extra vehicles is asked to leave them at the visitor center parking lot. Pets must be leashed and are not allowed on trails or in buildings.

SEASONS/AVOIDING THE CROWDS   Although the monument is open year-round, winters can be a bit harsh at this 6,500-foot elevation; the weather is best between late April and October. Because trail-head parking is limited and most people visit in June, July, and August, the best months to see the park, if your schedule permits, are May, September, and October.

RANGER PROGRAMS   Guided hikes and walks, evening campground programs, and talks at the visitor center patio are presented from spring through fall. Schedules are posted at the visitor center.

Seeing the Highlights

Natural Bridges National Monument probably won't be your major vacation destination, but you can easily spend a half- or full day, or even 2 days, here. For those who want to take a quick look, stop at the visitor center for a brief introduction, and then take the 9-mile loop drive to the various natural bridge overlooks. Those with the time and the inclination might also take an easy hike down to Owachomo Bridge; it's just a half-hour walk.

Outdoor Pursuits

Hiking is the number-one activity here. From the trail heads, you can hike separately to each of the bridges, or start at one and do a loop hike to all three. Be prepared for summer afternoon thunderstorms that can cause flash flooding. Although the possibility of encountering a rattlesnake is very small, you should still watch carefully. During the hot summers, all hikers should wear hats and other protective clothing, use sunscreen, and carry a gallon of water per person for all but the shortest walks.

The easiest hike—more of a walk—leads to **Owachomo Bridge** (.5 mile round-trip), with an elevation gain of 180 feet. Look toward the eastern horizon to see the twin buttes named Bear's Ears. Allow a half-hour.

The Sipapu and Kachina Bridge trails are both considered moderately strenuous—allocate about 1 hour for each. The trek to **Sipapu Bridge** has a 500-foot elevation change, climbing two flights of stairs with three ladders and handrails on a 1.2-mile round-trip trail. This is the steepest trail in the park, and it ends with a splendid view of the bridge about halfway down. The hike takes about 1 hour.

The 1.5-mile round-trip hike to massive **Kachina Bridge** has a 400-foot elevation change, descending steep slickrock with handrails. Under the bridge is a pile of rocks that fell in June 1992, slightly enlarging the bridge opening. Allow about 1 hour.

Those planning to hike the **loop to all three bridges** can start at any of the trail heads, although rangers recommend starting at Owachomo. The round-trip, including your walk back across the mesa, is about 9 miles. Although the trails from the rim to the canyon bottom can be steep, the walk along the bottom is easy.

Camping

A primitive 13-site campground has pit toilets, tables, tent pads, and fire grates, but no drinking water, showers, or other facilities. It's limited to vehicles no more than 26 feet long, and only one vehicle is allowed per site. Cost is $10; sites are allotted on a first-come, first-served basis.

HOVENWEEP NATIONAL MONUMENT

35 miles NE of Bluff; 122 miles S of Moab; 366 miles SE of Salt Lake City; 42 miles W of Cortez, Colorado

Located along the Colorado-Utah border, Hovenweep contains six separate sites with some of the most striking (and most isolated) **archaeological sites ★★** in the Four Corners area. These include castlelike towers, cliff dwellings, a kiva (a circular underground ceremonial chamber), stone rooms, walls, and petroglyphs. *Hovenweep* is the Ute/Paiute word for "deserted valley," appropriate because its inhabitants apparently left around 1300.

Essentials

No lodging, food, gasoline, supplies, or even public phones are available in the national monument; there are bathrooms with running water. The closest motels and restaurants are in Bluff (p. 292) and Blanding, Utah, or Cortez, Colorado.

GETTING THERE/ACCESS POINTS You can get to Hovenweep's Square Tower Site, where the visitor center is located, via paved roads from either Colorado or Utah. From Utah, follow U.S. 191, southeastern Utah's major north-south route, to Utah 262, between the towns of Blanding and Bluff. Head east on Utah 262 to Hatch Trading Post; then, watching for signs, follow paved roads to the monument. One option is to take Utah 163 east from Bluff toward the village of Aneth, turn north (left) onto an unnamed paved road, and follow signs to the monument.

From Cortez, Colorado, follow U.S. 491 (formerly U.S. 666) north to the community of Pleasant View and turn west (left) onto newly paved road, following signs to the monument.

VISITOR INFORMATION For advance information or questions about current road conditions, contact **Hovenweep National Monument,** McElmo Route, Cortez, CO 81321 (✆ **970/562-4282;** www.nps.gov/hove).

FEES, HOURS, REGULATIONS & SAFETY Entry to the national monument is $6 per vehicle or $3 per person. The monument is open 24 hours a day, but trails are open from sunrise to sunset only. The visitor center, with exhibits, restrooms, and drinking water, is open daily from 8am to 6pm in spring and summer and 8am to 5pm fall and winter.

Regulations are much the same here as at most National Park Service properties, with an emphasis on taking care not to damage archaeological sites. Summer temperatures can reach 100°F (38°C) and water supplies are limited; bring your own and carry a canteen, even on short walks. In late spring, gnats can be a real nuisance, so take insect repellent. Leashed dogs are permitted on trails.

Exploring the Monument

Hovenweep is noted for its mysterious and impressive 20-foot-tall sandstone towers, some of them square, others oval, circular, or D-shaped. Built by the Ancestral Puebloans (also known as Anasazi), the solid towers have small windows up and down the masonry sides. Archaeologists have suggested myriad possible uses for these structures—their guesses range from guard towers to celestial observatories, ceremonial structures to water towers or granaries. In addition to the towers, the monument contains the remains of cliff dwellings and a kiva, petroglyphs, stone rooms, walls, and a reconstructed dam.

Your walk among the 700-year-old buildings will take you through yucca, cactus, saltbush, juniper, and even some cottonwood trees. Watch for lizards, snakes, rabbits, hawks, ravens, and an occasional deer or fox.

The **Square Tower Site,** where the visitor center is located, should be your first stop. The other five sites are difficult to find, and you'll need to get detailed driving directions and check on current road conditions before setting out. (Ask about the **Cajon** site, a great place to snap sunset photos.)

At the Square Tower Site, the 2-mile **Square Tower self-guided trail** is a loop, the first part of which is paved and suitable for wheelchairs with assistance. The trail winds past the remains of ancient Puebloan buildings, including the impressive **Hovenweep Castle,** probably built around A.D. 1200. Once home to several families, this site contains two D-shaped towers plus additional rooms. A trail guide, based at the visitor center, discusses the ruins and identifies desert plants used for food, clothing, and medicine. Allow about 2 hours.

15

THE FOUR CORNERS AREA | Hovenweep National Monument

Camping

The 30-site Hovenweep Campground, at the Square Tower Site, is open year-round. It has restrooms, drinking water, picnic tables, and fire grills, but no showers or RV hookups. Most sites will accommodate short trailers and motor homes under 36 feet in length. Cost is $10 per night; reservations are not accepted, but the campground rarely fills, even during the peak summer season.

FOUR CORNERS MONUMENT

Operated as a Navajo Tribal Park (with the Colorado section owned by the Ute Mountain Tribe), a flat monument marks the spot where Utah, Colorado, New Mexico, and Arizona meet—or were thought to have met, until a 2009 survey found the marker to be up to 2½ miles away from the true intersection of the four states—on which visitors can pose for photos. Official seals of the four states are displayed, along with the motto FOUR STATES HERE MEET IN FREEDOM UNDER GOD. Surrounding the monument are the flags of the four states, the Navajo Nation and Ute tribes, and the United States. Despite its inaccurate location, which it owes to an 1868 survey, it's still legally recognized as the intersection of the four states (so says the Supreme Court), and makes for a good photo opportunity.

There are often crafts demonstrations here, and jewelry, pottery, sand paintings, and other crafts are for sale, along with T-shirts and other souvenirs. In addition, traditional Navajo food, such as fry bread, is available, and a small visitor center offers information on visiting the Navajo Nation.

A half-mile northwest of U.S. 160, the monument is open daily from 7am to 8pm from May through September and 8am to 5pm the rest of the year. It's closed on Thanksgiving, Christmas, and New Year's Day. Entry costs $3 per person. For information, contact the **Navajo Nation Parks and Recreation Department,** P.O. Box 2520, Window Rock, AZ 86515 (℡ **928/871-6647;** www.navajonationparks. org). Allow a half-hour.

EAST TO COLORADO & AN ADDITIONAL ARCHAEOLOGICAL SITE

The Four Corners region was once a bustling metropolis, the home of the Ancestral Puebloan people (also called Anasazi). The single best place to explore this ancient culture is Mesa Verde National Park.

Mesa Verde National Park

Mesa Verde ★★★ is the largest **archaeological preserve** in the United States, with more than 5,000 known sites dating from A.D. 600 to 1300, including the most impressive cliff dwellings in the Southwest.

The earliest-known inhabitants of Mesa Verde (Spanish for "green table") built subterranean pit houses on the mesa tops. During the 13th century, they moved into shallow alcoves and constructed complex cliff dwellings. These homes were obviously a massive construction project, yet the residents occupied them for only about a century, leaving in about 1300 for reasons as yet undetermined.

The area was little known until ranchers Charlie Mason and Richard Wetherill chanced upon it in 1888. Looting of artifacts followed their discovery until a Denver newspaper reporter's stories aroused national interest in protecting the site. The 52,000-acre site was declared a national park in 1906—it's the only U.S. national park devoted entirely to the works of humans.

A series of lightning-sparked fires has blackened over 50% of the park since 2000, closing it for several weeks one summer. Officials said that although the park's piñon-juniper forests were severely burned, none of the major archaeological sites were damaged. In fact, the fires uncovered some sites that officials were not aware existed.

ESSENTIALS

The entrance to Mesa Verde National Park is about 10 miles east of Cortez, Colorado; 56 miles east of Hovenweep National Monument; 125 miles east of Bluff; and 390 miles southeast of Salt Lake City. Admission to the park for up to 1 week for private vehicles costs $15 from Memorial Day weekend through Labor Day weekend and $10 the rest of the year; rates for motorcyclists, bicyclists, and individuals on foot are $8 and $5, respectively.

For information, contact Mesa Verde National Park, P.O. Box 8, Mesa Verde, CO 81330-0008 (© **970/529-4465;** www.nps.gov/meve).

The **Far View Visitor Center,** site of the lodge (described below), restaurant, gift shop, and other facilities, is 15 miles off U.S. 160; it's open from early April to mid-October only, from 8am to 7pm daily at the height of summer and closing at 5pm at the beginning and end of the season. **Chapin Mesa,** site of the park headquarters, a museum, and a post office, is 21 miles south of the park entrance on U.S. 160. The **Chapin Mesa Museum,** open daily year-round (8am–6:30pm from early Apr to mid-Oct, until 5pm the rest of the year), houses artifacts and specimens related to the history of the area, including objects from other nearby sites.

The cliff dwellings can be viewed daily, and, in summer, rangers give evening programs at Morefield Campground and Far View Lodge. In winter, the Mesa Top Loop Road, Spruce Tree House, and museum remain open, but many other facilities are closed. Food, gas, and lodging are generally available in the park from mid-April to mid-October only; full interpretive services are available from Memorial Day weekend through Labor Day weekend.

SEEING THE HIGHLIGHTS

Balcony House, Cliff Palace, and Long House can be seen up close only on ranger-led tours, which are offered only during the warmer months; tickets ($3) are available at the park visitor center and the Colorado Welcome Center at Cortez (see below). The **Cliff Palace,** the park's largest and best-known site, is a four-story apartment complex with stepped-back roofs forming porches for the dwellings above. Its towers, walls, and kivas are all set back beneath the rim of a cliff. Climbing a 32-foot ladder permits exploration of **Balcony House,** while **Long House,** on Wetherill Mesa, is the second-largest cliff dwelling at Mesa Verde.

From late spring through early fall, rangers lead **bus tours** that include a few short hikes to archeological sites along Mesa Top Loop Road and a hiking tour of Cliff Palace. The 4-hour **700 Years Tour** is a morning trip that costs $45 for adults and $34 for children under 12. The **Classic Pueblo Tour** is a 3½-hour afternoon tour that costs $35 for adults and $18 for children under 12. Tour tickets are available at Far View Lodge, Far View Terrace, Morefield Campground Store, and online at www.visitmesaverde.com.

Rangers lead free tours to **Spruce Tree House,** another of the major cliff-dwelling complexes, only in winter, when other park facilities are closed. Visitors can also explore Spruce Tree House on their own at any time.

Although the draw here is ancient cliff dwellings rather than outdoor recreation, you will have to hike and climb to reach the sites. None of the trails are strenuous, but the 7,000-foot elevation can make the treks tiring for visitors who aren't accustomed to the altitude. For those who want to avoid hiking and climbing, the 12-mile **Mesa Top Loop Road** makes a number of pit houses and cliff-side overlooks easily accessible by car. If you'd really like to stretch your legs and get away from the crowds, however, take one of the longer **hikes** into scenic Spruce Canyon; you must register at the ranger's office before setting out.

WHERE TO STAY & EAT

Only one lodging facility is actually in the park, Far View Lodge (see below), which has two restaurants and a bar. The company that runs the lodge also operates two other restaurants in the park—one near the campground and another near Chapin Mesa Museum. Numerous lodging and dining possibilities are in nearby Cortez. Stop at the **Colorado Welcome Center at Cortez,** Cortez City Park, 928 E. Main St. (🕿 **970/565-3414**), open daily from 8am to 6pm in summer, with shorter hours the rest of the year and closed Thanksgiving, Christmas, New Year's Day, and Easter. You can also contact the **Mesa Verde Country Visitor Information Bureau,** P.O. Box HH, Cortez, CO 81321 (🕿 **800/253-1616** or 970/565-8227; www.mesaverde country.com), or the **Cortez Area Chamber of Commerce,** P.O. Box 968, Cortez, CO 81321 (🕿 **970/565-3414;** www.cortezchamber.org). See *Frommer's Colorado* (Wiley Publishing, Inc.) for lodging and dining choices in the Cortez area.

Far View Lodge   Right in the heart of Mesa Verde National Park, Far View Lodge offers not only the most convenient location for visiting the park, but also the best views of any accommodations in the area. The facility lodges guests in 17 separate buildings spread across a hilltop. Rooms aren't fancy, and some are a bit on the small side, but all are well maintained and more than adequate, with Southwestern decor. The upscale Kiva rooms boast handcrafted furniture, one king-size or two double beds, CD players, and other amenities. Most standard rooms have one queen-size bed or two doubles, although a variety of bed combinations are available. Couples and singles may prefer the rooms with one bed—they seem less cramped than rooms with two beds. There are no TVs, but each unit has a private balcony and the views are magnificent in all directions. All rooms are nonsmoking.

The lodge restaurants serve three meals daily; from mid-May through late September, guided tours of the park are scheduled ($25 adults, $13 children under 12).

Mesa Verde National Park (P.O. Box 277), Mancos, CO 81328. www.visitmesaverde.com. 🕿 **800/ 449-2288.** Fax 970/564-4311. 150 units. $120–$152 double. AE, DC, DISC, MC, V. Closed late Oct to mid-Apr. Pets accepted only in standard rooms with two double beds with $50 deposit and $10 nonrefundable fee per pet per night. **Amenities:** 2 restaurants; Wi-Fi (in lobby only). *In room:* A/C (Kiva rooms only), CD player (Kiva rooms only), fridge, hair dryer.

Camping

Morefield Village, is site of Mesa Verde's campground, **Morefield Campground** (🕿 **800/449-2288;** www.visitmesaverde.com) has 365 sites, including 15 with full RV hookups. It's about 4 miles south of the park entrance station on the main park road (Colo. 10) and is open from mid-May to mid-October. The campground is set in rolling hills in a grassy area with scrub oak and brush. The attractive sites are fairly well spaced and mostly separated by trees and other foliage. Facilities include picnic tables and grills, modern restrooms, coin-operated showers and laundry (not within easy walking distance of most campsites), a convenience store, and an RV dump station. Basic sites (no hookups) cost $23 per night, and full hookup sites cost $33 per night. Reservations are accepted.

PLANNING YOUR TRIP TO UTAH

Once a dusty little desert corner, Utah has hit the big time, booming economically and demographically from the 1990s through today. It's no big secret why people are coming to Utah in greater numbers—its natural beauty is unrivaled and its communities are clean and relatively small, by East and West coast standards. But the increased tourism means that advance trip planning is essential. Hotels and restaurants fill up much more quickly than ever before, and traffic is thickening. But this wide-open state is still full of amazing, undiscovered surprises in literally every corner. Take the time, and drive the extra mile.

Utah is an easy state to visit—roads are good and generally uncrowded, and you can often expect to pay less for food and lodging than you would in other parts of the country. But once you leave the Wasatch Front—the area around Salt Lake City, Ogden, and Provo—distances between towns are long, with few services along the way. Plan your trip carefully and make reservations far in advance for popular areas such as the national parks, and for popular times, such as ski season.

The presence and influence of the Mormon Church—officially known as the Church of Jesus Christ of Latter-day Saints (LDS)—makes visiting Utah a unique experience, from ordering an alcoholic beverage to visiting a historic home with two identical bedrooms—one for each wife. To learn more about modern Mormonism, as well as Utah's history in general, see chapter 2, "Utah in Depth."

GETTING THERE

Utah's only major airport is **Salt Lake City International Airport** (© **800/595-2442** or 801/575-2400; www.slcairport.com), located just north of I-80 at exit 115, on the west side of the city. Its airport code is **SLC.**

Airlines serving Salt Lake City include **American Airlines** (www. aa.com), **Continental Airlines** (www.continental.com), **Delta Air Lines** (www.delta.com), **Frontier Airlines** (www.frontierairlines.com), **JetBlue Airways** (www.jetblue.com), **Southwest Airlines** (www.south west.com), **United Airlines** (www.united.com), and **US Airways** (www. usairways.com).

An alternative for visitors planning to go to southern Utah is to fly into **McCarran International Airport** in Las Vegas, Nevada (© **702/261-5211;** www.mccarran.com), which is only 120 miles southwest of St. George. Budget-conscious travelers should check airline and vehicle-rental prices at both airports to see which will provide the better deal for their particular circumstances.

By Car

About 80% of Utah's visitors arrive by car, in part because it's so easy: The state is accessed by **I-80** from the west or east, **I-70** from the east, **I-15** and **I-84** from the north, and **I-15** from the southwest. Salt Lake City is 600 miles from Albuquerque, 500 miles from Denver, 430 miles from Las Vegas, and 650 miles from Phoenix. Keep in mind that there will be long distances between services when traveling in and around Utah.

International visitors should note that insurance and taxes are almost never included in quoted rental car rates in the U.S. Be sure to ask your rental agency about any additional fees. They can add a significant cost to your car rental. While the minimum age for driving in Utah is 16, many car-rental agencies will not rent a vehicle to anyone under 25 years of age; others have a minimum age of 21.

By Train

There are four Amtrak stations in Utah along the **California Zephyr** line, which runs from Chicago to Emeryville, California: Salt Lake City, Provo, Helper, and Green River. Call © **800/872-7245** or visit www.amtrak.com for details. In state, **Trax** runs in metro Salt Lake City, and the **FrontRunner** train connects Salt Lake City and Ogden. Call © **888/743-3882,** or visit www.rideuta.com for additional information.

GETTING AROUND

By Plane

Attention visitors to the U.S. from abroad: Some major airlines offer transatlantic or transpacific passengers special discount tickets under the name **Visit USA,** which allows mostly one-way travel from one U.S. destination to another at very low prices. Unavailable in the U.S., these discount tickets must be purchased abroad in conjunction with your international fare. This system is the easiest, fastest, cheapest way to see the country. Inquire with your air carrier.

By Car

Most visitors to Utah travel the state in a car. In fact, in some areas, it's a necessity. Planes, trains, and buses do not cover many areas of the state.

Before you set out on a road trip, you might want to join the **American Automobile Association** (**AAA;** © **800/222-4357;** www.csaa.com for Northern California, Nevada, and Utah information), which has hundreds of offices nationwide. The Salt Lake City office is located at 560 E. 500 South (© **800/541-9902** or 801/364-5615), and is open Monday through Friday from 8:30am to 5:30pm. AAA also has offices in Ogden (© **801/476-1666**), Orem (© **801/225-4801**), St. George (© **435/656-3990**), and several other locations. Members receive excellent road maps and emergency road service, and AAA will even help you plan an exact itinerary.

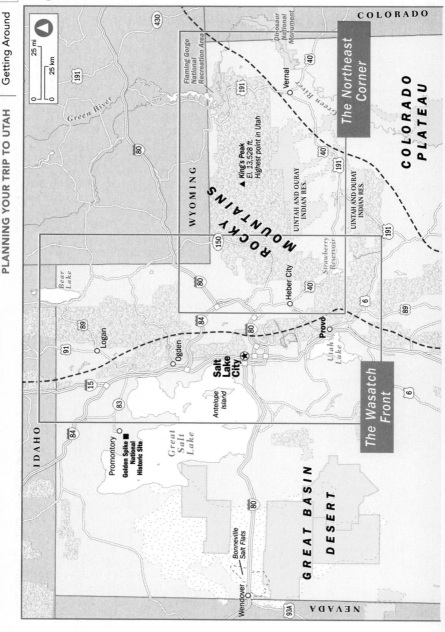

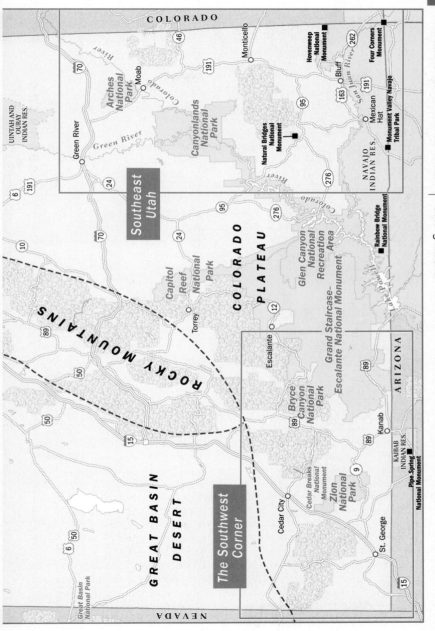

Gasoline taxes are already included in the printed price. At press time, the average price for a gallon of gas was $3.45. One U.S. gallon equals 3.8 liters or .85 imperial gallons.

If you're visiting from abroad and plan to rent a car in the United States, keep in mind that foreign driver's licenses are usually recognized in the U.S., but you may want to consider obtaining an international driver's license.

By Train

International visitors can buy a **USA Rail Pass,** good for 15, 30, or 45 days of unlimited travel on **Amtrak** (© **800/USA-RAIL** in the U.S. or Canada; © **001/215-856-7953** outside the U.S.; www.amtrak.com). The pass is available online or through many overseas travel agents. See Amtrak's website for the cost of travel within the western, eastern, or northwestern United States. Reservations are generally required and should be made as early as possible. Regional rail passes are also available.

By Bus

Greyhound (© **800/231-2222** in the U.S.; © **001/214-849-8100** outside the U.S. with toll-free access; www.greyhound.com) is the sole nationwide bus line. International visitors can obtain information about the **Greyhound North American Discovery Pass.** The pass, which offers unlimited travel and stopovers in the U.S. and Canada, can be obtained outside the United States from travel agents or through www.discoverypass.com.

TIPS ON ACCOMMODATIONS

Utah offers a variety of lodging options, from typical American chain motels to luxury hotels—primarily in Salt Lake City, Park City, and Deer Valley—plus delightful bed-and-breakfasts, rustic cabins, and pleasant and inexpensive mom-and-pop independent motels.

The chains here are the same ones you see everywhere else in America: Best Western, Comfort Inn, Days Inn, Embassy Suites, Hampton Inn, Hilton, Holiday Inn, Motel 6, Quality Inn, Sheraton, Sleep Inn, Super 8, Travelodge, and so on. They look about the same as those found elsewhere, and have the same levels of service. In most cases, their rooms are little more than boring boxes of various sizes, with beds and the appropriate plumbing and heating fixtures. If you're lucky, you'll get a decent view out the window. Because enjoying the magnificent *indoors* is probably not one of the main reasons you've come to Utah, these chains might be all that you require.

On the other hand, if you are exploring Temple Square and enjoying the numerous cultural offerings in Salt Lake City, the best choice for lodging would be the Inn at Temple Square. At Bryce Canyon National Park, go for one of the delightful Bryce Lodge cabins. And if you really want to be pampered after a hard day on the slopes, you can't beat the upscale properties at Park City and Deer Valley.

Another option is a B&B. Numerous bed-and-breakfasts are discussed throughout the book, and when you take into consideration the delicious breakfasts prepared at most of them, the rates are fairly reasonable. Why spend $90 for a boring motel room and then another $10 to $15 for breakfast when, for just a bit more, you can instead sleep in a handsome home, often uniquely decorated, and be served a delightful home-cooked breakfast?

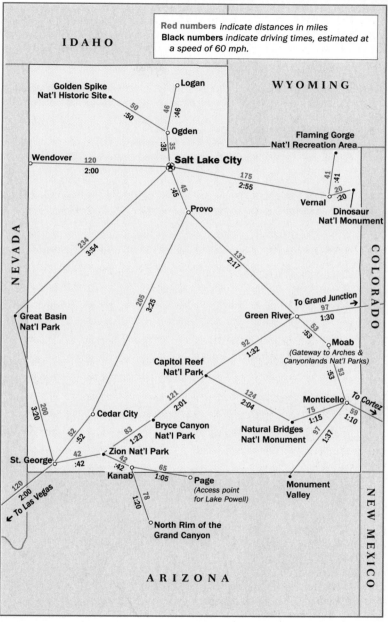

Other lodging choices in Utah include cabins and a handful of small independent motels. Both are usually fairly inexpensive, although they often lack the facilities, such as pools, spas, exercise equipment, and so on, that you'll find in most chains. The cabins and independents are still preferable because they're often a very good value, and the rooms usually have at least some personality (can anybody actually describe the decor of the last Super 8 or Days Inn he or she stayed at?)—and cabins, although sometimes a bit primitive, are often in beautiful settings.

In some areas, like the national parks, your options will be fairly limited: You can either camp, stay in one of the few in-park lodgings, or choose from one of the lodgings in a gateway town. You can save some money at Utah's numerous ski resorts by staying in a nearby town and taking a bus (often a free shuttle to the slopes). The accommodations in Salt Lake City are very reasonable, even in peak ski season, when the room rates at Snowbird and Park City go through the roof. The rates drop precipitously in the winter in southern Utah, and there are many nice days to be had in the national parks when the crowds are sparser and the weather mild.

For camping throughout Utah, you can make reservations through either **Utah State Parks** (© 800/322-3770; http://stateparks.utah.gov or www.stateparks.utah.gov) or the **National Parks Reservation Service** (© 877/444-6777; www.recreation.gov), depending on the park or recreation area. Keep in mind, however, that some campsites operate on a first-come, first-served basis.

To learn more about camping and bringing your RV through Utah, see chapter 4.

Saving on Your Hotel Room

The **rack rate** is the maximum rate that a hotel charges for a room. Hardly anybody pays this price, however, except in high season or during holidays. To lower the cost of your room:

- **Ask about special rates or other discounts.** You may qualify for corporate, student, military, senior, frequent flier, trade union, or other discounts.
- **Dial direct.** When booking a room in a chain hotel, you'll often get a better deal by calling the individual hotel's reservation desk rather than the chain's main number.
- **Book online.** Many hotels offer Internet-only discounts, or supply rooms to Priceline, Hotwire, Orbitz, Travelocity.com, Hotels.com, or Expedia at rates much lower than the ones you can get through the hotel itself. Comparison shop on hotel websites for great deals on hotel rooms and multiday packages.
- **Remember the law of supply and demand.** Resort hotels are most crowded and, therefore, most expensive on weekends, so discounts are usually available for midweek stays. Business hotels in cities are often busiest during the week, so expect big discounts over the weekend. Avoid holidays and school vacations, typically busy times for families and school groups.
- **Look for family-friendly pricing.** Many resorts and chain hotels entice families with big breaks on kids' costs, from letting kids under 12 stay free in a parent's room or promoting a "kids-eat-free" policy. Ski resorts often offer "kids-stay-free" or "kids-ski-free" incentives. Families looking for ways to cut costs can take advantage of these incentives or look for price breaks on ski-equipment rentals or lessons.

- **Look into group or long-stay discounts.** If you come as part of a large group, you should be able to negotiate a bargain rate. Likewise, if you're planning a long stay (at least 5 days), you might qualify for a discount. As a general rule, expect 1 night free after a 7-night stay.
- **Sidestep excess surcharges and hidden costs.** Many hotels have the unpleasant practice of nickel-and-diming their guests with opaque surcharges. When you book a room, ask what is included in the room rate, and what is extra. Avoid dialing direct from hotel phones, which can have exorbitant rates. And don't be tempted by the room's minibar offerings: Most hotels charge through the nose for water, soda, and snacks. Finally, ask about local taxes and service charges, which can increase the cost of a room by 15% or more.
- **Book an efficiency.** A condo or a room with a kitchenette allows you to shop for groceries and cook your own meals. This is a big money saver, especially for families on long stays.
- **Consider enrolling in hotel "frequent-stay" programs,** which are upping the ante lately to win the loyalty of repeat customers. Frequent guests can now accumulate points or credits to earn free hotel nights, airline miles, in-room amenities, merchandise, tickets to concerts and events, discounts on sporting facilities—and even credit toward stock in the participating hotel, in the case of the Jameson Inn hotel group. Perks are awarded not only by many chain hotels and motels (Hilton HHonors, Marriott Rewards, Wyndham ByRequest, to name a few), but also by individual inns and B&Bs. Many chain hotels partner with other hotel chains, car-rental firms, airlines, and credit card companies to give consumers additional incentive to do repeat business.

[Fast FACTS] UTAH

Area Codes The area code is **801** in the Wasatch Valley, which includes Salt Lake City, Provo, and Ogden. Most of the rest of the state is in the **435** area code.

Business Hours Banks are usually open Monday through Friday from 9am to 5pm, often until 6pm on Friday; some have hours on Saturday. Small stores are usually open Monday through Saturday, with some also open on Sunday afternoon. Most department stores, discount stores, and supermarkets are open daily until 9pm. Some supermarkets are open 24 hours a day.

Cellphones See "Mobile Phones," later in this section.

Crime See "Safety," later in this section.

Customs The Customs agency is **U.S. Customs & Border Protection** (CBP), 1300 Pennsylvania Ave. NW, Washington, DC 20229 (℡ **877/287-8667;** www. cbp.gov).

Disabled Travelers Disabled travelers can expect accessible lodgings and attractions throughout the state; some trails in the state and national parks are accessible and several ski resorts have programs for disabled guests.

Doctors Ask your hotel for references to local doctors. Also see "Hospitals," later in this section.

Drinking Laws Utah normalized its liquor laws in 2009; memberships are no longer required, and private clubs are a thing of the past. There are still two strengths of beer, 3.2% and 6%. You can buy 3.2% beer and malt coolers in supermarkets and convenience stores 7 days a week; stronger beer, wine, and hard liquor are available only at state-owned liquor stores and package agencies, which are closed Sundays and state holidays. Some establishments are licensed as taverns and can sell 3.2% beer only. The legal age for purchase and consumption of alcoholic beverages is 21; proof of age is required and often requested at bars, nightclubs, and restaurants, so it's always a good idea to bring ID when you go out. Do not carry open containers of alcohol in your car or any public area that isn't zoned for alcohol consumption. The police can fine you on the spot. Don't even think about driving while intoxicated.

Electricity Like Canada, the United States uses 110 to 120 volts AC (60 cycles), compared to 220 to 240 volts AC (50 cycles) in most of Europe, Australia, and New Zealand. Downward converters that change 220 to 240 volts to 110 to 120 volts are difficult to find in the United States, so bring one with you.

Embassies & Consulates All embassies are in the nation's capital, Washington, D.C. Some consulates are in major U.S. cities, and most nations have a mission to the United Nations in New York City. If your country isn't listed below, call for directory information in Washington, D.C. (☏ **202/ 555-1212**), or check **www. embassy.org/embassies**.

The embassy of **Australia** is at 1601 Massachusetts Ave. NW, Washington, DC 20036 (☏ **202/797-3000;** www.usa.embassy.gov.au).

Consulates are in New York, Honolulu, Houston, Los Angeles, and San Francisco.

The embassy of **Canada** is at 501 Pennsylvania Ave. NW, Washington, DC 20001 (☏ **202/682-1740;** www.canadainternational. gc.ca/washington). Other Canadian consulates are in Buffalo (New York), Detroit, Los Angeles, New York, and Seattle.

The embassy of **Ireland** is at 2234 Massachusetts Ave. NW, Washington, DC 20008 (☏ **202/462-3939;** www.embassyofireland. org). Irish consulates are in Boston, Chicago, New York, San Francisco, and other cities. See the website for a complete listing.

The embassy of **New Zealand** is at 37 Observatory Circle NW, Washington, DC 20008 (☏ **202/ 328-4800;** www.nzembassy. com). New Zealand consulates are in Los Angeles, Salt Lake City, San Francisco, and Seattle.

The embassy of the **United Kingdom** is at 3100 Massachusetts Ave. NW, Washington, DC 20008 (☏ **202/588-6500;** http:// ukinusa.fco.gov.uk). Other British consulates are in Atlanta, Boston, Chicago, Cleveland, Houston, Los Angeles, New York, San Francisco, and Seattle.

Emergencies Call ☏ **911.**

Family Travel Utah is a terrific family destination, from the museums to the

ski resorts. To locate accommodations, restaurants, and attractions that are particularly kid-friendly, look for the "Kids" icon throughout this guide.

Gasoline Please see the section "By Car," under "Getting Around," earlier in this chapter.

Health Utah's extremes—from burning desert to snow-covered mountains—can cause health problems for the ill-prepared. If you haven't been to the desert before, the heat, dryness, and intensity of the sun can be difficult to imagine. Bring a hat, strong sun block, sunglasses with ultraviolet protection, and moisturizing lotion for dry skin. Hikers and others planning to be outdoors should carry water—at least a gallon per person, per day.

Another potential problem for short-term visitors is elevation. There's less oxygen and lower humidity in Utah's mountains, which rise to over 13,500 feet. If you have heart or respiratory problems, consult your doctor before planning a trip to the mountains. Even if you're in generally good health, you may want to ease into high elevations by changing altitude gradually. Don't fly in from sea level in the morning and plan to hike 10,000-foot Cedar Breaks National Monument that afternoon. Spend a day or two at 4,000- or 5,000-feet elevation to let your body adjust. Also, get lots of rest, avoid large meals, and drink plenty of nonalcoholic fluids, especially water.

State health officials warn outdoor enthusiasts to take precautions against the hantavirus, a rare but often fatal respiratory disease first recognized in 1993. About half of the country's 200-plus confirmed cases have been reported in the Four Corners states of Colorado, New Mexico, Arizona, and Utah, and about 45% of the cases have been fatal. The disease is usually spread by the urine, feces, and saliva of deer mice and other rodents, so health officials recommend that campers avoid areas with signs of rodent droppings. Symptoms of hantavirus are similar to flu, and lead to breathing difficulties and shock.

Most cities in Utah have hospitals with 24-hour emergency rooms, but the smaller towns and less populated regions often have little in the way of health care. It is best to find out where the nearest medical facilities are to your specific destination.

Bugs, Bites & Other Wildlife Concerns Rattlesnakes, hobo spiders, and wood ticks are native to Utah, and each can inflict a nasty bite, the former two being venomous and the latter carrying a number of diseases. If you experience pain or swelling after a hike or camping, it could be a bug bite. Anti-itch cream will help diminish the itch, but time is the best medication—unless of course, the symptoms are dramatic, in which case you should seek medical attention or call *C* **911** immediately. While hiking or camping, insect repellent is always a good idea.

Respiratory Illnesses Air quality can be an issue on the Wasatch Front, where numerous cities have struggled to meet federal standards for various pollutants. For the daily air quality report, visit **www. airquality.utah.gov**.

High-Altitude Hazards For many people who live at or near sea level, the most common health issue is discomfort caused by Utah's high elevations. Altitude sickness is a process that can take a day or more to dissipate. Symptoms include headache, fatigue, nausea, loss of appetite, muscle pain, and lightheadedness. Doctors recommend that, until acclimated, travelers should avoid heavy exertion, consume light meals, and drink lots of liquids, avoiding those with caffeine or alcohol.

Sun/Elements/Extreme Weather Exposure In the desert area, extreme heat is common; wintertime in the Rockies can bring freezing temperatures and powerful blizzards. Depending on the time of year and your destination, it is best to be prepared with plenty of water and a wide range of layers for clothing. Symptoms of sunstroke include dizziness, clouded vision, and fainting. The best cure is shade, rest, and plenty of water. Seek medical attention if symptoms are dramatic.

Waterborne Illnesses Two waterborne hazards are *Giardia* and *Campylobacter,* with symptoms that wreak havoc on the human digestive system. If you pick up these pesky bugs, they might accompany you on your trip home. Untreated water from lakes and streams should be boiled for at least 5 minutes before consumption or pumped through a fine-mesh water filter specifically designed to remove bacteria.

Hospitals Salt Lake City has the state's most comprehensive medical facilities, including **LDS Hospital,** 8th Avenue and C Street (*C* **801/408-1100;** www.ldshospital. com), and **Salt Lake Regional Medical Center,** 1050 E. South Temple (*C* **801/350-4111;** www. saltlakeregional.com); both have 24-hour emergency rooms. Many of the national parks have clinics. For emergencies, dial *C* **911.**

Insurance For information on traveler's insurance, trip cancellation insurance, and medical insurance while traveling, please visit www.frommers.com/planning.

Internet & Wi-Fi

In Salt Lake City, Provo, Ogden, and Utah's major resorts, Wi-Fi is commonplace. It's generally not difficult to access the Internet in any urban area, but may be a little harder to find in some of the state's less populated areas.

Legal Aid

While driving, if you are pulled over for a minor infraction (such as speeding), never attempt to pay the fine directly to a police officer; this could be construed as attempted bribery, a much more serious crime. Pay fines by mail, or directly into the hands of the clerk of the court. If accused of a more serious offense, say and do nothing before consulting a lawyer. In the U.S., the burden is on the state to prove a person's guilt beyond a reasonable doubt, and everyone has the right to remain silent, whether he or she is suspected of a crime or actually arrested. Once arrested, a person can make one telephone call to a party of his or her choice. The international visitor should call his or her embassy or consulate.

LGBT Travelers

Although most Utahns are tolerant people, the Mormon Church has been criticized in the past for homophobia.

Mail

At press time, domestic postage rates were 28¢ for a postcard and 44¢ for a letter. For international mail, a first-class letter of up to 1 ounce costs 98¢ (75¢ to Canada and 79¢ to Mexico); a first-class postcard costs the same as a letter. For more information go to **www.usps.com**.

If you aren't sure what your address will be in the United States, mail can be sent to you, in your name, c/o General Delivery at the main post office of the city or region where you expect to be. (Call ✆ **800/275-8777** for information on the nearest post office.) The addressee must pick up mail in person and must produce proof of identity (driver's license, passport, and the like). Most post offices will hold mail for up to 1 month, and are open Monday to Friday from 8am to 6pm, and Saturday from 9am to 3pm.

Always include zip codes when mailing items in the U.S. If you don't know your zip code, visit www.usps.com/zip4.

Medical Requirements

Unless you're arriving from an area known to be suffering from an epidemic (particularly cholera or yellow fever), inoculations or vaccinations are not required for entry into the United States.

Mobile Phones

Just because your cellphone works at home doesn't mean it'll work everywhere in the U.S. (thanks to our nation's fragmented cellphone system). It's a good bet that your phone will work in major cities, but take a look at your wireless company's coverage map on its website before heading out. If you're not from the U.S., you'll be appalled at the poor reach of our **GSM (Global System for Mobile Communications) wireless network,** which is used by much of the rest of the world. Your phone will probably work in most major U.S. cities; it definitely won't work in many rural areas. And you may or may not be able to send SMS (text messaging) home from some of Utah's most secluded corners, either.

Money & Costs

Frommer's lists exact prices in the local currency. The currency conversions provided were correct at press time. However, rates fluctuate, so before departing consult a currency exchange website such as **www.oanda.com/currency/converter** to check up-to-the-minute rates.

Costs in Utah are moderate for the U.S. Lodging is lower than many comparable destinations, and there are more deals at ski resorts than neighboring Colorado, although Park City is comparable to Vail and Aspen in terms of lift ticket prices. Many hotels and motels have very low off-season rates.

THE VALUE OF US$ VS. OTHER POPULAR CURRENCIES

US$	Aus$	Can$	Euro (€)	NZ$	UK£
1	A$.97	C$1	€.73	NZ$1.27	£.62

WHAT THINGS COST IN UTAH	US$
Taxi from the airport to downtown Salt Lake City	20.00
Double room, moderate	100.00
Double room, inexpensive	50.00
Three-course dinner for one without wine, moderate	25.00–30.00
Bottle of beer	3.00–5.00
Cup of coffee	1.00–2.00
1 gallon/1 liter of premium gas	3.45/0.91
Admission to most museums	2.00–10.00
Admission to most national parks	10.00–20.00

For help with currency conversions, tip calculations, and more, download Frommer's convenient Travel Tools app for your mobile device. Go to www.frommers.com/go/mobile, and click on the Travel Tools icon.

Multicultural Travelers Most Utahns are tolerant people, but the Mormon Church has been criticized in the past for racism, although recent church initiatives have demonstrated more progressive attitudes. However, the state remains one of the least diverse in the United States, and strains of intolerance remain.

Newspapers & Magazines The state's two largest dailies, both published in Salt Lake City,

are the *Salt Lake City Tribune* (www.sltrib.com) and the *Deseret Morning News* (www.desnews.com). The *Salt Lake City Weekly* (www.slweekly.com) is the alternative weekly. Several other communities have daily newspapers, and many smaller towns publish weeklies. There are a few local magazines, *Salt Lake Magazine* (www.saltlakemagazine.com) among them.

Packing Weather changes frequently and abruptly in Utah; bring layers and be prepared to see winter and summer in one day. For more helpful information on packing for your trip, download our convenient Travel Tools app for your mobile device. Go to www.frommers.com/go/

mobile, and click on the Travel Tools icon.

Passports Virtually every air traveler entering the U.S. is required to show a passport. All persons, including U.S. citizens, traveling by air between the United States and Canada, Mexico, Central and South America, the Caribbean, and Bermuda are required to present a valid passport. *Note:* U.S. and Canadian citizens entering the U.S. at land and sea ports of entry from within the Western Hemisphere must now also present a passport or other documents compliant with the Western Hemisphere Travel Initiative (WHTI; see www.getyouhome.gov for details). Children 15 and under may continue entering with only a U.S. birth certificate, or other proof of U.S. citizenship.

Australia Australian Passport Information Service (*☎* **131-232;** www. passports.gov.au).

Canada Passport Office, Department of Foreign Affairs and International Trade, Ottawa, ON K1A 0G3 (*☎* **800/567-6868;** www.ppt.gc.ca).

Ireland Passport Office, Setanta Centre, Molesworth Street, Dublin 2 (*☎* **01/671-1633;** www. foreignaffairs.gov.ie).

New Zealand Passports Office, Department of Internal Affairs, 47 Boulcott St., Wellington, 6011 (*☎* **0800/225-050** in New Zealand or 04/474-8100; www.passports.govt.nz).

United Kingdom Visit your nearest passport office, major post office, or travel agency or contact the **Identity and Passport Service (IPS),** 89 Eccleston Sq., London, SW1V 1PN (*☎* **0300/222-0000;** www. ips.gov.uk).

United States To find your regional passport office, check the U.S. State Department website (travel. state.gov/passport) or call the **National Passport Information Center** (*☎* **877/487-2778**) for automated information.

Petrol Please see "By Car" under "Getting Around," earlier in this chapter.

Police Call *☎* **911** for emergency police help.

Safety Utah in general is a very safe vacation destination. Car accidents are more of a problem than crime in almost every corner of the state, and the biggest safety concerns apply largely to backpackers, skiers, rock climbers, and other adventurous types. As in any city, it's important to remain aware of one's surroundings in downtown Salt Lake City; South State Street is often highlighted as the most unsavory strip in all of Utah. In the backcountry of the state's numerous parks and forests, it's important to always carry plenty of water, a map, and a compass, and to let someone know of your plans in case something goes awry.

As you head into the great outdoors, also bear in mind that injuries often occur when people fail to follow instructions. Take heed when the experts tell you to stay on established ski trails, hike only in designated areas and carry rain gear, and wear a life jacket when rafting. Mountain weather can be fickle, and many beautiful spots are in remote areas. Be prepared for sudden changes in temperature at any time of year, and watch out for summer afternoon thunderstorms that can leave you drenched and shivering in minutes.

When visiting such historic sites as ghost towns, gold mines, and railroads,

remember that they were likely built more than 100 years ago, when safety standards were extremely lax, if they existed at all. Never enter abandoned buildings, mines, or rail cars on your own. When touring historic attractions, use common sense and don't be afraid to ask questions.

Walkways in mines are often uneven, poorly lit, and sometimes slippery due to seeping groundwater that can stain your clothing with its high iron content. In old buildings, be prepared for steep, narrow stairways, creaky floors, and low ceilings and doorways. Steam trains are wonderful as long as you remember that steam is very hot; oil and grease can ruin your clothing; and, at the very least, soot will make you very dirty.

Crime is relatively low in Utah in general and especially the parks, but Salt Lake City and the other cities have their share of incidents. Always keep a close eye on your wallet or purse and keep your wits about you when exploring unfamiliar neighborhoods.

Senior Travel Seniors can expect discounts at many attractions, including museums, restaurants, and ski resorts. The U.S. National Park Service offers an **America the Beautiful—National Park and Federal Recreational Lands Pass—Senior Pass** (formerly the

Golden Age Passport), which gives seniors 62 years or older lifetime entrance to all properties administered by the National Park Service—national parks, monuments, historic sites, recreation areas, and national wildlife refuges—for a one-time processing fee of $10. The pass must be purchased in person at any NPS facility that charges an entrance fee. Besides free entry, the America the Beautiful Senior Pass also offers a 50% discount on some federal-use fees charged for such facilities as camping, swimming, parking, boat launching, and tours. For more information, go to www.nps.gov/fees_passes.htm.

Smoking The Utah Indoor Clean Air Act prohibits smoking in any public building or office and in all enclosed places of public access. This includes restaurants but not private clubs, lounges, or taverns.

Taxes A combination of state and local sales taxes, from 6% to 8.5%, is added to your bill in all areas of Utah except Indian reservations. Local lodging taxes usually add an additional 3% to 6%. The United States has no value-added tax (VAT) or other indirect tax at the national level. Every state, county, and city may levy its own local tax on all purchases, including hotel and restaurant checks and airline tickets.

These taxes will not appear on price tags.

Telephones Many convenience groceries and packaging services sell **prepaid calling cards** in denominations up to $50. Many public pay phones at airports now accept American Express, MasterCard, and Visa. **Local calls** made from most pay phones cost either 25¢ or 35¢ and do not require the area code. Most long-distance and international calls can be dialed directly from any phone. **To make calls within the United States and to Canada,** dial 1 followed by the area code and the seven-digit number. **For other international calls,** dial 011 followed by the country code, city code, and the number you are calling.

Calls to area codes **800, 888, 877,** and **866** are toll-free. However, calls to area codes **700** and **900** (chat lines, bulletin boards, "dating" services, and so on) can be expensive—charges of 95¢ to $3 or more per minute. Some numbers have minimum charges that can run $15 or more.

For **reversed-charge or collect calls,** and for person-to-person calls, dial the number 0 then the area code and number; an operator will come on the line, and you should specify whether you are calling collect, person-to-person, or both. If your operator-assisted call is international,

ask for the overseas operator.

For **directory assistance** ("Information"), dial 411 for local numbers and national numbers in the U.S. and Canada. For dedicated long-distance information, dial 1, then the appropriate area code plus 555-1212.

Time Utah is in the **Mountain Standard Time Zone.** The continental United States is divided into **four time zones:** Eastern Standard Time (EST), Central Standard Time (CST), Mountain Standard Time (MST), and Pacific Standard Time (PST). Alaska and Hawaii have their own zones. For example, when it's 9am in Los Angeles (PST), it's 7am in Honolulu (HST),10am in Denver (MST), 11am in Chicago (CST), noon in New York City (EST), 5pm in London (GMT), and 2am the next day in Sydney.

Daylight saving time (summer time) is in effect from 1am on the second Sunday in March to 1am on the first Sunday in November, except in Arizona, Hawaii, the U.S. Virgin Islands, and Puerto Rico. Daylight saving time moves the clock 1 hour ahead of standard time.

For help with time translations, and more, download our convenient Travel Tools app for your mobile device. Go to www.frommers.com/go/mobile, and click on the Travel Tools icon.

Tipping In hotels, tip **bellhops** at least $1 per bag ($2–$3 if you have a lot of luggage) and tip the **chamber staff** $1 to $2 per day (more if you've left a big mess for him or her to clean up). Tip the **doorman** or **concierge** only if he or she has provided you with some specific service (for example, calling a cab for you or obtaining difficult-to-get theater tickets). Tip the **valet-parking attendant** $1 every time you get your car.

In restaurants, bars, and nightclubs, tip **service staff** and **bartenders** 15% to 20% of the check, tip **checkroom attendants** $1 per garment, and tip **valet-parking attendants** $1 per vehicle.

As for other service personnel, tip **cab drivers** 15% of the fare, tip **skycaps** at airports at least $1 per bag ($2–$3 if you have a lot of luggage), and tip **hairdressers** and **barbers** 15% to 20%.

For help with tip calculations, currency conversions, and more, download our convenient Travel Tools app for your mobile device. Go to www.frommers.com/go/mobile, and click on the Travel Tools icon.

Toilets You won't find public toilets or "restrooms" on the streets in most U.S. cities but they can be found in hotel lobbies, bars, restaurants, museums, department stores, railway and bus stations, and service stations. Large hotels and fast-food restaurants are often the best bet for clean facilities. Restaurants and bars in resorts or heavily visited areas may reserve their restrooms for patrons.

VAT See "Taxes" earlier in this section.

Visas The U.S. State Department has a **Visa Waiver Program (VWP)** allowing citizens of the following countries to enter the United States without a visa for stays of up to 90 days: Andorra, Australia, Austria, Belgium, Brunei, Czech Republic, Denmark, Estonia, Finland, France, Germany, Greece, Hungary, Iceland, Ireland, Italy, Japan, Latvia, Liechtenstein, Lithuania, Luxembourg, Malta, Monaco, the Netherlands, New Zealand, Norway, Portugal, San Marino, Singapore, Slovakia, Slovenia, South Korea, Spain, Sweden, Switzerland, and the United Kingdom. (**Note:** This list was accurate at press time; for the most up-to-date list of countries in the VWP, consult http://travel.state.gov/visa.) Even though a visa isn't necessary, in an effort to help U.S. officials check travelers against terror watch lists before they arrive at U.S. borders, visitors from VWP countries must register online through the Electronic System for Travel Authorization (ESTA) before boarding a plane or a boat to the U.S. Travelers must complete an electronic application providing basic personal and travel eligibility information. The Department of Homeland Security recommends filling out the form at least 3 days before traveling. Authorizations will be valid for up to 2 years or until the traveler's passport expires, whichever comes first. Currently, there is one $14 fee for the online application. Existing ESTA registrations remain valid through their expiration dates. **Note:** Any passport issued on or after October 26, 2006, by a VWP country must be an **e-Passport** for VWP travelers to be eligible to enter the U.S. without a visa. Citizens of these nations also need to present a round-trip air or cruise ticket upon arrival. E-Passports contain computer chips capable of storing biometric information, such as the required digital photograph of the holder. If your passport doesn't have this feature, you can still travel without a visa if the valid passport was issued before October 26, 2005, and includes a machine-readable zone, or if the valid passport was issued between October 26, 2005, and October 25, 2006, and includes a digital photograph. For more information, go to **http://travel.state.gov/visa**.

Canadian citizens may enter the United States without visas, but will need to show passports and proof of residence.

Citizens of all other countries must have (1) a valid passport that expires at least 6 months later than the scheduled end of their visit to the U.S., and (2) a tourist visa.

For information about U.S. visas go to **http://travel.state.gov,** and click on "Visas." Or go to one of the following websites:

Australian citizens can obtain up-to-date visa information from the **U.S. Embassy Canberra,** Moonah Place, Yarralumla, ACT 2600 (✆ **02/6214-5600**), or by checking the U.S. Diplomatic Mission's website at **http://canberra.usembassy.gov/visas.html**.

British subjects can obtain up-to-date visa information by calling the **U.S. Embassy Visa Information Line** (✆ **09042-450-100**) from within the

U.K. at £1.20 per minute, or ✆ **866/382-3589** from within the U.S. at a flat rate of $16 payable by credit card only) or by visiting the "Visas to the U.S." section of the American Embassy London's website at **http://london.usembassy.gov/visas.html**.

Irish citizens can obtain up-to-date visa information through the **U.S. Embassy Dublin,** 42 Elgin Rd., Ballsbridge, Dublin 4 (✆ **1580-47-VISA** [8472] from within the Republic of Ireland at €2.40 per minute; **http://dublin.usembassy.gov**).

Citizens of **New Zealand** can obtain up-to-date visa information by contacting the **U.S. Embassy New Zealand,** 29 Fitzherbert Terrace, Thorndon, Wellington (✆ **644/462-6000; http://newzealand.usembassy.gov**).

Visitor Information
For information on the state as a whole, as well as an official state map, contact the **Utah Office of**

Tourism, 300 N. State St., Salt Lake City, UT 84114 (✆ **800/200-1160** or 801/538-1030; www.utah.com). For information on Utah's national forests, contact the **U.S. Forest Service Intermountain Region,** 324 25th St., Ogden, UT 84401 (✆ **801/625-5306;** www.fs.fed.us/r4). The Utah State Office of the **U.S. Bureau of Land Management (BLM)** is at 440 W. 200 South, Ste. 500, Salt Lake City, UT 84145 (✆ **801/539-4001;** www.blm.gov/ut). For information on Utah's state parks, contact **Utah State Parks,** 1594 W. North Temple, Salt Lake City, UT 84114 (✆ **800/322-3770,** or 801/538-7220 for campground reservations; www.stateparks.utah.gov). You can find additional resources for planning your outdoor adventures in chapter 4.

Wi-Fi See "Internet & Wi-Fi," earlier in this section.

AIRLINE & CAR RENTAL WEBSITES

Airlines

American Airlines
www.aa.com

Continental Airlines
www.continental.com

Delta Air Lines
www.delta.com

Frontier Airlines
www.frontierairlines.com

JetBlue Airways
www.jetblue.com

Southwest Airlines
www.southwest.com

United Airlines
www.united.com

US Airways
www.usairways.com

Rental Cars

Advantage
www.advantage.com

Alamo
www.alamo.com

Avis
www.avis.com

Budget
www.budgetutah.com

Dollar
www.dollar.com

Enterprise
www.enterprise.com

Fox
www.foxrentacar.com

National
www.nationalcar.com

Hertz
www.hertz.com

Thrifty
www.thrifty.com

Index

Accommodations